Gifted Children

Psychological and Educational Perspectives

Abraham J. Tannenbaum
Teachers College, Columbia University

Macmillan Publishing Co., Inc.
NEW YORK

Collier Macmillan Publishers
LONDON

Macmillan Publishing Co., Inc.
866 Third Avenue, New York, New York 10022

Collier Macmillan Canada, Inc.

Library of Congress Cataloging in Publication Data

Tannenbaum, Abraham J.
Gifted Children.

Bibliography: p.
Includes index.
1. Gifted children—Education—United States.
2. Gifted children—United States—Psychology.
I. Title
LC3993.9.T36 1983   371.95   82-471 0
ISBN 0-02-418880-8

Printing: 2 3 4 5 6 7 8   Year: 5 6 7 8 9 0

ISBN   0-02-418880-8

שְׁמַע בְּנִי מוּסַר אָבִיךָ
וְאַל-תִּטֹּשׁ תּוֹרַת אִמֶּךָ
כִּי לִוְיַת חֵן הֵם לְרֹאשֶׁךָ
וַעֲנָקִים לְגַרְגְּרֹתֶיךָ

Listen, my child,
To instruction from your father,
And do not desert
The teachings of your mother;
For their wisdom can be worn
As priceless adornments about your head
And as exquisite ornaments around your neck.

Proverbs, 1:8-9

This book is dedicated
to my wife
Annette
and to my children
Alisa Judith
Moshe David
and
Nina Sara

To them I owe sincerest apologies for their having to endure my neglect while I devoted every spare moment to writing this book over a period of three years. I also owe them my deepest gratitude for encouraging me to remain on task through the many agonies of frustration that tortured me as I groped for ideas and for ways of expressing them. Their love gave strength to their loyalty even while they were denied so much of the attention they deserved from a husband and father. Tradition teaches us that unconditional love can be repaid only with unconditional love. I therefore assume my debt gladly in the earnest hope that I can repay it by learning to *express* as much love as I *feel* for Annette and the children.

Preface

Gifted Children: Psychological and Educational Perspectives is a combination textbook and think piece for undergraduate and graduate courses concentrating on the gifted. It is intended as an expository text in that it attempts to synthesize major theory and research in the field. There is also emphasis on generating new ideas and original interpertations, particularly in the critical commentary that constitutes the think-piece aspect of every chapter. In some instances I have introduced a point of view that is my own but that is also at odds with popular ones in the field. I hope thereby to stimulate a lively dialogue and a rethinking of widely held beliefs that are too often accepted uncritically.

Part I is a social history of concern about the gifted. It deals mainly with ambivalent attitudes toward encouraging the fruition of human talent. Pro- and anti-gifted feelings are presented in a historical context. This leads to a discussion of early research on gifted children as well as the cycles of devotion and indifference to their needs at school. The main focus is on the pendulum of public interest as it swings between extremes of egalitarianism and excellence, and its effects on the gifted. My discussion of historical trends ends with a projection into the future of how the gifted are likely to fare in school and society in the 1980s and beyond. The factual support I present comes from the American scene, but the interpretations and inferences I draw are meant to apply in all Western-type democracies.

Part II reviews various approaches to characterizing giftedness and ends with my own definition. All talents are clasified in four categories: (1) scarcity, (2) surplus, (3) quota, and (4) anomalous types of talent. A discussion of these typologies is followed by a review of sociocultural and utilitarian perspectives on defining giftedness. The most extensive review by far is devoted to the psychological perspective, which covers major theory and research in the field. This includes the work of Terman, Taylor, the U.S. Office of Education, Renzulli, Piechowski, Sternberg, and Tannenbaum, among others. The emphases move from the purely cognitive to combinations of cognitive and personality theory, then to information processing and componential theories, and finally to my own social-psychological approach that specifies five factors linking promise and fulfillment: (1) superior general ability, (2) special aptitudes, (3) nonintellective facilitators, (4) environmental influences, and (5) chance factors.

Part III deals extensively with the five linkages between promise and fulfillment, outlined at the end of Part II, and includes the relevant theory and research. The discussion of superior general ability summarizes and critiques the work initiated by Terman and Hollingworth and their associates, as well as the derivative research on IQ and giftedness. Special aptitudes are approached through the work of Thurstone and Guilford, among others, and there follows a review of contrasts among the following types of giftedness: scientific, mathematic, artistic, and social. Summaries and implications of research on personality correlates of achievement cover such topics as metalearning, cognitive styles, motivation, self-concept, and mental health, among others. Discussions of environmental facilitators include reports on influences of parents, peers, and teachers. Chance factors are analyzed as ranging from pure luck, or accident, to "making the breaks" for oneself. Part III ends with a detailed chapter on implications for understanding the dynamics of scholastic under- and overachievement among the gifted.

Part IV is an extensive critical review of the literature on creativity. Because of the enormous number of publications and unfounded claims about the nature, measurement, and nurture of creativity, I examined the research and rhetoric in an effort to organize a sober, original statement to counterbalance the growing mythology in the field. My intention was to sift the evidence objectively rather than take either a doctrinaire or cynical approach. What results is a statement that declares openly what is defensible and what is questionable about the "creativity movement." Topics include major theories of creativity, its development, its assessment, its relationship to IQ, personality dimensions, and experiments in cultivating it. A long list of references brings up to date the important recent literature without neglecting equally important traditional sources.

Part V deals with the education of the gifted and is divided into three subsections: (1) identifying the gifted, (2) educational enrichment paradigms, and (3) methods of evaluating programs for the gifted. The chapter on identification discusses the "state of the art" and ends with my own guidelines. There follows a chapter summarizing the most popular frameworks for curriculum enrichment. These include the works of Osborn and Parnes, Gordon, Williams, Renzulli, and others, and they are followed with an elaborate exposition of my own Enrichment Matrix. The concluding section offers practical guidelines and specially designed instruments for evaluating enrichment programs.

The book ends with an Epilogue consisting of ten rights of gifted children and a brief paragraph justifying and elaborating on each of these rights. The reason for a "Bill of Rights" is that too many educators seem to find it unnecessary to absorb these kinds of principles deeply into their belief systems. Without such all-out commitment they may eventually default on their leadership role in the field. If that happens, initiatives to honor the rights of the gifted will be assumed by concerned lay citizens, while professionals at best become reactive rather than active participants in these efforts. The lay citizen rightly expects the educator to be a self-starting innovator of enrichment, not just responsive to pressures to do something for the gifted, and innovation can grow only out of profound conviction that something *ought* to be done for them. To the reader, the message is straight-foward: Learning about the nature and needs of the gifted from this (or any other) book will be merely an academic exercise unless the special rights of these children are recognized fully.

In writing the book, I tended to use certain key terms for the sake of convenience and parsimony at the expense of precision. For example, the title, *Gifted Children,* should read *Potentially Gifted Children* since giftedness denotes *fulfillment,* but in the case of children we are dealing almost always with *promise.* I suggest that the reader accept the term *gifted* as an abbreviation of *potentially gifted* except when it refers to adults who already have histories of extraordinary accomplishment.

What adds to the trickiness of the label *giftedness* is a large body of literature that equates it with high IQ. Most modern writers on the subject deny the association as too simplistic, but many ignore their own denials by generalizing about giftedness on the basis of studies of high-IQ children. Of course, it is not easy to avoid such a trap since much of the published research has been conducted on this kind of population. Nevertheless, some caution has to be exercised or else we will be forever seduced by the "giftedness-equals-high-IQ" myth despite our protests to the contrary. I have therefore opted for precision in this case and refer to children with high IQ's as "high-IQ children," even when I cite research that calls them "gifted."

The term *creativity,* however, poses a somewhat different problem of semantics. Here, too, the label is meant to be a synonym, in this case for *divergent thinking,* especially in the literature pertaining to its measurement and cultivation. But unlike *giftedness* and *high-IQ, creativity* and *divergent thinking* seem to be widely accepted as interchangeable *in principle* as well as practice. What creates difficulties for me is that I am not yet convinced these terms refer to the same kinds of human functioning. If I were faithful to my doubts I would never use either of the words as a substitute for the other, even though most researchers who claim to be studying creativity in children assess it through tests of divergent thinking. Nevertheless, there are places where I apply the label *creativity* simply because it is the less awkward of the two, and to remind the reader of my true sentiments I place it in quotation marks. I also sprinkle the text with "divergent thinking" to reinforce the reminder.

Finally, I refer to my target population sometimes as "gifted," sometimes as "talented," not as "gifted *and* talented." My reasons for applying these labels interchangeably have nothing to do with brevity or simplicity of language. Instead, I feel the division into two subgroups is false and potentially dangerous. It creates an impression that the children within each group are alike but collectively different from those in the other group. The truth is that there is great variability among those called either "gifted" or "talented," far more than we sometimes care to admit.

A more serious problem in suggesting a gifted-talented dichotomy is that it can mislead people into taking sides as to which type of aptitude is more precious or vital to our interests. This might allow room for favoritism toward some children over others, depending on whether their special abilities classify them as gifted or as talented, a prospect that sounds like foolishness, but borders on prejudice. Nobody knows the extent of the problem, or even whether it is a problem at all. But much is at stake in our attitudes toward the varieties of excellence we encounter in our schools. I have therefore provided a means, through my evaluation instrument (Appendix C), of determining whether people consider these typologies real or contrived. In that instrument, the two labels are used separately, not as synonyms, in order to allow respondents to express their feelings about creating such subgroups and differential education for them. Elsewhere in the book, a single adjective (*gifted* or *talented*) describes the target population, beginning with the title and continuing throughout the text up to, but not including, Appendix C.

Of course, the most important issue concerning language usage revolves about my writing style and its appropriateness for the audience I want to reach. Although the book is meant primarily for psychologists and educators, its message is intended to be accessible to a much wider readership, in fact to *any* lay or professional person interested in the gifted. Perhaps it is impossible to find a mode of expression that communicates clearly to people with diverse backgrounds, but I made the attempt anyway. My guiding rule-of-thumb was to write in plain English wherever possible and in technical terms only where necessary. I am not sure how well I managed to follow this intention; the reader is the only one with a proper vantage point from which to judge such matters. All I ask is that the reader "tune in" to what I *tried* to communicate rather than to what might be read into my words and phrases. The professional has to acknowledge from the outset that simple language can express subtleties as well as banalities, and the lay person has to take neologisms in stride without fear or wonderment. In short, I want the book to be evaluated on the basis of three key questions: (1) What is the author trying to say? (2) How well does he say it? (3) Is it worth saying?

ACKNOWLEDGMENTS

The ideas in this book began to take shape as far back as 1954, when A. Harry Passow appointed me student research assistant to his newly formed Talented Youth Project at the Horace Mann-Lincoln Institute of School Experimentation, Teachers College, Columbia University. My responsibility at that time was to summarize the major literature on the gifted and to participate in disseminating the information to schools in different parts of the country. Besides introducing me to the world of the gifted, Harry also allowed me to share an office with

Miriam L. Goldberg, his research associate on the project. Miriam and I worked together for the five years I stayed with the project, and she served as my mentor at that stage of my career. We spent many hours discussing (and sometimes debating) virtually every issue pertaining to the gifted, and the outcomes of those dialogues are reflected throughout the text. Miriam deserves credit for so much of my thinking that I cannot thank her enough for her contribution to this book.

Another major influence in my professional life was the late Irving Lorge, whose masterful efforts on behalf of gifted children have been long appreciated by scholars in the field. I had the privilege of working closely with him as his student and then as a friend and advisee when I joined the staff of the New York State Education Department. He was always ready and willing to help me in my career in any way he could. In more recent years I worked closely with Reuven Feuerstein and Yaacov Rand, who helped me appreciate the modifiability of human functioning and the importance of mediating children's learning experiences if they are ever to realize their potentials.

Since the mid-1950s I have taught courses on the gifted continuously, even through the 1960s, when popular interest in these children was at a minimum. This has been an invaluable experience since it brought me into close contact with students whose challenges, curiosities, original ideas, and critical commentary have prevented me from ever becoming complacent about my convictions. So many of the ideas expressed in the book derive from our classroom discussions that I cannot lay claim to much of my commentary as strictly my own. In fact, the book is basically a collaborative effort involving my mentors, colleagues, and students. I take full responsibility for what I have written, but not full credit.

Several people ought to be singled out for special thanks because of the help they gave me in preparing this manuscript. Grace Lacy spent many hours distilling the literature on various enrichment paradigms and wrote first drafts of the summaries that appear in Chapter 20. She saved me countless hours of library work, and more than that, the material she assembled is invaluable. The list of books dealing with the joys and travails of gifted people (Appendix B) was developed during a brainstorming session I had with Martin Hamburger, whose career perspective has helped shape my thinking. Also, Donald J. Treffinger's bibliography of selected published material (Appendix A) is bound to be highly useful to classroom practitioners in need of "how-to-do-it" ideas and also to curriculum specialists assembling a library or planning enrichment activities for teachers of the gifted

Milton J. Gold read the first draft of the manuscript and provided me with insightful criticism throughout. His gentle, humorous approach to the text helped prevent me from taking my work (and myself) too seriously, a lesson that every author should learn. Finally, Brigid Coakley and Katharine K. Sheng came to my rescue when I faced the chore of putting together a bibliography. Katharine also prepared the indexes, without which the book would be thoroughly mystifying. The last stages of preparing the manuscript for typesetting were in some ways the most critical, requiring many hours of critiquing, proofreading, and editing. Rachel Blum-Zorman was always available to share this enormous task with me, and the value of her contribution is incalculable. I shall never forget the devotion and intelligence she displayed in helping me meet the final deadlines. To these helpers and to so many others who have lent a hand I extend my deepest gratitude. I sincerely hope the book proves worthy of their efforts on my behalf.

A. J. T.

Contents

Chapter 15.   Fulfilling Creative Potential   294

Chapter 16.   The Creative Personality   307

Chapter 17.   Creativity and Mental Health   320

Chapter 18.   Concluding Thoughts About Creativity   324

PART V.   Nurturing High Potential   341

Chapter 19.   Identifying the Gifted   342

History and the Gifted

For centuries school children and scholars alike have wondered whether the genius makes history or history makes the genius. It is the kind of puzzle that engenders endless speculation because the topic is lively and definitive solutions seem always beyond reach. Actually, the question is less tantalizing than deceptive. Instead of thinking in "either-or" terms, it would be more reasonable to assume that *neither* genius *nor* history predominates, the real relationship being rather an *interdependent* one. Great ideas are powerful enough to influence social and cultural change, and conditions in society help to shape the minds that produce great ideas.

Although the manner in which leaders and their times interact will always be a mystery, one fact seems clear: the work of seminal thinkers throughout the ages is so important that unless we learn to appreciate it we cannot hope to learn how the human family makes history.

Historical Concerns About the Gifted

Curiosity about the lives and works of gifted people probably dates back to the time when people first showed an interest in why they are different from each other. Whenever and wherever human beings excel in endeavors of cultural importance, they invariably arouse some degrees of public interest, suspicion, appreciation, or antipathy, depending on the temperament of their audiences. Some flash into prominence in their lifetimes but are devalued and forgotten after death; others live and die in anonymity but leave immortal legacies for later generations. There is no way of knowing for certain when (or if) public honor will be granted to an individual and how long it will last.

TRADITIONS OF PUBLIC AMBIVALENCE

Classical and Western cultures have been intrigued by the gifted, judging from the theories that have accumulated over centuries on the nature of genius and its impact on human affairs. Among ancient Greeks and medieval Europeans, for example, there existed a popular notion that great intellect is a divine gift, a touch of omniscience enabling one to penetrate to deep truths. A contrasting theory expressed widely by moderns as well as by ancients is that the genius is emotionally disturbed and can be carried into flights of creativity only on wings of madness. People have also believed that mental strength is often balanced by physical weakness in the form of disease or handicap. Broadly speaking, however, human-kind has always managed to show more interest in encouraging than in hampering the work of gifted individuals, but it has also had to moderate its support because of persistent undercurrents of suspicion and negativism.

Encouraging Influences

Any appreciation of talent must be expressed in a social context. The human family is capable of mastering countless skills, but it remains for society to determine which of them it wants to foster and honor. Such judgments are rooted in time and place, varying according to different historical eras and sociocultural settings. In Western civilization, basic conceptions of talent have been strongly influenced by biblical and classical traditions, both of which speak of the exceptionally able, although they refer to different kinds of talent. The Bible (Deuteronomy 17:11) extolls the saintly wisdom of prophets and learned elders from whom the masses seek guidance in interpreting divine will. Plato (1941) places the leadership reins of his ideal state in the hands of philosopher-kings who qualify for their high station in life by possessing the greatest measure of rational intelligence.

It is often believed, mistakenly, that the demise of classical civilization brought to a halt any new meaningful flowering of ideas in Europe until the so-called Dark and Middle Ages had passed. According to this myth, writes La Monte (1949), pre-Renaissance society was "blissfully ignorant of the 'spell of the classics' and interested only in theological speculation" (p. 553). But the fact is that great ideas in science, law, literature, philosophy, and art were actively expounded at that time. To the modern Westerner accustomed to a quick turnover of ideas in the arts and sciences, however, medieval Europe appears as a tradition-oriented society in which high-level talent was devoted primarily to the preservation, understanding, and enhancement of Church ideals. It seems that cultural innovation was not encouraged as expansively in that era as in later times, and there was little room for rational assessment of existing beliefs. Church tradition taught people that certain realms of inquiry were beyond human comprehension and also dangerous to enter, since the imperfect mind would only distort truth and lead people to stray from their faith. The wise person was, therefore, one who excelled in mastering the scriptures, clarifying their obscure, even mystical meanings, and communicating them to intellectural peers. Social and religious leadership often went hand in hand, and the Church bestowed honor on those capable of inspiring religious fervor among the masses and serving thereby as intermediaries between people and their Maker.

With the advent of the Renaissance, the Platonic conception of talent began to ascend in Western civilization. Humanists rebelled against what they considered to be the static, doctrinaire elements of medieval culture and introduced into the world of ideas a venturesome spirit that prevails to this day. Although the supernatural was not banished from their universe, humanists elevated the mind to a position of such stature that it was inevitable for the human family, not a deity, to become the measure of all things. This growing detachment from a spiritual and intellectual grounding in Church canon became evident in many aspects of Renaissance life. Among other things, it freed the talented to think, worry, and create more about humanity and the environment than did their medieval counterparts. It also inspired geniuses to flavor their conceptions of beauty, wisdom, ethics, and law with a touch of originality and daring unheard of in the preceding era.

As the audacious spirit in the realm of ideas became more and more pronounced, it signified a growing receptivity to new values, new disciplines, and a new-found optimism about the ability of the human race to determine its own destiny. The Renaissance awakening was, therefore, of pivotal importance in setting the direction in which Western culture was to foster high-level talent for centuries afterward (Brinton, 1953).

The growth of the Protestant spirit and ethic over the past five centuries and the conversion of the Western world from an agrarian to a highly commercial and industrialized society have exerted powerful influences upon our present-day concerns in the development of talent. People improved their efficiency in producing food to such an extent that they no longer had to be dispersed in rural areas. Instead, they could create urban communities and spend more leisure time building a "paper culture" replete with symbols and abstractions. In such an environment, people learned that the highest rewards in life could be attained through self-enlightenment and self-betterment with the help of an interchange of creative ideas. These conditions of life brought with them the seeds of universal education, scientific and technological curiosity, and an intense intellectual restlessness that has become ever more daring. Thus, the stage was set for humanity's energetic cultural activities so marked in the twentieth century.

Inhibiting Influences

From the voluminous literature on the history of Western civilization, it appears that two opposing currents have operated simultaneously in society's concern about human creativity. On the one hand, the public has demonstrated an almost insatiable demand for newness in the arts, sciences, and humanities and has consequently lavished encouragement and renown upon people with great ideas. On the other hand, it has manifested a tenacious will to remain culturally conservative and often views the creative spirit with suspicion and disdain.

Humankind has always tempered its enthusiasm for nurturing talent with negative attitudes toward the gifted, expressed not only in various forms of militant anti-intellectualism and pressures toward a middle standard in intellectual attainment but also through common belief that only a thin line separates genius from madness. Immortal thinkers from Aristotle to Freud, and beyond, have lent support to this widely accepted notion that nature unaccountably balances mental superiority with emotional or physical defects. In the late nineteenth century, the idea was supposedly given scientific credence when Lombroso (1891) and Nisbet (1891) published results of their studies of famous men in history, a disproportionately large number of whom had reportedly suffered from some kind of behavioral instability. Even Sir Francis Galton and William James, who had for many years denied any link between genius and abnormality, eventually reversed their positions and claimed considerable soundness for the theory. Psychoanalysts have gone so far as to characterize history as a summation of the sublimated neuroses of celebrated personages of all times (Witty and Lehman, 1930).

Suspicions about the emotional stability of gifted individuals have persisted in the scientific community but have never held sway over it. Of the many behavioral scientists who have fought against this kind of negativism, none were more persistent than Lewis Terman and his associates (1925) who dismissed as pure superstition the widespread belief that intellectual precocity is pathological. They also lamented the inhibiting effect that this kind of doctrine had exerted on previous research relating to the gifted. From his own examination of children with high tested intelligence, Terman concluded that they excel in a broad range of nonintellective traits, not just in cognitive functioning. These findings were then confirmed by Cox's retrospective study of famous people of the past (1926).

The work of Terman and his associates has not succeeded in settling the issue to the satisfaction of all. Witty and Lehman (1929a), for example, accepted Terman's evidence that those rating high in general intelligence tend to be emotionally stable, but they refused to support his claim that people who excel in any respected area of endeavor necessarily have higher IQs than do all but 1 to 3 percent of the general population. If giftedness can be associated with criteria other than the IQ, then generalizations about the mental health of high-IQ children would not necessarily apply to all the gifted. Psychologists often avoid using the term "genius," in part because it is charged with negative emotional connotations (Miles, 1954). Nevertheless, those labeled *talented* or *gifted* are still sometimes stigmatized as eccentrics and as strangely handicapped people suffering from some kind of developmental deficit.

EARLY SCIENTIFIC EFFORTS

The scientific examination of talent was initiated in the second half of the nineteenth century. Until that time, interest was focused on comparatively few individuals who made some claim to immortality and were regarded as qualitatively different from normal people (Jones, 1956). Relatively scant attention was given to the early earmarks of talent. Although there were some descriptions of the feats of *Wunderkinder* and how these prodigies fared in adulthood (Buckley, 1853), popular concern was chiefly with full-blown genius at the height of its creative power.

Beginnings of the Testing Movement

The earliest scientific investigations into the nature of talent began at about the time Darwin's and Mendel's studies of biological variations of species were joined by similar scholarly interest in mental, emotional, and social differences among humans. In 1869, Sir Francis Galton published *Hereditary Genius*, generally regarded as the first quantitative analysis of human ability. Surveying the achievements within highly reputed British families, Galton concluded that heredity is the prime determinant of intellectual functioning. Galton's observations touched off a lively debate among psychologists and sociologists on nature versus nurture that persists to this day, although later writers emphasized the interplay of both factors in the broad fulfillment of human potential (Olson and Hughes, 1942; Jones, 1954; Zigler, 1970). Galton, and later Yoder (1894), Ellis (1904), and Cox (1926), studied biographical material to discover characteristics that differentiated gifted from nongifted adults. However, it was Binet's work with Simon, resulting in the publication of their intelligence test in 1905, that paved the way toward investigation of the special mental qualities of gifted children. Further progress in mental and personality measurement aided researchers to enhance their understanding of the nature of talent. So intensively did psychometrists work at developing mental measurement instruments that by 1933 a comprehensive bibliography of available intelligence, aptitude, personality, and achievement tests and scales numbered thirty-five hundred titles (Hildreth, 1933).

Much of the success in studying and educating gifted children in the first two decades of the twentieth century was confined to the academically precocious and was stimulated largely by schools trying to provide classroom experiences commensurate with the abilities of rapid learners. This deepening concern among educators was reflected in two early yearbooks by the National Society for the Study of Education that dealt with the gifted and contained lengthy bibliographies of professional publications, concentrating mostly on how to locate the academically able and design programs for them (Henry, 1920; Whipple, 1924). However, far less headway was being made toward nurturing nonacademic talents, probably because they were much lower on the list of priorities in public education.

Volume I of the *Genetic Studies of Genius* by Terman and his Stanford University associates appeared in 1925. Nearly fifteen hundred California children, most of them coming from the upper elementary school grades with IQs of 140 and above, were studied in terms of racial origins, sex ratio, anthropometric measurements, health and physical history, school progress, specialized abilities, intellectual, social and play interests, and personality and character traits. The findings reported in this study and in the follow-up investigations form the core of scientific knowledge about high-IQ children. Quantifying the differences between the gifted and the less endowed on his own revision of Binet's scale of general intelligence, Terman demonstrated that the IQ can be used at an early age to predict superior adult achievement.

Another pioneer contributor whose work stands alongside that of Terman as basic in the field is Leta Hollingworth, who conducted research both as clinical psychologist and educator. Using approximately the same IQ criterion as Terman did in identifying gifted children, she organized special experimental classes for which she designed, taught, and evaluated such innovative enrichment curricula as *The Evolution of Common Things* and *The Study of Biography* (Hollingworth,

1938; Gray and Hollingworth, 1931). This work has had a strong influence on educators who emphasize enrichment in depth rather than rapid advancement over conventional subject matter for the gifted. No less important to the field is Hollingworth's study of children with IQs of 180 and above, issued in 1942, which remains among the most definitive investigations of its kind to this day.

The early major studies provided more than just valuable insights into the nature of talents; they also set the direction for related research in the field. Considerable efforts were therefore devoted to (1) elaborating on aspects of Terman's and Hollingworth's investigations of children with high IQs; (2) examining nonintellective factors associated with high-level achievement; (3) clarifying the conditions of home, school, and community that foster or inhibit the fruition of talent; and (4) evaluating various educational influences on the development of gifted children.

Recognizing Varieties of Giftedness

According to Cohn (undated), the acceptability of different kinds of talent as signs of excellence has changed over the years. As evidence, he cites a 1976 historical chart prepared by the New Zealand Council for Educational Research, which shows developments in conceptualizing talent since the last century when genius was uppermost in researchers' minds (see Figure 1-1). Interest in genius then broadened to include the high-IQ intellectually gifted; eventually, it expanded to take account of the creatively talented and, more recently, those possessing any one of a wide array of talents.

In interpreting trends, there is always a danger of oversimplifying and even distorting events to fit them into an understandable pattern. The New Zealand time line of developments runs that risk, too. It can create the impression that until midcentury giftedness denoted merely a capacity for intellectual endeavors and that multiple types of talent began to receive serious consideration only as late as the 1970s. Such an interpretation fails to conform to the facts. As far back as the 1920s, Hollingworth (1926) reported on special talents in a way that would reflect current views on the subject. She wrote that "a gifted child may be far more excellent in some capacities than in others. Such a child may even fall below the average in certain capacities, which are almost or utterly incoherent with ability in general throughout the species. These incoherent, or generally unrelated, capacities have been designated *special talents*. An intellectually gifted child may be of any status whatever in respect to one of these special talents, for they are independent of general intelligence" (p. 202). She even used a psychographic method of depicting one child's performance on a battery of twelve tests in order to show unevenness in his development (see Figure 1-2). Her expectation was that "As we gradually learn what capacities are most closely linked with success in various endeavors of practical life, the psychographic method of examination will become more and more highly developed" (pp. 218-219).

In the 1930s, Bentley (1937) also took note of the talented, whom he charac-

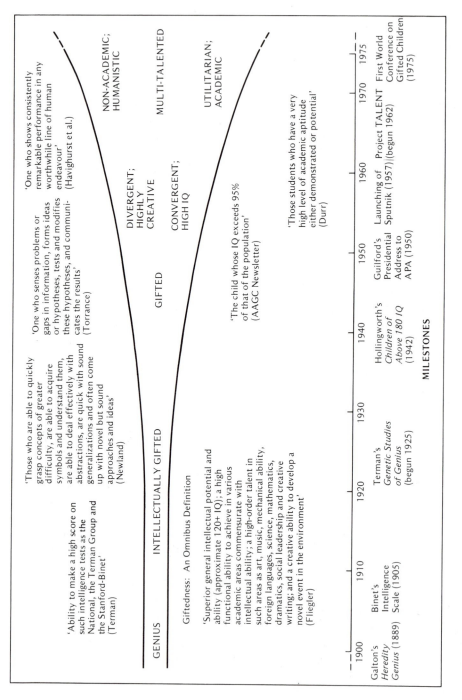

'One who shows consistently remarkable performance in any worthwhile line of human endeavour' (Havighurst et al.)

NON-ACADEMIC; HUMANISTIC

MULTI-TALENTED

UTILITARIAN; ACADEMIC

'One who senses problems or gaps in information, forms ideas or hypotheses, tests and modifies these hypotheses, and communicates the results' (Torrance)

DIVERGENT; HIGHLY CREATIVE

CONVERGENT; HIGH IQ

GIFTED

'Those who are able to quickly grasp concepts of greater difficulty, are able to acquire symbols and understand them, are able to deal effectively with abstractions and often come up with novel but sound generalizations and ideas' (Newland)

'The child whose IQ exceeds 95% of that of the population' (AAGC Newsletter)

'Those students who have a very high level of academic aptitude either demonstrated or potential' (Durr)

'Ability to make a high score on such intelligence tests as the National, the Terman Group and the Stanford-Binet' (Terman)

GENIUS   INTELLECTUALLY GIFTED

Giftedness: An Omnibus Definition

'Superior general intellectual potential and ability (approximate 120+ IQ); a high functional ability to achieve in various academic areas commensurate with intellectual ability; a high-order talent in such areas as art, music, mechanical ability, foreign languages, science, mathematics, dramatics, social leadership and creative writing; and a creative ability to develop a novel event in the environment' (Fliegler)

| 1900 | 1910 | 1920 | 1930 | 1940 | 1950 | 1960 | 1970 | 1975 |

Galton's *Heredity Genius* (1889)

Binet's Intelligence Scale (1905)

Terman's *Genetic Studies of Genius* (begun 1925)

Hollingworth's *Children of Above 180 IQ* (1942)

Guilford's Presidential Address to APA (1950)

Launching of Sputnik (1957)

Project TALENT (begun 1962)

First World Conference on Gifted Children (1975)

MILESTONES

Figure 1-1 Changing conceptions of giftedness (Cohn, undated)

8

SPECIAL TALENTS

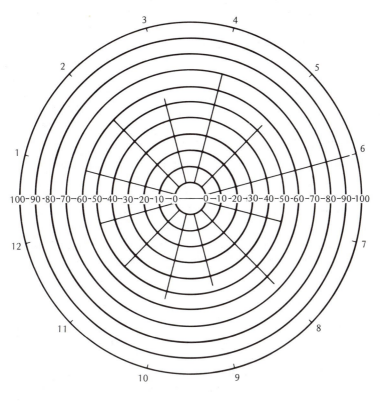

1. General Intelligence (Stanford-Binet)
2. Completion Test (Trabue)
3. Cancellation ⎤
4. Digit-Symbol ⎬(Pintner)
5. Opposites ⎦
6. Mechanical Ability (Stenquist)

7. Tonal Memory ⎤
8. Pitch ⎬(Seashore)
9. Time ⎥
10. Intensity ⎦
11. Pictorial Completion (Healy)
12. Grip in Hand (Smedley)

Figure 1-2 Psychograph of a boy, showing extent of various capacities, as measured by tests of specific appitudes. The traits measured, and indicated by numbers on the psychograph, are enumerated above. Scores are in terms of percentile status. (Hollingworth, 1926, p. 219)

terized as having "natural aptitude" and "susceptibility to advanced training" in a special field of activity, such as music, art, or mathematics. He argued forcefully that those who possess special talents be counted among the gifted despite his dour observation that "Talented individuals in ordinary life are often psychopathic, sometimes tyrannic, autistic, bohemian, and occasionally infantile in other modes of behavior" (p. 73).

In 1958, Witty anticipated future sentiments about the nature of giftedness when he cautioned against relying too heavily on the IQ as a means of identification. He also emphasized such factors as "drive" and "persistence," which he found difficult to measure. Such special talents as art, writing, and social leadership did not escape his attention either, but he felt that a child who possesses that kind of ability should prove it by actual performance rather than by some measure of potential because of the low predictive validity of such tests (Witty, 1958).

Finally, the federal definition of giftedness (Marland, 1971), which emphasizes multiple talents, seems to have been anticipated to a great extent by De Hahn and Havighurst as early as 1957. Although appearing a decade and a half apart, both definitions list nearly the same six domains of excellence. The only significant difference between the two is that the older one, surprisingly, is more explicit about the meaning of each domain, as follows:

1. *Intellectual ability*, which is related most directly to success in school subjects, encompasses the verbal, number, spatial, memory, and reasoning factors of the primary mental abilities. De Hahn and Havighurst (1957) regard combinations of these aptitudes as basic to other talents, such as fine arts, social leadership, science, and mechanics.
2. *Creative thinking*, which is revealed through some complex mental powers, such as the ability to recognize problems, to be flexible in thinking, to originate ideas or products, or to find new uses for old objects and materials.
3. *Scientific ability*, including skills in the use of numbers and algebraic symbols, arithmetic reasoning, curiosity about the natural world, and facility with the scientific method.
4. *Social leadership*, specifically the ability to help a group reach its goals and to improve human relationships within a group. Such skills are necessary for those who will eventually assume leadership positions in business and industry, labor unions, professional organizations, community groups, government, and international agencies.
5. *Mechanical skills*, otherwise known as "craft skills" and closely related to talents in the fine arts and in science and engineering. Success in this category depends on manipulative facility, spatial ability, and perception of visual patterns, details, similarities, and differences.
6. *Talents in the fine arts*, which are required of artists, writers, musicians, actors, and dancers.

Thus, we see how misleading it is to suggest that only in recent years has the definition of giftedness broken out of the restrictions imposed by the IQ and by narrowly conceived academic programs in our schools. It is important to know this not simply for purposes of correcting the record but rather to show the historical gap between what has been thought about multiple talents and what has been done about cultivating them.

In principle, behavioral scientists and educators have recognized for a long time that children can qualify as gifted if they possess any one of a substantial variety of talents. Even the predominance of the "g" factor in intelligence has been debated for many years. More than half a century ago, Thorndike and his associates (1926) advanced the idea that intelligence was made up of an infinite number of discrete aptitudes, and Spearman (1927) dealt with the relationships among specific, group, and general factors. However, *in practice*, educators have tended to equate gift-edness with superior performance on tests that measure general intelligence, as if children in *all* talent areas have to meet such standards. Of the children thus labeled gifted, only a small minority receive educational stimulation commensurate with their abilities. These enriched curricula have concentrated traditionally on the academic areas such as mathematics, citizenship, language, and science, as if they are the educational imperatives deserving first priority, while the arts, mechanical skills, and social leadership could only survive as educational electives that carry more appeal than importance in the schools. What we see, then, is not simple naïveté in the past about the *existence* of multiple talents but rather a hierarchy of educational preoccupations and value judgments about which talents have received *preferential treatment*.

The New Zealand report is probably more valid as a comment on increasing action rather than lip service on behalf of former frills in the curriculum. Guilford's pioneering efforts to assess creative thinking have been followed by the develop-ment of formal test batteries (Torrance, 1966; Wallach and Kogan, 1965) and exercises for practitioners to use with children (Noller, et al., 1976; Renzulli, 1974; Feldhusen and Treffinger, 1977). Educators are beginning to explore the advantages of exercises in brainstorming to supplement the conventional one-solution-per-problem requirements in programs for the gifted. They are also studying curriculum possibilities that may grow out of theories about the hierarchical complexity of cognition, as represented in Bloom's *Taxonomy* (1956) and Gagné's *Conditions of Learning* (1970). The tightening relationship of theory, measurement, and appli-cation is likewise reflected in Taylor's (1973) ideas about the existence of multiple talents that can be recognized through his *Biographical Inventory* (Institute for Behavioral Research in Creativity, 1978) and nurtured in such programs as Implode and Talents Unlimited. The growing trend, then, is not so much to conceptualize new and broader cognitive dimensions of giftedness as to measure them with greater efficiency than ever before and make them relevant to educational planning.

EARLY EDUCATIONAL EFFORTS

In a nation where compulsory education for all children and youth is a cherished principle, it is inevitable that providing adequately for the gifted should become a persistent and sometimes confounding problem. Years ago, when comparatively few children were given opportunities for formal study, many rare talents withered on the vine for want of schooling. Today, virtually *all* American youth, the poor along with the rich, the dull along with the bright, go to school for a good part of their early lives. A vital task of education has consequently become that of making the most of an unprecedented opportunity to identify and train the *total* population of gifted youth.

As the school's role in society grew more complex during the early part of the present century, educators showed increasing concern for training the "whole" child—not just academically, but socially, creatively, and vocationally as well. High schools began to expand course offerings to help make secondary schooling a meaningful experience for all youths. Thus, preparing the better-than-average for college and stimulating the gifted to make full and purposeful use of their capabilities emerged as but two of many objectives. Within the stream of these trends, schools set about making special administrative adjustments for the gifted.

The Beginnings of Special Programs

Beginning in 1868 with the acceleration of rapid learners in St. Louis schools, plans for flexible promotion were the most popular ones until the end of the nineteenth century (Bentley, 1937). Several such systems were initiated, the essential features of each being to arrange the promotion schedule for the academically advanced so as to allow them to complete their first eight years of schooling in less time, but without skipping over any parts of the curriculum sequence. The St. Louis plan served another function in taking bright children out of overcrowded lower grades and placing them in higher classes that were relatively depleted because of early dropouts. In 1886, Elizabeth, New Jersey schools divided each of the first eight grades into three sections, roughly according to the performance levels of the pupils. Those who demonstrated the ability to move to higher grades were given opportunities to do so without undergoing special examinations. Similar procedures were followed in Santa Barbara's Concentric Plan and in the Constant Group System in New York and Chicago.

Probably the best known flexible promotion system before the turn of the century was the Cambridge Double-Track Plan, developed in 1891. At first only the pupils in grades three through nine were affected, with the brighter ones being placed in classes that covered the six years' work in four years. Some twenty years later, the plan was revised to include the first eight grades, permitting rapid learners to complete the sequence in six years. Special teachers were appointed to coach the brighter pupils in the program. These adaptations are representative of the multiple-track plans instituted in the late nineteenth century. Variations of this system were devised in cities large and small throughout the country; still, such efforts were thinly scattered and affected only a small portion of able students in the nation's schools (McDonald, 1915).

Flexible promotion won increasing favor as a reward for high achievement during the first two decades of the twentieth century, although grade skipping also came into vogue at that time. In 1900, New York City established its first Rapid Advancement classes in a single school. This was the early version of what was to become the Special Progress classes, still in existence in that city, which permit pupils to complete three years of junior high school work in two. In 1901, Worcester, in Massachusetts, founded its preparatory school, generally regarded as the first special school for the academically able. Here, pupils from grades seven through nine were gathered from neighboring schools for special instruction in languages and mathematics for which credit was awarded toward a high school diploma. A similar plan was inaugurated in Baltimore in 1902. At about that time Stuyvesant High School was founded in New York City for boys superior in mechanical arts, mathematics, and science. Also making their appearance in the early 1900s, but only for a brief period, were the summer vacation schools, where children studied advanced subject matter enabling them to move quickly into higher grades.

According to Hollingworth (1926), one of the earliest experimental classes designed explicitly for bright children selected on the basis of mental test scores was organized in Louisville, Kentucky, in 1918. The children's Stanford-Binet IQs ranged from 120 to 168, with a median of 137. Working at its own pace, the class covered the prescribed elementary school program at about twice the ordinary rate without handicapping the pupils physically or emotionally. Similar encouraging findings were reached in subsequent experiments with high-IQ children conducted in New York City, Urbana, Illinois, Columbus, Ohio, and Berkeley, California, elementary schools. In almost every instance, the children profited by advancing rapidly through the curriculum in special classes rather than by skipping grades.

Other significant developments in the first two decades of the present century include the standardization and use of intelligence tests to identify the gifted in school; the initiation of studies at Stanford University (Terman, 1911) of children with high IQs, which later blossomed into the exhaustive work directed by Terman; and plans for individualizing instruction, which enabled rapid learners to progress at their own speed and at their own initiative in the classroom. These innovations formed an important prelude to trends in the 1920s and 1930s.

Programs from 1920 to World War II and Beyond

By 1920, earlier hints of change in American education had taken on sharp definition. The Progressive Education Movement, with its deep concern for human variability, began soon after World War I to exert powerful influence in schools around the country, particularly at the elementary level. In 1918, the Commission on Reorganization of Secondary Education issued its *Cardinal Principals of Secondary Education*, which took careful note of human differences and characterized the function of the high school program as college preparatory for some, terminal education for others. Much of the mounting interest in the unique individual was stimulated by the maturing sciences of psychology and sociology, which were shedding new light on laws of learning, personality development, and the impact of the group on the individual.

With respect to precocious learners, educators took serious account of their special qualities and the implications that could be drawn for their particular educational needs. It soon became apparent to all concerned that schools were capitalizing on the ability of these children to learn more rapidly than average students but were neglecting their capacity for broader and deeper understandings. Questions were raised as to the wisdom of removing them from agemates who share so many of their nonacademic interests and placing them in classes with older children simply to make competition at school stronger. To avoid these pitfalls, *enrichment* instead of *acceleration* became the preferred practice, with the gifted and nongifted grouped together in programs designed to accommodate individual differences (Bentley, 1937).

The so-called "contract" systems in Winnetka, Illinois, and Dalton, Massachusetts, outgrowths of an earlier individualized instruction plan in San Francisco, enabled bright children to work on special projects independently in a self-motivated, teacher-directed manner in the regular classroom. Hollingworth's successful experiments in Public School 165 and later in Public School 500 (The Speyer School) in New York City convinced her and her followers that an enriched program for the high-IQ children in the elementary grades was more meaningful to these children than was telescoping the conventional subject matter. Largely as a result of Hollingworth's experiments, New York City organized special classes in selected elementary schools that absorbed the gifted from neighboring schools and provided them with enriched experiences for the conventional eight years. Experimentation with special classes for the gifted in Los Angeles, beginning in 1915, likewise resulted five years later in the opening of "opportunity classes," where enrichment procedures were adopted. Other special programs organized in large cities included the Cleveland Major Work, the Detroit X,Y,Z, and New York City's Special Progress junior high school classes. Some of New York's specialized high schools for the gifted were also established during this period.

If the 1920s can be characterized as a time when the schools substituted ability grouping for acceleration as a favorite means of providing for the gifted, the 1930s and the war years might well be termed an era in which enrichment in special classes gave way to enrichment in the regular classroom.

The degree to which ability grouping was practiced in the 1920s is not clear. One 1929 survey reported by Otto (1944) of school systems of 2,500 to 25,000 populations indicates that fully two thirds had some form of ability grouping. To what extent the gifted were cared for in these schools is not reported. Another survey undertaken one year later (Heck, 1930) revealed that only 30 out of 762 cities with populations of over 10,000 had special classes or schools for gifted children. However, there can be no doubt about the decline of ability grouping in general and of special classes for rapid learners in particular soon after 1930. Surveys fairly comparable to the ones noted earlier were made in 1948 (National Educational Association, 1949) and gave unmistakable evidence of these trends. Heck (1953) reports one study showing that, out of 3,203 cities with populations of 2,500 or more, only 15 had special schools or classes for children with high tested intelligence.

Support for the battle to keep the rapid learners in the regular classroom came from specialists in child study (Keliher, 1931) who considered it impossible to effect homogeneous groupings even on the basis of ability alone. They considered the human psyche to be so complex that even those children who are capable of mastering subject matter with nearly equal rapidity show vast differences in their learning strengths and weaknesses. Moreover, human differences become still more marked when nonintellective traits are considered as well.

The 1930s and the war years saw some schools making valiant, if not always successful, efforts to provide enrichment in the regular classroom. For the most part, the existence of special opportunities of any kind for the gifted has never been widespread even in years when interest grew considerably. In 1941, the National Educational Association reported on the nature of education for the gifted in several hundred high schools throughout the country, but a subsequent check with many of these same schools thirteen years later indicated that most of the plans had long since been discarded for one reason or another. Interest probably reached its lowest ebb during World War II and immediately afterward. For the years 1942 to 1945, professional writing about the gifted suffered a decline (Witty, 1951), and by the 1950s, some increase in attention was becoming evident. In 1950, the Educational Policies Commission issued a policy statement in which powerful recognition was given to the social waste resulting from the neglect of mentally superior students, and proposals were made regarding their educational needs. A year later, the American Association for Gifted Children published a comprehensive volume entitled *The Gifted Child*, under the editorship of Paul Witty (1951), which received wide circulation. A national survey of secondary schools seemed to indicate that by 1954 more and more schools were becoming aware that the need to challenge the gifted educationally was urgent and that the holding power of high schools for rapid learners was growing stronger steadily (Jewett et al., 1954). Thus we see the beginnings of a swing back toward caring about gifted children and their education as America entered the 1950s.

_____

Chapter 2

Modern Trends
and Prospects

The five years following the launching of *Sputnik* in 1957 and the last half-decade of the 1970s may be viewed as twin peak periods of interest in gifted children. Separating the peaks was a deep valley of neglect in which the public fixed its attention more eagerly on the low-functioning, poorly motivated, and socially handicapped in our schools. It was not simply a case of bemoaning the plight of able and then disadvantaged learners, with each population taking turns as the pitied underdog or the victim of unfair play. Instead of *transferring* the same sentiments from one undereducated group to another, the nation found itself *transforming* its mood from intense anxiety to equally profound indignation—anxiety lest our protective shield of brainpower become weaker, rendering us vulnerable to challenge from without, followed by indignation over social injustice in the land, which could tear us apart from within. In the late 1960s, we began to experience a revival of earlier sensitivities to the needs of the gifted. Judging from these fluctuations in national temperament, it seems as if we have not yet succeeded in paying equal attention *simultaneously* to our most and least successful achievers at school.

The cyclical nature of interest in the gifted is probably unique in American education. No other special group of children has been alternately embraced and repelled with so much vigor by educators and laypersons alike. What this apparent faddism means and why it should recur so regularly can only be a matter of speculation. Gardner saw signs of public dilemma rather than fickleness when he commented that "the critical lines of tension in our society are between *emphasis on individual performance and restraints on individual performance*" (Gardner, 1961, p. 33, Gardner's italics). Such conflict would arise logically from a failure to reconcile our commitments to excellence and equality in public education. Fostering excellence means recognizing the right of gifted children to realize their potential, but it also suggests something uncomfortably close to encouraging elitism if the most able are privy to educational experiences that are denied to all other children. On the other hand, promoting egalitarianism will guarantee increased attention to children from lower-status environments who are failing at school. But as we concentrate more exclusively on raising the performance levels of these minorities, there is danger of discriminating against the minority of gifted students by denying their right to be challenged adequately on grounds that they are advantaged. Perhaps because we cannot live exclusively with excellence or egalitarianism for any length of time and tend to counterpose rather than to reconcile them, we seem fated to drift from one to the other like the fabled Flying Dutchman who was condemned to a lifetime at sea with only periodic visits ashore.

THE 1950s: PRE-*SPUTNIK*

From the current perspective, the 1950s are viewed as sedate, conservative years, at least in contrast to the convulsive 1960s. But this kind of hindsight is fairly myopic. While it is true that America was spared too much internal dissension, except for McCarthyism and some grumbling about our involvement in Korea, still it was the age of cold warfare at its worst, and its threat to the psyche seemed lethal. Two superpowers, determined to undo each other's political systems, possessed the ultimate weapon of destruction, and each feared that the other would use it as a deterrent if it imagined itself about to be attacked.

Unlocking secrets of the atom to produce the bomb represented a scientific as well as a military breakthrough and increased the dependency of armed power on the innovativeness of the scientist. Americans had grown confident that our country's leadership in science and technology was unchallengeable. We expected ourselves always to be the first in creating new gadgetry to make life and death easier, be it through sophisticated home appliances, computer systems, communications equipment, or explosives with the power of megatons of TNT. Imagine the shock, then, when this illusion was shattered with the orbiting of *Sputnik* by none other than our archenemy in the midst of a Cold War that at any moment could turn hotter than any conflict in history. *Sputnik* was not just a demoralizing technological feat; it had potential military applications, too. Suddenly, the prestige and survival of a nation were jeopardized because the enemy's greatest minds of the day had outperformed ours, and the Russians capitalized on this coup by broadcasting to every nation on earth its success in reducing America to a second-class power at long last.

Although the shock of *Sputnik* in 1957 triggered unprecedented action on behalf of the gifted, educators had already expressed their lament over public indifference to these children much earlier in that decade. But most of the attention was confined to regional and national surveys and public expressions of sentiment rather than the initiation of new enrichment programs. In 1950, the Educational

Policies Commission decried the schools' neglect of mentally superior children and the resulting decline of personnel resources in the sciences, arts, and professions. A year later, the Ohio Commission on Children and Youth revealed only 2 percent of the schools in that state having special classes for the gifted and a mere 9 percent reporting any kind of enrichment in the regular classroom.

Criticism of the elementary and high schools eventually spread to the academic community. In 1953, a historian (Bestor) published a sensational indictment of public education for practicing what he considered its special brand of fraudulence on America's children. He charged that schools were not governed by learned educators but rather by know-nothing "educationists," a term he used in referring to teachers, administrators, and those responsible for training them on college campuses. To his way of thinking, it was tragically ironic that "educationists" should exert nearly total influence on the content of curricula while caring so little about the world of ideas. How could anyone presume to dictate what should be taught at school if he or she is not immersed personally in any scholarly discipline? Because of what he regarded as a misplacement of power in the hands of educationists, Bestor was convinced that schools provided meager intellectual nourishment or inspiration, especially for the gifted, who often marked time in their studies until graduation released them from boredom.

Bestor was not alone in sounding the alarm. Lynd (1953) and Koerner (1963) concurred that education in our schools was a sham perpetrated by self-styled professionals who possessed little knowledge and imparted even less to their pupils. Particularly blameworthy were teacher-training faculties in colleges that emphasized easy, "how-to-do-it" courses in pedagogy, yet minimized the importance of substantive disciplines in the liberal and fine arts and sciences. Whatever the merits and faults of these criticisms, it is important to remember that they aroused attention throughout the country, touching off animated debates between detractors and defenders of the schools and, most of all, initiating pressures for reform that climaxed soon after *Sputnik*.

To some extent, the eagerness among educators to increase the nation's talent supply was probably influenced by politicians and economists who worried about our diminishing reservoir of high-level personnel in science and technology before *Sputnik* dramatized the problem. In a lengthy report prepared by the director of the Commission on Human Resources and Advanced Training (Wolfle, 1954), it was asserted that the United States had failed to prepare enough men and women in the natural sciences, health fields, teaching, and engineering. Only six of ten in the top 5 percent and only half of the top 25 percent of high school graduates went on to earn college diplomas. At the more advanced levels, a mere 3 percent of those capable of earning Ph.Ds actually did so. What made matters worse were expectations that the shortages would become even more acute in the late 1950s unless the schools succeeded in encouraging gifted students to continue on to advanced studies. These concerns were later echoed by the chairman of the U.S. Atomic Energy Commission when he warned the nation that its public schools were failing to maintain educational standards, especially for gifted students, thereby causing dangerous shortages of scientists and engineers and other technically trained individuals (*The New York Times*, November 27, 1955). He also charged that in the first half-decade of the 1950s the number of college graduates preparing to be high school teachers in science had dropped by 53 percent.

Statistics confirmed the existence of personnel shortages in some key professions (*The New York Times*, May 1, 1955). It was estimated that in 1954 American industry needed 30,000 engineers but that colleges and universities had graduated only 18,000. A mere 200 physicists earned diplomas in that year, and half chose not to enter the field of physics. Serious shortages existed also in industry, medicine, nursing, pharmacology, clinical psychology, and social work, among other important fields. Again, the cause of this alarming situation was attributed to the schools' commitment to deal with mediocrity rather than with superiority. Teachers were allegedly geared to work with average or even below-average students, with the result that the ablest were often disregarded. Many dropped out of school before graduation or refused to go on to college after four years of high school. The consequences of neglecting the brightest students were echoed clearly at the Ninety-third Annual Convention of the National Education Association (*The New York Times*, July 6, 1955). A committee report pointed out that each year 200,000 outstanding high school graduates did not enroll in college and that an equal number dropped out of college before graduation. The report went on to warn that an annual loss of 400,000 highly trained men and women could force the United States to lose its superiority to the Soviet Union in the realm of technology.

Aside from the exhortative statements and surveys dramatizing the failure to educate gifted children, there was also evidence of scholarly activity in the early part of the 1950s. Few people could forecast the impact of Guilford's paper, "Creativity," on subsequent research pertaining to the nature and measurement of productive thinking when it was first published in 1950. It encouraged psychometrists to abandon the assumption that tests of general intelligence such as those developed in the early part of the century by Terman could be used to locate the pool of children out of which virtually all the gifted would probably emerge. Instead, Guilford's model brought attention to multiple aptitudes, including divergent production or "creativity" as it is sometimes called. His ideas about creativity and its measurement were later adapted by Getzels and Jackson (1958) in their comparison of "high-creative, low-IQ" and "high-IQ, low-creative" students at the University of Chicago Campus High School. This study had a stunning influence on educational researchers because it announced a breakthrough in the use of so-called "creativity" measures to identify a talent resource that is supposedly overlooked by tests of general intelligence.

The question of whether instruments for assessing creativity can locate otherwise undiscoverable talent has never been fully settled (Crockenberg, 1972), but protagonists for the use of such tests have inspired widespread enthusiasm for them in identifying gifted children ever since. The rush to publish on the subject eventually picked up so much momentum that from June 1965 to June 1966 there were as many as 1,250 bibliographic entries on creativity in professional journals comprising fully two thirds of all studies of giftedness and talent in that year. This equaled the total output on creativity for all the preceding five years, for all the ten years before that, and for all the years from 1850 to 1950. Thus we see that in the early 1950s a foundation of sorts was laid for later research and advocacy on behalf of gifted children.

But despite the work of specialists on the gifted and the portents and premonitions concerning the Soviet Union's strides in building its talent reservoir, there was no serious action in America's schools until *Sputnik* was launched in 1957. At that time, the rhetoric started to become more strident and the research more abundant, and they either produced or accompanied radical changes in public education. The country was convinced that the Russians had slipped ahead of it in space technology because of its insufficient manpower to advance the sciences. Predictably, the schools were singled out as scapegoats, much as the Pearl Harbor military had been when America was caught napping at the time of another kind of surprise enemy attack. Here was an opportunity to denigrate public education as Bestor and Lynd had done only a few years earlier.

Prominent among the critics was Admiral Hyman Rickover, famous as the "father" of the atomic submarine and long an advocate of programs that would identify and educate an intellectual elite for leadership in our country. Rickover saw a deadly link between scientific advancement and military strength and warned that the Soviets were moving ahead menacingly on both fronts. Ennobling excellence was no longer just a means of improving the quality of life in a free society; it had also become a key to the survival of the free world. We were living through a period of national peril, and the only way to meet the Soviet threat, according to Rickover, was to stockpile brains in the sciences as rapidly as possible (Rickover, 1959). Before it could be accomplished, however, we had to overcome our traditional guilt about singling out the gifted for special opportunities at school. Rickover observed that "anti-intellectualism has long been our besetting sin. With us, hostility to superior intelligence masquerades as belief in the equality of man and puts forth the false claim that it is undemocratic to recognize and nurture superior intelligence" (Rickover, 1960, p. 30). America could no longer indulge in such a false sense of egalitarianism. Its task was to earmark superior students for an enriched education and to dedicate their abilities to the defense of their country.

Beyond the military advantages of producing knowledge in technology, there was also the prestige factor that Rickover saw clearly. "The biggest mistake we can make," he wrote, "is to look upon the Russian challenge as purely military. On the contrary, it affects every aspect of our way of life, even those we consider private. . . . Whatever the formal relationships between Russia and the free world may be at any given time, the technological race will not cease. I do not believe the Russians will *ever* stop trying to surpass us" (1960, p. 130). If anything, this forecast has proved to be an understatement, as evidenced by the ideological competition in every possible arena, including even the Olympics, that continues to grow in intensity.

Rickover lacked the formal credentials to qualify as an educator or educationist. This made his condemnation of the schools for failing to produce sufficient numbers of scientists unacceptable to many professionals in the field. It was difficult for them to concede that anyone who was not a "member of the lodge" should be taken seriously in such matters, particularly if his ideas about existing school programs were unflattering. Nevertheless, he reached a large and often sympathetic audience through his jeremiads even though he was expressing views about subjects outside his specialized field.

In retrospect, Rickover's thoughts are of historic importance because they were expressed by a man whose own career symbolized the marriage between science and the military. His criticisms of public schools were basically motivated by concerns about our national security. This coupling of education and defense became public policy through a significantly titled piece of legislation, the National Defense Education Act of 1958, which revealed a new and far more critical role for the schools than they had ever played before. While remaining obliged to produce an enlightened people capable of living together responsibly in a democratic system of government, schools were also in the business of protecting us from being buried ideologically, and perhaps militarily too, by a fearsome foreign power. The act provided funds to strengthen six components of American education, one of which was the identification of gifted children. In addition, it set aside money to help schools mount programs in science, mathematics, and foreign languages, which showed where the emphasis in high-level education was to be placed.

Meanwhile, the nation kept careful watch of scientific developments in the Soviet Union. Also monitored were the rates at which Soviet education was producing new scientists and the kind of training they received in the process. Invariably, invidious comparisons were made between the enemy's system and ours. One report claimed that, before graduating from a Russian high school, a student had to have completed five years of physics, biology, and a foreign language, four years of chemistry, one year of astronomy, and as many as ten years of mathematics (*Soviet Commitment to Education*, 1959). Our own graduates were woefully undereducated by comparison. Even worse, the young people in American colleges earning science degrees and committing their talents to defense-related professions did not compare in number with their counterparts in the Soviet Union.

It was essential to build up our supply of high-level human resources quickly or else risk seeing the national emergency deteriorate into a national catastrophe. In time, school officials began to acknowledge that something was wrong with public education and that there was much overhauling to be done. What moved them out of their complacency and made them more reform-minded were probably the mounting exposés of malpractice in the schools, capped by *Sputnik* and its ominous implications. Indeed, the reaction to *Sputnik* might not have been so swift and strong if the critics' cries for change in our schools had not had a cumulative effect.

THE 1950s: POST-*SPUTNIK*

When the educational community finally took action on behalf of the gifted, it did so with alacrity. Enormous public and private funds became available to assist in the pursuit of excellence, primarily in the fields of science and technology. Academic coursework was telescoped and stiffened to test the brainpower of the gifted. Courses that had been offered only at the college level began to find their way into special enrichment programs in high school and eventually in elementary school. Even the self-contained classroom, which had been a tradition in elementary education, gave way to limited departmental instruction in a pilot project called the Dual Progress Plan. Under this experiment, children were grouped as before with agemates of varied ability under a single teacher only in the social studies and language arts. These content areas were labeled "cultural imperatives," since all people require them for good citizenship and meaningful day-to-day communication with each other. However, for the "cultural electives," such as the fine arts and sciences, which are more important for careers than for survival, children were grouped according to ability, regardless of age, in a departmental program conducted by specialist instructors.

The heterogenous, self-contained classroom was rationalized for the cultural imperatives on the grounds that it reflects the heterogeneity of the society where these skills are needed in daily living. Not so for the cultural electives, which emphasize learning for the sake of specialization. Their best educational environments, according to the experimenters, were narrow-range classes taught by people qualified in specific subject matter areas, an arrangement many thought was particularly advantageous for the gifted.

The Dual Progress Plan never made it into the bloodstream of American education, but it is an example of the extent to which some educators were willing to part with tradition in servicing the gifted. It was by no means the only bit of imagination and daring that flashed into life briefly and passed on with hardly a trace. Attempts were made to introduce foreign language in the elementary schools, but that, too, did not last long after its auspicious beginning. Also making shortlived appearances were courses with such attractive titles as "The Mathematics of Science," "Opera Production," "Seminar in the Humanities," "Integration of the Arts," "World Affairs," "Structural Linguistics," and "Critical Thinking." Special efforts were even made to locate and nurture giftedness among the socially disadvantaged, most notably through the PS 43 Project in New York City, which later became the widely heralded but eventually ill-fated Higher Horizons Program. Interest spread also to school systems in rural areas and to colleges and universities where the gifted were provided with enrichment experiences never before extended to them.

There is no way of knowing precisely what percentage of our schools offered something special to the gifted in the years immediately after *Sputnik*. One reason is that most of the crash programs were never taken seriously enough by their sponsoring institutions to last long. But there were prominent exceptions that started out as enrichment experiences for the gifted and eventually changed the curriculum for all children. Much of what is taught today in mathematics and sciences, for example, is a legacy of post-*Sputnik* designs in educating the gifted. Similar influences can be felt in current secondary school programs that are comprehensive enough to accommodate human diversity without short-changing the gifted.

James B. Conant, a renowned chemist and public servant and a president of Harvard University, codified the sentiment of the post-*Sputnik* 1950s in a report entitled *The American High School Today* (1959). He offered a broad twenty-one-step plan for changing secondary education with special emphasis on core courses that were challenging in content and required of all students regardless of their career plans. His proposal also took special note of the academically gifted (defined as the upper 15 percent) and the highly gifted (defined as the upper 3 percent), and the tougher standards he suggested for them were far more acceptable to school officials than were those that had been recommended by Bestor, Lynd, and others. Perhaps the combination of the report's timeliness and Conant's personal credibility in the public schools enabled his message to get through and retain its influence to this day, while the earlier critics' ideas were taken less seriously.

In addition to the outpouring of special enrichment activities initiated in the schools during the late 1950s and early 1960s, there was massive research activity dealing with the characteristics and education of gifted children. Investigations in vogue at the time focused primarily on such topics as the relative effectiveness of different administrative designs, such as ability grouping, enrichment in regular classes, and acceleration; the social status of the gifted at school and its effect on their motivation to learn; the causes and treatment of scholastic underachievement among children with high potential; achievement motivation and other nonintellective factors in high-level learning; and the psychosocial correlates of divergent thinking processes. Professional journals were deluged with research reports and with exhortations to do something special for the gifted. So rapid was the buildup of literature in the field that one writer (French, 1959) claimed there were more articles published in the three-year period from 1956 to 1959 than in the previous thirty years.

Perhaps the most vivid recollection of the post-*Sputnik* years is that of the Great Talent Hunt. It was a time when every possible effort was exerted at federal, state, and local levels to identify gifted children and to educate them to the limits of their potential. So intense was the search for young brains, their nurture, and utilization that a parallel can be drawn between the way in which we dealt in the 1950s with high-level *human* resources and our approach to precious *natural* resources in the 1980s:

Human Resources (1950s)	**Natural Resources** (1980s)
Wherever there were possibilities of their existence, the potentially gifted were spotted by alert parents and teachers, while schools conducted elaborate testing programs to locate as many of them as could be identified.	Wherever there are possibilities of their existence, raw materials are extracted from the earth and deep seas or trapped in the atmosphere and then analyzed for their value.
Young children with high potential were then placed in enrichment programs to prepare them for professional careers.	Raw materials are then refined and processed in order to be converted from their naturally crude states to usable forms.
The gifted were counseled to major in fields of specialization where critical shortages existed, particularly in defense-related industries and professions.	The materials are categorized for various kinds of utilization and receive their final preparations and refinements to fulfill their special functions.

Human Resources (1950s)	**Natural Resources** (1980s)
The gifted were graduated, certified, or licensed with honors and then offered by their faculty sponsors for employment in jobs commensurate with their superior abilities and with the most sensitive needs of the nation.	The finished products are packaged and sold to the highest bidder or available customer.

Comparing the treatment of human and material resources is a way of illustrating several impressions of the Great Talent Hunt as it was conducted in the late 1950s. Just as we grasp at new energy sources today out of fear that we cannot continue to exist without them, so did we cast about frantically for signs of giftedness in the schools at that time. And just as we deal with natural resources in an objective, efficient manner, so did our talent hunt show signs of detachment and impersonality, as if gifted people's usefulness to society mattered more than their individualities and sensibilities as human beings.

High scholastic standards and standing, academic advancement, studiousness, and career mindedness were conspicuous themes in our schools when the bandwagon for the gifted was rolling. It became virtually unthinkable for a gifted child to bypass the tougher courses in favor of the less demanding ones. It certainly was no time for youths to do their own thing or to enjoy the privilege of doing nothing. Instead, they were brought up in a period of total talent mobilization, requiring the most able-minded to fulfill their potentials and to submit their developed abilities for service to the nation.

THE 1960s: A DECADE OF TURMOIL

The 1960s opened with John F. Kennedy's election to the presidency amid promises and dreams of a modern utopia. There was excitement in the air as the nation prepared itself to sweep away the stodginess of the 1950s and create a new age of excellence. Kennedy was particularly attractive to young people who saw in him (and his family) a refreshing blend of youthfulness, vitality, intelligence, idealism, and beauty. His earliest messages as president of the United States made it clear that brains and loyalty to the flag were among our most precious assets. He announced boldly his intention to put a man on the moon by 1970, a clear sign that we were accepting Russia's challenge for supremacy in space exploration and that the most brilliant scientists would be called upon to make such a feat feasible. This meant encouraging the largest possible number of able students to enroll in science programs that offered them the best possible specialized education. For who else but the gifted could yield forth from their ranks a cadre of scientists qualified to honor the president's commitment?

There were other hints of meritocracy in the air. Kennedy gathered around him some of the most precocious men (though few women) of his generation to advise him on governmental matters. Known then as the "Whiz Kids," some had earned their reputations as scholars at leading universities and others as promising idea men in industry. All of them projected an image of braininess with a zest for unraveling the chief executive's knottiest problems. They were gifted children grown up and enjoying the glamor of fame and power rather than living in relative obscurity as so many other gifted people have to do even in their most productive years. At last, able children had their own celebrity role models to emulate, much as budding athletes and entertainers have theirs. The nation's leaders were demonstrating by their own example that it pays to be smart at school if you want to get ahead in life. It certainly made good economic sense because the best paying jobs were going to the best educated.

It would, of course, be naïve to suggest that we had reached a point in history when brilliant students were taking their place alongside the sports stars as heroes on campus. Far from it. Research by Coleman (1962) and Tannenbaum (1962) demonstrated that acclaim among peers was achieved far more easily on the athletic field than on the honor roll. Still, the Kennedy years were making good on promises of social and economic rewards for those willing to cultivate their superior scholastic abilities despite the lack of enthusiastic cheering from schoolmates.

The bids were high for brains in the early 1960s, but there was a string attached. President Kennedy himself expressed it best in his immortal admonition to his countrymen: "Ask not what your country can do for you—ask what you can do for your country." It was a call for unselfish accomplishment, to dedicate the work of our citizens to the greater glory of the nation. Those with higher abilities had more to contribute and were therefore under pressure not to bury their talents or even to indulge in creative productivity that was impractical. The feeling during that Cold War period was that the scientist could better serve the nation than the poet.

Judging from the career plans of gifted children in the late 1950s and early 1960s, they evidently believed that the nation was worth serving. By far the largest number of students with high tested intelligence majored in the sciences, and many of them aspired to enter fields of technology that could somehow help the defense effort. Employment opportunities in these industries and professions were reinforced by the glamorizing of science as humanity's most exciting modern frontier. Yet the flurry of activity on behalf of the gifted left some unfinished business to haunt us ever since. Even the threat of *Sputnik* and the indulgence of excellence during the Kennedy era were not enough to guarantee that the needs of the gifted would be cared for perpetually at school. Instead, enrichment was considered a curricular ornament to be detached and discarded when the cost of upkeep became prohibitive. Then, too, the fervor with which guidance counselors ushered gifted youths into science programs backfired to some degree as large numbers of these students switched their academic majors by the time they reached their sophomore year in college (Watley, 1968), and many who did stay on to pursue careers mapped out for them became victims of the shaky fortunes of the aerospace industry.

On the other hand, little more than lip service was paid to the needs of the special breed of students not gifted academically but possessing exceptional promise in the arts, mechanics, and social leadership. Also, whatever work was done in defining and measuring divergent thought processes remained in the research laboratory; only a few people attempted to develop ways of cultivating this kind of ability. Finally, the national talent hunt failed to penetrate the socially disadvantaged minorities whose school achievement records were well below the national norm and whose children with high potential were much harder to locate because their environments provided too little of the requisite encouragement and opportunity to fulfill whatever promise they might have shown under other circumstances. A notable exception to the general neglect of talent among the underprivileged was the aforementioned PS 43 project in New York City, which was then modified to become the Higher Horizons Program (Landers, 1963). But these efforts were shortlived, coming to an end when a subsequent evaluation revealed no special accomplishments of the program, perhaps due to an underestimate of costs, personnel, curriculum planning, and just plain hard work needed to duplicate on a much larger scale the earlier successes of PS 43 (Wrightstone, 1964).

The gifted bandwagon of the late 1950s and early 1960s slowed down considerably, but it never came to a complete halt. The big-city programs in Los Angeles, Cleveland, and New York City, among other urban centers, had been started long before *Sputnik* and survived the changes in national priority. There is even evidence of the initiation of new efforts around the mid-1960s, such as the Georgia Governor's Honors Program in 1964 and the Louisiana Governor's Program in 1965, both of which were set in residential facilities and possibly inspired by the highly successful Governor's School in North Carolina. A few private corporations providing enrichment opportunities for the gifted also showed lasting power, a notable example being the Gifted Child Society of New Jersey, which conducts educational programs on Saturdays and during the summer months. Meanwhile, various advocacy groups at the national level, such as the American Association for Gifted Children and the National Association for Gifted Children, as well as local groups scattered throughout the states, continued to express their interests without letup during the lean years. But, for the most part, the vast majority of programmatic innovations triggered by *Sputnik* and sustained in the Kennedy era proved trendy rather than longlived despite their early promise.

Perhaps the decline of interest in the gifted would have been inevitable, considering how conflicted the public often feels about such children. Intimations of meritocracy can never fit easily into a democratic frame of reference. There will always be egalitarian-minded people who consider it necessary to withhold special opportunities that might aid the ablest to get far ahead of the pack. These critics often argue that bright children are advantaged and can fend for themselves, so why invest in them? The rationalization is a familiar one because it has circulated widely for a long time and is compatible with the popular notion of idealizing the norm, encouraging the deficient to reach as close to it as possible, and either ignoring or frowning on the efforts of the superproficient to move far beyond it. There has certainly been enough ambivalence about doing something special for the gifted to prevent campaigns on their behalf from sustaining their momentum indefinitely.

But it would be a mistake to assume that America merely grew tired of the gifted in the mid-1960s because its interest in them had been less than wholehearted all along. While attention might have declined, the fact is there were pressures forcing our preoccupation away from the gifted toward realities that seemed to be far more relevant to the events of those days. Among the most prominent were the civil rights movement, school integration, and compensatory education; Vietnam and the disenchantment of youth; and growing distrust of scientific discovery.

Focus on Underprivileged Minorities

The 1954 Supreme Court decision to desegregate public schools set off an inexorable movement toward updating the Constitution and the Bill of Rights. Once again, education became the linchpin of a national priority, this time for social justice, as it had formerly been for the Great Talent Hunt. Separatism and equality were declared an impossible combination and therefore unconstitutional. In 1955, Martin Luther King, Jr., began to emerge as a leader in the struggle for racial integration in all community institutions, including employment, housing, and transportation, as well as the schools, when he led his historic boycott of buses in Montgomery, Alabama, to protest the treatment of black passengers, an event that led to similar action throughout the country. His efforts placed the classroom in perspective as one of many battlegrounds in America's all-out campaign to raise the status of its underclasses. Educators learned quickly that pressures were mounting everywhere, not just in the schools, to take decisive action to eliminate even the subtle forms of discrimination that had hardly been noticeable over the years. It was the wave of those times and could not be ignored.

What became quickly obvious to everyone concerned was the fact that allowing blacks to sit with whites in the same classroom was a necessary but by no means sufficient step in the direction of equality. The two groups could not possibly compete with each other on a comparable footing under identical learning conditions; the disparity in readiness, motivation, and support systems at home were simply too great. The schools could not hope to meet their obligations to disadvantaged students without directing toward them an enormous amount of effort, some of it necessarily diverted from more advantaged populations, including the gifted. The cost for such an investment was staggering when judged by the standards of those times, but the investment was a good one according to Lyndon B. Johnson, who succeeded the fallen President Kennedy in the White House. Almost any monetary outlay was worthwhile since the new president's Great Society program derived from the idealistic expectation that solutions to the nation's social problems would be purchasable as long as there was general willingness to pay the price in cash.

In retrospect, Johnson's idealism may seem more like romantic naïveté, but the money was enough of a blandishment for some school administrators, college

professors, educational researchers, and curriculum specialists to become passion-
ately committed to the education of the disadvantaged. A great many other
professionals dedicated their talents similarly not for the sake of monetary gain or
for the thrill of riding a new bandwagon, but out of moral conviction that racism
and any form of inequality have a cancerous effect on the life of a democracy.

Whatever their motives, pragmatic or lofty, educators and social and behavioral
scientists placed the cause of disadvantaged children at the top of their priority list,
even ahead of the gifted. There was a new sense of urgency to avert internal unrest
by using every possible means to close the gap between the "haves" and the
"have-nots," and it was generally acknowledged that the schools would figure
prominently in the process. Attention was thus shifted away from the need to keep
our talent reservoir well filled for the sake of national defense and world prestige.
We felt that somehow these problems could take care of themselves unattended
whereas failure at school among the disadvantaged could not. In short, we were
more concerned about bolstering freedom and equality within our borders than in
playing the lead on the world stage, despite the unabated pressures of cold warfare
that brought confrontations between East and West in Europe, Southeast Asia,
and the Middle East.

In addition to diverting interest away from the gifted, the advocacy movement
for the socially disadvantaged actually contested at least two features of special
programs for the most able: (1) the use of IQ tests and other conventional measures
of mentality as a means of determining who deserves to be called gifted and (2)
grouping children in special classes for the gifted on the basis of their performance
on these kinds of assessments.

The IQ test, a major instrument for determining academic potential ever since
Terman initiated his monumental studies of genius in the early part of the century,
came under heavy attack for being biased against some racial minorities and the
socio-economically depressed. It was charged that the problem-solving tasks—
mostly verbal— favor the experiential backgrounds of children from higher-status
environments. Consequently, these students obtain higher scores, thus creating the
delusion that they are basically more intelligent and perhaps even born with
superior intellect. As a result of such charges, some urban centers with large racial
minorities, notably New York and Los Angeles, discontinued the use of IQ tests,
ignoring the arguments of some commentators (Lorge, 1953; Tannenbaum, 1965)
that the instruments per se are not prejudiced. Instead, they merely reflect fairly
accurately the biases of the society by assessing potentials of children growing up
in a system that fosters human inequality; therefore, eliminating the tests amounts
to removing a symptom rather than the cause and will accomplish nothing if
intergroup prejudice in the society remains uncorrected.

Nevertheless, there was strong opposition to the use of mental measures, not
only in identifying able children but for any purpose relating to human assessment.
The push toward greater egalitarianism aggravated a mild distrust of intelligence
testing that had always existed in the country. Many suspected that it is vaguely
antidemocratic to declare, on the basis of a test score, that a child is fated to
become an achiever or a failure, economically comfortable or uncomfortable, and
a high- or low-status person, even if such forecasts allowed broad limits of error.

Such an idea did not square with our traditional faith that in this country people are given the freedom and opportunity to make of themselves what they will. This residual aversion to testing intelligence on the grounds that it predestines inequality among *individuals* was compounded by charges that the measures discriminate against racial and socioeconomic *groups* as well. It was enough to threaten the use of instruments traditionally used for identifying gifted children.

Since racial minorities, such as Hispanics, blacks, Chicanos, and Native Americans, traditionally performed less well at school than did white majorities, it was logical to suspect ability grouping for the gifted as de facto racial segregation. Critics argued that schools were practicing blatant favoritism by creating special classes for children who were rated superior on conventional measures of intellect and also by offering the chosen few a kind of enrichment in their curriculum that was denied to everyone else. The objections were not necessarily against special ability grouping per se for the gifted, or even the enriched educational experience reserved for them because of their ability. What created the furor was the practice of denying enough children from disadvantaged subpopulations their rightful access to these classes. There was an overwhelming sentiment favoring the idea that high potential is distributed equitably among all races, privileged and underprivileged, but that life's circumstance in some groups is oppressive enough to cast a shadow over their innate competencies. And since nobody had ever devised a way in which to locate and nurture giftedness that was thus hidden from view, it was impossible to integrate special classes for the gifted with balanced racial quotas.

Some localities attempted to solve the problem by making standards of admission to special enrichment classes flexible enough to accommodate minority groups. Other communities eliminated scholastic aptitude testing altogether. The enriched curricula then had to be modified to bring meaningful education to newly devised classes of gifted children. However, even these adjustments were not enough to keep ability grouping from losing its popularity as a vehicle for enrichment. Eventually, a celebrated decision by U.S. Appeals Court Judge Skelly Wright (U.S. District Court for the District of Columbia, Civil Action #82-66) on June 19, 1967, ruled against ability grouping in the Washington, D.C., schools as a form of racial segregation. His reason may be summarized in an excerpt from his lengthy decision:

The aptitude tests used to assign children to the various tracks are standardized primarily on white middle-class children. Since these tests do not relate to the Negro and disadvantaged child, track assignment based on such tests relegates Negro and disadvantaged children to the lower tracks from which, because of the reduced curricula and the absence of adequate remedial and compensatory education, as well as continued inappropriate testing, the chance of escape is remote.

Thus we see that American education was not able to reconcile its interest in the gifted with its concern about the disadvantaged, nor could it design a satisfactory methodology for locating and cultivating giftedness among these minority groups. The dilemma was easy to resolve inasmuch as it reduced itself to a choice between battling for social justice as against pursuing excellence, and there was no doubt as to which of the two would better fit the mood of the 1960s.

Vietnam and Dissenting Youth

During the brief Kennedy era, the United States faced the communist world in three near-conflicts: the Berlin confrontation, the missile crisis in Cuba, and the Bay of Pigs. In each instance, we emerged with our self-image intact as the champions of the free world against forces of darkness. The subsequent adventure in Vietnam turned out to be disastrously different, despite the fact that President Johnson justified our entanglement on the same grounds that his predecessor defended his risks of war in Berlin and Cuba. However, what started out as a limited police action that was supposed to last only a short time, before the expected victory would be won and American troops returned home, degenerated into a nightmarish entanglement with staggering sacrifices of life and no end in sight. The leadership in Washington kept the public's hopes for a quick end to the war alive by issuing deceptive reports about successes on the battlefield. Eventually, the nation grew tired of war, suspicious of politicians' promises of a quick victory, and increasingly convinced that we were meddling in affairs of other nations rather than serving as a judge and enforcer of what was morally right in the world.

Among the many casualties of the Vietnam conflict was our perception of giftedness in political leadership. The Whiz Kids of the Kennedy years, many of whom had stayed on in the Johnson era to help formulate strategy for the war effort, eventually turned out to be *The Best and the Brightest* (Halberstam, 1972). While they were quick-minded, articulate, hard-working, and self-confident, they lacked wisdom and sensitivity to the feelings of the masses. Their cerebral artistry proved to be flashy rather than profound. They were rapidly losing their image as people who could become heroes in public life by virtue of their brainpower alone. In fact, their sad history seemed to prove that being supersmart scholastically was no guarantee of superunderstanding of humanity's most serious problems and how to solve them. Gifted youths on campuses throughout the country learned to despise them for their role in the Vietnam debacle rather than revere them as graduated honors students distinguishing themselves as national leaders.

A serious by-product of Vietnam was a growing unrest among students in the colleges. Many of them saw the war as an unprincipled adventure of the establishment in Washington and perhaps even of the senior generation over 30 who either did not care or did not understand how their actions were affecting the conscience of idealistic young people. Who were these malcontents, and how did they get to be that way?

It would be naïve to suggest that a simple set of differentiating characteristics explained their behavior in the middle and late 1960s. Kenneth Keniston, who studied them in great detail, made it quite clear that a complex mix of personal attributes, familial influences, peer associations, and school environments set them apart from their more conforming agemates (Keniston, 1971). However, it is noteworthy that a disproportionate number of disaffected youth on campus distinguished themselves in their studies at school and were frequently enrolled in some of the more enriched and prestigious programs. Their immediate targets were the colleges they were attending, which represented to them an establishment with archaic standards for success and unreasonable controls over their lives. Yet these same gadflies in centers of learning were themselves described in one study as possessing high degrees of intellectualism, defined as "Concern with ideas—desire to realize intellectual capacities—high valuation of intellectual creativities—appreciation of theory and knowledge—participation in intellectual activity (e.g., reading, studying, teaching, writing)—broad intellectual concerns" (Flacks, 1967, p. 70).

Some gifted college students took the retreatist rather than activist route and groped for new meaning in their lives privately or among groups of school dropouts; others acted more militantly by campaigning for an increase of student power in the administration of university life. The latter group could not wait to taste the privilege and independence usually reserved for adulthood and were willing to fight the older incumbents to make their presence felt. They were the ones who stormed the offices of college deans and school principals to insist on a greater voice in the governance of their educational experience. Their struggle, in short, was to get in. The retreatists, on the other hand, wanted out. They, too, saw themselves as victims of a world that threatened to suffocate rather than nurture the individual, but their response was a refusal to play the game by traditional rules, a willingness to withdraw from the rat race, sometimes with the help of drugs or some brand of bohemianism.

The unrest on campus underwent some dramatic changes over a relatively short period of time. As one observer remarked, "The key difference between the Berkeley riots of 1964 and the Columbia crisis of May, 1969 is that in the pre-Columbian case the major impetus for unrest stemmed from the perceived abuse or misuse of authority ('Do not bend, fold, or mutilate'), whereas the later protest denied the legitimacy of authority" (Bennis, 1970, p. 599). One might add that, when attention is called to the *misuse* of power, it is an expression of protest, but when there are doubts about the *legitimacy* of power, it is a sign of revolution.

The revolt was not only against institutions (educational or otherwise) and their leaders; it was also against a tradition of rationalism that sanctified ivory-tower scholarship. When Columbia rioters willfully destroyed a professor's research files, the act may have carried a message that goes beyond ordinary malicious mischief and vandalism. It seemed to imply that all the work invested in accumulating those files was a waste of the professor's talent, which ought to have been dedicated to building a better society rather than dabbling in esoterica. And to make matters worse, the educational establishment expected its brightest students to follow in the footsteps of professors like him.

Many questions were raised among gifted college students as to whether they ought to funnel their psychic energies into a life of the mind. Many were attracted to the sensitivity-training movements, which told them that "talking is usually good for intellectual understanding of personal experience, but it is often not effective for helping a person to *experience*—to feel" (Schutz, 1967, p. 11). Accordingly, the human being should not be seen simply as a thought machine but rather as a complex biological, psychological, and social organism that can fulfill itself through all these dimensions of being. Every part of the body has to be exercised to its fullest potential, which means building up the strength and stamina of its muscles, its sensory awareness and aesthetic appreciation, its motor control, and the gamut of its emotional and social feelings. Inhibiting other aspects of self for the sake of the intellect amounts to robbing life of its multidimensionality, so the task of individuals is to make something of their capacities, even if in so doing they cannot make the most of any of them.

What emerged in the late 1960s was a brand of anti-intellectualism that placed the mind in some kind of human perspective without discrediting it entirely. It also seemed to signal a partial decline of the familiar controlled, achievement-oriented youth faction that won the allegiance of many gifted individuals. To depict the change more clearly, it is useful to offer a slight adaptation of Bennis's (1970) paradigm for trends in America's cultural values at that time:

Achievement-Oriented Youth		Awareness-Oriented Youth
Self-advancement	⟶	Self-actualization
Self-control	⟶	Self-expression
Independence	⟶	Interdependence
Endurance of stress	⟶	Capacity for joy
Full employment	⟶	Full lives

This graphic representation of cultural trends is not intended to suggest that our youth had moved away from achievement orientation to embrace an awareness-oriented way of life. The traits listed as defining achievement orientation are embedded too deeply in our history to disappear or even fade appreciably. They form the essence of our Calvinist tradition that promises rewards for hard work and the self-made individual. However, while only a few young people succeeded in casting out the Horatio Alger dream from their life styles, a great many others tempered that dream with visions of "finding themselves" and indulging their sensibilities, not just their intellects, in free, creative ways that might have formerly been inhibited.

Significantly, a new utopia emerged in the form of Consciousness III, depicted by Charles A. Reich in his best-seller, *The Greening of America* (1971). One of the postulates of this new world was described by Reich as follows:

Consciousness III rejects the whole concept of excellence and comparative merit. . . . [It] refuses to evaluate people by general standards, it refuses to classify people, or analyze them. Each person has his own individuality, not to be compared to that of anyone else. Someone may be a brilliant thinker, but he is not "better" at thinking than anyone else, he simply possesses his own excellence. A person who thinks very poorly is still excellent in his own way. Therefore people are in no hurry to find out another person's background, schools, achievements, as a means of knowing him; they regard all of that as secondary, preferring to know him unadorned. Because there are no governing standards, no one is rejected. Everyone is entitled to pride in himself, and no one should act in a way that is servile, or feel inferior, or allow himself to be treated as if he were inferior. (p. 243)

Thus we see how life for campus dissidents became strangely paradoxical. Many of them espoused the habits of intellectualism generally associated with gifted students. At the same time they rejected excellence and its trappings as violations of democracy and too stultifying to the attainment of total joy and liberation.

Even those consenting to live the life of the mind learned an unforgettable lesson from the events in Vietnam. No longer could they be adjured to cultivate their talents for the sake of their country's prestige and need for survival. The war in Southeast Asia tarnished the nation's image enough to discourage such commitments among a large number of students who could potentially be counted among our high-level human resources. Besides, some may have felt it faintly dehumanizing to be treated like natural resources; it simply did not fit well with the new spirit of selfhood and individuality.

The Devaluation of Science

For many years, consuming or producing scientific knowledge was regarded as a human virtue, particularly if it helped to conquer nature in order to make humanity's life more comfortable. There was hardly much doubt that gifted children would derive great personal satisfaction and a certain measure of power and freedom if they became highly informed about the secrets of the universe or contributed significantly to unraveling some of these mysteries.

In the 1960s, however, serious doubts were raised about the value of scholarship as it had been traditionally transacted in the schools. Significant segments of campus youth began to sour on knowledge factories, and Herbert Marcuse, one of their most influential, though not so young, advocates, warned about the mechanizing, denaturalizing, and subjugating impact of knowledge (Marcuse, 1964).

Gifted youth in the age of *Sputnik* had been bombarded with the message that a lifetime devotion to achievement in science was not only in the interests of the state but of humankind in general. Such pursuits have their own built-in ethic, that any efforts at pushing back the frontiers of theory and research deserve the highest commendation because they attest to humanity's divinelike power of mastering its environment and creating its own brand of miracles. Suddenly the nation was told that science is as fallible as the one who advances it. Among the most vocal critics were the environment-minded scientists who warned that, in our enthusiasm for conquering nature, we may be destroying ourselves in the process unless we impose restraints on such activity (Bereano, 1969).

Perhaps the best known writer to forecast doom if science were to continue on its conventional course was the biologist, Barry Commoner, whose book, *Science and Survival* (1966), enjoyed wide circulation and influence. Commoner took the ecological point of view that the elements of nature are integrated, but our knowledge of these elements is so limited that we do not see their connectedness. Expressing deep concern about science's preoccupation with the elegance of its methods rather than the danger of its products, he directed much of his fire at the polluting effects of such symbols of technological giantism as nuclear testing and industrial waste. He acknowledged the need for brainpower to enrich scientific thinking, but he also warned that "no scientific principle can tell us how to make the choice, which may sometimes be forced upon us by the insecticide problem, between the shade of the elm tree and the song of the robin" (p. 104). With such caveats, it became more difficult to convince gifted children that a life dedicated to science is the kind of high calling it once was unless closer links were made between the intellect and the conscience.

Besides being tarnished because little account was taken of their human consequences, careers in science lost more of their glitter when the job market in various related fields began to tighten. The manpower crisis dramatized by *Sputnik* gradually calmed down when we began to overtake the Russians in the technology race and achieved a victory of sorts by transporting the first man to the moon in 1969. Personnel shortages in the various fields of science were no longer critical, partly because the flood of graduates in the early 1960s had filled available jobs and also because the Cold War was not considered serious enough to create new jobs through lucrative defense contracts. In fact, by the late 1960s, many Americans were suspicious of the so-called "military-industrial complex" for carving too much out of the tax dollar to support projects that they considered wasteful in times of peace. The primary need as seen then was to solve the problems of social unrest rather than to prop up our defense technology. Many would-be scientists and engineers began to realize that these professions attracted neither the prestige nor the occupational rewards that would have been guaranteed only a few years earlier. However, the supply of scientific talent did not slow down in accordance with the reduced demand, and as a result of the imbalance, many highly trained personnel found themselves either unemployed or working at jobs outside their fields.

THE 1970s: RENEWED INTEREST IN THE GIFTED

The decline of attention to the gifted in the 1960s is evident in the contrasting number of professional publications on that subject at the beginning and end of the decade. The number of entries under "Gifted Children" in the 1970 volume of *The Education Index* was less than half the number in the 1960 volume. Nevertheless, by the outset of the 1970s, there were unmistakable signs of a revival of interest. Probably the biggest boost came from a 1970 congressional mandate that added Section 806, "Provisions Related to Gifted and Talented Children," to the Elementary and Secondary Educational Amendments of 1969 (PL 91-230). This document expressed a legislative decision to include the gifted students among those receiving help from Titles III and V of the Elementary and Secondary Education Act and the Teacher Fellowship Provisions of the Higher Education Act of 1956. It also directed the commissioner to

1. Determine the extent to which special educational assistance programs are necessary or useful to meet the needs of gifted children.
2. Show which federal assistance programs are being used to meet the needs of gifted children.

3. Evaluate how existing federal educational assistance programs can be used more effectively to meet these needs.

4. Recommend new programs, if any, required to meet these needs.

The target population was defined as the upper 3 to 5 percent of school-aged children who show outstanding promise in six categories of giftedness: general intellectual ability, specific academic aptitude, creative or productive thinking, leadership ability, visual and performing arts, and psychomotor ability.

In response to the mandate, the then Commissioner Sidney P. Marland, Jr., issued a report of his findings and recommendations that set the stage for doing something significant about the deteriorated condition of programs for the gifted (Marland, 1971). He estimated that only a small percentage of the 1.5 million to 2.5 million gifted school children were benefiting from existing school services and that such services had a low priority at virtually all levels of school administration. Furthermore, even in those localities where there were legal or administrative directives to provide special offerings, little was accomplished due to other funding priorities, more threatening crises, and the absence of adequately trained personnel. Clearly, Marland saw the gifted as a deprived group whose talents were in danger of serious impairment unless appropriate intervention strategies were planned. He therefore declared his intention to initiate a series of major activities at the federal level with the hope of inspiring and pressing for more commitment on behalf of the gifted throughout the nation's schools.

As a result of federal encouragement and some public and private initiatives, the gifted were exposed to an increasing number of special educational experiences in the 1970s. While as late as 1973 fewer than 4 percent of the nation's gifted were receiving satisfactory attention at school, and most of the fortunate ones were concentrated in ten states, the nationwide picture improved considerably within the decade. Zettel (1979) reported the following outcomes of a survey conducted in 1977:

1. Nearly 75 percent of the states already had statutory definitions of gifted children.

2. Thirty-three (or 66 percent) of the states reported an aggregate increase of nearly 25 percent over the previous year in the number of gifted children served.

3. Thirty-one (or 62 percent) of the states increased their appropriations for the gifted by 50 percent.

4. Forty-two states reported sponsoring some kind of in-service training for persons interested in serving the gifted, a 110 percent increase over the previous year.

Leadership at the federal level also grew much stronger in the first half of the decade. After being in existence for a brief three-year period as an understaffed, temporary unit in the U.S. Office of Education, Bureau of the Handicapped, the Office of the Gifted and Talented was given official status by legislation in 1974. The Special Projects Act resulted in a 1976 appropriation of $2.56 million for developing professional and program resources in the field. The allocation was renewed for 1977 but did not rise dramatically above that modest level during the remainder of the decade.

There was talk about possible legislation that would change the Bureau of the Handicapped to the Bureau of Exceptional Persons, thus including gifted individuals as eligible for sustained support of their education, along with the handicapped. If this kind of move is ever made, it will go a long way toward erasing the image of gifted education as being only a periodic fad in the schools. It is admittedly a way of forcing attention on the ablest by tying their fortunes to those of the handicapped, for whom funding rarely abates appreciably. The public may never feel equally sympathetic to both groups, but it could be forced to reduce some of its favoritism toward one over the other if they are combined rather than separate recipients of support through legislation.

The thrust of activity for the gifted in the 1970s was mostly programmatic and promotional, with relatively little emphasis on research. Funding at all levels was invested in curriculum enrichment, teacher education, and training for leadership in the field. As part of their work on curriculum, many educators designed or adapted special instructional systems in order to offer experiences to the ablest that were uniquely appropriate for them, not just promising practices from which all children could derive benefits.

Some of the enrichment plans that enjoyed wide circulation include instructional adaptations of Benjamine S. Bloom's *Taxonomy of Educational Objectives: Cognitive Domain* (Bloom et al., 1956) and Mary Meeker's application of the Guilford Structure of Intellect model to classroom instruction (Meeker, 1969). Both approaches concentrate on the complex cognitive processes that the gifted are best equipped to handle. An even more popular design is the Enrichment Triad (Renzulli, 1977), which calls attention not only to higher-level intellective strategies but also to the need for introducing special curriculum content and for stimulating task commitment among able children.

Efforts initiated in the 1970s to develop distinctive curricula for the gifted may result in some lasting contributions to the field. Instructional aids that were created and distributed in many localities incorporate large numbers of divergent thinking exercises. This development reflects the foundational work of several prolific educators whose writings fairly dominated the field during the 1960s. Among the most widely influential persons has been E. Paul Torrance, who alone and with the help of occasional collaborators, was responsible for at least seven major books and monographs as well as a huge number of professional papers on the subject of creativity from 1960 to 1970. The popularity of research and materials development pertaining to divergent thinking has also had its impact on the classroom. It has clearly become a dominant theme in curriculum enrichment. However, it is not the only one that will vie for attention when inventories are taken of programs of the 1970s. Values clarification made its debut in that decade and has been gradually spreading in classes for the gifted. It introduces a new dimension in the curriculum by stimulating children to understand themselves better and to develop belief systems and behavior codes that they can justify as bases for some of the most important decisions of their lives.

Again, as in the post-*Sputnik* period, interest during the 1970s was expressed in gifted children with high social intelligence and in those especially talented in the visual and performing arts. It is hard to say whether educators were discussing the needs of such children more than their predecessors did two decades earlier. From all indications, it would seem that they only began to get beyond the lip-service level of commitment with the help of federal support. Even less fortunate were the gifted among the underprivileged minority populations who remained largely neglected, except in the arts, but not deliberately so. There is no doubt that many educators would gladly have initiated enrichment experiences for these children and that support was obtainable for such plans if they had stood a chance of success. However, the profession was stymied in its efforts to find a clear way of discerning high-level academic potential that was buried under a thick overlay of social and economic handicaps. In fact, it is hardly less difficult today to inspire the fulfillment of scholarly talent in the nation's underclasses.

In its desire to sustain interest in the gifted, the federal government funded projects designed to strengthen leadership in the field and to spread advocacy at the grass-roots level. The National/State Leadership Training Institute received federal funds to help state education departments develop viable plans for educating the gifted. In addition, Teachers College, Columbia University, was provided with support to coordinate efforts by seven universities in recruiting and training graduate students to become seminal figures in the field. It was seen as a long-range investment in the careers of men and women who had shown promise for making significant contributions in the 1980s and beyond. Besides these nationwide projects, the federal government, along with state, city, and private agencies, sponsored many regional and local programs for the gifted. The emphasis was mainly on enrichment practices, whereas research and experimentation received relatively little encouragement.

While benefiting from the work of dedicated professionals, the field was also victimized somewhat by crass promotionalism during the 1970s. There were highly skilled manipulators of audiences who organized public meetings for the gifted and turned them into revivalist sessions, filled with emotion but little substance. The interest of these opportunists was not in gifted children but rather in exploiting the real and latent enthusiasm of people who were willing to pay the fees to attend such conferences. Fortunately, this kind of slick salesmanship did not penetrate the more established advocacy organizations, but educators found it sometimes difficult to distinguish between the two.

Generally, the enrichment programs initiated in the 1970s are impressive in their variety, inventiveness, extent of their dissemination, and spirit and proficiency with which they have been implemented. The same cannot be said for research productivity. A review of the state of research for the years 1969 to 1974 reveals a fairly bleak picture (Spaulding, undated); only thirty-nine reports on the gifted had been published in that period. These efforts continued to be limited throughout the 1970s, but there are several major projects worth noting. They include Julian Stanley's (1976) studies of mathematical precocity, Halbert Robinson's (1979) investigations of the cognitive development of young able children, Pauline Snedden Sears' (1979) and Robert Sears' (1977) periodic assessment of the Terman population in their senior period of life, and George Vaillant's (1977) follow-up evaluations of the mental health status of adults who had been rated outstanding by their Harvard classmates in the 1940s and were in midcareer in the late 1970s.

What prompted the resurgence of activity in gifted education after nearly a decade of quiescence? A full answer probably will not come until future historians can view the 1970s in a proper time perspective. But the explanation that seems most obvious is America's backlash against awareness-oriented youth who turned excessively self-indulgent and against campus revolutionaries who attacked some sacred, scholarly traditions. Wagner (1976) published a scathing indictment of universities for compromising academic standards, inflating grades, and diluting degree requirements to fend off unrest among students. These were signs that the pendulum swung away from extreme egalitarianism in the direction of excellence. It is hard to imagine the youth of the late 1970s accepting the Consciousness III notion about brilliant minds not being better at thinking than anyone else and about poor thinkers necessarily being excellent in their own ways. That kind of argument may be too fantasy ridden to flourish successfully even in an egalitarian-minded society. However, there are legacies of the 1960s that were volatile enough in the 1970s to have prevented the gifted from making a comeback. They include the following realities:

1. Few personnel shortages continued to exist at the high-skill levels. The job market was glutted with Ph.D.s who could not find work in their fields of training. In 1976, the starting salary of college graduates was only 6 percent above that of the average American worker, whereas in 1969, a person with a college diploma could earn 24 percent more than the national mean.
2. The Cold War, while relentless, did not threaten any new surprises in the 1970s to shake our confidence in the nation's talent reservoir. There was even talk of moderating the confrontation between East and West through policies of detente and arms control.
3. It was not much easier in the late 1970s than in the late 1960s to persuade our ablest students that they had to work hard at school in order to serve their country in ways that only they could. National policies in Vietnam and in the civil rights movement had persuaded too many of them that the country was not worthy of such dedication. When the war in Vietnam came to an end, Watergate emerged to reinforce the cynicism and alienation of youth, including many gifted among them.
4. Quality, integrated education was as much a dream in the 1970s as it had ever been. A prodigious amount of work remained yet to be done before under-privileged children could begin to derive their rightful benefits from experiences at school. That kind of investment of effort in compensatory programs usually draws attention away from curricular enrichment for the gifted.
5. Science and scientists were still monitored critically for possible moral lapses. A growing controversy concerning value judgments in the scientific community

revolved around experiments in genetic engineering. Some gifted children may have chosen to avoid fields of science to keep their consciences clear about possibly opening any kind of Pandora's box in scientific discovery.

6. The 1970s experienced hard times and drastic cutbacks in expenditures for education. Programs for the gifted are usually the most expendable ones when budgetary considerations force cutbacks in services to children.

Despite the aforementioned lingering influences of the 1960s, the 1970s experienced a drift toward excellence after indulging egalitarianism for a while. However, the revival of interest was no more a sign of pure historical inevitability than was its decline a decade earlier. It was rather, in part at least, a sign of initiatives taken by people who believed in differentiated education at every ability level and who participated in vigorous campaigns to save the schools.

Prescriptive Teaching for All Children

When Frank Riessman published his highly influential book on the culturally deprived child in 1962, he reiterated a number of criticisms of the schools made some fifteen years earlier by Allison Davis and Robert Havighurst (1947). The charges were that the curriculum was excessively loaded with verbal content and therefore placed underprivileged children at a disadvantage; that the subject matter was irrelevant to the vital concerns of these children; that teachers espoused values and behavior codes that were oriented too narrowly toward middle-class living; and that schools were so preoccupied with teaching the disadvantaged how to become socially mobile that they were in effect trying to create a melting pot rather than striving to strengthen cultural pluralism. However, researchers did not take their lead from such charges. Instead of tampering with the old curriculum, they tried to create a learning environment that would enable the disadvantaged to meet the more conventional demands at school.

Among the most notable experiments at the time were those conducted by Martin Deutsch (1964) and his associates. They attempted to forestall educational retardation by intervening early in children's lives and equipping them with the readiness skills that they could not derive from their social milieu. This required developing elaborate ways in which to diagnose individual learning profiles and match instructional practices to them. It paralleled developments in special education for the handicapped, which emphasized prescriptive teaching based on increasingly sophisticated methods of diagnosing intellective processes. These approaches to instruction eventually led to the 1975 enactment of Public Law 94-142 and its requirement that every handicapped child have an individual diagnosis, prescription, and evaluation.

Attention to specific competencies among the handicapped dramatized the need to individualize education, with all children receiving a fair share of what is uniquely appropriate for them, regardless of how deficient or proficient they are in mastering curriculum content. It is logical, then, that the gifted should also receive special attention to accommodate their unique learning strengths and thereby demonstrate the educator's attention to human differences. Eventually, PL 94-142 may include the gifted, which would take us a long way toward actualizing the belief that democracy in education means recognizing how children are unlike each other, and doing something about it. Protagonists for the gifted have argued that the more sophisticated we become in discerning human individuality and the more inventive we are in providing for individual needs of the ablest, the more likely we are to achieve equality at school.

The Role of the Gifted in "Rescuing" Public Education

It is no secret that educators in the 1970s searched desperately for ways in which to maintain order in thousands of classrooms. This was especially true in big-city schools where 10 percent of the nation's pupil population was enrolled. The dismal picture was a familiar one: scholastic achievement levels were three, four, and even five years below norms; drugs, violence, vandalism, and truancy reached epidemic proportions; and costs climbed to such a height that there was always the danger of insufficient funds to pay the bills while maintaining an adequately staffed program. Many middle-class families fled the inner city in the 1970s or sought help from private schools in order to provide a meaningful educational experience for their children. This further aggravated the situation in urban centers.

School administrators became aware that one way in which to bring back the middle classes to the schools was to initiate special programs for the gifted. They therefore opened so-called "magnet schools" that offered enrichment activities in particular subject matter areas to interest sizable numbers of children who would otherwise have been studying elsewhere. The presence of the ablest began to make a difference in the total school atmosphere, which demonstrated that these children are capable of enhancing all education if their learning capacities are properly respected. This truism may turn out to be the most important lesson learned from our experience with gifted children in the 1970s.

A GLIMPSE AT THE 1980s AND BEYOND

The gifted are the natural enemies of George Orwell's "Big Brother" since they thrive on freedom to express their iconoclasm and to create alternatives in the world of ideas. If Orwellian predictions for the 1980s come true, it will be tragic proof of how ineffectual we have been in nurturing talent for the strengthening of selfhood in the human family. But even the failure of Big Brother to materialize is no guarantee that we will finally break the vacillation between public enthusiasm and apathy toward gifted children and continue to build on the hard-won gains of the late 1970s. Signs of the future are always difficult to read, whether they are used in forecasting the weather or conditions in society. The fortunes of the gifted are no less mysterious. There are, however, unmistakable trends that will probably impact in some ways on these children, although it is impossible to say precisely what the effects might be.

Demographic Changes

Perhaps the most important factors to influence the demand, nurturance, and supply of talent in the 1980s are basically demographic. An upsurge is expected in the number of new births as the large cohort of children born during the postwar baby boom come of age to contemplate parenthood. At the same time that the size of the 30-to 45-year-old age group increases dramatically there will be a sharp upsurge in the total number of people over age 65 and a proportional decline in the adolescent and young adult groups who were born at a time of low birthrates. The needs of the very young child, the maturing adult, and the senior citizen will therefore receive special consideration. Catering to the tastes of the youth culture may no longer be as important as it once was to budding artists. It is not easy for the tender ears of infants or of the aging adult to tolerate the stridency that had been associated with new music, theater, and poetry in the 1960s and 1970s. The kinds of social leadership, scientific research, medical care, political acumen, educational guidance, and mental health treatment may also have to change radically to make sense for the rapidly shifting age groupings of the population. These developments pose exciting problems for specialists in curriculum design who are dealing with educational enrichment for the gifted.

Along with the expected age redistributions, there is also likely to be a huge increase of highly trained personnel in the sciences and humanities (National Center for Education Statistics, 1976). Except for mathematics and statistics, which expect a 33 percent drop in earned doctorates from 1975-1976 to 1985-1986, all the other areas of concentration expect increases, including a modest 5 percent for the humanities and anywhere from 22 percent to 200 percent in the fields of education and various sciences.

As a result of a jump in numbers of people with advanced degrees, there may emerge a new class of brainworkers consisting of educators, social planners, policy makers, and communication experts. They are being mass produced at graduate schools and are beginning to assume important positions among political policy-makers and in the huge nonprofit foundations that subsidize the efforts of other brainworkers. There are also the technocrats in giant corporations who conduct market research and help to set policy. One of the most critical positions for people with advanced schooling is in the media centers where they can filter the flow of information and exert a strong influence on public reactions to issues. It may be the first time in modern history that a new power faction is emerging that can thrive mainly on its highly developed wits and remain independent of the proletariat left and bourgeois right. If such a group can gain visibility and maintain prestige as a mover of events in the nation, then it may serve as a reference group for gifted students to aspire toward joining someday. On the other hand, the emergence of an influential bloc of this kind may be resented by those who see it as a sign of the coming of meritocracy led by an intellectual elite. Any public backlash would then have a dampening effect on school programs for the gifted and on children's desire to excel.

New Sources of Talent

Even though it is impossible to determine whether events in years to come will encourage or inhibit the *realization* of early promise among children, there is good reason to expect that the pool of high *potentials* will become enlarged considerably. There are unmistakable signs of a major victory in the nation's battle against underachievement among gifted women, blacks, and various bilinguals who have perennially been victimized by minority group status. This population is so huge that any dramatic progress toward cultivating its abilities at the highest levels could have historic consequences, positive or negative.

There is always the prospect of an enormous talent pool creating a golden age of culture in America. Then again, a superabundance of brainpower may cause the supply of people with advanced training to exceed the demand by far and thus intensify the rivalry for placement in high-level occupations. And since the enlarged pool will probably attribute much of its growth to a sharp increase in the proportion and number of low-status people in its membership, the competition for jobs may not only be among individuals but also between representatives of minority and majority groups. The fierce struggle for work that ordinarily occurs when supply exceeds demand could then turn into vicious antagonism with sexist and racial overtones.

It is already apparent that women and low-status minorities are moving toward parity with middle-class white males in the extent and variety of their advanced education. Trends indicate a sharply rising representation of women in every creative field. Over the ten-year span from 1975 to 1985, only a 6 percent increase in first professional degrees is estimated for men, as compare with a huge 122 percent for women. During that same period, the estimated increase in earned doctorates among men is from slightly under 27,000 to about 28,000, or 4 percent, whereas for women the jump is from some 8,000 to about 14,000, or 75 percent. In the overall record of higher education, females earn half the number of degrees granted to males, an imbalance that is likely to change dramatically by 1990. In 1977 alone, women comprised 93 percent of the nation's enrollment growth in colleges, and in 1979 they succeeded in becoming a majority (52 percent) of undergraduates in the under-22 age group (McDonald, 1979).

Changes in the sex distribution among college students undoubtedly reflect a sharp change in the opportunity structure in the arts and sciences that once victimized women. We seem to be coming a long way from the early part of the century when Cattell (1906) included only 149 women among the 4,131 scientists (3.6 percent) listed in his biographical directory of American men of science. By

1921, the proportion of women scientists rose to 4.8 percent, a change of only 1.2 percentage points over a decade and a half (Rossiter, 1974). The story is told (Kevles, 1978) that the Harvard physics department voted against awarding an honorary degree to Marie Curie because of her gender. Also, Jane Dewey, daughter of the philosopher John Dewey, earned her doctorate in physics at MIT and spent two years working with Nils Bohr in his Copenhagen laboratory. Yet, when Karl Compton recommended her in 1929 for a faculty post at major American universities, he was turned down. A Berkeley physicist explained that his colleagues would not accept a woman on staff. In art, the creative powers of women have probably been neglected even more seriously. Germaine Greer's (1979) study of female artists reveals the tragedy of wasted, unfulfilled, and unrecognized talent in this huge segment of the population.

Considering the changing status of women in society, it is difficult to imagine that talent among them will continue to be suppressed as in former generations. Parents of school-age girls do not tolerate such biases as readily as the girls' grandparents would have, especially if the mothers of these children are themselves members of the new generation of women with advanced training and are in mid-career. Furthermore, opportunities for employment at all skill levels are increasing dramatically for women and will continue to do so in the foreseeable future. According to the U.S. Bureau of Labor Statistics, the number of men who will probably be added to the labor force from 1979 to 1995 is 8.1 million, not even half the 16.5 million figure for women. By 1995, more than 60 of every 100 women of working age will be employed, an increase from 43 per 100 in 1970. At that time they will constitute over 45 percent of the prime-age work force. Some of the professional occupations filled mostly by males possessing the requisite quota-type talents are now absorbing unprecedented numbers of women. These professions include engineering, law, medicine, dentistry, and the life sciences.

A similarly brightening future can be seen for the black population. In 1940, total black enrollment in postsecondary education was less than 50,000, and over 95 percent of that group was enrolled in traditionally Negro colleges (Pifer, 1978). By 1976, the number of blacks in colleges and universities had risen dramatically, to 1,062,000, and for the 1975-76 academic year alone, more than 83,000 blacks earned baccalaureate, masters, medical, law, and Ph.D. or Ed.D. degrees (Pifer, 1978; National Center for Education Statistics, 1978).

There is reason to expect the upward trend to continue as more and more blacks are accepted into the managerial, professional, and technical segments of the labor force. What women, blacks, and other minorities are expected to find in the high-skill labor market by the late 1980s is an increase of about 29 percent over the mid-1970s in the number of professional, technical, and kindred occupations. What they will also discover, unfortunately, is that the number of adults with advanced education will increase far more sharply, thus dimming the employment outlook for them. The total openings for Ph.D.s over the 1972-1985 period for growth and replacement is estimated at about 187,000. If present trends in awarding doctoral degrees continues, the supply of new Ph.D.s will number about 580,000 in the second half of the present decade. In all probability, doctoral recipients from all subpopulations will find it more difficult to locate work commensurate with their training. But the women and minorities are most vulnerable on account of age-old prejudices in our society, unless affirmative action practices can achieve a balance of opportunity in the lean years ahead.

Regardless of the opportunity structure, there can never be a surfeit of creative artists, scientists, writers, philosophers, and composers. Even so, the supply will depend at least to some extent upon public support for innovative activity. If past indicators of such support are also harbingers of the future, then what lies ahead does not seem promising. For example, in the sciences, public and private spending for research and development reached a peak of 3 percent of the gross national product in post-*Sputnik* 1964. By the end of the 1970s it slipped to 2.3 percent, and it supported more scientists' work on new weapons systems than on new-energy sources and increased food production combined (Brown, 1982). As might be expected, there has been a parallel decline in creative productivity among scientists. According to the National Science Foundation, in 1966 foreign countries granted American inventors 45,633 patents, while the United States gave only 9,567 to foreigners that year. However, in 1976 the number of American inventors granted patents abroad dropped by more than 25 percent, to 33,181, while the number of non-Americans earning U.S. patents almost doubled to 18,744. Predictably, too, opportunities for research scientists have diminished and, along with it, the flow of young blood entering scientific ranks in some fields. The share of American scientific papers published in the world has also dropped in chemistry, physics, engineering, biology, and psychology since the mid-1960s.

There is no way of forecasting how long the decline in investment in the creative aspects of science will continue since there are situational factors that can change the picture overnight. Nevertheless, the potential for innovative work will reach a new peak in the late 1980s when the nation will have in its midst the largest talent pool in history. It remains to be seen whether all these gifted persons will be given opportunities to produce and perform at their fullest capacity.

Trends in Diagnosing and Nurturing Excellence

Tactics for identifying children who might qualify for the talent pool of the future will probably undergo interesting change, some of it quite radical. There is no end in sight to the debate over the meaning of IQ, its measurement, and the nature-nurture issues that revolve about it, all of which arouse powerful emotions as well as scientific interest. Some behavioral scientists (Estes, 1976; Voss, 1976) have foreseen a decline in the concept of intelligence as a useful description of higher-level cognitive powers and expect it to be replaced by more diagnostic analyses of the patterns and processes of human functioning. This kind of orientation to the measurement of intellect conforms to the pioneering approach taken by Piaget (1952) in monitoring clinically the development of children's problem-solving behavior.

Feuerstein (1979) also opts for measuring the dynamics of human potential.

This means determining the extent to which children's functioning levels can be modified through what he calls mediation, or the examiner's use of appropriate helping tactics and practice materials. The idea of mediating the child's entering behavior in a test situation is novel in that it revises the role of the examiner from that of an objective observer to a participant observer who orients the child to the cognitive principles involved in the test experience. Feuerstein asserts that the organism is so modifiable that mediated learning affects not only the cognitive functioning of the individual but the structure of intellect as well. Such is the power of regulated encounters between the individual and the environment. It is a radically different point of view from that of Wilson (1978) whose theories on sociobiology are applied to humans and animals alike and who argues strongly for considering the impact of evolutionary processes in shaping our emotions and abilities. All higher-level mental activities, including altruism and morality, are regarded not as free, independently developed behaviors but rather as products of biology, specifically genetic impulses that can be traced back to the earliest of our human ancestors and to our closest primate relatives. We thus have a polarization of points of view about the origins of intelligent behavior represented by theories on mediated learning at one extreme and genetic causality at the other. The paradox is that both approaches seem likely to be leading themes in the 1980s and perhaps beyond.

One common concern of all theorists that will receive close attention is the problem of eliminating measurement error. Until now, performance testing of one kind or another has been used to assess cognitive abilities. Such a method is basically inferential since it does not monitor brain functioning directly and is therefore subject to cultural bias and imperfect reliability. The developing field of brain research eliminates inferential measures entirely and, instead, takes the shorter route to assessment of potential by direct monitoring of brain activity. Restak (1979) describes some neurometrics in which brain scientists are capitalizing on advances in computer technology and electroencephalography to measure what they call the brain's "evoked potentials." It involves a sensitive tracing of the electrical activity in the brain as it responds to external stimuli that can be administered experimentally in the laboratory. Neuroscientists expect that these electronic probes will provide more objective measures of decision-making ability, which is critical to social leadership. In a comparison of bright and dull children selected on the basis of IQ, Beck (1975) found that the visual evoked responses were consistently larger in the high-IQ group and that the bright children showed higher-amplitude responses in the right hemisphere than in the left whereas the dull children showed no such hemisphere differences. Among low-IQ, low-socio-economic groups, Beck (1975) discovered instances of the kind of hemispheric asymmetry revealed in high-IQ children, a sign that direct measurement of brain activity may shed light on underachievement in disadvantaged populations.

If brain research continues to show a relationship between neuroresponsiveness and general intelligence, the next step would be to attempt similar methods for assessing a wide variety of special aptitudes. The eventual, and most important, outcome would be a new wave of experiments in direct brain stimulation as a means of facilitating optimum cognitive potential among all children, including the gifted.

One method of stimulating the brain to function more proficiently is through drug injections. Bylinsky (1978) has reported the early stages of experimentation with a "creativity pill" to help people realize their creative potential. In preliminary field trials, writers who took the pill were able to produce more and better work. Similarly, National Institute for Mental Health scientists have found a hormone secreted by the pituitary gland that may improve cognitive functioning. Young college students who volunteered to take the drug in the form of a nasal spray improved their performance by 20 percent on various tests of memory functions that are critical to learning. These methods of enhancing human productivity and performance are nontraditional, to say the least. If they prove effective, they may hasten the advances in knowledge anticipated by Panati (1980), who has forecast such breakthroughs as developing new strains of bacteria that gobble up oil spills, discovering a vaccine against tooth decay, finding ways to prolong life, and enhancing clarity of thought at age 120.

Perhaps none of the knowledge breakthroughs will have as powerful an impact on our concerns about the gifted as will inventions in artificial intelligence. It is altogether possible that a symbiotic relationship between humanity and the computer will develop in the years ahead, with humans creating and caring for the machine while the machine ministers to many vital economic, social, and even personal needs of human beings. Microelectronics has become a multibillion-dollar industry with almost limitless possibilities of replacing the minds of many persons who are regarded as gifted. For example, one computer scientist has developed a program called ELIZA that enables the computer to vocalize questions and responses to a patient in a psychoanalytic dialogue. INTERNIST is a program that has stored within it all up-to-date information about certain physical illnesses. By questioning patients about their individual symptoms, it can utilize the responses to determine the best possible diagnoses. In another field, FRUMP has been programmed to "read" lengthy information about current events and write short summaries in grammatically accurate English, Spanish, and Chinese.

Of course, computers are subject to human intentions, and the knowledge they store is no better than the best ideas produced by the best minds. These machines are not able to initiate thought, but they have the potential for making optimal use of the most advanced thought in existence. They may therefore obviate the need to cultivate some kinds of human talent that are confined to implementing ideas created by other people. There may never be an oversupply of medical researchers and theoretical physicists, but artificial intelligence may someday compete with the special abilities of practitioners in medicine and in engineering who have traditionally been counted among the gifted. In other words, there is a good chance that the search for talent will eventually be restricted mostly to potential innovators rather than to highly skilled operatives.

It remains to be seen whether educators are prepared to adapt to radical changes in society and technology in the last years of the twentieth century. Those whose concerns are mainly on behalf of the gifted face a special challenge to reorient their thinking about the diagnosis and nurture of excellence. Plowman (1979) has expressed the view that they will be equal to the task and make appropriate changes, as shown in Table 2-1.

Less hopeful and probably more realistic is the expectation that no radical change will be introduced into the *nature* of educational enrichment. However, the *frequency* of implementing such special offerings will rise or fall sharply, depending on public sentiment that has tended to swing back and forth from positive to negative extremes. Federal, state, local, and private funds will probably continue

Table 2-1. Changes from the Present to the Future in Gifted Child Education

From	To
1. Partial or fragmented assessment and programming.	Thorough assessment and full development of individuals. Connected and holistic education.
2. Almost complete preoccupation with rational-linear thought.	Increased interest in fostering metaphoric, nonlinear thought.
3. Thinking of education as something accomplished mainly at school.	An educative society in which many persons and institutions assume responsibility for instruction and learning opportunities.
4. An educational fare devoid of aesthetic experiences.	Improving life satisfaction and even rationality through experiences in art, music, and drama.
5. Education involving mainly books, memorization, and lectures by credentialed teachers.	Education involving (a) many sources of knowledge; (b) use of knowledge as a requirement and means for fostering creativity, effective problem solving, and life fulfillment; (c) persons most capable of sharing and instructing—whether or not they hold a license.
6. Education as a means of fitting individuals into a predetermined (established) system for instruction and indoctrination.	Changing the system to meet the needs of individuals. Education that extends awareness, sensitivity, ideational fluency, adaptive flexibility, and rationality. Education that encourages making decisions upon prioritized lists of possible ways of proceeding or of solutions and consideration of data and information which transcend subject (content) fields.
7. Education as system based.	Education as life based.
8. Education as teacher-imparted truth.	Education as dialogical transactions in which teachers and students share their knowledge and discover deeper truths about themselves.
9. Education as a tool of the state.	Education as a tool of individuals.

Source: P. Plowman, "Futuristic Views of Gifted Child Education—Images of What Might Be." *Gate,* 1:153 (1979).

to support the development of appropriate methods and materials for use in the classroom, with the result that an already rich inventory of such resources should grow steadily. There is also an increasing number of newly trained specialists in the education of the gifted assuming key positions as leaders in the field. The presence of these special educators in the school world will make it more difficult for their professional colleagues to neglect the gifted. The continuous influx of "new blood" will also counteract intellectual incestuousness among veteran leaders who often spend more time reproducing each others' thoughts than creating new ones that may lead to dialogue or even debate.

In special or regular classes, enrichment curricula will probably continue to emphasize divergent thinking, higher cognitive processes, and unconventional topics of study. There exists already a huge number of teacher guides produced by school systems across the country as well as by commercial publishers, with the result that teachers have a wide collection from which to choose in planning their activities for the gifted. More will continue to come as pilot projects create new scopes and sequences for practical application. These innovative curricula will inevitably be challenged by professionals and laymen alike who either fear elitism in the schools or are not convinced that the contents of the programs are differentiated enough to be reserved only for the gifted. But if special curricula are implemented despite these objections, there may develop a tendency to expand further the opportunities for the gifted by calling upon local people in various professions to serve as mentors who can offer learning experiences that the school cannot provide because it lacks sufficient resources. IBM already has a larger education budget than does the state of Massachusetts.

In the last analysis, the survival of differentiated education for the gifted depends on how powerfully the community-based concerned groups can advocate their cause. Various lay organizations have persuaded legislators and school board members to vote for support of special enrichment, and that is what helps to keep interest alive and policymakers alerted to the needs of the gifted. If pressure from the lay community wanes, enrichment offerings will suffer and perhaps be dropped in most schools, inasmuch as these opportunities for the gifted seem still to be considered luxuries rather than necessities by vast numbers of educators.

References

Beck, E. C. "Electrophysiology and Behavior." In M. R. Rosenzweig and L. W. Porter, eds., *Annual Review of Psychology*, Vol. 26, pp. 233-262. Palo Alto, Calif.: Annual Reviews, Inc., 1975.

Bennis, W. "A Funny thing Happened on the Way to the Future." *American Psychologist*, **25**:595-608 (1970).

Bentley, J. E. *Superior Children*. New York: W. W. Norton & Company, Inc., 1937.

Bereano, P. L. "The Scientific Community and the Crisis of Belief." *American Scientist*, **57**:484-501 (1969).

Bestor, A. *Educational Wastelands*. Urbana: University of Illinois Press, 1953.

Bloom, B. S., ed. *Taxonomy of Educational Objectives: Cognitive Domain*. New York: David McKay Co., Inc. 1956.

Brinton, C. *The Shaping of the Modern Mind*. New York: American Library, 1953.

Brown, L. R. "R&D for a Sustainable Society." *American Scientist*, **70**:14-17 (1982).

Buckley, T. A. *The Drawings of Genius*. London: George Routledge & Sons, 1853.

Bylinski, G. *Mood Control*. New York: Charles Scribner's Sons, 1978.

Cattell, J. McK. "A Statistical Study of American Men of Science: The Selection of a Group of One Thousand Scientific Men." *Science*, New Series, **24**:658-665 (1906).

Cohn, S. J. "A Strategy for a Pluralistic View of Giftedness and Talent." Baltimore: Johns Hopkins University, Mimeo (undated).

Coleman, J. S. *The Adolescent Society*. Glencoe, Ill.: The Free Press, 1962.

Commoner, B. *Science and Survival*. New York: The Viking Press, Inc., 1966.

Conant, J.B. *The American High School Today*. New York: McGraw-Hill Book Company, 1959.

Cox, C. M., et al. *The Early Mental Traits of Three Hundred Geniuses*. Vol. II: *Genetic Studies of Genius*. Stanford, Calif.: Stanford University Press, 1926.

Crockenberg, S. B. "Creativity Tests: A Boon or Boondoggle?" *Review of Educational Research*, **42**:27-45 (1972).

Davis, W. A. and R. J. Havighurst. *Father of the Man*. Boston: Houghton Mifflin Co., 1947.

De Hahn, R. G., and R. J. Havighurst. *Educating the Gifted.* Chicago: University of Chicago Press, 1957.

Deutsch, M. "Facilitating Development of the Pre-school Child: Social and Psychological Perspectives." *Merrill-Palmer Quarterly,* 10:249-268 (1964).

Ellis, H. *A Study of British Genius.* London: Hurst & Blackett, 1904.

Estes, W. K. "Intelligence and Cognitive Psychology". In L. B. Resnick, ed., *The Nature of Intelligence,* pp. 295-305. Hillsdale, N.J.: Lawrence Erlbaum Associates, 1976.

Feldhusen, J. F., and D. J. Treffinger. *Teaching Creative Thinking and Problem Solving.* Dubuque, Iowa: Kendall/Hunt, 1977.

Feuerstein, R. *The Dynamic Assessment of Retarded Learners.* Baltimore, Md.: University Park Press, 1979.

Flacks, R. "The Liberated Generation: An Exploration of the Roots of Student Protest." *Journal of Social Issues,* 23 :52-75 (1967).

French, J. L., ed. *Educating the Gifted.* New York: Henry Holt and Co., 1959.

Gagné, R. M. *The Conditions of Learning.* 2nd ed. New York: Holt, Rinehart and Winston, Inc., 1970.

Galton, F. *Hereditary Genius.* London: Macmillian Publishing Co., Inc., 1869.

Gardner, J. *Excellence.* New York: Harper & Row, Publishers, 1961.

Getzels, J. W., and P. W. Jackson. "The Meaning of 'Giftedness'—An Examination of an Expanding Concept." *Phi Delta Kappan,* 40:75-77 (1958).

Gray, H. A., and L. S. Hollingworth. "The Achievement of Gifted Children Enrolled and Not Enrolled in Special Opportunity Classes." *Journal of Educational Research,* 24:255-261 (1931).

Greer, G. *The Obstacle Race.* New York: Farrar, Straus & Giroux, Inc., 1979.

Guilford, J. P. "Creativity." *American Psychologist,* 5:444-454 (1950).

Halberstam, D. *The Best and the Brightest.* New York: Random House, Inc., 1972.

Heck, A. O. *Special Schools and Classes in Cities of 10,000 Population and More in the United States.* Washington, D.C.: U.S. Government Printing Office, 1930.

———. *Education of Exceptional Children.* New York: McGraw-Hill Book Company, 1953.

Henry, T. S., ed. *Classroom Problems in the Education of Gifted Children.* Nineteenth Yearbook of the National Society for the Study of Education. Part II. Bloomington, Ill.: Public School Publishing Co., 1920.

Hildreth, G. H. *A Bibliography of Mental Tests and Rating Scales.* New York: The Psychological Corporation, 1933.

Hollingworth, L. S. *Gifted Children: Their Nature and Nurture.* New York: Macmillian Publishing Co., Inc., 1926.

———. "An Enrichment Curriculum for Rapid Learners at Public School 500: Speyer School." *Teachers College Record,* 39:296-306, (1938).

———. "What We Know About the Early Selection and Training of Leaders." *Teachers College Record,* 40:575-592 (1939).

———. *Children Above 180 I.Q., Stanford-Binet; Origin and Development.* New York: The World Book Company, 1942.

Institute for Behavioral Research in Creativity. "Preliminary and Research Manual, Biographical Inventory—Form U." Salt Lake City, Utah: The Institute, 1978.

Jewett, A., et al. *Teaching Rapid and Slow Learners in High Schools.* Bulletin No. 5. Washington, D.C.: U.S. Department of Health, Education, and Welfare, Office of Education, 1954.

Jones, E. "The Nature of Genius." In *Sigmund Freud: Four Centenary Addresses,* pp. 3-34.

New York: Basic Books, Inc., 1956.

Jones, H. E. "The Environment and Mental Development." In L. Carmichael, ed., *Manual of Child Psychology*, pp. 631-696. New York: John Wiley & Sons, Inc., 1954.

Keliher, A. V. *A Critical Study of Homogeneous Grouping, with a Critique of Measurement as the Basis for Classification*. Contributions to Education, No. 452. New York: Bureau of Publications, Teachers College, Columbia University, 1931.

Keniston, K. *Youth and Dissent: The Role of a New Opposition*. New York: Harcourt Brace Jovanovich, 1971.

Kevles, D. J. *The Physicists: The History of a Scientific Community in Modern America*. New York: Alfred A. Knopf, Inc., 1978.

Koerner, J. D. *The Miseducation of American Teachers*. Boston: Houghton Mifflin Company, 1963.

La Monte, J. L. *The World of the Middle Ages*. New York: Appleton-Century-Crofts, 1949.

Landers, J. *Higher Horizons Progress Report*. New York: Board of Education of the City of New York, 1963.

Lombroso, C. *The Men of Genius*. London: Robert Scott, 1891.

Lorge, I. "Difference or Bias in Tests of Intelligence." *Proceedings: Invitational Conference on Testing Problems*. Princeton, N.J.: Educational Testing Service, 1953.

Lynd, A. *Quackery in the Public Schools*. Boston: Little, Brown and Company, 1953.

Marcuse, H. *One-Dimensional Man*. Boston: Beacon Press, 1964.

Marland, S. P., Jr. *Education of the Gifted and Talented*. 2 vols. Washington, D.C.: U.S. Government Printing Office, 1971.

McDonald, K. "Women in Higher Education: A New Renaissance?" *The College Board Review*, no. **111**:10-13, 21 (1979).

McDonald, R. A. F. *Adjustment of School Organization to Various Population Groups*. New York: Teachers College, Columbia University, 1915.

Meeker, M. *The Structure of Intellect: Its Interpretation and Uses*. Columbus, Ohio: Charles E. Merrill Publishing Company, 1969.

Miles, C. C. "Gifted Children." In L. Carmichael, ed., *Manual of Child Psychology*, pp. 984-1063. New York: John Wiley & Sons, 1954.

National Center for Education Statistics. *Projections of Education Statistics to 1985-1986*. Washington, D.C.: U.S. Government Printing Office, 1976.

―――. *The Condition of Education, 1978* M.A. Golladay and J. Noell, eds., Washington, D.C.: U.S. Government Printing Office, 1978.

National Educational Association. *Education of the Gifted*. Research Bulletin of the National Educational Association, Vol. 19, no. 4. Washington, D.C.: Research Division, National Educational Association, 1941.

National Educational Association. *Trends in City School Organization, 1938-1948*. Research Bulletin of the National Educational Association, Vol. 27, no. 1. Washington, D.C.: Research Division, National Educational Association, 1949.

Nisbet, J. F. *The Insanity of Genius*. London: Kegan Paul, Trench, Trubner & Co. Ltd., 1891.

Noller, R. B., S. J. Parnes, and A. M. Biondi. *Creative Actionbook*. New York: Charles Scribner's Sons, 1976.

Olson, W. C., and B. O. Hughes. "The Concept of Organismic Age." *Journal of Educational Research*, **35**:525-527 (1942).

Otto, H. J. *Elementary School Organization and Administration*. New York: Appleton-Century-Crofts, 1944.

Panati, C. *Astonishing Advances in Your Lifetime in Medicine, Science, and Technology.* Boston: Houghton Mifflin Company, 1980.

Parnes, S. J. *Creativity: Unlocking Human Potential.* Buffalo, N.Y.: D.O.K. Publishers, 1972.

Piaget, J. *The Origins of Intelligence in Children.* New York: International Universities Press, 1952.

Pifer, A. "Black Progress: Achievement, Failure, and an Uncertain Future." Reprinted from the *1977 Annual Report,* Carnegie Corporation of New York, 1978.

Plato, *The Republic,* chap. iii. Translated into English by Benjamin Jowett. New York: Modern Library, 1941.

Plowman, P. "Futuristic Views of Gifted Child Education—Images of What Might Be." *Gate,* **1**:142-155 (1979).

Reich, C. A. *The Greening of America.* New York: Random House, 1971.

Renzulli, J. S. *The Enrichment Triad.* Mansfield, Conn.: The Creative Learning Press, 1977.

Restak, R. M. *The Brain: The Last Frontier.* Garden City, N.Y.: Doubleday & Company, Inc., 1979.

Rickover, H. G. *Education and Freedom.* New York: E.P. Dutton & Co., Inc., 1959.

———. "Don't Hamstring the Talented." *The Saturday Evening Post,* February 13, 1960, pp. 30, 126-130.

Riessman, F. *The Culturally Deprived Child.* New York: Harper Bros., 1962.

Robinson, H. B., et al. "Early Identification and Intervention." In A.H. Passow, ed., *The Gifted and Talented: Their Education and Development.* The Seventy-Eighth Yearbook of the National Society for the Study of Education, pp. 138-154. Chicago, Ill.: The University of Chicago Press, 1979.

Rossiter, M. W. "Women Scientists in America Before 1920." *American Scientist,* **62**:312-323 (1974).

Schutz, W. C. *Joy.* New York: Grove Press, 1967.

Sears, P. S. "The Terman Studies of Genius, 1922-1972." In A.H. Passow, ed., *The Gifted and the Talented: Their Education and Development,* The Seventy-eighth Yearbook of the National Society for the Study of Education, pp. 75-96. Chicago, Ill.: University of Chicago Press, 1979.

Sears, R. R. "Sources of Life Satisfactions of the Terman Gifted Men." *American Psychologist,* **32**:119-128 (1977).

Soviet Commitment to Education. Bulletin No. 16. Washington, D.C.: U.S. Department of Health, Education, and Welfare, Office of Education, 1959.

Spaulding, R. L. "Summary Report of Issues and Trends in Research on the Gifted and Talented." Mimeo (undated).

Spearman, C. E. *Abilities of Man: Their Nature and Measurement.* New York: Macmillan Publishing Co., Inc., 1927.

Stanley, J. C. "The Study of Mathematically Precocious Youth." *Gifted Child Quarterly,* **20**:246-283 (1976).

Tannenbaum, A. J. *Adolescents' Attitudes Toward Academic Brilliance.* New York: Teachers College Press, 1962.

———. "The IPAT Culture Fair Intelligence Test: A Critical Review." In D. Buros, ed., *Sixth Mental Measurements Yearbook,* pp. 721-723. Highland Park, N.J.: The Gryphon Press, 1965.

Taylor, C. W. "Developing Effectively Functioning People." *Education,* **94**:99-110 (1973).

Terman, L. M. "The Binet-Simon Scale for Measuring Intelligence: Impressions Gained by

Its Application upon Four Hundred Nonselected Children." *Psychological Clinic*, **5**:199-206 (1911).

———, et al. *Mental and Physical Traits of a Thousand Gifted Children* (preface). Stanford, Calif.: Stanford University Press, 1925.

Thorndike, E. L., et al. *The Measurement of Intelligence*. New York: Teachers College, Columbia University, 1926.

Torrance, E. P. *Torrance Tests of Creative Thinking*. Princeton, N.J.: Personal Press, 1966.

Vaillant, G. E. *Adaptation to Life*. Boston: Little, Brown, 1977.

Voss, J. F. "The Nature of the Nature of Intelligence." In L.B. Resnick, ed., *The Nature of Intelligence*, p. 307-315. Hillsdale, N.J.: Lawrence Erlbaum Associates, 1976.

Wagner, G. *The End of Education*. South Brunswick, N.J.: A.S. Barnes, 1976.

Wallach, M. A., and N. Kogan. *Modes of Thinking in Young Children*. New York: Holt, Rinehart and Winston, Inc., 1965.

Watley, D. J. *Stability of Career Choices of Talented Youth*. Evanston, Ill.: National Merit Scholarship Corporation, 1968.

Whipple, G. M., ed. *Report of the Society's Committee on the Education of the Gifted*. The Twenty-third Yearbook of the National Society for the Study of Education. Bloomington, Ill.: Public School Publishing Co., 1924.

Wilson, E. O. *On Human Nature*. Cambridge, Mass.: Harvard University Press, 1978.

Witty, P., ed. *The Gifted Child*. Lexington, Mass.: D.C. Heath & Company, 1951.

———. "Who Are the Gifted?" In N. B. Henry, ed., *Education of the Gifted*. The Fifty-seventh Yearbook of the National Society for the Study of Education, Part II, pp. 41-63. Chicago: University of Chicago Press, 1958.

———, and H. C. Lehman. "Religious Leadership and Stability." *Psychological Review*, **36**:56-82 (1929). (a)

———, and H. C. Lehman. "Nervous Instability and Genius: Poetry and Fiction." *Journal of Abnormal and Social Psychology*, **24**:77-90, 1929. (b)

———, and H. C. Lehman. "Nervous Instability and Genius: Some Conflicting Opinions." *Journal of Abnormal and Social Psychology*, **24**:486-497 (1930).

Wolfle, D. *America's Resources of Specialized Talent*. New York: Harper & Row, Publishers, 1954.

Wrightstone, J. W., et al. *Evaluation of the Higher Horizons Program for Underprivileged Children*. New York: Board of Education of the City of New York, 1964.

Yoder, A. H. "The Study of the Boyhood of Great Men." *Pedagological Seminary*, **3**:134-156 (1894).

Zettel, J. J. "Gifted and Talented Education over a Half-Decade of Change." *Journal for the Education of the Gifted*, **3**:14-37 (1979).

Zigler, E. "The Nature-Nurture Issue Reconsidered." In H. C. Haywood, ed., *Social-Cultural Aspects of Mental Retardation*, pp. 81-106. New York: Appleton-Century-Crofts, 1970.

PART II

Issues in Defining Giftedness

Among the miracles of the human psyche is its power to generate an almost endless variety of competencies, most of which rarely ever develop at all in a person's lifetime. Of the relatively few that are widely nurtured to any extent, most are either dulled or atrophied through neglect. And of the fewer still that are burnished to brilliance, some succeed in attracting public acclaim as signs of excellence, while other highly perfected aptitudes requiring no less braininess remain unheralded and sometimes unnoticed.

Chapter 3

Dimensions of Excellence

The Guinness Book of World Records reports on many people who perform superbly without being recognized publicly as truly eminent. There are even instances of individuals possessing dubious, if not dishonored, talent. One famous example is Mozart's operatic character, Don Giovanni (Don Juan), who is glorified by his servant, Leporello, in the famous "Catalogue Aria" for the impressive numbers of amorous conquests he has made all over Europe (especially in Spain). The Don's *tour de force* is a staggering display of social intelligence of sorts, if that is what it takes to become one of the world's greatest seducers of women. It may even have been enough to immortalize him as a tragic hero who, like so many others in classical and Western literature, was destroyed because he indulged in too much of a good thing. But it is hardly the stuff of which greatness is made, at least as the world acknowledges it in the history of ideas or service to humanity. Nor are Annie Oakley and Frank Butler, in Irving Berlin's *Annie Get Your Gun*, likely candidates for any Hall of Fame by virtue of the credentials they present in their one-upmanship duet, "Anything You Can Do I Can Do Better." School and society simply do not lavish honors on people for "long-distance spittin' " or the marksmanship required to "shoot a partridge with a single cartridge," despite the great psychomotor skills that are apparently involved in such feats.

Since the public valuates only some talents as evidence of excellence, it is fair to ask on what basis the choices are made. Why is ballet classified among the more celebrated art forms, whereas gymnastics, acrobatics, and figure skating never rise above the level of popular entertainment? What distinguishes between high-brow and low-brow creativity? Surely not the number of neural connections or size of audiences involved. Aesthetic values are not helpful either in clarifying the differences since they are so subjective; besides, all kinds of freakish exhibitionism may qualify on that basis.

Equating excellence with the ability to create beauty or to enhance the human condition is also problematic since it can lead to the logical adsurdity that pure mathematics should be excluded for failing to measure up on either count. It is a rare person who is sensitive enough to recognize artistry in mathematical abstractions or trusting enough to believe that what is theoretical and obscure in mathematics today could someday lead to practical outcomes. Still, the failure of renowned mathematicians to make sense aesthetically or practicably to all but a tiny handful of gifted colleagues has not prevented them from being revered by the masses for their intellect.

It is hard to know precisely why some extraordinary behaviors are considered gifted and others are not. Much depends on public tastes that are too subjective and ephemeral to be captured by rules of logic. But even though we rely so often on "gut feelings" rather than on clear rationales in deciding what belongs in the galaxy of high-level talent, there is remarkable consensus in most instances, and inexplicable disagreements in some. Dramatic theater, for example, is universally accepted as a major talent domain, whereas sports is far more controversial, despite the fact that both work hard at arousing pity and fear in their respective audiences. Pros and cons about the qualifications of athletics are hardly persuasive since they rely more on emotion than on reason. The same can be said about some types of human performance that attract *unanimous* pros *or* cons.

FOUR CATEGORIES OF TALENT

To understand where logic prevails in determining what is talent and where the interpretation is more arbitrary, it is useful to take a closer look at the way in which the concept is defined in contemporary literature. Khoury and Appel (1977) report what seems to be widespread disagreement about the meaning of giftedness. The lack of consensus may explain why so many exchanges of research findings in the field sound like confusion around a modern Tower of Babel, except that in this instance there is a single language with multiple referents, whereas the reverse seemed to be the case around the biblical Tower. But part of the problem may be cleared up by recognizing that there are various perspectives from which to study talent. Some educators view it in relation to the worlds of knowledge and human activity in which excellence is celebrated. Others deal with it in utilitarian terms, with emphasis on its service in the world of work. Others still focus on psychological powers that underlie exemplary performance and productivity. Every one of these perspectives basically recognizes four kinds of high-level ability, all of them extremely taxing to the brain in one way or another. They may be classified as (1) scarcity, (2) surplus, (3) quota, and (4) anomalous talents.

Scarcity Talents

Of the four categories of talent, those referred to here as *scarcity talents*, are forever in short supply. The world is always in need of people inventive enough to make life easier, safer, healthier, and more intelligible. Although it takes only a single Jonas Salk to achieve the breakthrough in conquering polio, there can never be enough talent like his for the great leaps forward that still need to be made in medical science. The same can be said for an Abraham Lincoln in political leadership, a Martin Luther King, Jr., in race relations, and a Sigmund Freud in mental health. Society will always venerate such talents as they appear, while thirsting for more and more since the shortage can never be filled, principally because its motives are more self-preserving than self-serving. It makes sense, therefore, to consider these special abilities as symbols of excellence.

Surplus Talents

While there is good reason for society to accept scarcity talents as examples of human excellence, the rationale is not always so clear for qualifying a second type, called *surplus talents*. Here, too, only a handful has the ability to excel, and some of them achieve celebrity status, which means that they are the most widely recognizable people in the eyes of the general public. Despite their fame and fortune, they are treated as "divine luxuries" capable of beautifying the world without guaranteeing its continued existence. Pablo Picasso, the artist, and Emily Dickinson, the poet, are examples of surplus talents who are more readily familiar to the layperson than are some major scarcity talents such as Alexander Fleming, the discoverer of penicillin, or the Bell Laboratory scientists who discovered the transistor. But even though fame is enough of a spur to stimulate neophytes toward careers in surplus talent fields, public encouragement clearly favors following in the footsteps of persons possessing scarcity talents and, it is hoped, going beyond the farthest reaches of their footsteps.

Of course, a Bach and a Monet are always welcome as cultural assets; in that sense theirs would appear to be scarcity talents. But the need represents a *craving* for ways in which to enhance the quality of life rather than a *demand* for finding means of preserving life itself. A craving can be satisfied, in this case, with what already exists in our cornucopia of talent. There is no compulsion to produce as many artists, musicians, actors, and writers as possible even if they are welcomed when they do appear. They should therefore be considered surplus (*not* superfluous) talent, unlike those recognized for their potential of someday contributing to global peace, conquering cancer, eliminating hunger, curing mental illness, and easing racial tensions.

The terms "scarcity talents" and "surplus talents" are not intended to express value judgments, as if one were inferior to the other. They are simply different in the *kinds* (rather than the *amounts*) of appreciation they elicit from society. Scarcity talents are treated as if they were vital commodities or natural resources that will always be in short supply as long as utopia is yet to be found. Their primary preoccupation is fathoming the unknown and even the unknowable, and modern Western society has committed itself to investing all it can to further such an enterprise. Surplus talents, on the other hand, are treated with deference for being precious in an intrinsic sense, not because the demand exceeds the supply. Instead of building knowledge to reveal the unknown, they create meaning to sweep away meaninglessness. The criteria for excellence among the surplus talents are not success oriented, as in scarcity talents, but rather are subject to value judgments by tastemakers. Critical acclaim determines who shall be regarded as gifted and also what kinds of human activities are highbrow or lowbrow. Even popularity is not always a reliable barometer of excellence. The media star who has become a celebrity in millions of households may be considered a person of modest abilities by the same critics who see signs of greatness in a relatively obscure performer.

Quota Talents

Quota talents fall somewhere between the first two categories. They include specialized, high-level skills needed to provide goods and services for which the market is limited. The job to be done is fairly clear; there are no creative break-throughs expected and no way of knowing precisely how long the opportunities for such work will last. Job openings for the relatively few who qualify depend on supply and demand, which can be irregular and geographically bound. Thus, a person with aptitudes for local political leadership has a chance of becoming elected only on the first Tuesday in November, provided that an appropriate vacancy in public office exists on that day. Physicians, teachers, engineers, lawyers, commercial artists, and business executives are but a few of the kinds of highly skilled people whose work is valuable but sought after in limited numbers. Some-times there are scarcities of such talents, as in the case of physicians needed in poverty-stricken communities, and sometimes there are surpluses, such as liberal arts Ph.D.s who are working at unskilled jobs because they cannot find faculty positions that may be filled by less capable people hired ahead of them and protected by tenure policies.

As in the case of scarcity talents, quota talents are subject to popular demand, but only up to the point where the public feels that its needs for such productivity are being met. For example, major symphony orchestras are kept alive by adoring audiences that crave first-rate performances played by first-rate musicians. Some-times there are vacancies to be filled in orchestral sections, and the search is on for candidates who qualify. But the number of such positions is necessarily limited to the number of orchestras the public is willing to support. Hence, we have a quota system against which to measure shortage and surplus.

The need for quota talents takes the form of both demands and cravings. But sometimes we fail to distinguish between formal credentials and performance qualifications for highly-skilled work. Even though long-term training is required before entering quota talent fields, the ability to do the job varies from one person to the next. Those who are certified as physicians, teachers, social workers, or clinical psychologists, and gain employment in their respective fields of work, are not necessarily talented. They may be formally educated for their jobs, but completing a course of study successfully is no guarantee that they are able to operate brilliantly in the field. Others with less aptitude to measure up to the book-learning requirements might have been able to develop the practical skills to serve just as competently as most qualified professionals. In fact, the skill demands of a professional task may sometimes be easy enough for *most* people to master, thus disqualifying it as proof of high-level talent. For example, those who are midwives and teacher aides do chores that are often associated with the work of professionals, and yet they are not considered gifted in the familiar sense of the term. Quota talents, therefore, have to be inventoried on the basis of needs for specific sophisticated services and products rather than through a head count of people licensed but often under- or overqualified to do such work.

Anomalous Talents

Finally, there are *anomalous talents*, which reflect how far the powers of the human mind and body can be stretched and yet not be recognized for excellence. They include many prodigious feats, some having practical value, others being appreciated for the amusement they provide. Speed reading, mastery of mountains of trivia, gourmet cooking, trapeze artistry, performance of complex mathematical calculations faster than a computer, and even the aforementioned records boasted in Mozart's *Don Giovanni* and Irving Berlin's *Annie Get Your Gun* are only a few examples of such talents. This is the only category that contains socially disapproved skills such as wily interpersonal behavior and demagoguery, which may require as much ingenuity as do leadership skills, except that they are detriments rather than benefits to humanity. In this category there are also "extinct" abilities such as oratory and various types of manual craftsmanship that would belong among the scarcity, surplus, or quota talents in another era, but can now be considered anomalous talents since they have become anachronisms.

What remains unaccountable are the bases for excluding many forms of great entertainment from the realms of excellence and thereby causing them to be grouped among the anomalous talents. Stardom in the circus or in sports may attract legions of fans and yet fail to be counted among the performing arts, whereas virtuosity on the concert stage is so regarded even though the adoring audiences are much smaller. There is no clear logical or psychological line of reasoning that explains these discriminations satisfactorily. Perhaps the best we can do in some instances is to ascribe such judgments to caprice or other such vagaries, knowing full well that by so doing we remove the possibility of having guidelines to help to define what is high-level talent. We will simply have to be satisfied with applying objective standards for talent belonging in the scarcity and quota categories and with the judgmental feelings of critics for those talents that are surplus and anomalous.

Chapter 4

The Eyes of Different Beholders

It is misleading to characterize talent as rare brainpower operating without temporal or cultural discipline. Talent needs to fit into its own *Zeitgeist* in order to be recognized and appreciated. In a particular period of Western history, architectural talent was devoted to designing functional huts to serve the housing needs of the "common folk" who predominated in the society of the time. Music and art were also of the folk variety that revealed the thoughts, emotions, and human relationships of a simple *Gemeinschaft*; and literature was exemplified by the Beowulfian epic, with its explorations of antiquity and the passions and conflicts that are vital to the folklore of a people. The gifted did not sign their names to the great architecture, art, music, or literature they produced because common folk in the aggregate rather than individuals talented or otherwise were the prime subjects of attention in that period.

In another era, architectural talent was devoted to the cathedral, art to spiritual representations, music to the Gregorian chant, literature to *Everyman*, and politics moved from the *Gemeinschaft* to church-state domination. Again, anonymity prevailed, this time because extraordinary performance or productivity was not meant to reflect on the greatness of its creator but rather on the sanctity of a Creator of all humankind. There followed a period in Western history when architectural genius was reflected not in functional huts or in the cathedral but in the palace, and the subject of art was not common folk or supernaturalism, but the portraiture of aristocracy by a Gainesborough, a Goya, and a Fragonard. Musical idioms had moved from folk song and dance and then the Gregorian chant to the Haydn quartet that was meant to please royal ears. Literature was represented by its classically elegant Alexander Pope couplet, a far cry from the turbulent epic or morality play, and politics was dominated by the monarchy. Gifted individuals could call attention to themselves through their great works since individuals had emerged out of the shadows of the *Gemeinschaft* and were becoming less and less dwarfed by an overpowering divinity. Humankind moved toward the center of its universe and the nobility celebrated the excellent among human beings as evidence of their perfectibility.

It is virtually unthinkable for a twentieth century gifted dramatist to write a morality play in medieval style or a composer to create an *Eine Kleine Nachtmusik* to entertain in the salons of aristocracy. There has to be a perfect match between a person's particular talent and the readiness of society to appreciate it. Otherwise, high potential will remain stillborn or mature to serve an unappreciating audience that may regard it either as anachronistic if it is a throwback to earlier times or as too avant-garde if the times are not yet ready for it. There is always room for wondering whether Einstein would have been able to make a contribution to theoretical physics, or whether the scientific world would have been ready for his kind of contribution, if he had been born only half a century before his actual birth. Perhaps, too, he would not have been capable of creating any spectacular new theories at all if he had been born in 1950 and others had formulated the theory of relativity ahead of him. This is pure speculation, but what does seem evident is that gifted individuals who achieve breakthroughs in the world of ideas do not operate simply as free spirits detached from the temper of their times.

SOCIOCULTURAL PERSPECTIVES

Those who view giftedness from a sociocultural perspective call attention to the domains of high-level productivity or performance. One example of this approach is Phenix's *Realms of Meaning* (1964), which, he believes, need mapping before the content of curriculum can be planned. There are six such realms, described as follows:

1. *Symbolics*, including basic forms of communication through ordinary language, mathematics, and such nondiscursive symbolic forms as gestures, rituals, and rhythmic patterns. These systems are structured according to socially accepted rules of formation and transformation and, as carriers of messages between human beings, they are the most basic of all realms of meaning since they have to be used to express ideas in each of the other realms.
2. *Empirics*, comprising the sciences of the physical and living world. Their content includes factual descriptions, generalizations, and theoretical formulations based on objective evidence in a world of matter, life, mind, and society. Hypotheses introduced into these realms are tested according to specified rules of evidence and verification before acceptable truths can emerge.
3. *Aesthetics*, including the various arts, such as music, painting, sculpting, theater, and literary creation. "Meanings in this realm are concerned with the contemplative perception of particular significant things as unique objectifications of ideated subjectivities." (pp. 6, 7)

4. *Synnoetics*, derived from the Greek word *Synnoesis*, meaning "meditative thought," or more specifically, a combination of *syn*, meaning "with" or "together," and *noesis*, meaning "cognition." Synnoetics therefore signifies insightful relationships between people or psychological understandings about people. It applies to other persons or to oneself in the sphere of *knowing*, just as sympathy relates to individuals in the sphere of *feeling*.

5. *Ethics*, which emphasizes moral meanings that are concerned with *obligation* instead of fact, what ought to be rather than what was, is, or will be. "In contrast to the sciences, which are concerned with abstract cognitive understanding, to the arts, which express idealized aesthetic perceptions, and to personal knowledge which reflects intersubjective understanding, morality has to do with personal conduct that is based on free, responsible, deliberate decision." (p. 7)

6. *Synoptics*, which embraces meanings that integrate history, religion, and philosophy comprehensively. The tools for building such meanings are empirical, aesthetic, and synnoetic, and the outcomes are new insights that amount to more than the sum of the parts from which they are derived.

The realms of meaning posited by Phenix were meant to be foundations for general curriculum design, but they can be viewed as spheres of activity in which excellence is rewarded. Giftedness would thus be defined as superior performance or productivity in any of these realms. Holmes, Lauwerys, and Russell (1961) suggest that the domains of activity for the gifted be categorized as moral, social, economic, and educational. Society arranges these domains in a prestige hierarchy in which the distances between them are not necessarily uniform. For example, if the social realm were ranked highest, followed by the economic, educational, and moral, in that order, it is possible that the educational would compare more prestigiously with the moral than would the social with the economic or the economic with the educational. To complicate the picture, distances between them are changing constantly; in fact, realms can change places in the hierarchy from one historical period to the next. There are also subcategories of specialized activity within each realm that have their own prestige hierarchy and are always on the move in the same way that the greater realms relate dynamically to each other. Finally, it is important to note that a specific area of specialization within a realm can be more highly acclaimed publicly than can one at a corresponding level of a higher realm. This applies even to the most prestigious talents in the various categories. It is therefore possible for the most renowned exponents of aesthetic expression to be more lionized than their counterparts in the scientific research even though empirics as a group may generally be more prestigious than aesthetics.

There is no way of knowing what accounts for society's seeming fickleness in preferring one sphere of activity over another. Public tastes may change partly because of the gifted individual's own iconoclasm and creativity, which are constantly revitalizing the world of ideas. Who could have anticipated ahead of time that sociobiology, biofeedback, microsurgery, and music for the synthesizer would become new fields of productivity and performance where giftedness could express itself in the 1960s, 1970s and beyond? With such surprising breakthroughs occurring constantly in all realms of meaning, it is difficult to design programs today to prepare the gifted for an unforeseeable tomorrow. These children may therefore need exposure to studies of futurism, as speculative as it may be, in the hope that it will help them inject more wisdom into their efforts to shape life in the next generation.

UTILITARIAN PERSPECTIVES

One of the better known definitions of giftedness suggests that "we consider any child gifted whose performance in a potentially valuable line of human activity is consistently remarkable" (Witty, 1958, p. 62). The term "worthwhile" would seem to restrict attention only to skills that are rewarded for social service of some kind and are therefore quantifiable. However, Witty's ideas were not so narrowly pragmatic; he also included abilities that are personally gratifying to their possessors and that provide uncommon pleasures for others. A fairly similar definition is offered by De Haan and Havighurst, as follows: "We shall consider any child 'gifted' who is superior in some ability that can make him an outstanding contributor to the welfare of, and quality of living in, society" (1961, p. 15). Here, too, the authors enumerate many kinds of human performance, not just the ones that are service oriented, as the definition would seem to imply.

From a strictly utilitarian point of view, talent is defined in terms of manpower needs for sophisticated kinds of work. For example, society requires specific numbers of legal authorities, educators, medical personnel, scientists, social service specialists, and organizational administrators. However, as Newland (1976) points out, these needs change in the course of time. In the late 1950s and early 1960s, there were visible shortages of scientists, teachers, and physicians, but as we moved into the 1970s, the ranks in some of these professions were filled, and demand increased for legal and social service personnel. These are examples of society's *explicit* needs. There are also *implicit* needs for personnel trained to provide special skills in newly emerging professions and in promising subspecializations that are only beginning to gain significance within traditional fields of inquiry. Finally, there is a *latent* need for surplus, quota, and even anomalous talents, particularly in the arts and in entertainment.

Taking into account all of society's requirements for gifted manpower, it is possible to ascertain what proportion of the work force has to function in that capacity. Assuming that x percent of employed persons are needed to fill high-level jobs, then schools would regard that fraction of the student population as targeted for advanced training. It would also be necessary to add another percentage, y, of backup students to fill in for those in the first group who turn out to be underachievers or are mistakenly qualified through measurement error.

From a utilitarian point of view, the size of targeted and backup groups required to perform advanced-level services in our society enables us to ascertain what fraction of the highest-functioning children may be considered gifted. Newland (1963) attempted to make such an estimate by tallying the numbers of persons engaged in the fifty-one occupations that constituted the top three occupational groups in 1950. With the help of a panel of judges, he then determined the proportion of personnel in every occupational category that would be required to operate at high conceptual levels. Results showed that 5 percent of the work force were so needed, along with another 3 percent to serve backup roles. If we take the simplistic view that tested intelligence is the *only* criterion for selecting children who have the potential to fill such top-level positions, then the cutoff would be somewhere between IQ 120 and 125 on a Binet-type instrument. However, as Newland points out, even if such an approach were scientifically sound, it would smack of totalitarianism, since it earmarks young children to serve specific societal needs without regard for their individualities, which may or may not resonate well with the careers chosen for them. A deterministic system of this kind would fit easily into a meritocracy, such as the one satirized by Young (1959), in which the talented are seen, more or less, as serving the needs of the state without much regard for their own sensibilities, rather than as free participants in a democracy that is always fine-tuning the balance between self and society.

Most important, existing measures for locating the potentially gifted are too primitive to help us make practical use of the utilitarian approach in defining talent. The most that can be accomplished from this perspective is to document the nation's need for high-level personnel and to evaluate educational policies accordingly. That is what Lorge (1954) did when he argued in favor of accelerating gifted children through school on the grounds that "saving a year for one percent of 25 million children in elementary and secondary school would mean an additional 250,000 man years of productivity, or an additional 6,500 for 40 professional years" (p. 5).

Lorge's figures may be contrasted to those published nearly two decades later by the U.S. Office of Education (Marland, 1971), which reported an elementary and secondary school population of 51.6 million children, of which 1.5 million to 2.5 million (3 to 5 percent) were estimated conservatively as gifted. According to the latter data, Lorge's calculation of person-years per calendar year of productivity would have to be doubled if we used his 1 percent figure to designate the talent pool and multiplied six to ten times if we applied the more recent U.S. Office of Education figures of 3 to 5 percent. This striking discrepancy shows how important it is to consider demographic changes over time when we deal with talent from a utilitarian perspective.

We also have to take into account the changes in age distribution from one era to the next. During a period of two decades, from the early 1950s to the early 1970s, the elementary and secondary school population more than doubled in size, thus increasing by 100 percent the number of gifted children in our schools, assuming that the percentile cutoff point on measures of potential to qualify as gifted is fixed. We would then expect a larger number of gifted children born during the baby boom era to grow up overtrained and underutilized occupationally, as compared with those born in a less fertile generation. Indeed, there is some peripheral evidence to show that this is so. A study of trends in the occupational distribution of college graduates reports a decline in the proportion of young college graduates in professional occupations from 1966, when the relatively small number of men and women born during World War II entered the labor force, until 1976, when the skyrocketing postwar baby population came of age (National Center for Education Statistics, 1978). These figures suggest that Newland's estimate of 5 percent of the working population being highly skilled has to be revised from time to time to take into account irregularities in population growth. Whatever these trends mean, one impression is clear: we do not know precisely how to characterize, recognize, and cultivate giftedness in the present era to satisfy the utilitarian needs of society in the next era. The sharp declines in birthrate during the 1970s and the aging of postwar babies in the 1980s will only serve to deepen the mystery in the decades ahead.

PSYCHOLOGICAL PERSPECTIVES

Talent is a psychological phenomenon. It refers to the powers of the mind as they become actualized in rare and precious human performances or products. Some may argue that the mind is a reflection of its accomplishments rather than vice versa, but either way, an effort has to be made to understand it before determining who is talented. To date, a great deal more is known about the extent of its strength than the essence of its functioning. For example, much of the literature has referred to gifted children in terms of their high "intelligence" (Miles, 1954). But the meaning of this term as it applies to such children is not much clearer today than it was more than a half-century ago when Boring (1923) defined intelligence as something that is measured by tests of intelligence. A similar circularity of meaning seems to have befallen creativity in efforts to assess it and to propose it as a dimension of giftedness. However, those who view talent from a psychological perspective are well aware that scores on tests of intelligence and creativity are intended to provide clues rather than understandings about superior potential.

Emphasis on Genius

The term "genius" originated in ancient Rome and referred to a private spirit or deity residing in the individual and living as a helpmate and protector from the cradle to the grave. Each male had his own genius, and each female her own Juno, which had a decisive influence on a person's character in all aspects of life, not just in the realm of mental functioning. The modern use of the term "genius," referring to the highest conceivable form of human accomplishment, did not appear until the eighteenth century. Even as late as that it was regarded as some kind of personological power that moved the individual to greatness. But gradually people themselves began to be labeled genius by virtue of their artistry, in contrast to the "talented" who were considered less able and whose achievement was more clearly the result of successful education and study.

When genius became the subject of scientific investigation in the late nineteenth century (Galton, 1869), the term denoted a degree of eminence that is rarely achieved. Galton devised a normal curve of ability ranging from idiocy at the lowest level to genius at the highest, with fewer persons categorized at either extreme than at any other fourteen intermediate points in the distribution. People were then rated according to the probability that contemporaries could do their jobs as well as they. For example, Galton placed prominent English judges and bishops at a level of eminence reached by no more than one individual in four thousand. The illustrious people, or geniuses, were those who could be singled out among millions as candidates for immortality.

Galton recognized genius as a matter of reputation for greatness, judged by contemporaries or by posterity, not as something revealed through psychometrics. Even though he was one of the earliest pioneers in formal mental testing, he never used his instruments to understand the nature of genius or to predict its emergence in young people. This is not surprising when we consider the relatively primitive kinds of tests developed in the nineteenth century to assess human functioning.

Near the turn of the century, Cattell (1890) summarized some of the work that he and Galton had done on measuring individual differences. He suggested that it could be accomplished by administering ten tests, four of which dealt with temporal functions and the rest with sensory acuity or simple motor skills. Kagan and Kogan (1970) contrast them to modern tests of ability that deal with language development, reasoning and classification skills, perceptual synthesis, and decision processes. It seems obvious, therefore, that Galton conducted his studies of genius too early in the history of mental measurement to collect meaningful formal data on the subject. Nevertheless, his insights into persons who had earned renown in science (1874) led him to the conclusion that these people were endowed with superior intellectual ability, tremendous energy, good physical health, a sense of independence and purposefulness, and exceptional dedication to their field of productivity. He also felt that they had vivid imaginations, strong, quick, and fluent mental associations, and a drive powerful enough to overcome many internal or external constraints. In short, Galton seemed to regard the genius as some kind of inspired mutant possessing exceptional characteristics, albeit in different combinations according to the respective fields in which greatness is achieved.

It is noteworthy that Galton's description of the personality traits of geniuses has been essentially confirmed by more than a century of subsequent research on biographies of famous historical and contemporary figures (Cox, 1926; Roe, 1953; McCurdy, 1960; Goertzel and Goertzel, 1962; Goertzel et al., 1978). What his successors have added, however, is a much better understanding of the environmental factors that contribute to career success. They have also devoted considerable attention to the childhood histories of the subjects under study.

Biographies of renowned people usually take for granted that those who become famous during or after their lifetimes necessarily deserve to be regarded as illustrious, whereas those who fail to rise from anonymity do not qualify. But there is evidence to cast some doubt on such an assumption. The *Times (London) Literary Supplement* asked a distinguished panel of writers, scholars, and artists to nominate the most underrated and overrated books and authors during the first three quarters of the twentieth century. Among those singled out for deflation were none other than Arnold Toynbee, Andre Malraux, George Orwell, Leo Tolstoy, Hermann Hesse, and André Gide. Sigmund Freud received high marks for his accomplishments, but the interpretations and extrapolations of his work were generally demeaned. Among those judged as underrated were such lesser lights as H. G. Wells, Carl Jung, and John O'Hara, along with some hardly knowns, including such writers as Barbara Pym and Jocelyn Brooke. In a far more elaborate and carefully designed study of Nobel prizes that have been awarded since 1901 in physics, chemistry, and the composite of physiology and medicine, Zuckerman (1978) discovered enough errors of omission and commission to suggest that fame can be mistakenly withheld or bestowed even in fields where the assessment of contributions is relatively objective.

Emphasis on Childhood Potential and the IQ

As risky as it is to define and describe talent fulfilled, it is far more precarious to speak with assurance about it in its period of promise when predictions have to be made about the gifted child's future development. Studying high-level potential among school-age children is of obvious interest to educators if there is some reason to hope that proper nurturance at school increases the chances of outstanding adult accomplishment. The first, and by far the largest-scale test of the hypothesis that such developmental linkages do exist can be found in the multi-volume *Genetic Studies of Genius* conducted by Lewis M. Terman and his associates (Terman et al., 1925; Cox et al., 1926; Burks et al., 1930; Terman and Oden, 1947; Terman and Oden, 1959).* Their methodology was two pronged: the first was to identify and conduct a longitudinal study of precocious elementary-school-age children for the remainder of their life spans; the second was to conduct a retrospective biographical study of three hundred historical figures judged eminent on the basis of the amount of space they occupied in biographical dictionaries. The key to giftedness was "general intelligence," which could be tested with an instrument developed by Binet and Simon in 1905 and revised in 1916 by Terman and his associates at Stanford University. The measure thus became known appropriately as the Stanford-Binet test, which yields an intelligence quotient (IQ) denoting a person's standing in relation to others in the population (see Table 4-1).

---

*Although Terman helped to prepare the 1959 volume, he died in 1957. Several additional follow-up studies have been reported by Melita Oden (1968), Robert Sears (1977), Pauline S. Sears and Ann Barbee (1977), and Pauline S. Sears (1979).

Table 4-1. Expected Occurrence of IQ Scores at or Above
Each Half Standard Deviation Above the Mean ($\sigma = 15$)

Standard Deviations Above the Mean	IQ	Approx. Expected Occurrence		
.0	100	50	in	100
.5	107	31	in	100
1.0	115	16	in	100
1.5	122	7	in	100
2.0	130	2	in	100
2.5	137	6	in	1,000
3.0	145	1	in	1,000
3.5	152	2.3	in	10,000
4.0	160	3	in	100,000
4.5	167	3	in	1,000,000
5.0	175	3	in	10,000,000
6.0	190	1	in	1,000,000,000

Terman felt justified in measuring general intelligence without formulating a theory about mental structure or process, just as physicists of his day thought it useful to measure electricity without knowing its exact nature. Along with his daring hypothesis about an isomorphic relationship between childhood promise and adult performance, he also pioneered the idea that the gifted—children and adults alike—differed from the nongifted in degree rather than in kind. His central argument was that greatness does not reflect a mysterious, freakish mutation; instead, it stems from an extraordinary ability to exercise sensitive judgment in solving problems, to adapt to new situations, and to learn from performing various tasks and experiencing various situations. Moreover, Terman hypothesized that all people have these abilities in varying degrees, except that the gifted excel in them and are therefore most successful in measuring up to the demands of school and society.

Even though the term "genius" appears in the title of Terman's massive work, he dropped it in favor of "gifted," which he defined as the ability to score in the top percentile on his test of general intelligence and which he distinguished from "talent," or specialized ability in a limited field. According to him, great talent could come to fruition only if it is combined with giftedness (Terman, 1954). He also regarded "creativity" as a personality factor that is independent of both giftedness and talent (Seagoe, 1975).

Since the Stanford-Binet produces a single score (in the form of an IQ), there seems to be an underlying assumption that intelligence is a general factor denoting mental power that can be channeled in any number of directions, depending on the individual's inclinations and the influences of the environment. Terman was apparently comfortable with this assumption and with the consequence that a single IQ score could denote signs of giftedness even though Galton, who otherwise had a strong influence on Terman's thinking, believed in a two-factor theory that suggested that individuals possess unique combinations of general abilities and special aptitudes. The two men did agree, however, that heredity exerts a much stronger influence on human intelligence than does environment, albeit from different basic premises: Galton cited his studies of the family trees of eminent personalities (1869), whereas Terman (1924) noted the relative stability of a person's IQ over time despite changes in life experiences. Results of the longitudinal studies involving a total sample of more than fifteen hundred children with minimum IQs of 135 for the high school subgroup and 140 for the elementary and preschoolers showed that tested intelligence was a key factor associated with success in scholastic studies and in careers after graduation. Cox's (1926) retrospective investigation of celebrated individuals, in which she estimated their IQs from biographical data, had an average IQ of 155, which was well over three standard deviations above the mean. Thus, the centrality of tested intelligence in high-level talent was confirmed, at least to the satisfaction of Terman and his team.

But the conclusion about IQ figuring indispensably in gifted performance has not been accepted universally. Probably none of the people in Terman's longitudinal study will ever qualify for listing among history's illustrious personalities as Galton defined them. In an unpublished paper quoted by Seagoe (1975), Terman himself is modest about the chances of any member of his group achieving immortality:

> Looking forward to the future, I regard it as unlikely that more than 50 or 100 of my 1300 subjects will become eminent in Galton's sense of the term. It would be surprising if a hundred years hence even one should be found among the thousand most eminent persons of recorded history. In sheer intellectual ability, however, I am sure that my group overlaps Cattell's thousand most eminent of history. Although the group probably contains no intellect at all comparable with that of Newton or Shakespeare, I believe it contains many who are intellectual equals of Washington, the nineteenth most eminent on Cattell's list, and some who are intellectual equals of Napoleon, the most eminent man of history. . . . I believe that several of my group are probably as well endowed with literary gifts as were Longfellow, Hawthorne, or George Sand. (pp. 227-228)

Realistically, it seems captious to fault the IQ for failing to lead Terman to a budding Shakespeare or Newton. Perhaps he could not find any because there was none to be found in the state of California where he collected his sample of gifted children in 1921 and 1922. A full listing of the longitudinal study population has never been published, but a few names have been leaked through word of mouth and into publications. They include Henry Cowell, one of the greatest American composers of the twentieth century, and Lee Cronbach and Robert Sears, two famous psychologists who have published widely. Even if their renown fades in years to come, it would be difficult to find a Californian of their generation who achieved comparable stature in the arts or sciences and yet was overlooked in Terman's search for gifted children. Nevertheless, the popular feeling is that general intelligence, as depicted by the IQ, is too narrowly conceived to capture the varieties of talents at school. Its value is reputedly limited to individuals like those in Terman's sample, who made their marks mostly in fields requiring superior academic achievement.

Terman's characterization of giftedness through IQ is criticized not only for being too *exclusive* with respect to the *types* of talent depicted but also too *inclusive* with respect to the *degree* of ability required to qualify a person as gifted. His cutoff point for the longitudinal sample may have been so low that it dipped into a population of mostly "also rans." In a follow-up study of children with superior tested intelligence, Lorge and Hollingworth (1936) found that those who scored at about Terman's cutoff point of IQ 140 had college records roughly comparable to the highest 25 percent of the collegiate population of the country. Those winning honors at a first-rate college had IQs of at least 160, and "the children who test at and above 180 IQ constitute the 'top' among college graduates. They are the students of whom one may confidently predict that they will win honors and prizes for intellectual work. . . . Perhaps this is the point at which the term *genius* begins to apply" (p. 226). "Gifted" or "talented" children are thus distinguished from "geniuses," albeit on the same factor, general intelligence, which would argue for more intellectual kinship between them than is often suspected.

Although the IQ figured most prominently in Terman's description of giftedness in children, the total picture he presented was by no means monochromatic. A huge amount of data was collected periodically on the children's health status, social development, emotional well-being, home environment, play interests, friendship choices, moral values, and achievement drives, and differences generally favored the gifted over their less able controls. Some of these sharp contrasts were later qualified by Bonsall and Stefflre (1955) and Smith (1962) who discovered that many temperamental differences between gifted and nongifted children were related more closely to socioeconomic levels than to IQ. Nevertheless, the evidence from Terman's California sample depicts gifted children as high IQ, stable personalities, whose nonintellective strengths complement their exceptional intellect. A replicative study of one hundred children in the Kansas City, Missouri, schools (Witty, 1930) showed results similar to those in the California investigation with respect to mental, physical, and social characteristics.

During the time that Terman was conducting his investigations on the West Coast, Leta S. Hollingworth initiated major research on the nature of giftedness in East Coast settings, specifically at Teachers College, Columbia University, and in the New York City public schools. Unlike Terman, who dealt primarily with mass data, Hollingworth was more interested in clinical and educational histories of gifted children. But she, too, characterized giftedness in terms of general intelligence, establishing the cutoff point at IQ 130. Those scoring above that level were admitted to her so-called "Terman Classes" as experimental subjects exposed to a special enrichment program that she designed and evaluated (1938). She agreed with Terman that potential leaders are recognizable by their superior tested intelligence and that children with high IQs are more likely to possess other traits necessary for leadership (1938). The kind of child she selected for her most intensive and compelling study was one who could be singled out as a nonpareil among a million peers. Again, she used the criterion of general intelligence to characterize such a child, but this time she set the qualifying level at IQ 180, which was so high that in twenty-three years of searching for a sample in the New York metropolitan area, she managed to assemble only twelve children. Her efforts were repaid by the revealing outcome that IQ makes a difference for the one in a million. The target group could be distinguished from the more "typical" 130 IQ precocious population by virtue of its incredibly rapid intellectual advancement and, conversely, by its painful problems in social and emotional development (1942).

Terman and his corroborators in different parts of the country established the primacy of tested intelligence as a means of defining giftedness. His influence was so great that the bulk of research on gifted children has been conducted on populations identified more consistently by IQ than by any other *single* device. Most of the existing empirical knowledge about the nature and nurture of giftedness derives from studies of that kind of sample. Those who have little confidence in the instrument but want to learn what research says about gifted children may therefore find themselves in the same predicament as the person who loses a valuable possession somewhere on a dark street but searches for it under a lamp post because the light is better there.

Besides creating what promises to become an endless debate over the value of IQ measures in distinguishing between gifted and nongifted children, Terman contributed to the field two major ideas that have since fallen into disfavor and at least two others that have been profoundly influential. One of the discredited conclusions has to do with the constancy of IQ scores and the inference that giftedness is basically a hereditary phenomenon. There is ample evidence from major longitudinal investigations, including the Harvard Growth Study (Dearborn and Rothney, 1941), the Berkeley studies (Honzik et al., 1948), and the Fels Institute Research (Sontag et al., 1958) that show dramatic shifts in IQ among individual children. But, while the patterns of growth tend to vary, the rates of growth show considerable stability during the school years. Bloom's (1964) summary of major longitudinal studies in which IQ tests were administered to children annually from their first through their seventeenth years of life reveals the extent to which each score correlates with the one administered at age 17. The signs are clear that coefficients tend to be low until about age 4, but thereafter they explain more than half the variance.

Although Terman believed that IQs did not change during childhood, thus proving the dominance of hereditary factors, researchers have tested the nature-nurture influences through studies of monozygotic (MZ) and dizygotic (DZ) twins. One of the largest samples ever investigated was made up of 687 MZ and 482 DZ twins drawn from the National Merit Scholarship Corporation files (Nichols, 1965). With high school achievement tests serving as criterion measures, Nichols found that heredity explains about 70 percent of the variance in language arts, social and natural sciences, and mathematics, a proportion comparable to what is reported in most twin studies (Jensen, 1969). However, conventional wisdom tends to suggest that heredity and environment combine to produce intelligent behavior in a way that is analogous to creating sound by clapping hands together. Just as it is a waste of time to argue about which hand contributes more to the sound, so it is nonsense to think of heredity and environment as competitors for supremacy rather than interactors that are indispensable to each other.

Another of Terman's legacies that has fallen into disfavor was his apparent belief in the indivisibility of the organization of mental powers. He never pretended to advocate a theory of intelligence, but his need for a single score and the way in which he obtained it implies an assumption that intelligence consists of one general factor. In the years following his revision of the Binet-Simon instrument, more and more theorists and researchers on the organization of intelligence have come to regard it as multifaceted (Thurstone, 1947; Guilford, 1967). But regardless of whether unifactor or multifactor theories predominate, Terman's belief that giftedness can be recognized on a continuum of abilities possessed by all people is accepted to this day. The gifted and nongifted are seen as having the same organization of abilities but differ in the extent to which they can cultivate some of them. Acceptance of Terman's assumptions about differences in degree rather than in kind means that studies of the nature and measurement of gifted performance can be subsumed under a general investigation of human mentality.

A second outcome of Terman's work that still endures is his conclusion that potential giftedness reveals itself even in childhood. "Early ripe, early rot" is a once-popular platitude that has been turned into a canard by his studies of gifted children growing up. There are occasional case histories written about aborted genius, such as the tragic case of William James Sidis who entered Harvard College in 1909 at age 11, lectured on higher mathematics within a year of his admission, graduated summa cum laude when he was 15, and spent the rest of his relatively short life in search of obscurity (Montour, 1977). However, this is undoubtedly an exception to the rule that children with ample mental abilities, reasonably stable personalities, and proper nurturance tend eventually to excel in their careers. And since greatness does not materialize suddenly and unaccountably in adulthood, but instead has its roots in the early years of growth, schools are in a key position to help gifted children realize their potential. It suggests the need for special educational programs for the gifted, an idea that would be irrelevant if there were no developmental connection between early promise and later fulfillment.

Emphasis on Differentiated Talents

The tendency to focus on giftedness in childhood has been paralleled in recent decades by efforts to examine specific talents and how they differ from each other. Much emphasis is placed on broadening the search for the kinds of high potential that would presumably be missed by IQ measurement. Renzulli (1978) describes this newer development as a move away from conservatism and toward liberalism in designating who should qualify for special enrichment programs. According to him,

there are very few educators who cling to the "great IQ" or purely academic influence of giftedness. "Multiple talent" and "multiple criteria" are almost the bywords of the present-day gifted student movement, and most educators would have little difficulty in accepting a definition that includes almost every area of human activity that manifests itelf in a socially useful form. (p. 181)

Renzulli's thoughts about an unwarranted dependence on the IQ to define giftedness echo the comments of Getzels and Jackson (1958), who suggest that this single metric is far too restrictive, "thus blinding us to other forms of excellence" (p. 75). On the basis of their own studies, they argue that many children can qualify as gifted because of their exceptional creativity, even though their IQs are not extremely high. Torrance (1962) likewise concludes from his research on children at all educational levels that over 70 percent of those in the upper 20 percent on measures of creative thinking would be unrecognized as gifted if tests of intelligence and scholastic aptitude were used exclusively. From another perspective, Robinson (1977) also deplores the exaggerated claims for the IQ in determining who is gifted. He credits Terman with exposing the myths of his day about the instability of genius but then charges him with creating his own myth by equating giftedness with IQ. The consequence of this deception is that

In the post-Terman era, it has indeed become possible to be a "gifted" individual without having any noticeable gift at all. We routinely categorize children as "gifted" if their IQ scores are above 125, 130, 140, or whatever cutoff score we happen to choose, in spite of the fact that they do not do better than average work in school or demonstrate in any other fashion an exceptional degree of talent. (p. 2)

Robinson's laboratory studies of extremely precocious preschoolers led him to doubt the validity of the general factor theory of intelligence. He found 2- and 3-year-olds earning what he called "modest" IQ scores of 117 or 137 but reading as effectively as children several times their age, whereas other children with much higher tested intelligence did not excel in reading. He therefore proposes that educators renounce the idea that giftedness is some kind of catch-all syndrome and stop the futile quest for traits that are supposed to typify all gifted children. Individuals should qualify as gifted only if they excel in something specific, such as the arts, sciences, mathematics, or whatever else is treasured by the society in which they live. But there is no reason to heap public honor on people just for performing remarkably well on IQ tests. Once we get away from the habit of looking at children as gifted in some vague sense and examine instead their special talents in worthwhile areas of activity, we will come to realize that individuals are as different from each other as are their specializations.

Important insights into the nature of young talent can be gained from monitoring Robinson's population as it matures through various stages of growth. Assuming that the opportunity structure in our society allows children to actualize their potentialities in any field they choose, are his spatially gifted 3-year-olds who excel in nothing else destined to achieve renown in fields related to their early promise? Will the high IQ per se prove to be a worthless indicator of any signs of giftedness? Probably not, according to Terman's findings. The childhood IQ cannot tell us precisely whether the person will become an economist, biologist, or any other kind of achiever. But it does show promise of a high-level adult career, albeit in an unspecified area of work. Perhaps the most serious misconception about the IQ is its acceptance as *both* necessary *and* sufficient to define excellence. But until data eventually show that it is neither a sufficient nor even necessary indicator of giftedness in any field, it would be premature to discard the general factor of intelligence as a valueless concept. At the same time, as Robinson points out, being gifted by virtue of high general intelligence has no practical meaning in itself. The child has to show talent that relates more directly to performance or productivity in the real world. And because talents are diverse, there is no basis for expecting all children who possess them to have some commonality of characteristics that defines giftedness.

Generally speaking, the movement away from exclusive reliance on IQ and its correlates to define giftedness is not intended simply to devalue the IQ. Instead, the argument is that IQ limits giftedness to traditional academics and is not helpful in distinguishing among different kinds of intellectual functioning. According to Taylor and Ellison (1971), intelligence tests encompass only about eight intellectual talents, which represent a small fraction of the well over one hundred that are known to exist. They suggest a "multiple talent" approach to seek out children who are not only learners and reproducers but also thinkers, producers, decision makers, communicators, forecasters, and creators.

Taylor (undated) hypothesizes that, as schools increase the kinds of distinctive talents they are willing to include in special enrichment programs, more and more children will qualify for these offerings. As evidence, he cites a study of some 4,000 public school children who where tested on his Biographical Inventory—Form U, which provides separate scores on academic potential, creativity, artistic aptitudes, leadership, vocational maturity, and attitudes toward formal education. Some children showed extremely uneven profiles but excelled in at least one test in the battery, thus qualifying them as gifted in the area represented by that specific measure. Many of them would presumably have been overlooked if scholastic aptitude were the only factor being measured. In another study of 1,254 children at the middle school level (Hainsworth, 1978), scores were obtained on the six subtests of the Form U Biographical Inventory and on four others that measure realistic decision making, remote forecasting, planning, and nonverbal originality. When the scores were tabulated, 47 percent of the children had scores in the top decile on at least one of the ten tests. This is an unusually high proportion of children to be designated as talented, perhaps larger than in any talent hunt ever conducted.

A definition of giftedness based on proficiency in a single mental operation taken from a wide array of possibilities seems to imply that the gifted are no longer a one-in-a-hundred minority, as perceived by Terman. Instead, the incidence of giftedness in the student population would appear to be directly proportional to the number of such specific skills that constitute the varieties of intellect. And since there may exist many more skills than people who possess them, it could bring about a democratization of excellence, with nearly every individual excelling in at least one of them. This is predicated on the assumption that such restricted mental functions are independent of each other and potentially amenable to measurement, so that a student who can score highly in one does not necessarily perform as well in another. Exceptional talents could then be spread thinly, allowing virtually every child to be counted as gifted in one way or another. But such a logical extension is probably as fanciful as it is utopian. Realistically, special aptitudes are arranged in relatively few clusters, thus limiting the number of children capable of excelling in any one of these group factors. A child who has outstanding potential as an artist, for example, is likely to shine in whatever specific skills *combine* to signify such promise, whereas a different group factor would relate to giftedness in science. It would therefore be overly optimistic to expect many children to possess the right combination of mental traits necessary to be potentially gifted in art, science, or any other valued activity.

Even if it were possible to imagine a spectrum of uncorrelated aptitudes, how significant could any one be in relation to the variety of mental powers necessary to achieve full-blown excellence? Each would be conceived so narrowly as to deny it any power in forecasting future achievment. It takes an aggregate of complex abilities in children to link early promise with eventual fulfillment, not just any one of multiple talents. Still, the idea of defining and measuring high potential in more talent areas than are usually considered in programs for the gifted would probably increase to some extent the number of children qualifying for special enrichment, provided that the talents being sought are varied enough to require markedly different combinations of mental traits.

Cohn (1981) offers two criteria for recognizing a separable domain of giftedness. First, it must be subject to assessment in ways that are empirically reliable and valid. Second, those who possess the specific talent need to live in a society that encourages its fruition through existing educational, social, and political systems. The implication is that a dimension of human ability should be specific enough to permit the planning of educational careers for those who excel in it. According to these standards, giftedness as we know it can be grouped in several domains, as shown in Figure 4-1. Those represented by the solid lines (i.e., intellectual, artistic,

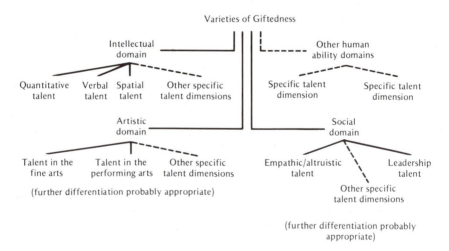

Figure 4-1 A proposed model for differentiating giftedness into specific talent dimensions within human ability domains (Cohn, 1981, p. 37; reprinted with permission of the publisher.)

and social, and some of their subdivisions) are already measurable and socially valued. The *intellectual* domain encompasses quantitative, verbal, and spatial talents, among others; the *artistic* domain includes talent in the fine and performing arts; and the *social* domain is represented by emphatic, altrustic, and leadership talent. Other talent dimensions are not yet explicated or encouraged and are shown by the broken lines.

Cohn's image of the varieties of giftedness seem to be a refinement of the multitalent definition proposed by the U.S. Commissioner of Education (Marland, 1971) as follows:

Gifted and talented children are those identified by professionally qualified persons who, by virtue of outstanding abilities, are capable of high performance. These are children who require differentiated educational programs and/or services beyond those normally provided by the regular school program in order to realize their contribution to self and society.

Children capable of high performance include those with demonstrated achievement and/or potential ability in any of the following areas, singly or in combination:

1. General intellectual ability
2. Specific academic aptitude
3. Creative or productive thinking
4. Leadership ability
5. Visual and performing arts
6. Psychomotor ability (p. ix)

Although the federal definition has been popular in schools throughout the country, it has been subjected to some vigorous criticism. Renzulli (1978) argues that it omits the nonintellective factors that are vital in characterizing giftedness. He also points to the nonparallel nature of the six catagories of giftedness in which two (specific academic aptitude and visual and performing arts) denote fields of accomplished performance, while the other four refer to cognitive processes that may be necessary to bring about superior achievement. Finally, there is a tendency for practitioners to treat the six categories as if they were independent of each other, and this results in the development of separate identification systems for each category. Gallagher (1979) also sees a possible overlap among the six types of giftedness. In addition, he argues that the listing of leadership and psychomotor abilities is not yet justified because we do not know precisely what they mean and we are not able to identify high potential in either one. Despite these reservations, the federal definition emphasizing various kinds of talent is accepted in many programs for the gifted. Psychomotor ability, however, has been dropped from the list.

Information Processing and Componential Theories

It may seem ironic, but despite its title, Terman's *Genetic Studies of Genius* was probably more instrumental than any other scientific work in *discouraging* investigations into the nature of genius. Instead, he moved his successors in the direction of characterizing potential giftedness and measuring it in children. There are occasions, however, when the more recent tradition is abandoned for the sake of the older one, popularized by Galton, that attempted to capture the essence of genius without relying on psychometrics. Ashby and Walker (1968), for example, agree with Galton on the potency of genetic factors in determining the emergence of genius, drawing their evidence from the strangely brilliant feats of *idiots savants* and the remarkable memories attributed to such immortals as Coleridge, Shelley, Goethe, and Freud. They also argue that originality is not the most crucial ingredient of genius on the grounds that it is entirely dependent on the observer, not on the performer, inasmuch as machines and animals can demonstrate it, too. As the authors point out,

> To one observer, the successive ticks of a watch may be mere repetitions; to another, who records the finest details, no two ticks may be identical. By changing observers, we can thus, it appears, change the watch from a device which cannot show originality to one which can. Of course, we do not really change the *watch* at all, but only the situation in which originality is to be judged. (p. 204)

Animal tracks in the snow may also be signs of originality since no two sets are alike, and it can be accomplished without high-level cognitive processing.

If genius is not comprehensible as originality in its most spectacular and celebrated form, what is it? To Ashby and Walker, it is manifested by an incredibly sophisticated excursion into *convergent* thinking, or a search for the single solution that no other person can fathom for a particular problem. A work of genius seems to have some kind of pre-existence that awaits conceptualization and discovery. The great product or performance is actualized by a process called *selection*, or the appropriate means to attain a goal that can be treasured for all time. Successful selection is accomplished through information processing whereby every alternative less than "the perfect" solution to the problem is eliminated. Thus, for example, Bach's *Well-Tempered Clavier* consists of notes, phrases, and rhythms selected by the composer from a universe of possibilities to make up the finished masterpiece. Bach could be regarded as a genius because only he had the ability to select the "bits" of information needed to solve his "problem." A parallel effort at information processing was exerted by Michelangelo through his high-speed, arduous elimination of alternatives to the strokes and color tones that constituted his great painting on the ceiling of the Sistine Chapel.

The function of originality in works of genius is not ignored altogether. Ashby and Walker acknowledge that it does have a place in problem solving to the extent that it prevents predictable and stereotyped searches for solutions, while seemingly improbable but fruitful leads are ignored. However, they emphasize mostly the powers of selection, which are convergent in nature, and the enormous investment of sheer physical energy needed to evaluate and discard inappropriate alternative solutions. What seems to be implied is that a mysterious "cosmic rightness" marks the work of genius and that it cannot be compromised even in the slightest way. Sometimes the movement toward perfection can almost be "read" by examining early versions of masterpieces, such as the next-to-last revision that Beethoven made of the famous opening chords of his Fifth Symphony, which featured the flutes a bit too prominently and thereby detracted from the power and mood of that musical statement.

An information processing approach to defining genius may sound vaguely Platonic and perhaps even bizarre to those who are accustomed to dealing with cognitive structures and the like. It reminds one of Eddington's (1927) conjecture that "If an army of monkeys were strumming on typewriters they *might* write all the books in the British Museum" (p. 72). But it also has a modern ring. With high-speed computers at his disposal, a physicist (Bennett, 1977) has been attempting to establish the probabilities involved in reproducing great literature through the application of "artificial intelligence." Specifically, how much information processing is necessary for a computer to put together the proper words and sentences to recreate Shakespeare's *Hamlet*? It is a heady question that challenges the imagination, but it cannot be ignored in the light of developing opportunities and adventures in productivity with the help of high-speed electronic information storage and retrieval systems.

The theory of genius expressed by Ashby and Walker is purely speculative, and they make no use of formal measures to verify it. A somewhat similar departure from the use of psychometrics is also apparent in Sternberg's (1981) "componential" theory of intellectual giftedness. Instead of dealing with stable factors, or products of performance, he emphasizes an understanding of how the organism responds conceptually to external stimuli. Intellectual giftedness may be understood in terms of superior functioning of what he calls "meta components," "performance components," and "acquisition," "retention," and "transfer components."

Meta components are processes used in executive planning and decision making preliminary to problem solving. They include (1) ordering, according to priority, alternative approaches to problems or deciding just what the problems are that have to be solved and their importance relative to each other; (2) establishing a knowledge base and tentative, sequential strategies that may eventually lead to a solution; (3) deciding on the strategies that are likely to work best for the individual problem solver; (4) representing information in ways that are most appropriate for the discipline being studied; (5) applying time, effort, and resources most economically; and (6) developing an approach that is flexible and open-minded enough to allow for midcourse adjustments.

Performance components are processes needed in the execution of the problem-solving strategy. They draw heavily on such competencies as (1) *encoding* the terms of the problem and gleaning information that will be needed for the solution; (2) *inferencing*, or building conceptual relationships and drawing conclusions; (3) *mapping*, or seeing commonalities between domains of knowledge; (4) *applying* knowledge by formulating predictions from a familiar to an unfamiliar domain; (5) *comparing* proposed predictions with alternative possibilities; (6) *justifying* the preferred prediction over the alternatives; and (7) *responding* to the problem by expressing the solution in terms that others can understand.

Acquisition components are skills needed to learn new information, *retention components* are skills involved in retrieving previously acquired information, and *transfer components* are the skills required for generalizing information from one context to another. Proficiency in these skills depends not only on the person's mental capacity but also on stimuli relevant to the targeted solution. For example, if the task at hand is to acquire complex information, success will depend partly on the number of times the information is encountered, the variability of contexts in which it is presented, its importance to the learner, and how it relates to other information stored in the learner's memory. Sternberg believes that giftedness can be characterized as superior access to all the aforementioned components and high proficiency in implementing them. Consequently, it is possible to train the gifted to build on their strengths through various exercises, although it remains to be seen whether the effects of training can generalize to unfamiliar contexts.

Intellective and Nonintellective Attributes

Most theories of giftedness from a psychological perspective, including those presented thus far, refer strictly to human abilities of one kind or another. Yet it obviously takes more than brainpower to be an exceptional producer or performer. Without the support of nonintellective traits, such as the capacity and willingness to work hard at achieving excellence, it is impossible to rise above mediocrity. Renzulli (1978) recognized the need for *both* inspiration and perspiration when he defined giftedness as consisting

of an interaction among three basic clusters of human traits—these clusters being above-average general abilities, high levels of task commitments, and high levels of creativity. Gifted and talented children are those possessing or capable of developing this composite set of traits and applying them to any potentially valuable area of human performance. Children who manifest or are capable of developing an interaction among the three clusters require a wide variety of educational opportunities and services that are not ordinarily provided through regular instructional programs. (p. 261)

The Renzulli concept is illustrated through three overlapping rings representing "above-average abilities," "task commitment," and "creativity," all of which are brought to bear on a large number of general and specific performance areas (see Figure 4-2). Although this framework is a relatively easy one for educators to translate into plans for identifying the gifted, it should be regarded as only a sketch of a complex psychological phenomenon. A more detailed picture would show that attribute combinations vary according to domains of performance and productivity. For example, there may be reasonably large numbers of people who are brilliant at classroom teaching or in social work and possess no more than moderately above-average general ability, as measured by IQ, but the minimal levels for outstanding thoretical physicists would probably be much higher. Additionally, the physicist and teacher could excel in their respective fields only if they possessed some entirely dissimilar aptitudes that have to be cultivated for the work they do.

Task commitment, of course, is a necessary requisite for excellence in any

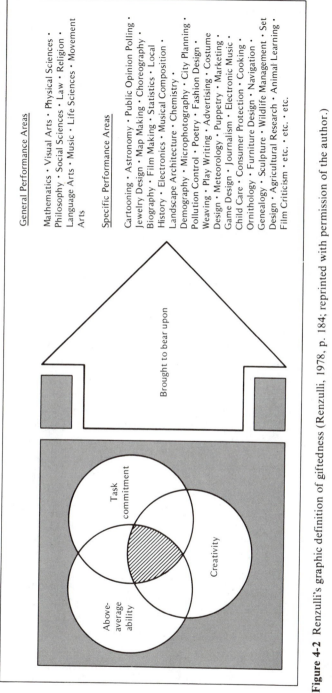

General Performance Areas

Mathematics • Visual Arts • Physical Sciences • Philosophy • Social Sciences • Law • Religion • Language Arts • Music • Life Sciences • Movement Arts

Specific Performance Areas

Cartooning • Astronomy • Public Opinion Polling • Jewelry Design • Map Making • Choreography • Biography • Film Making • Statistics • Local History • Electronics • Musical Composition • Landscape Architecture • Chemistry • Demography • Microphotography • City Planning • Pollution Control • Poetry • Fashion Design • Weaving • Play Writing • Advertising • Costume Design • Meteorology • Puppetry • Marketing • Game Design • Journalism • Electronic Music • Child Care • Consumer Protection • Cooking • Ornithology • Furniture Design • Navigation • Genealogy • Sculpture • Wildlife Management • Set Design • Agricultural Research • Animal Learning • Film Criticism • etc. • etc. • etc.

Figure 4-2 Renzulli's graphic definition of giftedness (Renzulli, 1978, p. 184; reprinted with permission of the author.)

worthwhile field of endeavor. But it would be a mistake to single it out exclusively and neglect other important nonintellective traits that facilitate great accomplishment, such as impulse control, tolerance for ambiguity and complexity, venturesomeness, and openness to experience, among others. Educators can be misled into believing that all it takes to be an achiever is a healthy mixture of ability and willpower, when in reality these psychological ingredients tell only part of the story. Finally, while a creativity factor has heuristic value for understanding giftedness in children, there are important questions yet to be answered concerning its true nature, its nurture, its measurement, and the value of so-called "creativity tests" in helping to predict the fulfillment of early promise.

In an elaborate adaptation of Renzulli's three-ring framework, Lamkins (undated) adds more flexibility and detail to the components of giftedness. One ring represents the special aptitudes necessary for mastery in a highly honored field of work. Thus, for example, the musically gifted would be recognized partly by their perfect pitch and rhythm, the intellectually gifted by their high IQs and superior achievement in various academic areas, and the psychomotoric whizzes by their agility, balance, strength, and physical endurance and coordination. As in Renzulli's definition, a second component represents the ability to find and solve problems in creative ways through the application of unique ideas. The third ingredient adds to task commitment several other nonintellective characteristics such as energy, acceptance of responsibility, ability to plan and organize, self-control and discipline, and self-confidence.

According to Lamkins (undated), the gifted are defined as those having all three attributes: (1) fundamental skills and knowledge, (2) creative problem-finding/solving skills, and (3) selected personal characteristics. There are also children labeled "talented" if they possess the necessary skills and personal characteristics but lack creativity. Thus, the academically talented are hard-working, well-organized, high achievers whose performance lacks evidence of innovative ideas. The talented in visual and performing arts are able to perfect their technical skills but with little imagination or daring. The other two possible combinations of attributes refer to those with some potential who fail to produce or perform with any distinction. Possessing the necessary skills and creativity while lacking the nonintellective traits for developing high potential can only result in underachievement. The combination of creativity and personal characteristics is also unlikely to facilitate much growth since it is not rooted in complex, basic skills.

In another approach to the understanding of giftedness through its intellective and nonintellective dimensions, Piechowski (1979) advances the concept of developmental potential (DP), defined as "the original endowment which determines what level of development a person may reach under optimal conditions" (p.28). DP is made up of special talents and abilities plus what Piechowski calls "overexcitability," an intense visceral reaction to experience that expresses itself in five forms: (1) the *psychomotor* mode, characterized by excessive physical energy, movement, restlessness, and action; (2) the *sensual* mode, of comfort and sensory delectation; (3) the *intellectual* mode, of logic, questioning, and the search for truth; (4) the *imaginational* mode, of dreams, fantasies, and images; and (5) the

Table 4-2. Forms and Expressions of Psychic Overexcitability

PSYCHOMOTOR

Surplus of energy
   Rapid speech, marked enthusiasm, fast games and sports, pressure for action, delinquent behavior

Psychomotor expression of emotional tension
   Compulsive talking and chattering, impulsive actions, delinquent behavior, workaholism, nervous habits (tics, nailbiting)

SENSUAL

Sensory pleasures
   Seeing, smelling, tasting, touching, hearing
Sensual expression of emotional tension
   Overeating, masturbation, sexual intercourse, buying sprees

INTELLECTUAL

Probing questions
Problem solving
Learning
   Curiosity, concentration, capacity for sustained intellectual effort, extensive reading
Theoretical thinking
   Thinking about thinking, introspection, preoccupation with certain problems, moral thinking and development of a hierarchy of values, conceptual and intuitive integration

IMAGINATIONAL

Free play of the imagination
   Illusions, animistic and magical thinking, image and metaphor, inventions and fantasy, poetic and dramatic perception
Spontaneous imagery as an expression of emotional tension
   Animistic imagery, mixing of truth and fiction, dreams, visual recall, visualization of events, fears of the unknown

EMOTIONAL

Somatic expressions
   Tense stomach, sinking heart, flushing
Intensity of feeling
   Positive feelings, negative feelings, extremes of feeling, complex feelings, identification with others' feelings
Inhibition (timidity, shyness)
Affective memory
Concern with death
Fear and anxiety
Feeling of guilt
Depressive and suicidal moods
Relationship feelings
   Need for protection, attachment to animals, significant others, perceptions of relationships, emotional ties and attachments, difficulty of adjustment to new environments, loneliness, concern for others (empathy), conflict with others
Feelings toward self
   Self-evaluation and self-judgment, feelings of inadequacy and inferiority

---

Source: M. M. Piechowski, "Developmental Potential," in N. Colangelo and R. T. Zaffrann, eds., *New Voices in Counseling the Gifted* (Dubuque, Iowa: Kendall/Hunt, 1979), p. 31.

emotional mode, of attachments to other people, empathy, and love. These forms of personal experience are the main channels of human perception and conception. Piechowski likens them to "color filters through which the various external impingements and internal stirrings reach the individual. They determine to what occurrences and in what way one is capable of responding" (p. 29). Table 4-2 details the five modes of overexcitability.

Chapter 5

A Proposed Psychosocial Definition

Judging from the many ways in which giftedness has been defined, there appears to be general agreement about some basic issues. First and foremost, there is no hesitation to focus on children, since precocity among the young is seen as a reliable forerunner of their future distinction. These children are not considered a "breed apart" with unfathomable mental powers or mindsets for finding and solving problems in ways that seem miraculous for others of their age group. Rather than being characterized as qualitatively different, they are singled out for having quantifiable gifts such as accomplishing unusual and important things faster, at a younger age than expected, with greater efficiency, and more imaginatively in comparison with their peers. Finally, the fact that gifted children are heterogeneous in the talents they possess is generally accepted without controversy although schools still nurture academic skills more ardently than any others.

There is a growing appreciation of diversity even within a particular talent domain. As Getzels (1979) concludes from his longitudinal studies of promising art students, profound personological differences are associated with the pursuit of careers in the fine arts, commercial arts, and art education. According to Nobel prize-winning zoologist Sir Peter Medawar (1979), scientists also come in a variety of temperaments. There are what he calls collectors, classifiers, and compulsive tidiers-up; detectives and explorers; artists and artisans; poet-scientists and philosopher-scientists; and even mystic-scientists. There is reason to suspect that, whatever nonintellective syndromes are associated with the way in which people create great art or science in their peak years, these syndromes have insinuated themselves into the personality structures of these people long before they become renowned, even as early as childhood.

Since it is generally agreed that there is evidence of giftedness in children as well as in adults, a clear distinction has to be made between them. Work accomplished during a person's maturity can be evaluated by objective standards if its aim is, for example, to prevent rejection of transplanted human organs. Or it can be subjected to critical review, as in the case of poetic composition, to determine whether it deserves to be disseminated and treasured. Not so with children's achievements. Although Lehman (1949) cites many cases of immortals who drew attention to themselves before age 21—especially concert artists—children who are usually identified as gifted would fail to attain greatness if they were judged on the basis of universal criteria. Instead, they have to be compared with others of their age for early signs of talent that is amenable to nurturance and that promises to live up to high expectations in the future.

Since there can never be any assurance that precocious children will fulfill their potential, defining giftedness among them is necessarily risky. One set of criteria may be *ineffective* because it excludes too many children who may grow up to be gifted; other qualifying characteristics may prove *inefficient* by including too many who turn out to be nongifted. There is inevitably a trade-off between effectiveness and efficiency, and educators invariably opt for a definition that enables them to cast the widest possible net at the outset to be sure not to neglect children whose high potential may be all but hidden from view.

Keeping in mind that developed talent exists only in adults, a proposed definition of giftedness in children is that it denotes their potential for becoming critically acclaimed performers or exemplary producers of ideas in spheres of activity that enhance the moral, physical, emotional, social, intellectual, or aesthetic life of humanity.

Outstanding contributors to the arts, sciences, letters, and general well-being of fellow humans tend often to show signs of promise in childhood. It is therefore reasonable to identify precocious children as the pool from which the most highly gifted are likely to emerge. But precocity only signifies rapid learning of ideas or about people, the ability to grasp abstractions quickly and efficiently, and generally to display skills far beyond those expected at the child's age level. Early schooling is reserved mainly for encountering, distilling, synthesizing, and *consuming* knowledge. *Producing* knowledge with great invetivness and impact, which is a sign of giftedness, comes later in a person's growth cycle.

Frequently, even voracious young consumers remain that way without ever becoming producers; instead, they grow up as superannuated precocious children. At cocktail parties they are easily recognizable as glib, superficial bores who have ready-made and forceful opinions about any issue under discussion and are always ready to unload their vast storehouses of trivia on audiences of almost any size. Truly gifted children, on the other hand, are sometimes far more limited in what they are capable of absorbing, and their marks on standardized and teacher-made tests show it. Yet, they could someday prove capable of making important contributions to the world of ideas. Generally speaking, however, renowned producers tend to have a history of extraordinary consumption, and they use their storehouse of understandings to great advantage in making original contributions.

Those who have the potential for succeeding as gifted adults require not only the personal attributes that are often mentioned in definitions of giftedness, but also

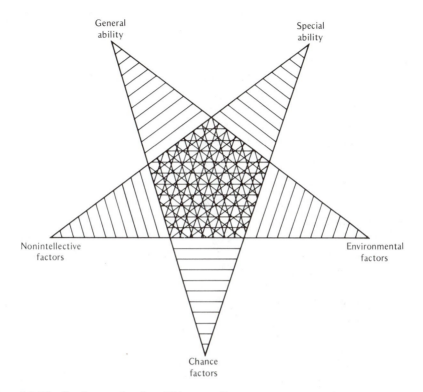

Figure 5-1 The five factors that "mesh" into excellence

some special encounters with the environment to facilitate the emergence of talent. The internal and external requirements may be illustrated in a starfishlike design, with giftedness produced by the overlap of all five factors (see Figure 5-1). These factors are characterized as follows:

General Ability. The "g" factor, or tested general intelligence, figures on a sliding scale in all high-level talent areas. This means that different threshold IQs are required for various kinds of accomplishment, higher in academic subjects than, for example, in the performing arts. There is no basis for making extreme assertions about the IQ, such as discounting its relevance to giftedness entirely or claiming that all those destined to become great producers or performers in any area of human activity need to score at the ninety-ninth percentile or better. Instead, positions along this continuum should be adjusted according to the talent area, which means taking a stance closer to one extreme for some kinds of giftedness and nearer the opposite extreme for others.

Special Ability. It is meaningless to regard children as gifted in general intelligence, even though the g factor may figure prominently in many kinds of outstanding performance and productivity. Giftedness means being exceptionally bright at doing something that is highly respected, and most people do not do many things equally well. Instead, they have special capacities and affinities for particular kinds of work. These aptitudes are becoming more and more recognizable in children, albeit not at the same chronological age. Musical talent appears as early as the preschool years, whereas insight into social and political structures develops much later in childhood. Whatever the aptitudes may be, it is necessary to assess them as soon as they become measurable so as to determine the extent of the child's special talents and whether to design appropriate curriculum modifications to cultivate these talents.

Nonintellective Factors. Ability alone cannot facilitate great accomplishment. It also requires a confluence of various nonintellective facilitators such as ego strength, dedication to a chosen field of productivity or performance, willingness to sacrifice short-term satisfactions for the sake of long-term accomplishment, and many others. These traits are integral to the achieving personality regardless of the areas in which talent manifests itself.

Environmental Factors. Many children show signs of giftedness only in response to pressure or even oppressiveness in their environments. For most of them, however, stimulating home, school, and community settings are indispensable not only for maximizing potentialities but also for helping to determine the directions they take. Parents serve as role models through their own achievement orientation while creating an enriched educational environment outside of school and urging their offspring to advance their studies to the fullest extent. The quality of classroom instruction also makes a difference, as do the attitudes of peers in and out of the classroom toward the life of the mind. As for the resources in the neighborhood, there are formal cultural institutions such as local museums, concert halls, and libraries as well as human resources that can inspire and instruct. Without proper stimulation in the human ecological structure, there is always the possibility, and often the likelihood, that children with outstanding mental endowment will "hide their lights under a bushel."

Chance Factors. Generally overlooked in the studies of the fulfillment of talent are the entirely unpredictable events in a person's life that are critical both to the realization of promise and to the demonstration of developed talents. It is not only a matter of being in the right place at the right time, although that is important, too. There are many unforeseen circumstances in the opportunity structure and in the prevalent life style that can make a big difference in the outlets for gifted performance. A brilliant medical researcher who is ready to achieve a breakthrough in disease control may suddenly and unpredictably be distracted by a personal crisis or by the lure of a social issue that is considered more relevant to human concerns. The "market" for lawyers may be so glutted that even those with freshly minted doctorates of jurisprudence who have leadership potential in the legal profession find that there is little room for them to get started in their practice. Chance factors can also serve as facilitators of achievement, as in the case of the gifted young singer or actor who happens to meet and study with the right coach and makes the most of the opportunity.

Thus we see that the proposed definition of giftedness as a potential for outstanding performance or productivity has meaning only if the complex mix of personal and situational facilitators are taken into account. These factors defy precise measurement because we have to rely on test instruments that lack perfect validity and reliability. Besides, the tests of intellective and nonintellective factors may be appropriate mainly for consumers of knowledge and far less so for potential producers or performers. As for the element of chance, it is by definition fortuitous and therefore unrelated to measurable antecedent conditions. A detailed review of these five linkages between promise and fulfillment is located in Part IV.

Finally, in view of the limited empirical evidence about the nature of giftedness and how to assess it, there will always be the question as to whether groping for definitions is useful or merely academic. Gallagher (1979) apparently thinks that it is premature to define anything before a good deal is known about it:

In education, it is natural for us to respond to the question "Who are you talking about?" by trying to state a definition. Scientists know that a definition of a concept is not the first thing to be completed, but quite literally the last. . . . The inadequacies of the definition are merely symptoms pointing to our incomplete knowledge about the relevant concepts. If we are to pass along a more coherent statement to the next generation, then we will need not only better rhetoric but more sustained research and development as well. (p. 31)

Without violating Gallagher's caveat, there are some defensible generalizations about the nature of giftedness that help us begin to understand what we are talking about when we look for it in children. First, we may regard it as extraordinary promise for productivity or performance in areas of work that are publicly prized; it is not a facility for consuming knowledge in abundance or at a rapid pace. Second, we may consider its parameters as encompassing surplus, scarcity, and quota talents, and perhaps some anomalous talents as well. Third, we may assume its existence in children to be a moderately reliable herald of their distinction as adults. Finally, there is enough empirical evidence to help us locate at least part of the "terrain" in a person's psyche and surroundings where factors associated with extraordinary potential and its realization are most likely to exist. These assertions derive from past theory and research on the meaning of gifted behavior in children and are useful to the extent that they can provide a basis on which to build further knowledge in the field.

References

Ashby, W. R., and C. C. Walker. "Genius." In P. London and D. Rosenhan, eds., *Foundations of Abnormal Psychology*, pp. 201-225. New York: Holt, Rinehart and Winston, Inc., 1968.

Bennett, W. R., Jr. "How Artificial Is Intelligence." *American Scientist*, **65**:694-702 (1977).

Bloom, B.S. *Stability and Change in Human Characteristics*. New York: John Wiley & Sons, Inc., 1964.

Bonsall, M. R., and B. Stefflre. "The Temperament of Gifted Children." *California Journal of Educational Research*. **6**:162-165 (1955).

Boring, E. G. "Intelligence as the Tests Test It." *The New Republic*, **34**:35-36 (1923).

Burks, G. S., D. W. Jensen, and L. M. Terman. *The Promise of Youth: Follow-up Studies of a Thousand Gifted Children*. Stanford, Calif. Stanford University Press, 1930.

Cattell, J. McK. "Mental Tests and Measurements." *Mind*, **15**:373-381 (1890).

Cohn, S. J. "What Is Giftedness? A Multidimensional Approach." In A.H. Kramer, ed., *Gifted Children*, pp. 33-45. New York: Trillium Press, 1981.

Cox, C. M., et al. *The Early Mental Traits of Three Hundred Geniuses*. Vol. II: *Genetic Studies of Genius*. Stanford, Calif.: Stanford University Press, 1926.

Dearborn, W. F., and J. Rothney. *Predicting the Child's Development*. Cambridge, Mass.: Science-Art Publishers, 1941.

De Haan, R. F., and R. J. Havighurst. *Educating Gifted Children*. Chicago: University of Chicago Press, 1961.

Eddington, Sir A. S. *The Nature of the Physical World*. Cambridge: Cambridge University Press, 1927.

Gallagher, J. J. "Issues in Education for the Gifted." In A.H. Passow, ed., *The Gifted and the Talented*, pp. 28-45. The Seventy-eighth Yearbook of the National Society for the Study of Education. Chicago: University of Chicago Press, 1979.

Galton, F. *Hereditary Genius*. London: Macmillan & Co. Ltd. 1869.

———. *English Men of Science, Their Nature and Nurture*. London: Macmillan & Co. Ltd., 1874.

Getzels, J. W. "From Art Student to Fine Artist: Potential, Problem Finding, and Performance" In A.H. Passow, ed., *The Gifted and the Talented: Their Education and Development.* The Seventy-eighth Yearbook of the National Society for the Study of Education, pp. 372-387. Chicago, Ill.: University of Chicago Press, 1979.

Getzels, J. W., and P. W. Jackson. "The Meaning of 'Giftedness'—An Examination of an Expanding Concept." *Phi Delta Kappan', 40*:75-77 (1958).

Goertzel, M. G., V. Goertzel, and T. G. Goertzel. *300 Eminent Personalities.* San Francisco: Jossey-Bass, 1978.

Goertzel, V., and M. G. Goertzel. *Cradles of Eminence.* Boston: Little, Brown and Company, 1962.

Guilford, J. P. *The Nature of Human Intelligence.* New York: McGraw-Hill Book Company, 1967.

Hainsworth, J. "A Teacher Corps Projection of Multiple Talents." In C.W. Taylor, ed., *Teaching for Talents and Gifts, 1978 Status,* pp. 85-89. Salt Lake City: Utah State Board of Education, 1978.

Hollingworth, L. S. "An Enrichment Curriculum for Rapid Learners at Public School 500: Speyer School." *Teachers College Record, 39*:296-306 (1938).

———. *Children Above 180 I.Q., Stanford-Binet. Origin and Development.* New York: The World Book Company, 1942.

Holmes, B., J. A. Lauwerys, and C. Russell. "Concepts of Excellence and Social Change." In G.Z.F. Bereday and J.A. Lauwerys, eds., *Concepts of Excellence in Education.* The Year Book of Education. New York: Harcourt, Brace & World, 1961.

Honzik, M. P., J. MacFarlane, and L. Allen. "The Stability of Mental Test Performance Between Two and Eighteen Years." *Journal of Experimental Education, 4*:309-324 (1948).

Jensen, A. "How Much Can We Boost IQ and Scholastic Achievement?" *Harvard Educational Review, 39*:1-123 (1969).

Kagan, J., and Kogan, N. "Individual Variation in Cognitive Processes." In P.H. Mussen, ed., *Carmichael's Manual of Child Psychology,* pp. 1273-1365. New York: John Wiley & Sons, Inc., 1970.

Khoury, T. J., and M. A. Appel. "Gifted Children: Current Trends and Issues." *Journal of Clinical Child Psychology, 6*:13-20 (1977).

Lamkins, A. W. *Guidelines for the Identification of the Gifted and Talented.* Albany, N.Y.: The University of the State of New York, undated.

Lehman, H.C. "Young Thinkers and Great Achievements." *Journal of Genetic Psychology, 74*:245-271 (1949).

Lorge, I. "Social Gains in the Special Education of the Gifted." *School and Society, 79*:4-7 (1954).

———, and L. S. Hollingworth. "Adult Status of Highly Intelligent Children." *Pedagogical Seminary and Journal of Genetic Psychology, 49*:215-226 (1936).

Marland, S. P., Jr., *Education of the Gifted and Talented.* 2 vols. Washington, D.C.: U.S. Government Printing Office, 1971.

McCurdy, H. G. "The Childhood Pattern of Genius." *Horizon, 2*:33-38 (1960).

Medawar, P. B. *Advice to a Young Scientist.* New York: Harper & Row, Publishers, 1979.

Miles, C. C. "Gifted Children." In L. Carmichael, ed., *Manual of Child Psychology,* pp. 984-1063. New York: John Wiley & Sons, Inc., 1954.

Montour, K. "William James Sidis, The Broken Twig." *American Psychologist, 32*:265-279 (1977).

National Center for Education Statistics. *The Condition of Education, 1978,* M.A. Golladay and J. Noell, eds. Washington, D.C.: U.S. Government Printing Office, 1978.

Newland, T. E. "On Defining the Mentally Superior in Terms of Social Need." *Exceptional Children*, **29**:237-240 (1963).

—————. *The Gifted in Socioeducational Perspective*. Englewood Cliffs, N. J.: Prentice-Hall, Inc., 1976.

Nichols, R. C. "The Inheritance of General and Specific Ability." *NMSC Research Report*, Vol. l, no. 1. Evanston, Ill.: National Merit Scholarship Corporation, 1965.

Oden, M. H. "The Fulfillment of Promise: 40-Year Follow-up of the Terman Gifted Group," *Genetic Psychology Monographs*, **77**:3-93 (1968).

Phenix, P. H. *Realms of Meaning*. New York: McGraw-Hill Book Company, 1964.

Piechowski, M. M. "Developmental Potential." In N. Colangelo and R.T. Zaffrann, eds., *New Voices in Counselling the Gifted*, pp. 25-57. Dubuque, Iowa: Kendall/Hunt, 1979.

Renzulli, J. S. "What Makes Giftedness? Reexamining a Definition." *Phi Delta Kappan*, **60**:180-184, 261 (1978).

Robinson, H. B. "Current Myths Concerning Gifted Children." *Gifted and Talented Brief No. 5*, pp. 1-11. Ventura, Calif.: National/State Leadership Training Institute, 1977.

Roe, A. *Making of a Scientist*. New York: Dodd, Mead & Company, 1953.

Seagoe, M. V. *Terman and the Gifted*. Los Altos, Calif.: William Kaufmann, 1975.

Sears, P. S. "The Terman Studies of Genius, 1922-1972." In A.H. Passow, ed., *The Gifted and the Talented: Their Education and Development*, pp. 75-96. The Seventy-eighth Yearbook of the National Society for the Study of Education. Chicago: University of Chicago Press, 1979.

—————, and A. H. Barbee. "Career and Life Satisfaction Among Terman's Gifted Women." In J.C. Stanley, W.C. George, and C.H. Solano, eds., *The Gifted and the Creative: Fifty-Year Perspective*, pp. 28-65. Baltimore, Md.: Johns Hopkins University Press, 1977.

Sears, R. R. "Sources of Life Satisfactions of the Terman Gifted Men." *American Psychologist*, **32**:119-128 (1977).

Smith, D. C. *Personal and Social Adjustment of Gifted Adolescents*. CEC Monograph No. 4. Washington, D.C.: The Council for Exceptional Children, National Educational Association, 1962.

Sontag, L. W., C. T. Baker, and V. L. Nelson. "Mental Growth and Personality Development: A Longitudinal Study." *Monograph of the Society for Research in Child Development*, Vol. 23 (Whole No. 68), 1958.

Sternberg, R. J. "A Componential Theory of Intellectual Giftedness." *Gifted Child Quarterly*, **25**:86-93 (1981).

Taylor, C. W. "How Many Types of Giftedness Can Your Program Tolerate?" Unpublished paper, 18 pp. (undated).

Taylor, C. W., and R. L. Ellison. "All Students Are Now Educationally Deprived." Paper presented at the Seventeenth International Congress of Applied Psychology, Liege, Belgium, 1971.

Terman, L. M. "The Physical and Mental Traits of Gifted Children." In G.M. Whipple, ed., *Report of the Society's Committee on the Education of Gifted Children*. The Twenty-third Yearbook of the National Society for the Study of Education, pp. 155-167. Bloomington, Ill.: Public School Publishing Co., 1924.

—————. "Scientists and Nonscientists in a Group of 800 Gifted Men." *Psychological Monographs*, Vol. 68, No. 7 (Whole No. 378), 1954.

—————, and M. H. Oden. *The Gifted Child Grows Up*. Stanford, Calif.: Stanford University Press, 1947.

————, and M. H. Oden. *The Gifted Group at Mid-Life*. Stanford, Calif.: Stanford University Press, 1959.

————, et al. *Mental and Physical Traits of a Thousand Gifted Children*. Stanford, Calif.: Stanford University Press, 1925.

Thurstone, L. L. *Multiple Factor Analysis: A Development and Expansion of "The Vectors of the Mind."* Chicago: University of Chicago Press, 1947.

Torrance, E. P., *Guiding Creative Talent*. Englewood Cliffs, N.J.: Prentice-Hall, Inc. 1962.

Witty, P. A. *A Study of One Hundred Gifted Children*. Lawrence, Kans.: Bureau of School Service and Research, 1930.

————. "Who are the Gifted?" In N.B. Henry, ed., *Education of the Gifted*. The Fifty-seventh Yearbook of the National Society for the Study of Education, Part II, pp. 41-63. Chicago: University of Chicago Press, 1958.

Young, M. *The Rise of the Meritocracy, 1870-2033*. New York: Random House, Inc., 1959.

Zuckerman, H. "The Sociology of the Nobel Prize: Further Notes and Queries." *American Scientist*, **66**:420-425 (1978).

PART III

Linkages Between Promise and Fulfillment

Great performance or productivity results from a rare blend of (1) general intelligence, (2) special aptitudes, (3) nonintellective facilitators, (4) environmental influences, and (5) chance, or luck. Each of these factors has a fixed threshold that represents the minimum essential for giftedness in *any* publicly valued activity. Research has not yet succeeded in revealing what thresholds are necessary for each of the five qualifiers of giftedness. But it is safe to say that whoever achieves some measure of eminence has to qualify by *all* these standards, and the person who is unable to measure up to just *one* of them cannot become truly outstanding. In other words, success depends upon a *combination of facilitators*, whereas failure results from even a *single deficit*. This truism should form the basis for understanding the relationship between promise and fulfillment.

There are children who seem to have superior brainpower and the desire to perform well in various academic disciplines, but they never rise above the level of mediocrity because their educational experience lacks richness and imagination. Others may be exposed to quality education and possess the intellectual power to perform with distinction, but are handicapped by insufficient motivation or sloppy work habits. It is therefore futile to look for a single explanation of why some children do or do not live up to high expectations. So-called underachievers cannot fit into only one typology.

For each of the five intellective, personological, and social-situational factors connecting potential with high-level accomplishment, there is also a threshold level that varies according to *specific* areas of excellence. Thus, for example, Getzels's (1979) sample of talented artists was able to demonstrate exceptional talent in various art forms even though their general academic abilities were no better than most other college students'. On the other hand, without high academic promise it is doubtful that many college students could become as distinguished as Roe's

(1953) creative scientists. We can speculate reasonably that the IQ, along with spatial and scientific aptitude thresholds, have to be different for artists and scientists. Those who fail to measure up to any of these minimum essentials for their respective fields of endeavor could never compare with the Getzels and Roe populations. By virtue of its "veto" power, then, every one of the qualifiers is a *necessary* requisite of high achievement, but none of them has *sufficient* strength to overcome inadequacies in the others.

From the foregoing comments, it seems as if the causes of extraordinary accomplishment can be described best as resembling some kind of not so clear, complex moving target. The number and variety of antecedent variables preclude any easy designation of a child as gifted on the basis of a few performance measures. Besides, the causes are not the same for all kinds of giftedness. Every area of excellence has its own mix of requisite characteristics, even though general ability, special aptitudes, nonintellective, environmental, and chance factors under which they are subsumed apply to all kinds of talent. These categories could be viewed as "common denominators" that are always associated with giftedness, no matter how it manifests itself. Yet, within each of them, the threshold levels, below which outstanding achievement is impossible, have to be adjusted to fit every talent domain, and that adds to the difficulty of making predictions about the fulfillment of promise.

Considering the elusive nature of causes of giftedness, there is no basis for stereotyped thinking on the subject. Such frequently heard statements as "Only children with IQs of 130 and above are truly gifted" and "IQ has no bearing on gifted performance" are equally naïve. One of the reasons these children are captivating cynosures to scholars and laypersons alike is that they resist stereotyping. Nevertheless, there is always the temptation to oversimplify what does and what does not make them function the way they do.

Chapter 6

General Ability

General ability can be defined roughly as the g factor, which is itself defined roughly as some kind of mysterious intellectual power common to a variety of specific competencies. Doppelt (1950) contends that the g factor is actually a composite of several competencies, including reasoning ability, speed, memory, perception, and rote skills. As the person matures, some specific competencies, such as rote skills and memory, seem to detach themselves from the general mass and may be identified as distinct abilities or factors. However, the underlying reasoning power tends to remain, along with various amounts of the other components. Reasoning ability itself is not well defined as a single entity; it is probably an amalgamation of applications of abstract thinking used in various contexts. Doppelt suggests that the best word that can be used to express the connotations of general reasoning ability is "intelligence."

FLUID AND CRYSTALLIZED INTELLIGENCE

Although it may seem to be a unitary phenomenon, Cattell (1963) argues that the g factor is represented by two kinds of ability: fluid (g_f) and crystallized (g_c) intelligence. The hypothesized existence of both entities has been tested in several studies that also clarify the distinction between them (Cattell, 1963, 1971; Horn and Cattell, 1966a, 1966b, 1967; Stankov, 1978, Horn, 1979). Fluid ability refers to success in adapting to new situations in which previously learned skills are of no advantage. It represents a form of intelligence that includes inductive, figural, and general reasoning. Crystallized ability, on the other hand, may be described as "breadth of knowledge, sophistication, the intelligence of experience, one's appropriation of the intelligence of his culture. Often this seems to be what people have in mind when they say that a person is intelligent" (Horn, 1979, p. 62). Before the person reaches biological maturity (age 15 to 20), individual differences in the discrepancy between g_f and g_c will result primarily from variations in cultural opportunities and interests. However, in adulthood, differences in age are critical, since g_c continues to grow with experience, whereas g_f declines gradually. The characteristic contrasts between the two may be summarized as follows:

Fluid Ability	Crystallized Ability
1. Reaches maximum development at about age 14 to 15 and declines continuously from about age 22 to old age.	1. Continues to develop at least until age 18, and even well into adulthood, depending on the individual's cultural experiences. It also begins to decline later and to a lesser extent than does fluid ability.
2. The distribution of scores is wide, resulting in a standard deviation of 24 to 25 points.	2. Formal instruction at school, which tends to slow the progress of bright pupils and accelerate the achievement of dull ones, brings about a compressed range of scores resulting in a standard deviation of about 12 to 16 points.
3. Hereditary factors contribute an overwhelming proportion of the variance, since g_f relies on biological and physiological determinants.	3. Environment and experience play a much larger role in shaping g_c.
4. Fluctuations in level of g_f are minimal over time.	4. Variations of intensity in exercise, training, and experience force sharper fluctuations in level of g_c over time.
5. The effect of general neurological impairment will be similar in both, but more pronounced in g_f. The effect of *local* brain damage will be always to lower g_f in proportion to the magnitude of the damage.	5. The effect of *local* brain damage will only be through the localized ability changes. Consequently, if g_c is estimated from a battery of test scores on cognitive operations not affected by that particular area of brain damage, there will be no noticeable effect in g_c.

(Cattell and Butcher, 1968)

One of the most important outcomes of Cattell's work is that the independent influence of general intelligence on learning is accounted for by both fluid and crystallized abilities. Schmidt and Crano (1974) used the nonverbal scale of the Lorge-Thorndike intelligence test to measure fluid ability. Its three subtests—Figure Analogies, Figure Classification, and Number-Series—are the kinds of measures that have been reported as loading heavily on g_f and negligibly or not at all on g_c (Cattell, 1971; Horn, 1968; Horn and Cattell, 1967). For the measurement of crystallized ability, Schmidt and Crano used the five subscales of the Iowa Test of Basic Skills: Vocabulary, Reading Comprehension, Language, Work Study

Skills, and Arithmetic. In the course of testing for giftedness through IQ, researchers generally introduce one kind of test bias (Flaugher, 1978) by using instruments that measure, at least in part, crystallized ability. That is the type of test administered by Terman and many other psychologists in their studies of gifted children.

In a critique of research on fluid and crystallized intelligence, Guilford (1980) argues that the concepts are "fanciful" and represent only a limited, vague approach to intellectual functioning. He finds methodological weaknesses in some of the studies, such as the use of only eighteen tests on a population ranging widely in age, education and occupation, which would tend to bias the results in favor of the theory. His own interpretation is that so-called "crystallized intelligence" is made up of several specific abilities, all of them having semantic content in common. "Fluid intelligence" consists of separate intellectual operations, most of them cognitive. Guilford's remarks are part of the ongoing debate among cognitive psychologists as to whether intelligence is a general ability or is made up of special aptitudes that are fairly independent of each other.

THE IQ AND HIGH IQ CHILDREN

The IQ score is an economical bit of information about several aspects of a person's functioning. As Zigler and Trickett (1978) point out, it measures "a collection of formal cognitive processes such as abstracting ability, reasoning, speed of visual information processing, and all those other formal cognitive processes that appear and reappear with regularity in factor-analytic studies of human intelligence-test performance" (p. 792). The IQ test also reveals something about the individual's past buildup of knowledge and how to retrieve it for solving problems. Finally, performance on intelligence tests is affected by all kinds of motivational strengths and directions.

It is well known that if students are distributed normally with respect to IQ and are given the same amount and quality of instruction and the same amount of time to learn, then IQ and achievement will correlate highly at the end of the instructional period. However, Carroll (1963) and Bloom (1974) hypothesize that, if the same students receive appropriate differentiated instruction and are allowed sufficient learning time, the majority will master the subject they are studying and the correlation between IQ and eventual achievement will approach zero. This would suggest that speed in cognitive processing is a vitally important entity measured by tests of general intelligence. There is also empirical evidence to show that the time it takes to learn correlates highly with IQ and with achievement (Spiegel and Bryant 1978; Gettinger and White, 1979). Children with high IQs are known to be rapid learners, which would also tend to confirm the Carroll and Bloom hypothesis, but the evidence so far deals with *mastery* learning or speed in *consuming* rather than in *producing* ideas. Both kinds of achievement are correlated positively though not perfectly (Oden, 1968).

It is fortunate that a great deal of evidence exists on the characteristics of high-IQ children, and Miles's (1954) summary of findings are generally as true today as they were in midcentury. She reports as follows:

Racial and Social Class Origin. High-IQ children can be found among all races and religious and ethnic groups. The subpopulations that are victims of racial and sociocultural discrimination tend also to be underrepresented by children with high scores on tests of general intelligence.

Sex Ratio. In most high-IQ groups there tends to be an excess of boys over girls, which Miles attributes to sex discrimination relating to opportunities for achievement at school and in high level careers afterwards. These differences may be diminishing in the last quarter of the twentieth century as women steadily achieve equal status with men in all societal institutions.

Heredity and Home Background. High-IQ children may come from impoverished or affluent homes. Socioeconomically, the parents of high-IQ children tend to belong mostly to the professional, semiprofessional, and business classes, and relatively few are semiskilled or unskilled workers.

Physical Traits and Health History. High-IQ children tend to score better than their age peers on anthropometric measures, including height, weight, general physical development, and muscular energy. They walk, talk, and cut their first teeth earlier than do children with average ability and reach pubescence somewhat earlier, too.

School Progress. High-IQ children often enter school early, advance rapidly, enjoy their education, and show special interest in the more theoretical subjects. Judging by their mental age and tested educational accomplishment, they are often far below appropriate grade placement. They excel mostly in subjects that require verbal comprehension and language usage and are least proficient in subjects that have low correlations with tested intelligence, such as physical training, sewing, drawing, sculpturing, and shop work. In short, their strengths are in work requiring abstract thought, and their relative weakness is in activities that involve manual coordination or dexterity.

School Achievement. High-IQ children consistently earn superior achievement scores, although their deviation from the norm in achievement is not as great as their relative standing in IQ tests. As for the effects of special programs on their development, acceleration through conventional subject matter generally proves beneficial, while enrichment in depth is much more difficult to evaluate with exiting standardized measures.

Extracurricular Pursuits and Interests. Large numbers of high-IQ children engage in some kind of learning activity outside of school. Among their extracurricular

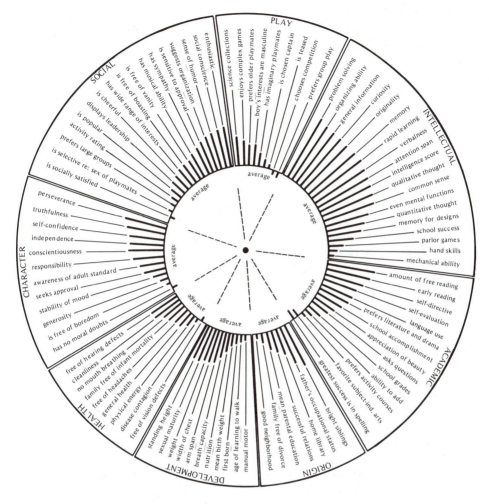

Figure 6-1 Schematic profile of high-IQ compared with characteristics of "average" IQ children (Freehill, 1961, p. 80; reprinted with permission of the author.)

studies are music, drawing, dancing, and foreign language. Reading is their favorite pastime as well as their best liked and easiest subject at school. Many learn to read before starting their formal education. They also engage in many hobbies that involve making collections, such as stamps, rocks, coins, and bottle tops.

Play Activities. High-IQ children tend often to prefer playmates who are older than themselves, and their play interests are generally similar to those of their less gifted peers, except that they lean somewhat in the direction of "thinking games."

Personal and Social Character Traits. On tests of personal and social standards and ideals, high-IQ children show far more favorable social preferences and social attitudes, more desirable preferences, less boastful exaggeration, less cheating, and considerably greater trustworthiness under stress. They are more stable emotionally and tend to be free from psychoneurotic trends. Their strengths lie mostly in intellectual, volitional, emotional, moral, physical, social, and special-ability characteristics and least in fondness for large groups, freedom from vanity, and cheerfulness. They are often called upon for leadership responsibilities, although they are not quite as distinguished for their popularity.

Freehill (1961) presents graphic evidence on differences between high- and average-IQ children in various aspects of their functioning (see Figure 6-1). Note that while the high-IQ children have superior ratings on almost all of the traits measured, the margin of superiority is not uniform. For example, they excel to a much greater extent intellectually than socially. Although the cumulative data on which these generalizations are based are more than twenty years old, subsequent studies have tended to confirm these findings.

Extremely High-IQ Children

Defining precisely what is meant by extremely high IQ is somewhat like judging precisely how high is "up". Researchers vary widely in assigning cutoff points on tests of general intelligence, and the insights they gain are usually based on clinical studies of single or small numbers of subjects (see Jones, 1923; Witty, 1930; Jenkins, 1943; Zorbaugh et al., 1951; Montour, 1977). There are also clinical investigations of prodigies who perform with incredible proficiency in specific talent domains such as music or chess rather than on IQ tests (Révész, 1970; Feldman, 1979). These studies may be contrasted to those of idiots savants who, by definition, can perform exceptionally well in certain skill areas but are below average in tested intelligence (Minogue, 1923; Roberts, 1945; Anastasi and Levee, 1960; Lindsley, 1965).

Several investigations seem to indicate that children who score at or beyond the upper tenth of 1 percent in IQ are distinguishable even from those who are labeled gifted by virtue of their testing at the ninety-eighth or ninety-ninth percentile in general intelligence. Lewis (1943) identified children with IQs of 145 and higher and compared them with those rating between 125 and 144 in a population of forty-five thousand pupils from grades four to eight inclusive. Teachers described the higher-IQ group as being unusually ambitious, dependable, energetic, friendly, honest, investigative, capable of being leaders, liking jokes, and being original, polite, and tidy. However, these children also showed somewhat greater maladjustment than did those slightly below them in intelligence, but only a few of the maladjusted showed signs of aggressive behavior. Instead, teachers found them to be daydreaming, nervous, moody, depressed, unhappy, overly sensitive about self, overly critical of others, suggestible, inattentive in class, lazy, and self-conscious.

Another large-scale study contrasting extremely high-IQ and moderately high-

IQ elementary school children is reported by Barbe (1964). The subjects were 130 children throughout Ohio in grades three through six, half of them with IQs of 148 and above, with the comparison group having IQs of 120 to 134. A huge amount of information was accumulated concerning the children's scholastic development, personal, social and educational adjustment, and family backgrounds. Results show that, although few children were in special classes, the higher-IQ group achieved at a significantly higher level in basic skills and scored better on creativity measures than did the comparison group. Much of the difference is attributed to the performance of girls, who were fewer in number; they earned better scores than did the boys in the younger grades, but the boys showed signs of catching up by grade six.

Regarding adjustment and self-concept, standardized measures revealed that the higher-IQ children were more exuberant, talkative, happy-go-lucky, cheerful, quick, and alert. However, more behavior irregularities were listed by parents for this group than for their moderately able counterparts, sibling rivalry being the difficulty mentioned most frequently. Parents also reported that the higher-IQ children preferred adult companions and were relatively less free from nervous habits. Given the opportunity to state three wishes, these children proved to be more self aggrandizing in contrast to their lower-IQ peers who seemed to be more socially oriented. The higher-IQ children's parents were more likely to be college-educated professionals or attached to managerial occupations, while earning more money and living in more affluent neighborhoods.

The most elaborate study of extremely high-IQ children was conducted by Leta Hollingworth (1942) who established IQ 180 as her cutoff point. Unfortunately, she died before reporting her findings on the follow-up study of these children, which would have included a description of their adult status. However, the original report was finally completed and published by her husband, Dr. Harry L. Hollingworth. Her observations convinced her that these children are probably the most able students at school and likely to win top academic honors at college. For them, ordinary schooling is a waste of time, viewed either with sheer indifference or positive distaste, especially if the demands are no more imaginative than requiring mastery of the multiplication table and all the drudgery that goes with it. To make matters worse, they seem to be tortured by universal problems of good and evil and the general menaing of life. Hollingworth (1942) writes, "the higher the IQ, the earlier does the pressing need for an explanation of the universe occur; the sooner the demand for a concept of the origin and destiny of the self appears" (p. 281).

Probably because of their incredible mental powers, children at the upper extreme of the IQ scale find it difficult to relate socially to their agemates. Hollingworth observed that her sample lacked the ability to make close, congenial friendships. Their play interests were different, and too often they felt that, if they developed socializing habits, they would have "to suffer fools gladly" (1942, p. 299). It was therefore difficult for them to keep from becoming isolates with extremely negative attitudes toward authority.

Terman and Oden (1947) confirmed Hollingworth's findings on the educational superiority and adjustment problems of high-IQ children. Their sample was drawn from their population of fifteen hundred high-IQ children and consisted of forty-one males and thirty-four females with IQs of 170 or above. Compared with children having lower IQs, parents of those at the upper extreme were more likely to be college graduates, engaged in professional work, and members of the highest occupational status groups. The children learned to read earlier and earned slightly higher marks than did the others in Terman's population, although not in proportion to their excess in IQ. They also graduated from high school at a younger age, and the likelihood of their earning an "A" average in college was twice that of the lower-IQ students designated by Terman as "gifted." However, they had serious adjustment problems that the researchers attributed to the large discrepancy between intellectual and social development. The incidence of their being rated poor in social adjustment was twice that of their less able peers, which showed how isolated they could be despite their excellent records at school. What comes through clearly in the Hollingworth and Terman samples is the impression that extremely high-IQ children exist in such small numbers that they rarely have the opportunity to form close relationships with children their own age who can provide the intellectual stimulation that they crave.

Stability of the IQ

Educators are interested in developmental factors associated with exceptionality in children. Where the targeted group is handicapped, insights into etiologies of behavior or learning disorders are considered essential first steps toward prevention. In the case of gifted children, a fostering and facilitating type of intervention is sought, and that, too, can be made possible by examining early signs of superior ability. If a child's IQ is regarded as a sign of giftedness, the question arises as to whether these scores remain stable throughout childhood and beyond. Otherwise, how can we rely on any one score yielded by such a test?

Periodic IQ measurements of individuals at various points in their lifetimes provide information about the long-range stability and growth of tested intelligence. In a study of 252 unselected children from an urban community, Honzik, MacFarlane, and Allen (1948) found that from ages 6 to 18 nearly 60 percent of the group showed IQ changes of fifteen points or more, although the shift of average IQ for the total sample never exceeded five points (118 to 123). Gallagher and Moss (1963) also report wide fluctuations during the first ten years of life, as evidenced from a variety of investigations. In a study of older samples, Bradway and Thompson (1962) found that intellectual functioning can change even after age 16, its rise or decline depending on the quality of a person's learning experiences. Where there is improvement from adolescence to adulthood, it is greater in abstract reasoning and vocabulary than in rote memory and practical reasoning.

In their study of 933 men and women, ages 25 to 64, Birren and Morrison (1961) likewise found that performance on tests measuring the g factor is more related to education than to age. According to Corsini and Fassett (1953), who administered the Wechsler-Bellevue to a sample of San Quentin prisoners for each five-year period from ages 15 to 74, performance subtest scores tend to decline faster with age than do verbal subtest scores, a finding that would confirm the importance of practice in basic communication skills in helping to sustain adult IQ levels. However, a study by Bilash and Zubek (1960) using tests of factorially "pure" mental abilities administered to 634 subjects, ages 16 to 89, revealed that generalized intellectual ability, based on a composite of the eight subtests, declined progressively from the teens to the seventies. The decline was gradual until the forties and very steep after the forties. Differences between the teens and twenties, twenties and thirties, and thirties and forties were all statistically significant. Abilities that held up well with age were comprehension, verbal fluency, and numerical and spatial skills. Those that declined rapidly were reasoning, memory for names and faces, perception, and dexterity. Perhaps these findings are at variance with other studies of age and intelligence because the criterion measures used here were highly speeded, which therefore penalized older adults more than younger people.

Studies of age and intelligence have also been conducted exclusively with high-IQ adults, and the results tend to confirm the findings with more randomized populations. Ghiselli (1957) observed the relationship between intelligence test scores and age of adults under optimal conditions. He hypothesized that the performance of superior adults on very-high-level intellectual tasks without time pressure would suffer little or no deterioration with age. Results show no change in average score from the 20- to 60-year-olds in a population sample of over fourteen hundred. Although the general ability of older people was found to be equivalent to that of the younger ones, with increasing age there was some decrease in variability, so that the older subjects were more alike than were the younger ones. The fact that testing was conducted under optimal conditions may have contributed to the results.

In a somewhat similar study, Owens (1959) retested 127 men in 1950 on the same test (Army Alpha, Form 6) they had taken for college entrance in 1919. He then compared the differential effects of age by initial ability levels and found no tendency for subjects scoring at the top in 1919 to show any special gains or losses by 1950. Thus, it would seem that, from ages 20 to 50, able adult males do not improve their tested intelligence as a result of added years of experience and learning, and they do not regress toward the mean any more than do agemates whose tested abilities in early adulthood had been closer to the national norm.

In a study of high-IQ women, on the other hand, Norman and Daley (1959) found a general downward trend in Wechsler-Bellevue scores associated with age, although the decline was less than for average-ability persons of both sexes reported in Wechsler's standardization sample. A comparison was also made between the older and younger women, all of whom were divided into subsamples of ages 19 to 29 ($N = 75$), 40 to 49 ($N = 25$), 50 to 59 ($N = 25$), and 60 and over ($N = 25$). The groups were roughly equivalent in general ability and years of formal schooling. Results revealed significant differences associated with age, the combined older groups proving superior to the youngest subjects in verbal scores but significantly inferior to them on the performance measures. The older women tended to perform better on tests of Information, Arithmetic, Similarities, and Vocabulary, while the younger ones excelled in Picture Arrangement, Picture Completion, Block Design, and Digit Symbols. It would not be warranted to draw generalizations from this study, considering its small sample, but it does suggest that the relationship between age and general ability may have to be examined separately for both sexes. If sex is a powerful independent variable, then it would be useful to monitor it closely as women's status, roles, aspirations, and opportunities undergo change in the course of time.

In addition to examining the fluctuation of scores obtained for individuals tested repeatedly over a period of years, researchers have investigated the stability of IQ by intercorrelating these intraindividual ratings. Bradway and Thompson (1962) examined 111 adults, ages 27 to 32, who had been tested on the Stanford-Binet as preschoolers in 1931, again in 1942, and finally in 1956 when they took the Wechsler Adult Intelligence Scale (WAIS). Results show a correlation between preschool and adult tested intelligence of .59 on the Stanford-Binet and .64 on the WAIS; coefficients between adolescent and adult scores were .85 on the Stanford-Binet and .80 on the WAIS. It would therefore appear that IQ scores obtained as early as the preschool years are valid predictors of IQs in adolescence and in adulthood.

Much less valid are the IQs obtained in the earliest years of life. Evidence from the Berkeley growth study (Bayley, 1955) shows that we cannot predict later intelligence from scores on tests made in infancy. These assessments are limited by the small range of behaviors that can be observed and recorded. The only measurable infant behaviors include sensory functioning in reaction to stimuli, motor coordination, memory, and recognition of differences. By the second and third years of life, the child can begin to show goal-directed behavior. It is only with the development of language skills during the preschool years that IQ-type tests with heavy verbal content can be administered to obtain scores that correlate highly with later performance on such measures.

By factor analyzing Bayley's data, Hofstaetter (1954) confirmed that sensorimotor alertness predominantly accounts for children's intelligence test performance up to the age of 20 months. From 20 to 40 months, the dominant source of intelligence test variance is *persistence*. From age 40 months on, the factor of sensorimotor alertness contributes almost nothing to the variance of mental age scores, but beginning in month 48 of life, most of the variance is accounted for by the factor of manipulation of symbols. In the second decade of life, the manipulation of symbols accounts for nearly all the variance.

The radical development change that seems to occur at age 4 may explain Bloom's (1964) findings on relationships among a person's infancy and childhood IQ scores. He reports that in the Berkeley study, as well as in others of its kind, IQ tests were administered to children every year after birth until age 17, and the last score in the series was correlated with each of the previous 16. Results show that scores obtained in the first years of life correlate negligibly with the score at age 17; afterward the coefficients climb abruptly to .7 and beyond and remain at that level. (See Figure 6-2.)

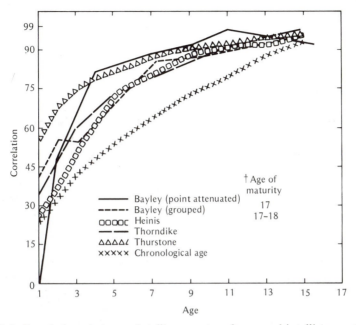

Figure 6-2 Correlations between intelligence at each age and intelligence at maturity† contrasted to select growth curves for intelligence (Bloom, 1964, p. 64; reprinted with permission of author.)

Confirmation of the Berkeley growth study evidence was obtained on high-IQ children in the Collaborative Perinatal Study at Boston Children's Hospital (Willerman and Fiedler, 1974, 1977). In these studies of over four thousand children tested at 8 months, at 4 years, and at 7 years of age, seventy girls and forty-four boys yielded Stanford-Binet IQ scores of 140 or above at age 4. One hundred of these had been administered the Collaborative Research Form of the Bayley Scales of mental and motor development at 8 months. From the evidence collected, it appears that data on mental and motor development, birth weight, and birth order did not differentiate the precocious children from the total population. These results, like the ones obtained in the Berkeley growth study, might be interpreted as evidence that a child's cognitive abilities are more malleable in the first three or four years of life than in the school years and beyond. However, it is equally reasonable to argue that the apparent unconnectedness between levels of infant and childhood performance is basically an artifact of the two ability measures. One is necessarily loaded with sensorimotor content, which is the only kind of performance obtainable for infants. The other kind of test is heavily saturated with cognitive abstractions, many of them transacted verbally. If the two instruments could somehow measure the same skills and yet maintain the same face validity and reliability, the relationship between them would probably be much stronger. But performance measures of any kind are necessarily limited by the subject's environment and repertoire of behaviors, both of which change radically from infancy to childhood. Perhaps a direct assessment of human potential through monitoring brain wave activity will someday bring us closer to the ultimate test of cognitive stability within individuals.

IQ and Mental Age

IQ is a ratio between mental age (MA) and expected mental age (i.e., chronological age, or CA). Since mental age reflects the child's functioning level, the question arises as to why not use that bit of information, instead of IQ, to determine the kinds of nurturance that are most appropriate? In other words, is not a 10-year-old with an MA of 15 comparable in ability to a 15-year-old with the same MA and therefore eligible for the same kind of education? Fortunately, comparisons have been made among children of different CAs, but matched for MA, and the evidence suggests wide variations in the way in which their cognitive abilities are organized.

Kolstoe (1954) examined differences in performance on intellectual tasks between twenty-nine third- and fourth-grade children with IQs of 116 and above, whose MAs were matched with those of twenty-nine eighth- and ninth-grade students with IQs of 82 or below. Results favored the dull group on the WISC subtests of Comprehension and Coding, the Symbol Copying test scored for speed, and the PMA subtest, Number. The bright children, on the other hand, excelled on the subtest Digits and on the Symbol Copying test scored for accuracy. Both groups performed equally well only on the subtests Picture Arrangement, Block Design and Object Assembly. These results suggest that chronological age should be taken into account in assessing the primary abilities of children who are comparable only in MA.

The evidence is even more dramatic when the measurement criteria are reading skills. Bliesmer (1954) assembled groups of high- and low-IQ children whose mental and chronological ages were the same as Kolstoe's samples, respectively, except that in this study the high-and low-IQ children were compared on a battery of reading tests rather than on cognitive aptitudes. Significant differences were found in five of the subtests, and they all favored the bright group. These children excelled in location or recognition of detail, recognition of main ideas, drawing inferences and conclusions, total comprehension ability, and listening comprehension. No differences were observed in word meaning, word recognition, and reading rate, but score discrepancies on memory for factual details and perception of relationships among definitely stated ideas approached significance in favor of the bright children. The results imply that bright children are significantly superior to dull children of comparable mental ages with respect to the relatively more complex language skills. This suggests that mental age is not just a quantification of general tested abilities but also has qualitative meaning that relates to the chronological age at which an MA score is obtained.

In addition to comparing different age groups matched on MA, researchers have investigated the organization of mental abilities of children who are high-, average-, and low-IQ, but are comparable in chronological age. Lucito and

Gallagher (1960) examined patterns of intellectual strength and weakness in the WISC subtests for seven samples of children and adults: three with IQs of 125 to 145, one with IQs of 90 to 110, and three with IQs of 40 to 75. In each of the samples, the mean weighted subtest ratings for the group were ranked, and the high-IQ children's scores intercorrelated at a moderately positive level (.83, .44, and .47); for the low-IQ children, the rank-order correlations also showed fairly high coefficients (.72, .77, and .46). However, correlations between high- and low-IQ samples were consistently negative, with three coefficients significant at the .05 level. Indeed, to some extent the patterns of intellectual development for the two groups were mirror images of each other.

The outstanding strengths of the high-IQ children appeared, for the most part, in tests of similarities, vocabulary, and information. These children benefited from their large fund of past information and their ability to associate abstract concepts. The researchers felt that enrichment for the high-IQ children could best be served by an analytic, evaluative curriculum rather than by one restricted to acquiring facts, skills, and information. The low-IQ groups, on the other hand, were relatively strong in their capacity to use structured, concrete visual materials on tasks where most of the elements necessary for problem solving are presented to the examinee and only modest reorganization and association skills are required for success. These results were confirmed in a replicative study by Thompson and Finley (1962) with much larger samples of 400 high-IQ and 309 low-IQ children.

Thus we see that tested intelligence, which represents a relationship between an individual's *actual* and *expected* mental age, is more than just a barometer of general intellectual power. It also carries implications about *relative* strengths and weaknesses that are different for high-IQ as compared with average- and low-IQ children. This would tend to qualify Terman's belief that high-IQ children differ from their less able peers in degree rather than in kind.

Longitudinal Studies of High-IQ Children

A good way to validate the importance of superior general ability as a factor in giftedness is to look at what happens to high-IQ children in later years of life. Several investigations of this type have been reported on samples of various sizes, and results show consistently that such children tend to grow up relatively healthy, wealthy, and wise. Terman's study, of course, has produced the best known and most complete set of findings. But there are others that are important in their own right, even if they serve mostly to test the reasonableness and generalizability of some of Terman's conclusions.

MacDonald, Gammie, and Nisbet (1964) conducted a follow-up study of high-IQ British children who had been tested over a five-year period (1950-1954) for transfer from primary to secondary education. Two samples were identified, one consisting of 125 boys and 67 girls with IQs of 130 and above, the second of 38 boys and 34 girls with IQs 125 and 129. Results indicate that 65 percent of the first sample entered a university, as compared with 56 percent of the second group and

20 to 25 percent of the comparison group of 14,000 11-year-olds (average IQ between 104 and 105) examined during the five-year period in the same city where the high-IQ groups had been tested.

The children who went on to university were more likely to come from the male subsample and from homes where the fathers' occupations were nonmanual and relatively prestigious. Twenty-nine of the 125 males and 34 of the 67 females did not enter a university. Thirteen of them, including 9 sons and daughters of manual workers, had had adequate qualifications for admission but elected not to attend. The remaining 50 were not qualified, but took up a wide variety of careers, many of which also involved further education of a high standard. The lack of a one-to-one correspondence between IQ and the pursuit of higher education, in addition to the fact that home background and sex factors also made a difference, show clearly that general ability on its own is only a tentative predictor of eventual success at school. The chances are that special educational opportunities offered to the high-IQ children in this sample after they reached their eleventh birthday may also have had something to do with preparing and encouraging them to continue on to advanced studies.

Sumption's (1941) follow-up study of children who had attended Major Work Classes in Cleveland suggests that special education per se makes a difference in the lives of able children. Questionnaires were sent to a large number of graduates from Cleveland public schools, 25 percent of whom responded. These were divided into three groups, one of them with a mean IQ of 127.6 for those who had studied from four to twelve years in Major Work Classes, a second with a mean IQ of 127.2 consisting of those who had spent two or three years in Major Work Classes, and a third with a mean IQ of 126.5 for those who had not spent any time in Major Work Classes. An analysis of the questionnaires revealed that the two experimental samples exceeded the control in response to the question, "Have any awards, scholarships, citations, or any other honors been conferred on you since leaving our public schools?" (p. 80).

Another follow-up study of graduates of the Major Work Classes was conducted by Barbe (1955, 1957). In this investigation, there was a 77 percent return on questionnaires sent to all graduates of the program over a fifteen-year period, thus producing a sample of 456 adult subjects. The respondents reported that 91 percent of the men and 53 percent of the women had attended college for at least one term. Forty-four percent of the total group already held college degrees, and about one fifth did not attend college, nearly half of them for lack of financial means. The respondents generally reported having a wide range of interests, many of which involved activities with other people, and their social adjustment seemed to be exceptionally healthy, as evidenced by their joy in participating in numerous community and school activities.

The predictive validity of scholastic aptitude was tested further in an eight-year follow-up study of Merit Scholars (Nichols and Astin, 1966). The scholarship winners were those who turned out to be the most promising students based on a two-stage screening process that subjected them to a test of educational development, the Scholastic Aptitude Test of the College Entrance Examination Board, and a review of all application materials, including high school records, recommendations, and test scores. Information was obtained in 1964 on all but 75 of the 3,106 subjects who had been named as Merit Scholars from 1956 through 1959. Results show that 95 percent of the 1956 group had earned bachelors' degrees, and of the 16 percent of the 1959 sample who had not yet completed their undergraduate studies, almost all were planning to do so eventually.

In the Nichols and Astin study, as in others that have monitored the development of high-IQ-type children, the results show a higher dropout rate for females than for males in advanced education; only 69 percent of the girls as against 87 percent of the boys entered a graduate or professional school. An overwhelming majority of the scholars reported being heavily involved in intellectual pursuits and dedicating their abilities to the fulfillment of self and service to society. However, the researchers report that "over two thirds of the scholars had made major changes in their career plans since entering college. The net effect of these changes was to reduce the proportion of scholars planning careers in scientific research and engineering, initially the most popular fields, and to increase the range and diversity of career choices" (p. 18). Such changes in career aspirations were probably accompanied by emotional conflicts in many instances, or at least some adjustment problems.

Studies of the educational histories of high-IQ children grown up do not mean to suggest that college enrollment represents a fulfillment of early promise. Few college students go on to become distinguished producers of ideas or outstanding performers in the arts or in any service professions. However, posthigh school education is necessary, albeit rarely sufficient to qualify an individual for nearly any high-level career. Moreover, high-IQ children who go on to advanced schooling have a much better chance of achieving prominence than do their equally able peers who do not and their less able peers who do. This was borne out by Burt's (1962) case histories of nearly three hundred children with IQs of 135 and over, most of whom eventually enrolled in universities or in some other form of posthigh school education. Only 16 percent failed to bear out the predictions of career success implicit in the initial assessments.

A comparison of Terman's so-called "A" and "C" groups (Olden, 1968) provides even more dramatic evidence that IQ is not a perfect predictor of success in the arts and professions and that college attendance is a good forerunner of accomplishment among adults who had possessed superior test intelligence as children. The A's and C's had comparable IQs and achievement scores in elementary school, but the A's started to pull ahead early in high school, and by the time of graduation, the slump of the C's was quite marked. Even in 1940, when the two groups consisted of people ages 25 and older, there were only moderate differences between them in intelligence test scores. Nevertheless, 97 percent of the A's entered college and 90 percent graduated, whereas only 68 percent of the C's enrolled and 37 percent earned diplomas. As would be expected, the A's were more likely to achieve "life success," which Terman defined as the extent to which the subjects have made use of their superior intellectual ability, regardless of earned income. By 1960, when the average age of the samples was 50, the career differences between them seemed to be even wider (Oden, 1968), with the A's far surpassing the C's in self-ratings on ambition for excellence in work, recognition for accomplishments, and vocational advancement.

The C group represents only a small minority that deviated from the norms for accomplishment in Terman's population. On the average, even this handful of men had better scholastic and work histories than did their contemporary generation in general. By 1960, 62 percent were in retail business, clerical jobs, or skilled trades, 13 percent in official, managerial, or semiprofessional positions, and 5 percent in various professions, while only 15 percent had either full-time semiskilled occupations or were employed less than full time. The median income for the group was nearly 50 percent higher than that of white male workers at the time. It is evident, therefore, that the superior tested intelligence they exhibited from childhood to middle age worked for them too, despite some psychosocial handicaps that apparently prevented them from achieving the kinds of success they would otherwise have achieved.

As for Terman's total sample, the follow-up data make it clear that a large proportion of these high-IQ children have excelled as adults. Oden (1968) reports that in 1960, when they were in midcareer, 46.6 percent of the men were in professional occupations and another 40 percent were in official, managerial, and semiprofessional work. Among the women, more than 45 percent were housewives, and of those with full-time employment, some 64 percent were in professional and semiprofessional occupations and another 37 percent in the business world. It is interesting to note that the careers favored most frequently clustered around law, engineering, teaching, science, and responsible positions in business. The modest influx into the arts and politics may have been due to the relatively few openings in these fields. Or, perhaps the IQ, which figured so prominently in the selection of the original sample, is too restrictive a measure to discern talents other than those related directly to scholastic aptitude. Nevertheless, it would be a mistake to assume that these grown-up high-IQ individuals distinguished themselves only in rapid and high-volume mastery learning and in finding solutions to problems that others had found before, but did not distinguish themselves in innovative work of lasting value. Terman and Oden (1959) report that at midlife seventy-seven of the eight hundred men surveyed were listed in *American Men of Science* and thirty-three in *Who's Who of America*. An estimate of the men's productivity showed that it was anywhere from ten to thirty times as great as expected, the output including some sixty-seven books, more than four hundred short stories and plays, and over fourteen hundred professional and scientific papers. Women, of course, showed a far more modest record of creative accomplishment because so many of them were spending full time taking care of home and family. At the next follow-up in 1960, when the group had reached its fiftieth birthday or close to it, Oden (1968) again saw signs of exceptional productivity through its long list of publications, patents, and other professional and business accomplishments, as well as the many recognitions and honors bestowed upon its members.

The Terman population has had an exemplary record not only in school and career accomplishments but also in psychosocial development. Serious mental illness and personality problems have been reported less often than one might expect in a nongifted population, and criminal records exist hardly at all. Most of the men and women have found time to participate actively in promoting civic welfare efforts and generally fulfilling the obligations of good citizenship. Oden (1968) concludes: "Now after 40 years of careful investigation, there can be no doubt that for the overwhelming majority of subjects the promise of youth has been more than fulfilled" (p. 51).

Longitudinal investigations of Terman's subjects did not end in their peak years with the follow-up studies of the 1950s and 1960s. In 1972, a half-century since the first set of data was collected, questionnaires were returned by some nine hundred respondents who constituted a large majority of subjects still alive at the time. They were entering their retirement years and had an opportunity to look back on their careers and life experiences in general. This time, separate reports were issued about the men (Sears, 1977) and women (Sears and Barbee, 1977). Results show that in comparison with male controls, the better educated among the men were more likely to continue their full-time employment, enjoy higher occupational status, and achieve greater success in their careers from ages 30 to 50. Thirty years earlier, they rated themselves highly persistent and successfully integrated in their work, and twelve years earlier, they reported real satisfaction with the kinds of occupations they had entered and rated themselves more ambitious than other men. Interestingly, though, there was little relationship between job satisfaction and income.

In 1940 there were already two key indicators of how the men would feel about their careers as they looked back upon them in 1972. One factor at average age 30 was the self-rating on persistence and planning about work activities, and another had to do with whether the occupation at that time had been entered out of choice or by simply drifting into it. In the next two decades, important forecasters of occupational satisfaction included the person's feelings about his chosen work, his health, his estimate of how well he lived up to his potential, and how he rated himself on career ambitions. It is noteworthy that such seemingly important variables as occupational status, income, and education had no predictive value. As for their marital status, the men who had in earlier years reported close attachments to their parents and affectionate relationships with them, especially with their mothers, were more likely to keep their marriages intact.

As for the women, income workers were compared with homemakers, and the self-reports reveal that those who had been employed outside the home expressed satisfaction with their work, particularly if they were heads of households, whereas the homemakers were less satisfied with theirs. However, the married women rated themselves higher than did the single and divorced women on "general satisfaction 5," which Sears and Barbee (1977) defined as "covering the five areas of occupational success, family life, friendships, richness of cultural life, and total service to society" (p. 56). Parents' career levels and choices were not related to the women's careers or with the satisfaction they expressed in the work they had chosen for themselves. Rather, the women's own level of education, occupation, health, and ambition related positively to their satisfaction with life and work.

Whereas the subjects' earlier relationship with their parents did not relate to how they eventually felt about their careers, it figured prominently as a forerunner of "general satisfaction 5" and joy in living. What made an important difference, according to the subjects, was their parents' understanding and helpfulness, parents' encouragement of their independence, and the general admiration subjects express- ed for their parents. Other predictors of "general satisfaction 5" and joy in living were the subjects' earlier ambition for excellence in work and vocational advance- ment and high self-ratings on self-confidence and persistence.

In comparing the general life satisfaction scores between men and women, Sears (1979) found the men clearly superior in occupational satisfaction, the women more pleased with friends and cultural activities, and both sexes achieved greater than expected satisfaction in family life, with no difference in ratings between men and women. As for next steps in the study, Sears speculates

How long will the research continue? Into the foreseeable future, in any event, for on actuarial grounds, there is considerable likelihood that the last of Terman's gifted children will not have yielded his last report to the files before the year 2010! And of course, on the same grounds, it is most likely that the last one will be *her* report, not *his*! (p. 96)

Criticisms of the Terman Studies

Some sharp attacks have been leveled against Terman's research methods, and hence his conclusions in the longitudinal study. Hughes and Converse (1962) have summarized a number of weaknesses discovered by many critics. For example, there is a suspicion that the original sample represents only a small proportion of the many children who might have qualified with IQs of 140 and above and were somehow missed in the selection process. The main experimental group of 643 was obtained from canvassing a school population of 159,812 children, of whom 1,758 should have been in the top 1.1 percent (IQ of 140 or above) instead of the 643 discovered by Terman and his associates. By lowering the cutoff point to 135, an additional 1,600 cases should have been found, thus raising the total to 3,358. This is over five times the 643 that Terman actually located.

Hughes and Converse also summarized misgivings about the selection process that started with teacher nominations and went through group testing before the "finalists" who had completed these earlier stages received the individually admin- istered IQ test. This procedure led to a disproportionately high representation of advantaged racial groups and socioeconomic classes. It also placed too much confidence in the acumen of teachers who are notoriously deficient in recognizing high-IQ children through observation of their classroom performance. (See Chapter 19 for a more detailed discussion of teachers' skills in identifying giftedness in their pupils.) Even at the stage where the Stanford-Binet was administered, criticism was leveled at the bias introduced by such an instrument, not just discrimination against low-status racial and socioeconomic groups, but against the varieties of talent that would allegedly be ignored by such a test. Laycock (1979) charges that the Stanford-Binet is mainly a school-related test measuring potential for academic performance while ignoring other relevant indicators such as motivation and imagination. According to him, Terman's children succeeded in fields that are tied mostly to schooling and are therefore restrictive when compared with the wide varieties of equally important careers in which success does not depend heavily on high scholastic aptitude.

Laycock feels that Terman's use of group comparisons rather than matched pairs in order to determine how the gifted differ from the general population hampered the precision of his analyses. A far more serious methodological limitation is the fact that cross-sectional data on successive samples of high-IQ groups representing childhood, adolescent, and adult age levels at different points in time were never collected to compare with the results of the longitudinal study. This kind of temporal control might have shown that high-IQ people are different from each other in some important ways depending on whether they reached their fortieth birthday in 1950, 1970 or 1980.

Despite the limitations in Terman's methodology, his data are so abundant and the message they carry about the high-IQ individual over much of the life span is so powerfully consistent that it would be naïve to gainsay the importance of general intellectual abilities as measured by the IQ test in the development of giftedness. It would be equally naïve to say that every person with a potential for greatness in any line of human endeavor that society prizes needs to have an IQ of at least 135, as did Terman's group. The cutoff point for IQ is undoubtedly not fixed for the many forms of excellence that are known and appreciated, but it is easy to imagine that at least above-average general ability is necessary for those whom our society values highly.

PROCESSES OF COGNITION

Assessment of general abilities in high-IQ children and adults has been confined mostly to monitoring various forms of intellective powers that are not necessarily understood but do correlate to some extent with various kinds of individual accomplishment. Because research evidence is geared heavily in this direction, much is known about how well those with high IQs function in the work they do, but there is little information concerning the qualitative development of what Piaget calls "intellectual structure," as it applies to the gifted.

Piaget's interest in qualitative development led him to divide the growth of intelligence into a number of stages that occur in a fixed sequence and can be distinguished clearly from each other. Their interrelationship is also "cumulative" in the sense that the intellectual structures defining the earliest stage are incorporated into those of the next stage and so on until the developmental periods have been completed. For the first two years of life, the human organism goes through its sensory motor period in which it develops the ability (1) to focus visually on sources of sound, (2) to be guided by auditory, visual and tactile cues,

(3) to recognize that objects still exist and may be located even after they disappear from view, and (4) to exhibit goal-directed behavior that is governed from the outset by conscious intention. There follows the preoperational period, from age 2 to 7, which Piaget finds somewhat puzzling. The child's intellectual ability can be underrated because of frequent failures in solving simple logical problems; yet, sensible and logical behavior are usually evident in free-play situations.

During the school years, from age 7 to 11, the child is at the stage of concrete operations in which formal thought processes follow rules of logic more easily. The child can solve problems having to do with comparisons of sizes, numbers, classes and subclasses of objects, and distances between objects. In essence, there are signs of some beginning understanding of time, space, number, and logic. However, such advanced performance indicators as mastering the scientific method by holding control variables constant while manipulating experimental variables one at a time are not developed until the next stage, that of formal operations, which begins at age 11. At that point, the child can begin to understand some basic ideas about causal relationships and deductive thinking (Piaget, 1952, 1954; Piaget and Inhelder, 1969).

The sequence of Piagetian developmental periods tends to be invariate, except perhaps for children with severe mental handicaps. However, the production of Piaget-type tests that could yield quantified scores based on formal standardization has had a relatively short and difficult history, much of it beginning in the 1970s (Tuddenham, 1971; Sharp, 1972; Tyler, 1976). Experimental tests do not yet provide clear indications about the developmental stage that an examinee has successfully reached, the correlations among same-stage items often ranging only between .10 and .40.

Tuddenham (1971) expresses the pessimistic view that "the evidence thus far obtained has about extinguished whatever hope we might have had that we could place each child on a single developmental continuum equivalent to mental age, and from his score predict his performance on content of whatever kind" (p. 75). Nevertheless, correlations between this kind of measure and IQ tend to be impressive, though far from perfect. Kaufman (1971), for example, obtained correlations of more than .6 between a Piaget-type test and both the Lorge-Thorndike and Gesell tests administered to a group of kindergarten children. These findings were substantiated by later evidence reported by Zigler and Trickett (1978) that showed that the correlations between the two types of tests tend to hover around .70. In a follow-up study of Kaufman's kindergarten sample, it was found that both the Piaget and Lorge-Thorndike instruments had similar correlations of better than .60 with first-grade achievement. The evidence is therefore fairly clear that Piaget-type measures tend to assess the kinds of scholastic aptitudes that are revealed through the administration of IQ instruments but that they are not yet efficient in yielding qualitative insights into the child's functioning at a particular developmental stage.

Thus far, there is little evidence about high-IQ children's movement through the Piagetian periods of development. One major effort in this direction is reported by Keating (1975) in a study of early adolescents (fifth- and seventh-graders), with each age group divided into subsamples of bright and average pupils, based on scores obtained on Raven's Standard Progressive Matrices. When Piagetian tasks were administered to the four groups, results showed that the brighter children outperformed their average peers on the formal operational tasks. No significant difference on total score was obtained between the bright seventh- and fifth-graders, but the important fact is that the bright fifth-graders outperformed the average seventh-graders. Keating suggests that, where growth is tied more closely to physiological maturation, as in the child's moving from one developmental period to the next, there is less evidence of precocity than where growth depends more on interaction with the environment. This would confirm the findings by Webb (1974) and Lovell (1968) who report that rapid acceleration is more clearly evident within stages than across stages.

Kaufman (1968) also found IQ a factor in the performance of third-and fourth-graders on conservation tasks. In his study of low (IQ 81 to 99) middle (IQ 100 to 110), and high (IQ 114 to 133) functioning children, he found that, whereas the coefficients were .7 and .5, respectively, for the third and fourth grade samples, they were close to zero for second- and fifth-graders. His results led him to speculate that

all children within a given Piagetian stage do not perceive the conservation tasks in the same way and may well be attacking the problems from different developmental levels regardless of their performance on the tasks. Thus, IQ may be quite an important ingredient in the conceptual ability of a child of a certain optimum age who attacks a particular problem in his characteristic way; but IQ may be unrelated or less related to a younger or older child's conceptual ability since their modes of attacking a problem may be quantitatively different. (p. 6)

COGNITIVE HIERARCHIES

The idea of cognitive hierarchies is not only associated with theories of development, such as Piaget's; it has also been posited as a comprehensive index, arranged in order of complexity, of the ways in which the intellect can function in a learning or creative experience. Of these, the most widely used as a guide in developing higher-level thinking exercises for the gifted is the cognitive domain of the *Taxonomy of Educational Objectives*, developed by Bloom and his associates (1956). The hierarachy consists of six gradations of complexity in cognitive processing, each of which is further divided into more finely distinguished levels of sophistication within each category. From lowest to highest, the hierarchial divisions and subdivisions are as follows:

1.00 Knowledge
"Includes those behaviors and test situations which emphasize the remembering, either by recognition or recall, of ideas, material, or phenomena" (p.62).
1.10 Knowledge of Specifics

        1.11 Knowledge of Terminology
        1.12 Knowledge of Specific Facts
     1.20 Knowledge of Ways and Means of Dealing with Specifics
        1.21 Knowledge of Conventions
        1.22 Knowledge of Trends and Sequences
        1.23 Knowledge of Classifications and Categories
        1.24 Knowledge of Criteria
        1.25 Knowledge of Methodology
     1.30 Knowledge of the Universals and Abstractions in a Field
        1.31 Knowledge of Principles and Generalizations
        1.32 Knowledge of Theories and Structures

2.00 Comprehension

"Includes those *objectives*, *behaviors*, or *responses*, which represent an understanding of the literal message contained in a communication" (p. 89).

     2.10 Translation
     2.20 Interpretation
     2.30 Extrapolation

3.00 Application

"A demonstration of 'Comprehension' shows that the student *can* use the abstraction when its use is specified. A demonstration of 'Application' shows that he *will* use it correctly, given an appropriate situation in which no mode of solution is specified" (p. 120).

4.00 Analysis

"Comprehension emphasizes the grasp of the meaning and intent of learning content, and application denotes bringing to bear appropriate generalizations or principles to further understanding. Analysis involves the breakdown of the material into its constituent parts and detection of the relationship of the parts and of the way they are organized" (p. 144).

     4.10 Analysis of Elements
     4.20 Analysis of Relationships
     4.30 Analysis of Organizational Principles

5.00 Synthesis

"This is a process of working with elements, parts, et cetera, and combining them in such a way as to constitute a pattern or structure not clearly there before" (p. 162).

     5.10 Production of a Unique Communication
     5.20 Production of a Plan, or Proposed Set of Operations
     5.30 Derivation of a Set of Abstract Relations

6.00 Evaluation

"Making of judgments about the value, for some purpose, of ideas, work, solutions, methods, material, et cetera. It involves the use of criteria as well as standards for appraising the extent to which particulars are accurate, effective, economical, or satisfying." (p. 185)

     6.10 Judgments in Terms of Internal Evidence
     6.20 Judgments in Terms of External Criteria

In another formulation of a six-level hierarchy, Gutman (1961) offers the following gradations of behavior from lowest to highest: (1) vegetative, (2) reflex, (3) conditioned response, (4) learned behavior, (5) problem solving, and (6) creative activity. On the *vegetative*, or physiological, *level*, input consists of food, water, and oxygen, and output is made up of various waste products and secretions. On the *reflex level*, the input is from a well-defined single stimulus in the form of energy of one kind or another, and output is a single response in which energy is expanded. In *simple conditioned response*, stimuli are paired, associations are formed, and responses are made to stimuli that did not have the power to elicit them previously. At the *learning level*, input is represented either by a series of stimuli or a complex stimulus situation, and output consists of a series of responses and a more complex behavior pattern. In *problem-solving behavior*, input is made up of circumstances which constitute obstacles to need gratification and requires the organism to engage in complex cognitive processing in order to solve the problem efficiently. At the highest level of human functioning, *creative activity*, individuals impose a new order on their environment.

Newland (1976) proposes a hierarchy of what he calls "cognitive styles," or variations in the ways in which people apply their abilities. These "styles" may be viewed as intellective processes, not unlike those posited in Bloom's taxonomy, and are reflected in the following kinds of behaviors: (1) discovering, (2) organizing, (3) describing, (4) evaluating, and (5) creating. Newland cautions that, even though these behaviors are listed separately, they interact to a greater or lesser extent, depending on the nature of the activity. A describer organizes and evaluates in the course of production, and the creator also harmonizes these processes but in a unique and imaginative manner. However, people tend to favor the use of one or two cognitive styles over the others and should be educated to expand their repertoires. These processes are defined by Newland (1976) as follows:

1. *Discovering*: locating and/or identifying data, phenomena, and/or interrelationships of a relatively minor conceptual magnitude among phenomena—the "bits and pieces" (relatively) of which our world is constituted. Probably we should include here the recognizing of relationships among such givens or "discovereds," the integrations and principles which are necessary to but not of the same inclusiveness as a science, or the "subthemes" in musical productions. This kind of behaving can be related to Guilford's "cognition" kind of intellectual operation.
2. *Organizing*, of both ideational and social phenomena: as in effecting a well-integrated research undertaking; in effecting structure to implement some form of social welfare, union, or (even) criminal program; in structuring a philosophy or a philosophy of science, a major work in music or in the theater. In terms of social outcome, this well may be superordinate to the function of discovering and recognizing conceptual structures, although equally "high intelligence" is essential to both.
3. *Describing*: setting forth what has been discovered, how the discovery was made, and/or how the organization was effected. Given the productions of 1 and 2 above, there is a need to communicate them verbally to lay persons or to other specialists in the same or other, possibly related, fields. This is essentially an expository function but necessitates high-level comprehension and high verbal skill.
4. *Evaluating*: determining whether elements or structures (probably provided by other persons as described above) are new, different, relevant, or contributive. This is a necessary adjunct to the other manners of functioning. It obviously is related to Guilford's "evaluative thinking."
5. *Creating*: the manipulating of givens, whether symbolic or physical, with a view to

producing something that is new, productive, and relevant to some goal or objective. This kind of functioning is apparent in producing novel relationships among words (literature), sounds (music), ideas (science, philosophy, religion), and operations among components of a social or mechanical structure (new welfare and educational programs, new motors, or whatever). (pp. 67-68)

MAXIMIZING THE USES OF GENERAL ABILITY

A different kind of approach to describing higher cognitive processes is in the context of ways in which people use their brainpower to achieve full potential. According to Fletcher (1978), formal education is often oriented toward emphasizing what he calls minimum skills and competencies. This is inevitable in school and society, where the norm in human variability is treated as if it were the ideal. Fletcher argues instead that education should adopt as a major goal the stretching of the human mind to its outer limits, with every child having a personal standard based on capacity to learn rather than on some vague notion about how much accomplishment is necessary in order to get by. According to Fletcher, human educability can be maximized by the use of the following cognitive capacities:

Capacities to Assimilate Experience. This involves increasing the efficiency of the five senses, possibly through hypnosis, medication, and diet, and even through various altered states of consciousness or guided fantasy. It also includes mobilizing additional senses that the human organism possesses through the use of the entire body as a receptor. There are vestigial senses comparable to those used by other animals that can be developed with the help of various forms of biofeedback. Then, there is extrasensory perception, or psi phenomena, which may add a new dimension to human experience if experimenters can help to produce such events on demand. Finally, there is the process of looking inward and achieving some enlightenment through meditation and contemplation. In this connection, Fletcher suggests two lines of inquiry, Jung's investigation of the "Collective Unconscious" and Grof's work on evoking prenatal, preconception "past-life" experiences. The work of both these psychotherapists relates to the ageless idea that all knowledge can be found by searching within oneself.

Capacities to Process (Store, Combine, Synthesize) Experience. Within the constraints imposed by age/stage sequences in cognitive development, it is possible to expand the means by which the organism deals with reality. One way is to elevate to the conscious level those powerful subconscious patterns that affect the way in which the person perceives the world and the behavior that is a consequence of that perception. Another way is to cultivate means of processing that are not necessarily logical and linear. This would involve making use of offbeat mental exercises, such as training people to organize material in patterns and arrays, to make use of analogies, to employ myth and metaphor, and to fantasize intention, purpose, and personification to inanimate objects. Finally, there is the need to maximize creativity through practice in synthesizing ideas, developing innovative ways to deal with existing and anticipated problems, and introducing newness in products or performance.

Capacities to Take Action. An inventory of extraordinary human behavior past and present can help to provide a perspective on how high or deep are the *proven* reaches of the brain. In some instances, these limits are approached through individual effort, in others with the help of positive group synergy in which a team inspires the performance of its members. It would therefore be helpful to understand the special social and professional climates that existed in such groups as the Bauhaus, the Vienna Circle, and even Weight Watchers, Alcoholics Anonymous, and assorted championship athletic teams. To exercise one's full capacity to take action, it is also necessary to exploit to one's advantage various critical events in life, such as marriage, birth of a child, loss of a job, a major promotion, a major illness, or retirement. The achievement of superior states of health can keep the energy level high, even among people whose abilities would ordinarily decline in their retirement years.

Capacities to Determine or Create Purpose. With the help of developing methodologies by futurists, it is possible to begin to understand the meaning of social indicators and the way in which they connect with the stream of important historical events. A better analysis of trends is a first step toward exercising some control over them. That kind of power, in turn, places a responsibility on individuals to develop a conception of what they would like the future to be. It also leads to clarifying conceptions of the good life and the social significance of enhancing personal development.

MAPPING THE COGNITIVE FUNCTIONS OF THE BRAIN

There is a suspicion with ancient origins about a duality in human experience that involves (1) knowing and (2) appreciating. But it was not until past the middle of the present century that a significant amount of research evidence has begun to suggest that this duality in modes of thought reflects a concentration of different mental abilities in the right and left cerebral hemispheres of the brain. At the lowest levels of information processing, the two hemispheres perform the same function, albeit in a mirror-image fashion. The left hemisphere absorbs through the senses those stimuli that originate primarily from the world on the right side of the body, and the right hemisphere senses the world on the left.

With respect to more complex cognitive processes, the two hemispheres operate quite differently. The great majority of right-handed people (95 percent) and a smaller proportion of left-handers (64 percent) have their dominant language functions located in the left hemisphere. This part of the brain is heavily involved in the processing of language and rational planning behavior. It is also responsible for short-term memory that figures so prominently in any kind of dialogue around a particular subject, since participants have to retrieve from their memory banks whatever content is shared in the course of verbal exchange in order to sustain conversation. We use the left hemisphere for the expression of language through speech and writing, and for mathematical concepts as well. We rely on it also for our linear-sequential reasoning, particularly the convergent production of ideas to solve problems for which there are predetermined solutions and which require the learner to exercise powers to discriminate, differentiate, and classify.

The right hemisphere, on the other hand, dominates our appreciation of spatial relationships and patterns, imagery, fantasy, dreams, music, and body language, including the interpretation of facial expressions. It may also exercise control in divergent thinking processes requiring multiple solutions of problems for which there is no one right answer. In addition, it seems to play an important part in aesthetic judgment through its sensitivity to beauty and harmony.

Although it is tempting to assume there is a need to integrate left- and right-hemisphere functioning in order to maximize human performance, the evidence is not yet abundant enough to be conclusive. However, there may be considerable credence in Scheffler's (1976) belief in the need to develop children's "cognitive emotions," or, as Rubenzer (1978) describes it, to bridge the gap between "unfeeling knowledge" (primarily left-hemisphere development) and "mindless arousal" (primarily right-hemisphere development only). More data are needed to clarify how the two hemispheres interact, and with what effect. Judging from the content of the school curriculum and the relative importance placed on various kinds of subject matter, one fact seems clear: our schools seem preoccupied with left-hemisphere functioning. This emphasis may be part of the legacy of our scientific revolution and the secularization of Calvinist codes. Moreover, the intellectual competencies governed by the brain's left hemisphere seem to be measured most efficiently by the conventional IQ, which may explain why such tests are widely used in measuring potential for success at school.

CONCLUSIONS ABOUT THOUGHT PROCESSES AND THE IQ

If the proverbial visitor from a remote planet wanted to carry back home a single earthly artifact to reveal the modes of thinking emphasized in the modern classroom, there could be no better choice than the IQ test. The reason is that, in most of their educational transactions, teachers and pupils are constantly "IQ-ing." Their inquiry and dialogue are couched in the same thought processes tapped by this instrument. In fact, the basic rules for problem solving are so widely understood that, if children in our schools are asked to explain what causes rain, they know that a scientific solution is expected of them, not one that involves the will of deities, as would be the case in other societies. The IQ, therefore, reveals as much about educational values as it does about the status of a particular kind of rational behavior exhibited by the examinee under test conditions. As a mirror of existing priorities in education, the IQ can serve us valuably by reflecting back to us the limitations of our curricular objectives and by revealing those students who stand a good chance of excelling in our existing school programs. However, the danger of such an instrument lies in its power to "dictate" what *ought* to be valued in children's thought processes and, by inference, in the school curriculum. In other words, the test takes on an inflated importance only when teachers spend most of their time teaching to the test and when behavioral scientists equate giftedness with superior performance on such measures.

Chapter 7

Special Abilities

The idea of a general factor in intelligence has stirred up considerable controversy, some of it concerning its very existence. Spearman (1927) recognized the g factor as an intellectual force that is necessary for every kind of problem solving. He also discovered specific abilities that share common variance with the g factor and are partly independent of it. These aptitudes presumably relate to narrow areas of specialization. Later, his data convinced him that special abilities combine into clusters, each of which shares a common variance, and he called them *group factors*. This three-tier pyramid consisting of general, group, and specific factors was eventually confirmed by Vernon's (1950) investigations, and he likewise emphasized the importance of the g factor in various kinds of human performance. In fact, Vernon (1965) argues that the predictive validity of the g factor is at least as strong as any primary aptitude in intelligence testing. To the extent that g figures prominently in any particular kind of performance, it is necessary to channel it to meet the challenge of that specialization. Thus, for example, the writer exercises not only the requisite verbal aptitude, but also the more general reasoning ability that figures in music, mathematics, social science, or any other worthwhile area of accomplishment.

Vernon (1950) divides g into two major group factors: *v:ed*, denoting verbal-educational aptitudes, and *K:m*, referring to spatial, mechanical skills (see Figure 7-1). The major group factors could be subdivided into minor group factors that show more specific abilities in the two major categories and finally break down into specific factors that relate directly to the content of school subjects.

At the opposite extreme is the view of Guilford, who is convinced "that the 'group' factors, which Spearman relegated to minor roles, are the most significant components of intelligence and the existence of a g component is extremely doubtful" (Guilford, 1973, p. 632). To support his contention, he cites over seven

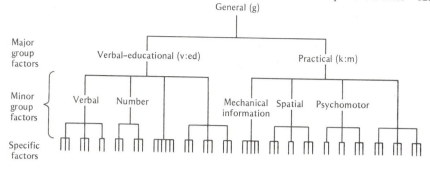

Figure 7-1 Model of a hierachical organization of abilities (Vernon, 1960, p. 22; reprinted with permission of the publisher.)

thousand correlations among numerous measures of intellect with as many as 17 percent of the coefficients hovering around zero. These outcomes seem to be in line with Anastasi's (1970) report of low correlations between tests of general intelligence and various special abilities. In a high-IQ population, Wilson (1953) found no correlation between IQ and musical memory, artistic ability, and mechanical aptitude, although this may have been due partly to the restricted IQ range of the sample. Such data suggest a possible alternative to the assertion that excellence in a particular field involves a commitment of superior general ability that might apply just as well to other areas of specialization. Contrary to Spearman's argument that tests of intellect share some common variance, some believe mental strength flows exclusively from specific aptitudes that relate to a person's area of accomplishment.

FACTOR ANALYTIC CLASSIFICATION

The use of factor analysis to demonstrate the existence of distinguishable special abilities was developed and applied originally by Thurstone (1947). His work led him eventually to identify seven primary factors that can be recognized as separate entities, though partially related to each other as well as to an overall g factor (see Figure 7-2). They include V (verbal meaning) in vocabulary tests and scrambled sentences, W (word fluency) in anagrams and word naming, N (number ability) in arithmetical exercises, M (memory) in rote learning, S (spatial relations) in various figural forms and structures, P (perceptual speed) in visual discrimination, and R (reasoning ability) in inductive and syllogistic analyses. Eventually, the Primary Mental Abilities Tests were produced (Thurstone, 1958), which yield separate scores on V, N, S, P, and R as well as an extrapolated estimate of an overall IQ. This enables psychometricians to map intellectual profiles that show relative strengths and weaknesses within individual children and, of course, to compare children with each other.

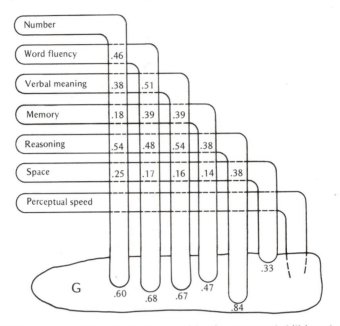

Figure 7-2 Thurstone's multiple-factor theory, with primary mental abilities ralated to each other and to a general capacity (Bischof, 1954, p. 14)

Undoubtedly, the best known multifactor theory of intelligence is Guilford's Structure of Intellect (1959, 1967). He defines *intellect* as information processing and *information* as anything the organism can discriminate in its field of perception. *Intelligence* is a qualitative tag referring to the proficiency with which the intellect functions. The Structure of Intellect model is usually presented in the form of a cube to show that it has three dimensions: operations, contents, and products (see Figure 7-3). Operations is the engineering dimension denoting the alternative ways in which the organism can process any kind of informational content and develop out of it products that take any form. There are five categories under operations, five under contents, and six under products. Altogether, 150 factors are identified, and they consist of every possible combination of categories representing the three rubrics.

To illustrate how the three categories modify each other, circles are drawn around divergent production of semantic units, classes, relations, systems, transformations, and implications merely to illustrate 6 of the 150 possible combinations, their definitions, and the kinds of tests used to measure them.

Operations	Contents	Products
C cognition	F figural (Visual + Auditory)	(U) units
M memory	S symbolic	(C) classes
(D) divergent production	(M) semantic	(K) relations
N convergent production	B behavioral	(S) systems
E evaluation		(T) transformations
		(I) implications

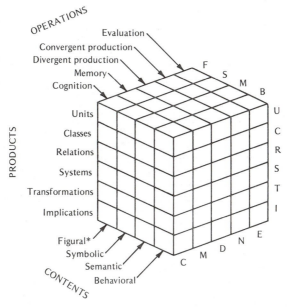

Figure 7-3 The Structure of Intellect model and definitions of its categories (Michael, 1977, p. 153; reprinted with permission of the publisher).

*In a subsequent presentation of his model, Guilford divided figural content into auditory and visual, thus increasing the number contents from four to five.

OPERATIONS	CONTENTS	PRODUCTS
Major kinds of intellectual activities or processes; things that the organism does with the raw materials of information, information being defined as "that which the organism discriminates."	Broad classes or types of information discriminable by the organism.	Forms that information takes in the organism's processing of it.
C *Cognition.* Immediate discovery, awareness, rediscovery, or recognition of information in various forms; comprehension or understanding.	**F** *Figural.* Information in concrete form, as preceived or as recalled possibly in the form of images. The term "figural" minimally implies figure-ground perceptual organization. Visual spatial-information is figural. Different sense modalities may be involved, e.g., visual kinesthetic.	**U** *Units.* Relatively segregated or circumscribed items of information having "thing" character. May be close to Gestalt psychology's "figure on a ground."
M *Memory.* Retention or storage, with some degree of availability, of information in the same form it was committed to storage and in response to the same cues in connection with which it was learned.	**S** *Symbolic.* Information in the form of denotative signs having no significance in and of themselves, such as letters, numbers, musical notations, codes, and words, when meanings and form are not considered.	**C** *Classes.* Conceptions underlying sets of items of information grouped by virtue of their common properties.
		R *Relations.* Connections between items of information based upon variables or points of contact that apply to them. Relational connections are more meaningful and definable than implications.
D *Divergent Production.* Generation of information from given information, where the emphasis is upon variety and quantity of	**M** *Semantic.* Information in the form of meanings in which words commonly become attached, hence most notable in verbal	**S** *Systems.* Organized or structured aggregates of items of information; complexes of interrelated or interacting parts.

OPERATIONS	CONTENTS	PRODUCTS
output from the same source. Likely to involve what has been called transfer. This operation is most clearly involved in aptitudes of creative potential. N *Convergent Production.* Generation of information from given information, where the emphasis is upon achieving . . . conventionally accepted best outcomes. It is likely the given (cue) information fully determines the response. E *Evaluation.* Reaching decisions or making judgments concerning criterion satisfaction (correctness, suitability, adequancy, desirability, etc.) of information.	thinking and in verbal communication but not indentical [sic] with words. Meaningful pictures also often convey semantic information. B *Behavioral.* Information, essentially non-verbal, involved in human interactions where the attitudes, needs, desires, moods, intentions, perceptions, thoughts, etc., of other people and of ourselves are involved.	T *Transformations.* Changes of various kinds (redefinition, shifts, or modification) of existing information or in its function. I *Implications.* Extrapolations of information, in the form of expectancies, predictions, known or suspected antecedents, concomitants, or consequences. The connection between the given information and that extrapolated is more general and less definable than a relational connection.

DMU - *Divergent production of semantic units* (ideational fluency). Production of many ideas appropriate in meaning to a given idea (e.g., list consequences of unusual event, such as no babies born for one year; list as many uses as possible for a common brick or wooden pencil).

DMC - *Divergent production of semantic classes* (spontaneous flexibility). Production of many categories of ideas appropriate in meaning to a given idea (e.g., arrange given words into different meaningful groups).

DMR - *Divergent production of semantic relationships* (associational fluency). Production of many relationships or associations appropriate in meaning to a given idea (e.g., write as many synonyms as possible for common words).

DMS - *Divergent production of semantic systems* (expressional fluency). Ability to produce a variety of ideational systems from a known set of idea units (e.g., write many different four-word sentences, the first letter of each word being given).

DMT - *Divergent production of semantic transformations* (originality). Production of a number of changes of interpretation, neither immediate nor obvious, that are appropriate to a general requirement (e.g., list *remote* consequences that others would not think of as possible results of an unusual situation such as people not needing or wanting sleep).

DMI - *Divergent production of semantic inferences* (elaboration). Production of a number of antecedents, concurrents, or consequents of given information (e.g., add detailed operations needed to make a briefly outlined plan succeed).

After postulating the existence of 150 abilities, Guilford then applied factor analysis methods to determine their existence empirically. However, despite the fact that the Structure of Intellect model has had a strong impact not only on understanding the nature of giftedness in children but on current theories about human mental functioning generally, it has not been free from criticism. For example, Carroll (1968) argues that the factor analytic evidence presented by Guilford and his associates is not decisive because the statistical techniques they use provide little opportunity to reject their hypotheses. Carroll's suspicion is reinforced by Horn and Knapp (1973), who concede that Guilford's model has considerable heuristic value but are doubtful about the empirical supports. They express skepticism over an approach to factor analysis, such as the one used by Guilford, which confirms hypotheses in 93 percent of the tests. By applying what they call "Procrustean" methods of factor analysis to Guilford's own data, they found that, in fully 84 percent of the cases where a variable was designated *randomly* as a marker for a factor, it was possible to produce a solution in which the variable loaded highly on the factor hypothesized beforehand. They charge that Guilford used similar arbitrary procedures to force solutions in support of his Structure of Intellect paradigm, when in fact, such an approach makes it possible to promulgate an arbitrary theory about factor structures.

But even if the Structure of Intellect had the necessary empirical underpinnings, there are still those who would question its practical value. As McNemar (1964) remarks caustically, fractionating and fragmentizing ability into what he calls "more and more factors of less and less importance" may reflect nothing more than some special sign of "scatterbrainedness." He goes on to conclude that

general intelligence has not been lost in the trend to test more and more abilities; it was merely misplaced by a misplaced emphasis on a hope. . . that in turn was based on a misplaced faith in factor analysis: the hope that factors, when and if measured, would find great usefulness in the affairs of society. By the criterion of social usefulness, the multiple aptitude batteries have been found wanting. (pp. 875-876)

Guilford's factors remain yet to be tested fully for their concurrent and predictive validity. Perhaps none of the factor measures correlates with accomplishment in a specific line of activity any more than does a test of general intelligence. It may even turn out that a small handful of subtests in the Guilford battery provides a good estimate of IQ, as do the Differential Aptitude Tests' (DAT) Verbal Reasoning and Numerical Ability subtests, which together correlate highly with IQ, thus supporting the DAT manual's contention that the two subtests can serve most of the purposes for which a general ability measure is usually given. It should be kept in mind, however, that Guilford never intended to compete with the IQ in measuring human potential but rather to define the variety and organization of human ability. He attempted to show mental functioning as represented by an aggregate of special competencies that can be discerned and described. Such a conceptual framework is especially valuable for the educator who wants a clear perspective on the range of special aptitudes that ought to be cultivated at school and also wants to inventory those that are and those that are not neglected. In all probability, only a few of Guilford's 150 special abilities receive more than just passing attention in any curriculum, even in special ones for the gifted.

DIFFERENCES IN INFORMATION PROCESSING

The factor analytic studies of intellect conducted by Guilford and his associates represent by far the most ambitious investigations of their kind. A different approach to mapping the full range of special abilities is taken by Carroll (1976) who uses an information processing construct to posit what he calls "a new structure of intellect" consisting of twenty-four cognitive processes. He suggests fewer factors than does Guilford, but he deals in much greater detail with the strategic operations open to the learner in the course of solving problems.

Carroll's twenty-four factors are as follows: (1) *spatial scanning*, which involves a visual search for connectedness of lines and spaces, such as finding the right path through a maze as quickly as possible; (2) *length estimation*, requiring a comparison of distances; (3) *perceptual speed*, or a quick visual search through a field for specified figural elements; (4) *flexibility of closure*, in which a figure is recognized in relation to a surrounding visual representational field; (5) *spatial orientation*, in which a visual image is rotated mentally; (6) *visualization*, which requires further problem solving after spatial orientation solutions have been obtained; (7) *figural adaptive flexibility*, which requires solutions to problems built on those categorized under "flexibility of closure"; (8) *memory span*, involving the storage and retrieval of information; (9) *associative rote memory*, an elaboration of memory span tasks; (10) *speed of closure*, which requires a retrieval from memory of an intact image to match a partial stimulus cue; (11) *word fluency*, which involves retrieval of word meanings or structures from the memory bank to associate in some meaningful way with stimulus graphemes, phonemes, or whole words; (12) *fluency of expression*, which emphasizes grammatical structures and syntactical patterns of phrases and sentences; (13) *associational fluency*, or the elaborate use of semantic associations; (14) *verbal comprehension*, or the ability to retrieve the correct meaning of words from the memory bank; (15) *number facility*, involving the retrieval of appropriate number associations and algorithms and using them to perform serial operations on stimulus materials; (16) *induction*, involving the development of hypotheses on the basis of previously mastered logical operations; (17) *syllogistic reasoning*, which requires the retrieval of meanings and algorithms from the memory bank to develop the required relationships with various kinds of content; (18) *general reasoning*, with special emphasis on the logical characteristics of semantic and mathematical content; (19) *ideational fluency; (20) originality*; (21) *semantic redefinition*, which resembles various aspects of Guilford's divergent thinking processes, involving the production of various plausible solutions to problems; (22) *semantic spontaneous flexibility*, also related to divergent thinking processes, which refers to category shifts in brainstorming solutions to problems; (23) *sensitivity to problems*, involving a logical analysis of causalities and consequences of actions; and (24) *mechanical knowledge*, including special aptitudes for analyzing the operational properties of different kinds of machines.

PEOPLE WITH EXTRAORDINARY APTITUDES

A question arises as to how early in a child's life do aptitudes become differentiated and measurable. Actually, there are many records of *Wunderkinder* (wonder children) who have proven by their own accomplishments that it is possible to become highly specialized even during the early childhood years. For example, Karl Witte learned to read German, French, Italian, Latin, and Greek by the age of 9, enrolled at the University of Leipzig soon afterward, and was awarded the Ph.D. degree with distinction before reaching his fourteenth birthday. William James Sidis performed brilliantly in mathematics before reaching adolescence. And there is hardly a lover of serious music who has not heard about the extraordinary performances of child prodigies such as Yehudi Menuhin and Ruggiero Ricci. Actually, a person who does not show special aptitude for the violin and receive appropriate training in early childhood is unlikely ever to qualify for performance on a concert stage. Yet the same cannot be said for cellists, who can take up their instruments sometimes as late as adolescence and, with proper studies, eventually achieve world renown for solo performances.

In one of the earliest attempts to measure and cultivate special abilities in children as young as four and one half to five and one half, Davis, French, and Lesser (1959) developed the Hunter Aptitude Scales for the gifted and experimented with them at the Hunter College Elementary School (New York City). The tests focused separately on Vocabulary, Number, Reasoning, Science, and Space. When the battery was administered to a sample of 110 children, the average correlation among the subtests was .44, an indication that the five intellectual abilities are related only loosely to each other. A group of 27 preschoolers, selected on the basis of high scores on the aptitude tests, enrolled in the Hunter College Elementary School and constituted an experimental class. The average IQ for these children was 132. Another preschool class, admitted on the basis of the Stanford-Binet with an average IQ of about 153, served as the control class. Pretesting on the Thurstone Primary Mental Abilities Test (PMA) was also conducted on the experimental and control groups, and the results generally favored the experimentals on all measures, except Number, despite a 21.2-point difference in IQ favoring the controls.

As a supplement to the usual school program, efforts were made to provide special emphasis in the five areas in which the experimental class was selected. It was hypothesized that, by matching educational experience to each child's special strengths, there would be an increase in general participation and productivity in the areas that the children demonstrated exceptional ability. Again, the PMA was administered as a posttest at the end of the year, and again the experimentals outperformed the controls on all but the Number tests. The results add credence to the idea that, within a restricted range in tested intelligence, where IQs are mostly in the upper 2 or 3 percent of the general distribution, discrepancies of as many as twenty-one IQ points reveal little about rates and directions of intellectual growth, whereas special ability tests apparently do. This study also suggests that aptitude structures of high-IQ children may be measurable even in the preschool years. Indeed, Robinson (1977) reports on children with extraordinary special abilities even at ages 2 and 3. Some have highly developed verbal skills even before reaching their second birthdays; others as young as ages 2 or 3 can assemble complex puzzles and draw maps of their immediate surroundings; and there are 3-year-olds with memories of minute details of events they have experienced.

Whether specialized abilities become more differentiated with age is a matter of considerable speculation. Russell (1956) quotes conflicting data on the question but personally supports the hypothesis that a general factor can be elicited in most mental tests and that specific abilities become more and more differentiated as children grow older. These developmental processes seem evident in people who excel in their own separate ways. In each case it is clear that we need to consider both *general* and *specific* abilities as contributors to giftedness in various fields of specialization. The importance of the two kinds of intellect can be illustrated through evidence on such diverse types as idiots savants, scientists, mathematicians, artists, and the socially gifted.

Idiots Savants

One way in which to show how independent special and general abilities can be of each other is to examine a sampling of reports on so-called "idiots savants" classified as mentally retarded and yet capable of performing incredible mental feats of a specific nature. Lindsley (1965) dismisses what he considers several myths about idiots savants including the beliefs that (1) they are schizophrenics whose developmental history is not sufficiently understood, (2) the single talent these retarded persons demonstrate may be impressive in the handicapped population but not among normals, (3) the skills have no practical value, and (4) because of their rarity, these cases should be considered unsolved mysteries. Lindsley considers this kind of thinking "an unnecessary concession to the doctrine of unitary behavioral ability. Happily, retarded geniuses still exist, but unitary behavior skill does not" (p. 227).

Lindley presents the case of Kiyoshi Yamashita, a boy with an IQ of 68 who nevertheless displayed superior artistic skills. Yamashita received formal art instruction and produced paintings that were so noteworthy that, when he was 35 years old, an admiring critic published a booklet describing his work, including photographs of outstanding compositions. Lindsley offers the novel theory that in this case and in others, where there are sharp discrepancies between levels of general and specific abilities, deficits may actually be an advantage, since a limited symbolic repertoire seemingly spares idiots savants the distractions of irrelevant and time-wasting hypotheses when they are in the midst of solving a problem.

Yamashita's success in achieving some measure of renown is unique among the small number of idiots savants described in the professional literature. The others remained obscure despite their special talents, and although they constitute too small a sample from which to draw generalizations, their record suggests that an extraordinary single aptitude does not constitute giftedness unless it is reinforced by other mental strengths. The published reports about such cases are usually in the form of brief descriptions without any attempt at clinical analysis.

For example, Jones (1923) reports on an adult male with an IQ of 74 who demonstrated a poor memory for designs and a deficiency in the use of verbal material but was nevertheless capable of memorizing thousands of trivial facts such as the populations of all cities with more than five thousand people and names and numbers of rooms in about two thousand leading American hotels. Jones discredits the theory that an idiot savant has any exceptional aptitude; instead, he regards such a person's interest and drive as a compensation for physiological, social, and intellectual handicaps.

There is also a theory that the idiot savant is endowed with extraordinary eidetic imagery. Bousfield and Barry (1933) reached this conclusion after observing an adult male prodigy add up three- and four-place numbers more quickly than an adding machine and give the log of any number to seven places. Anastasi and Levee (1960) reached similar conclusions after studying a 38-year-old male with a WAIS IQ of 73 who had suffered epidemic encephalitis that had caused permanent brain damage during infancy. Yet he was capable of recalling a written passage verbatim after only one or two readings. In addition, he showed musical ability that was advanced enough for him to receive lessons from outstanding musicians and to be allowed to practice with famous orchestras. But even though he showed signs of knowing musical theory, the extent of his understanding could not be ascertained.

One of the best known and most detailed studies of an idiot savant is reported by Scheerer, Rothman, and Goldstein (1945). Their subject was a 19-year-old male whose IQ at age 6 was 86, but by ages 11 and 15 his IQ had dropped to 50. he was incapable of understanding what he read and failed at any tasks requiring comprehension or reasoning. The special ability he showed was in calculations covering any date in the years 1880 to 1950. He could remember the day and date of his first visit to a place and also the names and birthdays of those he met there. His immediate auditory memory was good (seven digits forward and six backward), and he could add up ten to twelve two-place numbers instantaneously. At age 4 he counted rapidly by sixteens and later developed the ability to spell words backward and forward with great facility but did not care at all about their meanings. During his preschool years he never asked "why" questions; he was emotionally indifferent to other children; and he displayed many rigid fears and habits that remained with him throughout adolescence. When tested for eidetic imagery, he demonstrated subnormal ability on visual tasks and, in general, had poor visual-motor coordination. His ability to deal with abstractions was impaired, and, possibly due to these deficiencies, he was strongly driven to excel in some mental tasks to come to terms with a world beyond his grasp.

The sparse literature on idiots savants provides little understanding about the organization of their abilities. However, it does show that parochial aptitudes can develop unilaterally, while the others remain profoundly deficient. Although hardly anyone can demonstrate such near-magical feats, they usually amount to little more than anomalous trifles that may be entertaining but hardly of much consequence. If an idiot savant's aptitudes were represented graphically, the profile would show an inordinately tall, narrow single peak amid exaggerated depressions. One peak can produce dazzling cognitive effects, but the depressions will prevent the effects from enriching the lives of any audience. Giftedness requires both: it has to startle with its brilliance and edify with its profundity.

Scientists

In his summary of research on cognitive factors associated with achievement in science, Cole (1979) points out that measured intelligence is as influential for success in scientific careers as it is for job status in the total American stratification system. Its effect on the status of a person's occupation is greater than father's background, father's education, or family size. Although it is not a vital factor in forecasting the initial placement of a scientist in the prestige hierarchy of the profession, it is of critical importance later on. After the scientist's first job, IQ influences positional recognition directly, regardless of first job prestige, educational background, and scholarly performance.

Roe's (1953) retrospective study of eminent scientists also shows the influential effects of IQ. The total sample in this investigation consisted of sixty-seven subjects, including roughly equal-sized groups of biologists, physical scientists, and social scientists, who were between 31 and 60 years of age and were judged by their peers as distinguished contributors to their fields. The background data of the subjects resemble closely some of the outcomes of Terman's longitudinal study of high-IQ children. As in the Terman sample, a disproportionately large number of scientists were born to professional parents, were first born in the family, excelled in elementary and secondary school, and enjoyed their education. The median IQ was 166, at least one standard deviation above that of Terman's group.

The biologists, physical scientists, and social scientists seemed to show marked variations in their personal development. Although they all valued learning for its own sake, their interests were directed differently. Physical scientists were preoccupied early with gadgets of all kinds, social scientists with literature and the classics, and biologists with a number of subjects, most of them outside of natural history. Many physical scientists expressed early feelings of social isolation, but the social scientists came from families where relationships were relatively close. In response to projective measures, the latter group showed more aggressiveness toward other people than did biologists and physicists.

Equally important were the differences in the way in which scientists think. Roe found that their visual aptitudes, auditory-verbal skills, imageless thought, and kinesthetic abilities were directly relevant to the type of science fields or subjects they pursued. Also, geneticists and biochemists obtained higher scores on nonverbal tests than did the physiologists, botanists, and bacteriologists who made up the rest of the biological sciences sample. Also, the anthropologists were relatively low in mathematical ability as compared with the psychologists and the social science group. As for the physicists, those dealing more with theory in their respective fields scored higher on verbal tests, in comparison with the experimentalists who excelled on the spatial measures.

Roe's data did show some relationship between specific cognitive strengths and areas of specialization in science. Yet it would be difficult to justify counseling young students on which branches of science they should enter, or even whether they should concentrate on science at all, on the basis of cognitive measures alone, for several reasons: (1) existing tests may not be adequate for such purposes; (2) special aptitudes are not sufficiently measurable until after childhood in order for such prognoses to be made; or (3) tests of cognition only reveal whether the person has the intellectual power to qualify for careers in science, but whether such careers will be pursued has little to do with the intellect.

One of Terman's follow-up studies of gifted children reported in 1954 showed that nonintellective factors may be more critical than is suspected. In an effort to discover why scientists and politicians could not work harmoniously in government, he compared his gifted children who grew up to be scientists with those who eventually elected to major in law, the humanities, and the social sciences. Since a great deal of data had been accumulated on these subjects over the years, it was possible to search for whatever developmental differences may have existed between the two subsamples.

Of the many variables on which comparisons were made, 108 yielded significant differences. The first had to do with an early and persistent interest in science. As 11-year-old children in 1922, those who were later to fall in the science group were already showing a far higher tendency toward interests in science than were those who were to go on to other careers. Moreover, these inclinations were still evident eighteen years later in 1940 when the subjects were already launched on their careers. Since the differences between the two groups in 1940 were in most cases similar to those in 1922, it would seem that educational concentration and vocational experience were not the sole factors in shaping interest patterns during adulthood. Even in later years, the interest patterns were surprisingly constant. Of the 250 men taking the Strong Vocational Interest Test as college freshmen and again twenty years later, few showed appreciable changes in their scores, and such changes as occurred bore little relation to the kind or amount of involvement in their respective fields in the interim.

Furthermore, comparisons between the two groups on their interests in business occupations showed sharp differences, with the nonscience groups favoring such pursuits far more strongly than did their scientific counterparts. Commenting on this, Terman points out that physical scientists, engineers, and biologists are the ones who do most of the secret research for the government and are compelled to operate under rules laid down by a Congress composed mainly of lawyers and business executives. Although it would be oversimplifying the matter to assume that the difficulties of these contrasting groups in trying to understand each other are explained merely by their different interests per se, personality factors can be critical in such circumstances.

Finally, an analysis of the data revealed that nonscientists scored higher than did scientists in social relations. There were various degrees of social adjustment and social understanding within each group, but overall, Terman's scientists tended to resemble Roe's in showing relatively little need for strong interpersonal ties to accomplish their work successfully.

Terman's follow-up study of high-IQ children who entered fields of science reveals little about specific cognitive factors that may have qualified them to pursue such careers. It is possible that some measure of differential aptitudes would have helped to forecast major fields of productivity at least from the time the children were of high school age, if not earlier. In the absence of these kinds of data, noncognitive and environmental factors loom large. There is general agreement in the Roe and Terman studies on the nature of these characteristics, and there is further confirmation in MacCurdy's (1954) survey of six hundred men and women who had earned honorable mention or better in the Science Talent Search of 1952 and 1953. In the latter study, comparisons were made between the superior science students and their contemporaries in general education who had outstanding scholastic ability. MacCurdy found that, with respect to personality, the science students had a strong curiosity about causality in relation to natural phenomena. Their thoughts often took the form of daydreaming or mental puzzle solving, and they often enjoyed symbolic art and classical music. They tended to prefer activities that were solitary or nearly so; yet they did not enjoy the role of a spectator who was entertained by the accomplishments of others. Preferences for independent activities led them to read science, take nature walks, tinker with gadgets, practice photography, and build radios. Typically, their activities in high school were scholarly, with much emphasis on scientific problem solving. There is also an important place for an inspiring science teacher who helped them to determine the course of their professional lives.

In addition to the studies by Roe, Terman, and MacCurdy, which were conducted on adult populations, there have also been investigations of elementary and high school children gifted in science. Anderson, Page, and Smith (1958) report on their study of high school seniors in Kansas who scored in the upper 10 percent on any of the following measures: science, mathematics, English, social studies, and IQ. Out of a total population of 1,445 students tested, 98 males and 47 females scored in the upper 10 percent in science. An examination of the mathematics, social studies, English, and IQ scores of this group revealed that they placed at the forty-third, fifty-sixth, fortieth, and fifty-seventh percentiles, respectively. The relatively modest relationship between ranking in science and in other tested abilities, particularly intelligence, suggests that this aptitude is partially independent of any other. Even the overlap between science and mathematics scores seems less than is often expected.

The question of whether there exists a specific science aptitude was also addressed in Brandwein's studies of more than one thousand students from a single New York City high school (1951, 1953, 1955). Brandwein doubts the existence of "science talent" as something that is transmitted hereditarily; instead, he attributes high-level ability in science to the following indicators:

1. The *genetic factor*, defined as high IQ (at least 130 or above) and such correlated special abilities as verbal, numerical, and abstract reasoning. These kinds of intellective strengths seem to be especially important for excellence in science.
2. The *predisposing factor*, which is marked by persistence, or determination to get work done, and a questing attitude that can only be satisfied with better solutions to complex problems. Children who are highly predisposed to success in science are willing to spend extra time and free hours to complete a task, even if it means withstanding discomfort along the way. They are also willing to face failure while realizing the virtues of patience in the quest for success. Underlying any serious task commitment is a dissatisfaction with existing ways to explain the workings of the world and a need to find new understandings that will clarify them better and better.
3. The *activating factor*, in which the inspired, competent science teacher plays a key role. Brandwein's intensive study of twenty-two high school teachers confirms the findings of Knapp and Goodrich (1952) concerning the influence of mentors on scientists' careers. The most distinguishing characteristics associated with teacher effectiveness include advanced study and frequent publication in science and education; affiliation with a local or national professional organization; active involvement in formulating courses of study in science; interest in a wide range of extracurricular activities and hobbies; a personal demeanor marked by vigor, decisiveness, and a sense of humor; a love for teaching and a commitment to stay in the profession; success in projecting the image of a guide, a counselor, a friend, guardian, and "father-confessor" to students; and an expressed need for self-improvement in the profession.

Brandwein's study emphasizes motivational and inspirational factors associated with high school students' success in science. He does not differentiate specific cognitive factors, except to say that the ability to deal with abstractions at a high level is an important prerequisite. Nevertheless, there has been an attempt to determine the specific nature of science aptitudes and how to measure them.

Lesser, Davis, and Nahemow (1962) constructed a test to assess children's mastery of science material that had been learned previously and also their ability to combine elements into principles and to apply the scientific method. The scientific aptitude instrument addressed itself to the following behavioral objectives:

1. Ability to recall information
   a. Knowledge of scientific vocabulary
   b. Knowledge of scientific principles

    c. Knowledge of tools and scientific instruments

    d. Knowledge about the natural environment

2. Ability to assign meanings to observations

    a. Formulation or verbalization of a principle to explain an effect described

    b. Identification of crucial elements of a problem

3. Ability to apply new principles in making predictions

    a. Utilization of available information in novel situations

    b. Utilization of a scientific principle in a familiar situation

    c. Analysis of the factors influencing predictions

4. Ability to use the scientific method

    a. Planning steps leading to a solution

Lesser and his associates administered the test to fifty-eight third-graders at the Hunter College Elementary School. The children ranged in age from 6 years, 9 months to 7 years, 9 months, and their Stanford-Binet IQs ranged from 136 to 171, with a mean score of 151.4. The predictive validity of the Science Aptitude Test proved to be extremely high. One form of the measure correlated .77 with a battery of seven science achievement tests, and the other form correlated .74 with the same science achievement battery. Performance on the aptitude tests also proved to be closely associated with teachers' ratings of the children. In fact, the aptitude scores were much better predictors of the children's accomplishments in science than were the IQs. The researchers suggest that a reason for the weak relationship between verbal intelligence and science achievement may stem from the fact that IQ scores were obtained from one to three years earlier than were the science achievement scores, while the science aptitude test was administered just before the school year, during which the validating information was gathered.

Another possible explanation of the poor predictive validity of IQ is that the scores of the Hunter College sample may have been high enough to exceed the threshold level for excellence in science. This would mean that beyond, say, IQ 140, any increment denotes the kind of additional intellective power that is not specific enough to the requirements of science to make much difference. Besides, the reliability of scores at either extreme of a normal distribution tends to be weaker than those closer to the middle. Despite the 35-point range in IQ, the children's scores were beyond two standard deviations above the mean and well within a narrow band of less than 3 percent of the normal distribution. In such a restricted sample, one can hardly expect relatively unreliable IQ scores to correlate highly with science achievement, even if IQ were strongly associated with achievement potential in that subject across the entire ability range.

It would seem, therefore, that at some point in the IQ distribution there is a threshold beyond which IQs are no longer predictive of achievement in science. At that point, IQ should probably give way to assessment of special aptitudes. Such tests are valuable, either because they provide new insights into the *nature* and *extent* of a child's scientific aptitudes, or because they measure the same cognitive power that the IQ test does, except that they are better at differentiating among children who are more or less capable of *using* that power to excel in science.

Mathematicians

As do physical scientists, mathematicians tend to reveal their promise relatively early in childhood, reach their peak years relatively early in adulthood, and stop creating newness in science relatively early in their senior years. Since mathematical talent develops rapidly, it is not difficult to find instances of great mathematicians displaying remarkable precocity even in childhood. Charles Babbage, Carl Friedrich Gauss, Gottfried Wilhelm Leibnitz, Blaise Pascal, and Norbert Weiner are only a few who have attracted attention as child prodigies. Those who are outstanding in mathematics at school are fortunate, not only because teachers recognize their talents relatively easily, but also because the school curriculum features mathematics among its major subjects. While special programs are not often designed for budding mathematicians, the mathematically precocious can race through the conventional sequence into the electives and begin planning original work at their own pace if school policy makes such allowances. The same cannot be said for children with potential for becoming playwrights or politicians. Their kinds of talent are hidden so deeply in the psyche as to escape easy detection. Even if children's playwriting or political skills were as recognizable as were their potential in mathematics, there would be no comparison in the amount of educational opportunities offered at school in these disciplines. The conventional curriculum does not stress drama or social leadership enough to provide special stimulation for children who could benefit most from it.

Despite the fact that mathematical precocity often reveals itself in the early school years, it is still difficult to predict the degree and kind of success a child will eventually have in later life. As Aiken (1973) observes,

Obviously, the findings of the correlational, descriptive studies . . . are at best suggestive. Not only do they fail to account for the wide variation in creative abilities among mathematicians, but somewhat different results would undoubtedly be obtained on cross-validation. And even if personality assessment devices were vastly improved, situational and contingency factors undoubtedly play as large a role as personality traits in stimulating and fostering creativity. For example, what child psychologist, equipped with all of the personality assessment devices that 20th century psychometrics has . . . could predict that the boy Isaac Newton would be one of the most creative geniuses of our time? (pp. 418-419)

Nevertheless, there are certain consistencies in research findings with respect to mathematical precocity. Sherman (1980) summarizes these factors as general intelligence and/or verbal skill; spatial visualization; confidence in learning mathematics; perceived attitude of mother, father, and teacher toward one as a learner of mathematics; perceived usefulness of mathematics; effective motivation in mathematics (a kind of joy in problem solving); and for girls only, the extent to which mathematics is perceived as a sex-neutral rather than a male domain.

As in the case of scientific talent, the cognitive underpinnings of mathematical ability include general intelligence and appropriately facilitating special aptitudes. Language skills are also critical in learning mathematics. Aiken (1972) cites several studies to show that problem-solving abilities relate more closely to reading comprehension than to computational facility. Verbal arithmetic problems are particularly saturated with a conceptual density factor, containing verbal, numerical, and literal symbolic meanings in a single task. Of course, language skills are applied in a special way in solving mathematical problems. The reading rate is slower than for narrative materials, eye movements have to be varied to include some regressions, and attention must be paid to the special uses of common words.

Support for Aiken's hypothesis concerning the importance of verbal reasoning aptitudes come from the well-known "Study of Mathematically Precocious Youth" (SMPY). Fox's (1974) study of SMPY participants' achievement in special classes found that performance on the verbal tests, when adjusted for age, related positively to learning rates in mathematics. Those with lower verbal scores, which were still high for SMPY students' age, tended to progress at a slower pace than those with equivalent math aptitude scores but with higher verbal ratings. However, Aiken (1972) points out that the correlation of mathematical and verbal ability may decrease when their joint relationship to general intelligence is partialed out. This is understandable, since IQ is heavily saturated with abstract reasoning, which, in turn, figures prominently in mathematical and verbal comprehension.

A study of Structure of Intellect factors associated with achievement in mathematics among ninth-grade pupils is reported by Petersen et al., (1963). They wanted to determine which specific intellectual functions are required for success in mathematics in order to facilitate prediction of achievement. Aware that research evidence demonstrates a strong relationship between verbal reasoning and mathematical skills, they assessed the children's cognition of semantic units, cognition of semantic systems, and evaluation of semantic relations. However, they hypothesized that symbolic factors would be even better predictors. They therefore measured cognition of symbolic relations, systems, and implications; memory of symbolic implications; divergent production of symbolic relations; and convergent production of symbolic relations, systems, transformations, and implications. Of the six hundred ninth-graders taking the test earlier in the school year, some were enrolled in general mathematics and others in algebra courses. Near the end of the school year, the children took an achievement test in mathematics that served as the criterion measure. A regression analysis revealed the relative importance of different factors. Results confirmed the independent predictive validity of symbolic factors. Not only did the special abilities forecast achievement in mathematics better than did measures of verbal facility, but they also succeeded in discriminating between above-average algebra and general math students with considerable accuracy.

The evidence presented by Peterson and his associates is in line with their theory that human abilities are highly differentiated. Anastasi (1970) offers further evidence on intellective trait patterns among groups differing in sex, ethnicity, socioeconomic level, type of educational program, age, and cognitive ability. Among other things, her data show differences in aptitude profiles among various ethnic groups and between males and females. Also, a greater differentiation of special abilities is associated with higher (versus lower) social class membership, enrollment in departmentalized (versus self-contained) classes, and reaching late adolescence (versus early childhood). Perhaps most important, she cites evidence to support a positive relationship between level of intellectual functioning and degree of differentiation of special abilities, although most of the studies deal with populations that are not exceptionally high in tested general intelligence. Nevertheless, her conclusion concurs with that of Ferguson (1954), which she quotes as follows: "As the learning of a particular task continues, the ability to perform it becomes gradually differentiated from . . . other abilities" (Anastasi, 1970, p. 905).

Research associated with SMPY focuses on children who are exceedingly precocious in mathematics (Keating, 1974; Fox, 1974). Evidence presented on these "radical accelerates" in mathematics, particularly their performance on the Raven's Progressive Matrices, Concept Mastery Test, and Academic Promise Test, indicates that they were also well advanced for their age in general intellectual ability. At their high performance levels, one would expect a tendency toward greater differentiation of special aptitudes, as suggested by Anastasi (1970).

Results of the testing program show that intellectual development was indeed uneven. The Verbal SAT mean score of 546, while well above average for junior high school children, was nearly half a standard deviation lower than the mean Mathematics SAT score. Such a sharp discrepancy may be explained, in part, by the familiar statistical phenomenon of regression toward the mean. Since the children were selected on the basis of scores in mathematics that were well above average for junior high school students generally, it would therefore be expected that scores on a second test, such as one on verbal ability that correlates highly with mathematics in a random population, would be closer to the mean of that age group. However, Keating (1974) suggests that the discrepancy in this case "may also be indicative of something a bit deeper. Verbal precocity may be rather rarer than the quantitative variety. Mathematics may be, in some psychologically meaningful sense, a closed system, whereas vocabulary and perhaps verbal reasoning may be somehow 'open-ended,' more dependent on accumulated experience" (p. 39). He also points out that the intraindividual variability was such that correlations between the Mathematics subtest of the SAT with either the Verbal SAT or the Ravens Progressive matrices were not significantly different from zero. Since low correlations would be expected in a sample as restricted in range as the SMPY group, assessments of different cognitive functions clarify different dimensions of mathematical talent.

As would be expected, there are noncognitive traits that may be partly the cause and partly the consequence of mathematical precocity. In their study of sixty-three mathematicians with Ph.D.s who were divided into comparison groups of creatives and noncreatives on the basis of peer nomination, Helson and Crutchfield (1970) found several sharp personality differences between the subsamples despite the fact that they did not differ in tested intelligence. Evidence from a variety of formal measures indicated that the creatives were significantly lower in self-control and higher in flexibility. They also performed better on a test of originality and expressed less commitment to religious values.

Helson and Crutchfield also compared the total sample of mathematicians with a group of research scientists and architects and found sharp differences here, too. Although the groups had fairly comparable IQs—135 on the Wechsler Adult

Intelligence Scale for the mathematicians and 133 and 130 for the scientists and architects—there were distinctive personality traits associated with each area of specialization. Compared with the scientists, the mathematicians had relatively little need to understand and control the natural environment. They also did not have as much self-assurance as did the scientists and architects, but they seemed to show a greater measure of humanitarian conscience and adaptive autonomy. Generally, Helson and Crutchfield found that mathematicians tend to be reserved, sensitive, conscientious, and highly individualistic in spirit, although conventional in behavior. Intellectually, they seem able to reconcile the contrasting traits of flexibility and precision within themselves.

The Helson and Crutchfield study yielded evidence on personality structures of adult mathematicians that seem to apply also to adolescents with mathematical precocity. Haier and Denham (1976) studied the nonintellective traits of SMPY subjects, ages 12 to 14. Their sample consisted of seventy-five junior high school boys who scored at least 640 on the Mathematics sections of the SAT tests and twenty-five girls with scores of 600 and above. The objective of the study was to investigate the children's interpersonal effectiveness, emotional stability, social adjustment, values, vocational interests, and self-images.

Results show that the boys were as capable of mature social interaction as were their mathematically less able agemates. They scored high on independence and flexibility, which the authors regard as compatible with their cognitive styles. The results for the girls were similar, but they were also pictured as nonconforming. As in the case of adult studies by Helson and Crutchfield, the children examined by Haier and Denham scored high on flexibility and low on self-control. Basically, the children appeared to be a well-adjusted group, tending not to be neurotic or especially extroverted. They are described as passive, careful, thoughtful, peaceful, controlled, reliable, even-tempered, calm, introspective, serious, planful, fond of books, and reserved except with friends. Such traits are intimately aligned with the children's cognitive individualities and will probably remain permanent among those who continue to advanced study and careers in mathematics.

Artists

Research on the relationship between precocity in the visual arts and general intellectual ability is sparse and inconclusive. This is understandable in view of the difficulties involved in measuring artistic talent through formal means of assessment that are not as reliable and valid as tests of academic potential. Goodenough (1926) analyzed children's drawings for the clues they gave to complexity of concept development, rather than to their aesthetic appeal, and concluded that they reflect levels of general intelligence. However, when drawings were evaluated for their accuracy in representing real objects, evidence showed that scores do not correlate with general intelligence (Hollingworth, 1926). Analytical drawing, symbolic drawing, and caricature, on the other hand, combine a high degree of tested intelligence and special talent, but these skills are no more valid than the facility for representational drawing as early signs of giftedness in the visual arts. Instead, Hollingworth suggests the following cognitive traits as relating to such talent: the abilities "to notice visually and to remember forms, areas, silhouettes, spatial relations, and colors; to control and direct movements of the hand; to invent artistic combinations; to judge the beautiful; and, in case of colored drawings, to discriminate accurately among colors" (p. 210).

There is other evidence of low correlations between various measures of art talent and tested intelligence. Lewerenz (1928) experimented with the Los Angeles tests in the fundamental abilities of visual art, which were developed to discern aesthetic aspects of intelligence, and found ratings on these tests to be fairly independent of IQ scores. Similar results were obtained in studies by Hurlock and Thomson (1934) and by Tiebout and Meier (1936) who used other means of assessing artistic talent. In a study of high-IQ adolescents, Holland (1961) found tested intelligence unrelated to creative performance in the arts, but in this case the restricted IQ range may account for the low coefficients. However, Welsh (1975) reported on a number of studies showing a low correlation between his Revised Art Scale and IQ for populations of various ages and ability levels. Welsh also cited several studies in which the revised art scale and the instrument from which it is derived, the Barron-Welsh Art Scale, proved moderately effective in distinguishing between more and less creative adults and adolescents in the arts.

It is noteworthy that measures of artistic aptitude are notoriously weak in discerning artistic aptitudes in children. Part of the reason may be implied in a comment that the late Irving Lorge once made to this author. He observed that, if a universal moratorium were declared on verbal communication, and people were allowed to exchange ideas with each other only through the media of the arts, the result would be the greatest flowering of artistic productivity our world has ever known. Since aptitude in art can only be revealed through performance, the fact that so few people practice it regularly makes it difficult for them to reveal, even to themselves, whether they have extraordinary undeveloped abilities of that kind. It is analogous to the problem of finding the potential champion dart thrower in a neighborhood where such activity is not popular. The persons with championship caliber may be hidden from view until they spend some time at least in dabbling in it. Otherwise, it does not make sense to measure potential through performance of people who never aimed a dart at a target. The same can be said for assessing the artistic precocity of those who have rarely, if ever, faced a canvas with paintbrush in hand. The world-famous orchestral conductor, Sir Thomas Beecham, is reputed to have nominated his washerwoman as possessing the greatest female singing voice he had ever heard, but he quickly explained that she had never been trained to sing and therefore had never performed on stage.

In a society in which the mental activity that engages most people's attention is of verbal-linear-sequential-analytic variety, it is easiest to get valid readings of human variability in that kind of potential. But in art activity, which is practiced by some and neglected by most, it is hard to imagine a reliable and valid normal distribution of scores on any test that pretends to measure special aptitudes.

In the absence of good measures of artistic precocity, alternative approaches have been taken, with inconclusive results. One is the product review, as practiced in the Gifted Child Program of Portland, Oregon (Wilson, 1959). This method requires that the children in the upper elementary grades engage in a series of practice exercises in preparation for producing the works that will eventually be evaluated. These works consist of a crayon drawing and a painting on such topics as "Saturday Fun," "This Is My House," "My Favorite Story," and "Company for Dinner." The children also complete five partial pencil drawings that are presented to them. Each child's portfolio is then judged by a committee of teachers trained for such purposes. There is no empirical evidence on the effectiveness of this procedure or of the mental structures of children who qualify through it. However, in a study of over five hundred men and women (Wallach and Wing, 1969), a comparison was made between the art attainments of so-called "high-intelligence" and "low-intelligence" groups. The quality of a painting, drawing, or sculpture depended on whether it had won an award in artistic competition, or had been an also-ran in competition, or had merely been exhibited but never competed with other people's works. The results show no difference in art attainment, although it should be noted that the sampling was skewed toward the upper extreme of the normal curve in general intelligence. The mean score was 619.12 on the Verbal SAT and 644.88 on the Mathematical SAT, and since the standard deviation on both measures was about 17, those labeled "low" in intelligence probably exceeded the norm for the population on which the instrument was standardized.

Artistic talent and tested intelligence are not expected to correlate highly at the upper extreme of either distribution, since the range of scores is necessarily limited; still, intelligence can serve as a threshold variable in the same way that it does in the academic disciplines, except at a lower level. The reason for the difference is that measures of intelligence emphasize the rational manipulation of semantics and symbols, as in the sciences, mathematics, and language fields, whereas the arts require the creation of visual figures in space and tonal figures in time. The only commonality between the arts and academics that is relevant to intelligence is that they both require extraordinary abstract reasoning ability. Those who measure up to threshold expectations in abstract reasoning may still never "make it" because of deficits in special aptitudes in their respective fields.

Another approach to the understanding of artistic aptitude has been taken by Getzels and Csikszentmihalyi (1976) in their study of 321 students in fine art, advertising art, industrial art, and art education. Instead of evaluating performance on an art-related task, the researchers developed a systematic way of examining the processes by which artistic products are developed. Before doing this, they tested a sample of their target population on a battery of demographic and psychological instruments. Results show that the artistically talented did not differ from the general norm for college students on cognitive measures. Nevertheless, this would probably place the young artists at least in the upper one third of their normative age group in IQ. They also performed well on creativity tests, scoring at or above the eighty-ninth percentile on college norms.

Where they distinguished themselves most clearly was on such noncognitive measures as the Allport-Vernon-Lindzey Study of Values, a personality test (e.g.,

16 PF), projective measures such as the Sentence Completion and Thematic Apperception tests, and on autobiographical and family questionnaires. The future artists scored higher than the norms in Aesthetic value and lower in Economic and Social values. They also made impressive showings on Theoretical values. Personality data showed the art students to be more introspective, alienated, imaginative, radical, self-sufficient, and socially reserved than college students of their age and sex. Males tended to score higher than the norms on feminine characteristics, whereas females exceeded the norm on masculine traits. The various noncognitive measures distinguished not only between the young artists and college students generally but also between subsamples of the target population. For example, those concentrating on fine art had higher Aesthetic values, the advertising and industrial arts students had higher Economic values, and art education students higher Social values. The young fine artists were also distinguishable from the other art students by virtue of their imaginativeness, unconventionality, self-sufficiency, and alienation.

Having examined the correlates of artistic talent, the researchers proceeded to investigate the processes. At the outset, they observed every young artist at work and then devised a way of determining proficiency in what they called "problem finding." They accomplished this by furnishing a studio with two tables, an easel, paper, and a variety of drawing media. On one table they placed approximately thirty still-life objects and then asked each of thirty-one male fine art students to use as many objects as he wished to put together a still-life composition on the second table and then to make a drawing of the composition. In the course of performing the tasks, the artists were observed closely for signs of distinctive ways of working. First, a count was taken of the number of objects handled. Second, observations were made of how they interacted with the objects, since some simply picked up the items, transferred them to the second table, and immediately began to draw, while others lingered over the items, rolling them in their hands, tossing them in the air, holding them against the light, smelling them, biting them, feeling their texture, moving their parts, or turning them upside down. Finally, a record was made of the uniqueness of objects selected by each of the young artists. Some items were used by only one or two students, others by most of the group. Thus, the researchers obtained insights into the artists' orientation to discovery, or problem finding, at the stage of problem formulation.

It was expected that artistic talent would be associated with the number of objects chosen to be examined, the uncommonness of these choices, and the thoroughness with which the examination was conducted. To test the hypothesis, the researchers obtained ratings of the artists' drawings from a panel of judges who examined the overall aesthetic value, originality, and craftsmanship of the products. Results showed that the combined problem-finding process variables correlated as highly as .40 with ratings of aesthetic value and .54 with originality. The coefficients were statistically significant, but the third correlation of .28 with craftsmanship was not. Even more impressive was the predictive validity of problem-finding scores when they were correlated with the status ratings of twenty-four out of the original sample of thirty-one student artists during a follow-up study seven years later. The coefficient was .30, which is impressive after a hiatus period of such length.

The idea of recognizing special aptitudes through so-called problem-finding behaviors, or idiosyncratic strategies surrounding a person's act of creation, opens up new possibilities for the study of talent. Traditionally, human potential has been inferred from the quality of work *completed* rather than from performances or products in the *making*. Getzels and Csikszentmihalyi have demonstrated that artists reveal their potentialities not only by *what* they accomplish in their formative years, but also by *how* they use their tactical repertoires to create works of art. A similar approach to the study of process variables in creativity may also apply to other kinds of talent, if ways can be found to set the stage for problem finding for young composers, writers, mathematicians, scientists, and social leaders with raw materials as appropriate for their respective fields as were the still-life objects placed on the table before the young artists. Each field of specialization probably dictates its own ways of finding problems, since each has its own conceptual system and media with which the practitioner has to work. What may also prove evident is that, within a particular field of specialization, those who excel may practice problem solving differently from those who do not. In that case, a qualitative dimension would be added to the meaning of special aptitudes and how they figure in giftedness.

Socially Gifted

In the case of scientific, mathematical, and artistic aptitudes, the question that is generally addressed is how well the individual relates to the symbols inherent in these disciplines. Social aptitudes are different in the sense that they involve an individual's interaction with people rather than with concepts and media. They therefore have to be approached from at least two perspectives: one is an external view of the individual socializing with the group; the other is from the point of view of the group assessing the individual's impact on it. The group may regard an individual as excelling either as its leader or its head, and the difference between leadership and headship is described by Gibb (1969) as follows:

(1) Domination or headship is maintained through an organized system and not by the spontaneous recognition by fellow group members, of the individual's contribution to group locomotion.
(2) The group goal is chosen by the head man in line with his interests and is not internally determined by the group itself.
(3) In the domination or headship relation there is little or no sense of shared feeling or joint action in the pursuit of the given goal.
(4) There is in the dominance relation a wide social gap between the group members and the head, who strives to maintain this social distance as an aid to his coercion of the group.
(5) Most basically, these two forms of influence differ with respect to the sources of authority which is exercised. The leader's authority is spontaneously accorded him by

his fellow group members, and particularly by the followers. The authority of the head derives from some extra-group power which he has over the members of the group, who cannot meaningfully be called his followers. They accept his domination, on pain of punishment, rather than follow. (p. 213)

There is a positive relationship between talent in social leadership and general intelligence. This is not surprising since so much of the leader's behavior involves some kind of cognitive problem solving. However, here again, general intelligence is not enough; it must be combined with special aptitudes. As Mann (1959) points out: "Considering independent studies as the unit of research, the positive association between intelligence and leadership . . . is found to be highly significant. . . . However, the magnitude of the relationship is less impressive; no correlation reported exceeds .50 and the median correlation is roughly .25" (p. 248). A somewhat higher relationship between verbal intelligence and leadership behavior is reported by Bass (1960) who reviewed some twenty-four studies and estimated an average coefficient of about .30.

In all likelihood, the correlation varies with the criterion of leadership. Studies by Cattell and Stice (1954) show that problem-solving leaders score higher on tests of intelligence than do nonleaders and also higher than do those regarded as leaders by other criteria. Perhaps the most important fact about the intelligence of leaders and their followers is the magnitude of difference between them. As Gibb (1969) points out,

One of the most interesting results emerging from studies of the relation between intelligence and leading is the suggestion that leaders may not exceed the non-leaders by too large a margin. Great discrepancies between the intelligence of one member and of others militate against his emergence into and retention of the leadership role, presumably because wide discrepancies render improbable the unified purpose of the members concerned and because the highly intelligent have interests and values remote from those of the general membership. The evidence suggests that every increment of intelligence means wiser government but that the crowd prefers to be ill-governed by people it can understand. (p. 218)

Studies of young children show that social skills may develop early in life as separate aptitudes. Abroms and Gollin (1980) selected a group of twenty 3-year-olds with a mean IQ of 134 and watched them interact with other children during free play in a nursery school setting for ten four-minute periods on ten different days. In these observation sessions, the following prosocial behaviors were monitored: (1) *sharing* materials and work space with others, (2) *helping* others physically or verbally, (3) *reacting* to another child's distress, and (4) showing *affection* for another child. Correlations between IQ and prosocial behavior proved statistically significant, but they were independent enough of each other to suggest the possibility that giftedness is plural almost from birth.

An effort has also been made to assess the relationship between tested intelligence and social power in elementary school children (Zander and Van Egmond, 1958). The experimental sample came from a population of 638 pupils in sixteen second-grade and sixteen fifth-grade classrooms in a medium sized city. Separate categories of boys and girls were divided on the basis of IQ (upper versus lower third of their class). Thus, four subgroups were formed: (1) high-IQ, high social power; (2) high-IQ, low social power; (3) low-IQ, high social power; and (4) low-IQ, low social power. The scores for social power were obtained from the children themselves. Every child rated each classmate on four characteristics: social power, attractiveness, ability in schoolwork, and ability to threaten others. The children were then divided randomly into four small groups, each of which worked on assigned problems requiring group decision. Teachers observing these groups did not know to which IQ or social power category any child belonged. Their task was to rate each child in relation to specific group dynamics criteria during the work sessions.

Results showed that social power was significantly but not highly correlated with intelligence; the coefficient for boys was .20 and for girls, .28. Boys and girls who were attributed high social power were seen as more attractive by their classmates than were those low in power, regardless of their intelligence. Girls with greater power were rated as more able in schoolwork than were girls low in power, irrespective of their intelligence. Among the boys, however, only those high in power and intelligence were described as more able in schoolwork. As for their behavior in small groups, the highly intelligent boys and girls behaved about the same regardless of whether they were high or low in social power. The differences associated with the extent of social power could be found among those with lower IQs. The high-power boys revealed a relatively vigorous, consistent, and competitive pattern of behavior, and the high-power girls were more often successful in their influence attempts and more positive in their remarks about the behavior of others than were their low-power counterparts. It is therefore evident that the aptitude for social power is distinguishable from other human abilities, and it is probably useful to develop and validate measures that will help to identify children who have the potential for exercising power in a group with great effectiveness.

An attempt to develop an assessment device for so-called social intelligence in youthful populations has already been made (O'Sullivan et al., 1965). It is based on the Structure of Intellect theory, which, according to Guilford (1959) posits four kinds of intelligence, including social intelligence. The other three include figural intelligence (later split between visual and auditory), symbolic intelligence (involving pure mathematics and languages), and abstract intelligence (incorporating logical abstractions). Social intelligence is defined as (1) knowing or understanding people's behavior and (2) coping with that behavior. At the level of knowing or understanding, we deal with such psychological constructs as social sensitivity, perception, and empathy. The questions addressed are "Do we apprehend the other person's state of mind?" "Do we sense other people's attitudes toward us?" "Do we recognize what they really want?" "What are they likely to do next?"

The attempt at measuring the knowledge and understanding aspects of social intelligence was made on a sample of white, upper-middle-class eleventh-graders with a mean IQ of about 118 (O'Sullivan et al., 1965). What emerged were six factors, all of them involving behavioral cognition, as follows: (1) *CBU*, the ability to understand facial expressions; (2) *CBC*, the ability to recognize different modes of expressions, gestures, postures, and faces; (3) *CBR*, understanding dyadic relations; (4) *CBS*, the ability to comprehend a social situation or sequence of events; (5) *CBT*, the transformation or redefinition factor indicating the ability to reinterpret a gesture, a facial expression, a statement, or a whole social situation; and (6) *CBI*, the ability to make predictions about what will happen following a given situation of social content. Interestingly enough, the pattern of factor loadings suggests that general reasoning is not essential for knowing or understanding people's behavior.

Another investigation involving Guilford's Structure of Intellect deals with a second major aspect of social intelligence, that of coping with the behavior of others (Hendricks et al., 1969). Specific coping behaviors include abilities to influence other people's behavior, organize defenses against their aggression, win them over to a particular point of view, and cause them to take actions that they would not ordinarily take.

To determine the existence of special aptitudes for social problem-solving skills, the researchers administered a battery of Structure of Intellect instruments to 110 boys and 82 girls, mostly middle-class whites in grades ten to twelve. Results show that, although IQ does not figure in this kind of ability, divergent production factors relating to behavior are closely involved. They include *DBU* (e.g., *alternate picture meanings*: write many different things that a person might say if he or she felt as the person in a given picture does; *alternate social meanings*: read the description of a person's action and write many different interpretations, each showing how the person might think or feel); *DBC* (e.g., *alternate face groupings*: group given facial photographs in many different ways, so that each subgroup of at least three photographs expresses a different thought, feeling, or intention; *multiple behavioral grouping*: organize a list of comments into many different subsets according to the thoughts, feelings, or intentions they express); *DBR* (e.g., *creating social relations*: in response to the illustrated expressions of two people, write many different things that the second person might be saying to the first one; *varied emotional relations*: from many pictures of individuals, choose many different sets of two pictures, each set showing a cause-effect relationship); *DBS* (e.g., *writing behavioral stories*: given a photograph of three people in a social situation, write many different stories describing how the people feel, what they are thinking, and why; *multiple cartoon fill-ins*: given the first and last frames of a cartoon strip, write what might have happened between them so that the explanation involves the feelings, thoughts, and intentions of the characters in all the frames; *DBI* (e.g., *alternate social solutions*: given a described social situation, list many different social solutions for the situation; *multiple social problems*: given two members of a typical family, such as brother and sister, write many different personal problems that they might have with each other; the problems should involve the feelings, thoughts, and attitudes of the two people).

It should be remembered that the researchers' attempts at identifying the coping behaviors associated with social intelligence were in the form of pencil-and-paper tests. There is obviously room for questioning whether this kind of instrument can measure the wits a person needs in real-life situations to influence other people or to face a multitude of day-to-day social challenges. Keating's (1978) search for social intelligence among 117 college students also involved the use of various pencil-and-paper measures, and the results are far less encouraging than were those reported by Hendricks, et al. Commenting on his failure to locate social intelligence through the academic and social problems tests that he used, Keating states,

In particular, it may be that the very format of such measures (i.e., paper-and-pencil format with delimited response options) activates an academic framework so constraining that relevant social skills contribute little true variance to the resulting scores. Accurate assessment of social competence may require a different approach to measurement, presumably one that capitalizes on systemic in situ observation. (p. 222)

It would therefore seem that social intelligence probably exists as a special aptitude, but it is difficult to differentiate through conventional assessment formats.

CONCLUSIONS RELEVANT TO THE GIFTED

The choice of scientific, mathematical, artistic, and social abilities for discussion is intended merely to illustrate the diversity of their psychosocial concomitants. Those who excel in these four areas of specialization are strikingly different from each other in the way in which they think and behave. Even the stereotypes attached to them satirically or offensively are fairly distinctive for every kind of highly developed aptitude. Yet there appears to be an intellectual common denominator among them in the sense that each requires its own modicum of reasoning ability as measured by tests of general intelligence. Nobody knows what minimum essential, or threshold level of general ability is necessary to achieve distinction in any area of specialization, but from the research evidence thus far, it would be reasonable to hypothesize that the thresholds at above-average levels of tested intelligence do exist and that they vary for the four fields of accomplishment depicted here, as they do for every other field that is socially valued. In addition to the abilities common to all kinds of achievement, there are also unique skills that distinguish one type of excellence from the next, and every aptitude has its own threshold that is pertinent to its specific area of acomplishment. The idea of thresholds in general and special abilities exposes the futility of comparing the brainpower needs of one profession against another. What does it mean, for example, to say that mathematics requires greater mental strength than does politics? The IQ and number skill thresholds may be much higher for virtuoso mathematicians, but by the same token it takes far more social intelligence and administrative acumen to become a great politician.

Among children who show high potential in a specific area of performance or productivity, there is some evidence to show that they are often superior in tested intelligence and occasionally possess several exceptional talents. Liddle (1958) reports a study of 1,015 public school children in late childhood and early adolescence who were tested for maladjustment, social leadership ability, artistic talent, and intellectual ability. He found that the three kinds of ability were interrelated positively and that none of them was associated with any of the maladjustment characteristics. Miller (1962) also conducted a large-scale investigation of children with WISC IQs of 120 and higher for a five-year period from grades four to eight. Along with their schoolmates, these children were tested on skills in writing, drama, music, and symbolic thinking and on two of the Getzels and Jackson tests of creativity.

Results showed that the high-IQ children were overrepresented in the five talent areas examined but that a few children of lesser intellectual ability also received high ratings in these areas. Also, some high-IQ children demonstrated talent in several lines of endeavor, an important finding, since it shows that we cannot always enlarge the pool of potentially gifted children by increasing the number of special talents that we accept as signs of giftedness. Finally, the highest creativity scores were not necessarily associated with the highest tested intelligence, but artistic products of greatest value were usually developed by children with unusual intellectual gifts.

Thus we see that, at the high-IQ levels, special aptitudes can be differentiated sharply, probably more so than near the middle of the general IQ range. The likelihood is that, at the upper extreme of the IQ distribution, correlations between IQ and special aptitudes are negligible. The intelligence test is therefore a poor instrument for determining precisely in what way the child excels; that can be determined only through some assessment in a substantive area.

Since it is important to identify exceptional specific abilities in children, the question arises as to how early in a child's life do these aptitudes emerge. It is true that people become more and more specialized as they grow older, probably as a result of their learning experiences, educational and career predilections, and opportunities to major in fields of their choice. Prior to their adolescent stage, however, children are often viewed as possessing intellectual abilities that are not yet differentiated. Giftedness is equated with superior tested intelligence, which is reflected in a single test score and weighted heavily with verbal and abstract reasoning abilities. Yet, there is ample evidence that even at the preschool stage children can already show signs of becoming specialists. Robinson, Roedell, and Jackson (1979) cite their own and other behavioral scientists' research to show that preschoolers have distinctive profiles that seem to be more easily recognizable among those who are intellectually precocious. However, there is no evidence as yet of a relationship between early signs of specific precocity and later accomplishment in supposedly related fields. Should such linkages ever be found, educators will face new dilemmas about the preferred design of elementary curricula.

Traditionally, the common branch subjects taught in elementary schools have been presented, cafeteria-style, with children sampling the basics of a variety of disciplines. All subjects are taught by one teacher, who serves as a generalist without necessarily having intensive training in any one content area. Such an approach is understandable if it is based on an assumption that precocious young children are themselves generalists who eventually excel in a particular discipline because their learning experiences inspire them toward that direction rather than because they are endowed with the necessary aptitudes for specialization even early in their school years. The children are therefore exposed to the widest possible variety of subject matter to prepare them to choose their majors wisely. If they make their choice by the time they reach secondary school, they are then given an opportunity to work under subject matter specialists in elective courses that can satisfy their interests.

There are probably other reasons for a common branch curriculum that have to do with the need to synthesize rather than compartmentalize subject matter. However, it may be a good idea to reconsider this practice if it is justified largely by assumptions about how children's intellect is organized. The little that is known already about aptitude profiles in children suggests that the precocious among them are uneven in their development and can benefit from instruction that is tailored to their respective strengths. It is even conceivable that the greater use of subject matter specialists at the elementary level may help to strengthen the relationship between specific forms of early precocity and eventual excellence. In that case, educators would be faced with the dilemma of trading off one educational benefit for another. On the one hand, a narrowly focused, in-depth concentration on areas in which precocious children excel can satisfy obvious intellectual needs, but at the expense of broader exposure to the world of ideas. On the other hand, a widely based curriculum that attempts to do justice to many disciplines may succeed in its synthesis and comprehensiveness, but at the expense of delving into the manysidedness of a single discipline.

CHAPTER 8   ————————————————————————

Nonintellective Facilitators

Conceptually, it is easy to distinguish between intellective and nonintellective factors in human functioning. One denotes the mental powers and processes needed to master or create ideas; the other refers to the social, emotional, and behavioral characteristics that can release or inhibit the full use of a person's abilities. Problems in separating both psychological domains do arise, however, when they have to be assessed. Mental measurement, for example, is accomplished inferentially, through tests of performance, which are always "contaminated" by nonintellective factors.

We may think it possible to determine the level of a child's intelligence from an IQ, when in reality the score is partially affected by the child's feelings about self, success, the examiner, the test, and the testing situation generally. We may also think that tests of divergent thinking measure different abilities from those that assess convergent thinking. Yet both instruments could be addressing largely, though not completely, similar functions, except that one is more comfortable in the hands of an examinee who is playful with ideas, has a sense of humor, and enjoys brainstorming and tinkering with ambiguities, whereas the other type of test is welcomed more by a serious-minded, straightforward examinee who wants to strip a problem of its complexity rather than savor it for a while.

Since these life-style variations may contribute to differences in scores on tests that purportedly assess intellectual functioning, it is difficult to determine the organization of intellect from such measures. What may seem to be a special ability, separable from all others, may actually reflect clusters of intellective and nonintellective traits that usually go together. If it were possible to separate the two types of characteristics, then some of the seemingly independent aptitudes would perhaps be more closely interrelated. Indeed, even the entire structure of intellect might look different under such circumstances.

The nonintellective factors that facilitate various kinds of gifted performance are not only the familiar helping behaviors, such as persistence and dedication, but also particular life styles and seemingly unrelated skills. These ancillary characteristics enable the talented to call attention to themselves and their work and help to make it possible for them to maximize their impact on audiences, patients, or clients. For example, in a longitudinal study of fine artists Getzels and Csikszentmihalyi (1976), much is made of the artist's loft in showcasing works of real promise. If the artist is unable or unwilling to acquire the social habits required in the loft for self-promotional purposes, the chances of public recognition may be dimmed.

Getzels (1979) described how these nonintellective traits figure in success or failure:

Although the loft, or its equivalent, has become almost an essential first step to certify the former art student's commitment as a fine artist, the requirement entails serious difficulties for the young artist. He is temperamentally withdrawn, introverted, sensitive, self-sufficient, and he holds the conventional economic and social values in low esteem. These values and traits are functional, since they make for tolerance and even enjoyment of the solitary and subjective condition under which works of art are created. But a loft requires the artist to be entrepreneurial and sociable, a salesman and a master of ceremonies. It often demands behavior that is at odds with the most basic aspect of his character. And so, too, do many of the other modes that have evolved presumably to help art students become artists. Some of the students negotiate the difficulties, while others do not. (p. 384)

Thus, while the personal qualities needed to adapt to what might be called the "culture of the loft" are uninvolved in the production of great art, and perhaps even antithetical to it, they do arouse the attention of critics, patrons, and appreciators in general, who ultimately determine the value of artistic production and performance. By inference, then, it is impossible to imagine great accomplishment in the absence of beneficiaries or appreciators, even though they may materialize long after the work comes into existence. Talent that is obscured from everybody's attention forever is as meaningless as the musicianship of an instrumentalist performing in a vacuum where sound does not carry. The movement of the musician's lips or fingers on the instrument may be inspired, but the effect is stillborn in an environment of soundlessness. Unfortunately, we know little about the ancillary, nonintellective traits, comparable to the ones artists need in the culture of the loft, that enable the gifted in other fields to gain recognition for their work. Most of the research deals, instead, with the facilitative characteristics that help to close the gap between potential and fulfillment. Our discussion, therefore, has to focus primarily on them.

META-LEARNING ORIENTATION

As used here, the term "meta learning" refers to a person's mind set or intellectual impulse that is advantageous in the earliest preparation for accomplishment. These are not simply detour tactics that substitute cleverness for insight and make it possible for a person to achieve without real effort or understanding. Instead, they are unspoken understandings about the "rules of the game" of cognition in a society oriented toward the scientific method. As such, they are indispensable to success in intellelctual activity, although they do not tax the powers of intellect heavily.

There probably exist strong cultural and subcultural differences in learning how to learn, and these variations may often be mistaken for cognitive deficits. It stands to reason that an improper alignment of meta-learning habits tends to thwart the use of intellectual powers, even those that are substantially intact. Thus, when a building contractor asks a construction worker to build an alcove from floor to ceiling in a new house in order to insert bookshelves, the contractor's expectation is that the shelves will be cut in uniform size to fit perfectly into that space. The worker, on the other hand, may be satisfied with a fairly close approximation of the width and depth dimensions that have been requested. In that case, every shelf would have to be cut to a slightly different size, depending on precisely where it is to be fitted in the alcove.

Faced with the costly prospect of paying a carpenter to cut each shelf to separate specifications, the builder may dismiss the worker for ineptitude and look for a more talented replacement to blueprint the alcove exactly as requested. Yet, what caused the problem may have nothing to do with the worker's intellectual or spatial aptitudes. Instead, there is a possibility that the learning assumptions of both parties are mismatched. The builder sees the alcove walls as having to be perfectly parallel to each other and perpendicular to floor and ceiling, as confirmed by objective instrumental calibrations. The worker, on the other hand, may have been raised and trained in a part of the world where success at fulfilling such an assignment is determined by the naked eye rather than by exact measurements. Thus, we see how important the meta-learning agreement can be in regulating cognitive performance. The worker in this illustration is no more backward than the child in a far-off country who interprets the causes of rain in terms of favors from local gods rather than in scientific terms.

Even among people coming from the same cultural background there can be mismatches in meta-learning orientations, as in the accompanying Peanuts cartoon.

© 1981 United Feature Syndicate, Inc.

"The answer lies within the heart of all mankind" may be appropriate in a house of meditation, whereas in a school building the "name of the game" is arithmetic and the answer is in the form of a number. Being aware of the "name of the game" does not help directly in figuring out the right solution, but it does help to form an impression of what kind of solution is acceptable. In this case, each building requires a different answer to the same question; the first child's answer is merely misplaced, not stupid. But among the gifted, such disorientation is a rarity because part of their intellectual "killer instinct" is to have their wits about them in addition to keeping them sharp at all times. These children make it their business to find out what "building" they are in, what "game" they are playing, and above all, what standards of excellence are expected of them by their audiences (e.g., teachers, patrons, sponsors, and critics).

Meta learning should not be confused with what DeCecco (1968) called "entering behavior" and Gagné (1970) described as "learning sets." Their formulations refer to prerequisite cognitive mastery in one form or another. For example, for children to learn how to read an old-fashioned nondigital clock, they have to study beforehand how to distinguish between the long and short clock hand, recognize the number to which each clock hand is pointing, and know how to count up to 60 by 1's and by 5's. Gagné's (1970) learning sets arrange the entering behaviors in an appropriate hierarchy of complexity, but here, too, the antecedent conditions of success are purely cognitive. Even Ellis's (1965) concept of "learning to learn," which emphasizes repeated practice as a mneans of improving speed and accuracy in solving new problems, is basically a cognitive means of gaining cognitive mastery.

Meta learning is also a kind of mastery, but at the level of adapation rather than complex, abstract reasoning. In the process of fine-tuning their readiness for success in an achievement-oriented society, potentially gifted children realize quickly and clearly that, before they initiate problem finding or solving, they should determine in advance whether they are dealing with semantic, symbolic, or figural material. They see the advantages of making preliminary estimates about parameters within which solutions will be located and beyond which there can only be bizarre or impossible solutions. They have to assume in advance that, in the case of solving differential equations, for example, single, exact, or multiple relevant solutions are expected, not general approximations. They understand that it is helpful to try to reduce data to manageable proportions by eliminating facts and ideas that can only delay or spoil outcomes. They also develop the habit of deferring judgment until all the relevant data are sifted, rather than jumping to hasty solutions. In other words, they are aware of the need to know the road to excellence before testing whether they can make the journey.

All these adaptive postures are necessary, though not sufficient, for achieving excellence. That is, if meta-learning rituals are followed, achievement will depend on whether the student has the requisite kinds and amounts of cognitive power; if they are not, then cognitive power alone cannot mobilize a person toward high-level productivity or performance. Sometimes it is tragic that children with exceptional mental strength particularly those coming from socially disadvantaged backgrounds, are denigrated for cognitive deficits when in reality the fault is traceable to poor meta-learning habits that prevent proper release of potential.

APPROACH BEHAVIORS

Meta learning precedes action. It is a mental pose or stance that enables the learner to tune in to the task ahead with the adaptive impulses of a homing pigeon returning to base. In some contexts, it expresses itself as a need for developing and testing hypotheses and for precision and accuracy in data gathering. In other situations, it is an "automatic" felt need to engage in fantasizing and brainstorming. The next step is to take preliminary strategic action that paves the way for maximum use of intellectual powers. One of the approach strategies that has been researched extensively relates to conceptual tempo.

Kagan (1965) developed special instruments to distinguish between children who are deliberate and reflective and those who are impulsively rapid in their responses to problems. The reflective child tends to avoid situations that can lead to harm or humiliation, whereas the high-risk child is more interested in quick success than in avoiding failure. There is no clear empirical evidence on the relationship between conceptual tempos and intellective functioning. Kagan warns teachers to avoid an understandable inclination to associate reflectiveness with high ability despite his finding that relatively reflective first-graders with superior verbal ability as measured by the WISC make fewer reading errors than do impulsive children. Research information is not yet sufficient to reveal how conceptual tempo makes a difference in performance, and on what kinds of tasks. However, it is conceivable that every act of excellence has its own requirements. Preparing oneself for intervention in social crises or leading a country toward peace or war may involve more of a willingness to take the risks of quick action than would be necessary in precision cutting a precious stone.

In another study of strategies that children use to approach problem-solving situations, Kagan (undated) examined children's preferences for analytic versus relational responses to visual stimuli. The child is asked to pick out two pictures that are alike or go together in some way. If the response is *analytic*, the pairings are based on similarities among objective attributes that the child sees in the stimulus material (e.g., "animals with their tongues out," "objects with a leg missing"). A *relational* response, on the other hand, involves pairings based on a functional relationship between the stimuli (e.g., "the dog goes into the doghouse," "the man wears the watch," "the man and woman are married").

Kagan administered the Conceptual Style Test to over eight hundred children in the elementary grades in an effort to relate preferred modes of conceptualization to performance on a variety of cognitive and projective measures. Results show that an analytic attitude generalizes across different task requirements, such as classification of ink blots, the WISC Picture Arrangement subtest, and a hidden figures test, but it was relatively independent of vocabulary level. An analytic attitude was also associated with delay of impulsive responses, which shows a tendency to reflect upon thoughts and events and to analyze experiences in the course of learning. Kagan recommends a search for the antecedents of analytic and relational inclinations in children's approaches to problems.

The contrasts between reflection and impulsivity and between analytic and relational forms of thinking may be aspects of a larger conceptualization of cognitive styles, which Witkin and associates (1962) describe as field dependence versus field independence. People who perceive objects or experience information as separate from the organized context of which it is a part are considered field independent, whereas those whose perception is dominated by the overall organization of the field are considered field dependent. Witkin (1967) has made a strong case for the theoretical importance of these styles in relation to the educative process. He also contends that knowledge of children's cognitive styles can be at least as useful as knowledge of their IQs in diagnosing how they function and what their learning needs are.

In his critical review of relevant literature, Borland (1978) summarized the psychological correlates of field independence and dependence, as reported by Witkin et al., (1954, 1962) in the following manner:

Field dependence is associated with

1. General passivity in dealing with the environment.
2. Lack of self-awareness and poor control of impulses, with accompanying fear of aggressive and sexual impulses and high anxiety.
3. Low self-esteem including low evaluation of the body and a primitive body image.
4. Use of repression and denial as psychological defenses.
5. Tendency to change stated views on social issues in the direction of the attitudes of an authority.
6. Sociability and sensitivity to the feelings and needs of others.

Field independence is associated with

1. Active dealing with the environment.
2. Awareness of "inner life" and effective control of impulses, with low anxiety.
3. High self-esteem and relatively mature body image.
4. Use of sublimation and intellectualization as psychological defenses.
5. Independence of judgment and opinion.
6. Social autonomy, sometimes to the point of being "strikingly isolated . . . overcontrolled, cold and distant, and unaware of their social stimulus value." (Borland, 1978, p. 5).

Zigler (1963) and Vernon (1972) argue that tests of cognitive style, such as those developed by Witkin, do not add anything beyond the insight supplied by measures of cognition to the understanding of school achievement. However, Busse (1968) succeeded in separating a factor of cognitive style from general intelligence among boys. Satterly (1976) likewise demonstrated the separability of cognitive style from general ability. In a study of over two hundred boys, ages 10 and 11, he showed significant residual correlations between field independence and mathematics achievement after intelligence was held constant. Nevertheless, the evidence presented thus far is not conclusive.

Buriel (1978) points out that studies showing a significant relationship between cognitive style and scholastic performance generally rely on a single measure of field dependence and independence. But when several such measures are used, they tend not to correlate significantly with each other or, in combination, with achievement at school. In his own study involving forty Anglo-American and forty Mexican-American children from grades one through four, he examined inter-relationships among three measures of field dependence: Portable Rod-and-Frame Test (PRFT), Children's Embedded Figures Test, and the WISC Block Design subtest. He also determined the relationship between these measures and reading and math achievement scores of the two populations. His results generally *failed* to support previous assertions that (1) Mexican-American children are more field dependent than are Anglo-American children, (2) intercorrelations between the three field-dependent tests are significant and comparable for members of both cultural groups, and (3) field dependence is of substantial importance in school achievement among Anglo-American and Mexican-American children.

Although it is unclear whether field independence and dependence relate to levels of *general* scholastic achievement, there is some indication that they are associated with specific areas of accomplishment. For example, in a large-scale longitudinal study of 787 men and 761 women who were followed through their undergraduate years at college, Witkin and Goodenough (1977) examined their preliminary choices of academic majors at the time of college entrance as well as their majors in undergraduate and graduate programs. Results showed that the relatively field-independent students favored impersonal domains of inquiry such as the sciences, whereas the relatively field-dependent students leaned toward interpersonal domains of specialization, such as elementary education. There was also a tendency for entering students who chose a field of study that was incompatible with their cognitive styles to make a more appropriate shift in their academic programs by the time of graduation or entrance into graduate school, whereas students who concentrated in fields that were more congruent with their cognitive styles were likely to remain with their choices. Equally important, students performed better in domains that were compatible with their cognitive styles. On the basis of this investigation and others relevant to it, Borland (1978, p. 53) lists the following career interests among relatively field-dependent and field-independent individuals:

Field Dependent	Field Independent
Clinical psychology	Experimental psychology
Psychiatric nursing	Surgical nursing
Psychiatric practice with an interpersonal relationship with patients	Psychiatric practice with impersonal forms of therapy
Business personnel director	Business production manager
Business education teacher	Natural science teacher
Social studies teacher	Industrial arts teacher
Elementary teacher	Art students with "formal" style
Art students with "informal" style	Systems engineer
Nonsystems engineer	Naval student pilots
Nonpilot naval students	

Goodenough (1976) likewise found that learning style is related to the nature rather than to the extent of achievement. In his review of relevant studies, he found that field-independent people seem particularly successful under discrimination learning conditions when stimulus cues are relevant and that field-dependent individuals respond better to conditions involving incidental learning of social stimuli. However, he points out that "the great majority of studies show relationships between measures of field dependence and learning effectiveness that are low and insignificant. It is clear from these results that field-dependent and field-independent people differ more consistently in how the learning or memory process occurs than in how effective the process is" (p. 688).

MOTIVATION

According to Renzulli (1978), task commitment is one of only three major factors that figure prominently in giftedness, the other two being above-average ability and creativity. Yet, Bolles (1978) observes ruefully that theoreticians and researchers have been losing interest in the concept of motivation. He argues that motivational ideas were originally introduced into psychology to counterbalance some of the mechanistic, passive, and structuralistic views of the organism. As the more dynamic and functional approach to understanding human behavior gained dominance, the need for motivational concepts gradually disappeared. Bolles argues that behavioral scientists seem to have adopted an assumption that the organism is intrinsically active in directing its behavior toward certain goals. They therefore consider it unnecessary to invoke motivational concepts in order to understand how or why the organism acts as it does.

Nevertheless, research on the gifted shows that precocity often goes hand in hand with a powerful desire for self-advancement. When Terman's (1925) elementary school sample was evaluated by parents and teachers on twenty-five traits, the ratings favored the high-IQ children over controls on each criterion. As might be expected, the greatest discrepancy was on intellectual attributes, followed by volitional, emotional, moral, physical, and social traits, in that order. Similar evidence showing the high IQ child's striving toward success was noted in a follow-up study of this group five years later (Burks et al., 1930). High levels of motivation can also be found among adults who have achieved renown for their accomplishments.

After studying biographical data on three hundred geniuses, Cox (1926) concluded that these geniuses distinguished themselves not only through their extraordinary accomplishments but also in three aspects of personality: (1) persistence of motive and effort, (2) confidence in their abilities, and (3) strength of character. But, while motivation is clearly evident in exemplary performance among children and adults, more needs to be known about the intrapsychic and external forces influencing these outstanding individuals to engage in a particular kind of activity.

Among the most extensively researched theories of motivation is the need for achievement (n Ach) as developed by McClelland and his associates (1953). It refers to a fundamental inclination toward accomplishment in any situation whenever the opportunity arises. To measure n Ach, researchers use Murray's Thematic Apperception Test (TAT) as a projective technique to reveal voluntary and even involuntary preoccupation with achievement. Winterbottom's (1953) study of antecedent factors influencing n Ach showed that achievement motivation in children is related to (1) early independence training, (2) the amount of contact and degree of affection between parent and child, and (3) the extent to which parents use psychological techniques of reward and punishment, such as withdrawal of love or isolation.

In a further study of origins of n Ach, Rosen and D'Andrade (1959) found that it results from the following socialization practices in the home: (1) *achievement training*, in which the parents set high goals for the child to attain, parents have a high regard for the child's competence to do a task well, and parents impose standards of excellence that they expect the child to meet; (2) *independence training*, in which the parents indicate that they expect the child to be self-reliant and to assume responsibility for success or failure; and (3) *rewards and punishments* employed by parents to ensure that their expectations are met and that proper behavior is reinforced. The researchers also discovered differences in levels of achievement motivation between social classes, due in part to differential class emphases upon achievement and independence training. Middle-class parents are more likely than are lower-class parents to stress self-reliance, economy, and success in problem-solving situations, particularly those representing standards of excellence. They tend to recognize and reward signs of achievement and are more sensitive to and act more punitively toward indications of failure.

Rosen (1956) regards the achievement syndrome as consisting of several elements, of which n Ach is only one. The others include aspiration levels, denoting degrees of satisfaction with different occupational choices, and achievement value orientation, which builds on parent-child early interactions associated with n Ach and denotes specific beliefs along the following continua:

1. *Activistic-passivistic orientation*, denoting one's perception of control. Those who are activistic or internally oriented reject the fatalistic view that success is in the cards but are instead convinced that they can manipulate the environment and shape their destinies.
2. *Individualistic-collectivistic orientation*, which offers the choice between self-sufficiency as against close physical proximity to family and responsiveness to group ties and incentives. The highly motivated tend to prefer individual over collective effort and often reject the idea that the best job is accomplished by the organization pulling together, even if there is no individual credit. They choose to work at a task they like, even in the company of people they dislike, rather than to work with people they like at a task they dislike.
3. *Present-future orientation*, denoting the choice between immediate gratification versus planning for the future even if it means sacrificing present gains. The

highly motivated take a more optimistic view of their chances of eventual success, whereas the less motivated tend to believe that things hardly ever work out, so why make long-range plans?

In his study of Italian and Jewish life styles, Strodtbeck (1958) identified those values that were most responsible for differences in occupational achievement in his immigrant samples. The factors he identifies overlap considerably with those in Rosen's achievement syndrome; they also bear a close resemblence to aspects of the Protestant ethic as promulgated through the Calvinist tradition. Emphasis is placed on a sense of personal responsibility in relation to the external world, the need to loosen ties with the family if they inhibit opportunities for self-advancement, the belief in the perfectability of the individual, a movement away from the idea that "each man is his brother's keeper," and the need to recognize that a person-to-person relationship does not operate at the extremes of a "for me-against me" or "over me-under me" polarity.

Despite the emphasis on individualism and self-direction, motivation may have a conformance component as well. Gough (1964) reports a study on the relationship of scholastic achievement and two types of achievement motivation: achievement via independence (A-I) and achievement via conformance (A-C). A-I seeks to reflect the kind of achievement motivation that accentuates independence, divergent thinking, and creation of method rather than the observance of method. A-C attempts to calibrate that aspect of the achievement motive in which self-discipline, acceptance of rules, and convergent thinking predominate. The subjects of this study consisted of 204 males and 137 females attending four Italian high schools from different parts of that country. Both motivation scales correlated significantly with scholastic performance, thus confirming the cross-cultural relevance of these measures. However, the evidence indicated that abled children respond more to an inner urge toward independence than to conformity pressures.

In a study by Lucito (1964), fifty-five high-IQ and fifty-one low-IQ sixth-graders were asked to compare the length of several lines drawn on a chart against a given standard. Before reacting, the children saw what they thought were responses recorded by their peers but were really erroneous answers placed there by the examiners. In responding to the stimuli, the brighter children seemed better able to resist the influence of what they thought were peer judgments and offer independent responses. It would seem, therefore, that bright children have more confidence in themselves and in their powers of discernment.

The independence of high-IQ children should not be confused with rebelliousness. Although they often apply their own rules to their work, they also show a need to relate closely to people they can admire and emulate. Ringness (1965) compared the motivational patterns of eighty-eight high-, eighty-five average-, and eighty-eight low-achieving eighth-grade boys with IQs of 120 or above. He discovered that the high achievers were motivated to excel in school and to gain satisfaction from their scholastic activities. They were independent and often showed leadership skills while enjoying their relationships with peers without being dependent on peer group support. Yet, they tended to identify more with parents, authority figures, and cultural norms and usually behaved in a manner that was socially acceptable. The low-achievers, on the other hand, were seen as rejecting parental and school values, resenting authority, employing less socially accepted behavior, deviating from the norms of the peer group, yet tending to lean on the peer group for support.

Judging from the gifted child's need for independence and affiliation, it would seem that achievement motivation originates both from within and outside the individual. Maslow (1970) seems to imply this in his hierarchy of basic human needs, which he lists, from lowest to highest, as follows:

1. Physiological
2. Safety
3. Belongingness and love
4. Esteem
5. Self-actualization

According to Maslow even if the physiological, safety, belongingness, and esteem needs were satisfied, there would still be a feeling of restlessness among individuals to fulfill the need of self-actualization. There is an inner urge for human beings to become what they can be. Musicians have to make music, artists have to paint, and poets have to write in order for them to achieve peace within themselves. Perhaps that is what the mountain climber meant when he said that he had to conquer Mt. Everest "because it's there."

In the same vein, Newland (1976) has distinguished between two kinds of motivation that energize an individual's outgoing tendencies. One type is *extrinsic*, a condition "in which stimuli are brought to bear on the individual in order to get him to 'employ' that outgoingness in responding in a certain way—this response being mostly or entirely a reaction to such externally applied stimuli" (p. 105). The other type is *intrinsic*, a condition "in which the individual, on his own and largely or totally in the absence of . . . external motivating stimuli, reacts in the desired manner. In this latter case, the conditions immediately predisposing to such action are regarded as residing within the individual" (p. 105). Unfortunately, not enough is known about extrinsic and intrinsic types of motivation to determine whether they mix differently for people excelling in various fields of accomplishment, such as fine art versus commercial art, theoretical science versus applied science, and social leadership versus mathematics.

Little is known also about the circumstances under which achievement motivation influences school performance. Atkinson and Raynor (1974) comment that in light of the contradictory evidence, there is a "now you see it, now you don't" (pp. 200-201) relationship between people's energy and persistence and their school grades. Perhaps some of the research that deals with the social contexts in which motivation is measured can help to explain these apparent contradictions. Veroff (1969) distinguishes between what he calls autonomously oriented achievement motivation, which is the prime mover of children's desire to perform well during their early years at school, and social comparison orientation, which predominates at the time a child reaches the middle grades. In the period of life when autonomous factors operate strongly, children establish achievement standards based on bettering their own previous performance; later, self to others' comparisons begin to predominate.

Veroff (1969) presents empirical support for his hypothesis. Further confirmation is reported by Ruhland, Gold, and Feld (1978), but their evidence suggests that the relationship is not strong. In their own study of 154 second- and fifth-graders, they hypothesized that achievement motivation would be related positively to scholastic performance under two conditions: high peer acceptance (popularity) and low role conflict, which exists when the child's teacher and peers pressure for adherence to fairly similar behavior codes. Both hypotheses were strongly supported by the data on fifth-graders, but the results for second-graders were ambiguous. Nevertheless, it would seem that achievement motivation has to be understood in the context of social realities, particularly the child's status among peers. A strong desire to excel can be nullified by conformity demands that distract from the goals of achievement.

Distractors can also be in the form of competing achievement objectives. A student who has the capacity, motivation, and opportunity to head in the direction of immortality in science needs to follow such a strict regimen of study and experimentation that there is not enough time to cultivate an equally high potential in other academic disciplines. Even an Arthur Rubenstein could not rise to preeminence during the early stages of his concert career when a rich social life competed with his immersion in great music. One social scientist whose extensive research focuses mainly on achievement motivation (Atkinson, 1978) also emphasizes the importance of singleness of purpose in maximizing achievement. In commenting on Thomas Edison's alleged claim that genius is 1 percent inspiration and 99 percent perspiration, he suggests that the research evidence on factors associated with achievement probably credits inspiration with about 25 percent of the variance, perspiration with some 50 percent, and the avoidance of alternative distracting activities with the remaining 25 percent (Atkinson, 1978).

As for the overall message that can be gleaned from research on achievement motivation, Atkinson comments as follows:

When all of the rest of it has blown away, the single most important implication of a quarter of a century of work on achievement motivation will stand: its demonstration of the ubiquity of the interactive effects of personality and situational determinants of behavior. This implies, stated boldly, that neither the study of individual differences, ignoring the role of variations in situational conditions, nor the study of the effects of systematic variations in the environment, ignoring the role of differences in personality, will ever yield a science of motivation because the theoretically significant result so often lies in the interaction. (p. 240)

What can parents and teachers make of the evidence on achievement motivation? It is useful to keep in mind that both the home and the school can create conditions that affect children's desire to excel and thereby influence the fulfillment of promise. This may be self-evident, but it should be understood in the proper perspective. Among the linkages between potential and fulfillment—general ability, special aptitude, nonintellective, environmental, and chance factors—there are only a few that lend themselves to systematic influence at home and at school. Parents and teachers can cajole, pressure, and inspire children to make the most of themselves, and of course, they can provide the necessary educational support systems. But powerful as these influences are, many more remain beyond the reach of people responsible for nurturing children's abilities.

Assuming that early signs of giftedness exist, there are so many distractors with the power to seduce that there is no way of predicting with assurance what path the child will take. Some of the distractions are peer inspired and mediated; others materialize predictably and still others fortuitously in the widening world of the child. Parents and teachers cannot often control these competing influences, and even when they can, they are not always willing. There is always the painful value judgment to be made as to whether the child with the potential for excelling in a particular field should be helped to become "well-rounded" but relatively shallow, or to plunge deeply into that restricted domain of ideas and remain relatively ignorant of the surrounding domains, to say nothing of distant ones. Existing knowledge about motivation would suggest that this is a Hobson's choice that forces the sacrifice of one for the other.

SELF-CONCEPT

A person's individuality may be delineated from two perspectives: the evaluation of others and the perception of self. According to phenomenological psychologists (Snygg and Coombs, 1949), the self-concept is at the core of personality. It is the subjective image we each have of ourselves and that we spend our lives maintaining and enhancing. It may seem contradictory to maintain and enhance these images at the same time since one impulse represents a need to resist personal change while the other is a need to encourage it. But even though we withstand any external effort to change the image we each have of ourselves because it may result in a distortion of a picture that must remain clear if we are to preserve our identity and mental health, there is also an inner urge to modify that image, provided that it is for the better. We can never satisfy what Maslow calls our need for self-fulfillment without striving to become smarter, stronger, more attractive, more creative, and more ethical, despite the fact that our familiarity and comfort with the persons we think we are have a restraining influence. Thus, Jones (1973) quotes many studies showing people's desire to receive messages from others that embellish rather than confirm their self-image, and he offers the following poem to summarize his conclusions:

> *I am good*
> *You love me*
> *Therefore you are good.*
> *I am bad*
> *You love me*
> *Therefore you are truly beautiful (p. 198)*

One of the salient hypotheses of phenomenological psychology is that we tend to act in accordance with our self-concept even if that image is at variance with the way in which others see us and with objective evidence about our attributes. If we *think* of ourselves as gifted, we will try to *act* as if we were, to match our projections with our perceptions of ourselves. However, the effects are circular: the quality of performance influences the self-image of the performer and the self-image of the performer affects performance. It is therefore important to examine empirical evidence on the relationship between the two.

In a large-scale study of 1,050 seventh-graders in four junior high schools, Brookover, Peterson, and Thomas (1962) found a significant correlation between self-concept and achievement (males .42, females .39) when IQ was partialed out and a low correlation (.17) between self-concept and IQ when achievement was partialed out. This shows that measures of self-concept and of IQ assess different aspects of human potential.

In another study of junior high school students, restricted in this case to children with high IQs, Dean (1977) investigated the relationship of self-concept to performance on verbal recall and paired associate learning tasks among high-IQ seventh- and eighth-graders. The sample consisted of twenty-four males with a mean IQ of 148 and twenty-four females with a mean IQ of 139, all taken from an ungraded enrichment class for the gifted and divided into subsamples of high and low self-concept on the basis of Coopersmith's Self-Esteem Inventory. Results show self-concept related to learning across tasks but independent of intelligence. Also, children with high self-concepts were most likely to use relatively sophisticated learning strategies. It is especially noteworthy that, for this high-achieving, high-IQ sample, self-esteem scores were unrelated to grade-point average or tested intelligence. A restricted IQ range may account for its low correlation with scores on the Coopersmith instrument.

Similar results were obtained in a study of 159 Israeli children, grades four through eight, with a mean WISC IQ of 140 (Milgram & Milgram, 1976). In this study, the children were divided into two subsamples, those with IQs of 125 to 140 and the comparison group with IQs of 140 and above. Still, the analysis of variance yielded significant differences associated with IQ on only three of the twenty nine measures of self-concept. Since the low- as well as high-IQ children were all well within the highest decile of the normal distribution in intelligence, the absence of sharp differences between the two samples in IQ may explain the lack of contrast in self-concept ratings. For such a high-potential group, information on how the children feel about themselves may add insights into whether or in what way they will work hard enough in the long run to fulfill their promise eventually.

Over the wide range of potential, there is no doubt about a positive correlation between academic achievement and various self-concept measures (Purkey, 1970). Although the relationship between the two is at least partially reciprocal, there is little evidence as to which of the two has greater influence over the other. The issue is important inasmuch as educators want to know how much effort to invest in enhancing children's feelings about themselves as a means of influencing the quality of their schoolwork.

The largest-scale study of this question was conducted on 556 adolescents ranging widely in ability (Calsyn and Kenny, 1977), and the findings may or may not apply to a gifted population. Nevertheless, the results of their analysis of data from grades eight to twelve suggest that achievement in the form of grade-point averages is causally predominant over self-concept of ability, particulary among females. Nevertheless, as the investigators themselves point out, grade-point average is at least in part a measure of the teacher's subjective evaluation of the student rather than a purely objective measure of achievement.

Since our self-concepts are strongly influenced by our perception of what others think of us, the grade-point average may represent that perception to the student and therefore exercises an inordinately strong influence on the student's self-concept. Perhaps more impersonal, objective assessments would be less influential. In the case of high achievers, their desire to measure up to standards they think worthy of themselves may help to give them a seemingly slight but critical edge in the pursuit of excellence. If Heifetz had the slightest doubt that he could "conquer" his immensely difficult instrument, his performance might have been "merely" tidy and precise, but would have lacked the daring and spontaneity that can make a world of difference on the concert stage.

Some people who think well of their own abilities tend to "play it safe" and avoid opportunities to prove themselves again and again for fear of failure and the consequent threat to their self-images. Beery (1975) and Covington and Beery (1976) propose a theory of achievement behavior in which students protect their self-concepts of high ability by exercising little effort to learn. They refuse to submit themselves to a test where the demands are high, to avoid the risk of failure and the implication that their potential is not as high as they think it is.

In a study of 360 college freshman, Covington and Omelich (1979) presented evidence to support the theory that school achievement behavior is affected by feelings of personal competency and efforts to preserve a sense of self-worth. In pressured problem-solving situations, the students tended to give up their pursuit of solutions with the familiar refrain "nothing ventured, nothing lost." The investigators concluded,

Little wonder that excuses are such a permanent part of the school scene. There emerges from this complex interplay among students, peers, and teachers a "winning" formula when risking failure which is designed to avoid personal humiliation and shame and to minimize teacher punishment: try, or at least *appear* to try, but not too energetically and with excuses always handy. It is difficult to imagine a strategy better calculated to sabotage the pursuit of personal excellence. (p.178)

It appears, therefore, that high self-regard has to be actualized through risk-taking behavior; otherwise, it amounts to little more than empty bravado or self-delusion. Sometimes, the gifted who are endowed with strong egos pay social penalties for appearing to be arrogant, but if they did not believe their abilities were exceptional, they could never prime themselves for maximum effort when they are called upon to confirm their giftedness through yet another extraordinary accomplishment.

In an attempt to determine what kinds of self-reports are associated with academic motivation, Doyle and Moen (1978) asked more than six hundred college undergraduates to report on their beliefs about themselves as students. Results showed that academic motivation could be defined along nine dimensions, which included self-reports about their desires, enjoyments, and resentments. It is noteworthy that the desire for self-improvement and for esteem (factors 1 + 3) explained nearly 46 percent of the common variance in the drive toward scholastic achievement and that antischool feelings (factor 2) accounted for another 23 percent. Paradoxically, perceiving oneself as interested in learning and enjoying the world of ideas is no guarantree that the rules and routines of school are appreciated. Table 8-1 lists the nine factors, including the illustrative items with the highest loadings and the percentage of common variance accounted for by each factor.

Table 8-1. Factors of Academic Motivation with Illustrative Items, Percentages of Common Variance, and Scale Reliabilities

Factor	Illustrative Highest-Loading Items (loadings)	% Common Variance	Scale Internal Consistency
1. Desire for self-improvement (15 items)	I hope school will make me feel able to handle whatever comes up (.78) I hope school will help me become a better person (.65) I hope school will teach me better ways of handling conflicts with people (.65)	33.8%	.87
2. Antischool (17 items)	School gives me a feeling of insignificance that I hate (.61) Grade or degree requirements put restrictions on me that I hate (.55) I dislike most schoolwork (.55)	22.7	.82
3. Desire for esteem (14 items)	I worry that others might think something I do or say in class is stupid (.54) I hope what I learn in school will make others pay more attention to me (.52) I worry that others might think badly of me if it seems I don't try to do my best in school (.52)	12.0	.81
4. Enjoyment of learning (11 items)	It is very important that my classes make me use my mind (.55) I enjoy reading most books and articles my teachers assign (.50) I just really enjoy learning new things (.45)	9.6	.77
5. Enjoyment of assertive interactions (7 items)	I enjoy matching wits with others in school (.60) I sometimes enjoy having a good hot argument in class (.57) I enjoy looking for the flaws in an argument (.48)	6.5	.71

Table 8-1. (Cont.)

Factor	Illustrative Highest-Loading Items (loadings)	% Common Variance	Scale Internal Consistency
6. Resentment of poor teaching (3 items)	I resent being given assignments which I think are purposeless (.57) Poorly done lectures, books, etc., really irritate me (.54) I get upset by teachers who will not seriously consider other points of view (.38)	4.3	.58
7. Desire for academic success (4 items)	I am enthusiastic about trying to get high scores or grades (.49) If I have started on something, it is very important for me to complete it (.41) I try to do my very best on all my schoolwork, even on things I don't find interesting (.45)	4.1	.63
8. Desire for career preparation (4 items)	I need high scores, high grades, or a degree to help me get the position I want (.42) I am in school because I expect to learn things that will make me better at the job I want (or one I already have) (.40) School is a way of preparing myself so I can accomplish significant things (.30) Preparation for a career is not one of my main objectives in school (-.56)	3.6	.61
9. Enjoyment of passive interactions (5 items)	I like to learn by hearing what other students think (.57) An important part of school is being around people I like (.50) It is very important for me to be able to feel friendly with my instructors (.30)	3.3	.52

Source: D. O. Doyle, Jr., and R. E. Moen, "Toward the Definition of a Domain of Academic Motivation," *Journal of Educational Psychology,* **70**(2): 234 (1978).

PERSONAL IDIOSYNCRASIES

The relationship between various nonintellective and intellective traits may seem clear, but it is not necessarily exclusive or even direct. For example, Terman's (1925) study of the medical histories of his high-IQ children show that they were healthier than the controls. It is also known that socioeconomic status (SES) is correlated positively with physical health and with IQ too. The question then arises as to whether high-IQ and good health go together because they reinforce each other or because high socioeconomic status is a passport to better health and to higher scores on IQ tests; control for SES and the relationship between physical health and IQ may be nullified. Since relatively few studies exercise such experimental controls, it is not easy to interpret the research literature on emotional and social concomitants of giftedness.

In one large-scale study (Bonsall and Stefflre, 1955), great care was taken to control for background variables, and the results seem to differ from those in other studies of high-IQ children. From a population of more than thirteen hundred male high school seniors, the experimenters compared subsamples of high- and average-IQ students on the Guilford-Zimmerman Temperament Survey. Results showed that the boys with superior tested intelligence were also rated better in a variety of traits, including thoughtfulness and emotional stability, as expected. However, when the comparison was restricted to high- versus average-IQ children from the upper socioeconomic levels, the contrasts in nonintellective traits were all but wiped out. The investigators raise serious questions about Terman's data showing multiple superiorities of high-IQ children that they attribute to the advantages of middle- and upper-SES upbringing rather than to scores on IQ tests.

Nevertheless, there is evidence to show that high-IQ youngsters possess distinguishable nonintellective traits that are not associated with SES. Nichols (1966) reports a large-scale follow-up study of National Merit Scholarship finalists and scholars who had reached their senior year in college. They were then compared on a number of characteristics with a group of representative college seniors coming from similar socioeconomic backgrounds. The differences were extensive and dramatic. Among the able students there were larger percentages of males, Jews, first-borns, and members of small families; on the other hand, there were smaller percentages of Catholics and blacks. The two groups also differed in their interests and career plans, with the more able students leaning more in the direction of intellectual and artistic activities and away from social activities. Their career choices probably reflected the temper of the times, as they frequently expressed the desire to become scientific researchers, college professors, writers, attorneys, and physicians, while their less able counterparts opted more often for careers as businessmen and as elementary or secondary school teachers. However, if such a study were repeated periodically, changes in the labor market might bring about other differences in career choices, and it is conceivable that at times the two groups would resemble each other in their choices.

Self-ratings and assessments by teachers and peers all agreed in characterizing Merit finalists more frequently than less able students as independent, assertive, idealistic, unconventional, cynical, rebellious, and argumentative. They were less frequently seen as friendly, sociable, easygoing, obliging, cooperative, and submissive. Yet they were described as more mature, dependable, well adjusted, and honest than average students.

The Merit finalists tended to be extremely involved in campus political activities, they held more than their share of organizational leadership positions, and they conducted more discussions of political, social, and religious issues with teachers and peers than did the control group. This involvement in idealistic strivings apparently diminished their interest in dating, parties, and socializing with peers. Again, as with career differences, contrasts in personal traits may be a reflection of life on campus in the mid-1960s.

The contentiousness and independence of the more able college students proba- bly placed them at the forefront of rebellious movements. But what happens to their equally able successors at different moments in time? If they change along with the times, in what ways are they consistently distinguishable from their less able peers? Perhaps the most defensible and frequently ignored generalization about them is their variability. The Nichols study (1966) is only one of many that attempt to reveal their collective uniqueness, but it would be naïve and misleading to use the data to sterotype them. Whatever central tendencies may be observed in the personality traits of gifted children, it is important to remember that there is a wide range of individualities among them and that no single member of the group should be expected to conform to any single set of descriptors that are supposed to "typify" the group as a whole. Beyond the threshold level of every qualifier, there is considerable room for individual differences. Roedell (1978) discovered such differences in the social development of intellectually advanced children of pre- school age. She concludes, "One of the most striking findings in each set of these measures of social development is the wide range of performance within the group. Certainly it would be difficult, if not impossible, to compile an adequate profile of 'the gifted child' from these data" (p. 9).

As might also be expected, shifts occur over time in the normative personality characteristics of the gifted as a group, and there are also changes within individuals. Nichols (1965) reported on the nature of these developments in a study of 1,177 National Merit finalists in the course of their college careers. The instruments used included several personality questionnaires and vocational preference indices. Results were as follows:

1. There were signs of a decline in anxiety, tension, and guilt over a four-year period. However, the scholars reported an increased recognition of their own hostility, dependency, and irrationality.
2. Academic interests increased significantly. However, the scholars were less enthusiastic about most other things and seemed less confident and less eager to take on difficult problems.
3. There was a decline in sociability and interest in being with other people. However, the scholars showed an increased interest in marriage and family life.
4. The scholars seemed less conventional in their moral standards and less con- cerned with following socially prescribed standards.
5. The scholars were less suspicious and less likely to blame others for their difficulties.

As a group, then, these outstanding college students seemed to become more aware of their own shortcomings and negativism during their period of under- graduate study. They also became less dependent on external standards for their behavior while their motives and interests became more specific and differentiated. Finally, correlations between scores on the test instruments at the beginning and end of college attendance were low compared with the test-retest coefficients when the instruments were administered within a much shorter time. This shows that maturation and experience produce significant changes in a large variety of personal attributes among the gifted. Evidently, time has its effect on the characteristics of the gifted, not only in relation to the era in which they live but also as a result of their growing older and exposing themselves to the influences of different environments in which they find themselves.

Even though changes in personality patterns among the gifted may be expected to change from one era to the next and in the course of their maturation, there are also consistencies that are independent of these temporal contexts. In a study of National Merit Scholars of the mid-1950s, Warren and Heist (1960) discovered distinguishing traits similar to some located by Nichols (1966) and his mid-1960s Merit Scholars sample. The subjects of the earlier study were 918 finalists who were compared during their college years with 388 University of California and 453 Michigan State University students representing all four undergraduate years. On the basis of a large battery of personality inventories and attitudinal scales, the investigators obtained the following results:

1. The National Merit Scholars scored higher on measures of ego strength, indicating that they operate at a higher level of personal affectiveness and are more self-confident, resourceful, and independent than are less able college students.
2. The Merit Scholars showed greater individual independence and a tendency toward original and unconventional ways of responding to the environment as well as a greater tolerance of ambiguity and potential for creativity. This tendency toward nonconformity has been seen in much younger high-IQ samples, as was noted by Lucito (1964) in his study of responses to group influence among high-IQ sixth-graders.
3. In addition to being relatively independent, the Merit Scholars proved themselves confident and generally mature in their interactions with the external world. As compared with the normative groups, they had more complex perceptions and reactions. They were less authoritarian and more willing to become "risk takers" in the world of ideas. Most of them reacted with extraordinary imagination and resourcefulness to the stimulations of the testing experience.
4. The attribute that most sharply differentiated the Merit Scholars from the other college students was their strong disposition toward intellectual activity. Specifically, they preferred reflective and abstract thought, chose a rational-cognitive approach to reality, and preferred a positive-functional approach to scholarly pursuits.
5. Accompanying the Merit Scholars' high scholastic aptitude and strong attraction to intellectual activity was a high level of aesthetic awareness and appreciation. Highest aesthetic scores were exhibited particularly by the females, which indicates a special receptivity toward sensory experiences that are notable for their beauty and harmony.
6. The Merit Scholars valued theoretical and aesthetic orientations relatively high and economic, or utilitarian, orientations relatively low, as compared with the other college students.

7. The investigators concluded that the personality structures and ways of thinking demonstrated by gifted students, especially their intellectual rebelliousness, originality, ego strength, and potential for creativity, are conducive to superior intellectual achievement.

There is further evidence of consistency of personal traits among able students over time. Niemiec and Sanborn (1971) investigated the value structures of forty-eight high school senior boys who were college bound and ranked in the top 5 percent nationally in achievement and IQ. Each individual in the sample rank ordered the following four values on the basis of relative importance: (1) *material* accomplishments and rewards, (2) *public recognition* or acclaim, (3) *social service* in the form of helping others to improve and develop, and (4) *personal development*. Several sources of information were used independently to appraise the order of preferences for each student. One source was the student's cumulative record combined with a structured senior year interview administered and interpreted by a school counselor. Another counselor evaluated the same cumulative record and structured interview, as did the principal investigator, to determine the extent of interjudge agreement. Finally, each student ranked the values independently.

Results show strong consistency among the different perceptions of the students' value preferences. Moreover, in analyzing the value hierarchies over the four years, the investigators found that the students' value patterns were crystallized by the ninth grade and were likely to remain stable thereafter. It is therefore possible to recognize consistencies over time in nonintellective traits among the gifted, even though they are not entirely immune to the temper of the times. As individuals they may be fairly unchanging in some ways, but they are also so diverse that whatever distinguishes them as a group does not apply to every member.

Signs of diversity in interpersonal values are apparent in high-IQ students at least from junior high school into college. For example, Bachtold (1968) found that seventh-, eighth-, and ninth-graders scoring in the top 2 percent on measures of general ability and scholastic achievement tended to believe more in personal independence and nonconformity than did average achievers at their school. Yet there was also considerable overlap between the two groups with respect to these values, and the group differences should not obscure the importance of the overlap.

In addition to evidence on personality traits that characterize a population with high general intelligence, it is also apparent that there are nonintellective attributes associated with various areas of specialization. Haggard (1957) conducted an elaborate longitudinal study of forty-five children at the University of Chicago Laboratory School, monitoring their progress for five years from grades three through seven. He discovered that, by the time they arrived in grade three, the high achievers who performed exceptionally well on all tests of general ability were sensitive and responsive to socialization pressures, had largely accepted adult values, and were striving to live up to adult expectations. They saw their parents as somewhat overprotective, pressuring for achievement, and lacking in emotional warmth. The children were adept at emotional control and fairly tense, competitive, and aggressive. Yet they got along better with their parents, teachers, and peers and showed a greater level of overall adjustment than did their lower-achieving classmates who nevertheless scored well above the national norm on scholastic measures.

By grade seven, some changes had taken place in high achievers. Although they continued to respond to the socialization pressures of adults and to strive for adult standards of behavior, they had developed strong antagonistic attitudes toward adults. At the same time, they showed a marked increase in their level of anxiety and a corresponding decrease in intellectual originality and creativity. They became more aggressive, persistent, hard-driving, and competitive, and they showed signs of willingness to be destructive in order to defeat other people. Nevertheless, they retained a high degree of mental flexibility and spontaneity, particularly in their ability to manipulate abstract symbol systems. They also began to emerge as the social leaders among their peers while serving on important class committees and holding important class offices.

High achievers in reading had seemingly withdrawn into themselves and viewed their world and the people in it from a distance. The reaction to their parents and other authority figures was mildly negative. These children were intent on maintaining their sense of integrity, and they defined it by exercising independence of thought and action. Although generally sensitive to others, they felt rejected and tended to become hostile or withdraw rather than conform to the ways of others. These children had difficulty in expressing either affection or hostiltity openly, and they lacked the facility for developing and maintaining close relationships with peers.

The high achievers in spelling and language tended to view parental and other authority figures as omnipotent, rejecting, and generally punitive, not as sources of emotional support. Although these children were dependent upon their parents, they seemed unable to show real affection or to establish warm emotional relationships with them. They were also markedly passive and dependent upon outside sources for direction of their thoughts and actions. They showed a bland emotional life, appeared to be incapable of giving or receiving much affection, and were equally inhibited in expressing hostility. Their fantasy life was relatively barren, and they seemed to lack the necessary emotional strength to act with initiative.

The high achievers in arithmetic tended to see their environment as being neither threatening nor overwhelming. They viewed it with curiosity and felt capable of mastering any problems they might encounter. In relating to their parents and other authority figures, they showed less strain than did the high general achievers and the high achievers in reading and greater independence than did the high spelling achievers. They had the best developed and healthiest egos, both in relation to their own emotions and mental processes and in their greater maturity in dealing with the outside world of people and things. They could express their feelings freely and without anxiety or guilt and were capable of integrating their emotions, thoughts, and actions. Their intellectual processes tended to be spontaneous, flexible, venturesome, and creative. In their relations with authority figures and peers, they were more assertive, independent, and self-confident than were the children in other subgroups. Generally, they related well to others, but if they felt that attempts were being made to impose undue restrictions upon them, they tended to respond with hostility and self-defense to maintain their independence and autonomy of thought and action.

A follow-up study reported two years later, when the children had finished grade nine (D'Heurle et al., 1959), revealed no change in the children's personal attributes. Again, the high general achievers conformed to parental values, performed consistently well in school, participated effectively in group activities, and showed independence and self-confidence. On the other hand, the high reading achievers continue to have difficulty in expressing their feelings openly and in relating to adults and peers. They were the most intensely anxious of any group and showed the greatest fear of parental rejection and deprivation. While lacking self-confidence, they showed a high degree of competitiveness and ill-feeling toward their siblings. The high spelling achievers seemed to be less anxious than the other groups and expressed few guilt feelings and negative reactions to their parents. They were also extremely cooperative with teachers and peers. The high arithmetic achievers continued to be spontaneous and free in their behavior, worked well with others, were effective in group activities, and tended to occupy positions of leadership at school. In their relationship with the adult world, they showed less strain than did the high general achievers and the high achievers in reading and greater independence than did the high spelling achievers.

On the basis of their seven-year study of the relationships between intellectual functioning and personality structures among able children, D'Heurle, Mellinger, and Haggard (1959) reached the following conclusions:

1. Children with exceptional imaginations and spontaneity perform better on mental tests consisting of problems that cannot be solved by previous learning.
2. Children who are dependent and passive, or tense and strained, perform well on tests that consist of familiar material. These children often have parents who are overprotective or exert excessive pressures on them for academic achievement.
3. Children who seem inhibited in expressing their feelings do better on verbal tests, whereas those who are more free and active in their behavior and fantasy perform better on tests requiring the manipulation of objective data.
4. By examining the behavior ratings, a tentative continuum could be formed ranging from rigidity and constriction to labile expressiveness. At one extreme are the highly verbal children who seem tense and constrained in their behavior; then there is the reasoning group, independent and effective in classroom interactions; finally there are the children who are especially advanced in the basic skills of arithmetic, are more expressive, self-confident, and spontaneous in their demeanor than are most of the others.

Despite the fact that the University of Chicago Campus School sample was relatively small, with only forty-five children out of a total of seventy-six staying throughout the seven-year study period, a considerable amount of data on intellective and nonintellective factors was gathered over the course of the study. Equally important, the results were probably not affected by social class factors, since most students attending that school at the time came from middle- and upper-status homes. The school population from which the samples were drawn was also narrow in range with respect to scholastic performance, with few students scoring below the highest decile for the normative population in tests of scholastic potential and achievement. Since the school population is fairly homogeneous in SES and scholastic functioning, these factors could not account for major differences in trait clusters that were associated with the various special abilities.

In another study involving a population that was narrow in range with respect to SES and academic records, Borgen (1971) attempted to predict the career choices of more than one thousand male scholarship winners from scores on the Occupational and Basic Interest Scales of the Strong Vocational Interest Blank. He discovered that interests play a larger part in career choice for high-ability men than they do for the typical college student. These results may help to dispel a frequently held belief that the intensity of a child's interest in learning is a valuable clue to the existence and nature of giftedness in that child. Actually, intense interest does not make up for a lack of superior ability, but it is probably helpful in actualizing the potential of a person who possesses high potential.

MENTAL HEALTH

Psychodynamic variables are associated with achievements, as demonstrated in a series of studies by Stern, Stein, and Bloom (1956). On the basis of these investigations, the researchers developed several synthetic typologies of college freshmen in an effort to synthesize purely hypothetical personality syndromes that would have predictive validity with respect to scholastic achievement and general social adjustment. One such model was labeled stereopath; another was called nonstereopath. The *stereopath* can be characterized as a hypothetical individual who tends to accept authority unquestioningly, exercises strong control over impulses, and adheres to rigid standards of orderliness and conformity. Such a person's childhood is often controlled by at least one strict parent whose authority is absolute and to whom the child submits overtly while repressing strong feelings of hostility. The *nonstereopath*, on the other hand, is capable of close interpersonal relationships, rejects authority figures, allows for spontaneous and creative expression of impulses, and espouses behavior codes that are flexible enough to include nonconformity. In such a person's upbringing, self-importance is established early in a permissive, nurturant environment at home.

The major personality differences between the stereopath and nonstereopath may be summarized as follows:

Stereopath	Nonstereopath
1. Reactions to Others	
Depersonalization of relationships. Perception of authority figures as omnipotent, threatening, and impregnable.	Highly personalized relationships. Perception of authority figures realistically, frequently as overprotective or overpossessive.

Stereopath	**Nonstereopath**

2. *Coping Mechanisms*

Submission to authority. Overwhelming unconscious hostility, displaced externally. Aggression expressed extrapunitively in attempted dominance and control.	Identification with cathected objects. Conscious rebellion and overt rejection of negative or ambivalent cathexes. Aggression expressed freely and directly in attempt to maintain inviolacy, autonomy, and independence. Generally characterized by maintenance of good contact and rapport with others.

3. *Impulse Acceptance*

Inhibition and denial of id impulses. Depersonalized sexuality.	Acceptant of id impulses. Capable of direct sentient and sexual representations, as well as their sublimations.

4. *Impulse Control*

Strong, punitive superego structure, not necessarily internalized. Anxiety and guilt associated with unconscious hostility. Control of unacceptable impulses in order to avoid criticism or disapproval of parent or parent-surrogate is incomplete, resulting in impulse-ridden physical outbursts. Such explosions are noncathartic, only increasing anxiety and guilt.	Balanced ego-id-superego demands. Anxiety associated with conscious hostility more focused, more readily verbalized and dissipated. Internalized superego. Conflict conscious and verbalized. Capable of responsibility and emotional maturity.

5. *Energy Level*

Ineffectual liberation of effective tension and continual free-floating anxiety drains off energy otherwise available for goal-directed activity. Compensated for by autistic thinking in goal-behavior and fantasied achievement.	Capable of sustained effort for remote goals.

6. *Autonomous-Homonomous Balance*

Predominantly exocathective-extraceptive: manipulating things and people as external objects through practical, physical action. Conformity and adaptation to reality as given for more or less immediately tangible ends, emphasizing money and property. Countercathective rejection of sensuality, introspection, intraception and verbal-emotional-artistic expressiveness. Egocentric (infantile) perception: animism, anthropormorphism, mysticism, superstition.	Predominantly other-directed, placing great emphasis on interpersonal relationships. Identification with "underdog," and capacity for dramatic, idealistic social action. Sensuous, introspective, intraceptive. Verbal-emotional-artistic sublimations.

7. *Self-maintenance*

Repression, inhibition, projection, paranoia, escapism, masochism, sadism. Denial of negative aspects of self. Concern with physical symptoms, appearance.	Counteraction. Exhibitionism and self-dramatization. Capacity for realistic self-appraisal, introspection.

Stereopath	Nonstereopath

8. *Organization and Integration*

Sphincter morality, emphasizing obedience, order, punctuality. Despite stress on arrangement and detail, activities tend to be diffused and conflicted due to uncontrolled anxiety. Rigid set and outlook; inaccessible to new experience. Resistance to departure from tradition. Rigid and compulsive. (Stern et al., p. 190)	Behavior plastic and labile. Capacity for spontaneity, impulsiveness. Mobile and intense emotional responsiveness. Flexible, adaptable to changing circumstances. (Stern et al., p. 193)

Since the stereopath and nonstereopath were hypothetical characters, the investigators proceeded to locate students who would fit the descriptions. To do so, they developed an instrument that required respondents to accept or reject ideological statements concerning feelings toward ideas and intellectual abstractions, social groups, interpersonal relations, and the self. Having identified eighty-one college freshmen in each of the two samples, the investigators proceeded to make critical comparisons. Results on the American Council on Education Psychological Examination, a test of general intelligence, show that the stereopaths and nonstereopaths, respectively, scored below and above the average for their total class and that the mean difference between the two experimental groups was highly significant. Another evaluation was made of the students' performance on placement tests and on initial measures of achievement for subsamples of sixty-one cases in each group matched on ACE scores. Differences were found in Humanities, Social Sciences, English, and Language I (defined as analysis of language as a symbolic system), and they all favored the nonstereopaths. The two groups performed comparably, however, in foreign language, biological and physical sciences, and mathematics.

The investigators speculate that a possible reason for no differences in achievement in freshman-level foreign languages and sciences is that these courses deal with basic skills rather than with high-level abstractions that come later in the sequence, whereas the intellectual demands of courses in which differences were found may have been more sophisticated. Another possible explanation is that personality syndromes, such as those contained in descriptions of stereopaths and nonstereopaths, actually relate to success in specific fields of study rather than to high-level achievement across the board.

The contrast in specialized abilities between the two groups seems to be confirmed somewhat by their vocational preferences. Over two thirds of the interests cited by the stereopaths are described as "instrumental activities," including such occupations as accounting, engineering, business, law, and medicine. On the other hand, more than two thirds of the interests expressed by the nonstereopaths reflected "consummatory activities," such as psychology, sociology, teaching, music, art, and literature. It should be remembered that these preferences were expressed during the students' freshman year in college and that changes in outlook could have occurred by the time they graduated. Nevertheless, the data indicate some value in investigating the ways in which clinical syndromes facilitate *both* levels and kinds of achievement.

Judging from the characteristics of the stereopath, it would come as no surprise if such a person were beset by emotional problems that prevent the realization of potential. Indeed, the investigators found that instructors rated such students significantly lower than nonstereopaths on such variables as open-mindedness, emotional adjustment, extensive classroom participation, type of classroom participation, and academic potential. Their classroom behavior was seen as predominantly critical and hostile, which may account for the instructor's responding in kind. The college atmosphere is simply not a comfortable place for those who show signs of rigidity, conventionality, dependence, and anxiety. Small wonder that the dropout rate during the first year of college was 23 percent for the stereopaths and only 1 percent for the nonstereopath.

As logical as it may seem that handicaps—physical as well as mental—prevent the flowering of talent, there are persistent suspicions that they sometimes serve as facilitators. Blind Milton, deaf Beethoven, suicidal Schumann, and dyslexic Flaubert, Yeats, and Edison are only a few examples of genius prevailing over adversities of the body and spirit. In his sociological study of the relationship between genius and madness, Becker (1978) uncovered a variety of traditional beliefs regarding this issue. They are as follows:

1. *Genius as disequilibrium.* Embodied here is the still-popular idea that nature somehow balances off extraordinary mental powers with physical or mental weaknesses.
2. *Genius as degeneracy.* Although less popular today than it was in the late nineteenth and early twentieth centuries, this concept may still have its adherents who interpret aspects of evolutionary theory to mean that genius reflects a reversal of a highly complex organism to an earlier, simpler biological state. The same can be said for criminals, prostitutes, anarchists, and pronounced lunatics, all of whom display their own kind of inferiority by deviating from the norm in one way or another. The special characteristics of the genius are said to be smallness of body, pallor, emaciation, stammering, precocity, sterility, originality, along with behavioral disorders that plague other degenerates as well.
3. *Genius as a neurasthenic condition produced by overwork.* According to this view, mental exhaustion combined with various kinds of social stress become so intense that they somehow release within the individual a miraculous reservoir of creative ability.
4. *Genius as product of pathological state produced by genetic conflict or outside agents.* Conflicting hereditary tendencies create some kind of innate disequilibrium that propels the individual away from ordinary occupations and pleasures of life toward extraordinary accomplishments in order to achieve inner peace. Sometimes this restless, compensatory activity results from outside agents such as drugs, intoxicants, and crippling ailments.
5. *Genius as pathological by virtue of the selective granting of fame.* This point of view does not equate genius with insanity. However, the contention is that an

emotionally disturbed individual with special abilities is particularly susceptible to fame and to popular regard as a genius, whereas a mentally healthy person who becomes renowned is not as likely to be labeled "genius."

6. *Genius as criminally disposed.* Those who subscribe to this point of view regard the genius as an iconoclast with extreme hostility toward social structures, organizations, and traditions. The tendency of the genius is to destroy the existing order and pressure to construct a better one to replace it. Sometimes genius takes the form of lawful bohemianism; at other times it resorts to illegalities in its war against society.

7. *Genius as sublimation and substitute gratification.* In contrast to the criminal or pervert who is controlled by the libido, the genius is seen as sublimating infantile fantasies by becoming preoccupied with aesthetic or intellectual concerns. Those who subscribe to this point of view do not agree as to whether such a rechanneling of libidinal energies enables the genius to avoid neurotic tendencies or whether it leads inevitably toward neurosis, which in turn becomes the source of great performance and productivity.

Becker (1978) points out that the currently powerful labeling theory in the social sciences depicts the genius as a hopeless victim of stereotyping. Accordingly, the problem lies within our society of labelers whose prejudices have to be expunged rather than among the labeled, who are seen as innocent targets of intolerance. Becker raises serious questions about this point of view and presents evidence from his own historical research that "the genius was clearly not the helpless 'victim' of philistine labelers — he not only contributed heavily to his 'victimization,' he even, to a degree, instigated it" (p. 129). The genius's "antic disposition" is often just an attention-getting device of a rule breaker in a world of conformists. Sometimes it is the pose of an effete romantic, like the one described by W. S. Gilbert in his libretto for the operetta, *Patience*:

> *If you're anxious for to shine*
> *In the high aesthetic line*
> *As a man of culture rare,*
> *You must get up all the germs*
> *of the transcendental terms*
> *And plant them ev'rywhere.*
> *You must lie upon the daisies*
> *And discourse in novel phrases*
> *Of your complicated state of mind.*
> *The meaning doesn't matter*
> *If it's only idle chatter*
> *Of a transcendental kind.*
> *And ev'ryone will say,*
> *As you walk your mystic way,*
> *"If this young man expresses himself*
> *In terms too deep for me,*
> *Why what a very singularly deep young man*
> *This deep young man must be."*

Evidence brought to support the belief that genius is usually accompanied by real or feigned psychological disorders is generally in the form of anecdotal material about famous historical figures. There is little clinical information about contemporaries, except in isolated instances such as the psychoanalytic data Sigmund Freud himself collected about his patient, Gustav Mahler, the renowned composer and conductor, in the early part of this century. Nor do these theories suggest an inverse relationship between intellect and mental health. Instead, their concern is only with the few-in-a-generation immortals who have attracted attention not only to their accomplishments but to their personal lives as well. It is therefore inappropriate to compare this kind of evidence with the direct studies of stereopaths and nonstereopaths (Stern et al., 1956) that show that higher-achieving college students, none of whom would qualify as geniuses, enjoy better emotional stability.

It seems that, wherever research reports generally good mental health among gifted adults, the reference is to individuals who have no pretensions toward immortality. Most of Terman's high-IQ children went on to excel at college and in their subsequent careers and showed signs of better psychosocial development than did members of their group whose promise was never entirely fulfilled (Terman and Oden 1947, 1959). A more clinically oriented follow-up study of successful college students (Vaillant, 1977) produced similarly encouraging results. Unlike the Terman sample that was originally selected on the basis of high-IQ scores, Vaillant's 268 male Harvard graduates qualified for the long-range study on account of their apparent emotional stability and academic records as undergraduates. Their tested intelligence was only slightly higher than their classmates'; yet 61 percent of them graduated with honors, in contrast to only 26 percent of their fellow graduates. Also, more than three quarters of them went on to graduate school, and by the time they reached their middle-forties, their average income and social standing equaled that of a successful businessman or professional, as did Terman's group. They also compared favorably with the Terman sample with respect to their representation in *Who's Who in America* and in *American Men of Science*.

Psychologically, the Harvard graduates fared about as well as the Terman sample, only 9 percent of whom had shown "serious maladjustment" and only 3 percent had been hospitalized for mental disorders. At comparable periods of their lives, both groups had similarly low rates of drinking to excess and criminal convictions, and their mortality rate was lower than what would be expected for white American cohorts. Thus, it would appear that a sharp difference exists between evidence on the mental health status of the one-in-a-million as compared with the one-in-a-thousand. It is unfortunate that the two populations have unnecessarily been pitted against each other by Terman and his critics.

Terman (1925) disputed what he considered a traditional belief that childhood precocity and psychopathology frequently go together, but the opinion he contradicted referred to adult geniuses, not to high-IQ children. On the other hand, Witty and Lehman (1930) questioned Terman's conclusions about the superior mental health of high-IQ children on the grounds of psychoanalytic evidence that, according to them, depicts the genius as being often neurally unstable, superensitive and overresponsive to stimuli, and a marvelously complex and delicately vulnerable organism. This may be true of the mature genius who is either destined to achieve immortality or has already achieved it. But those who are a cut or two below the genius level and a cut or two above their peers in accomplishment probably come closer to filling the descriptions of the nonstereopath.

The generally superior mental health of high-IQ, high-achieving adults is also evident in able children and adolescents. Hildreth (1938) matched high-IQ and average-IQ children on age, racial background, and SES and found that teachers ascribe five times as many favorable ratings to those in the intellectually advanced group. In his review of Rorschach studies of high-IQ children, Mensch (1950) found that the responses of this group were quantitatively and qualitatively superior to those of less able subjects. The pattern of responses corresponded with the positive ratings by teachers of the children's maturity. In another study involving the Rorschach test, administered this time to children with IQ's no lower than 150, Gallagher and Crowder (1957) found only two out of the thirty-five elementary school children examined showing signs of serious emotional problems. These results were confirmed by Liddle (1958) in a larger-scale study of elementary school children who were tested on a variety of instruments for aggressive and withdrawal tendencies.

Among older students, too, there is an association between mental health and academic superiority. Warren and Heist (1960) conducted a large-scale study of the personality characteristics of more than nine hundred men and women who had either won or reached the semifinals of the National Merit Scholarship competition. The results on MMPI scores showed that these advanced students were relatively free of serious maladjustment. Thus, we see at all age levels an assocation between scholastic aptitude and mental health, as diagnosed by conventional measures. This generalization is necessarily equivocal on two counts: first, the relationship seems to break down at the utmost extremes of tested ability (Hollingworth, 1942); second, achievement and adjustment may relate more to social class membership than to each other in a cause-effect way, and perhaps the reason they both seem to go together is that the tests and procedures used to measure them favor the higher-status groups (Bonsall and Stefflre, 1955).

What remains open is the question of whether children's mental health not only accompanies but also contributes to their achievement at school. It would appear that it does make a difference. However, the evidence is basically peripheral since it is derived from research on so-called "underachievers" who are usually recognized on the basis of discrepancies between expected and actual scholastic standing. Although the results of research are by no means consistent, studies comparing nonintellective traits between high-IQ-achieving and high-IQ-non-achieving students often show differences in psychosocial adjustment. This is apparently true for students ranging from middle elementary to college levels who have been diagnosed by a wide variety of instruments and found to differ with respect to feelings of adequacy, alienation, nervousness, maturity, hostility, independence, and social sensitivity (Horrall, 1957; Shaw and Grubb, 1958; Drake, 1962; Ringness, 1965; Bachtold, 1968; Propper and Clark, 1970). The implication is that mental health status contributes to part of the variance in school success, at least for some students.

Since adjustment apparently affects achievement, it is important to know the incidence of emotional handicap among able children. Definitive statistics are probably impossible to obtain, considering the wide varieties of disorders and means of diagnosing them. However, incidence reports do exist for fairly sizable samples. One of them (Haarer, 1966) examined records of 1,135 institutionalized delinquents in Michigan. Results showed that 4.4 percent of the 665 boys and 2.3 percent of the 407 girls had IQs of 120 or above, rates considerably lower than the expected 12.6 percent on the Stanford-Binet test.

However, another investigation of some 540 elementary and secondary school children with IQs of 130 and above shows less encouraging results (Schauer, 1976). In this study, delinquents were excluded from the various categories of maladjustment; instead, the investigator examined the children's records for evidence of emotional difficulties based on referrals to psychiatric clinics, feelings of insecurity, peer and social adjustment problems, enuresis, parental problems, underachievement, fears and conflicts preventing functioning at full capacity, and miscellaneous behavior disturbances. The records revealed that as many as 30 percent of the high-IQ children had emotional handicaps that were associated with learning difficulties in the great majority of cases. The investigator cites other studies along with his own to confirm his conclusion that emotional conflict can often be responsible for underachievement among able students.

Although there are no definitive figures on the extent to which behavioral disorders inhibit the realization of high potential, they often figure in accounts of the familiar tragedy known as talent wasted. The sources of maladjustment are both mysterious and manifold, and they may be discerned everywhere in the child's environment, even at school. As Strang (1951) observes, "Maladjustment in gifted children may grow out of a curriculum that does not challenge their ability or provide education in interpersonal relations, self-understanding, and family living, in addition to the usual academic subjects" (p. 153). What is at stake, therefore, in developing an enrichment program for gifted children is not only mastery and creativity but also the emotional supports for productive thinking.

Chapter 9 _____

Environmental Influences

Human potential cannot flourish in an arid cultural climate; it needs nurturance, urgings, encouragement, and even pressures from a world that cares. The child lives in several worlds, the closest of which are the family, peer group, school, and community, while the remotest are the various economic, social, legal, and political institutions. These environments all help to determine the *kinds* of talent that society is willing to honor as well as the *amount* of investment that it is willing to make in cultivating them. Societal conditions are therefore critical in stimulating the gifted child's pursuit of excellence.

Needless to say, there is no simple connection between extraordinary accomplishment and a favorable environment. Many people have to overcome all kinds of adversity to distinguish themselves in the crowd. They seem to succeed *because* of the pressures, not just *despite* them. Hardships that discourage most people from achieving somehow challenge a few to "beat the odds" and "make it big." Their drive toward excellence may be basically an act of defiance against what they consider hostile, inhibiting forces in the world. But they constitute a minority among people with high potential, most of whom need a supportive environment and would wither on the vine if they did not have it.

AMERICAN CULTURAL TRADITIONS

Giftedness today is in some ways different from that of preceding or succeeding eras because it is shaped by the special needs and sanctions of a society existing in the last quarter of the twentieth century. Every social structure and every period in history responds differently to human potential, and many individuals earn renown as a result of the special "chemistry" between their talent and the milieu that nurtures it. That milieu is transitory to some extent, but it also reflects long-standing traditions that are often as contradictory as they are pervasive.

For example, in America, Laski (1948) detected a social legacy that he called "the quintessence of a secularized Puritanism" (p. 42). This has otherwise been referred to as the "Protestant ethic" (Weber, 1948), but it is applied singularly to the American condition. It extols effort and the belief that success is its inevitable consequence. In a pioneering society, it is praiseworthy to take risks, show courage, innovate and adapt, and even engage in "rugged individualism" to build and maintain a modern society. It takes so much ingenuity and hard work to get the job done that there is hardly much time to cultivate the arts. Indeed, artistic life is a luxury that few can afford when so many shoulders have to be put to the wheel.

Only later—when the pioneering days were over and political, social, and economic institutions were established—could increasing numbers of people allow themselves to turn to the life of the mind. Great political theory and science flourished earliest in the post-pioneer years because they were rooted in the necessities of the pioneer period; great drama and music began to appear much later, also as symbols of hard work and self-perfection in conformance with the Protestant ethic.

Thus, we have the tradition of the perfectability of human beings and their constant need to prove it through productivity and performance. On the other hand, there is the restraining idea that while talent and effort are precious human attributes, they should be dedicated to the betterment of the masses and not to self-indulgence through creative arts and letters.

In his massive study of the achieving society, McClelland (1961) showed evidence of a relationship between the Protestant character of a country and its need for achievement (n Ach) in that persons high in n Ach tend to seek out situations in which they can derive satisfaction from successful accomplishment. They are expected to set achievement standards for themselves rather than depend on extrinsic incentives, and they seem to try harder to measure up to these standards. They choose experts over friends as working partners, are more resistant to social pressure, and participate actively in college and community activities.

In linking n Ach with aspects of Protestantism, McClelland suggests that nations strong in such traditions enjoy superior economic and technological development, and this, in turn, is probably associated with high-level educational activity, at least in the applied sciences. Empirical evidence seems to lend support to this hypothesis. For example, Knapp and Goodrich (1952) found that Protestant groups in America tend to produce disproportionately large numbers of scientists. These findings suggest the view that high regard for rational empiricism and the scientific method are important ingredients of the value systems of these populations. Roe's (1953) discovery that fifty-nine out of the sixty-five eminent scientists she studied were from Protestant homes apparently lends further credence to the theory that Protestant values help to stimulate at least one kind of high-level mental activity.

Other research, however, holds that no single religious, national, or traditional ethnic group has a monopoly on desire for success through achievement. In their study of tiny Jewish communities in Eastern Europe (i.e., the *Shtetl*) Zborowski and Herzog (1952) reported on the high value placed on education and intellectual attainment by these subsocieties. In the *Shtetl*, brainpower was considered a person's greatest gift, far more prestigious than physical skill or strength. Children began their formal studies when they reached their third birthdays. Soon they found themselves spending long hours at school in a program consisting exclusively of the scriptures, the Talmud, and their commentaries. The most precocious young scholars were treated with deference by adults and peers alike. Teachers tried to instill in their students a love of learning for its own sake rather than for material benefits. Indeed, nobody thought about this kind of study as being potentially profitable except in the sense that it perpetuated the Jewish cultural heritage from one generation to the next. In the hope of achieving cultural continuity, Eastern European Jewry encouraged its prodigious young scholars to devote their lives entirely to learning and provided for their material sustenance even after they married and had children.

Strodtbeck (1958) recognized the *Shtetl* traditions as sources of achievement motivation among American Jews whose parents or grandparents had emigrated from the *Shtetl*. When the Eastern European Jews reached the New World, they retained their Old World love of learning, but devotion was no longer restricted to religious Jewish thought, except in a small proportion of families. Instead, their interests shifted to the entire range of up-to-date, secular ideas. Indeed, their cultural interests now resemble those of inheritors of the Protestant ethic. Underlying these motivations are beliefs that (1) the human being is perfectible, (2) the human being is also capable of exercising rational mastery of the world and is therefore responsible for its well-being, (3) loyalty to self and society takes precedence over filial obedience and accepting parental authority, (4) each person is his or her brother's (sister's) keeper, and (5) individuals can serve in subordinate positions without having to act or feel as if they were being dominated by their superiors.

Strodtbeck's (1965) studies of adolescent boys from third-generation Jewish-American, Italian-American, and Japanese-American homes confirmed his hypothesis that Jewish-Americans espouse the cause of individualism, hard work, and achievement. These attitudes also seem to make a difference among school-aged children. Getzels (1958) reports data to show that the work-success ethic and belief in the autonomous self are expressed more often by successful achievers in high school than by their less able schoolmates. These orientations toward individualism are reminiscent of what Reisman (1950) describes as "inner-directed" traditions in America that encourage the Horatio Alger dream of success through virtue and hard work. However, "other-directedness" is also prominent in our society since it represents sensitivity to the norms of group living and to the skills that are adaptive in social settings. The norm becomes something of an ideal that counteracts inclinations toward deviance of any kind, even creativity. Thus, we live with the contradictions of "inner-" and "outer-directedness" in which rugged individualism and the onward and upward motives operate against group consensus that always threatens to become group tyranny.

Allegiance to societal norms implies belief in the common man. Taken to its logical extreme, it represents a fear and distrust of elitism, intellectual and artistic as well as social and economic. As Krutch (1954) points out, a dangerous outcome of this tradition is that the common denominator begins to function as the standard of excellence, and instead of encouraging common people to become as uncommon as possible, we regard their commonness a virtue and often praise them for being undistinguished. It is perhaps this convergence upon a common ground of mediocrity that De Tocqueville (1954) had in mind when he wrote, "a middling standard is fixed in America for human knowledge. All approach as near to it as they can; some as they rise, others as they descend" (p. 55) De Tocqueville made this comment in the 1830s, and more than a century later Mead (1954) had a similar observation: "The pressures for keeping on all fours with one's classmates, neighbors, business associates, which are increasing in American life, tend to be particularly felt in the school age groups, especially in the case of the child who shows intellectual or artistic gifts" (p. 211).

Besides being subjected to pressures toward conformity, creative intellectuals are sometimes regarded as eccentrics, out of touch with conventional values and behaviors. Some are feared as dangerous radicals promoting the overthrow of popular social and political doctrines. There are those who are viewed as lazy ivory-tower dwellers who lack the practical intelligence to deal with day-to-day problems. There are even traditions attributed to the influence of Marx and Freud that belittle the power of rational thought in controlling the human being's behavior or destiny. Still, the strongest influence in this country is in the direction of learning, achievement, self-advancement, and self-betterment. The pursuit of excellence has caused the professional classes to grow much faster than the general population since the Republic was established more than two centuries ago. These traditions continue to have their strong impact on precocious children, even though there are forces in society that try to inhibit the flowering of excellence.

SOCIAL CLASS AND THE FAMILY

The relationship between social class and giftedness has been well documented. In his large-scale study of American men of science, Cattell (1906) reports that, in the early part of the century, the chances were 14 to 1 that the fathers of eminent scientists would be in professional careers rather than in any other occupation. He also notes that the probability changes dramatically when other status factors are taken into account. Thus, at that time, a white boy from the professional classes in New England had a million-to-one advantage over a black girl from the southern cotton fields to become distinguished in the sciences.

Terman (1925) discovered similarly that children he identified as gifted on the basis of IQ were overrepresented among the middle and upper socioeconomic classes. This apparent association between scholastic aptitude and social status was later confirmed in a comparison between more than three hundred Merit Scholars and randomly selected classmates during their freshman year in college (Astin, 1964). Results show that Merit Scholars tended to come from higher socioeconomic backgrounds than did the comparison group and also excelled in academic, scientific, literary, and artistic achievement. However, these differences in performance could not be attributed entirely to social class because they remained to some extent even after the Merit Scholars were matched with another group of freshmen on such independent variables as sex, high school class size, father's level of education, and father's occupation. What accounted for the contrast in performance were probably some ability and motivational factors on which the samples were not matched. Still, social class seems to make a difference in personal development, even within groups of children designated as gifted. Frierson (1965) compared upper- and lower-class gifted samples from several elementary schools and found several differences between them. The upper-status children showed more interest in reading after school hours, chose better quality materials to read, expressed better attitudes toward school, and were more aware of their parents' desires to have them continue on to college.

One reason for the high educational motivation in middle- and upper-class families is that they regard formal schooling as a means of staying ahead or getting ahead in the socioeconomic world. However, some students from lower-class families are also encouraged by their families to succeed scholastically, and the effects are often positive. Kahl (1953) reveals that, when fathers of highly able adolescent boys were satisfied with "getting by," the boys were less apt to consider going to college than were boys in families where the fathers were concerned with "getting ahead." These findings suggest that, within a given socioeconomic stratum, a family's attitudes and values have a greater influence on the aspirations of their sons than does the actual class membership.

The mother's identification with academic life is important, too. In a study of 360 mothers of children identified as gifted, Groth (1975) discovered that nearly half these women had baccalaureate degrees, as compared with only 7.2 percent of the general population. They also earned six times more masters and doctoral degrees than would be expected in a random sample of women in this country. However, there may be a difference in the extent to which mothers' and fathers' levels of education relate to their offspring's scholastic performance.

Benbow and Stanley (1980) collected data from nearly nine hundred 11- and 12-year-olds who had participated in the 1976 talent search for the Study of Mathematically Precocious Youth (SMPY) and whose SAT Verbal and Mathematical scores equaled or exceeded the norms for children four or five years older. Although an investigation of family profiles confirms previous findings that social class correlates positively with scholastic aptitude, there is also some indication that the children's SAT scores were more directly associated with fathers' than with mothers' levels of education. Nevertheless, the mother served as an influential role model for her offspring, and this fact may take on new importance in the years ahead when college attendance among females is expected to rise dramatically.

Studies of relationships between parents' and children's feelings about education suggest that the intellectual climate in the home reveals much about motivation at school. In a study of fifth-graders stratified according to socioeconomic status, Wolf (1966) hypothesized a positive correlation between what he called "process variables" and performance on measures of scholastic ability and suggested that these coefficients are higher than the ones between "status variables" and scholastic performance. Status variables are conventional indices of socioeconomic levels, which, according to Wolf, correlate only about .40 with children's IQ scores. Process variables, on the other hand, refer to various means through which parents encourage and provide opportunities for children to engage in learning experiences outside of school.

There are three such variables, each having several specific subcomponents, as follows:

1. *Press for Achievement Motivation*
   a. Nature of the child's intellectual expectations.
   b. Nature of parents' intellectual aspirations for the child.
   c. Amount of information parents have regarding the child's intellectual development.
   d. Nature of parental rewards for the child's intellectual development.
2. *Press for Language Development*
   a. Emphasis on use of language in various situations.
   b. Opportunities provided for enlarging the child's vocabulary.
   c. Emphasis on correct usage of language.
   d. Quality of language models available in the home.
3. *Provisions for General Learning*
   a. Opportunities provided for the child to learn at home.
   b. Opportunities for learning outside the home and school.
   c. Availability of learning materials at home.
   d. Availability of books at home and a public library nearby and parents' encouragement to use them.
   e. Nature and amount of assistance in learning provided by the parents.

Wolf measured the process variables through a questionnaire administered to mothers of his sample population. Results showed a startlingly high correlation of .69 between mothers' response to the total instrument and the targeted children's Henmon-Nelson IQ scores. An even more impressive coefficient of .80 was obtained in relation to *Metropolitan Achievement Test* results. In a subsequent replication of this study, Trotman (1977) noted similarly high correlations between the process variables and IQ for white as well as black ninth-graders in a middle-class suburban school system. However, Longstreth (1978) warns against drawing easy cause-and-effect inferences from these data. The temptation is to conclude that home environment exerts a powerful influence on IQ and achievement scores, but "is it not even more likely that the parents, discovering that they have a bright child in the family, react to that information in various ways, such as encouraging good study habits, planning and preparing for a college education ... [e.g., by engaging in the kinds of behaviors covered in Wolf's maternal interview schedule?"] (p. 470). Logically, however, the influences would seem to go both ways. Children probably achieve better as a result of parental encouragement, and parental encouragement is affected by how well children perform.

What we have to guard against is the simplistic idea that behind *every* great person there is a loving, culturally rich family background. There are famous people in history who enjoyed a supportive upbringing, but there are also others who did not. McCurdy (1959) examined the childhood home life of twenty-seven geniuses selected from Cox's (1926) list and found that twenty of them received considerable amounts of affection and intellectual stimulation from their parents, whereas only three suffered comparative neglect or abuse. On the other hand, in their study of over four hundred famous twentieth-century men and women, Goertzel and Goertzel (1962) cited case after case of great people whose childhoods were agonizing and who came from troubled homes where the mothers were either "smothering" or dominating and the fathers were failure prone.

It is difficult to know who will actually be galvanized to greater and greater achievement *despite* an unhappy home life. Nor is it easy to imagine parents actually reacting negatively to their children's desire to excel in something that is publicly prized. This kind of mismatch between parents' and children's desires vis-a-vis accomplishments is fortunately either rare or is rarely prolonged. One side usually falls into line with the other, and young talent is either strengthened or stifled, depending on which side prevails.

Perhaps because much of the research on parental stimulation has been conducted on young children, it seems that the stimulation is most powerful during the child's early years of life. Dennis (1960), Hunt (1961), and Bloom (1964) offer evidence that environmental conditions are especially influential from ages 1 to 5 and that the effects seem to be carried over to the later years. Clark-Stewart (1973) interviewed thirty-six mothers on the degree of acceptance and social stimulation they provided their children, ages 9 to 18 months. Results show that the infants' cognitive, language, and social development related significantly to maternal care. Verbal stimulation from the mother had an especially strong effect on the offsprings' ability to comprehend and express language. Also, a close relationship was noted between the complexity of infants' play and the amount of time the mothers spent playing with them and acting as mediators of the physical environment. Noteworthy, too, is the observation that the reciprocal mother-child influence on social interaction became evident in the course of the experiment. The more the child looked at the mother, approached and vocalized to her, or shared objects with her, the more affectionate and attached the child became. This maternal responsiveness to social signals from infants probably enhances their later intellectual and social performance.

Of particular interest to researchers has been the effect of maternal warmth on the development of young children. In a study of fifty-two lower-class mothers and their 4-year-olds, Radin (1971, 1974) hypothesized a positive correlation between maternal warmth and children's IQ and responsiveness to a compensatory pre-school program. The mothers were interviewed in their own homes with children present, and thirty minutes of mother-child interactions were scored for the mothers' use of physical or verbal reinforcement, their tendency to ask the children to share in decision making, and their sensitivity in anticipating the children's requests or feelings. Stanford-Binet and Peabody Picture Vocabulary tests were administered to the children at the beginning and at the end of the school year in order to assess possible IQ changes. In addition, each teacher filled out a Pupil Behavior Inventory that assessed academic motivation, classroom conduct, and teacher dependence. Results showed that maternal warmth correlated significantly with the children's growth in IQ and on the behavior ratings.

In a subsequent analysis of the data, Radin (1974) reports that maternal nurturance ratings were significantly correlated with IQ scores for girls but not for boys. These results tend to confirm the findings on mother-daughter relationships reported earlier by Bayley and Schaefer (1964). However, the Bayley-Schaefer study found that the effects of maternal warmth on daughters' behavior was evident only in the first four years of life, whereas for their sons, the impact seems to have become apparent in the later years of childhood. These long-range effects of mothers on their sons are borne out in a study of 135 women and 108 men selected from Mensa, an organization consisting of people with IQs of 130 and above (Groth, 1971). The subjects were asked to circle highest academic degrees earned and to recall the extent of parental warmth toward them during their first seven years of life. Results showed that the number of college degrees earned by men was associated positively with maternal, but not paternal, warmth. However, women's achieving college degrees related to the warmth of their fathers *and* mothers. The outcomes of these various studies are difficult to interpret, and the exact influence of child-rearing practices on children's eventual performance at school remains to be ascertained. The little evidence of an opposite-sex effect that exists has to be verified through more research on different age groups and through more uniform methods of collecting data on early child-parent relationships.

PEER INFLUENCES

The question of whether giftedness makes a child unpopular among peers has been of interest to parents and educators of the gifted and even to the well-known satirist, Jules Feiffer (see the cartoon). Gallagher (1975) cites several studies to show a positive relationship between IQ and social status, namely, that in face-to-face associations with schoolmates, children with high IQs generally fare better than do those who perform less well on such tests. However, the relationship between tested intelligence and popularity seems not to be perfectly linear. In a study of sociometric ratings of high-IQ junior high school students in the Toronto secondary schools, up to IQ 150, the higher the intelligence quotient, the greater

the likelihood of achieving high social standing (Association of Heads of Guidance Departments, Research Committee, 1955). The number of cases with IQs above 150 was too small to draw a definitive conclusion, but the tendency was for the status ratings to drop beyond this IQ level.

It is difficult to determine where the IQ-social acceptance relationship breaks down. The likelihood, though, is that a breakdown *does* occur somewhere in the highest extremes of IQ. Miller (1956) likewise discovered a positive correlation up to certain limits of the intellectual continuum between social status and tested intelligence. He concludes, however, that high social status is conferred on the gifted, not because of their IQ but because of certain personality traits that they seem capable of acquiring with greater ease than do children with lower IQs.

In a laboratory school, where the average IQ was in the highest decile according to national norms, it was found that the high-achieving seventh-graders began to emerge as social leaders (Haggard, 1957). According to Haggard, these children were more respected than liked by their peers. Furthermore, they were in a school atmosphere in which motivation and achievement were generally high; in a more "typical" classroom, there is probably a greater chance that they would be snubbed as "grinds" and "bookworms."

Research has also been reported on peer attitudes toward children designated as highly creative on the basis of their performance on a divergent thinking test. Kurtzman (1967) divided samples of 80 boys and 71 girls, all ninth-graders, separately into subgroups of high, middle, and low creatives on the basis of instruments taken from the Educational Testing Service Kit of Reference Tests for Cognitive Factors. All the children were high achievers, having scored at or above the eighty-fourth percentile on the School and College Abilities Test. Every English class containing one or more of the subjects rated them on a social distance scale to determine degrees of acceptance/rejection. It was found that the high-creative girls were less well accepted than were the middle- and low-creative boys, and the high-creative boys received the best peer acceptance ratings of all six groups.

Kurtzman speculates that the high-creative boys may have been rated most favorably because they tended to be exceptionally secure and stable, as indicated by their scores on the Cattell 16 PF Personality Measure.

A positive relationship between academic and social status seems evident from research on various age groups, although it is not clear which of the two has the greater impact on the other. In a study of elementary school children, Williams (1958) found a positive correlation between academic performance and acceptance of and by peers. These results tend to confirm other findings on elementary school samples (Bonney, 1944; Grossman and Wrighter, 1948). Interestingly enough, in the Williams study, children with the highest academic potentials accepted their classmates more readily than their classmates accepted them. Among adolescents, too, there is evidence of a connection between school achievement and status among peers. Nason (1958) reports a study showing that high school students with above-average IQs who were performing well in high school enjoyed better social status than did those with comparable IQs but poor scholastic records. In a survey of several hundred students in a suburban senior high school, more than two thirds of whom were college bound, Ryan and Davie (1958) found a slight positive relationship between social acceptance and school grades and an even slighter apparent relationship between social acceptance and scholastic aptitude as measured by the American Council on Education Test. According to the investigators, these findings cast doubt on the old supposition that social isolates turn to intensive schoolwork for compensation.

Whether or not giftedness helps children to win favor with their classmates is not easy to determine on the basis of peer ratings, because the reactions may be to a constellation of traits, not just to ability. When people express opinions about each other, they may be thinking about physical characteristics, social habits, personal mannerisms, and emotional states as well as intellect, all of which form a *Gestalt* as either acceptable or unacceptable, depending on the tastes of each person. To isolate feelings about extraordinary ability per se, several studies have focused on attitudes toward hypothetical rather than real people.

In one such investigation of stereotypes, Tannenbaum (1962) developed eight imaginary high school students, each of whom was described in three sentences. The first sentence referred to the student's academic ability, (either brilliant or average); the second to effort in schoolwork (studious or nonstudious); and the third to sports-mindedness (athletic or nonathletic). The two alternative characteristics in each sentence appeared in every possible combination, thus resulting in eight separate imaginary adolescents with the following attributes: (1) brilliant, studious, athletic; (2) average, nonstudious, athletic; (3) brilliant, nonstudious, athletic; (4) average, studious, athletic; (5) brilliant, nonstudious, nonathletic; (6) average, nonstudious, nonathletic, (7) brilliant, studious, nonathletic; and (8) average, studious, nonathletic.

In a large, urban, comprehensive high school, 615 eleventh-graders rated each of the stimulus characters on the basis of a list of fifty-four traits, some desirable, others undesirable, and a few neutral. The results presented in Figure 9-1 show the brilliant, studious, nonathlete ranking significantly lower than all other characters

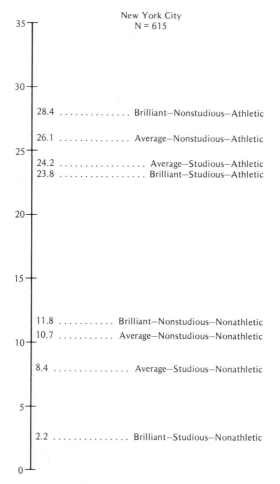

Figure 9-1 Social acceptance scores ascribed to the eight stimulus characters (Tannenbaum, 1962, p. 36; reprinted by permission of the author.)

on the trait ratings. The only other significant gap separating any two successively ranked characters was between the lowest-rated athlete and highest-rated non-athlete. In a comparison of *all* athletes versus *all* nonathletes—the two groups matched character for character with respect to academic ability and effort in schoolwork—the difference proved to be enormous, in favor of the athletes. The high school juniors also showed preference for the aggregate of nonstudious over studious characters, the characters in one group and their counterparts in the other having the same academic ability and degree of sports-mindedness. However, when the stimulus characters were paired on effort at school and sports-mindedness, no differences were found in ratings on the four described as "brilliant" as compared with the "average."

It may therefore be concluded from these data that brilliance in and of itself is regarded as fully acceptable as average ability. Academic standing alone seems to have little effect on a person's status among peers, but it does make a difference depending on what other attributes are combined with it. In this study, brilliance or average ability did not matter either way, provided that the stimulus character was also athletic minded. A display of academic brilliance by one described as studious and indifferent to sports constituted a definite status risk. This may mean that the brilliant student is an exceptionally prominent target for teenage pressures to conform to popular behaviors and values. If so, there is a danger that young people possessing outstanding abilities will deliberately mask their talent to relieve these pressures.

The Tannenbaum investigation was conducted in a New York City public high school. Some ten years later, Mitchell (1974) replicated the study in Calgary, Canada, where his sample consisted of 213 eleventh-graders. In addition to conducting his analyses on the total group, Mitchell also attempted to determine whether there would be differences in reactions according to the adolescents' membership in academic, fun, and delinquent subcultures. The overall findings on attitudes toward the different stimulus characteristics singly and in combination were the same as those of the earlier study. In addition, the data provided only slight support for the hypothesis that respondents' attitudes vary according to adolescent subculture. However, another replication by Morgan (1981) attempted to assess the attitudes of high school students in an academically oriented suburban community and also to ascertain whether attending a school that offers special programs for the gifted affects a student's attitudes toward the stimulus characters. Results showed a more positive feeling about brilliance and studiousness among these eleventh-graders than among the Tannenbaum and Mitchell samples. The outcomes were consistent regardless of whether the school offered differential education to the gifted. The latter finding should help to allay the often-heard fear that special enrichment classes tend to exacerbate charges of elitism in the schools.

In another study of stereotypes, Solano (1977) asked ninety-five average-ability ninth-graders to react to descriptions of precocious adolescents. The stimulus characters consisted of descriptions of male and female students who performed exceptionally well in the study of Mathematically Precocious Youth (SMPY). Average-ability eighth- and ninth-graders rated the stimulus characters by ascribing to them personality-relevant adjectives from the Gough and Heilbrun Adjective Check List (ACL). Results show no significant differences between the overall scores that respondents ascribed to themselves as compared with those they attributed to the stimulus characters. In other words, the average-ability children perceived the high-achieving boys as being neither better nor worse than themselves.

However, a closer look at the data reveals qualitative differences in the subjects' reactions. The favorable traits they chose for themselves were "friendly" and "active," whereas for the male-stimulus characters they chose the following traits: "alert," "clever," "intelligent," "dependable," and "clear-thinking." On the neutral adjectives, the contrast was between "determined," "civilized," "anxious," "talkative," and "cautious" for the average-ability raters and "determined," "self-confident," "sophisticated," "sharp-witted," "serious," and "cautious" for the gifted males. On the negative adjectives, the respondents rated themselves as "impatient," "argumentative," "complaining," "careless," and "loud," but saw the gifted boys as "dull," "opinionated," "conceited," "self-centered," and "boastful."

As for the ratings of female-stimulus characters, the respondents were as favorably disposed to them as to themselves. Also, the females attracted the same positive adjectives as did the males. But on the neutral and negative adjectives, the peer attitudes were clearly hostile. "Agressive" was the most frequently chosen neutral adjective, and the unfavorable traits included "aloof," "bossy," "careless," "conceited," "snobbish," "show-off," "dull," "apathetic," "self-centered," and "fickle." Compared with the unfavorable adjectives chosen to describe gifted boys, those associated with gifted girls were much more negative. Furthermore, the favorable traits ascribed to both females and males are almost identical to the ones attributed to the brilliant, studious, nonathlete in Tannenbaum's investigation.

Where large numbers of school children stereotype giftedness negatively, are those with high potential affected by it? Maybe so, according to Coleman (1960) who addressed this question. He asked a group of boys from several high schools to answer the question, "How would you most like to be remembered in school: as an athletic star, a brilliant student, or most popular?" Results showed a tendency to select "star athlete" over either of the other alternatives. The boys were then asked to indicate which of the three descriptions most typify members of the leading crowd at school, and again the responses were directed away from the ideal of the brilliant student. Asked to react to a similar questionnaire—but with "brilliant student," "leader in extracurricular activities," and "most popular" as the trio of choices—a group of adolescent girls likewise tended to select "brilliant student" less often than either of the others. Most important, Coleman found a direct relationship between the frequency with which each of several school populations mentioned "good grades" as a means of getting into the leading crowd and the degree to which the average IQs of the "straight A" students exceeded the mean IQs for the total student body in the respective schools. Coleman concluded that in high schools where students are encouraged by peers to direct most of their energies into athletics and social activities, it is unlikely that intellectual pursuits will be attractive even to the most able among them.

THE EFFECTS OF SCHOOLING

There will probably always be people who believe that talent is irrepressible in some children and impossible to nurture in others. It is often said that those who have it in them to reach the top will make it, even without help from an enriched curriculum; conversely, if they cannot make it on their own, no amount of intervention at school will matter at all. Why, then, invest in special programs for the gifted? Some people raise the question openly in their cynicism about differentiating education for anybody, except the handicapped. Many more are skeptical rather than cynical about the need for providing "extras" in the progam. They will do it under pressure of public opinion or advocacy groups, but not wholeheartedly. There is always the suspicion that partiality to the gifted in any form is not only undemocratic but unnecessary.

Do Teachers Make a Difference?

Perhaps educators and laypersons alike often have doubts about the benefits of programs for the gifted because research evidence is not always powerful enough to overcome popular prejudices. For example, there is a question as to whether variations in the way in which teachers do their jobs in the classroom make a difference in pupil progress. According to Veldman and Brophy (1974), most of the relevant research has been unproductive because it focuses primarily on the influence of presage variables such as years of teaching experience and highest degree obtained. On the basis of such studies, it has been concluded that only the quality of the student body, not the school or its teachers, makes a difference in students' success in learning. In their own study of 115 second- and third-grade teachers with five or more consecutive years of experience in the classroom, they found that practitioners vary in their impact on pupil achievement. The conclusion, therefore, is that teachers *do* make a difference. However, *what* they do to make the difference is not known. Nor can we be sure that their impact on the potentially gifted is as significant as it was on the unselected sample in this study.

A much more elaborate investigation of teachers' behavior and its effect on pupil achievement is reported by McDonald and Elias (1976), whose target group consisted of children in ninety-seven second- and fifth-grade classrooms representing forty-five schools in eight different school districts. For an entire school year, two separate classroom observation systems, along with work diaries, were used to collect data on teacher performance, which was then analyzed in relation to pupil gains in reading and mathematics achievement. Some of the important results may be summarized as follows:

1. As in the Veldman and Brophy study (1974), teachers made a difference in pupils' progress over the school year. When spring scores (with fall scores partialed out) and mean gain scores were regressed on teaching performances, the correlations ranged from .33 to .80, all statistically significant.

2. Teacher behaviors that correlated significantly with changes in pupil achievement were different by subject matter and by grade level. In other words, no single method proved to be equally effective in both the second and fifth grades in both reading and mathematics.

3. No single approach to teaching correlated highly enough with pupil achievement to be considered critical for effective instruction.

The data suggest that a pattern of teaching performance, rather than a single strategy, is most likely to affect achievement and that these effects vary according to subject matter and grade level. However, this study reveals only how teachers help unselected children to become more proficient in acquiring two kinds of academic skills. It says nothing about whether teachers make a difference in enabling high-achieving children to become producers or performers in the world of ideas.

Enrichment in Regular and Special Classes

Research on teacher effectiveness with the gifted deals mostly with adjustments in curriculum content rather than with instructional strategies. In adding substance to the conventional course of study, the educator has the choice between going the route of enrichment or acceleration. According to Stanley (1976), enrichment can be relevant or irrelevant, depending on whether it is uniquely suitable for gifted children, not simply reserved for them. Enrichment is considered irrelevant if it is lateral in nature, as in those instances when a foreign language and touch-typing are added to the regular elementary school program and are made available only to the gifted, even though they are taught at a beginner's level of instruction. Conceivably, though, such offerings can be relevant if they are meaningful enough to those who are able to meet the additional challenge. Whereas most children will find it burdensome to add more than one or two courses to their program, a few of their classmates will thrive on the exposure to new fields of interest while maintaining their excellent records at school. In other words, singly the "extras" are too elementary to fit the *special* needs of the gifted; in the aggregate, however, they provide a breadth of experience that only the gifted may appreciate.

More clearly relevant is the kind of enrichment that challenges the gifted and is too recondite for the nongifted. While pitched at a high level, this is not a telescoped version of a conventional program and neither a supplement nor an elaboration of it. The gifted, therefore, remain in lockstep with their agemates instead of accelerating through the grades and finishing school earlier. According to Daurio (1979), relevant enrichment is exemplified best by curricula designed for special schools and classes for the gifted. He notes that there are also fast-paced classes such as those described by Wilson (1959) where year-long or semester-long courses are covered as scheduled, not sooner. However, they are taught at a rapid pace only three days a week, leaving the remaining two days for lateral enrichment. Stanley (1976) cautions that irrelevant enrichment will only postpone the gifted child's boredom at school unless it eventually gives way to an acceleration of subject matter or grade placement.

Evaluations of enrichment programs have not produced consistent results, probably because the programs vary in content, relevance, sample populations, and criteria for success. Despite these limitations, there is reason to believe that well-planned enrichment does make a difference. As Gallagher (1975) observes, "Although program evaluation has not been given a major emphasis in gifted programs, the results now available suggest that where definable programs with clear goals are instituted the results are generally favorable" (p. 295).

Perhaps the most comprehensive evaluation of special programs for the gifted was reported by Martinson (1961) and involved nearly a thousand students (478 boys and 451 girls), grades one through thewlve, with a mean Stanford-Binet IQ of 143. All subjects came from rural, semirural, and urban areas in various geographic locations, and nearly all were from the middle and upper socioeconomic classes. All had benefited from some kind of enrichment or acceleration and were matched with control groups on the basis of age, IQ, sex, and social class. A battery of criterion measures contained sixteen indicators of how the subjects grew intellectually, emotionally, and socially.

Results were impressive in every way. In comparison with the controls, children exposed to special programs performed better on scholastic achievement tests without penalty to their popularity at school or to the number of friendships they enjoyed. Those who participated in special senior and junior high school programs showed better gains in personal and social maturity than did nonparticipants. In explaining these successful outcomes, Martinson (1971) comments as follows:

The highly significant gains in the special groups in academic, social, and psychological areas at all grade levels were attributed to careful preservice and inservice preparation of teachers, the assignment of special full-time consultants, appropriate learning opportunities (both in and out of school), the use of a wide variety of community resources, close inter-school liaison, and close collaboration with parents. (p. 851)

As might be expected, the nature and degree of impact the program has on the gifted depends on the kind of enrichment that it offers. Goldberg, Passow, Camm, and Neill (1966) reported a three-year study of mathematics enrichment for nearly 1,500 junior high school students with IQs of 120 or higher and two or more years ahead of grade level in reading and mathematics achievement. Initially, fifty-one seventh-grade classes were involved in the evaluation, but due to normal attrition, the number dropped to thirty-seven by the end of the ninth grade, thus reducing the sample to 868 subjects. The experiment involved a comparison of six different programs differentiated according to content (standard versus contemporary) and teaching-learning pace (enriched versus accelerated). The contemporary programs consisted of those developed by the School Mathematics Study Group (SMSG) and the University of Illinois Committee on School Mathematics (UICSM).

Year-by-year results showed little change in the relative effectiveness of the programs. The ones that produced the greatest gains in mathematical achievement (as measured by the ETS Developed Mathematical Abilities Test and the Mathematics Achievement Test, as well as teacher-made measures) were produced by accelerated versions of the SMSG and UICSM programs, which clearly exceeded the effects of the standard program, regardless of whether it was accelerated or supplemented with lateral enrichment. Teacher factors, such as the amount of mathematical preparation, degrees earned, and experience in teaching mathematics related significantly to pupils' success at the end of the seventh grade, accounting for about 20 percent of the variance in pupil achievement. However, the researchers reported that teacher factors had little effect in the ninth grade, possibly because teachers at that grade level were more homogeneous with respect to subject matter preparation and competence than were their colleagues working with seventh-graders. Also assessed were the effects of achievement on pupil's attitudes toward mathematics, and the results showed no such relationship. Neither the nature of the mathematics program nor the level of pupil achievement in any of the programs seemed to affect the pupils' appraisal of their own abilities, their assessment of the nature and importance of mathematics, and their interest in careers in mathematics. In fact, the contemporary program, which tended to produce the best scholastic progress, was associated with the most negative attitudes, whereas the reverse was true for the standard programs. These apparent inconsistencies are surprising and remain unexplained.

Since the different mathematics programs varied in nature, the relevant advantages and disadvantages could be revealed meaningfully, especially since the criteria for effectiveness related directly to program objectives. These conditions were not quite so clear in an evaluation of graduates of four New York City high schools that offered enrichment to the gifted in presumably different ways (Abramson 1959). The groups were matched for IQ at three levels (115 to 124, 125 to 134, 135 to 160) and compared on grade-point average at the end of their freshman and sophomore years in college. Each of the groups had completed a different high school program. One had attended a specialized high school for the gifted; the second had been in an honors school within the regular school where they took a complete honors program; a third had attended honors classes at a regular school where students were allowed to enroll in honors classes only in those subjects in which they excelled; and the fourth came from heterogeneous classes in a school that had no special program for the gifted. Results showed no difference between the groups in their college records, but the higher-IQ graduates clearly outperformed those with lower IQs in college, regardless of the enrichment program or high school they had attended. It would seem, therefore, that it does not matter how a high-IQ student's program is enriched in secondary school, or even whether it is enriched at all, if we judge high school education for the gifted by how well it prepares them to excel in college. Yet there is no clear indication of precisely how the *content* of the four curricula varied, for even though they were *labeled* differently, without a full description of the subject matter covered in high school, it is impossible to know which (if any) of the enrichment programs should have prepared the students to perform better in college. Nor is it entirely clear that grade-point average in the sophomore year of college should be relevant to special enrichment experiences in high school. Besides, the "extras" absorbed in high school may be important to educational growth even if they are not reflected in a college grade-point average.

It is likewise difficult to interpret the effects of ability grouping without knowing precisely what is happening in these classrooms. Simply organizing special schools or classes exclusively for able children does not guarantee that anything at all will be done to enrich the curriculum. Perhaps that is the reason the effects of such an administrative adjustment are inconsistent from one study to the next. As Findley and Bryan (1971) conclude from their review of research on the subject, "Ability grouping, as practiced, produces conflicting evidence of usefulness in promoting improved scholastic achievement in superior groups, and almost uniformly unfavorable evidence for promoting scholastic achievement in average or low-achieving groups" (p. 7). At one extreme, there are the highly encouraging data reported by Martinson (1961) that show how well high-IQ children can perform in special classes if all aspects of the program are well planned and expertly administered. At the other extreme, there are the failures of ability grouping to make a difference when no formal attempt is made to adjust the curriculum content accordingly.

Such was the case when Goldberg, et al. (1965) investigated the scholastic and personal development of high-, moderate-, and low-IQ children grouped in classes where the IQ ranges varied from extremely narrow to extremely wide. The study involved about twenty-two hundred fifth-and sixth-graders attending eighty-six classes in forty-five schools. The entire sample was divided into five IQ groups: (1) 130 and above, (2) 120 to 129, (3) 110 to 119, (4) 100 to 109, (5) 100 and below. Children fitting these levels were combined to produce fifteen different kinds of classes, some consisting exclusively of high-, middle-, and low-IQ groups, while others accommodated at least two and as many as all five IQ levels. All classes were kept intact from the beginning of the fifth to the end of the sixth grades, which allowed the pre- to posttesting period to cover two full years. When growth gains were assessed over the course of the experiment, results were generally unimpressive. None of the class organizations made an appreciable difference for children at any of the IQ levels. It therefore seems that grouping patterns per se do not necessarily bring about differentiated instruction in a classroom, at least not enough to make an impact on rapid learners.

Acceleration Through The Conventional Curriculum

When something special *does* happen in a classroom, and tests that measure growth relate directly to what is being taught, the effects can then be seen far more easily. Evidence for this can be found in evaluations of children who are accelerated through conventional subject matter. Administratively, acceleration can take several forms, including early admission into elementary school, high school, and college; rapid advancement classes; admission to college with advanced standing; and grade skipping. Those who favor this kind of intervention are less enthusiastic about grade skipping than about the other plans (Pressey, 1954), but they argue that any approach is better than lockstep progress since it eliminates boredom in class and enables the gifted to begin their careers as early as possible. The supportive evidence cited is both massive and impressive.

For example, Worcester (1955) reviewed a variety of programs in different parts of the country in which large numbers of precocious children were admitted to elementary school at an early age. Even though the children averaged eight months below the regular age of admittance, the study showed no significant differences in physical development when compared with older classmates of average ability. In academic work, the accelerants equaled or surpassed their older peers not only in the first grade but in every subsequent grade where comparisons were made.

Judging from teachers' ratings, the children seemed well adjusted, were accepted by their classmates, and expressed positive feelings toward school.

Another study (Robeck, 1968) involving two school districts in California evaluated the effects of acceleration among children already in elementary school. Those nominated by their teachers to participate in the experiment had high IQs and were making exceptionally rapid progress in the second grade. They were then allowed to continue their studies in summer classes to prepare themselves for admission into the fourth grade the following fall. Evaluations of the program on two sites showed that the children were not at a disadvantage after skipping the third grade; in fact, they outperformed their older classmates, related well to them socially, and continued their superior showing when they were reexamined the following year. At the junior high school level, Justman (1954) matched two groups of high-IQ, high-achieving students representing two different programs in the New York City schools. The experimental sample (N = 74) attended so-called "Special Progress" classes in which they completed the three-year junior high school program in two years, while the control groups (N = 82) was comparable in ability but was enrolled in the conventional program. At the end of their junior high school years, the groups were compared in academic achievement as well as in personal and social adjustment. Even though they differed by one year in age, the accelerants outperformed the controls in mathematics, science, and social studies achievement without penalty to their personal or social development. Finally, at the senior high school level, Daurio (1979) summarizes several studies involving large populations to show that acceleration, either in the form of early admission to college or admission to college with advanced standing, has been overwhelmingly advantageous to students with the proper academic qualifications.

Perhaps the most ambitious of all studies is a longitudinal investigation of mathematically precocious children born between 1955 and 1961 who have been helped to accelerate their progress in mathematics since 1971 and are slated to be studied closely until the end of the century. All 250 subjects were selected on the basis of their advanced mathematical reasoning ability that placed them in the upper 1.5 percent of their age group in mathematical aptitude, and in a subsequent administration of a Stanford-Binet, almost all of them scored 140 or above, two of them as high as 212. After their initial acceptance into the program during the junior high school years, they were encouraged to accelerate their educational progress, especially in the mathematical and physical sciences, with the help of the project staff that placed them in various programs that would facilitate their rapid advancement.

Based on early evaluations of the program, Stanley (1976) concludes that the students benefited in the following ways:

1. Better educational advancement than would otherwise be expected, especially in mathematics.
2. Enhanced feelings of self-worth and accomplishment.
3. Less boredom at school and generally a more positive attitude toward education.
4. Reduction of egotism and arrogance.

5. More time to explore hobbies, specialties, and career options.

In a subsequent follow-up reported by Cohn (1980), 200 of the 202 locatable participants in the project's first three talent searches responded to a survey questionnaire concerning their learning experiences in high school and college. Results show sharp differences between the sexes. Whereas the girls used few accelerative alternatives to the age-in-grade lockstep, the boys progressed through higher grade levels and more advanced subject matter much faster than their average-ability agemates and much faster than the SMPY girls. In reviewing several background and personal factors associated with the degrees of acceleration, Cohn notes that few of the concomitants investigated applied to the girls since they hardly availed themselves of opportunities to accelerate. However, the results are dramatic among the boys. For them, the extent of acceleration was significantly associated with parents' levels of education, positive attitudes toward school, scores on screening measures in mathematics administered early in the experiment, and preference for investigative careers in the sciences, mathematics, and philosophy rather than for earning lots of money. Also, the boys showed excellent development in academics as well as their social skills, whereas the girls seemed more willing to sacrifice academic stimulation for satisfying peer group relationships.

Despite the overall benefits of acceleration, it seems to be a far less popular administrative device for satisfying the needs of the gifted than is some form of ability grouping, which has much shakier evidence to support it. Educators often express the feeling that acceleration places an inordinately heavy work load on children, encourages speed and superficiality rather than depth of understanding, and ignores the need for socializing with agemates who share similar interests. On the other hand, arguments often heard on behalf of ability grouping for the gifted suggest that (1) it facilitates easier, richer instruction by reducing the difficulties of providing for individual differences; (2) it allows more opportunities for impact of gifted mind upon gifted mind; (3) it eliminates unfair competition and resulting poor attitudes between rapid and slower learners; and (4) it opens new leadership opportunities for the nongifted who no longer have to defer to the gifted. These arguments are apparently persuasive enough to account for the widespread practice of ability grouping outside regular classrooms, as reported by Findley and Bryan (1971) in their review of practices throughout the country.

There is also evidence to show that teachers *believe* that they adjust their instructional methods according to the ability levels of their classes. Pfeiffer (1967) reports on a study of high school instructors, each of whom taught eleventh-grade English to two classes at different ability levels. Six successive sessions of each of the ten classes were monitored closely to determine the extent to which teachers restricted (or expanded) students' freedom to communicate ideas during class discussion and also the extent to which higher-level cognitive processes were stimulated in the classroom. In addition, the teachers themselves were asked to comment on whether they acted differently with respect to these two criteria depending on the ability levels of their classes.

The results indicate that the teachers were practicing self-deception. All were convinced that they had adjusted their teaching to each group's abilities, but these impressions were not confirmed by the observers' reports, which saw no difference in content or method in the two kinds of classes. If the progress of the high-ability children had been evaluated, the chances are that those in wide-range classes would have performed just as well as their counterparts in narrow-range groups. It would, therefore, be a mistake to expect teachers to respond in any special way to the gifted simply "because they are there." Instead, it takes conscious planning and execution of enrichment that is addressed to individual differences among the gifted. This is demonstrated amply within narrow- or wide-range classes where rapid learners are accelerated at a pace that is comfortable for them.

Concluding Comments

Unlike acceleration, which makes it possible to cover conventional content within less time, the other forms of enrichment have to be evaluated program by program, since the subject matter varies from one to the next. Sometimes, two kinds of intervention are not mutually exclusive, as in the case of an experiment in which fifty-one seventh-and eighth-graders with exceptionally high Verbal SAT scores were organized into two groups, depending on whether they elected to enroll in a social science or in a creative-writing course designed especially for them by the researchers as a one-year enrichment experience (McGinn et al., 1980). Both courses could be regarded as forms of acceleration since they covered topics that were normally at a college level. Although the experimental design was limited by the fact that there were no control groups, results showed a significant increase in verbal intelligence, as measured by the Concept Mastery Test (CMT), designed for use with Terman's (1956) gifted sample in adulthood. Interestingly enough, the subjects also covered the Productive Thinking Program, designed for children two or three years *younger* than they (Covington et al., 1974). Even though this intervention seemed *decelerative*, it offered practice in divergent thinking, which the children had never experienced previously, and this may account for their improvement in thinking skills.

From the growing evidence on special programs for the gifted, it is easy to see that lateral enrichment and acceleration make a difference in the growth and development of these children. We are also beginning to discover some of the things a teacher can do in the classroom to make that difference. It is true that some children will overcome the effects of mediocre teaching or a sterile program and achieve distinction nonetheless. There are people like Abraham Lincoln and Thomas Edison who had hardly any kind of formal schooling and yet were immortalized in their respective fields. Real-life histories will always make it difficult for some people to believe in the value of extra efforts for the gifted. Still, there is enough empirical evidence to prove that such efforts do pay off when they are exerted with skill and imagination. Of course, there are children who do not require extra assistance. Such cases are probably much rarer than are those in which talent withers on the vine for lack of proper nurturance.

Chapter 10

Chance Factors

Elements of luck, or chance factors in the environment, are usually ignored in discussions about talent and its fruition. Instead, social scientists focus on influences that are more easily observable, measurable, and perhaps eventually controllable. This bias is understandable, because what is there to say about luck, except that it exists and that it can make the difference between success and failure? Nobody knows what forms it will take or when or how often it will strike. We treat it almost as if it were a supernatural force, inscrutable and therefore outside the pale of science.

It is true that we cannot characterize luck and its essential ingredients, but our lack of attention to it should not obscure the fact that it has a powerful influence on achievement. In his study of personal opportunity in America, Jencks (1972) suspects that luck has at least as much influence on income levels as does competence, and in order to neutralize the effects of luck, he has devised an economic plan whereby those who are favored by it subsidize the less fortunate ones. Atkinson (1978) seems to ascribe all of human behavior and accomplishment to

two crucial rolls of the dice over which no individual exerts any personal control. These are the accidents of birth and background. One roll of the dice determines an individual's heredity; the other, his formative environment. Race, gender, time and place of birth in human history, a rich cultural heritage or not, the more intimate details of affluence or poverty, sensitive and loving parents and peers, or not, all of them beyond one's own control, have yielded the basic personality: a perspective on the life experience, a set of talents, some capacities for enjoyment and suffering, the potential or not of even making a productive contribution to the community that could be a realistic basis for self-esteem. (p. 221)

According to Austin (1978), there are four kinds of chance factors. The first is the stroke of good luck that befalls a person who is basically in a passive state. This means being ready to take advantage of an unforeseen situation by being in the right place at the right time. To use a personal example, this writer was lucky enough to have "timed" his birth and education so as to be ready and qualified when his university was recruiting for a faculty member. It is quite possible that any one of several younger scholars who are his former students could outperform him in the position he fills, if it were available today. However, the opening cannot materialize at least for as long as the incumbent remains on the job. A far worse misfortune for the young scholars would be an absence of appropriate opportunities anywhere to coincide with their readiness for highly productive careers. If they have to settle for work outside their own fields for lack of alternatives, this chance factor would make it impossible for them to live up to their professional potentialities.

At the second level of chance, a person increases the likelihood of being struck with good fortune by setting the mind and body into constant motion. The activity is ill defined, restless, and aimlessly driven. Even though it is mostly wasteful, it gives the person an edge to stumble upon a good idea. Of course, this seemingly aimless activity has to be located in places where the unexpected can happen. For example, the Sahara is a good place in which to chance upon new insights into land erosion, not marine biology. The basic idea is to overcome inertia by stirring the "pot of random ideas" constantly so that they can collide and mostly repel each other, and perhaps a few will connect in new unanticipated combinations. As Austin (1978) observes, "Motion yields a network of new experiences, which, like a sieve, filters best when in constant up-and-down, side-to-side movement; . . . its premise is that *un*luck runs out if your persist" (p. 73).

Then there is the third level of chance, which connects an unforeseen experience with a person who is uniquely equipped to grasp its significance. The experience and the right person for it are rarities unto themselves; how probable is it that they will come together at all, much less with prodigious effect! As an example of how chance favors the prepared mind, Austin describes Sir Alexander Fleming's reactions to a chance occurrence in his laboratory, as follows: (1) I noticed that a mold had accidentally fallen into my culture dish; (2) the staphylococcal colonies residing near it stopped growing; (3) therefore, the mold must have secreted something that destroyed the bacteria; (4) this brought to mind a similar experience I once had; and (5) maybe this mysterious ingredient, the mold, could be used to destroy staphylococci that cause human infections.

It is interesting to note that the "similar experience" Fleming remembered was his suffering from a cold some nine years earlier, and his own nasal drippings accidentally fell on a culture dish, killing the bacteria around the mucus. He followed this lead with further experimentation but got nowhere until the accident with the mold reminded him of the nasal drippings, but this time he was on to a most celebrated medical discovery. The finding was truly serendipitous, although it is also possible to experience serendipity at the second level of chance.

Finally, there is a fourth level of chance, which involves more focus than initiative and personal idiosyncrasy compared to the first three levels. Here, too, activity and sagacity are required, but there is also a need for what Austin calls "altamirage,"

Table 10-1.   Various Aspects and Kinds of Good Luck

Term Used to Describe the Quality Involved	Good Luck Is the Result of	Classification of Luck	Elements Involved	Personality Traits You Need
	An accident	Chance I	"Blind" luck. Chance happens, and nothing about it is directly attributable to you, the recipient.	None.
Serendipity	General exploratory behavior	Chance II	The Kettering principle. Chance favors those in motion. Events are brought together to form "happy accidents" when you diffusely apply your energies in motions that are typically nonspecific.	Curiosity about many things, persistence, willingness to experiment and to explore.
	Sagacity	Chance III	The Pasteur principle. Chance favors the prepared mind. Some special receptivity born from past experience permits you to discern a new fact or to perceive ideas in a new relationship.	A background of knowledge based on your abilities to observe, remember, and quickly form significant new associations.
Altamirage	Personalized action	Chance IV	The Disraeli principle. Chance favors the individualized action. Fortuitous events occur when you behave in ways that are highly distinctive of you as a person.	Distinctive hobbies, personal life styles, and activities peculiar to you as an individual expecially when they operate in domains seemingly far removed from the area of the discovery.

Source: J. H. Austin, *Chase, Chance, and Creativity* (New York: Columbia University Press, 1978), p. 78.

or a facility for becoming lucky because of the highly individualized action taken by a person (see Table 10-1).

In other words, it is the kind of good luck "experienced only by *one* quixotic rider cantering in on his own homemade hobby horse to intercept the problem at an odd angle" (p.77). Such rare individuals are not only distinctive but often eccentric in their hobbies, personal life styles, and motor behaviors, but when they succeed in some spectacular way, it seems as if fate has smiled upon them unexpectedly, when in truth they were somehow able to force a smile by tickling fate. There is no point in trying to disagnose "what makes them tick" in such a special way because it is hidden from view at all times except when they make the great leap forward to discovery.

The most difficult problem in dealing with chance factors is that they are unpredictable and always create an element of mystery in forecasting the fulfillment of early promise. As educators, parents, and members of the helping services, we have to realize that our best laid plans and actions can be enhanced or nullified by circumstances over which we have no control. Even when a person seems to be a sure bet for success or failure, luck can turn matters around unexpectedly. This happens all the time to a greater or lesser extent, as Getzels (1979) discovered in his longitudinal study of young adult art students.

After collecting considerable data on backgrounds, abilities, personalities, and processes by which they executed a creative work of art, he conducted a follow-up study five to six years after their graduation in order to see how well earlier signs of talent led to subsequent success in the field. Of the thirty-one former fine arts students, seven could not be located and were considered as either having abandoned a career in art or were not visibly successful in it. Of the twenty-four who could be found, eight had abandoned art as a career, seven were only marginally involved, and the remaining nine had achieved various levels of success as fine artists. Evidently, chance played an important part in the careers of these subjects. As Getzels reports,

There were idiosyncratic accidents and exigencies determining each artist's life and achievement that could not be reflected in the group data—for example, a personal event that turned one highly talented student from art to social action, a move in residence from one part of the country to another that unexpectedly caused a disconcerting change in another artist's palette. (p. 385)

Obviously, whatever information that could be gathering about these subjects as individuals during their years in art school revealed only a little about prospects for future success in the field. Too much depended on events in the lives of the budding artists which the researcher could not have anticipated. The existence of chance factors may help to explain why it is easier to predict success at school than at work in the years after graduation. In the school world, the rituals and requirements for success are fairly straightforward. There are few surprise changes in the "rules of the game," and the children know who calls the shots along the way. Life in the world of work is far more complex, with surprises happening all the time to boost the chances of some and to distract and discourage others from making it successfully. The unexpected can originate anywhere, in the economy, the social milieu, the workplace, the family, and even within the body itself when there is a sudden change in a person's health status that can affect a career. Therefore, the instruments used for measuring children's abilities are designed to predict performance in a predictable environment, namely, the school. But whatever these instruments measure in the organism and the environment cannot anticipate happenings or conditions of chance in a person's later career. Both the knowable and unknowable interact in a mutually dependent way: without intimations of high potential, no amount of good fortune can help the person achieve greatness; conversely, without some experience of good fortune, no amount of potential can be truly realized.

Chapter 11

Implications for Under- and Overachievement

Under- and overachievement are defined easily as discrepancies between expectations and performance. It is far more difficult to reach a consensus on who qualifies in either category since measurement criteria are arbitrary and varied. Of the two phenomena, underachievement has attracted far more attention from educators who find it a difficult problem to solve and from behavioral scientists who seem tantalized by it, judging from the huge body of research they have published on its nature and remediation.

Since the linkages between promise and fulfillment are fairly well documented, it would seem obvious that underachievement is caused by an absence or breakdown in at least one of these connections. Unfortunately, however, the evidence is not always clear on specific causes and concomitants. In their review of more than ninety empirical studies conducted between 1931 and 1961, Raph and Tannenbaum (1961) could find no definitive way of explaining why some so-called "gifted" children do not measure up to their potentialities. Traits that seem to inhibit scholastic success in one report fail to do so in another. Added together, the studies yield a tangle of conclusions that are more puzzling than revealing. Despite the voluminous research conducted during that thirty-year period, there is no clear profile of attributes to distinguish underachievers from achievers matched on academic potential. Raph and Tannenbaum interpret the evidence to suggest that perhaps only one characteristic differentiates *all* underachievers from *all* achievers: the fact that one group succeeds at school and the other does not.

In a subsequent review of research on over- and underachievement, Asbury (1974) also noted that results tend to be conflicting and inconclusive. He pointed to a frequent lack of sound methodology, misinterpretation of findings, neglect of possible interactions among cognitive and noncognitive factors, and failure to take into account the possibility that cognitive organization differs by race and sex.

A major problem derives from the fact that no uniform definition of under-achievement exists to guide all researchers in judging who fits the description and who does not. In some cases the definition is so broad as to include almost anybody suspected of not measuring up to expectation. For example, in the New York State commissioner's regulations (Article xxiii, Section 187-a, 1965), a child listed as an underachiever "is one who, on the basis of the teacher's or teachers' judgment(s), has not achieved for a year in accordance with his capacity." With the possibilities so wide open for interpreting a child's "capacity" and success at measuring up to it, researchers can choose their experimental samples almost at will and produce results that would vary accordingly.

Thorndike (1963) argues that what may seem to be "over-" and "under-achievement" are often misnomers and reflect under- and overprediction instead. Instruments are not precision tooled enough to assess accurately the predictor and what is being predicted. This is complicated by the fact that usually what is being predicted consists of various criteria, not just one. Thus, for example, if we are trying to forecast a student's grade-point average made up of scores in a variety of subjects such as math, English, art, and political science, it is difficult to imagine a single measure that can correlate equally well with all these disciplines. Also problematic is the fact that predictors are limited in scope and constitute only part of the determinants of success in any achievement area. The influences are too many and varied to be measured by any single instrument. Finally, prediction involves forecast over time during which any number of personal experiences can intervene either to foster or diminish the chances of success.

Thorndike (1963) offers the following general questions to help researchers avoid pitfalls in measurement before labeling children as over- or underachievers:

(1) Have I an appropriate procedure for determining expected achievement?
   a. Have I taken account of statistical regression?
   b. Have I used the best *team* of predictors to establish expected achievement? Have I included aptitude? Initial achievement? Other appropriate factors?
(2) Do I have a criterion measure of achievement that has the same meaning for all cases?
   a. Have I procedures to check for criterion heterogeneity?
   b. Have I a plan to deal with heterogeneity if it is found?
(3) Am I aware of the effect of errors of measurement on my study: (a) in reducing sensitivity? (b) in producing bias? (p. 65)

Besides the difficulty of finding error-free ways of measuring predictor and predicted variables, there is also the problem of inconsistency among researchers in deciding who qualifies as an over- or underachiever. These disagreements in applying the labels may account for at least some of the contradictory findings on why children deviate from expectations. Farquhar and Payne (1964) reviewed the various techniques of selection and discovered that they fall into four distinct categories: (1) *central tendency splits*, in which children with extremely high general ability and extremely low achievement scores are considered undera-chievers, those rated relatively low or relatively high in both are par achievers, and the extremely low-ability, high-achieving students are overachievers; (2)

arbitrary partitions, the same as central tendency splits, except that the middle group of par achievers is removed; (3) *relevant discrepancies splits*, in which the children are ranked separately on achievement and general abilities scores and over- and underachievers are identified by a discrepancy in rank; and (4) *regression model selection*, in which achievement is predicted by general ability test scores and performing above or below expectation determines who is an over- or underachiever.

Since these selection methods are so varied, the child who is labeled on the basis of one of them would not necessarily meet the other three criteria. Annesley, Odhner, Madoff, and Chansky (1970) actually tested such an hypothesis with 157 first-graders who had taken the Metropolitan Achievement Test and the Kuhlman-Anderson Intelligence Test. Significant differences were found in the numbers of adequate achievers as well as over- and underachievers identified according to the various approaches to labeling.

To complicate further the problem of generalizing across groups identified by different criteria, there is evidence to show that underachieving children vary according to the levels at which they are expected to function. Ziv (1977) reports a study of sixty-seven Israeli children with IQs of 140 and above, twenty-three of whom were in the lower 75 percent of their class in school grades. Another group of sixty-one children with IQs of 110 to 115 was divided into two subgroups, depending on whether they had above- or below-average grades. Four samples were thus formed, including those called "gifted achievers" and "gifted underachievers" with IQs of 140 or over and those called "bright achievers" and "bright underachievers" with IQs of 110 to 115. The children filled out a semantic differential questionnaire that asked them to describe themselves in relation to eighteen pairs of antonyms (e.g., strong-weak, shy-outgoing, slow-quick). Parents were asked to rate their children on the same questionnaire.

Results revealed some unexpected significant differences. The bright achievers reported a higher self-image than did the bright underachievers, but conversely, the gifted underachievers rated themselves higher than did the gifted achievers. Parents' assessments of their children similarly favored the bright achievers and gifted underachievers. Ziv speculates that, since bright underachievers receive low grades, their self-esteem is threatened by pressure from teachers, rejection by peers, and parental disappointment. Gifted underachievers, on the other hand, may remain unnoticed because their grades are acceptable by general standards. What boosts the egos of these children could be the joy of success in widely ranging activities outside of school. Thus, it seems that loose definitions of underachievement and imprecise methods of measuring it contribute greatly to the heterogeneity among those alleged to be its victims. It can also swell the ranks of those meeting the various criteria to the point where one reviewer of research estimates that approximately half of all males and a quarter of all females with above-average ability may be considered underachievers (Weiss, 1972).

To establish a single standard for identifying over- and underachievers, Farquhar and Payne (1964) suggest that labels be attached to children only if the difference between their predicted and actual achievement equals or exceeds ±1.00 standard error of estimate. Researchers often take lightly the burden of proof in designating students as discrepant achievers and assume that the only way to explain the gaps is in terms of personal, social, or emotional influences. Curiously enough, the factors hypothesized as affecting academic achievement seem powerless to interfere with performance on measures of potential.

ATTEMPTS AT SYSTEMATIZING THE RESEARCH EVIDENCE

Some reviewers of past research have found no psychosocial factors consistently associated with discrepant achievement (Raph and Tannenbaum, 1961; Asbury, 1974; Ziv, 1977). Others, however, interpret the evidence differently and conclude that distinctive personality and behavior patterns do exist. In her summary of Taylor's (1964) evaluation of studies of over- and underachievers at elementary, high school, and college levels, Whitmore (1980) noted the following characteristics as consistently discriminating between the two groups:

1. *Academic anxiety*, which the overachiever can control more consistently and direct more easily toward the attainment of a goal.
2. *Self-value*, with the overachiever feeling more adequate, optimistic, confident, and personally and intellectually efficient.
3. *Authority relations*, with the underachiever acting defensively either through compliance, evasion, and escape or through blind rebellion and negativism, which may reflect a displaced hostility toward parents.
4. *Interpersonal relationships*, with the underachiever tending to feel rejected and isolated while sometimes giving the impression of outward composure.
5. *Independence-dependence conflict*, another problem in interpersonal relations, in which the underachiever appears uninterested, apathetic, or critical of others.
6. *Activity patterns*, with the underachiever more interested in social activities than academics, while the reverse is true for the overachiever.
7. *Goal orientation*, with the underachiever setting unrealistic goals that perpetuate a sense of failure.

Other reviewers of previous research recognize sample error as well as personality and social factors contributing to underachievement. Purkey (1970) noted that these children lack self-confidence and perseverance, fail to express themselves adequately, have a poorly organized belief system, and are unable to establish good social relationships. Zilli (1971) pointed to inadequate motivation, social pressure or maladjustment, poor educational stimulation, and problems in the home environment as some of the reasons that gifted children fail to measure up to expectations. Summaries of the literature reported by Whitmore, Purkey, and Zilli generally agree with each other and also with an extensive one reported by Clark (1979).

Thus we see a basic difference in interpretation of evidence on contributors to underachievement. Some argue that the findings are ambiguous and contradictory and therefore difficult to interpret, while others consider the evidence persuasive enough to reveal the causes clearly. No meta analysis has ever been done on data accumulated in past investigations, nor is it easy to conduct one in view of the disparity of criteria by which children are labeled underachievers in these studies. Probably because researchers have not been bound to a single set of criteria, they cannot agree even on the age at which a child begins to perform below expectations.

For example, Shaw and McCuen (1960) traced the scholastic records of high school students back to the first grade in an effort to determine how early signs of underachievement could be discerned. The experimental sample had IQs of 110 or above on the Pinter General Abilities Test (Verbal Series, a group measure), and they were designated as achievers or underachievers depending on whether their grade-point averages were above or below the class mean. Results showed that the differences in performance at school did not become significant until the third grade for boys and as late as the ninth grade for girls. Yet Karnes et al. (1961) reported an experiment involving children described as underachievers as early as the second grade! In this study, the IQs were 120 or higher on the Stanford-Binet, and scores on standardized achievements tests were at least one standard deviation below what would be expected of children at these IQ levels. Whitmore (1980) likewise reported a study of underachieving boys and girls, some of them second-graders with Stanford-Binet IQs ranging from 130 to 155 and standardized achievement scores as low as 1.6 and as high as 2.7. The children studied by Karnes and Whitmore were different scholastically from those investigated by Shaw and McCuen. In both the Karnes and Whitmore studies it appears that children can show signs of underachievement *before* reaching the third grade.

INTERVENTION THROUGH COUNSELING

Attempts at reversing the patterns of underachievement have produced mixed results, due probably to the variations in labeling and strategies of intervention. Counseling is by far the most widely used technique, but research reports are usually not detailed enough to clarify precisely what transpires in the course of these sessions or how competent the counselors are in executing their plans. Nevertheless, there is evidence of success as well as failure of such efforts with different age groups designated as underachievers by a variety of criteria and exposed to any number of individual and group guidance methods.

On the positive side, there is a study of twelve 13-year-old underachievers with IQs of 116 and above who were divided into three matched groups: (1) an experimental counseling sample participating in individual and small group interviews for periods ranging from twenty to forty minutes over a period of six months and taking various diagnostic tests along the way; (2) a "placebo" sample that received no counseling but was tested on the diagnostic measures; and (3) a control sample that merely took the initial screening and final tests (Shouksmith and Taylor, 1964). Counseling was generally nondirective, with individual and group sessions kept as informal as possible. When an impasse was reached, the counselor took a more directive line. Encouragement and help were also given whenever it appeared that a child was in need of direct support. Each session was concluded by the counselor giving a generalized summary of the discussion and making arrangements for future meetings. Parents of the counseling sample were seen twice, once at the outset of the experiment and again at the end of the program. Results showed a significant effect of the intervention efforts, with eight out of the twelve children in the counseling sample no longer classified as underachievers and all but two of the placebo and control groups retaining their labels.

Encouraging results were also obtained in a study of freshmen honors students known as James Scholars at the University of Illinois who were failing to maintain a "B" grade-point average, the minimum permissible grade for continuation in this special program. Of the 255 students, 118 comprised the counseled group and 137 the noncounseled group. In addition, there were 28 students who had been invited for counseling but did not appear at the sessions, and there were also 20 noncooperative students among the controls so designated because they had failed to fill out the initial intake questionnaire (Ewing and Gilbert, 1967).

Intervention consisted of (1) general counseling to assist students in dealing with any problems they voiced and (2) focused counseling aimed especially at assisting students to achieve better grades. The experimentals were requested to participate in a maximum of four counseling interviews, which proved to be moderately effective. There was a significant difference in posttreatment grade-point averages in favor or the experimentals when they were compared with the combined cooperative *and* noncooperative controls. However, differences between cooperative experimentals and controls were not significant.

McCowan (1968) investigated thirty-two male tenth-graders with WISC IQs ranging from 110 to 125 whose academic average in grades eight and nine were below 75 percent. The samples were divided into eight subgroups, the four in each group matched for IQ, age, achievement, reading level, and socioeconomic status. In one group the experimental treatment involved counseling for students and their parents; in a second group, only the students received counseling; in a third group, only the parents received counseling; and the fourth group served as a control, with neither parents nor students being counseled. During the first semester of the school year, forty-five minute sessions were held once a week for those in the student counseling groups. The major effort was to assist individuals in modifying their attitudes so that they could deal more effectively with their problems. Particular emphasis in these nondirective sessions was placed upon growth and development in the affective domain. As for parent counseling, sixty minute sessions were held once a week for twelve weeks, with the same nondirective methods used to help parents achieve a better understanding of their children.

Posttesting showed that parent counseling was effective in improving academic achievement and that the improvement lasted at least through the period of the study. The combination of student and parent counseling also improved the children's adjustment at home. However, counseling of students alone was not enough to raise their school grades. These latter results are somewhat less encouraging than those obtained by Perkins and Wicas (1971) in a fairly similar study of 120 bright underachieving ninth-grade boys who received counseling in small groups, in some cases with their mothers and in other cases without them. Five male counselors provided ego supportive group sessions with significantly positive effect. All experimental groups showed increases in grade-point average and self-acceptance, although when counseling was administered to the mothers, with or without their children, the impact was equal to or greater than when it was administered only to the underachievers.

In an effort to reinforce the effects of counseling on underachievement, Wittmer (1969) combined it with tutoring services administered by a group of ninth-graders to eighteen underachieving seventh-graders. The experiment lasted for ten weeks, with each underachiever receiving one-and-a-half hours of tutoring and an hour of individual counseling every other week. Before and after the experimental period the subjects were rated by their teachers on a nine-point scale of attitudes toward school, self, and authority and for their general outlooks on life. Pre- and post-experiment grade-point averages were also compared. Results show a positive change in attitude for sixteen underachievers and a decline in only two of them. As a group, they also produced significant gains in their grade-point averages. Wittmer concluded that this kind of intervention in the sixth grade may avert failure among some students who find it difficult to make the transition between elementary and junior high school.

Unfortunately, there are also instances where counseling efforts have failed to turn underachievers into achievers. Mink (1964) administered a counseling program to four eighth-graders and four seventh-graders who had IQ scores of 116 or higher on the Lorge-Thorndike Test but were doing below-average or failing work in three or more subjects. The experimentals were matched with high achievers for grade placement, IQ, and sex. The school psychologists worked exclusively with the students in eleven forty-five-minute group sessions during which the children were lectured on study skills and participated in discussions concerning their relationships with parents, academic and general interests, and plans for the future. In addition, the guidance counselor met with the parents of the experimentals for two sessions lasting two hours and one hour, respectively, and devoted to discussions of such topics as college attendance, children's aptitudes, and vocational opportunities. Results showed that, while the parents of the experimentals seemed to take a much more active interest in their children and began to understand them better, there was no measurable effect on the grades and teacher ratings of offspring.

Mink suggests that further research efforts concentrate on the relative effectiveness of alternative treatment procedures, such as multiple counseling with peers, parents, teachers, and students, as opposed to counseling efforts restricted only to parents and underachievers.

This failure to effect change by counseling parents and children was also experienced by Ohlsen and Gazda (1965) in their eight-week-long study of fifth-graders with tested intelligence similar to that of Mink's sample (IQ 116 and over) and achievement levels at least one grade below expectation. Here, too, researchers were critical of their own experimental design and expressed the hope that better results would have been obtained if sample selection and treatment had been planned more carefully.

In another study of elementary school children, Winkler, Teigland, Munger, and Kranzler (1965) selected as their target group of underachievers eighty-six males and thirty-five females with IQs ranging from 84 to 144 and classroom grades well below expectation. The subjects were randomly assigned to one of five treatment conditions: individual counseling, group counseling, reading instruction, Hawthorne effect, and control. Counseling was conducted by six males assigned at random to meet with their groups for fourteen half-hour sessions, one per week for the first eight weeks and two for each of the following three weeks of the experiment. The basic counseling approach was client centered and role playing. In both the individual and group counseling samples, the reading instruction group concentrated on the Science Research Associates Reading Laboratory, while the Hawthorne effect group received no treatment except listening to records and having stories read to them. Results show no significant gain for experimentals over controls either in grade-point average or in measured personality variables. The researchers found that underachievement is not a surface phenomenon that can be remedied easily.

Experiments with counseling in high schools have produced mixed results similar to those in the elementary school. Finney and Van Dalsel (1966) evaluated such a program for ninety-two sophomores who scored at or above the seventy-fifth percentile on the Differential Aptitude Test Battery (DAT) and whose freshmen grade-point average was below the mean for all students at their DAT level. Students were divided according to sex and were randomly assigned to eight counseling groups (four female, N = 52; four male, N = 40) and paired also by sex with eight control groups (four female, N = 46; four male, N = 58). The groups averaged twelve members each but actually varied in size from five to fifteen members.

The experimental subjects met weekly during the school days from the late fall of their sophomore year until May of their junior year. Attendance varied from session to session, and by the end of the study, the counseling sample had been reduced to sixty-nine and the control group to eighty-five. The fourteen regular high school counselors, ranging in experience from none to two years, conducted the group counseling sessions during the four semesters of treatment.

Results showed no significant difference between the counseling and control groups in grade-point averages and in scores on the California Study Methods Survey. However, the students receiving counseling were rated by their teachers as more cooperative and less restive in class. The underachievers also exhibited an increased willingness to seek assistance and to accept suggestions from teachers. They improved their attendance records as well as increased their enjoyment of learning for its own sake. Their scores on the California Psychological Inventory administered at the end of the fourth semester of counseling showed an improvement on eight scales, particularly those that measure social development, self-acceptance, and intellectual mindedness. The researchers concluded that, while the data do not support the hypothesis that counseling would result in improved grades, the changes that did occur involved personal characteristics and could be assets in later stages of life if the unsolved academic problems and poor grades would not permit admission to college.

In still another study of high school underachievers, Goebel (1967) compared the relative effectiveness of three types of counseling procedures. In one treatment, the students received individual counseling during four fifty-minute sessions; a second treatment was similar in frequency and length but focused on group counseling; and in the third type of treatment, students participated in two group sessions followed by one or two meetings for individual counseling. The target sample consisted of thirty-six students divided randomly into three groups of eight experimental subjects assigned to the different treatments and twelve controls who received no counseling.

Results show no short- or long-term effects among treatment groups and between experimentals and controls on any of the four criteria: grade-point average, Iowa Tests of Educational Development, success in earning academic diplomas, and signs of continuing education after high school.

At the college level, evidence on the effects of counseling is likewise unimpressive. Winborn and Schmidt (1961) reported on an attempt to improve the academic performance of thirty-four male and twenty-five female freshmen with scores at or above the eightieth percentile on the American Council of Education Psychological Examination but with grade-point averages of 1.50 or below. Two counselors with substantial prior experience in the field were responsible for working with students in six one-hour sessions extending over a period of two months. As a result of the short-term intervention, differences in grade-point average between the experimental and control groups were found to be significant in favor of the control group. However, these differences were wiped out by the end of the next semester. The futility of short-term counseling for underachievers in the first year of college is substantiated by Semke's (1968) study of some fifty-five students who failed to benefit from eight one-hour sessions of "structured" and "unstructured" guidance.

In general, the literature on intervention through counseling is difficult to interpret. Any number of possible intervening variables may account for the contradictory results from experimentation. Neither the successful nor the unsuccessful studies are uniform enough in design to suggest that a particular counseling technique for students showing specified signs of underachievement is likely to succeed, whereas a different counseling strategy or the same one for students with different symptoms of underachievement is just as likely to fail. We do not even have a clue as to which age groups seem to be most responsive to any of these types of intervention. Perhaps success depends on some kind of "goodness of fit" between counselor and client, an idiosyncratic relationship that is not yet understood and therefore is impossible to plan in advance.

EDUCATIONAL INTERVENTION

Although relatively few efforts have been made to evaluate special instruction for underachievers, some of those on record are described in considerable detail. Karnes et al. (1962) reported an experiment in which twenty-five underachievers (nineteen boys and six girls), constituting approximately equal numbers of second-, third-, fourth-, and fifth-graders, were placed in homogeneous classes with high achievers at their respective grade levels for two to three years. A control group of twenty-three children (fourteen boys and nine girls) attended heterogeneous classes for the same period of time. All subjects had Stanford-Binet IQs of 120 or above, with the mean for the experimentals (IQ 144.8) significantly higher than that of the controls (IQ 135.8). Underachievement was defined on the basis of scores at least one standard deviation below expected levels in reading and arithmetic, as estimated by the Horn (1941) formula.*

Results proved to be almost consistently encouraging, as the experimentals outgained the controls in achievement test scores over the course of the experiment. Similarly significant discrepancies favored the experimentals in one of the four measures of divergent thinking (i.e., fluency) and in the children's perceptions of being accepted and valued by their parents. Only their perceptions of acceptance by peers were unaffected by placement in either homogeneous or heterogeneous groups. The researchers concluded that placing gifted underachievers in classes of equally able achievers can be beneficial, particularly in the elementary grades.

Another kind of educational intervention is reported to be similarly rewarding for younger children. Rather than relying just on a special grouping arrangement to reduce symptoms of underachievement, Whitmore (1980) also adjusted the curriculum and provided intensive clinical services for twenty-seven underachievers (twenty males and seven females, ages 5 to 9) over a period of one to three years. Nearly all the children had Stanford-Binet IQs of 140 or above and were labeled underachievers by exhibiting at least ten of the following traits, including all of those asterisked:

—*exhibits poor test performance,
—*is achieving at or below grade-level expectations in one or all of the basic skill areas: reading, language arts, mathematics,
—*turns in daily work that is frequently incomplete or poorly done,
—*has superior comprehension and retention of concepts when interested,
—*exhibits vast gap between qualitative level of oral and written work,
—possesses an exceptionally large repertoire of factual knowledge,
—exhibits vitality of imagination, creative,
—exhibits persistent dissatisfaction with work accomplished, even in art,
—seems to avoid trying new activities to prevent imperfect performance; evidences perfectionism, self-criticism,

---

*According to Horn (1941) a child's expected achievement in reading and arithmetic may be estimated as follows: reading = $(2 MA + CA)/3 - 5$; arithmetic = $(2 MA + CA)/2 - 5$.

—shows initiative in pursuing self-selected projects at home,
—*has a wide range of interests and possibly special "expertise" in an area of investigation and research,
—*evidences low self-esteem and tendencies to withdraw or be aggressive in the classroom,
—does not function comfortably or constructively in a group of any size,
—shows acute sensitivity and perceptions related to self, others, and life in general,
—tends to set too unrealistic self-expectations, goals too high or too low,
—dislikes practice work or drill or memorization and mastery,
—is easily distractible, unable to focus attention and concentrate efforts on tasks,
—has an indifferent or negative attitude toward school,
—resists teacher efforts to motivate or discipline behavior in class,
—has difficulty in peer relationships; maintains few friendships. (Whitmore, 1980, p. 237)

Teachers, counselors, and school psychologists referred appropriately qualified children to the Under-achieving Gifted Program (UAG), which was administered in special classes for these pupils. The children remained in the UAG classes for one year in the primary grades and two years in the intermediate grades before entering the Extended Learning Program (ELP) for gifted children. The objectives of the UAG program were to help children to (1) reduce self-degrading invidious comparisons with high achievers; (2) learn to accept themselves through acceptance of others with similar problems; (3) enjoy intellectual stimulation through a curriculum centered on their strengths; (4) acquire a sense of genuine success; and (5) develop social skills and potential for leadership.

To achieve the program objectives, the UAG classes resembled Hewett's (1968) "engineered classroom," except that it was student centered rather than teacher centered. Under this plan, the children were allowed considerable freedom to enter into self-directing activities in a classroom environment that emphasized flexible controls. Yet their instruction in the basic skills was highly structured, following a prescriptive, individualized method resembling the kind of instruction administered to handicapped learners. The curriculum content, however, was sharply different from what is usually found in classes for the handicapped: whereas the handicapped focus is mainly on basic language and numbers skills, the UAG children concentrated on advanced thought processes, including analysis, synthesis, evaluation, and divergent production. No less important was the enhancement of social skills, self-understanding, and feelings of self-worth through specially planned activities in and out of the classroom. Whitmore's (1980) description of the UAG program is lengthy and vivid enough to reveal precisely what kind of approach was taken to help young children overcome the problems of underachievement.

Of the eighteen children completing the first year (1968-1969) of the UAG program, all scored at or above grade level in language skills, twelve scored above grade level in mathematics, and twelve gained a year and a half to three years in reading ability, while only three remained below grade level in reading or mathematics. By the end of the second year, the six students remaining in the UAG class continued to accelerate in achievement, and the new students made gains similar to those enrolled in the previous year. Nonacademic progress included more enthusiastic participation in school activities, better work habits, more realistic goal setting and self-evaluations, and improved social behavior. In 1972-1973, a follow-up comparison was made between UAG graduates and controls who had initially been recommended for the program but did not participate in it. Results show significant differences favoring the experimentals, their attitudes toward self and school, and in teachers' ratings of behavior and academic skills. A second follow-up in 1975 indicated that the program effects noted three years earlier were being sustained.

The Whitmore study demonstrates that an intensive psychoeducational program in a class consisting only of young underachievers can be successful. Unfortunately, however, somewhat similar efforts on behalf of underachieving students in a high school for boys failed to produce such gratifying results. Raph, Goldberg, and Passow (1966) identified thirty-one pairs of tenth-year students matched on the bases of IQ and ninth-year grade averages. All were labeled underachievers with IQs of 120 or higher on two group tests and ninth-year grade averages below 80 percent. Personality assessments yielded a considerable amount of additional data about students' out-of-school interests, their feelings about the transition from junior to senior high school and about school life in general, and their attitudes toward teachers, parents, peers, and themselves.

One of the two matched groups was organized into a special class that combined homeroom and social studies for two periods each day under the same teacher. The students in the other group served as controls and did not stay together as a unit but were assigned instead to various other sections of tenth-grade social studies. The teacher of the experimental class informed his students that their academic potential was expectionally high but that they needed help in improving their school performance. He expressed his genuine interest in them as individuals and made himself available to discuss any personal or academic problems they wished to raise.

At the end of the first semester, the grade-point averages were higher than they had been in junior high school, with the controls improving significantly more than the experimentals. No difference was found in social studies grades, but the teacher of the experimental class expressed confidence that his students had benefited greatly from their association with each other and that his work with them would have a positive effect on their future performance.

Realizing that a single semester is a short time in which to expect improvement, the researchers kept the experimentals intact as a group to continue the homeroom-social studies schedule with the same teacher for the remainder of the year. Final grades showed a closing of the gap between experimentals and controls with neither group outperforming the other in any subject area or in overall grade-point average. Yet the teacher of the experimental class felt that the final grades did not reflect how much the children benefited from working together with him for a year. According to him, a warm, accepting atmosphere had been established in class, and that was balanced by the high standards of effort and achievement to which the group was held. The teacher expressed genuine interest in the class, and the class members assisted each other admirably in their work. A few benefited dramatically from the experience, but the effect was not contagious enough to produce significant, observable changes in the entire group.

In the eleventh grade, it was decided that the experimentals would continue as a separate class, this time in a social studies honors course with a female teacher who had previously been successful in working with honors classes. She was advised by the experimenters not to relax her usual high expectations, even though the students' work had previously been judged mediocre by such standards. The results of her brooking no nonsense proved to be ineffectual for courses other than social studies and disastrous for social studies, with the experimentals receiving significantly lower grades than the controls.

A comparison of the two groups in overall averages from the end of grade ten to the middle of grade eleven showed that both had lost ground, the special class's decrement having been significantly greater than that of the control group. The teacher expected her children to "toe the mark" and would tolerate no sloppy or tardy work at any time. These high expectations, which had been eminently useful in honors classes over the years, were completely inappropriate in this situation. The boys resisted the pressure, cut corners in their assignments, performed poorly, and introduced many behavior problems into the classroom. It is a matter of speculation as to whether the severe setback in the third semester was caused by sudden demands for honors-level work or by an unhappy mix between a teacher who was demanding and female and adolescents who were underachieving and male and perhaps burdened with unresolved oedipal conflicts.

For the last semester of the two-year study, the experimentals were again retained as a unit for social studies under a male teacher other than the one in grade ten. Twenty-eight of the original thirty-one students remained, the other three having failed the first semester of social studies. After hearing about the experiences of the previous two teachers, the third one did not expect the group to measure up to honors' class expectations. He found the group lacking in emotional stability and self-control, with any attempt at humor sending the students into fits of uncontrolled laughter, which made it difficult to maintain a serious, work-oriented atmosphere in the classroom. However, skillful classroom management helped the boys to reorganize themselves into a unit that functioned fairly smoothly and cooperatively. Homework of a factual nature was completed and handed in on time, but any assignment that required independent thought was often handed in after the due date or not at all.

Yet the teacher was able to steer a middle course between control and permissiveness. He also showed an interest in the students' individual problems and concentrated on teaching them much needed study skills. But despite the turnabout in group morale and task-orientedness, the experimentals' end-of-term grades did not differ significantly from those of the controls in any subject. The grade average of the special class was a mediocre 73, only two points higher than the controls. By the time of graduation, the majority of underachievers were not accepted by the colleges of their choice; many had withdrawn from the academic stream and made no plans to continue their education beyond high school; and a few had already dropped out of school. These patterns were similar in both groups, although each contained three or four students whose achievement improved greatly.

Comparing the successes of Karnes and associates (1962) and Whitmore (1980) with the failure of Raph, Goldberg, and Passow (1966) to intervene successfully with underachievers, the immediate impression that comes to mind is the difference in age between the experimental samples. The Raph, Goldberg, and Passow study dealt with a high school population that may be far more resistant to change than the younger groups treated in the other studies. It is easy to hypothesize that, by the time a child reaches adolescence, it may be too late to overcome the inhibitions to successful work at school; hence the need to identify symptoms of underachievement early in life and to eradicate them before the child reaches high school. As attractive as this hypothesis may be, there are other possible reasons for the contradictory outcomes, including differences in criteria for labeling underachievers and variations in approaches to educating and counseling them. Perhaps the only way to know for sure what makes a difference (and with whom) is to replicate the success stories with samples similar to those in the original experiments and then on other age groups with different symptoms and etiologies of underachievement.

CONCLUSIONS

Overachievement is probably far easier to explain than underachievement. If an individual performs beyond our expectations, the straightforward meaning is that something is wrong with our expectations. The measures we have used to estimate potential are fallible and can sometimes lead us to expect more than we should from people. In other words, overachievement is an illusion resulting quite clearly from underprediction. To believe that it really exists would amount to accepting the possibility that we can absorb or perform beyond our true capacity. It would be analogous to believing that a gallon of liquid can somehow fit in a liter-sized container.

Underachievement, on the other hand, is a mysterious, elusive phenomenon that can be explained only partially in terms of measurement error. Some children's abilities are indeed overestimated, but there are others who perform inadequately at school even after we take into account the difficulties in estimating their potential. It is certainly reasonable to assume that any number of personality and environmental factors can thwart productivity or performance and produce the same signs of failure at school. It would therefore be appropriate to approach an understanding of underachievement in the same way that physicians interpret a skin rash. Although the surface appearance of skin rashes may resemble each other, at least to the unpracticed eye, the underlying causes can vary widely. Some people break out because of disease, while others are allergic to food they eat or things they touch. Similarly, underachievement should be regarded as a single symptom representing diverse etiologies. One type of underachiever fails to measure up to expectations because of overestimated general abilities; a second type possesses inadequate special aptitudes of any kind; a third type does not have the necessary drive, mental health, meta-learning habits, or any other personality supports; a fourth type lacks the proper nurturance at home, at school, and in the community; and a fifth type sinks into mediocrity through a series of misfortunes or distractions beyond anybody's control. Thus, the five factors that serve as links between potential and fulfillment are also clues to potential and failure. But it would be a mistake to assume that *all* underachievers suffer from all five handicaps. Each kind of deterrent can by itself make the difference between success and failure.

The existence of five broad categories of underachievers may help to explain the inconsistencies in research findings on the nature and needs of these children. Studies of underachievement show variations not only in symptoms but in etiology as well. Without taking these differences into account, we would expect researchers to disagree in their findings, and indeed they do. For example, in one experimental sample (Pringle, 1970), a disproportionate number of underachievers had access to only one parent, while another sample (McGillivray, 1964) was not atypical in this way. One study (Pierce and Bowman, 1960) showed that high dominance among mothers is associated with their daughters' achievement at school, while another study (Groth, 1971) reports that a "warm mother" is significant for high achievement among women. Gowan (1957) found clear evidence of maladjustment among underachievers; Ringness (1965), on the other hand, found no such symptoms in his experimental group.

What could have happened to produce the contradictory evidence is that in every pair of studies the two groups were underachieving for different reasons even though the surface signs were similar. It would therefore be futile to generalize about underachievers on the basis of mass data alone. Each sample has to be diagnosed clinically in order to understand the separate syndromes within the group. Such an in-depth examination of every child's individuality seems to have taken place in Whitmore's (1980) study and may account for her success in matching intervention strategies to the special needs of her sample.

References

Abramson, D. A. "The Effectiveness of Grouping for Students of High Ability." *Educational Research Bulletin*, **38**:169-182 (1959).

Abroms, K., and J. Gollin. "Developmental Study of Gifted Preschool Children and Measures of Psychological Giftedness." *Exceptional Children*, **46**:334-343 (1980).

Aiken, L. R. "Ability and Creativity in Mathematics." *Review of Educational Research*, **42**:405-434 (1972).

———. "Language Factors in Learning Mathematics." *Review of Educational Research*, **43**:359-385 (1973).

Anastasi, A. "On the Formation of Psychological Traits." *American Psychologist*, **25**:899-910 (1970).

———, and R. Levee. "Intellectual Defect and Musical Talent: A Case Report." *American Journal of Mental Deficiency*, **64**:695-703 (1960).

Anderson, K. E., T. C. Page, and H. A. Smith. "Study of the Variability of Exceptional High School Seniors in Science and Other Academic Areas." *Science Education*, **42**:42-59 (1958).

Annesley, F., F. Odhner, E. Madoff, and N. Chansky. "Identifying the First Grade Underachiever." *Journal of Educational Research*, **63**:459-462 (1970).

Asbury, C. A. "Selected Factors Influencing Over- and Under-Achievement in Young School-Age Children." *Review of Educational Research*, **44**:409-428 (1974).

Astin, A. W. "Socioeconomic Factors in the Achievements and Aspirations of the Merit Scholar." *Personnel and Guidance Journal*, **42**:581-586 (1964).

Atkinson, J. W. "Motivational Determinants of Intellective Performance and Cumulative Achievement." In J.W. Atkinson and J.O. Raynor, eds., *Personality, Motivation, and Achievement*, pp. 221-242. New York: John Wiley & Sons, Inc., 1978.

———, and J. O. Raynor, eds. *Motivation and Achievement*. Washington, D.C.: Hemisphere Publishing Corp., 1974.

Austin, J. H. *Chase, Chance, and Creativity*. New York: Columbia University Press, 1978.

Bachtold, L. M. "Interpersonal Values of Gifted Junior High School Students." *Psychology in the Schools*, **5**:368-370 (1968).

Barbe, W. B. "Interests and Adjustments of Adults Who Were Identified in Childhood as Gifted." *Progressive Education'*, **32**:145-150 (1955).

———. "What Happens to Graduates of Special Classes for the Gifted?" *Ohio State University Educational Research Bulletin*, **36**:13-16 (1957).

———. *One in a Thousand: A Comparative Study of Highly and Moderately Gifted Elementary School Children.* Columbus, Ohio: The F.J. Heer Printing Company, 1964.

Bass, B.M. *Leadership, Psychology, and Organizational Behavior.* New York: Harper & Bros., 1960.

Bayley, N. "On the Growth of Intelligence." *The American Psychologist*, **10**:805-818 (1955).

———, and E. S. Schaefer. "Correlations of Maternal and Child Behaviors with the Development of Mental Abilities." *Monographs of the Society of Research in Child Development*, **29**:1-96 (1964).

Becker, G. *The Mad Genius.* Beverly Hills, Calif.: Sage Publications, 1978.

Beery, R. "Fear of Fairlure in the Student Experience." *Personnel and Guidance Journal*, **54**:190-203 (1975).

Benbow, C. P., and J. C. Stanley. "Sex Differences in Mathematical Ability: Fact or Artifact?" *Science*, **210**:1262-1264 (1980).

Bilash, I., and J. P. Zubek. "The Effects of Age on Factorially 'Pure' Mental Abilities." *Journal of Gerontology*, **15**:175-182 (1960).

Birren, J. E., and D. F. Morrison. "Analysis of the WAIS Subtests in Relation to Age and Education." *Journal of Gerontology*, **16**:363-369 (1961).

Bischof, L. J. *Intelligence: Statistical Conceptions of Its Nature.* Garden City, N. Y.: Doubleday & Company, Inc., 1954.

Bliesmer, E. P. "Reading Abilities of Bright and Dull Children of Comparable Mental Ages." *Journal of Educational Psychology*, **45**:321-331 (1954).

Bloom, B. S. *Stability and Change in Human Characteristics.* New York: John Wiley & Sons, Inc., 1964

———. "An Introduction to Mastery Learning Theory." In J.H. Block, ed., *Schools, Society, and Mastery Learning*, pp. 3-14. New York: Holt, Rinehart and Winston, Inc., 1974.

———, ed. *Taxonomy of Educational Objectives: Cognitive Domain.* New York: David McKay Co., Inc. 1956.

Bolles, R. C. "What Happened to Motivation?" *Educational Psychologist*, **13**:1-13 (1978).

Bonney, M. E. "Relationships Between Social Success, Family Size, Socioeconomic Home Background, and Intelligence Among School Children in Grades III to V." *Sociometry*, **7**:26-39 (1944).

Bonsall, M. R., and B. Stefflre. "The Temperament of Gifted Children." *California Journal of Educational Research*, **6**:162-165 (1955).

Borgen, F. H. "Predicting Career Choices of Able College Men from Occupational and Basic Interest Scales of the SVIB." Evanston, Ill.: National Merit Scholarship Corporation, 7(9), 1971.

Borland, J. "Field Dependence-Independence and Cognitive Performance: A Review." Mimeo. New York: Center for the Study and Education of the Gifted, Teachers College, Columbia University, 1978.

Bousfield, W., and H. Barry. "The Visual Imagery of a Lightning Calculator." *American Journal of Psychology.* **45**:353-358 (1933).

Bradway, K. P., and C. W. Thompson. "Intelligence at Adulthood: A Twenty-five Year Follow-up." *Journal of Educational Psychology*, **53**:1-14 (1962).

Brandwein, P. F. "Origin of Science Interests." *Science Education*, **35**:251-253 (1951).

———. "Developed Aptitude in Science and Mathematics." *Science Teacher*, **20**:111-114 (1953).

———. *The Gifted Student as Future Scientist*. New York: Harcourt, Brace & World, 1955.

Brookover, W. G., A. Peterson, and S. Thomas. *Self-concept of Ability and School Achievement*. Cooperative Research Project 845. East Lansing, Michigan: Office of Research and Publications of Michigan State University, 1962.

Buriel, R. "Relationship of Three Field-Dependence Measures to the Reading and Math Achievement of Anglo American and Mexican American Children." *Journal of Educational Psychology*, **70**:167-174 (1978).

Burks, B. S., D. W. Jensen, and L. M. Terman. *The Promise of Youth: Follow-up Studies of a Thousand Gifted Children*. Stanford, Calif.: Stanford University Press, 1930.

Burt, C. L. *The Gifted Child*. New York: Harcourt, Brace & World, 1962.

Busse, T. V. "Establishment of the Flexible Thinking Factor in Fifth-Grade Boys." *Journal of Psychology*, **69**:93-100 (1968).

Calsyn, R. J., and D. A. Kenny. "Self-concept of Ability and Perceived Evaluation of Others: Cause or Effect of Academic Achievement?" *Journal of Educational Psychology*, **69**:136-145 (1977).

Carroll, J. B. "A Model of School Learning. *Teachers College Record*, **64**:723-733 (1963).

———. "Review of the Nature of Human Intelligence by J.P. Guilford." *American Educational Research Journal*, **73**:105-112 (1968).

———. "Psychometric Tests as Cognitive Tasks: A New 'Structure of Intellect'." In L.B. Resnick, ed., *The Nature of Intelligence*, pp. 27-56. Hillsdale, N.J.: Lawrence Erlbaum Associates, 1976.

Cattell, J. McK. "A Statistical Study of American Men of Science. III: The Distribution of American Men of Science." *Science, New Series*, **24**:732-742 (1906).

Cattell, R. B. "Theory of Fluid and Crystallized Intelligence: A Critical Experiment." *Journal of Educational Psychology*. **54**: 1-22 (1963).

———. *Abilities: Their Structure, Growth, and Action*. Boston: Houghton Mifflin Company, 1971.

———, and H. J. Butcher. *The Prediction of Achievement and Creativity*. Indianapolis, Ind.: The Bobbs-Merrill Co., Inc., 1968.

———, and G. F. Stice. "Four Formulae for Selecting Leaders on the Basis of Personality." *Human Relations*, 7:493-507 (1954)

Clark, B. *Growing Up Gifted*. Columbus, Ohio: Charles E. Merrill Publishing Company, 1979.

Clark-Stewart, K. A. "Interactions Between Mothers and Their Young Children: Characteristics and Consequences." *Monographs of the Society for Research in Child Development*, **38**:1-109 (1973).

Cohn, S. J. "Two Components of the Study of Mathematically Precocious Youths' Intervention Studies of Educational Acceleration: Chemistry and Physics Facilitation and Longitudinal Follow-up." Unpublished doctoral dissertation. Johns Hopkins University, Baltimore, Maryland, 1980.

Cole, J. R. *Fair Science*. New York: The Free Press, 1979.

Coleman, J. S. "The Adolescent Subculture and Academic Achievement." *American Journal of Sociology*, **65**:337-347 (1960).

Corsini, R. J., and K. K. Fassett. "Intelligence and Aging." *Journal of Genetic Psychology*, **83**:249-264 (1953).

Covington, M. V., and R. Beery. *Self-worth and School Learning*. New York: Holt, Rinehart and Winston, Inc., 1976.

————, R. W. Crutchfield, L. B. Davies, and R. M. Olton. *The Productive Thinking Program: A Course in Learning to Think.* Columbus, Ohio: Charles E. Merrill Publishing Company, 1974.

————, and C. L. Omelich. "Effort: The Double-Edged Sword in School Achievements." *Journal of Educational Psychology,* **71**:169-182 (1979).

Cox, C. M., et al. *The Early Mental Traits of Three Hundred Geniuses. Stanford, Calif.: Stanford University Press, 1926.*

Daurio, S. P. "Educational Enrichment versus Acceleration: A Review of the Literature. In W.C. George, J.S. Cohn, and C.J. Stanley, eds., *Educating the Gifted,* pp. 13-63. Baltimore, Md.: Johns Hopkins University Press, 1979.

Davis, F. B., E. French, and G. S. Lesser. "The Identification and Classroom Behavior of Elementary School Children Gifted in Five Different Mental Characteristics." Mimeographed Research Report, Hunter College, N.Y., 1959.

Dean, R. S. "Effects of Self-concept of Learning with Gifted Children." *Journal of Educational Research,* **70**:315-318 (1977).

DeCecco, J. P. *The Psychology of Learning and Instruction: Educational Psychology.* Englewood Cliffs, N.J.: Prentice-Hall, Inc., 1968.

Dennis, W. "Causes of Retardation Among Institutional Children: Iran." *Journal of Genetic Psychology,* **94**:47-59 (1960).

De Tocqueville, A. *Democracy in America.* New York: Vintage Books, Inc., 1954.

D'Heurle, A., J. Mellinger, and E. A. Haggard. "Personality, Intellectual, and Achievement Patterns in Gifted Children." *Psychological Monographs,* Vol. 73, no. 13, 1959.

Doppelt, J. E. *The Organization of Mental Abilities.* New York: Bureau of Publications, Teachers College, Columbia University, 1950.

Doyle, K. E., Jr., and R. E. Moen. "Toward the Definition of a Domain of Academic Motivation." *Journal of Educational Psychology,* **70**:231-236 (1978).

Drake, L. "MMPI Patterns Predictive of Underachievement." *Journal of Counseling Psychology,* **9**:164-167 (1962).

Ellis, H. *The Transfer of Learning.* New York: Macmillan Publishing Co., Inc., 1965.

Ewing, T. N., And W. M. Gilbert. "Controlled Study of the Effects of Counseling on the Scholastic Achievements of Students of Superior Ability." *Journal of Counseling Psychology,* **14**:235-239 (1967).

Farquhar, W. W., and D. A. Payne. "A Classification and Comparison of Techniques Used in Selecting Under- and Over-Achievers." *Personnel and Guidance Journal,* **42**:874-884 (1964).

Feldman, D. "The Mysterious Case of Extreme Giftedness." In A.H. Passow, ed., *The Gifted and the Talented: Their Education and Development.* The Seventy-eighth Yearbook of the National Society for the Study of Education, Part I, pp. 335-351. Chicago: University of Chicago Press, 1979.

Ferguson, G. A. "On Learning and Human Ability." *Canadian Journal of Psychology,* **8**:95-112 (1954).

Findley, W. G., and M. Bryan. "Ability Grouping: 1970 Status, Impact, and Alternatives." Athens: Center for Educational Improvement, University of Georgia, 1971.

Finney, B. C., and E. Van Dalsel. "Group Counseling for Gifted Underachieving High School Students." *Journal of Counseling Psychology,* **16**:87-94 (1966).

Flaugher, R. L. "The Many Definitions of Test Bias." *American Psychologist,* **33**:671-679 (1978).

Fletcher, J. L. "The Outer Limits of Human Educability: A Proposed Research Program." *Educational Researcher,* **7**:13-18 (1978).

Fox, L. H. "A Mathematics Program for Fostering Precocious Achievement." In J.C. Stanley, D.P. Keating, and L.H. Fox eds., *Mathematical Talent: Discovery, Description, and Development*, pp. 101-125. Baltimore, Md.: Johns Hopkins University Press, 1974.

Freehill, M. *Gifted Children: Their Psychology and Education*. New York: Macmillan Publishing Co., Inc., 1961.

Frierson, E. C. "A Study of Differences Between Gifted Children from Upper and Lower Status Communities." *Science Education*, **49**:205-210 (1965).

Gagné, R. M. *The Conditions of Learning*. 2nd ed. New York: Holt, Rinehart and Winston, Inc., 1970.

Gallagher, J. J. *Teaching the Gifted Child*. 2nd ed. Boston: Allyn & Bacon, Inc., 1975.

———, and T. Crowder. "The Adjustment of Gifted Children in the Regular Classroom." *Exceptional Children*, **23**:306-312, 317-319 (1957).

———, and J. W. Moss. "New Concepts of Intelligence and Their Effects on Exceptional Children." *Exceptional Children*, **30**:1-4 (1963).

Gettinger, M., and M. A. White. "Which Is the Stronger Correlate of School Learning? Time to Learn or Measured Intelligence?" *Journal of Educational Psychology*, **71**:405-412 (1979).

Getzels, J. W. "The Acquisition of Values in School and Society." In F.S. Chase and H.A. Anderson, eds., *The High School in a New Era*, pp. 146-161. Chicago: University of Chicago Press, 1958.

———. "From Art Student to Fine Artist: Potential Problem Finding and Performance." In A.H. Passow, ed., *The Gifted and the Talented: Their Education and Development*. The Seventy-eighth Yearbook of the National Society for the Study of Education, Part I, pp. 372-387. Chicago: University of Chicago Press, 1979.

———, and M. Csikszentmihalyi. *The Creative Vision: A Longitudinal Study of Problem Finding in Art*. New York: John Wiley & Sons, Inc., 1976.

Ghiselli, E. E. "The Relationship Between Intelligence and Age Among Superior Adults." *Journal of Genetic Psychology*, **90**:131-134 (1957).

Gibb, C. A. "Leadership." In G. Lindzey and E. Aronson, eds., *The Handbook of Social Psychology*, Vol. 4, pp. 205-282. 2nd ed. Reading, Mass.: Addison-Wesley Publishing Co., Inc., 1969.

Goebel, M. E. "A Comparison of the Relative Effectiveness of Three Types of Counseling with High School Underachievers." *Dissertation Abstracts*, **27**:(9-A): 2827 (1967).

Goertzel, V., and M. G. Goertzel. *Cradles of Eminence*. Boston: Little, Brown and Company, 1962.

Goldberg, M. L., A. H. Passow, D. W. Camm, and R. D. Neill. *A Comparison of Mathematics Programs for Able Junior High School Students*. Project No. 5-0381. Washington, D.C.: U.S. Office of Education, Bureau of Research, 1966.

———, A. H. Passow, J. Justman, and G. Hage. *The Effects of Ability Grouping*. New York: Bureau of Publications, Teachers College, Columbia University, 1965.

Goodenough, D. R. "The Role of Individual Differences in Field Dependence as a Factor in Learning and Memory." *Psychological Bulletin*, **83**:675-694 (1976).

Goodenough, F. L. *The Measurement of Intelligence by Drawing*. Yonkers, N.Y.: The World Book Company, 1926.

Gough, H. "Cross-Cultural Study of Achievement Motivation." *Journal of Applied Psychology*, **48**:191-196 (1964).

Gowan, J. C. "Dynamics of the Underachievement of Gifted Students." *Exceptional Children*, **24**:98-101 (1957).

Grossman, B., and J. Wrighter. "The Relationship Between Selection-Rejection and Intelligence, Social Status, and Personality Amongst Sixth Grade Children." *Sociometry*, **11**:346-355 (1948).

Groth, N. J. "Differences in Parental Environment Needed for Degree Achievement for Gifted Men and Women." *Gifted Child Quarterly*, **15**:256-259 (1971).

———. "Mothers of Gifted." *Gifted Child Quarterly*, **19**:217-222 (1975).

Guilford, J. P. "Three Faces of Intellect." *American Psychologist*, **14**:469-479 (1959).

———. *The Nature of Human Intelligence*. New York: McGraw-Hill Book Company, 1967.

———. "Theories of Intelligence." In B.B. Wolman, ed., *Handbook of General Psychology*, pp. 630-643. Englewood Cliffs, N.J.: Prentice-Hall, Inc., 1973.

———. "Varieties of Creative Giftedness, Their Measurement and Development." *Gifted Child Quarterly*, **19**:107-121 (1975).

———. "Fluid and Crystallized Intelligences: Two Fanciful Concepts." *Psychological Bulletin*, **88**:406-412 (1980).

Gutman, H. "The Biological Roots of Creativity." *Genetic Psychology Monographs*, **64**:417-458 (1961).

Haarer, D. L. "Gifted Delinquents." *Federal Probation*, **30**:43-46 (1966).

Haggard, E. A. "Socialization, Personality, and Academic Achievement in Gifted Children." *The School Review*, **65**:388-414 (1957).

Haier, R. J., and S. A. Denham. "A Summary Profile of the Nonintellective Correlates of Mathematical Precocity in Boys and Girls." In D.F. Keating, ed., *Intellectual Talent, Research and Development*, pp. 225-241. Baltimore, Md.: Johns Hopkins University Press, 1976.

Helson, R., and R. S. Crutchfield. "Mathematicians: The Creative Researcher and the Average Ph.D." *Journal of Consulting and Clinical Psychology*, **34**:250-257 (1970).

Hendricks, M., J. P. Guilford, and R. Hoepfner. "Measuring Creative Social Intelligence." *Psychological Laboratory*, No. 42. Los Angeles: The University of Southern California, 1969.

Hewett, F. M. *the Emotionally Disturbed Child in the Classroom: A Developmental Strategy for Educating Children with Maladaptive Behavior*. Boston: Allyn & Bacon, Inc., 1968.

Hildreth, G. H. "Characteristics of Young Gifted Children." *Pedagogical Seminary and Journal of Genetic Psychology*, **53**:287-311 (1938).

Hofstaetter, P. R. "The Changing Composition of 'Intelligence': A Study of t Technique." *Journal of Genetic Psychology*, **85**:159-164 (1954).

Holland, J. L. "Creative and Academic Performance Among Talented Adolescents." *Journal of Educational Psychology*, **52**:136-147 (1961).

Hollingworth, L. S. *Gifted Children: Their Nature and Nurture*. New York: Macmillan Publishing Co., Inc., 1926.

———, *Children Above 180 IQ, Stanford-Binet; Origin and Development*. Yonkers, N.Y.: The World Book Company, 1942.

———, and M. V. Cobb. "Children Clustering at 165 IQ and Children Clustering at 146 IQ Compared for Three Years in Achievement." In G. M. Whipple, ed., *Nature and Nurture: Their Influence Upon Achievement*. The Twenty-seventh Yearbook of the National Society for the Study of Education, Part II, pp. 3-33. Bloomington, Illinois: Public School Publishing Company, 1928.

Honzik, M. P., J. MacFarlane, and L. Allen. "The Stability of Mental Test Performance Between Two and Eighteen Years." *Journal of Experimental Education*, **4**:309-324 (1948).

Horn, A. "Uneven Distribution of the Effects of Specific Factors." In *Educational Monographs*. Los Angeles: University of Southern California, 1941.

Horn, J. L. "Organization of Abilities and the Development of Intelligence." *Psychological Review*, **75**:242-259 (1968).

———. "The Rise and Fall of Human Abilities." *Journal of Research and Development in Education*, **12**:59-78 (1979).

———, and R. B. Cattell. "Age Differences in Primary Mental Ability Factors." *Journal of Gerontology*, **21**:210-220 (1966)(a).

———, and R. B. Cattell. "Refinement and Test of the Theory of Fluid and Crystallized Intelligence." Journal of Educational Psychology, **57**:253-276 (1966)(b).

———, and R. B. Cattell. "Age Differences in Fluid and Crystallized Ingelligence." *Acta Psychologica*, **26**:107-129 (1967).

———, and J. R. Knapp. "On the Subjective Character of the Empirical Base of Guilford's Structure-of-Intellect Model." *Psychological Bulletin*, **80**:33-43 (1973).

Horrall, B. "Academic Performance and Personality Adjustments of Highly Intelligent College Students." *Genetic Psychology Monographs*, **55**:3-83 (1957).

Hughes, H. H., and H. D. Converse. "Characteristics of the Gifted: A Case for a Sequel to Terman's Study." *Exceptional Children*, **29**:179-183 (1962).

Hunt, J. McV. *Intelligence and Experience*. New York: The Ronald Press, 1961.

Hurlock, E. B., and J. L. Thomson "Children's Drawings: An Experimental Study of Perception." *Child Development*, **5**:127-138 (1934).

Jencks, C. *Inequality*. New York: Basic Books, Inc., 1972.

Jenkins, M. D. "Case Studies of Negro Children of Binet IQ 160 and Above." *Journal of Negro Education*, **12**:159-166 (1943).

Jones, A. M. "The Superior Child." *Psychological Clinic*, **15**:1-8, 116-123 (1923).

Jones, S. C. "Self- and Interpersonal Evaluations: Esteem Theories versus Consistency Theories." *Psychological Bulletin*, **79**:185-199 (1973).

Justman, J. "Academic Achievement of Intellectually Gifted Accelerants and Non-Accelerants in Junior High School." *School Review*, **62**:142-150 (1954).

Kagan, J. "Preferred Modes of Conceptualization: Consistency and Significance of an Analytic Attitude." Mimeo. Yellow Springs, Ohio: Fels Research Institute, undated.

———. "Reflection-Impulsivity and Reading Ability in Primary Grade Children." *Child Development*, **36**:609-628 (1965).

Kahl, J. A. "Educational Aspirations of 'Common Man' Boys." *Harvard Educational Review*, **23**:186-203 (1953).

Karnes, M. B., G. F. McCoy, R. R. Zehrbach, J. P. Wollersheim, H. F. Clarizio, L. Costin, and L. S. Stanley. *Factors Associated with Underachievement and Overachievement of Intellectually Gifted Children*. Champaign, Ill.: Champaign Community Unit Schools, Department of Special Services, 1961.

———, G. F. McCoy, R. R. Zehrbach, J. P. Wollersheim, and H. F. Clarizio. *The Efficacy of Two Organizational Plans for Underachieving Intellectually Gifted Children*. Champaign, Ill.: Champaign Community Unit Schools, Department of Special Services, 1962.

Kaufman, A. S. "A Child's I.Q.: How It Relates to a Child's Performance on and Perceptions of a Conservation of Mass Experiment." Mimeo. New York: Teachers College, Columbia University, 1968.

———. "Piaget and Gesell: A Psychometric Analysis of Tests Built from Their Tasks." *Child Development*, **42**:1341-1360 (1971).

Keating, D. P. "The Study of Mathematically Precocious Youth." In J. Stanley, D. Keating, and L. Fox, eds., *Mathematical Talent*, pp. 23-46. Baltimore, Md.: Johns Hopkins University Press, 1974.

————. "Precocious Cognitive Development at the Level of Formal Operations." *Child Development*, **46**:276-280 (1975).

————. "A Search for Social Intelligence." *Journal of Educational Psychology*, **70**:218-223 (1978).

Knapp, R. H., and H. B. Goodrich. *Origins of American Scientists*. Chicago: University of Chicago Press, 1952.

Kolstoe, O. P. "A Comparison of Mental Abilities of Bright and Dull Children of Comparable Mental Ages." *Journal of Educational Psychology*, **45**:161-168 (1954).

Krutch, J. W. *Is the Common Man Too Common?* Norman: University of Oklahoma Press, 1954.

Kurtzman, K. A. "A Study of School Attitudes, Peer Acceptance, and Personality of Creative Adolescents." *Exceptional Children*, **34**:157-162 (1967).

Laski, H. J. *The American Democracy*. New York: The Viking Press, 1948.

Laycock, F. *Gifted Children*. Glencoe, Ill.: Scott, Foresman and Company, 1979.

Lehman, H. C. "Young Thinkers and Great Achievements." *Journal of Genetic Psychology*, **74**:245-271 (1949).

Lesser, G. S., F. B. Davis, and L. Nahemow. "The Identification of Gifted Elementary School Children with Exceptional Scientific Talent." *Educational and Psychological Measurement*, **22**:349-364 (1962).

Lewerenz, A. S. "I.Q. and Ability in Art." *School and Society*, **27**:489-490 (1928).

Lewis, W. D. "Some Characteristics of Very Superior Children." *Pedagogical Seminary and Journal of Genetic Psychology*, **62**:301-309 (1943).

Liddle, G. "Overlap Among Desirable and Undesirable Characteristics in Gifted Children." *Journal of Educational Psychology*, **49**:219-223 (1958).

Lindsley, O. R. "Can Deficiency Produce Specific Superiority—The Challenge of the Idiot Savant." *Exceptional Children*, **31**:226-231 (1965).

Longstreth, L. E. "A Comment on 'Race, IQ, and the Middle Class' by Trotman: Rampant False Conclusions." *Journal of Educational Psychology*, **70**:469-472 (1978).

Lovell, L. "Some Recent Studies in Cognitive and Language Development." *Merrill-Palmer Quarterly*, **14**:123-138 (1968).

Lucito, L. J. "Independence-Conformity Behavior as a Function of Intellect: Bright and Dull Children." *Exceptional Children*, **31**:5-13 (1964).

————, and J. J. Gallagher. "Intellectual Patterns of Highly Gifted Children on the WISC." *Peabody Journal of Education*, **38**:131-136 (1960).

MacCurdy, R. D. *Characteristics of Superior Students and Some Factors That Were Found in Their Background*. Unpublished Ed.D. dissertation. Boston University, Boston, Massachusetts, 1954.

MacDonald, B., A. Gammie, and J. Nisbet. "The Careers of a Gifted Group." *Educational Research*, **6**:216-219 (1964).

Mann, R. D. "A Review of the Relationships Between Personality and Performance in Small Groups." *Psychological Bulletin*, **54**:241-270 (1959).

Martinson, R. *Educational Programs for Gifted Pupils*. Sacramento: California State Department of Education, 1961.

————. *Education of the Gifted and Talented*. Vol. 2: *Background Papers*. Washington, D.C.: U.S. Department of Health, Education, and Welfare, August 1971.

Maslow, A. H. *Motivation and Personality*. 2nd ed. New York: Harper & Row, Publishers, 1970.

McClelland, D. C. *The Achieving Society*. New York: The Free Press, 1961.

————, et al. *The Achievement Motive*. New York: Appleton-Century-Crofts, 1953.

McCowan, R. D. "Group Counseling with Underachievers and Their Parents." *The School Counselor*, **16**:30-35 (1968).

McCurdy, H. C. "The Childhood Pattern of Genius." *Smithsonian Report for 1958.* Washington, D.C.: The Smithsonian Institution, 1959.

McDonald, F. J., and P. Elias. "Report on the Results of Phase III of the Beginning Teacher Evaluation Study; an Overview." *Journal of Teacher Education*, **27**:315-316 (1976).

McGillivray, R. H. "Differences in Home Background Between High-Achieving and Low-Achieving Gifted Children: A Study of One Hundred Grade Eight Pupils in the City of Toronto Public Schools." *Ontario Journal of Educational Research*, **6**:99-106 (1964).

McGinn, P. V., M. C. Viernstein, and R. Hogan. "Fostering the Intellectual Development of Verbally Gifted Adolescents." *Journal of Educational Psychology*, **72**:494-498 (1980).

McNemar, Q. "Lost: Our Intelligence—Why?" *American Psychologist*, **19**:871-882 (1964).

Mead, M. "The Gifted Child in the American Culture of Today." *Journal of Teacher Education*, **5**:211-214 (1954).

Mensch, I. M. "Rorschach Study of the Gifted Child—A Survey of the Literature." *Journal of Exceptional Children*, **17**:8-14 (1950).

Michael, W. B. "Cognitive and Affective Components of Creativity in Mathematics and the Physical Sciences." In J.C. Stanley, W.C. George, and C.H. Solano, eds., *The Gifted and the Creative: A Fifty-Year Perspective*, pp. 141-172. Baltimore, Md.: Johns Hopkins University Press, 1977.

Miles, C. C. "Gifted Children." In L. Carmichael, ed., *Manual of Child Psychology*, pp. 984-1063. New York: John Wiley & Sons, 1954.

Milgram, R. M., and N. A. Milgram. "Personality Characteristics of Gifted Israeli Children" *Journal of Genetic Psychology*, **129**:185-194 (1976).

Miller, R. V. "Social Status and Socioempathic Differences Among Mentally Superior, Mentally Typical, and Mentally Retarded Children." *Exceptional Children*, **23**:114-119 (1956).

———. "Creativity and Intelligence in the Arts." *Education*, **82**:488-495 (1962).

Mink, O. B. "Multiple Counseling with Underachieving Junior High School Pupils of Bright-Normal and Higher Ability." *Journal of Educational Research*, **58**:31-34 (1964).

Minogue, B. "A Case of Secondary Mental Deficiency with Musical Talent." *Journal of Applied Psychology*, **7**:349-352 (1923).

Mitchell, J. O. "Attitudes of Adolescents Towards Mental Ability, Academic Effort and Athleticism." Unpublished Masters of Arts thesis. The University of Calgary, Department of Sociology, Calgary, Alberta, Canada, 1974.

Montour, K. "William James Sidis, The Broken Twig." *American Psychologist*, **32**:265-279 (1977).

Morgan, H. "Adolescent Attitudes Toward Academic Brilliance in the Suburban High School." Mimeo. Boulder: University of Colorado, 1981.

Nason, L. J. "Academic Achievement of Gifted High School Students." *University of Southern California Educational Monograph*, Series 17 (1958).

Newland, T. E. *The Gifted in Socioeducational Perspective.* Englewood Cliffs, N.J.: Prentice-Hall, Inc., 1976.

Nichols, R. C. "Personality Change and the College." *NMSC Research Report*, Vol. 1, no. 2. Evanston, Ill.: National Merit Scholarship Corporation, 1965.

———. "The Origin and Development of Talent." *NMSC Research Report*, Vol. 2, no. 10. Evanston, Ill.: National Merit Scholarship Corporation, 1966.

———, and A. W. Astin. "Progress of the Merit Scholar: An Eight-Year Follow-up."

Personnel and Guidance Journal, **44**:673-681 (1966).

Niemiec, C. J., and M. P. Sanborn. "Identifying Values of Superior High School Students." *School Counselor,* **18**:237-245 (1971).

Norman, R. D., and M. F. Daley. "The Comparative Personality Adjustment of Superior and Inferior Readers." *Journal of Educational Psychology,* **50**:31-36 (1959).

Oden, M. H. "The Fulfillment of Promise: 40-Year Follow-up of the Terman Gifted Group." *Genetic Psychology Monographs,* **77**:3-93 (1968).

Ohlsen, M., and G. Gazda. "Counseling Underachieving Bright Pupils." *Education,* **86**:78-81 (1965).

O'Sullivan, M., J. P. Guilford, and R. De Mille. "The Measurement of Social Intelligence." *Report from the Psychological Laboratory,* No. 34. Los Angeles: University of Southern California, 1965.

Owens, W. A., Jr. "Is Age Kinder to the Initially More Able?" *Journal of Gerontology,* **14**:334-337 (1959).

Perkins, J. A., and E. A. Wicas. "Group Counseling Bright Underachievers and Their Mothers." *Journal of Counseling Psychology,* **18**:273-278 (1971).

Petersen, H., J. P. Guilford, R. Hoepfner, and P. R. Merrifield. "Determination of 'Structure-of-Intellect' Abilities Involved in Ninth-Grade Algebra and General Mathematics." *Report from the Psychological Laboratory,* No. 31. Los Angeles: University of Southern California, 1963.

Pfeiffer, I. L. "Teaching in Ability Grouped English Classes: A Study of Verbal Interaction and Cognitive Goals." *Journal of Experimental Education,* **36**:33-38 (1967).

Piaget, J. *The Origins of Intelligence in Children.* New York: International Universities Press, 1952.

———. *The Construction of Reality in the Child.* New York: Basic Books, Inc., 1954.

———, and B. Inhelder. *The Psychology of the Child.* New York: Basic Books, Inc., 1969.

Pierce, J. V., and P. H. Bowman. "Motivation Patterns of Superior High School Students." *The Gifted Student,* Cooperative Research Monograph 2. Washington, D.C.: U.S. Government Printing Office, 1960.

Pressey, S. L. "That Most Misunderstood Concept—Acceleration." *School and Society,* **79**:59-60 (1954).

Pringle, K. M. L. *Able Misfits.* London: Longman Group Limited, 1970.

Propper, M. M., and E. T. Clark. "Alienation: Another Dimension of Underachievement." *The Journal of Psychology,* **75**:13-18 (1970).

Purkey, W. W. *Self-concept and School Achievement.* Englewood Cliffs, N.J.: Prentice-Hall, Inc., 1970.

Radin, N. "Maternal Warmth, Achievement Motivation and Cognitive Functioning in Lower-Class Preschool Children," *Child Development,* **42**:1560-1565 (1971).

———. "Observed Maternal Behavior with Four-Year-Old Boys and Girls in Lower Class Families." *Child Development,* **45**:1126-1131 (1974).

Raph, J. B., and A. J. Tannenbaum. *Underachievement: Review of Literature.* Mimeo. Talented Youth Project, Horace Mann-Lincoln Institute of School Experimentation. New York: Teachers College, Columbia University, 1961.

———, M. L. Goldberg, and A. H. Passow. *Bright Underachievers.* New York: Teachers College Press, Columbia University, 1966.

Renzulli, J. S. "What Makes Giftedness? Reexamining a Definition." *Phi Delta Kappan,* **60**:18-24 (1978).

Révész, G. *The Psychology of a Musical Prodigy.* Westport, Conn.: Greenwood Press, 1970.

Reisman, D. *The Lonely Crowd.* New Haven, Conn.: Yale University Press, 1950.

Ringness, T. A. "Emotional Adjustment of Academically Successful and Nonsuccessful Bright Ninth Grade Boys." *Journal of Educational Research,* **59**:88-91 (1965).

———. "Identification Patterns, Motivation, and School Achievement of Bright Junior High Boys." *Journal of Educational Psychology,* **58**:248-253 (1966).

Robeck, M. C. *California Project Talent: Acceleration Programs for Intellectually Gifted Pupils.* Sacramento: California State Department of Education, 1968.

Roberts, A. "Case History of a So-called Idiot-Savant." *Journal of Genetic Psychology,* **66**:259-265 (1945).

Robinson, H. B. "Current Myths Concerning Gifted Children." *Gifted and Talented Brief No. 5,* pp. 1-11. Ventura, Calif.: National/State Leadership Training Institute, 1977.

———, W. Roedell, and N. Jackson. "Early Identification and Intervention." In A. H. Passow, ed., *The Gifted and the Talented: Their Education and Development.* The Seventy-eighth Yearbook of the National Society for the Study of Education, Part I, pp. 138-154. Chicago: University of Chicago Press, 1979.

Roe, A. *Making of a Scientist.* New York: Dodd, Mead & Company, 1953.

Roedell, W. C. "Social Development in Intellectually Advanced Children." Paper presented at the symposium, *Intellectually Advanced Children: Preliminary Findings of a Longitudinal Study.* Annual Convention of the American Psychological Association, Toronto, 1978.

Rosen, B. C. "The Achievement Syndrome: A Psychocultural Dimension of Social Stratification." *American Sociological Review,* **21**:203-211 (1956).

———, and R. D'Andrade. "The Psycho-Social Origins of Achievement Motivation." *Sociometry,* **22**:185-218 (1959).

Rubenzer, R. "The Left-Right Hemisphere Model for Information Processing: Possible Implications for Education." Mimeo. New York: Teachers College, Columbia University, 1978.

Ruhland, D., M. Gold, and S. Feld. "Role Problems and the Relationship of Achievement Motivation to Scholastic Performance." *Journal of Educational Psychology,* **70(6)**:950 (1978).

Russell, D. H. *Children's Thinking.* Lexington, Mass.: Ginn and Company, 1956.

Ryan, F. J., and J. S. Davie. "Social Acceptance, Academic Achievement, and Academic Aptitude Among High School Students." *Journal of Educational Research,* **52**:101-106 (1958).

Satterly, D. J. "Cognitive Styles, Spatial Ability, and School Achievement." *Journal of Educational Psychology,* **68**:36-42 (1976).

Schauer, G. "Emotional Disturbance and Giftedness." *Gifted Child Quarterly,* **20**:470-477 (1976).

Scheerer, M., E. Rothman, and K. Goldstein. "A Case of 'Idiot Savant': An Experimental Study of Personality Organization." *Psychological Monographs,* Vol. 58, no. 4, 1945.

Scheffler, I. "In Praise of the Cognitive Emotions." Paper presented at the Annual Meeting of the American Psychiatric Association, Brooklyn College, Brooklyn, New York, 1976.

Schmidt, F. L., and W. D. Crano. "A Test of the Theory of Fluid and Crystallized Intelligence in Middle- and Low-Socioeconomic-Status Children: A Cross-Lagged Panel Analysis." *Journal of Educational Psychology,* **66**:255-261 (1974).

Sears, P. S. "The Terman Studies of Genius, 1922-1972." In A.H. Passow, ed., *The Gifted and the Talented: Their Education and Development,* pp. 75-96. The Seventy-eighth Yearbook of the National Society for the Study of Education. Chicago: University of Chicago Press, 1979.

————, and A. H. Barbee. "Career and Life Satisfaction Among Terman's Gifted Women." In J.C. Stanley, W.C. George, and C.H. Solano, eds., *The Gifted and the Creative: A Fifty-Year Perspective*, pp. 28-65. Baltimore, Md.: Johns Hopkins University Press, 1977.

Sears, R. R. "Sources of Life Satisfactions of the Terman Gifted Men," *American Psychologist*, **32**:119-128 (1977).

Semke, C. W. "A Comparison of the Outcomes of Case Study Structured Group Counseling with High Ability, Underachieving Freshmen." *Dissertation Abstracts*, 29(1-A), 128 (1968).

Sharp, E. *The IQ Cult*. New York: Coward, McCann & Geoghegan, Inc., 1972.

Shaw, M. C., and J. Grubb. "Hostility and Able High School Underachievers." *Journal of Counseling Psychology*, **5**:263-266 (1958).

————, and J. T. McCuen. "The Onset of Academic Underachievement in Bright Children." *Journal of Educational Psychology*, **51**:103-106 (1960).

Sherman, J. "Mathematics, Spatial Visualization, and Related Factors: Changes in Girls and Boys, Grades 8-11." *Journal of Educational Psychology*, **72**:476-482 (1980).

Shinn, E. O. "Interest and Intelligence as Related to Achievement in Tenth Grade." *California Journal of Educational Research*, **7**:217-220 (1956).

Shouksmith, G., and J. W. Taylor. "The Effect of Counseling on the Achievement of High-Ability Pupils." *British Journal of Educational Psychology*, **34**: 51-57, (1964).

Snygg, D., and A. Coombs. *Individual Behavior*. New York: Harper Bros., 1949.

Solano, C. H. "Teacher and Pupil Stereotypes of Gifted Boys and Girls." *Talents and Gifts*, **19**:4-8 (1977).

Spearman, C. E. *Abilities of Man: Their Natures and Measurement*. New York: Macmillan Publishing Co., Inc., 1927.

Spiegel, M. R., and N. D. Bryant. "Is Speed of Processing Information Related to Intelligence and Achievement?" *Journal of Educational Psychology*, **70**:904-910 (1978).

Stankov, L. "Fluid and Crystallized Intelligence and Broad Perceptual Factors Among 11 to 12 Year Olds." *Journal of Educational Psychology*, **70**:324-334 (1978).

Stanley, J. C. "The Study of Mathematically Precocious Youth." *Gifted Child Quarterly*, **20**:246-283 (1976).

————, D. P. Keating, and L. Fox, eds. *Mathematical Talent*. Baltimore, Md.: Johns Hopkins University Press, 1974.

Stern, G. S., M. I. Stein, and B. S. Bloom. *Methods in Personality Assessment*. Glencoe, Ill.: The Free Press, 1956.

Strang, R. "Mental Hygiene of Gifted Children." In P. Witty, ed., *The Gifted Child*, pp. 131-162. Lexington, Mass.: D.C. Heath & Company, 1951.

Strodtbeck, F. L. "Family Interation, Values, and Achievement." In D. C. McClelland, A.L. Baldwin, U. Bronfenbrenner, and F.L. Strodtbeck, eds., *Talent and Society*, pp. 135-194. Princeton, N.J.: D. Van Nostrand Co., 1958.

————. "Commentary on 'Motivation to Achieve,' by Richard Alpert." In M.J. Aschner and C.E. Bish, eds., *Productive Thinking in Education*, pp. 122-127. Washington, D.C.: National Education Association, 1965.

Sumption, M. R. *Three Hundred Gifted Children*. Yonkers, N.Y.: The World Book Company, 1941.

Tannenbaum, A. J. *Adolescent Attitudes Toward Academic Brilliance. Talented Youth Project Monograph*. New York: Bureau of Publications, Teachers College, Columbia University, 1962.

Taylor, R. G. "Personality Traits and Discrepant Achievement: A Review." *Journal of*

Counseling Psychology, **11**:76-82 (1964).

Terman, L. M. *Mental and Physical Traits of a Thousand Gifted Children*. Stanford, Calif.: Stanford University Press, 1925.

————. "Scientists and Nonscientists in a Group of 800 Gifted Men." *Psychological Monographs, Vol. 68, no. 7 (whole no. 378), 1954.*

————. *Concept Mastery Test*. New York: The Psychological Corporation, 1956.

————, and M. H. Oden. *The Gifted Child Grows Up*. Stanford, Calif.: Stanford University Press, 1947.

————, and M. H. Oden. *The Gifted Group at Mid-Life*. Stanford, Calif.: Stanford University Press, 1959.

Thompson, J. M., and C. Finley. "A Further Comparison of the Intellectual Patterns of Gifted and Mentally Retarded Children." *Exceptional Children*, **29**:379-381 (1962).

Thorndike, R. L. *The Concepts of Over- and Underachievement*. New York: Bureau of Publications, Teachers College, Columbia University, 1963.

Thurstone, L. L. *Multiple Factor Analysis: A Development and Expansion of "The Vectors of the Mind"*. Chicago, Ill.: University of Chicago Press, 1947.

Thurstone, T. G. *SRA Primary Mental Abilities*. Chicago: Science Research Associates, Inc., 1958.

Tiebout, C., and N. C. Meier "Artistic Ability and General Intelligence." *Psychological Monographs*, **48**:85-94 (1936).

Trotman, F. K. "Race, IQ, and the Middle Class." *Journal of Educational Psychology*, **69**:266-273 (1977).

Tuddenham, R. D. "Theoretical Regularities and Individual Idiosyncracies." In D.R. Green, M.P. Ford, and G.B. Flamer, eds., *Measurement and Piaget*, chap. 4. New York: McGraw-Hill Book Company, 1971.

Tyler, L. E. "The Intelligence We Test—An Evolving Concept." In L.B. Resnick, ed., *The Nature of Intelligence*, pp. 13-25. New York: John Wiley & Sons, Inc., 1976.

Vaillant, G. E. *Adaptation to Life*. Boston: Little, Brown and Company, 1977.

Veldman, D. J., and J. E. Brophy. "Measuring Teacher Effects on Pupil Achievement." *Journal of Educational Psychology*, **66**:319-324 (1974).

Vernon, P. E. *The Structure of Human Abilities*. New York: John Wiley & Sons, Inc., 1950.

————. *The Structure of Human Abilities*, rev. ed. London: Methuen & Co., Ltd., 1960.

————. "Ability Factors and Environmental Influences." *American Psychologist*, **20**:723-733 (1965).

————. "The Distinctiveness of Field Independence." *Journal of Personality*, **40**:366-391 (1972).

Veroff, J. "Social Comparison and the Development of Achievement Motivation." In C.F. Smith, ed., *Achievement-Related Motives in Children*, pp. 46-101. New York: Russell Sage Foundation, 1969.

Wallach, M. A., and C. W. Wing, Jr. *The Talented Student: A Validation of the Creativity-Intelligence Distinction*. New York: Holt, Rinehart and Winston, Inc., 1969.

Warren, J. R., and P. A. Heist. "Personality Attributes of Gifted College Students." *Science*, **132**:330-337 (1960).

Webb, R. A. "Concrete and Formal Operations in Very Bright 6 to 11 Year Olds." *Human Development*, **17**:292-300 (1974).

Weber, M. *The Protestant Ethic and the Spirit of Capitalism*. New York: Charles Scribner's Sons, 1948.

Welsh, G. S. *Creativity and Intelligence: A Personality Approach*. Chapel Hill: Institute for

Research in Social Science, University of North Carolina at Chapel Hill, 1975.

Whitmore, J. R. *Giftedness, Conflict and Underachievement.* Boston: Allyn & Bacon, Inc., 1980.

Willerman, L., and M. F. Fiedler. "Infant Performance and Intellectual Precocity." *Child Development,* **45**:483-486 (1974).

————, and M. F. Fiedler. "Intellectually Precocious Preschool Children: Early Development and Later Intellectual Accomplishments." *The Journal of Genetic Psychology,* **131**:13-20 (1977).

Williams, M. F. "Acceptance and Performance Among Gifted Elementary School Children." *Educational Research Bulletin,* Vol. 37, No. 8, 1958.

Wilson, F. T. "Some Special Ability Test Scores of Gifted Children." *Pedagogical Seminary and Journal of Genetic Psychology,* **82**:59-68 (1953).

Wilson, J. A. "Some Results of an Enrichment Program for Gifted Ninth Graders." *Journal of Educational Research,* **53**:157-160 (1959).

Wilson, R. C. *The Gifted Child in Portland.* Portland, Ore.: Portland Public Schools, 1959.

Winborn, B., and L. G. Schmidt. "Effectiveness of Short-Term Group Counseling upon the Academic Achievement of Potentially Superior but Underachieving College Freshmen." *Journal of Educational Research,* **55**:169-173 (1961).

Winkler, R. C., J. J. Teigland, P. F. Munger, and G. D. Kranzler. "The Effects of Selected Counseling and Remedial Techniques on Underachieving Elementary School Students." *Journal of Counseling Psychology,* **12**:384-387 (1965).

Winterbottom, M. R. "The Relation of Childhood Training in Independence to Achievement Motivation." Unpublished doctoral dissertation. University of Michigan, Ann Arbor, Michigan, 1953.

Witkin, H. A. "A Cognitive Style Approach to Cross-Culture Research." *International Journal of Psychology,* **2**:233-250 (1967).

————, R. B. Dyk, H. F. Paterson, D. R. Goodenough, and S. A. Karp. *Psychological Differentiation.* New York: John Wiley & Sons, Inc., 1962.

————, and D. R. Goodenough. "Field Dependence and Interpersonal Behavior." *Psychological Bulletin,* **84**:661-689 (1977).

————, et al. *Personality Through Perception.* New York: Harper & Bros., 1954.

Wittmer, J. "The Effects of Counseling and Tutoring on the Attitudes and Achievement of Seventh Grade Underachievers." *The School Counselor,* **16**:287-290 (1969).

Witty, P. A. *A Study of One Hundred Gifted Children.* Lawrence, Kans.: Bureau of School Service and Research, 1930.

————, and H. C. Lehman. "Instability and Genius: Some Conflicting Opinions." *Journal of Abnormal and Social Psychology,* **24**:486-497 (1930).

Wolf, R. "The Measurement of Environments." In A. Anastasi, ed., *Testing Problems in Perspective,* rev. ed., pp. 491-503. Washington, D.C.: Council on Education, 1966.

Worcester, D. A., *The Education of Children of Above Average Mentality.* Lincoln: University of Nebraska Press, 1955.

Zander, A., and E. Van Egmond. "Relationship of Intelligence and Social Power to the Interpersonal Behavior of Children." *Journal of Educational Psychology,* **49**:257-268 (1958).

Zborowski, M., and E. Herzog. *Life Is with People: The Culture of the Shtetl.* New York: Schocken Books, Inc., 1952.

Zigler, E. "A Measure in Search of a Theory?" *Contemporary Psychology,* **8**:133-135 (1963).

————, and P. K. Trickett. "IQ, Social Competence, and Evaluation of Early Childhood

Intervention Programs." *American Psychologist*, **33**:789-796 (1978).

Zilli, M. C. "Reasons Why the Gifted Adolescent Underachieves and Some of the Implications of Guidance and Counseling to This Problem." *Gifted Child Quarterly*, **15**:279-292 (1971).

Ziv, A. *Counselling the Intellectually Gifted Child*. Toronto: The Governing Council of the University of Toronto, 1977.

Zorbaugh, H., R. K. Boardman, and P. Sheldon. "Some Observations of Highly Gifted Children." In P. Witty, ed., *The Gifted Child*, pp. 86-105. Lexington, Mass.: D.C. Heath & Company, 1951.

PART IV

Creativity: A Tantalizing Phenomenon

A funny thing happens to some scholars on their way to forums on creativity— they become victims of enchantment. Scientists who ordinarily analyze other psychological phenomena, such as "intelligence" or "motivation," in measured, prosaic language suddenly become grandiloquent in referring to creative persons, processes, and products. Instead of dealing with creativity as an *objectively* describable construct, they tend to approach it *projectively*, as if to a Rorschach-type figure, and respond with all kinds of protean images. Occasionally, the sentiment is so florid that it borders on hyperbole. Consider, for example, the following definition:

Creativity, as the unique combination of elements of meaning and significance ... is the searching for and finding of the definite, valid expression in time and space and yet the eternal doubt about and dissatisfaction with the validity and definiteness of this very expression. . . . [It] is the very symbol of the fusion of heterogeneous elements, of the irreducibility of innumerable variables, of the union between subjective action . . . and objective worth. In his creativity, man poses the question of the meaning of existence, of his existence and of existence in general. By his creativity he attempts to provide the answers, reaching for the unreachable, expressing the inexpressible, displaying in the creative act the defeat of his resourcefulness and the triumph of his limitations. (Hacker, 1965, p. 35)

Hacker's perspective may be breathtaking, but he is not alone in glorifying the awesome power of creativity. In his *Study of History* (1934), Toynbee regards creative activity as nothing less than a life-sustaining force of civilization. Creative individuals who respond successfully to the challenges of history in each era can "rescue" society from what would otherwise be an inevitable life cycle of infancy, youth, maturity, and decay, similar to that of biological organisms. Toynbee's optimism about the capacity of society to *sustain* life indefinitely through the efforts of its greatest minds is as much a tribute to human intellect as is Hacker's confidence in humankind's potential to *understand* life. Both Toynbee and Hacker are referring to near-miracles that can be wrought by the process of creative thinking, which is sometimes equated with mobilizing mental resources totally and employing them to their fullest extent.

As one researcher (Ghiselin, 1963) suggests, creativity is an exercise of the configurative powers of the *whole* psyche, involving *all* its substance and the play of its *entire* energy. From his psychoanalytic orientation, Storr (1972) attaches equally profound importance to creativity in making life's experiences not only fathomable but livable as well. He sees a natural split between the inner and outer worlds of human beings, and the need to bridge that gap is the source of creative endeavor. No wonder that Gutman (1961) places this kind of behavior at the very top of his hierarchy of intelligent activity, declaring it the means "by which man imposes a new order upon his environment" (p. 421).

Chapter 12

Theories of Creativity

The sententious statements made about creativity reveal much about the significance of the phenomenon but little about its essence. Nothing is nobler in human nature than the mind working at full capacity, in the way it contemplates, innovates, and communicates. These qualities are universally revered because they represent the outer reaches of intelligent thought and action, setting humans apart from all other living creatures. If such is the heady stuff out of which creativity is made, it deserves to be viewed both telescopically and microscopically. The advantage of a distant perspective is that it makes the big picture intelligible and prevents us from becoming distracted by trivia. It certainly enables us to appreciate why people react to creativity with so much fervor. On the other hand, close-up magnification from all angles particularizes the elements in some detail, thus revealing the complexities as they exist. It is therefore useful to examine the various dimensions of creativity, its development, the mental processes that characterize it, its measurement, and the conditions for cultivating it.

MULTIFACET THEORIES

According to Anderson (1965), creativity represents the emergence of something unique and original. With this assumption in mind, he offers ten propositions about the dynamics of creative activity, as follows:

1. *Creativity as product and as process.* The traditional emphasis on a tangibly original product, such as a painting, sculpture, sonnet, or invention, tends to draw attention away from the way in which these works come into being. Creativity should be understood not only as an outcome of human endeavor but also as the endeavor itself. While the product can be described, discussed, and admired, the process is usually obscure, even to the person in the act of creating. It is important that we try to understand whatever phases of planning activity seem to be fairly consistent among people engaged in important original work.

2. *Creativity as a quality of protoplasm.* The quality of uniqueness, which is so important to the creative act, exists in every biological element. The cell, which is the essence of life itself, is unique in the sense that no two cells are identical. The same is true for human beings, each of whom consists of an aggregate of cells that are unlike each other and unlike those of any other human being. "As an individual interacting with other humans in his environment, he is a moving, growing, changing, flowing uniqueness. As is true for his cells, the uniqueness of his total organization and harmony of purpose, or integration, with other humans are basic necessities for his optimum development" (p. 47).

3. *Creativity as spontaneous behavior.* Creative activity is an expression of individual differences and originality. It emerges from the person's own perceiving, thinking, knowing, feeling, and acting. These processes are relatively free of environmental threat or coercion and are therefore spontaneous. In fact, the extent to which creativity can emerge depends on the degree of the absence of threat or coercion from the environment.

4. *Creativity as harmonious interacting at a social level.* "Under-the-skin" individuality is important, but it also has to be understood in the way in which it interacts with the environment. This kind of rapport can be accomplished when the individual feels secure and engages others in a "mutual and reciprocal interweaving of spontaneities . . . and free interplay of differences" (p. 48).

5. *Creativity in the moment of now.* It is impossible to define, describe, or predict a creative product until it has been completed. But while the product exists only in the closed past, the process takes place in the instantaneous present. Completing an innovative work means reaching closure in a series of plans, experiences, and acts. But the process continues as the person functions constantly in the nonrepeatable edge of time between the historic past and the unborn future.

6. *The product of creativity exists only in the past.* Our vast storehouses of knowledge and invention are legacies of creative activity that has already been exercised. As Einstein was arriving at his famous formula for energy, he was living through a particular creative experience. Once his famous equation was produced, it could be validated, evaluated, reproduced, and recorded by others, thus adding it to society's bank of ideas. The arts and sciences are generally treasures of the creative moments of individuals whose work is acknowledged for its excellence. Such moments cannot be relived even by those who appreciate the product for what it is worth, nor is it easy to judge from the product precisely what kinds of struggle, imagination, frustration, persistence, and endurance were involved in creating it. In fact, the created product often gives the illusion of being simple enough to have been produced without effort.

7. *Creativity is based upon an awareness of the past.* Reports describing the work of creative people consistently suggest that the process of producing something novel and valuable is enhanced by solid knowledge and experience, along with special skills, dedication, and hard work. But applying answers of the past to problems of the present results in stereotypes rather than creativity. The creative individual reorganizes the past in order to interact spontaneously with conditions of the present. This is how old knowledge paves the way to new understanding.

8. *Creativity as a developmental process.* At birth, the infant interacts freely with the environment. This uninhibited interplay continues through the early years of life as children become curious investigators, experimenters, explorers, improvisors, and inventors. They are refreshingly open-minded and adventuresome and seem to be interested in practically everything that touches their five senses. But as they develop their ability to communicate and to become more mobile, the human environment closes in on them with a complicated system of demands, taboos, and requirements for acculturation. Then come the rules and routines of the school, with special attention to a curriculum that encourages mastery of old ideas and the development of new ones. Small wonder that in early childhood creativity is universal, and by the time a person reaches adulthood there are many social constraints that have an inhibiting effect on the playful, innovative mind.

9. *Creativity embraces a wide range of activities.* It is therefore found in varying degrees in all people of all ages. There is no need to worry that by meaning everything creativity signifies nothing. Rather, it resembles the concept of learning that does not lose its significance despite the many ways in which it is characterized. In the last analysis, creativity as a process is important in that it represents the essence of life itself.

10. *Creativity emerges from the depths of the unconscious.* Poets, scientists, and artists often report that consciousness by itself is inadequate in producing works of lasting value. There is also a need to elicit truth from the unconscious self and to formalize its beauty and harmony. The external world is often intolerant of ideas that spring out of a person's inner being, and the result is that individual integrity is sacrificed for a veneer of conformity. Moments of inspiration require casting off the irrelevancies of the culture to allow unconscious truths to reach the surface of awareness, because "creativity is to live truthfully" (p. 51).

Anderson's many-sided view of creativity suggests that consciousness and subconsciousness are somehow catalyzed through sheer inspiration in response to the challenge of human experience. The product of a creative act, then, provides contemporaries with insight into what is unique and enduring in the mind of its creator as well as in the temper of the times in which creativity is exercised. But the psychological processes leading to such an act are not yet understood. Nor do we know what neurochemical and neurophysiological changes occur in artists, composers, inventors, playwrights, and poets during their creative states. Perhaps because the seminal mind is at once so precious and mysterious, there has been wide-open speculation about its exact nature.

A Classification of Characteristics

In her review of theories of creativity, Clark (1979) suggests that it has been characterized in four ways: (1) thinking, (2) intuiting, (3) feeling, and (4) sensing—and she encompasses these views in the form of a circle (as shown in Figure 12-1).

Those who perceive creativity as a function of *rational thinking* tend to describe it as a separate entity from what is popularly known as general intelligence. Guilford (1959) suggests that it be seen as a group of divergent thinking abilities requiring such special aptitudes as fluency, flexibility, originality of thought, sensitivity to problems, and skills in redefining and elaborating on existing ideas. Torrance (1962) regards creativity as "the process of sensing gaps or disturbing missing elements; forming new hypotheses and communicating the results, possibly modifying and retesting the hypotheses" (p.16). Parnes (1967) sees it as a function of knowledge and imagination, with the underlying processes involving the abilities to *find* facts, problems, ideas, solutions, and the acceptance of solutions. Similarly, Williams (1968) emphasizes the importance of knowledge, along with mental processes based on cognition, divergent-productive and associative thinking, evaluative behaviors, and communicative skills.

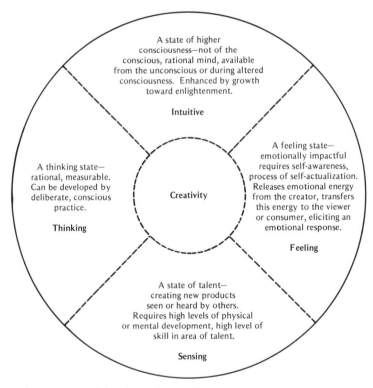

Figure 12-1 Clark's creativity circle (Clark, 1979, p. 245)

In general, creative individuals may be described as having the following *rational* attributes:

—self-disciplined, independent, often anti-authoritarian.
—zany sense of humor.
—able to resist group pressure, a strategy developed early.
—more adaptable.
—more adventurous.
—greater tolerance for ambiguity and discomfort.
—little tolerance for boredom.
—preference for complexity, asymmetry, open-endedness.
—high in divergent thinking ability.
—high in memory, good attention to detail.
—broad knowledge background.
—need think periods.
—need supportive climate, sensitive to environment.
—need recognition, opportunity to share.
—high aesthetic values, good aesthetic judgment.
—freer in developing sex role integration; lack of stereotypical male, female identification.
  (Clark, 1979, p. 248)

The *intuitive* approach to creativity emphasizes irrationality and the mechanisms of exploring the unconscious and subconscious states of mind. Clark (1979) cites various researchers who "examine the use of drugs, trances, hypnotism, meditation, chanting, dreams, fantasies, and daydreams for clues to lead to the intuitive, creative spark" (p. 257). Prominent among them is Krippner (1968) who regards alternative levels of awareness as important to the release of creative behavior. This is in essential agreement with Koestler (1964), who also suggests that conscious controls over one's own thoughts and actions may be necessary as a means of achieving self-discipline but that they can also impede creative spontaneity. Creativity at the highest levels can be accomplished only through a relaxing of controls exercised by verbal logic and by dogmas that are popularly known as common sense. Taylor (1963) likewise describes the creative process as "most likely preconscious, nonverbal or preverbal, and it may involve a large sweeping, scanning, deep, diffused, free and powerful action of almost the whole mind" (p.4).

According to Clark (1979), individuals considered creative from this point of view would

—have their energy field accessible.
—have ability to tap and release unconscious and preconscious thought.
—be able to withstand being thought of as abnormal or eccentric.
—be more sensitive.
—have a richer fantasy life and greater involvement in daydreaming.
—be more enthusiastic and impulsive.
—often show abililties of synesthesia (e.g., tasting color, seeing sound, hearing smells).
—show different brain wave patterns than the less creative, especially during creative activity.

—when confronted with novelty of design, music, ideas, get excited and involved (less creative people get suspicious and hostile).

—when given a new solution to a problem, get enthused, suggest other ideas, overlook details and problems (less creative students analyze the defect rather than explore potentials). (Clark, p. 258)

Those who emphasize the *feeling* aspects of creativity deal primarily with emotional health and realizing one's potential as a total human being. To Maslow (1959) it denotes the self-actualizing qualities that provide meaning, purpose, and fulfillment to a person's life. Actualizing potential means more than just solving problems and making products; it also requires supreme self-understanding, a sense of mission, and a harmony among personal attributes. Similar sentiments are expressed by Rogers (1959) who also recognized people's tendencies to actualize themselves by fulfilling their potentialities as the basic source of creativity. To Fromm (1959), creativity denotes an awareness of realities in the environment and the ability to respond to them. May (1959) and Moustakas (1967) regard being creative as an intensely personal experience in which we search within ourselves and draw upon our own resources, capacities, and roots as we encounter the world.

In summarizing the views of Maslow and Fromm concerning the special nature of self-actualizers, Clark (1979) notes the following characteristics:

—a special kind of perception.

—more spontaneous and expressive.

—unfrightened by the unknown, the mysterious, the puzzling; often attracted to it.

—resolution of dichotomies, selfish and unselfish, duty and pressure, work and play, strong ego and egolessness.

—able to integrate.

—more self-accepting, less afraid about what others would say, less need for other people, lack of fear of old emotions, impulses, and thoughts.

—have more of themselves available for use, for enjoyment, for creative purposes; they waste less of their time and energy protecting themselves against themselves.

—involved in more peak experiences, integration within the person and between the person and the world, transcendence.

—capacity to be puzzled.

—ability to concentrate.

—ability to experience self as creative, as the originator of one's acts.

—willingness to be born every day.

—ability to accept conflict and tension from polarity rather than avoiding them.

—courage to let go of certainties, to be different, to be concerned with truth, to be certain of one's own feelings and thoughts and trust them. (p. 253)

Those theorists who perceive creativity from a *sensing* perspective emphasize talent as reflected in the products of invention. Maslow (1959) believes that creative productivity can be accomplished only through self-discipline and hard work. Rogers (1959) suggests that a product qualifying as both novel and rational grows out of the uniqueness of an individual interacting with an extraordinary combination of materials, events, people, or circumstances of life. According to May (1959), creating something of value is a sign of self-actualization and represents the highest degree of emotional health. The key ingredient is inventiveness, while its objective is to reveal the profoundest truths of life.

Clark (1979) describes the inner conditions and characteristics of a creative individual from a *sensing* point of view as follows:

—openness to experience, new ideas.
—an internal locus of evaluation.
—an ability to toy with elements and concepts.
—perceiving freshly.
—concern with outside and inside worlds.
—ability to defer closure and judgment.
—ability to accept conflict and tension.
—skilled performance of the traditional arts.
—high theoretical and aesthetic values. (p. 256)

A Range of Characteristics

In his analysis of various approaches to creativity, Gowan (1971) shows how widely theories range concerning its nature and cultivation. At one extreme is the Osborn-Buffalo school, which regards as creative even such commonplace matters as knowing where to locate a light switch in order to turn on the lights in a dark room. According to this point of view, techniques for creative problem solving are basically rational and pragmatic and can be taught to anyone. At the other extreme, there is the psychedelic point of view that sees superrational powers in creativity summoned through the use of psychedelia, hypnosis, religious or meditational exercises, drugs, mysticism, and the like. However, Gowan notes that, regardless of what meaning is attached to creativity, it is a "turn-on" phenomenon and cannot be developed fully without careful stimulation and nurturance.

In his survey of the literature on creativity, he found five characterizations of creative personalities along the rational-psychedelic continuum, as follows: (1) the cognitive, rational, and semantic problem-solving views represented by Osborn (1953) and Guilford (1967); (2) theories focusing on personality traits and environmental conditions, with special emphasis on such characteristics as originality, energy, and positive self-concept, along with focus on child-rearing practices; (3) the mental health views of Maslow (1954,1959) and Rogers (1959), which deal mostly with self-actualization and openness to experience; (4) psychoanalytic theories dealing with oedipal conflicts, pleasure, and the preconscious (Kubie, 1958); and (5) the psychedelic view, which emphasizes existential, nonrational, and cosmic consciousness factors (Tart, 1969).

Antonymous Characteristics

Some theorists believe that creativity is a matter of inner conflict resolution. Contrasting impulses push a person's beliefs and behaviors in opposite directions, thus causing tensions that have to be pacified. The creative individual is one who

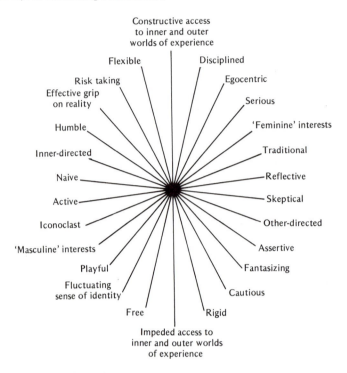

Figure 12-2 The roots of creativity (Austin, 1978, p. 116)

possesses these conflicts and is able to balance them rather than settle for a compromise between the extremes.

There are many pairs of antithetical traits that figure in creativity; taken together, they provide a comprehensive description of the processes involved. Bruner (1960) refers to the reconciliation of such paradoxical variables as detachment and commitment, passion and decorum, and immediacy and deferral. Schachtel (1959) notes the contrast between autocentrism, with the accompanying need to reduce tension, as against allocentrism, with its urge to sustain it. According to Maslow (1954), the individual's progress toward self-actualization requires a balance between defense and growth as well as safety and venturesomeness. Jung (1971) also perceives creativity as a reconciliation of opposites: conscious-unconscious, rational-irrational, sensation-intuition, thinking-feeling, extroversion-introversion, and collectiveness-individualism. From a different psychodynamic point of view, Rank (1932) distinguishes between two traumas that dominate the human personality. There is the trauma of birth brought on by separation from the womb, which in turn, produces fear of independence, of conspicuousness in the crowd and the burdens of life itself, and a craving for a return to the safety and nurturance of the womb. Conversely, there is the trauma of death, or the fear of anonymity and the failure to leave any trace of self through a creative act.

In illustrating the inner contradictions that seem to characterize a creative personality, Austin (1978) depicts a series of crosswires stretched tautly by opposing forces (see Figure 12-2). The opposing traits balance each other, and each of them figures in some way in creative activity. To perform creatively, a person has to live with these centrifugal forces and achieve some kind of balance among them.

Rothenberg (1979) describes the cognitive tensions between antithetical ideas as "janusian thinking," after Janus, the Roman deity who was variously portrayed as having two, four, or six faces and was therefore capable of looking in various directions at the same time. As a cognitive process, janusian thinking denotes a person's capacity to conceive and utilize several opposite or contradictory ideas, concepts, or images simultaneously. It can be accomplished only through a creative leap that reaches beyond the boundaries of conventional logic. What emerges is not simply a blending of antagonistic elements but, rather, a newly conceived coexistence among them. This kind of thought process operates in various domains of creativity, including the visual arts, literature, music, science, and philosophy. Rothenberg justifies his theory through studies of the work and testimony of more than fifty creative artists and scientists, some of whom had already achieved immortality. In the course of interviewing some subjects and examining biographical records of others, he discovered that janusian thinking appears at crucial points in the development of great works, but rarely in the final products per se. For example, in the course of developing his theory of relativity, Einstein made the startling observation that, if a person falling from a roof of a house releases some objects, the objects will remain in a state of rest relative to the person in the course of descent. He then concluded that the person recognizes no gravitational field in the course of falling and is therefore in a state of rest and motion at the same time. Einstein regarded this flash of insight as the happiest thought of his life since it led to the kinds of complex formulations that resulted in his great scientific breakthrough.

In Eugene O'Neill's play *The Iceman Cometh,* Rothenberg recognizes three contradictory identities: the Iceman is death, Christ, and a sexually potent adulterer. Contradictions figure also in the discovery of the double helix, in the successive sketches of Picasso's mural, *Guernica,* and in the works of da Vinci, Van Gogh, Mozart, and Conrad. These creative thinkers did not achieve greatness simply by associating incompatible elements; instead, they perceived the contradictions in a new way and then allowed themselves to conceive the inconceivable. In janusian thinking, much depends on which opposites are selected and what is made of them. Creative artists deal with those antitheses that reflect personal as well as universal meanings, experiences, and sensitivities. Scientists deal with contradictions that are derived from the world of natural events and are significant at a particular time in the development of theory and knowledge.

UNIFACET THEORIES

The comprehensive views of creativity illustrate how the concept can be approached by theorists representing different fields of inquiry. No attempt has been made to synthesize these orientations and to emerge with anything resembling a unified theory. Indeed, it may be futile to search for such a synthesis. Perhaps creativity is not a single *phenomenon* with different facets or dimensions, but rather a single *term* meaning entirely different things to different people. Either way, it is important to examine separately some of the vantage points from which creativity is perceived and interpreted.

Psychoanalytic Views

In some of his earliest writing, Freud (1908) developed a concept of sublimation from his studies of writers and artists, especially Leonardo da Vinci. Sublimation, or the ability to divert sexual energy in other directions, is a powerful facilitator of creative activity. According to Freud, persons who are frustrated in their pursuit of sexual gratification and other instinctual goals may fulfill these needs by turning to fantasy and shaping it into a new reality. Later, Freud (1915) extended his view of sublimation as figuring prominently not only in the individual's creative process but also in the evolution of a culture. To him, sublimation enabled higher mental processes to advance scientific, artistic, and ideological activities and thereby make important contributions to civilization as a whole. Also contributing to his understanding of creativity was the notion that it originates within rather than outside the individual and that it reflects unconscious imagery after it is monitored and modified by the ego.

Jung (1971) also recognized the function of the unconscious as a source of creative thinking, but not the only one. He saw the process occur in two modes: the visionary and the psychological. Of the two, Jung was far more concerned about the visionary mode, which yields creative ideas from what he called "the collective unconscious," a source of primordial memories originating in the forgotten past and transmitted from generation to generation. These experiences are not alway understandable, but they are reawakened and find expression in a great work of art. They infuse the masterpiece with substance that transcends its creator's personality or the historical period in which it is conceived. By thus resisting adaptation to the environment and relying instead on inner resources, the creative individual is able to invest a work of art with universal significance rather than anchor it in the here and now.

In the psychological mode, creative products are drawn from human consciousness as it relates to people, places, ideas, events, and emotions. Here, creativity is drawn from a person's active encounter with the world rather than from atavistic impulses that surface involuntarily. In short, the psychological mode deals with the realm of the understandable and directs creative activity toward conscious, purposeful goals.

In a movement away from Freud's and Jung's strong emphasis on the unconscious, Kris (1952) placed greater importance on ego psychology in understanding the creative process. The key to creativeness is a relaxation, or regression, of ego functions. Ego regression is prominent both in psychotic and creative behavior, but there is a fundamental difference in these processes. In creativity, regression services the ego, which overwhelms the id, whereas psychotic episodes result from an inability to keep primary processes in check, as the id overwhelms the ego. Schafer (1958) expands on Kris's theory by describing psychological factors that facilitate and inhibit creative regression. Favorable conditions include a secure sense of self, a relative mastery of early trauma, relative flexibility of defenses and controls, a history of adequate trust in interpersonal relations, and a self-awareness that facilitates effective communication with others. Hampering conditions include the ego's failure to function autonomously because of pressure from the id, and the superego's suppression of fantasy life that is so necessary for regression in the service of the ego.

Kubie (1958) goes so far as to deny the importance of unconscious forces in contributing to creativity; if anything, their effect may be negative. Instead, he argues that the essential ingredient is preconsciousness that is influenced by conscious processes, or reality, as well as unconscious forces. Neither conscious nor unconscious forces can have a direct, positive influence on creativity since both are too rigid to allow freedom for the imagination.

Humanistic Theory

Although humanism owes much to psychoanalytic thought, it rejects Freud's notion that creativity can stem from psychopathological origins in the psyche. Instead, humanists see mental health as the source of creative impulses. They generally believe in the basic goodness of human beings but regard society's pressures as posing a threat to human virtues. This optimistic view about the nature of humankind carries with it the belief that every person possesses creative potential that can be fulfilled through self-actualization. According to Maslow (1959), self-actualizing creative people are distinguishable by their independence, autonomy, and self-directedness. They overcome their fear of learning about their inner selves and can function independently in a society that attempts to control and regulate their behavior.

Rogers (1959) considers human autonomy and resistance to excessive social controls as necessary conditions for creative activity. He points out that

the mainspring of creativity appears to be the same tendency which we discover so deeply as the curative force in psychotherapy—*man's tendency to actualize himself, to become his potentialities.* By this I mean . . . the urge to expand, extend, develop, mature, the tendency to express and activate all the capacities of the organism, to the extent that such activation enhances the organism or the self. (p. 72).

Creativity, therefore, requires an openness to experience, an internal locus of evaluation, and a facility for toying with ideas. Society can encourage creative endeavor by accepting the individual unconditionally and free of external critical evaluation. As Moustakas (1967) suggests, the creative individual is oriented toward the future and faces it in a constant state of "becoming," which means acting with self-determination in the course of growth and development.

Humanists often regard creativity as resulting from a mutually beneficial interaction between the person and the environment. For example, Rogers (1959) who seems to infuse his humanistic theories with a strong social consciousness, characterizes creativity as an "emergence in action of a novel relational product, growing out of the uniqueness of the individual on the one hand, and the materials, events, people, or circumstances of his life on the other" (p. 71). Although Rogers recognizes the inner drive toward self-actualization as the propelling force toward creativity, he is also aware that society has to provide the latitude and freedom for creative persons to explore new ideas. Moreover, he believes that "unless man can make new and original adaptations to his environment as rapidly as his science can change his environment, our culture will perish" (p. 70). Rogers's vision of persons reaching toward the ultimate goal of self-actualization with the help of a supportive environment is compatible with Adler's (Ansbacher and Ansbacher, 1956) belief that creative power is the force within an individual that dominates every other aspect of personality. Creativity makes life meaningful by positing its goals and the ways of attaining them. The ultimate objective is to bring forth a perfect society, and this can be accomplished only if the self is sensitive to its surroundings and uses its creative powers altruistically. This dedication to perfecting self and society is described eloquently by Arieti (1976):

> [Creativity] may be explained in terms of a complicated neurology susceptible of infinite combinations. It may be interpreted . . . as the function of a finite center that tends toward infinity. Man alone is aware of his finitude and of the infinite, and of his need to cope with both. When he tries to decrease the unknown with his creativity, he remains surrounded by transcendence, mystery, . . . He runs and runs toward an ultimate goal which always escapes.
>
> Is this another version of the myth of Sisyphus? Is man doomed forever to roll heavy stones to the summits of mountains . . .? The answer is no. Contrary to Sisyphus, the creative man does not start from the foot of the mountain again, but from where other people have left off. It is true that the infinite cannot be conquered, and therefore even when he reaches the peak of a mountain with his heavy burden, he will discover that there are other and higher mountains to climb. But another human being will take over the task. Creative man is Sisyphus in reverse, and has to climb and climb and climb *ad infinitum*. The infinity is not in time only, but within the goal itself. . . .
>
> Sisyphus-in-reverse is not at all like the greedy king of Corinth of the old myth. Whatever he gets, he gives to others; whatever he gives to others, he retains. Although he will not reach the peak of the ultimate mountain, the horizons that open before his eyes are vaster and vaster. And he rejoices in his heart, knowing that his labor has not been in vain, since those horizons will be shared by millions of brothers and sisters, not just today, but as long as people will live on earth.
>
> Thus, what remained unfinished as a cognitive ascent finds an end as an act of social love. (pp. 413-414)

Social Perspectives

According to Rogers (1959), the best social milieu for creativity is a permissive one. Murphy (1958) describes what he calls "creative eras" as periods of history in which pressures toward conformity were at a minimum and individuality was encouraged. In such times and places, people were fairly isolated from surrounding status-striving societies, thus allowing for the emergence of immortal works of art, social philosophies, and political structures. Murphy points to ancient Athens and India as well as to the European renaissance as examples of the historical flowering of great ideas. Mead (1959) dealt with the effects of freedom and the control of creativity from an anthropological point of view. From her studies of the Samoan, Manus, Arapesh, and Bali cultures she concluded that creativity was affected by variations in the degrees of social control exercised among these groups.

But a permissive environment is not enough to encourage innovativeness and a free flow of ideas; there also have to be active influences in the person's milieu, especially during childhood. In his study of famous musicians and athletes, Pressey (1955) discovered conditions for facilitating creativity that were consistent in every subjects's environment. First, the musicians and athletes under study spent their early years in the company of family and friends who encouraged them to develop their skills. Second, special instruction and guidance came early in life, and the quality of educational experiences was consistently superior. Third, there was opportunity for the precocious children to practice their skills as much as necessary and to progress at their own pace. Fourth, the children had extensive contact with people who shared their interests and who could participate in their creative activities. Finally, as the children grew older, they received accolades for their accomplishments from a steadily widening audience that constantly stimulated them to reach new heights of creativity. These conclusions were later confirmed in a study of 120 individuals renowned for their excellence in artistic, cognitive, and psychomotor fields by the age of 35 (Bloom and Sosniak, 1981).

With respect to the broad social and political forces and their effect on talent fruition, there is a popular belief that the gifted can best realize their potential in a culture where they are accepted and where their work is encouraged unconditionally. Who would deny that it is far more reasonable for a golden age to emerge out of freedom in Athens than out of oppression in Sparta? The argument is persuasive because it is both logical and morally compelling. It makes sense for a supportive society to be the best possible cradle for creativity; more than that, such a society *deserves* to benefit best from its creative minds. But the fact is that wishing and expecting assumptions to be confirmed objectively is no guarantee that they can be.

The work of artists and scientists has achieved world renown under the worst of tyrannies, even in Stalinist Russia and Hitler Germany. In some cases, as with Werner von Braun, the Nazi regime encouraged creativity in science, provided that it helped to produce a miracle weapon to use against the enemy. In communist Russia, Shostakovitch was allowed to create his own idiom as a composer so long as he did not pander to what tastemakers in his country considered decadent bourgeois inclinations. More remarkable still is the galaxy of great minds that achieved immortality despite suffering the worst possible persecution under despots in many countries and periods of history.

What seems to be critical in the release of creative potential is nurturance from people who touch the gifted child's life directly, not the political and social powers who are relatively remote from the scene. It is always difficult, and often impossible for a dictator to stifle the influence of individuals who can inspire and guide the young to fulfill themselves creatively. There are also creative individuals who are loyal to despotism and dedicate themselves to enhance it through their productivity or performance. Generally speaking, it would be naive to assume that creativity could only thrive in a laissez-faire atmosphere. The fact is that constraints are often placed on the gifted, even in a free society, as evidenced by those who work frequently under some kind of patronage. Benefactors who can afford to pay individuals to create "on order" influence not only the nature of personal accomplishment but public taste as well. How much do we owe Lorenzo Medici for Michaelangelo's art? Could "Papa" Haydn have been as prolific as he was and composed the kind of music that he did if he were not satisfying the tastes of the Esterhazy family? What does it mean to be freely creative when a patron can regulate the quantity and style of an artist's work without seeming to diminish its quality? It seems paradoxical that whoever commissions a new work of art, sponsors an exhibit, or produces a stage performance can simultaneously control and release extraordinary human potential. Patrons and artists interact in mysterious ways, and the interpersonal "chemistry" between them attests to their need for each other.

Personal Attribute Theory

It is sometimes convenient to think of "creativity" as a unitary construct consisting of some kind of broad, indivisible characteristic. However, Guilford and Merrifield (1960) argue that it is a composite of separable aptitudes and possibly some nonaptitude traits of personality. Based on his Structure of Intellect model, Guilford (1975) hypothesizes four creative thinking abilities: fluency, flexibility, originality, and elaboration. The element of operation for all these abililties is basically divergent, and it can apply theoretically to all content areas, although most of the interest thus far has focused on semantics. Even within the semantic domain, children can excel in any one of the functions (i.e., fluency, flexibility, originality, elaboration) while failing to distinguish themselves in any of the others.

Fluency. All divergent production tests are essentially assessments of *fluency*, each of which lends itself to measurement and evaluation. *Ideational fluency* (divergent semantic units) denotes the ability to generate quantities of ideas in response to problem-solving situations. Examples of this competency include skills in writing large numbers of acceptable plot titles for untitled literary works and imagining many consequences of a change in the environment or in the conditions of life. *Associational fluency* (divergent semantic relations) is the ability to produce many relationships or meaningful associations to a given idea. It is evidenced by the quantity of synonyms a person can attach to any familiar word that has many meanings. *Expressional fluency* (divergent semantic systems) refers to skills in juxtaposing words to meet sentence structure requirements. A person who excels in such tasks is able, for example, to write many sentences while being limited to a uniform number of words and a single set of initial letters for the words in each sentence.

Flexibility. *Flexibility* denotes the skill to discontinue an existing pattern of thought and shift to new patterns. Two subskills can be recognized, each having a different content and product. *Spontaneous flexibility* (divergent semantic classes) deals with changes in direction of thinking when a person is not instructed to do so. For example, in listing the various uses of a brick, the flexible individual tends to produce ideas relating not only to the weight of the object but also to its size, color, shape, texture, and so on. *Adaptive flexibility* (divergent figural transformations) also deals with changes in direction of thinking to solve problems. However, in this case, the content is figural, such as geometric forms that the person uses to make as many objects as possible or match sticks arranged in a design that has to be altered in a specific way by removing a given number of matches, and in some cases *any* number. Another example of adaptive flexibility is planning air maneuvers, which requires the person to indicate the most efficient path in "sky-writing" letter combinations.

Originality. *Originality* (divergent semantic transformations) resembles ideational fluency, except that here the emphasis is on products that are offbeat, unexpected, and sometimes amusing. For example, the "consequences" problem is intended to elicit responses that are either indirectly or remotely associated with a given problem situation. For plot titles, what counts is the number of responses judged to be clever, witty, and pithy.

Elaboration. *Elaboration* (divergent semantic implications) is relevant to skills in planning and organization. For example, the person demonstrates the ability to fill in all the various details necessary to make a briefly outlined activity, such as preparing to mount a stage play effectively.

Guilford (1959) emphasizes the importance of nonintellective traits in creativity, too. The prominent ones include exceptional interest in exercises in convergent and divergent thinking processes, aesthetic appreciation and expression, tolerance of ambiguity, and reflective, rigorous, and autistic thinking. Individuals who perform well on tests of associational fluency tend to seek out adventurous experiences and are extraordinarily capable of tolerating ambiguity. Those who score high in ideational fluency are likely to be more impulsive, more ascendant, and more self-confident. They also have an unusually high appreciation of creativity. Expressional fluency tends to be associated with fairly high amounts of impulsivity, an appreciation of aesthetic expressiveness, and a tendency to enjoy reflective thinking. A person characterized as original tends to possess more self-confidence and a tolerance of ambiguity and enjoys reflective and divergent thinking as well as aesthetic expression. However, contrary to expectation, such an individual is not necessarily inclined to adopt attitudes of unconventionality or to reject cultural conformity any more than most people do.

Guilford also cites evidence to show that people high in spontaneous flexibility are likely to have a strong need for variety and to be free from perseveration in solving problems. Adaptive flexibility reflects a freedom from persistent uses of previously learned, futile approaches to the search for solutions. "This raises the question as to whether the flexibility-rigidity factors in thinking should be classified in the modality of aptitudes or in the modality of temperament traits or whether in these instances we have traits with both temperamental and aptitudinal aspects, depending upon how one looks at them" (Guilford, 1959, p. 150).

The issue has wide ramifications that extend far beyond the meaning of flexibility and pertain even to such global concepts as creativity and giftedness. It is surely easier and far more popular to treat these phenomena as purely intellective powers, ignoring the emotional, attitudinal, motivational, learning style, and life-style elements inherent in them. Measures of cognitive functioning cannot help but be "contaminated" by nonintellective variables. "Purifying" the test so that it focuses only on cognition will only restrict the scope of its portrayal in relation to the total picture. There is no question about the presence of nonintellective factors in any kind of high-level performance or productivity. What has to be resolved about creative behavior, however, is a question similar to the one Guilford poses for flexibility. Is it a special kind of ability, different from all others, or is it a combination of idiosyncratic "temperament traits" that differentiate this type of giftedness from any other?

Barron's (1963a) hypotheses concerning the nature of creativity clearly emphasize the importance of nonintellective characteristics. According to him, (1) creative people have exceptionally good observational powers; (2) they are content to express only part-truths; (3) they tend to see things not only as other people do but also as others do not; (4) they value the fact that their cognitive faculties are independent; (5) their achievement is motivated by their special talents and values; (6) since they are capable of handling several ideas simultaneously, it is possible for them to make extraordinary comparisons and syntheses of ideas; (7) sexually as well as physically, they are more vigorous and more sensitive; (8) their lives are more complex and they see the universe as exceedingly complex; (9) they are deeply aware of their unconscious motives and fantasy life; (10) they possess strong egos that allow them to regress and return to reality; (11) sometimes they allow the distinction between subject and object to disappear; and (12) they enjoy maximum freedom of their organisms, and their creativity is a function of that freedom. The important cognitive component of creativity is the process of devising uncommon solutions or unusual adaptive responses to problems. In other words, the key intellective trait is originality, but intellect is only part of the story.

In their review of factors associated with creative performance, Taylor and Holland (1964) distinguish among the intellectual, motivational, and personality variables that are important in the creative process. Under intellect, they list memory, cognition, evaluation, convergent production, and divergent production. Motivational factors include drive for accomplishment, dedication to work, resourcefulness, striving for general principles, desire to bring order out of disorder, and the desire for discovery. Included among the personality variables are independence, self-sufficiency, tolerance for ambiguity, femininity of interests, and professional self-confidence.

Torrance (1962) also summarized investigations of traits associated with creativity, and the list he compiled includes eighty-four characteristics that differentiate between highly and moderately creative persons. It is noteworthy that some traits are desirable, others are nonconforming, and others still appear to be negative. The desirable ones include altruism, high levels of energy, industriousness, persistence, self-assertiveness, and versatility. Nonconformance is revealed through attraction to the mysterious, defiance of convention, independence of judgment and thought, odd habits, and radical beliefs. Negativism is revealed through discontentment, a tendency to disturb organization and to be a fault-finder, stubbornness, and a temperamental disposition. All in all, the adjectives that trait theorists use to describe creativity are both intellective and nonintellective, adaptive and divergent, and popular and unpopular.

Developmental Stage Theory

Gowan's (1979) synthesis of growth stage theories of Erikson, Piaget, and Freud provide what is probably the most comprehensive view of how creativity develops in the various periods of a person's maturation. According to Gowan, these stages are actually the transformation of energy from one locus of tension to another, beginning with "the world," then "I," and finally "thou" (see Figure 12-3). This represents the development of the psyche outward toward the world, then inward toward the self, and finally toward another human being with love. The sequence is from the third to the first and eventually to the second personal pronoun.

Gowan speculates that this tripartite sequence of stages is experienced in each of three major periods of a person's life. The infant, youth, and adult must all come to terms with "the world" (the infant through trust, the youth through industry, and the adult through generativity), "the ego" (first through autonomy, then identity, and finally ego-integrity), and "the other" (beginning with initiative, followed by intimacy, and perhaps culminating in "agape love,"* which, according to Gowan, embraces all of humankind). In the early stages of development, the person is immersed in the world of the senses and world experiences; later, the person experiences a period of introspection and withdrawal; last, there comes a time when the person can relate to another human being in such a way as to enable both of them to share their discoveries about themselves and about each other.

Gowan (1979) believes that creativity is born, not fostered, in the "thou" or

---

*Gowan is not sure of the existence of a developmental stage that might be characterized as "agape love," but if it does exist, then it would represent an extension of the "initiative" and "intimacy" stages during which there is a broadening of love relationships from narcissistic self-love through oedipal love of parents to a more general heterosexual love. This leads to a deeper fixation on a particular individual and finally to a love of the human family.

Attentional Modes ——→	Latency	Identity	Creativity
Developmental Levels	3. it, they The World	1. I, me The Ego	2. thou The Other
Infant — Erikson (affective) / Piaget (cognitive)	Trust vs. mistrust ① Sensorimotor vs. chaos	Autonomy vs. shame and doubt ② Preoperational vs. autism	Initiative vs. guilt ③ Intuitive vs. immobilization
Youth — Erikson (affective) / Piaget-Gowan (cognitive)	Industry vs. inferiority ④ Concrete operations vs. nonconservation	Identity vs. role diffusion ⑤ Formal operations vs. dementia praecox	Intimacy vs. isolation ⑥ Creativity vs. authoritarianism
Adult — Erikson (affective) / Gowan (cognitive)	Generativity vs. stagnation ⑦ Psychedelia vs. conventionalism	Ego-integrity vs. despair ⑧ Illumination vs. senile depression	

Figure 12-3 Gowan's periodic developmental-stage chart, incorporating theories of Erikson and Piaget (Gowan, 1979, p. 62)

"other" stage through the experience of love relationships during periods of initiative (ages 4 to 6) and intimacy (ages 18-25). In other words, a love relationship is a requisite for creativity. As Gowan states, "Love and hence creativity may enter our lives environmentally at any time, and to the degree that one is found in abundance the other is likely to be present" (p. 64). Creativity first develops when the young child (ages 4 to 6) initiates control over the environment by actively entering into an affectionate relationship with the opposite-sex parent. In the period of intimacy (ages 18-25), a similar process occurs, this time through a love relationship with a person of the opposite sex. One may conjecture that, in the final stage of "agape love," creative inspiration flows from a spirit of idealism or possibly religious fervor.

The oedipal relationship is crucial to the development of creativity. If the affection of the opposite-sex parent is full and close, then the child's fantasy conceptualization of the world becomes more distinct from the real world. Parental love and affection prevent a nightmarish fantasy from developing, which would make the child feel helpless in the environment. Gowan believes that this success in winning the affection of the opposite-sex parent provides the oedipal fantasies of this period with some semblance of reality. Thus, children who are given a sense of security and approval during their preschool years feel relatively free to delve into their preconsciousness, to play uninhibitedly, and to draw from past experiences without fear. They begin to master the differences between what exists (i.e., a strong relationship with parents) and what they long to achieve (i.e., a fantasy relationship).

The importance of love, support, approval, and encouragement of ideas and creative activities cannot be overestimated. During the initiative stage of development, gifted children may be influenced to become adaptive, conflictive, or creative, depending on the kind of stimulation that parents offer. If children become too frightened by their errors and parental admonitions, they will conform and adapt to acceptable modes of behavior; they may even become too docile to take any kind of meaningful initiative. Stronger children who persist in reaching out for new experiences without parental support become conflicted. This implies that an overly strict or disciplined environment can stifle creativity in children, forcing them either to adapt or to remain conflicted and laden with destructive feelings of guilt and shame. On the other hand, gifted children who have the love and guidance of opposite-sex parents develop their creativity freely and joyously. They have ready access to their preconscious states and are able to become more relaxed, more imaginative in their play activities, in closer touch with the earlier experiences in their lives, and mentally healthier.

Creativity not only seems to undergo stages of maturation but also shows unmistakable signs of growth during childhood, albeit at an irregular pace. Torrance (1964a) cites evidence to show that, in the United States, one peak of development is apparently reached at age 4½. It drops at age 5 when the child enters kindergarten and grows steadily through first, second, and third grades, only to decline sharply in the fourth grade. This is followed by a period of recovery, particularly among girls, in the fith and sixth grades, but there is another drop at the end of elementary school and into junior high school. Torrance feels that the shape of the developmental curve differs from one society to the next and may be affected by variations in cultural continuity.

Right and Left Brain Theory

Rapidly developing areas of theory and research on creativity relate to the special powers located in the two hemispheres of the brain. Those who have investigated existing evidence tend to believe that divergent thinking processes in its various forms can be conceptualized as aspects of the same underlying cognitive style based in the right hemisphere.

Katz (1978) notes that highly creative people become innovators by involving two kinds of thought processes: the first utilizes the right hemisphere to perceive familiar problems in a new way, rearrange old ideas, and achieve a novel synthesis; the second relies on the left hemisphere to confirm, elaborate, and communicate the earlier insight systematically. Thus, both parts of the brain are used in the process of creativity, except that each has its own "specialization," or preference for domains of knowledge and ways of appreciating and enhancing them.

The left brain regulates the critical and inquiring nature of thought. It takes major responsibility for mastery of reading, language, and mathematical computation and specializes in thinking strategies that are often described as rational, analytic, linear, and sequential. Right-hemisphere activity, on the other hand, is closely associated with creating music, art, and mathematical concepts. It deals with metaphor, synthesis, intuition, and perceptual coherence, processes that are generally associated with creativity. These discrepancies in brain activity are being noted by educators who see possible implications for changing the school curriculum.

For example, Kane and Kane (1979) argue that appropriate programs can assist a child in utilizing both brain hemispheres when they seek the best possible solutions to problems. Initial instruction, however should incorporate the child's preferred cognitive style and modality in order to facilitate easier success. Boys in the primary grades are more visually and spatially oriented and therefore require right-hemisphere stimulation, whereas girls appear to be biased toward left-hemispheric processes and should receive greater emphasis on language during instruction. The more we understand about the two parts of the brain and how they relate to each other, the easier it will be to tailor education to the strengths of children.

There is some evidence that stimulating right-hemisphere activity may enhance divergent thinking. In a study of adults who were highly susceptible to hypnosis, Gur and Rayner (1976) found that those who were hypnotized performed better than did controls on Torrance's figural tests of creativity though not on the verbal measures. Since hypnosis proved effective only with figural problems, the results are interpreted as demonstrating the effects of right-hemisphere stimulation. Another study involving hypnosis (Dave, 1979) reports further tentative evidence that this kind of treatment can help adults to overcome blocks to creative problem solving. Direct stimulation of the right hemisphere has also been atttempted through experiments with the use of marijuana. In a study of cognitive functioning as a result of smoking cannabis in the form of marijuana, eighty-four male college students participated in the experiment (Weckowicz, 1975). Some received high dosages while others were given low dosages of the drug. These groups were then compared with each other as well as with placebo and control groups. Results show relatively poor convergent thinking among those smoking cannabis, regardless of dosage. However, the low-dose smokers performed best on some tests, mainly those measuring divergent thinking. It is noteworthy, too, that the high-dose group performed worst on these tests. Here again,the results show the possibility of shifting into a different cognitive mode while altering the state of consciousness.

An entirely different approach to improving divergent thinking through stimulating right-hemisphere functioning was taken by Reynolds and Torrance (1978). Subjects consisted of two hundred high school students participating in the Career Awareness Component of the Georgia Governor's Honors Program (GHP). This group received indirect training in the context of the curriculum. Students spent two hours each day for six weeks working in their areas of specialization. The remainder of the day was taken up with interdisciplinary activities emphasizing career education, current problems, futurism, and special interest groups. Deliberate and systematic attempts were made to help students see clear relationships among the different disciplines and between their own areas of specialization and future careers.

A second sample, consisting of sixty-eight graduate students in a creative thinking course taught by Torrance received lectures and readings in creative thinking and intensive training in creative problem solving. The class met four hours each week for eleven weeks, and the students spent additional time outside class engaged in various creative experiences as part of the course. It is assumed, then, that part of the course concentrated on specialized functions of the right cerebral hemispehre.

On the first day and during the last week of their respective training sessions, both groups filled out an instrument called Your Style of Learning and Thinking (SOLAT). On the basis of these self-reports, the researchers were able to classify students according to right or left brain preferences. There were also those categorized as "integrated" (i.e., utilizing styles showing primarily cerebral complementarity in information processing) or "mixed" (i.e., showing no clear preference for any of the styles). Pre- and posttest differences showed changes in the hypothesized direction, with the high school students increasing sharply in the direction of the integrated category and the college students moving toward right-hemisphere preferences. Reynolds and Torrance conclude that it is possible to modify individuals' preferred style of learning and thinking over a relatively short period. Not only are changes possible, but apparently the general direction of change can also be controlled. These results also suggest that hemisphere preferences may be a key to creative functioning, and further tests of such an hypothesis are warranted.

Chapter 13 ─────────────────────────────

Creative Processes
and Abilities

In his classic investigation into the meaning of creative thought, Wallas (1926) cites a theory by the German physicist Helmholtz that there are three steps to developing a new idea. The first may be called *preparation*, in which a problem is investigated in every possible way. The second is the stage of *incubation*, during which no conscious thought is given to the problem, but the ideas and materials collected during the period of preparation are somehow stored below the conscious level of the psyche. They are then organized, elaborated upon, and reorganized in mysteriously new ways. Finally, there is the stage of *illumination* when the "Aha" feeling is suddenly experienced, often unexpectedly, and the creative thought emerges as if by intuition. Wallas himself adds a fourth stage, *verification*, in which the new idea is evaluated on the basis of its creator's own standards, which may be sharply different from the public's or critics' tastes.

Interestingly, the first and last steps of the process, preparation and verification, require convergent mental powers, as Guilford defines them. What is sought after initially is the only set of substances out of which the final outcome can be fashioned, and the ultimate product or performance can be judged only by criteria acceptable to the person who creates it. If these criteria are also adopted by an influential circle of critics who then apply them to the newly created work and evaluate it as excellent, it will be treasured as a masterpiece. But sandwiched between the two convergent operations that produced it are the equally important incubation and illumination stages that should probably be linked with aspects of divergent thinking. The Wallas stage theory has been tested empirically in studies of poets, artists, and scientists, and the evidence tends to substantiate it (Patrick, 1935, 1937, 1938).

In a large-scale investigation of the productive thinking of inventors, Rossman (1931) discovered a seven-step process that begins with an awareness of a problem

Table 13-1. Steps in Invention, Creative production, and problem Solving as Perceived by Rossman, Wallas, and Dewey

Rossman (1931) (invention)	Wallas (1926) (creative production)	Dewey (1910) (problem solving)
1. Observation of need or difficulty (problem situation, area of concern)		1. Felt need or difficulty observed
2. Analysis of need; problem formulated and defined		2. Difficulty or problem situation located and problem defined (formulated)
3. Survey of all available information	1. Preparation (information obtained)	
Rudimentary incubation (unconscious work) possible, depending on problem complexity		
4. Formulation of many possible (objective) solutions		3. One or more possible solutions suggested
5. Critical analysis and examination of these solutions for their advantages and disadvantages		4. Consequences considered and evaluated
Sustained and ongoing incubation (unconscious work) probable, particularly for complex problems	2. Incubation (unconscious work occurring)	
6. Birth and formulation of new ideas, invention, or solution to problem	3. Illumination (one or more solutions emerging)	
7. Testing of most promising solution and selection and perfection of final embodiment of solution by some or all of the previous steps; more or less final acceptance of revised solution	4. Verification (solutions tested, judged for appropriateness, and elaborated upon)	5. Solution accepted at least tentatively

Source: W. B. Michael, "Cognitive and Affective Components of Creativity in Mathematics and the Physical Sciences," in J. C. Stanley, W. C. George, and C. H. Solano, eds., *The Gifted and the Creative: A Fifty-Year Perspective* (Baltimore, Md.: Johns Hopkins University Press, 1977), p. 157.

and ends with validating an innovative solution. Michael (1977) notes that Rossman's steps toward invention parallel Wallas's steps toward creative production and Dewey's (1910) steps toward Problem Solving (see Table 13-1). He also finds that it resembles Guilford's (1967) Structure of Intellect problem-solving model (SIPS).

In the SIPS process a tension is created in the organism when it senses a problem arising either internally or externally. The psyche then becomes activated to filter these initial sensory inputs and to retrieve from its memory bank whatever figural, symbolic, semantic, and/or behavioral information may be relevant to the newly acquired stimuli. The effort may be terminated at this point if it is felt that no more investment is worthwhile because the problem is either negligible in importance or overwhelming in difficulty. On the other hand, if the decision is made to pursue a solution, new information is acquired, filtered, and evaluated and a more informed judgment can then be made about the gravity of the problem and what (or whether) further action should be taken. By this time, the organism can become more discriminating when it selects additional data from its internal and external environments and from what has previously been committed to memory. Having completed this winnowing process, the organism is ready to apply its convergent and/or divergent powers to put together a solution which is then tested for its viabililty. It is possible, of course, to reach closure at this point, provided that the individual is satisfied with the solution. However, there are times when the problem is so complex that additional steps have to be taken.

The next phase is a period of apparent inactivity, or incubation, during which the assembled data may be subjected to various kinds of change through redefinition or modification. In the midst of this suspended activity, a sudden flash of insight brings about a restructuring or reconceptualization of the original problem, and this in turn leads to a new solution. Finally, the evaluation process takes over to determine precisely what accomplishments were intended, how well they were realized, and whether they were worth realizing in the first place.

As a result of his extensive work in developing principles and procedures of creative problem solving, Osborn (1963) concluded that creativity is a three-step process, each step of which incorporates two substages and the process bears a close resemblence to those formulated by Wallas and Rossman. He outlines them as follows:

1. **Fact-Finding**
   Problem-Definition: Picking out and pointing up the problem.
   Preparation: Gathering and analyzing the pertinent data.
2. **Idea-Finding**
   Idea-Production: Thinking up tentative ideas as possible leads.
   Idea-Development: Selecting from resultant ideas, adding others, and pre-processing by means of modification, combination, etc.
3. **Solution-Finding**
   Evaluation: Verifying the tentative solutions by tests and otherwise.
   Adoption: Deciding on implementing the final solution. (Osborn, 1963, p. 111)

A graphic summary of what seems to be consistent in all the theories presented thus far is contained in Von Fange's (1955) illustration of the creative process (see Figure 13-1). It indicates that, when a problem is first encountered, it should be defined as well as the person's initial understanding allows it to be. There follows an investigation of various methods that could lead to a solution. Each method has to be evaluated for its practicality as well as its effectiveness in defining and addressing all dimensions of the problem. These successive trials bring the person closer to understanding and perhaps to the point where the problem can be solved.

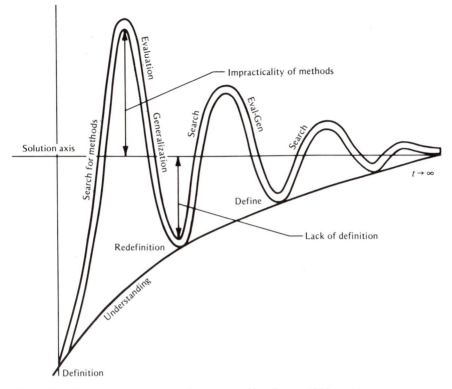

Figure 13-1 Understanding the creative process (Von Fange, 1955, p. 54)

For some problems, new circumstances arise constantly, and it is only possible to find solutions for a particular time and place, thus forcing the search-evaluation-generalization sequence to repeat itself forever.

According to Taylor (1975) the Wallas-type theory of steps toward creative accomplishment is valid, but we also have to realize that there are hierarchical levels of creativity. From lowest to highest, they arrange themselves as follows: (1) *expressive creativity*, or the development of a unique idea with no concern about its quality; (2) *technical creativity*, or proficiency in creating products with consummate skill, as in shaping a Stradivarius violin, without much evidence of expressive spontaneity; (3) *inventive creativity*, or the ingenious use of materials to develop new use of old parts and new ways of seeing old things, possibly through novel plots or cartoons or the inventions of an Edison, a Bell, and a Marconi whose products are novel and appropriate but do not represent contributions of new basic ideas; (4) *innovative creativity*, or the ability to penetrate basic foundational principles of established schools of thought and formulate innovative departures, as in the case of a Jung and Adler building their theories on Freudian psychology or a Copernicus extending and reinterpreting Ptolemaic astronomy; and (5) *emergentive creativity*, a rarely attained quality of excellence since it incorporates "the most abstract ideational principles or assumptions underlying a body of art or science" (Taylor, 1975, p. 307), as in the work of an Einstein and a Freud in science and a Picasso and a Wright in art.

Stein (1953) takes a somewhat unique approach to creative processes, apparently regarding them as comparable to what goes into scientific inquiry. Prior to taking the first step in the sequence, the person has to be (1) highly sensitive to ambiguities that constitute problems in the environment and (2) willing to live with them until they are resolved. It is then necessary to proceed through the stages of generating hypotheses on how to solve a problem, testing the hypotheses, and communicating results to others. Stein points out that the outcomes of the creative process have to be accepted as tenable or useful or satisfying for other people at some point in time. This means that even though tastes may change—and the work of creation once appreciated falls into disfavor, or once rejected by contemporaries is eventually revived with accolades, even temporarily—it still qualifies as something of value, however briefly in the history of ideas. In other words, creativity requires just a moment "in the sun," not immortality.

Useful as it is to conjecture about the processes of creativity, whatever supportive evidence we have is strictly inferential, most of it collected after a creative act has taken place. Perhaps the only attempt to observe directly what happens just *prior* to the creative act was made by Getzels and Csikszentmihalyi (1976) whose study of what they considered to be problem-finding behavior involved recording the ways in which art students selected, handled, and arranged materials that were to become subjects of their still-life drawings. But here, too, the thoughts and feelings of the artists would have to be inferred, although this time from their behaviors rather than from post hoc recollections by them or interpretations by others.

The picture could not become entirely clear unless there were *direct* evidence on changes taking place internally in the person who was about to act creatively. Some of the most important clues are probably embedded in the functions of the brain, which remain a mystery to a great extent. In effect, at this stage of brain research, we are a long way from understanding the basic mechanisms of thinking, even at its lowest levels, to say nothing of creativity with all its lofty meanings. We have yet to determine precisely what regions of the brain play a part in the organism's formulation of a new idea. When these regions are eventually discovered, there will still be a need to collect other kinds of physiological data before the creative process can be fully understood. It will be important to discover, for example, whether the organism undergoes chemical changes and shifts in blood pressure and breathing patterns at the moment of inspiration. Furthermore, does the organism function in the same special way no matter whether it is engaged in artistic, scientific, literary, or mathematical activity, so long as it is creative? Is there a similar pattern of internal functioning among all organisms that are engaged in the same kind of creative activity? As long as these questions go unanswered, there will continue to be important gaps in our knowledge of the creative process. In this case, a little bit of knowledge can be a dangerous thing if it leads to premature generalizations.

Perhaps it is unrealistic to expect that physiological changes and a sequence of stages are the same for all creative acts. Vinacke (1952) may have been correct in pointing to basic differences in the ways in which poets, artists, and playwrights, respectively, give birth to their great ideas. Any sampling of biographies and autobiographies of immortals reveals such obvious variations in their work habits and temperaments that it is hard to imagine them following the same path toward creative accomplishment. There are the tinkerers and toilers, the sloppy and the meticulous, the agonized and the tranquil, the misanthropes and altruists, all seemingly unlike each other in every way except for their success in achieving greatness. An even more serious mistake that can be made in generalizing from our limited knowledge of creative processes is to assume that they apply in the same way to children as well as adults. Too often, what is known or suspected about creativity in adults is applied uncritically to children. Yet the processes may be quite different, or even if they are the same, they may denote different qualities of intellective functioning. Perhaps Rollo May (1975) was right when he wrote, "Creativity is not merely the innocent spontaneity of our youth and childhood; it must also be married to the passion of the adult human being, which is a passion to live beyond one's death" (p. 31).

Chapter 14 _____

Problems in Assessing Creativity

Any attempt at assessing creativity is fraught with obstacles from the outset. For a test to have good face validity, its content must resemble in some way the essential phenomenon it is measuring. This would be especially difficult to demonstrate in tests of creativity, considering the multidimensionality of the concept, how it develops in the human psyche, and the mental processes involved in activating it. Before determining that a test qualifies as a measure of creativity, two obvious questions would have to be answered affirmatively. First, can we expect high scores on such a test from people who are generally regarded as creative in their fields of work? Second, if the instrument is supposed to be measuring creative potential in children, how well can it forecast the eventual fulfillment of that potential? These are standard questions, similar to those asked about measures of intelligence or of any kind of special ability.

Thus far, many so-called "creativity tests" have appeared, but validation studies are rarely reported, and in cases where studies of predictive validity have been made, the results are not yet conclusive. Petrosko (1978) analyzed over one hundred instruments for elementary school children, using thirty-six criteria of educational and psychometric quality to assess the value of these tests. The results showed that there is little information about reliability and even less evidence about their validity. Petrosko acknowledges that it is too early to judge these measures, considering the small amount of relevant empirical research conducted thus far. However, he speculates that it may be futile to expect creativity tests to meet the standards of quality advocated by measurement experts. Perhaps the main difficulty in producing such instruments is trying to standardize a way of capturing what may be considered a nonstandard behavioral product. Yet, despite the lack of substantial evidence as to the value of the instruments, there is widespread use of them in identifying giftedness in children. It is therefore important to examine some of the more popular ones, the kinds of psychological functions that they attempt to reveal, and some critical comments about them.

VALIDITY OF PERFORMANCE MEASURES

The Guilford Battery

Rekdal (1979) reports an increase in th use of biographical or personality inventories in order to locate creative-productive thinkers. Such instruments are administered primarily to adult populations. As for children, the emphasis has been on tests derived from measures of performance such as those developed by Guilford and his associates (Guilford, 1966; Merrifield et al., 1963; Merrifield et al., 1964) in their studies of the Structure of Intellect. Merrifield, Guilford, and Gershon (1963) conclude from research on sixth-graders that the special abilities associated with creativity for this age group are similar to those of creative adults, at least in the vitally important area of divergent thinking with semantic content. These childhood-adulthood similarities are also evident in the fifth- and seventh-graders (Merrifield et al., 1964). Therefore, if there is an ontogenetic differentiation of abilities during childhood, it probably occurs prior to the fifth grade. The instruments used to assess creativity in these studies include measures of *ideational fluency* (DMU), *associational fluency* (DMR), *expressional fluency* (DMS), *originality* (DMT), *sensitivity to problems* (EMI), and *conceptual foresight* (CMI). Somewhat weaker indicators are tests of *spontaneous flexibility* (DMC) and *semantic elaboration* (DMI).

Merrifield et al. (1963) also found that the factors characteristic of academic aptitude and achievement were for the most part distinguishable from the factors associated with creativity, as measured by the Guilford battery. This would seem to indicate that current tests of mental age used for assessing scholastic potential reveal at best only some dimensions of individual differences, at least at the fifth grade level and higher. The question of whether these results are generally confirmed by other studies is part of the broader issue concerning the relationship between tested creativity and tested intelligence and will be discussed later (See pp. 283-293). However, for our present purposes of understanding Guilford's measures of creativity, it is important to inquire about the intercorrelations among the separate tests in his battery. If the scores "hang together," then they would seem to be revealing a single set of human attributes, which Guilford chooses to call "creativity." If, on the other hand, the scores are independent of each other, then it is difficult to lump together the disparate human attributes under any kind of rubric. In his review of this issue, Wallach (1970) presents considerable evidence showing low intercorrelations among tests in the Guilford battery, with average coefficients rarely reaching as high as 0.3, even in separate studies of the fluency-flexibility subbattery.

Since the test scores are largely independent of each other, and in varying degrees are unrelated also to performance on convergent thinking measures, the small amount of common variance suggests, at best, something of a weak second-order or group factor that may be labeled "creativity." This would raise questions about the proper use of the term as denoting a global, unitary phenomenon. Perhaps there exists, instead, several kinds of discrete creative functions, each helping to facilitate separate types of accomplishment. Thus, for example, creative powers applied to writing poetry might be basically different from those involved in scientific investigation. As plausible as this hypothesis may seem, it has yet to be confirmed through the use of a Guilford-type battery or subtests in it. In other words, the evidence is not yet clear enough for us to make even such obvious generalizations as (1) high expressional fluency scores are important in the making of a journalist or novelist, and (2) ideational fluency connects in some meaningful way with inventiveness in business, industry, and some of the professions.

Research is not only fragmentary and inconclusive, but the little that is reported deals mostly with concurrent rather than with predictive validity and for the total battery rather than for separate subtests. Some studies show signs of a relationship between specific factors and judges' ratings on several kinds of creative performance; others do not. On the encouraging side, there is Barron's (1963a) investigation, which found a correlation of .55 between the ratings Air Force officers received for originality and the scores they made on a battery of tests, including some of Guilford's instruments, that measured divergent production. Similarly encouraging results were found in a study of advanced undergraduate and graduate students of arts and sciences whose creativity ratings by independent judges correlated .33 with scores on Guilford's originality tests (Drevdahl, 1956). Still another positive finding was communicated by Elliott (1964) who reported that semantic divergent production tests distinguished between public relations personnel rated high as against those rated low by their superiors.

On the other hand, there is evidence, particularly in studies of artists, that raises doubts about the validity of Guilford tests. One investigation of students at a school of design yielded low correlations between artistic achievement and scores on three types of divergent thinking: redefinition, semantic spontaneous flexibility, and associational fluency (Skager et al., 1967). These results tend to substantiate the outcomes of a similar study by Beittel (1964), which also failed to show a clear relationship between scores on divergent thinking tests and artistic performance. In a similar investigation of architects rated highly creative by experts in their field, MacKinnon (1961) found that neither the quality nor the quantity of responses to the Guilford divergent production test related in any way to creativity in architectural design. Similar results were obtained by Gough (1961) in his study of highly acclaimed research scientists whose creativity ratings by peers correlated from −.27 to .27 on a variety of Guilford tests.

While it is impossible to know for sure why the attempts at validating Guilford's tests have been unconvincing, the following guesses at an explanation might be considered:

1. The kinds of test questions contained in these instruments have little or nothing to do with creative productivity or performance. In other words, it is naïve to assume that divergent thinking encompasses the complex processes of creativity. Consequently, if there is no face validity, it would be unrealistic to expect high concurrent or predictive validity.
2. The reliability of these instruments is low, too, and, according to Guilford (1966), "reflects the general instability of functioning of individuals in creative ways . . . and therefore, high levels of predictive validity should not be expected" (p.189).
3. Since the Guilford battery seems to be measuring separate, unrelated abilities, it is possible that the subtests vary in their validity across different areas of human accomplishment.
4. The tests are restricted to measuring cognitive operations, when in reality nonintellective factors may be at least as important in creative functioning.
5. Since the criteria for determining creative human accomplishment are often so subjective and variable, it is impossible to verify the validity of *any* instrument that purports to measure creativity.

The Torrance Battery

The Torrance Tests of Creative Thinking (Torrance, 1966) are probably the most widely used measures for children at the elementary school levels. Based primarily on the Guilford battery, these instruments provide a single index of creativity based on a summation of scores for fluency, flexibility, originality, and elaboration on figural and verbal tasks. The battery includes an *ask-and-guess test* in which the subject is shown a picture and is required to (1) write as many questions as possible; (2) list all the possible causes of a situation that is depicted; and (3) list all the possible consequences of the illustrated situation. In the *product improvement task*, the respondent is shown a stuffed animal and is asked to list all the cleverest and most unusual ways of changing it so that children can have even more fun playing with it. The *unusual uses task* asks the child to imagine as many interesting and unusual users of a familiar object as possible. Then there is a request to raise as many *unusual* questions as the child can imagine. The *just suppose task* requires the child to imagine as many things as possible that would happen as a result of an improbable situation such as clouds having strings attached and hanging down to earth. *Picture construction* is a figural task in which the child is given an egg-shaped slip of paper and is asked to paste it anywhere on a black page and draw something clever and unusual that incorporates the shape into an overall picture. Another figural task is to take drawings of *incomplete figures* and add as many imaginative details as possible to finish the pictures. Finally, there is the *parallel lines figural task*, which has the same rules as *incomplete figures*, except that all the line forms from which the child works are the same, whereas the given figures in the previous test are varied.

Table 14-1. Product-Moment Coefficients of Correlation Between Creativity Predictors Established in 1959 and Criterion Variables Established in 1966 and 1971 (N = 46 for 1966 and 52 for 1971)

| | Criterion Variables | | | | | |
| | Quality | | Quantity | | Motivation | |
Predictors	1966	1971	1966	1971	1966	1971
Flexibility (TTCT)	.48*	.59*	.44*	.58*	.46*	.54*
Originality (TTCT)	.43*	.49*	.40*	.54*	.42*	.51*
Fluency (TTCT)	.39*	.53*	.44*	.54*	.34	.49*
Intelligence test	.37*	.45*	.22	.46*	.32	.41*
Elaboration (TTCT)	.32	.40*	.37*	.43*	.25	.41*
Achievement (ITED)	.20	.47*	.09	.38*	.15	.46*
Peer nominations	.13	.34*	.13	.39*	.18	.38*

*Significant at the .01 level.

Source: E. P. Torrance, "Creatively Gifted and Disadvantaged Gifted," in J. C. Stanley, W. C. George, and C. H. Solano, eds., *The Gifted and the Creative: A Fifty-Year Perspective* (Baltimore, Md.: Johns Hopkins University Press, 1977), p. 180.

A study of discriminant validity (i.e., interrelatedness among the subtests) found a high average correlation of .77 among scores on fluency, flexibility, and originality, whereas elaboration seems unrelated to the other three measures (Cicirelli, 1965). On the other hand, intercorrelations among individual Torrance tests with respect to trait consistency (i.e., the extent to which fluency scores on one subtest correlate with fluency on the other subtests) are fairly low compared with average intercorrelations among IQ subtests (Crockenberg, 1972).

Despite the limited amount of evidence concerning the relationship among the various subtests in Torrance's battery, data are presented on predictive validity based on a longitudinal study of 392 high school students who had been assessed in 1959 on several predictor variables, including IQ, the Torrance Tests of Creative Thinking, and peer judgments of their ability to generate high-quality, original ideas (Torrance, 1977). The criterion variables for follow up studies conducted in 1966 (N = 46) and 1971 (N = 52) were indices of the quantity and quality of creative achievements, which Torrance (1977) characterizes as follows:

An index of Quantity of Creative Achievements was developed from self-reports based on responses to checklists of creative achievements in the following categories: poems, stories, songs written/published; books written/published; radio and television scripts/performances; music compositions produced/published; original research designs developed/executed; in-service training for coworkers created/executed; research grants received/completed; scientific papers presented/published; business enterprises initiated; patentable devices invented/produced; awards or prizes for creative writing, musical composition, art, leadership, research, etc.

An index of Quality of Creative Achievement was obtained by having five judges (all advanced students of creativity) rate on a ten-point scale the originality/creativeness of the most creative achievements described. (p. 178)

In summarizing the results (see Table 14-1), Torrance observes that his tests are not only equal and perhaps superior to measures of intelligence in forecasting creative achievements later in life but that the predictive validity of these instruments grows stronger as the examinees mature. One possible reason for the general rise in coefficients from 1966 to 1971 is that the subjects became more and more differentiated as they moved closer to realizing their potentialities. It is also noteworthy that the creativity tests administered in high school were better at predicting creative achievements in writing, science, medicine, and leadership than in music, visual arts, business, and industry. (This was also true of the other predictors.)

Another longitudinal study is reported by Cropley (1972), who administered the Seeing Problems, Consequences, Symbol Production, Hidden Figures, Tin Can Uses, and Circles tests to several hundred seventh-graders in 1964. Nearly five years later, he located 111 of these subjects and collected data on their out-of-school achievement in art, drama, literature, and music. After combining the six divergent thinking scores into a single "creativity" rating and the four criterion scores into a single achievement rating, he correlated the two and obtained a coefficient of .51 for the full sample, .52 for the boys and .46 for the girls. He concluded that divergent thinking measures possess reasonable and encouraging long-range predictive validity. However, a reanalysis of the data led Jordan (1975) to contradict these inferences, on the grounds that Cropley's procedure for determining predictive validity is flawed and that the correlations between "creativity" and achievement ratings are statistically not significant.

In what is probably the longest-range and largest-scale investigation of tested creativity, Torrance (1981) reports a follow-up study of all pupils enrolled in grades one through six in two elementary schools who were tested on the Torrance battery from 1958 to 1964. Follow-up data of adolescent and adult creative behavior were obtained in 1979-1980 from 211 subjects (116 women and 95 men, ages 24 to 32) out of the 400 originally tested for three or more years. The follow-up questionnaire elicited five indices of creative achievement, as follows: (1) number of high school creative achievements; (2) number of publicly recognized achievements after finishing high school; (3) number of "creative style of life" achievements that have not been recognized publicly; (4) quality of the highest creative achievements; and (5) ratings of the creative quality of career aspirations and images. Correlations between the creativity index in each of the five criteria proved significant at or beyond the .001 level, ranging from .38 for the number of high school creative achievements to .58 for ratings of the quality of highest creative achievements. A stepwise regression analysis yielded a multiple correlation of .62 (see Table 14-2).

Torrance's reports of follow-up studies of elementary and high school populations are the only ones that contain consistently encouraging evidence that his (or any other) tests of creativity can forecast various kinds of accomplishment in adulthood. Replications of his research therefore ought to be conducted with a large sample stratified for age, sex, and socioeconomic status. Also, new follow-up studies should determine whether there is a consistent, predictable relationship between scores on specific tests and specific criteria for creative accomplishment.

Table 14-2. Predictive Validity of the Torrance Tests of Creative Thinking for Males, Females, and Total Sample for Five Criteria of Achievement*

Criteria of Creative Achievement	Males (N = 95)	Females (N = 116)	Total (N = 211)
Number of high school creative achievements	.33	.44	.38
Number of post high school creative achievements	.57	.42	.46
Number of creative style of living achievements	.42	.48	.47
Quality of highest creative achievements (ratings)	.59	.57	.58
Quality of future career image	.62	.54	.57

*All coefficients of correlation are significant at the .001 level.

Source: E. P. Torrance, "Predicting the Creativity of Elementary School Children (1958-60)—and the Teacher Who 'Made a Difference'," *Gifted Child Quarterly*, *Vol.*, 25(2): 60 (1981).

In other words, can we generally expect that scores on verbal inventiveness and on flexibility in imagining consequences in improbable situations will forecast success in creative writing with correlations on the order of .6, as Torrance discovered for his 1960 sample? Equally important, how much of the variance in these relationships can be explained independently by measures of divergent thinking? What would happen to Torrance's .6 coefficients if assessments of convergent thinking, such as IQ, were partialed out?

Cicirelli (1965) reports on controlling for IQ in his study involving validation of the Torrance tests with a population of six hundred sixth-graders. He found most of the correlations reaching .2 or better before partialing out IQ, and below .2 after partialing it out. However, his criteria were various aspects of school achievement rather than success in creative work comparable to the kinds outline by Torrance. A fairly similar study by Yamamoto and Chimbidis (1966) also shows little relationship between scores on the Torrance battery and performance on a standardized achievement test, with IQ partialed out. As in the Cicirelli report, the evidence presented by Yamamoto and Chimbidis must be regarded as limited, since it restricts itself to conventional scholastic criteria.

Developing a valid measure of creativity can be particularly frustrating because the concept is so complex and elusive. Torrance himself (1975) seemed slightly unsure about expecting strong predictive validity in such tests and expressed his doubts in the following way:

When confronted by the fact that creative functioning involves a variety of phenomena which occur simultaneously and interact with one another, how much weight should we expect measures of general creative abilities to carry? Research evidence indicates that the motivation of the subject, his early life experiences, the immediate and long-range rewards, the richness of the environment, and other factors are all important enough to make a difference in creative functioning and furthermore that these phenomena interact with one another. (p. 285)

An intriguing addendum to the issue of test validity is suggested by reports on factors affecting test performance. Torrance (1975) cites several studies to show that there is no evidence of heritability or of racial and socioeconomic bias in the abilities measured by his instruments. This has curious implications, for it amounts to saying that some of the most powerful elements of the genotype and of the phenotype have no bearing on creativity. It is hard to imagine any test of creative performance, let alone potential, in which the results are entirely unaffected by hereditary factors or by forces in the environment that are so prominent in determining racial or socioeconomic status. What else is there to account for human variability? Torrance does not specify these factors, but he implies that, while they are potent enough to account for individual differences in test performance, they do not discriminate against racial and socioeconomic groups and thus preserve the bias-free nature of the measures.

The problem is that there has to be a trade-off between test bias and test validity. If an imperfect world causes some racial and socioeconomic groups to be underrepresented among the creative achievers, that imperfection is inevitably reflected in measures of creative potential; otherwise, the tests will overpredict for the lowest-status groups or underpredict for highest-status populations. Torrance regrets the fact that "thus far, the findings concerning the lack of heritability of creative abilities and the lack of racial and socio-economic bias have stimulated no visible enthusiasm" (1975, p. 289). Perhaps the reason for the indifference is that such an assertion raises more questions than it settles concerning the validity of his tests.

The Wallach and Kogan Battery

The Torrance battery and the one developed by Wallach and Kogan (1965) share several common features, as follows: they can be administered to young children; their subtests are restricted to measuring divergent thinking; and they include both verbal and visual content. All the Wallach-Kogan subtests are scored separately for number and uniqueness of responses. The first of three verbal measures is called Instances (e.g., "Name all the things you can think of that will make a noise"); the second is Alternate Uses (e.g., "Tell me all the different ways in which you could use a newspaper"); and the third is Similarities (e.g., "Tell me all the ways in which a grocery store and a restaurant are alike"). The visual tests include Pattern Meanings, in which the child indicates the kinds of images that may be suggested by a series of drawings, and Line Meanings, which require the same kinds of responses as Pattern Meanings, except that the stimulus material is in the form of nondescript line drawings.

As in the case of "creativity" measures developed by Guilford and by Torrance, the Wallach-Kogan battery has been subjected to several kinds of validation studies with mixed results. These investigations have focused on the interrelatedness among subtests, the association between total creativity and IQ ratings, the concurrent and predictive validity of the total creativity score, and the effects of test conditions on test performance. Wallach and Kogan (1965) determined that frequency of associations occur early, that uniqueness of associations appear late in the series of examinee's reponses, and that both kinds of performance should be highly correlated. A fixed time limit would reduce such a correlation by curtailing the emergence of unique responses. Therefore, to obtain proper readings of the two key performance indicators, the authors allowed the responses to run their course without any time constraints. They then administered the battery under these conditions and in a gamelike atmosphere to 151 10-and 11-year-olds, mostly from professional and managerial families.

Results proved to be highly encouraging. Although intercorrelations among subtests ranged from as low as .07 to as high as .74, all but two of the coefficients were significant beyond the .05 level, with forty-one beyond the .01 level. Even the correlation between verbal and figural subbatteries was highly significant, thus indicating that what the tests measure is a unitary phenomenon rather than just a collection of diverse skills. Scores on the total battery could then be correlated legitimately with those on IQ tests to determine whether the two kinds of measures assess separate intellective entities.

In their statistical analysis, Wallach and Kogan correlated ten subscores from their battery with subscores on the WISC and SCAT "ability" measures as well as the STEP "achievement" indicators. Results show that only ten out of the one hundred correlations were significant beyond the .01 level, with an additional eleven beyond the .05 level, and no coefficient exceeding .23. The low correlations between tests of divergent and convergent thinking show that these are two different types of thought processes, especially since the subtests measuring each of them are highly related among themselves. The authors conclude that through their instrument and technique of measurement they "have been able to provide an operational definition of creativity that does justify conceiving of it as substantially independent of the intelligence concept and as possessing a goodly degree of generality" (1965, p. 48).

There is, however, some criticism of the Wallach and Kogan research that tends to compromise their conclusions, at least to some extent. In his review of the literature on approaches to administering creativity measures, Hattie (1977) cites conflicting evidence on the efficacy of testing under untimed gamelike conditions. His interpretation of the pros and cons led him to doubt the advantages of either approach. His own investigation (Hattie, 1980) compared the following three conditions for administering both the Torrance and the Wallach-Kogan batteries: (1) untimed gamelike, (2) conventional testlike, and (3) administration of the measures under testlike conditions on two adjacent days, using the second testing as the predictor. Results showed that the conventional testlike conditions appeared to produce optimal test results.

Actually, issues surrounding test conditions would be relatively unimportant if the Wallach-Kogan battery proved to be highly valid under some form of test administration. However, various studies seem to suggest that the scores correlate better with concurrent than with future accomplishment. Wallach and Wing (1969) conducted a study of over five hundred entering college freshmen with average Scholastic Aptitude Test (SAT) scores in the highest decile for college-bound high school seniors (Verbal = 619.12, Mathematical = 644.88). The group then took the Wallach-Kogan tests, and the results were correlated with the students' retrospective reports about their achievements outside the classroom in high school. These accomplishments included *leadership* (e.g., participated as an active member of one or more student organizations); *art* (e.g., created artwork such as painting, drawing, sculpturing, cartooning, or photography, not as part of a course); *social service* (e.g,, participated actively in programs sponsored by community or religious groups, such as scouts, 4-H clubs, etc.); *literature* (e.g., wrote original poems, plays, stories, articles, or essays, not as part of a course); *dramatic arts* (e.g., participated in activities of speech, debate, or dramatic group); *music* (e.g., performed music with school or community group); or *science* (e.g., participated as a member of a science club or reading and discussion group). Results showed that performance on the Wallach-Kogan battery was significantly associated with these out-of-classroom activities, whereas SAT scores were not, although it may be difficult to justify some of the extracurricular experiences as necessarily "creative."

Similar positive results on concurrent validity were obtained for elementary school populations. In their study of 7-year-old children, Rotter, Langland, and Berger (1971) reported a significantly positive relationship between performance on the Wallach-Kogan battery and the children's self-reported participation in various innovative activities outside the classroom, including creative writing and composition, reading and writing, life sciences, and dramatics. However, unlike the Wallach and Wing (1969) results with an older population, the findings for the 7-year-olds showed no close association between creativity scores and involvement in the physical sciences and arts and crafts. In their investigation of third- and fourth-graders in an inner-city school, Wallbrown and Huelsman (1975) found Wallach-Kogan scores accounting for 45 percent and 52 percent of the variance, respectively, in originality and effectiveness of expression ratings ascribed by four judges to the children's crayon drawings and clay products. Another study using direct evaluations of the subjects' work as signs of creative output was conducted with undergraduate college students and showed that also at this age level there is a significant correlation between Wallach-Kogan test scores and ratings of the student's writing (poetry or short story), artwork, ideas for two inventions, and a creative teaching strategy (Bartlett and Davis, 1974).

While the evidence on concurrent validity is consistently positive, a different picture emerges for predictive validity. Kogan and Pankove (1972) administered the Wallach-Kogan tests to fifth-graders in several schools and then obtained records of the children's extracurricular participation (i.e., leadership, art, social service, writing, dramatic arts, music, and science) in the tenth grade. Over this five-year period between fifth- and tenth-grade testing, the rate of attrition for the sample group was 37.5 percent, and the results were mixed for those who remained. The creativity tests showed significant concurrent and predictive validity in the smaller school system, but not in the larger one. Another follow-up study was conducted two years later, and the researchers (Kogan and Pankove, 1974) reported that, for the smaller school system (N = 22), there were no significant correlations between fifth-grade Wallach-Kogan scores and twelfth-grade nonacademic attainments and that only two out of the eight correlations between Wallach-Kogan ratings in the tenth grade and nonacademic attainments in the twelfth grade were significant at the .05 level. Results for the larger school system (N = 46) were even more discouraging, as none of the coefficients were significant. Oddly enough, intellective-aptitude tests, which are designed to reflect academic potential, showed some modest strength in forecasting nonacademic attainments in the children's senior year in high school. At least as surprising is the fact that in the smaller school system intellective-aptitude scores in the fifth grade were better predictors than were those obtained in the tenth grade.

Needless to say, the Kogan and Pankove studies have to be replicated on a much larger scale before firm generalizations can be made about the predictive validity of the Wallach-Kogan tests. The small samples and high attrition rates in these investigations make it difficult to speculate as to why school system size made a difference in some of the results. Perhaps a larger-scale investigation of intact groups would provide a more encouraging picture. Nevertheless, to say that an instrument's predictive validity has not been disproven conclusively is a long way from confirming that it is valid. The burden of proof is with the test constructor, and subsequent research should supply further support of data. These conditions remain yet to be met consistently in research on creativity.

A Final Comment on Performance Measures

The instruments developed by Guilford, Torrance, and Wallach and Kogan are by no means the only ones used in measuring creative potential in children, but they represent the kinds that are most widely in vogue in programs for the gifted. All three share a heavy emphasis on the assessment of divergent thinking skills. What is also common among them is their exclusion of a quality criterion in scoring the tests. Children's responses are not evaluated for their aesthetic appeal, ingenuity, or usefulness. These are admittedly difficult to score with a high degree of reliability, but the absence of such judgments in the scoring procedures may account partly for the questionable predictive validity of the instruments.

In one study where an attempt was made to reanalyze Torrance test protocols on the basis of aesthetic reactions of judges, it was found that the individuals rated high for the aesthetic quality of their work were not necessarily the most fluent, flexible, original, and elaborative in their performance (Feldman et al., 1971). Crockenberg (1972) suggests, however, that, even if such tests were scored for quality of response, little would be accomplished toward improving the degree of congruence between conceptual and operational definitions of creativity.

This being the case, a reasonable resolution of the discrepancy between what the so-called creativity tests measure and a conceptual definition of creativity is to alter the labels we give to these tests. Perhaps creativity tests should be referred to as measures of fluency and originality as Torrance suggests, or as measures of ideational productivity or associational fluency in Wallach's terms. (Crockenberg, 1972, p. 42)

VALIDITY OF SELF-REPORTS

One approach to assessing creative potential that takes into account the quality of performance, along with nonintellective indicators, is the use of a biographical inventory. Such instruments are unlike those developed by Guilford, Torrance, and Wallach and Kogan, which were designed to estimate creativity levels through a person's responses to divergent-type problems; instead, they are questionnaires that elicit self-reports on personal characteristics and past experiences, from which an individual's abilities can be inferred. One representative instrument of this kind is Taylor's Biographical Inventory—Form U. (Institute for Behavioral Research in Creativity 1978). It contains 150 multiple-choice items (or questions) about child-hood activities and experiences, sources of derived satisfactions and dissatisfactions, academic experiences, attitudes and interests, value preferences, and various kinds of self-descriptions. From this information, the following six assessments are made:

1. *Academic performance.* Students report their school grades and evaluate themselves on such specifics as solving math problems, reading with speed and comprehension, study and concentration habits, and work speed.
2. *Creativity.* Students report on levels of interest in independent thinking and learning and on individual, self-selected activities outside of school. They also describe their inclinations to try out new ideas and to develop a variety of hobbies during their spare time.
3. *Artistic potential.* Students report on the extent to which they appreciate and are involved in artistic activities, including music and the visual arts. They estimate the levels of their desire to practice or study in an artistic area during their free time, their preference for art exhibits or ballet as entertainment, and their plans to major in artistic areas in college.
4. *Leadership.* Students report on the extent of their involvement in organized groups at school and in the community. They also describe how well they can elicit cooperation from peers, how well they get along with other people, and how well they manage to get their own ideas recognized.
5. *Career maturity.* This is a measure of the students' awareness of future careers and willingness to plan for them. They report on the extent to which they have discussed these matters with counselors, teachers, and people actually working in jobs of interest to them. They also show how much they know about the education, training, and experience necessary for the jobs they are considering. They take into account the influence of jobs on their lives, how their hobbies and interests might affect a job choice, and how jobs may change in the immediate and distant future.

6. *Educational orientation.* This is a measure of the importance of education to the student. Respondents estimate the number of hours they spend on homework, the regularity of their independent studies, and their motivation to work toward future goals. They evaluate their school, their schoolwork, and their desires to do advanced studies.

The test manual for the Biographical Inventory—Form U reports mean scores for samples in grades as low as four through six, as well as for grades seven through nine and ten through eleven. No studies of mean differences between age groupings are noted, but the expected rise in scores from one grade level to the next does not seem evident. For example, tests administered to a Utah population of over thirty-eight hundred pupils, grades four to twelve, showed an overall mean raw score of 95.7, with a standard deviation of 8.2; yet the means for each subpopulation were remarkably close, with fourth- to sixth-graders averaging 96.9, seventh- to ninth-graders 94.8, and tenth- to twelfth-graders 96.5. Even in *Career Maturity*, which showed the best improvement of scores from lowest to highest grade levels, the difference between fourth- to sixth-graders and tenth-to twelfth-graders was a fairly modest 5.1, where the overall standard deviation was 7.45. Reliability coefficients were about the same for each age group, the coefficients ranging from .77 to .91 on the various subtests.

Even though the instrument is reportedly used with elementary school children, its reliance on self-reports probably makes it most applicable to high school and college populations who can describe a longer, richer history of personal experiences. Indeed, the validation studies described in the test manual were conducted on older samples. These investigations deal with cross-validities and report the following results: Academic Performance correlated .6 to .7 with scholastic achievement and IQ measures for high school students and college freshmen; Creativity correlated .4 to .5 with performance ratings of scientists and engineers; Artistic Potential correlated .4 to .6 with differentiating levels of artistic performance among high school students; and Leadership showed cross-validities as high as .7 in relationship to other evaluations of leadership qualities among students in a special high school for the gifted. Career Maturity and Educational Orientation subscales were examined for relevance of content and judged to be highly adequate for their purposes. As for the instrument's usefulness in forecasting later accomplishment "there is no direct evidence that the present format is valid against representative criteria. All that can be said is that the items, in general, have been highly selected, and, on the basis of the extensive past research evidence, could be expected to have predictive utility in identifying talents" (IBRIC, 1978).

There is good reason to expect high concurrent validity in biographical inventories, considering the nature of supportive evidence. The positive correlation between self-ratings and ratings from external sources merely confirms the well-known fact that people perceive themselves at least partly on the basis of how others perceive them. When examinees are asked to assess their own academic performance, creativity, artistic potential, leadership, career maturity, and educational orientation, they will respond to some extent in accordance with a variety of performance indicators, such as grades at school, IQ scores, and various judgments by people they respect, except in the relatively few instances when they engage in fantasy or self-deception. It is therefore not surprising to find that the subjectivity in biographical data conforms fairly well with a more general consensus about accomplishments thus far.

Since the self-report reflects a significant amount of what others already know about an individual, it is important to determine whether such an instrument also adds some insights about ability and potential that cannot be obtained elsewhere. The resolution of this issue, not yet reached, will help considerably in determining the value of biographical inventories for identifying talent in our schools. Similarly, it makes sense to consider the usefulness of "creativity" tests for children developed by Guilford, Torrance, and Wallach and Kogan, only on the condition that these measures reveal what would otherwise be hidden and neglected human attributes. If, indeed, tested creativity is even partly unlike any other tested ability, and is worth nurturing, then its measurement and cultivation can enhance programs for the gifted. Furthermore, the validity of tests purporting to measure creativity can be evaluated best in an environment that enables creativity to flourish. Although some research has dealt with the question of how independent tested creativity is of other evidence of human potential, particularly tested intelligence, much more remains to be done. These new investigations will, it is hoped, help to clarify the extent to which such measures contribute to an overall assessment of potential giftedness.

RELATIONSHIPS AMONG TESTED CREATIVITY, INTELLIGENCE, AND ACHIEVEMENT

Categorical Studies

Probably the most influential attempt to prove the value of creativity measures in helping locate talent that IQs would fail to reveal is the Getzels and Jackson (1958, 1962) study of 449 adolescents in a midwestern university secondary school. Every subject took at least one of three possible IQ tests: the Stanford-Binet, the Wechsler, or the Henmon-Nelson, and the results from the latter two measures were converted into comparable Stanford-Binet scores. The creativity battery consisted of five subtests, as follows: Word Association, which requires the examinee to provide as many synonyms as possible for a list of words with multiple meanings; Uses of Things, which requires the examinee to state as many different and original ways to make use of a familiar object, such as a brick; Hidden Shapes, which is basically a perceptual test that calls for the location of a simple geometric figure hidden in one of several complex figures; Fables, in which the examinee is asked to give "moralistic," "humorous," or "sad" endings to unfinished fables; and

Make-up Problems, which is basically a mathematical task requiring the examinee to derive many possible problems from a paragraph containing a series of numerical statements. Two comparison subsamples were then organized, with each group representing the highest 20 percent of the school population in one of the two test batteries (i.e., IQ or creativity) but not the other. As a result of this selection process, the high-IQ, low-creativity group had an average IQ of 150, whereas the mean IQ for the high-creativity, low-IQ sample was 23 points lower.

Despite the huge difference in IQ, the two groups were comparable with each other in scholastic achievement and superior to the rest of the school population with respect to this criterion. Otherwise, there were sharp differences favoring the high creatives on nearly all measures of imaginative and innovative work. Teacher preference ratings showed that the high-IQ group ranked significantly above the general school population, whereas the high creatives did not.

Getzels and Jackson (1958) conclude that "high academic performance of . . . creative children coupled with the related lack of recognition which they may receive from teachers points to the core of the problem of expanding the present conception of 'Giftedness,' and of breaking the bonds that the IQ has on this concept in the school situation" (p. 77). They interpret the results of their study to mean that the pool of gifted children can be expanded considerably by including those who qualify on the basis of creativity tests, even if they would fail to qualify by virtue of IQ alone.

Because of its dramatic implications, the Getzels and Jackson study has been replicated and the results reanalyzed by several researchers. Hudson (1962) investigated a sample of ninety-five English pupils, ages 15 to 17, and determined that IQ and creativity tests are associated with various personality differences. He also discovered that boys specializing in history and English literature are strong on the open-ended tests and relatively week in IQ, whereas the reverse is true for those concerntrating in the physical sciences. However, majors in the classics, modern languages, and ecology seem to be distributed between these two extremes. Torrance (1963) reports that he and his associates undertook fifteen partial replications of the Getzels and Jackson study, and the results were similar only in schools where students were taught in such a way that they had a chance to use their creative thinking ability in acquiring traditional educational skills or where the avarage IQ for the total school population was exceptionally high. Furthermore, the creative puplis "overachieved" in the sense that their educational quotients were considerably higher than were their intelligence quotients.

Torrance and Wu (1980) also conducted a twenty-two-year follow-up study of elementary school children divided according to their IQ and creativity test scores. In 1958, Torrance began administering various forms of his tests and several IQ measures to children from grades one through six in two elementary schools. On the basis of these data he organized his experimental groups as follows: (1) twenty-six high-creative, low-IQ children whose creativity index was in the upper 20 percent of the total sample but not in the upper 20 percent in IQ; (2) twenty-six high-IQ, low-creative children scoring in the upper 20 percent in IQ but not on creativity tests; and (3) ten high-IQ, high-creative children scoring in the upper 20

Table 14-3. Comparisons of Three Groups of Gifted Elementary School Children on Adolescent and Adult Creative Achievements

Criteria of Creative Achievements	High Creative		High IQ		High IQ High Creative		F Ratio
	Mean	*SD*	*Mean*	*SD*	*Mean*	*SD*	
Quality of creative achievements	19.4	3.7	17.0	4.7	19.5	4.4	2.46*
Quality of career image	19.7	3.9	16.6	5.9	20.7	3.3	3.95†
High school creative achievements	7.9	7.3	4.5	2.3	7.2	6.0	2.62*
Posthigh school creative achievements	24.1	21.7	13.6	15.3	19.8	19.7	1.99
Creative style of life achievements	10.3	5.6	6.3	3.3	6.9	2.9	4.54†

*Significant at .10 level.

†Significant at .05 level.

Source: Torrance, E. P. and T. Wu. "A comparative Longitudinal Study of the Adult Creative Achievement of Elementary School Chidlren Identified as Highly Intelligent and as Highly Creative." *Creative Child and Adult Quarterly*, 6: 74 (1980).

percent on both measures. At the time of the follow-up, the mean age of all subjects originally tested was 27.5. Criterion measures included number of high school and posthigh school creative achievements, number of creative style of life achievements, quality of highest creative achievements, and creativeness of future career image.

Results show some differences among the sample groups (see Table 14-3). The two high-creative groups tended to possess somewhat better quality future career images than did the high-IQ, low-creative sample. Also, the low-IQ high-creative group scored significantly better than did the other two groups on a measure of creative style of life achievements. No differences at the decimal .05 level or better were found on the other criterion measures. From these outcomes, Torrance feels justified in his concerns that the children he calls "creatively gifted" sometimes fall short of being identified as gifted even though they equal or excel over those who qualify on the basis of IQ alone.

Other replications of the Getzels and Jackson study have failed to confirm the hypothesis that creativity and IQ measures are equally valid in distinguishing high from low scholastic achievers. Edwards and Tyler (1965) administered the School and College Achievement Test (SCAT) and the two subtests from Torrance's battery to 181 ninth-grade students. Two experimental samples were then organized as follows: a high-SCAT group, consisting of students scoring in the upper third of SCAT but not on creativity (estimated mean IQ, 123) and a high-creativity group, consisting of students scoring in the upper third on creativity but not on SCAT (estimated mean IQ, 102). Results showed that the high-SCAT group was superior on both grade-point average and Sequential Tests of Educational Progress (STEP) batteries. In another variation of the Getzels-Jackson design, Flescher (1963) divided a sample of 110 sixth-graders into four groups, instead of two, as follows: (1) High-IQ, low-creativity, (2) high-creativity, low-IQ, (3) high-creativity, high-IQ, and (4) low-IQ, low-creativity. Results of these four-way comparisons showed no evidence that creativity is as closely related to scholastic achievement as is IQ. Flescher attributed these negative results to (1) the high correlation between IQ and achievement tests, (2) the extremely low correlation between his creativity measures and IQ (.09), and (3) the uncertain validity of so-called "creativity" tests.

Since the Getzels and Jackson study has not always been replicated successfully, it is difficult to be certain that divergent thinking measures aid in discovering dimensions or levels of human potential that would otherwise remain obscure. What may account for the inconsistent findings are basic flaws in the original design. Marsh (1964) reanalyzed the original data, using a simple chi-square technique, and concluded that it is a mistake to regard creativity as entirely independent of the general factor of intelligence. Another challenge to the results of the first study has to do with intercorrelations among the critical variables. Although Getzels and Jackson justify summing the scores across subtests in the creativity battery by pointing to significant positive intercorrelations among them, Thorndike (1963) notes that the range of coefficients (i.e., .159 to .420 for boys and .197 to .525 for girls) is not much different from the range of correlations between IQ and the *total* creativity battery (i.e., .131 to .178 for boys and .115 to .393 for girls). Wallach (1970) argues further that even the small discrepancy between average intra- and interbattery correlations might have been eliminated if the IQ test had been administered at the same time that creativity measures were taken. These criticisms raise some doubts as to whether Getzels and Jackson dealt with two completely separate kinds of intellect.

Aside from the problems of measurement, limitations in the original study's sampling procedures may account for the failure of other researchers to obtain similar results. Although there was a mean difference of twenty-three points between so-called "high"- and "low"-IQ subgroups in the Getzels and Jackson sample, the "low" IQs averaged 127, which placed them at about the ninety-fifth percentile according to the test norms. Hasan and Butcher (1966) have speculated that only in such a biased sample is it possible to distinguish "creative" from "intelligent" children, whereas in a relatively unselected group, measures of convergent and divergent thinking largely overlap. They based these conclusions on their own studies of 175 Scottish students ranging widely in ability and attending the second year of high school. Three out of the four possible creativity-IQ combinations were compared (omitting the "low-lows"), and the results were as follows: the group that rated high in verbal reasoning outperformed the high-creativity group on measures of English and arithmetic; students rated high in both creativity and verbal reasoning scored highest of all in English; the highest teacher ratings on "desirability as a pupil" went to those who scored best in creativity and verbal reasoning, followed by the high-verbal-reasoning, low-creativity and high-creativity, low-verbal-reasoning groups, respectively; and there was considerable overlap between creativity and verbal reasoning.

Other studies dealing exclusively with high-IQ populations, as did the Hasan and Butcher (1966) investigation, tend to confirm the Getzels and Jackson results. Rekdal (1979) agrees that creativity measures can effectively complement IQ-based information on signs of giftedness. As evidence, he cites investigations by MacKinnon (1962) and Johnson and Fogel (1974), all of which were restricted to samples in the upper extremes of tested intelligence. Rekdal further notes Torrance's (1962) assertion that IQ tests miss as many as 70 percent of those who score in the top 20 percent on creative thinking measures.

Since the Getzels and Jackson study seems to have been replicated more successfully with high-IQ populations than with randomly selected groups, there may exist an IQ threshold, with creativity-IQ correlations low above that point and high below that point. Indeed, there is agreement among some researchers, including Torrance (1962), Guilford (1968), and Barron (1969a), on an IQ cutoff level, presumably around 120. In accordance with the theory, it would be possible that high creativity scores make a difference in the scholastic achievement of people scoring above but not below the IQ 120 threshold. Part of the hypothesis was tested by Yamamoto (1964) in his study of high school students selected from the upper quintile in creativity scores and divided into three groups according to IQ (i.e., above 130, 120 to 129, and below 120). Results show no difference in scholastic standing between the two higher-IQ groups, but those scoring below IQ 120 tended to achieve at a significantly lower level than did the others. In another investigation, this time involving nearly eight hundred fifth-graders with a mean IQ of 110 (Yamamoto and Chimbidis, 1966), general intelligence correlated significantly with scholastic achievement for subgroups both above and below IQ 120; when IQ was partialed out, the correlation between creativity and achievement approached zero for the higher- and lower-IQ samples. It would therefore seem from these studies that creativity tests do not add much to IQ in identifying superior scholastic potential.

An even more direct test of the threshold hypothesis was reported by Cicirelli (1965) in his study of more than six hundred sixth-grade pupils ranging in IQs from 70 to 162 who were categorized into eight levels of IQ, as follows: 70 to 79, 80 to 89, 90 to 99, 100 to 109, 110 to 119, 120 to 129, 130 to 139, and 140+. Low, medium, and high creativity levels were established by dividing the population into approximate thirds on the Torrance battery. A factorial design made it possible to evaluate simultaneously the relationship of IQ and creativity with academic achievement. Results show significant IQ main effects on all twelve achievement criteria and significant creativity main effects on seven of the twelve. There was no interaction between IQ and creativity as they affected academic achievement, except in one case (arithmetic achievement). No evidence could be found for a minimum IQ threshold beyond which creativity would begin to distinguish individuals with respect to their academic achievement. There is also little evidence of a maximum IQ threshold beyond which the relationship between IQ and achievement would be negligible.

In still another investigation (Edwards and Tyler, 1965), conducted with a small group of ninth-graders, good performance on creativity tests not only failed to predict what the students achieved at school, but it proved to be somewhat of an impediment. The two comparison groups rated high on SCAT but varied in creativity; yet the low creatives not only scored as well as the high creatives on standardized achievement tests but actually outperformed them on grade-point average. As a possible explanation of these unexpected results, the researchers refer to some comments made by Torrance about the difficulties creative students have in coping with school requirements, curricula, and interpersonal relationships. Overall, Edwards and Tyler conclude from their results "that the *generalizability* of the Getzels and Jackson and the Torrance Findings about the relationship of creativity scores to academic achievement is limited. They apparently do not apply to all kinds of students, all kinds of schools, and all kinds of intelligence and creativity tests" (p. 99).

Correlational Studies

The various categorical studies of the type conducted by Getzels and Jackson provide no consistent support for Rekdal's (1979) assertion that "creativity enhances achievement" (p. 849). Another approach to testing the assertion is by determining first whether divergent and convergent processes relate to different kinds of accomplishment and whether they reinforce each other in affecting the same kinds of accomplishment. Wallach and Wing (1969) and Torrance (1977) have connected some specific types of productivity and performance with divergent thinking, but what would happen to such relationships if IQ were partialed out? Would the creativity measures retain their strength or a substantial part of it? More generally, to what extent do tested creativity and tested intelligence correlate with each other and represent distinguishable factors in human intellect? Thus far, considerably more research effort has been devoted to determining the relationship between divergent- and convergent-type abilities than to clarifying the areas of human accomplishment that depend heavily on the kinds of skills assessed by measures of divergent thinking.

As noted earlier, Wallach and Wing (1969) discovered that scores on tests of divergent thinking relate better than IQ to various kinds of creative performance. The study excluded the middle third of the distribution on divergent thinking scores and focused only on students performing at the upper and lower extremes. However, Milgram and Milgram (1976a) extended the design to include a full range of divergent thinking scores made by 145 seniors in an Israeli high school known for its high academic standards. An adapted version of the Wallach-Kogan battery was administered, along with an Israeli measure of intelligence and a self-report questionnaire on creative performance in nine activity areas. The internal consistency of the divergent thinking test was extremely high with respect to ideational fluency and unusual responses. On the other hand, the self-reports did not intercorrelate highly, although there was strong association between the quality and quantities of activities reported in the nine categories. Results showed a significant relationship between perceived creative performance and scores on divergent thinking tests when intelligence was partialed out (.35 for males and .21

for females). On the other hand, neither intelligence test scores nor school grades correlated much above zero with self-reports on creativity when divergent thinking scores were partialed out. Equally important is the agreement between findings in this study and in the investigation of college freshmen by Wallach and Wing (1969). Both found positive relationships between divergent thinking and accomplishments in science, art, writing, and social leadership, but no association with drama or music. These results lend credence to the idea that, at least among older adolescents whose IQs are fairly restricted in range and skewed toward the top of the normal distribution, divergent thinking measures may denote some kinds of specialized talent fairly independently and consistently.

The possibility of a unique relationship between divergent thinking tests and creative performance has also been investigated at the elementary school level. Wodtke (1964) administered the Lorge-Thorndike and Torrance batteries, along with a test of creative writing, to about 100 fourth-graders and about 130 fifth-graders selected from schools in and around a large urban community. Although test-retest reliability coefficients for the Torrance measures were low, the battery contributed significantly to the prediction of scores in imaginative writing at both grade levels. The tests designed to assess verbal creativity uniquely accounted for about 4 percent of the variance of the total imaginative writing score in grade four and between 9 and 10 percent in grade five. An examination of the first order correlations indicated that the IQs were closely associated with writing scores among fourth-graders but that IQ and verbal creativity predicted equally well in the older group. Lorge-Thorndike and verbal creativity coefficients were .57 and .40, respectively, but adding them together produced a somewhat higher multiple correlation of .60 with imaginative writing in the fourth grade. In the fifth grade, the Lorge-Thorndike and verbal creativity coefficients were .37 and .38, and the corresponding multiple correlation was .46. Thus, despite the high degree of common variance between IQ and verbal creativity, the latter type of measure apparently had a unique relationship with writing judged for its organization, sensitivity, originality, imagination, psychological insight, and richness of ideas. In other words, the two kinds of tests were mutually reinforcing when facility in language usage reflected both convergent and divergent thinking skills. The reinforcement in Wodtke's study is not strong, but it is statistically significant.

It undoubtedly makes good sense for all students to spend far more time than they do now in learning how to brainstorm solutions to open-ended problems. If such thought processes were given the attention they deserve, instruments for measuring them would probably also rise in importance. As a self-fulfilling prophecy, scores on divergent thinking tests ought to relate *independently* to achievement in any course of study where the emphasis is on divergent thinking skills. The association not only makes good sense, but there is also some evidence to support it.

In his study of creativity and academic achievement among seventy-five graduate students at the University of Minnesota, Bentley (1966) used the Miller Analogies Test (MAT) to estimate traditional academic ability and a Torrance test to assess creativity. Achievement levels were determined by weekly tests requiring the application of the following mental processes taken from Guilford's Structure of Intellect: memory, cognition (discovery, recognition), divergent thinking (seeking many possible answers), and evaluation (critical thinking and decisions as to the suitability, goodness, and adequacy of given information). Another criterion for achievement was success in formulating a "new idea in personality development and mental hygiene." This was graded for creativity and usefulness (divergent thinking) as well as for ability to follow directions as to form, content, and so on (convergent thinking).

As expected, scores on the creative thinking tests correlated higher with divergent and evaluative achievement than with memory and cognitive achievement. On the other hand, the MAT scores correlated highly with memory and convergent thinking. The creativity and MAT scores correlated almost identically with total achievement, thus demonstrating that, when there is a balanced stress on divergent and convergent thinking skills, both types of measures may be equally valid.

Research evidence is more abundant but less encouraging with respect to the contribution of creativity tests in predicting "conventional" scholastic achievement that presumably relies far more on convergent than on divergent thinking skills. As mentioned earlier, a large-scale study of nearly eight hundred fifth-graders (Yamamoto and Chimbidis, 1966) showed nearly zero correlations between creativity and standardized achievement test scores when IQ was partialed out. For the total sample, the coefficient rose only from .56 to .57 when creativity was added to IQ as a predictor. In the subgroup consisting of children with IQs above 120, the correlation improved slightly from .22 to .27, and among those with IQs below 120, it remained the same at .56 regardless of whether creativity scores were added to two IQs as predictors of achievement in basic skills. Similarly, in a study of 265 ninth-graders, Mayhon (1966) correlated creativity and IQ scores with achievement in basic skills and found that creativity failed to contribute significantly to the variance in any of the subtests of a standardized achievement battery.

Aliotti and Blanton (1973) investigated the interrelationship among creativity, IQ, and scholastic aptitude in another way. In their study, eighty-three white first-graders took three batteries of tests consisting of the Torrance Tests of Creative Thinking, the California Test of Mental Maturity, and the Metropolitan Readiness Tests. Sixty measures were obtained from these batteries, and the intercorrelations produced three distinct factors, as follows: (1) an index of readiness and intelligence incorporating classroom success skills, which include ability with numbers, copying, alphabet, word meaning, language intelligence, nonlanguage intelligence, and picture interpretations; (2) an index of creative thinking ability applied to figural content; and (3) an index of verbal creativity based on scores in verbal fluency, verbal flexibility, and verbal originality. Thus, creativity factors remained independent of each other and of measures of intelligence and school readiness. Particularly noteworthy is the fact that even verbal creativity failed to contribute to the intelligence-school readiness indicators.

Other researchers, however, report more positive relationships between creativity and scholastic success. For example, Feldhusen, Treffinger, and Elias (1970) reviewed previous literature on the subject and concluded that creativity and intelligence measures are equally efficient in predicting academic achievement. In their own study, they administered to seventh- and eighth-graders a battery of tests consisting of eighteen predictor variables that included tests of divergent and convergent thinking, self-ratings of creative abilities, scholastic achievement, and anxiety. Ninety-seven of these students were then retested four years later when they were high school seniors in order to determine the predictive powers of the independent variables. A stepwise multiple regression analysis showed that from 44 percent to 83 percent of the variance in school achievement was accounted for by the combined batteries administered in junior high school. Also, important predictors included all major convergent thinking, divergent thinking, and personality variables that were part of the study.

The conclusions reached by Feldhusen, Treffinger, and Elias (1970) seem consonant with those reported by Bruininks and Feldman (1970) in their study of thirty-six boys and thirty-six girls (80 percent black) from a rural area considered economically disadvantaged. These third-and fourth-graders averaged slightly under 10 years of age, with a mean IQ of about 86. The instruments administered included the Stanford-Binet, the Peabody Picture Vocabulary Test, part of the Torrance battery, and the Metropolitan Achievement Tests.

Correlations between IQ and creativity scores turned out to be positive, though low. The Stanford-Binet correlated highly with academic achievement, but the Torrance scores did not. However, it was found that a combination of the verbal intelligence and creativity measures was a better predictor of written language achievement than was the IQ alone. The researchers felt that the creativity score acts as a "suppressor variable" by removing from the IQ scores some unexplained variance that is either not related or is negatively related to achievement. Apparently, some of the variance shared by intelligence and creativity is independent of the variance shared by IQ and achievement. Any part of the IQ score that is unrelated to academic performance may, in effect, be removed when the creativity scores are combined with IQ to predict verbal achievement. In their conclusions, Bruininks and Feldman suggest that vocabulary and knowledge acquisition skills may be more important than intellectual flexibility and ideational fluency. However, instructional methods should be developed to take advantage of the relationship between creativity and intelligence to facilitate better performance at school among socially disadvantaged children with low IQs.

The most direct approach to asssessing the relationship between creativity and IQ has been through correlational and factor analytic studies. Results sometimes vary widely, as might be expected when evidence is drawn from different instruments, age groups, and ability levels. In his investigation of architects, MacKinnon (1961) found a correlation of minus .08 between experts' ratings of creativity in architecture and scores on the Terman Concept of Mastery Test (CMT), a measure of adult intelligence. Similar near-zero coefficients between rated quality of work and CMT scores were discovered by Barron (1963) in his study of creative artists. Although MacKinnon and Barron dealt with adult samples, Wallach and Kogan (1965) generally confirmed their findings in a study of an elementary school population. Estimates of general intelligence were derived from subtests of the

WISC, SCAT, and STEP batteries, and the correlation with the Wallach-Kogan creativity test was only .09, even though the intercorrelations among creativity scores (.41) and among intelligence scores (.51) were highly significant. Divergent thinking measures also proved to be independent of tested intelligence and scholastic achievements in a study of 129 second-graders whose scores on the Wallach-Kogan, Primary Mental Abilities, and Iowa Basic Skills tests were subjected to factor analysis (McKinney and Forman, 1977).

Cropley's (1968) study of Australian university students also showed high intercorrelations among the Wallach-Kogan tests and low correlations between this battery and conventional IQ measures. However, when the entire intercorrelational matrix was factor analyzed, there emerged a large general factor on which both the creativity and intelligence tests loaded highly. Since both types of measures could be arrayed along one rather than two dimensions, Cropley raised some doubt as to whether the creativity tests measure a new and separate mode of intellectual functioning. His conclusions about the Wallach-Kogan instrument seem to differ from those expressed by Wallach and Kogan (1965) when they inferred from their own data that "creativity as herein defined—the ability to generate many cognitive associates and many that are unique—is strikingly independent of the conventional realm of general intelligence, while at the same time being a unitary and pervasive dimension of individual differences in its own right" (pp. 64-65).

Studies of other widely used divergent thinking measures likewise failed to provide conclusive evidence that tested creativity and IQ are independent of each other. Wodtke's (1964) research on the Torrance battery administered to children in grades three, four, and five showed total creativity correlations with verbal and nonverbal parts of the Lorge-Thorndike test ranging from .36 to .46. These coefficients are higher than the ones reported by Torrance (1962), whose study of elementary school samples yielded correlations with various intelligence tests ranging only from .16 to .32. In his study of 272 high school students, Yamamoto (1964b) found a low but statistically significant correlation of .3 between Torrrance and Lorge-Thorndike scores. Yamamoto (1965) also discovered that low test reliability and restrictions in the range of scores can depress the correlation between IQ and creativity. In his large-scale study of fifth-grade children, he corrected for attenuation and produced coefficients as high as .88. This led him to conclude that creativity tests should not be regarded as measuring aspects of human intellectual behavior that are exclusive of those assessed by IQ.

Cropley (1966) draws similar inferences from his factor analytic study of six tests of convergent thinking and seven tests of divergent thinking administered to 320 seventh-graders. Results showed that the two largest factors were defined by both types of tests, respectively. Although the divergent measures indicated a separate factor, "creativity," it showed a significant correlation of .514 with the general factor designated by the more conventional tests of intelligence. Cropley points out that the presence of a large general factor accounting for 76 percent of the common variance makes it "unacceptable to think of creativity as a separate basic intellective mode" (p. 264). He concludes from his findings that divergent and convergent thinking are probably not identical, but the fact that scores on tests measuring both kinds of functioning tend to be interrelated "supports the suggestions that conventional skills may provide the basis upon which creative productions rest . . . " (p. 264).

A FINAL COMMENT ON THE RELATIONSHIPS

From the research produced thus far, it is impossible to draw a clear picture about the relationships among tested creativity, IQ, and achievement. Perhaps further refinement of these performance measures and of the curricula currently in vogue in our schools will help matters considerably. Until then, we will have to be content with more speculation than closure in dealing with these relationships.

Existing evidence can be summarized briefly as follows:

1. We are far from certain that divergent thinking tests can help us to discern talent that other instruments would overlook. The categorical-type studies intitiated by Getzels and Jackson do not support this hypothesis consistently. Furthermore, some correlational studies confirm while others deny an *independent* relationship between creativity test scores and academic achievement when IQ is partialed out. However, such an association appears to exist in instances when educational programs and their achievement criteria are heavily weighted with divergent thinking processes.

2. Correlations between creativity test scores and IQs vary from near-zero to moderately positive and significant. McNemar (1964) attempts to explain this discrepancy through a "fan-shaped" hypothesis that suggests a wide range of creativity scores at high-IQ extremes but much less scattered at average and below-average IQ levels. However, attempts to test the hypothesis in adult and adolescent populations have failed to divulge such a curvilinear relationship (Mednick and Andrews, 1967; Dacey and Medaus, 1971).

3. Correlations between IQ and proficiency in the different divergent thinking skills vary widely. Wallach (1970) cites a considerable amount of data to show that ideational fluency is far more independent of general intelligence than is word fluency, flexibility, or originality.

4. Depite the finding by Wallbrown, Wallbrown, and Wherry (1975) that creativity and intelligence measures define entirely separate cognitive entities, other factor analytic studies generally agree that creativity and IQ are only partly distinguishable from each other (Thorndike, 1963; Ward, 1966; Cropley, 1966). However, there is no evidence to suggest that the two types of mental processes overlap entirely. Thorndike (1966) is probably right in his observation that there exists a broad domain of human abilities describable as "divergent" or "creative" thinking that is unrelated to thought processes measured by conventional intelligence tests.

Chapter 15

Fulfilling Creative Potential

It is self-evident that creative potential needs a proper environment in which to flourish. Given the right conditions, there can be extraordinarily rich outcroppings of genius concentrated in short historical periods and in geographically restricted areas as, for example, Berlin's Bauhaus and Paris' Left Bank, where so much great art was produced during the early part of this century. Nobody knows precisely what causes such convergences of greatness, nor is it possible to determine just where or when they are going to occur. It may be tempting to speculate about these matters from a post hoc perspective, but generally speaking the hard evidence on conditions that foster creativity is gathered from fairly restricted settings that can be studied more systematically than can a complex communitywide incubator of genius such as the Athens of a Pericles or the Vienna of a Beethoven.

INFLUENCES IN THE HOME

One place where the nurture of creativity can be monitored with some degree of precision is the home. Most of the available evidence derives from biographies dealing with the growing up years of eminent men and women (see Pressey, 1955; McCurdy, 1960; Goertzel and Goertzel, 1962; Goertzel et al., 1978; Bloom and Sosniak, 1981). No clear picture emerges from the various investigations, except that children destined for greatness vary widely in their relationships with parents. In some instances the home provides them with enthusiastic encouragement and opportunities to develop their talents; in other cases they have to overcome the ill effects of living with "smothering" or dominating mothers, failure-prone fathers, or generally troubled homes. Sometimes, parents show ambivalent feelings toward their children's creativity (Hitchfield, 1973). On the positive side, they are proud of what the children accomplish and enjoy taking part of the credit. Yet they feel somewhat embarrassed by the link between creativity and nonconformity and would like their children to be less distinguishable from their agemates in the way that they think and behave.

Child-Rearing Practices

Are there measures that parents can take consciously to enhance their children's creative performance? Roe (1953) expresses an optimistic view, suggesting that the family can have considerable influence in promoting or inhibiting creativity, depending on how flexible or rigid the parents are in their reactions to children's desire to engage in exploratory activity, intellectual as well as manual. Datta and Parloff (1967) explored these parental influences in their study of 1,039 male high school seniors who had scored above the eightieth percentile on a science exam and had competed in the 1963 and 1965 Westinghouse Science Talent Searches. They discovered that the main influence on early scientific creativity was autonomy versus parental control. The less creative students reported higher levels of enforcement and lower levels of autonomy than did their more creative counterparts. Datta and Parloff conclude that while autonomy/control is relevant to creativity, the issue is not one of permissiveness versus authority. Rather, the differences seem to be associated with the kinds of the achievement expectations children absorb from the home environment. Parental demands enforced in authoritarian ways may be associated with scholastic attainment and the need to achieve by conformity, while creative behavior may result from parents communicating to children a sense of trust in their ability to choose rationally, thus enhancing their desire to achieve by independence. These results confirm Nichols's (1964) study of child-rearing attitudes expressed by mothers of 796 males and 450 female National Merit finalists. The Parental Attitude Research Instrument (PARI) was administered to the mothers and scored for three factors: authoritarian-control, hostility-rejection, and democratic attitudes. Students in the sample were assessed by a variety of inventory scales, self-ratings, interest and activity checklists, high school performance measures, and teacher ratings. Results indicated that students whose mothers reported authoritarian child-rearing practices lacked originality and were more conforming in their thoughts and ways of expressing them. However, in comparison with children of nonauthoritarian mothers, they tended to make better grades in high school, and their behavior was rated more favorably by teachers. It would therefore seem that authoritarian child-rearing practices help lead to conformity and approved behavior, but stifle creativity.

It is possible, however, that in some instances, what appears to be autonomy granted by parents is really a case of parental rejection. Siegelman (1973) cites evidence of little warmth between creative individuals and their parents. Perhaps this is due to rebelliousness against rejecting parents that leads the child to independent thought and action. On the other hand, loving parents may influence the child's acceptance of parental orientations and thus encourage conformity to society's values and behaviors. Siegelman notes further that, although the maternal factor of "love-reject" appears stronger than the paternal in influencing creativity, the father's role should also be considered seriously. He refers to his own study of 418 college students in which he assessed their retrospective reports of early parental behavior. A factor analysis of these recollections yielded three consistent factors: love-reject, casual-demand, and protect. The Sixteeen Personality Factor Questionnaire (16 PF) was also administered and analyzed with specific attention to creativity and independence factors.

In relating the 16 PF results to self-reports on early relationships with parents, Siegelman found that sons and daughters with creative potential more often reported rejecting parents, whereas students with less creative potential were more likely to describe loving parents. Also, parents' casual or demanding child-rearing practices did not appear to influence creative personality traits in their children. As for parental protectiveness, only females responded creatively when this trait was demonstrated by their fathers. In other cases, being a protective parent did not seem to be a significant factor in encouraging or discouraging creativity.

According to Siegelman, the finding that children's creative potential is independent of parental casual-demand and protective approaches to child-rearing agrees with some previous research and is contradicted by other studies. He speculates that extremely casual or demanding home environments may foster creativity because, instead of conforming to their parents' expectations, the children respond to overprotecting or authoritarian parents with rebellion and independence. It is also possible that specific kinds of parental encouragement and rewards rather than more general orientations of casualness or demand, as measured in this study, account for children's autonomy and the fostering of their creative potential.

The inconsistencies in research evidence on stimulating creativity through child-rearing practices may be due partly to inconsistencies in research methodology. The studies vary widely in their definitions of creativity, its measurement, the ages of experimental samples, the specific fields in which creativity is demonstrated, the kinds of child-rearing practices, and the ways of collecting information about these practices. These variables have to be sorted out and controlled in a large-scale program of coordinated research that would lead to a better understanding of the dynamics of parent-child interaction and their effects on different kinds of productivity.

Parents' and Children's Creativity

There is also no definitive evidence on the relationship between divergent thinking in children and the creativity interests of parents. Domino (1979) compared forty-three mothers of creative boys with forty-three mothers of controls on a semistructured interview to determine parental attitudes and home environments in which the boys were being raised. The children, selected from grades four to six, were placed in the experimental and control groups on the basis of teacher nominations and scores on seven divergent thinking measures. Only those who came from intact families took part in the study. Results of the interview show that mothers of boys who scored well on divergent thinking tests were more deeply involved in creative pursuits, received greater public recognition for their attainments, and were more ready than control mothers to accept regressive behavior of their children. Control parents, while not being as involved personally in creative pursuits, encouraged their children to a greater extent to take part in cultural activities, provided their children with more varied learning materials and better facilities, and generally valued creativity more than did the mothers of creatives. It is therefore difficult to determine how the mothers of creatives influenced their children's creative pursuits.

Another attempt at obtaining clues from the home environment was made by Wallinga and Sedahlia (1979) in their investigation of a possible relationship between creativity of children and that of their parents. Their subjects were forty fifth-grade boys and twenty-five girls with a mean age of just under 11. Also participating were their mothers (N = 65) and their fathers (N = 56). The Torrance Tests of Creative Thinking were administered to both the children and adults to determine relationships and differences between the two groups. Results showed that children's scores correlated significantly with those of their fathers on the three total and on three verbal factor scores but did not correlate with any of their mothers' ratings. Children outscored their parents significantly on verbal scores, and parents outscored their children significantly on figural scores. With respect to their overall ratings on the test batteries, the children outperformed their fathers but not their mothers.

The Wallinga and Sedahlia study illustrates the difficulties that researchers have had in clarifying how the home influences children's performance on divergent thinking tests. It is difficult to draw meaningful conclusions from these data or even to use them in developing hypotheses for derivative investigations. But the same lack of consistency exists in the general research literature on home environments for children with creative potential regardless of how creativity is defined or measured and no matter whether the studies are retrospective or prospective. Whatever seems *logically* essential in child-rearing practices for the nurturance of creativity often fails to be confirmed *empirically*. The inconsistency of the picture suggests that perhaps there are no generalizations, except that much depends on the special "chemistry" between person and parent. For one child, a particular nurturance at home may inspire creative work; for another child, the same parental influence may have an adverse effect, or none at all. Generally, there is a need to determine what kinds of home environments and childhood individualities constitute the best "matches" in fostering creativity in children.

EFFECTS OF SCHOOL-BASED PROGRAMS

A great deal more effort has been expended on researching the influences of creativity programs at school than on isolating the critical factors in the community and the home. In school-based studies, experiments are generally conducted with programs designed to stimulate divergent thinking, and the criterion measures assess this type of skill. It remains to be demonstrated conclusively, however, that divergent thinking and creativity are synonymous and that so-called "creativity tests" have strong predictive validity. Given these basic limitations, the evidence on program effectiveness tends to be favorable, though sometimes mixed.

On the positive side, there is a review by Torrance (1972) of 142 evaluations of creativity programs, as many as 72 percent of which have proven successful (see Table 15-1). However, a sampling of studies for each of the nine types of

Table 15-1. Summary of Successes in Teaching Children to Think Creatively According to Type of Intervention

Types of Intervention	Number of Studies	Number of Successes	Percentage of Successes
1. Osborn-Parnes CPS and/or modifications	22	20.0	91%
2. Other disciplined approaches	5	4.0	92
3. Complex programs involving packages of materials	25	18.0	72
4. Creative arts as vehicle	18	14.5	81
5. Media and reading programs	10	7.8	78
6. Curricular and administrative arrangements	8	4.0	50
7. Teacher-classroom variables, climate	26	14.4	55
8. Motivation, reward, competition	12	8.0	67
9. Facilitating testing conditions	16	11.0	69
Total	142	101.7	72%

Source: Torrance, E. P. "Can We Teach Children to Think Creatively?" *Journal of Creative Behavior,* **6**: 114–141 (1972).

intervention shows how difficult it is to interpret the results. In most instances, the treatment consisted of exercises in divergent thinking, and the tests used to assess gain over the experimental period focused on the same thought processes, thus suggesting that experimenters were evaluating the effects of "teaching to the test."

There is, of course, also a possibility that children exposed to such programs perform exceptionally well not only on creativity tests but also on tasks requiring inventiveness, such as creative writing, art production, scientific research, or various kinds of stage performance. Or else they may be especially skillful at finding problems, not just solving them, brainstorming ideas, not just absorbing them, projecting consequences of events, not just planning or experiencing them, and trying to conceptualize and achieve what might be, rather than remaining satisfied with the status quo. There is no clear indication of how students apply their training in divergent thinking programs to broader fields of inquiry where such skills may be important.

Torrance's optimism about the values of creativity training is not shared by Mansfield, Busse, and Krepelka (1978) after their review of seventy-two evaluation studies. In addition to questioning whether improvement in divergent thinking enhances real-life creative accomplishments, they point out several methodological weaknesses in the research, as follows:

1. Creativity training programs may be successful only because they strengthen children's motivation and alert them to the fact that original and clever responses are wanted in both the instructional sessions and in the test periods.
2. Since few teachers participate in any one experiment, there is always the danger that the treatment effects may be confounded by instructional competence, not by the content of the program.
3. The "halo effects" are usually felt in such experimentation and can influence results significantly.
4. Students are often not assigned randomly to treatment and control conditions.
5. Instructional tasks bear a close resemblance to items on the criterion measures.
6. Individual scores rather than classroom means are used as the unit of statistical analysis.
7. Several univariate analyses are used rather than a single multivariate analysis.

In their review of evaluations of the Productive Thinking Program (Covington et al., 1972), Mansfield, Busse, and Krepelka acknowledged that evidence exists to support the program's effectiveness. However, results are far less encouraging when they are obtained from criterion measures that do not resemble the training materials. Besides, the largest training effects have been found in small studies with methodological flaws, whereas better designed investigations using large samples provide far less dramatic evidence of the programs' value.

Considerable evidence also exists on the efficacy of the Purdue Creativity Training Program (Feldhusen et al., 1970), and the results are generally supportive. But here, too, Mansfield et al. (1978) find methodological limitations due to the use of individual scores rather than classroom means as units and also because of the similarities between content in the program and on the criterion measures. It may be of interest to practitioners to know that, if there are advantages to the Purdue program, most of them can be gained by administering it through a self-instruction method, which is relatively easy for the teacher to implement (Huber et al., 1979).

Studies of other programs, such as the Myers-Torrance Workbooks (1964, 1965, 1966a, 1968) and the Khatena Training Method (1970, 1971a, 1973), also report evidence on exceptional gains of divergent thinking tests, but these instruments measure the same thought processes that are stressed in the training programs. What remains to be seen in any of these evaluations is whether there are long-term effects on solving and finding problems in broad, vital domains of knowledge.

From the vast amount of evaluative evidence reported thus far, it would seem that creativity training is a matter of "ya gets what ya pays for." In other words, children who receive practice in divergent thinking exercises generally perform better in them than do children who do not receive such instruction, provided that the groups are compared on a test battery that closely resembles the creativity training program. But as Anderson and Anderson (1963) conclude from their study of sixth-graders, the skills may not transfer automatically to insight problems in other contexts. This means that teachers have to infiltrate divergent thinking into all areas of the curriculum rather than restrict it to a self-contained unit of study or a time-out period of fun and games.

Administrative Adjustments

Experiments have been conducted on the relative effectiveness of different kinds of grouping arrangements to stimulate creativity under laboratory and classroom conditions. Among the more popular questions is whether groups perform better than do individuals working separately on brainstorming solutions to divergent-type problems. The research evidence that exists thus far pertains to adult populations, and the conclusions to be drawn from it are not entirely clear. Osborn's (1957) experiences in experimenting with various brainstorming techniques convinced him that individuals can generate more creative ideas by working together than by working alone. However, research by Taylor, Berry, and Block (1958) and Dunnette, Campbell, and Jaastad (1963) shows that brainstorming groups are more prone to pursue a rigidly single line of thought for extended periods of time than are individuals operating under similar conditions. Moreover, the rules to avoid criticism during brainstorming do not always help group members to overcome inhibitions about expressing any ideas that come to mind.

Perhaps the key lies in the kinds of groups that are engaged in brainstorming and how they are trained. For example, Cohen, Whitmyre, and Funk (1960) found that pairs of brainstormers with prior training in such processes and cohesive pairs, whose members preferred each other as partners for brainstorming, were more effective than were pairs without these attributes and also more effective than individuals. Ziller, Berringer, and Goodchilds (1962) also confirmed the importance of group organization in creative problem solving. In their experiment, they discovered that so-called "open groups" in which there is a change of membership tend to perform better on various creativity tasks than do "closed groups" that retain their membership intact during the course of creative problem solving. Thus, we see that it is not simply a matter of determining whether creativity is accomplished better by groups or by individuals; instead, what has to be determined is the nature of grouping arrangements and the prior training given to groups and individuals that will produce optimum results.

The limited empirical evidence on the influence of environments on creativity also makes it difficult to determine what kinds of classroom settings are likely to enhance such thought processes in children. Haddon and Lytton (1968) investigated British children in primary schools and discovered that those who were studying in relatively informal, permissive classrooms performed better on divergent production tests than did those who were taught in more formal classrooms. A follow-up study four years later showed that these differences were maintained (Haddon and Lytton, 1971). A somewhat similar study by Wilson, Stuckey, and Langevin (1972) showed that 11- and 12-year-olds attending an open school program for six years performed better on five out of eighteen creativity measures than did children in a newly established open school and those in two traditional schools.

Less conclusive are the results of another comparison between open and traditional schools (Ramey and Piper, 1974), which showed that children in the open school performed better on figural creativity and that traditionally taught children were superior in verbal creativity, as measured by the Torrance instruments. However, Ward and Barcher (1975) reported different findings in their comparison of high- and low-IQ elementary students in open and traditional classes. Their results show that, among high-IQ children, those in traditional classes scored higher on figural creativity tests than did those in open classes. For low-IQ children, type of classroom did not figure significantly in the children's performance on either verbal or figural creativity measures.

Even more discouraging results are reported by Wright (1975), who studied fifth-grade students attending open and traditional classes for three years and found no differences between them on the Torrance battery. These results were confirmed in a study of 129 second-graders with continuous educational experience in either open or traditional self-contained classrooms in three school systems (Foreman and McKinney, 1978). The children representing both types of classes scored at about the same level on the Wallach and Kogan tests. Interestingly, however, those in traditional classrooms performed consistently higher than did those in open classrooms on measures of vocabulary, reading, and mathematics achievement. These results suggest that it may be easier to create a classroom environment for children to advance in convergent-type mastery learning than in divergent-type productivity.

Open and traditional classes are not the only possible settings that deserve to be explored. Programs for the gifted have traditionally experimented with a variety of grouping arrangements that would enable children with extraordinary abilities to work closely with comparably able peers. Most of the evidence on the effects of ability grouping pertains to academic performance, while little attention is given to creativity. A notable exception is Bachtold's (1974) investigation of the verbal productivity of fifty-eight fifth- and sixth-graders with scores at or above the ninety-eighth percentile on an individualized intelligence test. The children were divided randomly and placed in three settings, as follows: (1) a special class program (SCP), a self-contained, full-day class providing extensive variation from the regular curriculum; (2) an enrichment program (EP) designed to develop special interests and provide in-depth experiences beyond the regular curriculum offerings; and (3) a learning center program (LCP) supervised by specially assigned teachers and designed for the free flow of interaction with volunteer parents and older students. The main objective of these programs was to encourage creative self-expression, openness to new experiences and ideas, flexibility, and adaptability. Comparisons among the groups were made on the Torrance battery, and results showed a greater increase in verbal creativity and in total verbal scores for the LCP over the other two samples and no significant differences between children in the SCP and EP classes. These results may be of interest to school administrators interested in establishing an atmosphere that encourages creative activity.

However, there is need for far more evidence than now exists to determine what or even *whether* special administrative arrangements make much difference. *How* children are grouped for creativity seems far less important than *what* they experience in these groups since so much depends on the nature of pupil-teacher interaction. Only after we know a good deal about the relationship between specific classroom practices and creativity can we begin to explore alternative school environments that make it possible for teachers to be most effective.

Direct Instruction

Since there is reason to believe that divergent thinking skills are amenable to cultivation, it is useful to know what specific strategies are useful in the nurturing process. Research has revealed the positive effects of various types of stimulation, mostly direct and occasionally indirect. A popular approach is through practice in brainstorming, which seems to result in the production of more and better ideas. For example, Turner and Rains (1965) addressed the question of whether both high and low creatives profit equally from brainstorming instructions, or are high creatives already working at a level that cannot be raised even through such practice sessions. Subjects consisted of thirty high-creative and twenty-nine low-creative college freshmen selected on the basis of two creativity measures. Both groups were given instructions to write as many ideas that come to mind regardless of how impractical or silly they may seem. As a result of these exercises, the high and low creatives achieved significantly higher scores, although the gap between them did not close.

Length of time devoted to brainstorming seems to affect the rate at which ideas are produced. Parnes (1961) compared the outputs of high and low creatives in a college-age population and discovered both groups producing more and better ideas in the second half of an extended brainstorming session than in the first. There was also a significant relationship between quantity and quality of ideas, and the high and low producers had similar proportions of good ideas in the second half of the total production period. These findings were recorded for subjects who had previous experience in brainstorming as well as for those who had no such earlier practice. There is also evidence to show that instructions on how to brainstorm have a beneficial effect on performance and that so-called "nominal groups" consisting of persons who brainstorm individually and later pool their responses are more successful than are "actual groups" in which members interact and cooperate from the start (Arici, 1965).

In another approach, Torrance (1970) cites four studies of 5-year-olds, fifth-graders, and college students on the effects of dyadic groupings on divergent production. Members of the dyads were seated side by side and called out their responses to each other as they wrote them. They were encouraged to listen to their partners' responses and to "hitchhike" on them so that the members of each pair could be mutually stimulating. In all these studies, the dyadic approach significantly increased the quality and quantity of creative responses.

A unique method of encouraging creative thought is reported by Taylor (1970) who provided five intensive weeks of sensory stimulation to a small group of 17-year-olds with a mean IQ of 158 and superior records in social adjustment and academic achievement. The exercises included a high-frequency signal from an oscillator, a phosphorescent Archimedes spiral wheel, pungent incense, a floor vibrator, and percussion-type music. In addition, there were several group sessions that included experiments in independent judgment and training. The results, based on judgments of students' drawings before and after sensory stimulation, showed that the experience of the experimental group had a significant effect on the aesthetic quality and psychological openness of their drawings.

Another study (Feldhusen et al., 1975) also tested the effects of nonverbal stimulation, although in this case training was conducted through pictorial (not auditory) images. These visual stimuli were related somewhat to questions derived from Guilford's Consequences Test and presented to a sample of undergraduate students. Another sample of undergraduates received similar experimental treatment, except that the stimuli were verbal.

All 125 subjects answered several of Guilford's Consequences Test questions, such as "What would be the results if everyone suddenly lost the ability to read and write?" Results show that (1) verbal stimuli associated with remote responses introduced during a divergent thinking task increased originality responses, although pictorial stimuli did not; (2) neither type of stimulus (verbal or pictorial) affected fluency; and (3) time of introducing the stimuli (either at the beginning or midway through the tasks) made no significant differences in the originality of the responses. It therefore appears that verbal stimuli may enhance the uniqueness of responses to verbal content, just as visual and auditory stimuli may help to improve artistic performance (Taylor, 1970).

Stratton and Brown (1972) have reported that two of the most widely used strategies for solving verbal problems creatively lead to conflicting results: training in the evaluation of completed solutions (judgment training) increases quality but reduces productivity, and training in idea-generating techniques (production training) increases productivity but reduces quality. The researchers therefore combined the two seemingly incompatible techniques and administered them to a sample of forty-five college students. The experimental group was then compared with samples operating under three other conditions: production training, judgment training, and a no-training control. Results show that, in comparison with separate or no training, combined training procedures increased productivity, solution quality, and judgment accuracy. These outcomes suggest that educators have to define precisely the kinds of creativity skills they seek to stimulate in children. If they want their pupils to generate sheer quantities of ideas, then nonevaluative production training procedures may be most appropriate. On the other hand, if solutions to problems are judged by quality rather than by quantity, then some form of judgment training is warranted. "In other words, a form of production training gets more ideas out of reluctant contributors while a form of judgment training increases the probability of the success of each solution. A practical consequence of the combined training is that both productivity and probability of success can be increased" (Stratton and Brown, 1972, p. 397).

Hershey (1979) evaluated a method of creativity stimulation that is somewhat indirect in that it emphasizes relaxation techniques in addition to guided fantasy. Fifty-one fifth- and sixth-graders with scores above the ninety-fifth percentile on achievement tests were divided into two groups, one taking part in relaxation/ guided fantasy sessions and the other serving as a control and participating in "just for recreation" activities in arithmetic, such as games, puzzles, and riddles. After eight half-hour sessions, both groups took the Torrance tests to assess creative thinking ability and submitted written compositions that were rated for creative writing skills. Results showed significantly higher scores for the exper- imentals on the Torrance tests at both grade levels; however, the outcomes on creative writing were inconclusive, due perhaps to low interrater reliability in scoring the compositions.

An even more indirect method of improving performance on divergent thinking tests is the use of humor as a stimulus. Ziv (1976) organized 282 Israeli tenth- graders into experimental and control groups in a study that assessed the effects of listening to a recorded performance of a comedian. Pre- to posttest differences on the Torrance battery were greater for the experimentals than for the controls on total score and three subscores, including fluency, flexibility, and originality. Besides being of practical value to educators seeking to upgrade divergent produc- tion among children, these results raise an interesting question about the role of humor in tested creativity.

Getzels and Jackson (1962) also found that adolescents scoring high on creativity measures had exceptionally good senses of humor. Is this trait, then, a nonintel- lective concomitant or part of the essence of creative functioning? Perhaps it signifies that divergent production is at least partly a turn of mind rather than just a special power of intellect. That is, instead of measuring only the *ability* to solve problems in unconventional ways, the Guilford- and Torrance-type tests may also (or primarily) be useful in assessing *sensitivity* to the unconventional, the absurd, the bizarre, the offbeat, and the unexpected ways of looking at the world, all of which are strongly reflected in humor. Stimulating humor in children could therefore positively affect their performance on so-called "creativity measures."

A similar case can be made for increasing children's capacity to live with frustration and lack of closure in scholastic activities. A study by MacDonald and Raths (1964) evaluated the extent to which more and less creative elementary school children (ages 9 to 12, N = 72) differed in their reactions to "open tasks," which encouraged varieties of responses in problem-solving situations, and "closed tasks," which required all children to respond alike. The experimental groups were also subjected to various frustrating curriculum tasks. Results show that the children's reactions to different kinds of classroom assignments were associated with scores on the Torrance tests. High creatives tended to perform exceptionally well on open and frustrating tasks and more often disliked closed tasks than did low creatives. This predilection for freewheeling and open-ended thought seems to characterize those who score well on divergent thinking tests, and nurturing such nonintellective traits may be crucial to the development of divergent mind sets in children.

Shaping the Learning Environment

Besides experimenting with direct instruction and the ways of creative thinking, researchers have also tested the effectiveness of manipulating the learning environment. Torrance (1964b) cited evidence on the responsiveness of children in grades four through six to three types of evaluation of their work on divergent thinking exercises: (1) criticism and correction, (2) suggestion of constructive possibilities, and (3) a combination of criticism and constructiveness. No differences were found as a result of these three types of evaluated practice. However, when peers applied the evaluation, the constructive approach proved more effective than did criticism and correction for children in the upper elementary grades. It is noteworthy, too, that the responsiveness to adult evaluation depended on how frequently it was communicated to the children. The least often evaluated groups seemed most productive, suggesting that evaluative treatment beyond a certain degree may inhibit creativity.

A possible key to the effectiveness of different types, sources, and degrees of evaluation is the extent to which they *motivate* rather than *train* creative thought processes. A study by Halpin (1973) assessed the effects of testing seven male and fifty-five female college students on the Torrance battery under conditions designed to increase motivation. Results show that the experimental treatment produced higher than expected scores in verbal fluency, flexibility, and originality. A somewhat similar investigation, conducted with 475 undergraduates showed that, when people were told they had reputations of being original thinkers, a mental set was created that upgraded their problem-solving effectiveness (Colgrove, 1968).

Competitiveness may also have a positive effect on motivation and consequently on divergent thinking. Raina (1968) informed an experimental group of high school students that cash prizes would be awarded to the three highest scorers on several subtests of the Torrance battery. As a result, the experimentals outperformed the matched controls in ideational fluency and flexibility of ideas, thus suggesting that competition can lead people to discover within themselves resources they had not known to exist.

These findings may come as a surprise to teachers who assume that children's creativity flourishes best in a permissive classroom environment. Indeed, Wodtke and Wallen (1965) tested the hypothesis that high teacher control, as opposed to permissiveness, would suppress the development of creative functioning among fourth- and fifth-graders scoring high on the Torrance tests. Results did not support the hypothesis, at least not for the short period of experimentation. Perhaps a much longer exposure to strict, authoritarian instruction would have the expected stifling effect on creativity. That remains to be seen, however, as research evidence continues to produce new insights into classroom social climates and how they relate to the nurturance of children's learning strengths and styles.

Chapter 16

The Creative Personality

Creativity is often portrayed in the professional literature as a unique cognitive power, exclusive of any other, or as an amalgam of general and specific abilities. Nonintellective traits that correlate with it are seen as facilitators of its fruition rather than as part of its essence. Yet a case can be made for personality as playing more than just an ancillary role in the process.

MacKinnon (1962) goes so far as to draw the following conclusion from his studies of creativity in adults: "Our data suggest . . . that if a person has the minimum of intelligence required for mastery of a field of knowledge, whether he performs creatively or banally in that field will be crucially determined by nonintellective factors" (p. 493). To the extent that this extreme generalization is justified, it may apply only to people who have already earned reputations for being highly creative in a particular field (i.e., architecture) studied by MacKinnon. For those who are only showing potentiality, not fulfillment, or even fulfillment in domains of productivity or performance other than architecture, nonintellective attributes may be less crucial in characterizing creativity. Indeed, after extensive research on the cognitive dimensions of creativity in science, Bloom (1963) seems to have reached a more even-handed conclusion than did MacKinnon when he stated "rather reluctantly that personality and motivational factors are at least as important as aptitude in determining performance" (p. 252). Although MacKinnon and Bloom differ on how much importance to attach to dispositional characteristics, both apparently agree that such attributes are essential to creative functioning.

Two methods have been used in investigating personality correlates of creativity. One is through the study of biographical data on persons who have achieved renown, and the other is through the analysis of responses to questionnaires administered to individuals who show either promise or success in their creative endeavors. Both types of research, the retrospective and the prospective, have already yielded a considerable amount of information that is consistent enough to clarify the nature of the creative personality to some extent.

In their review of empirical studies conducted over a fifteen-year period on nonintellective traits of gifted people, Barron and Harrington (1981) report a fairly stable set of characteristics that emerge repeatedly. Included among them are "high valuation of aesthetic qualities in experience, broad interests, attraction to complexity, high energy, independence of judgment, autonomy, intuition, self-confidence, ability to resolve antinomies or to accommodate apparently opposite or conflicting traits in one's self-concept, and, finally, a firm sense of self as 'creative' " (p. 453). These are designated as "core traits" because they tend to be common among people in various fields of creativity, including the arts, music, science, and writing. However, it is not known which of the attributes are *responsible* for creative achievement, which are merely *associated* with it, and which are *by-products* of it.

HETEROGENEITY AMONG CREATIVES

The reappearance of certain personality traits in study after study of creatives representing different fields suggests the existence of commonalities among these diverse populations. In other words, such persons resemble each other in some ways by virtue of their creativity, at least in the few areas of accomplishment investigated closely. There are also personality traits that distinguish creatives in one field from those of any other. One extensive study that illustrates consistencies and contrasts among various types of specialists was reported by MacKinnon (1960) who administered several cognitive and personality measures to samples of twenty writers, forty architects, forty-five research scientists, and forty-one female mathematicians. Responses to the Myers-Briggs Type Indicator showed that between 90 and 100 percent of the creatives in these groups characterized themselves as "intuitives" rather than as "sense-perceptives" in contrast to only 25 percent of the general population characterizing themselves in this way. However, groups differed in their preferences between "feeling" and "thinking." The writers favored "feeling" strongly, and the architects were divided evenly in their choice of one or the other of these two functions. On the other hand, the research scientists and mathematicians felt more attuned to "thinking."

MacKinnon (1961) administered the California Psychological Inventory to a group of creative architects and found that the most distinctive traits included self-confidence, aggressiveness, flexibility, self-acceptance, little concern with social restraints or other people's opinions, and strong motivation to achieve in situations requiring independent thought and action rather than conformity. A strong need for independence and assertiveness was also found in studies of creative research scientists (Roe, 1953; Stein, 1956) and artists (Roe, 1975).

However, Roe (1975) also pointed to some basic differences in the personality structures of artists and scientists. To an extent even greater than among scientists, artists were seen as entirely on their own and in need of a great deal of self-discipline. While the scientist strives for comprehensiveness and elegance in explaining natural phenomena, the artist aspires and struggles to create beauty. Although painters do not often show overt homosexual tendencies, a frequent pattern among them is passivity and almost feminine submissiveness, which is partly related to a rich responsiveness to the external world, especially to sensual stimuli. In the relatively few instances in which aggressiveness is expressed, it can usually be seen as defensive and fraught with considerable conflict. Scientists are also generally nonagressive, but they lack the basic passivity associated with fine artists. For both groups, perhaps the strongest impulse is the need to create. As Roe (1975) stated, "Creativity, as seen in both artists and scientists, does not come from any sudden inspiration invading an idle mind and idle hands, but from the labor of a driven person" (p. 168).

In a study of 740 male scientists, Chambers (1964) compared eminent creative chemists and psychologists with lesser known professionals in these fields on various personality inventories. The creative researchers emerged as strongly motivated individualists who are self-propelled and whose interests are channeled away from social and civic activities and directed toward their own individual research problems. They were also described as being more dominant and as having stronger initiative than their less creative counterparts. The comparison between creative psychologists and chemists indicated that the psychologists were more bohemian, introverted, unconventional, and imaginative in their thinking and behavior.

By far the greatest differences in Chambers's (1964) investigation were found in comparisons of creatives with noncreatives. He showed that creative scientists are not overly concerned with other persons' views of them or with obtaining approval for the work they are doing. They do not wait for someone else to tell them what to do but would rather take action on their own with little regard for convention or current fashion. They are prepared to face the consequences of making unpopular decisions or pursuing unconventional paths in their search for evidence relating to nature's laws. Despite their self-sufficiency, they do not tend to engage in schizophrenic-type behavior or experience severe emotional problems.

In an examination of the nature of relationships between personality variables and creative productivity, Gilchrist (1970) studied 112 female and 81 male college students majoring mostly in the arts and architecture. She found a correlation of .28 between the scores on the Creative Interest Scales of the Zimmerman-Guilford Interest Inventory and ratings of creative productivity. Although highly significant for a sample of this size, the correlation indicates a relatively small degree of overlap between creative attitudes and creative productivity. It was also found that students scoring high on both these scales saw themselves as unconventional, impulsive, prepared to take risks, observant, imaginative, idealistic, concerned with beauty, and subject to emotional conflicts. High scores on creative attitudes alone were correlated positively with traits denoting self-actualization and controlled regressive experiences. High scores on creative productivity alone were related to neurotic symptoms and lack of self-control.

Gilchrist concluded that respondents who actually engage actively in creative pursuits tend to be impractical, lack self-control, and are subject to neurotic disorders. She speculated that a sublimation theory of creativity that emphasizes the impulse to solve problems and resolve neurotic conflicts may be more valid than Maslow's theory of self-actualization. MacKinnon (1975) likewise reported traces of psychopathology among creative architects, but at the same time there is evidence of ego strength and the courage to be open to experiencing the inner life.

In their study of the 153 artists and writers, Drevdahl and Cattell (1958) used the Cattell 16 PF test, which provides estimates of sixteen independent and objective personality characteristics. Results show that, in comparison with the population on which the test was standardized, the experimental sample was somewhat more intelligent, dominant, adventurous, bohemian, radical, self-sufficient, and emotionally mature and sensitive. As for comparisons between creative artists and writers, the researchers concluded from their data that differences between these two groups were associated more clearly with personality than with intellect. Artists are more bohemian and less intelligent than writers, perhaps because artistic talent and creativity depend more on emotional expression than on cognitive power. Science fiction writers appear to be somewhat more radical and less emotionally sensitive than nonscience fiction writers and artists. This may reflect their involvement in a world that has no present-day counterpart in "reality." The fact that they also have greater degrees of dominance and surgency may likewise help them to conceptualize and convey radically different and unusual stories or points of view.

Halpin, Payne, and Ellett (1973) reported an elaborate study on 360 junior and senior high school students participating in the Georgia Governor's Honors Program, an eight-week summer educational experience for the academically and artistically gifted. The purpose of the investigation was to determine differences among adolescents displaying special aptitudes in mathematics, science, English, foreign language, social science, drama, music, and art. Those with exceptional artistic ability were required to achieve at least a fiftieth percentile rank on the Cognitive Abilities Test (CAT), while those with academic talents had to place at least at the ninety-fourth percentile. In addition, the students had overall grade averages of "B" or better, attained high scores in achievement and aptitude tests, and showed strong interests in special areas of study. All responded to a questionnaire, "What kind of person are you?," a fifty-item forced-choice creative personality inventory. Data on the validity of this instrument suggest that scores are significantly related to skills in producing original stories, tendencies to be "creatively oriented," and inclinations toward majoring in creative arts such as speech, drama, and fine art.

In making comparisons among the subsamples, the researchers found differences among gifted individuals in various areas of specialization. Those in the social and natural sciences and fine arts had significantly higher mean scores in their creative personality traits than did the music and foreign language groups. The scientifically and artistically gifted seemed to be more curious, energetic, independent, determined, and willing to take risks. They also liked to work alone, preferred complex tasks, and resisted accepting ideas on face value. Children designated as musically gifted scored lowest on the criterion measure, possibly because they were chosen for their technical development rather than artistic interpretations or inventiveness.

Thus we see the similarities and differences among people, mostly adults, who have "made it" in various creative endeavors. Despite the differences in samples and measuring devices, a creative individual emerges as a person with enduring interest in imaginative activity, some mistrust of personal relationships, tendencies toward impulsivity and rebelliousness and investment in an inner life, and strong independence of judgment and originality. Yet there are also ways in which creative scientists, writers, musicians, artists, and any others who excel through productivity or performance in their separate ways can be distinguished by personal characteristics associated with their separate areas of specialization. These idiosyncracies seem to predispose an individual to achieve distinction in a particular field, while others with comparable creative ability may be moved by their own character structures to find other paths to accomplishment.

Because of the difficulty in predicting adult creativity from childhood performance on cognitive measures, it may be useful to examine personality traits to help in making prognoses for the future. Dellas and Gaier (1970) draw evidence from various studies to show a similarity of nonintellective characteristics among younger and older populations rated high in creativity. Since these attributes develop fairly early in life, they may help in the early identification of potential. Unfortunately, however, the similarities have to be extrapolated from separate studies of childhood and adult samples since there is no large-scale longitudinal study of creative development comparable to Terman's work with high-IQ children.

One of the few large-scale follow-up investigations focusing on aspects of personality development of young creatives is reported by Schaefer (1973), whose initial sample consisted of 800 high school students from higher socioeconomic backgrounds and selected from schools noted for their outstanding academic achievement records. These adolescents reported on their self-concepts through the Adjective Check List (ACL), and 390 of them were retested on the same instrument five years later. Subjects identified as "creative" on the basis of teacher nominations and scores on Guilford's Alternative Uses and Consequences Tests were compared pre and post with the rest of the sample, which served as a control.

In the first administration of the ACL Scales, the creatives scored higher on measures related to openness to both external and internal experience and self-assertiveness and rated themselves as relatively low on inhibition of impulses and social acceptance. The report on the pretest results (Schaefer, 1969) also showed that the creative adolescents' traits, as revealed on the ACL, were in many ways similar to those associated with adult creatives. Specifically, the children reported themselves to be creative (imaginative, artistic, ingenious, original), independent (unconventional, individualistic), uninhibited (spontaneous, impulsive), iconoclastic (assertive, outspoken, rebellious), complicated (complex, reflective, cynical, idealistic), and asocial (aloof). Members of the control group, on the other hand, saw themselves more often as dependable, cooperative, contented, conventional, and quiet.

The follow-up findings indicate that the creatives continued to report high self-concepts, although in comparison with the controls they distinguished themselves more dramatically during early adolescence than five years later. In fact, the self-concepts of creative science and mathematics students did not remain distinctive over the five-year period. However, those in the writing and art fields remained consistently superior over control in three ways: (1) their willingness to live with complexity and to reconcile the cynical and idealistic forces in their nature; (2) their impulsivity and craving for novelty; and (3) their preference for working alone in recognition of their need for autonomy and self-assertiveness. Judging from the results of this study, and from another reported earlier by Schaefer (1972), it would seem that similar nonintellective traits are found among adult and adolescent creatives and that to some extent these characteristics remain stable for at least part of a person's lifetime. Nevertheless, such stability may exist in some fields of specialization, but not in others. It would also be interesting to determine the possibility of discerning these self-concepts before a person reaches adolescence.

Despite the evidence showing similarities in personal characteristics between younger and older creatives, several misconceptions have evolved regarding creativity in children and adults. Dudek (1974) cites several myths that are sometimes found in the professional literature:

1. Creativity is universal among young children, but it fades as they grow older.
2. Creativity in young children disappears as a result of society's pressures toward conformity.
3. Children are naturally creative and only require the right atmosphere in which to manifest it.
4. A child creates at will and at a moment's notice.

In her own longitudinal study, Dudek (1974) followed a group of twenty-seven children from grade one through grade six. Each child in the sample was rated for creativity on Torrance's battery, while personality was measured by psychiatric evaluation, teachers' classroom ratings, and Cattell's Children's Personality Questionnaire. Results show signs of partial stability and some change over the period of the study. On the Children's Personality Questionnaire, factors of outgoing, conscientious, venturesome, and tender-minded were related significantly to divergent thinking scores in grade one. The factor structure changed in grade four, but in the fifth grade no significant correlation between personality and divergent thinking scores was obtained. There was also a significant positive relationship between the psychiatrist's evaluation of mental health and creativity scores in the first grade, but this relationship was no longer evident by the time the children reached the fourth grade.

Dudek notes that creativity measures taken at an early age are not predictive of future performance, but it is reasonable to hypothesize that, if a child shows high creative ability that is then fostered and encouraged, these talents will continue to develop into the adult years. She also views creativity as a process, not as the making of material products, and the distinguishing characteristic is the individual's openness to varied experiences and to one's own thought and feelings. It therefore relies heavily on a constellation of nonintellective traits, not simply on some kind of cognitive ability.

The exact relationship between personality variables and creative performance or productivity is an empirical question, not yet fully resolved. What we have thus far is considerable information about the traits that distinguish creatives from noncreatives. We know, for example, that the creatively endowed seem to have stronger motivation toward achieving excellence; they are attracted to unusual and unconventional jobs and kinds of accomplishments; they possess considerable independence of judgment, which allows them to tolerate ambiguity, delay closure in finding and solving problems, and harbor doubts about existing truisms, even those they arrive at themselves; and they prefer a life of "divine discontent" rather than one of comfort, "normality," conformity, complacency, and happiness. Yet, we lack data on which of these or any other nonintellective traits exhibited in childhood can help to predict creative achievements in adulthood. The only way in which to examine such issues systematically is through large-scale longitudinal studies that focus on the regression effects of relevant variables singly and in combination.

Barron and Harrington (1981) express the hope that the Murray Research Center for the Study of Lives, founded at Radcliffe College in 1979, will produce much needed insight into the development of creative individuals. The outcomes of such studies could parallel those dealing with the prediction of scholastic achievement from measures of personality and IQ (Warburton, 1961, 1962a, 1962b; Barton et al., 1972).

The results of the latter investigations may be summarized as follows: (1) measures of both IQ and personality are superior to either type of measure taken singly in predicting various kinds of achievement; (2) some personality factors seem to be related to achievement only at particular age levels, not at others; and (3) some personality factors are related specifically to individual areas of accomplishment, but not to others, and the same is true for individuals with high IQs. Perhaps an assessment of selected personality traits in children can help to predict future levels and even fields of creativity. These measures may be particularly valid in combination with assessments of intellectual functioning, either convergent or divergent, or both. Such issues can be resolved through longitudinal investigations aimed, in part at least, at determining how best to forecast creativity in adults from data collected on children.

SELF-ACTUALIZATION AND SELF-CONCEPT

Maslow's (1959) belief in a positive relationship between creativity and self-actualization is generally supported by research evidence. For example, in Vernon's (1970) study of over more than two hundred adolescent boys and girls, the Mednick Remote Associates Test (RAT) and an inventory of biographical information were used to measure creativity, while self-actualization was assessed by the Shostrom Person Orientation Inventory (POI). The latter instrument is based on the humanistic-existential definition of self-actualization, which is characterized by the person who functions more fully and lives a more enriched life than do most people. Those who achieve self-actualization are seen as developing and using all their unique capabilities or potentialities, relatively free of inhibitions and emotional turmoil.

A correlational analysis involving creativity and self-actualization scores showed a close association between the two variables. Furthermore, comparisons of subpopulations categorized by high and low creativity and IQ revealed that students high in IQ and creativity did not differ significantly in ego strength from students high in creativity alone but were significantly higher in ego strength than were students high in IQ alone.

In their review of past research, Murphy, Dauw, Horton, and Fredian (1976) also concluded that there is a positive relationship between creativity and self-actualization. In their own study, they tested this hypothesis on a sample of eighty-eight seminarians majoring in philosophy and theology and eighty-nine business majors at a local university. Creativity was assessed by the Torrance battery and self-actualization by the POI. Results showed no strong relationship between creativity and self-actualization. Although seminarians scored significantly higher on the creativity measures than did the business students, there was no difference between the levels of self-actualization for these two samples.

The authors explained their results by suggesting the following possibilities: (1) subjects were not in fact self-actualizing according to Maslow's definition, but were individuals who possessed positive mental health; (2) if a more obviously creative group had been sampled, such as exceptionally productive artists or architects, then more significant differences might have been found; and (3) the instruments utilized in the study may not measure the concepts under investigation accurately enough. Thus, we see that, despite the logical relationship between creativity and self-actualization, there may still exist conceptual and measurement problems to be resolved.

The self-concept of adults acknowledged by their peers as highly creative has also been a subject of investigation. One intensive study was reported by MacKinnon (1963) on 124 American architects divided into three groups according to their ratings as creative in their profession. Each subject was asked to indicate on the Gough Adjective Checklist (ACL) of three hundred adjectives which ones he judged to be most descriptive of himself and then to indicate the ones describing him if he were the person he would like to be. The two images thus obtained were, first, that of the real self and, second, that of the ideal self or ego ideal.

With respect to the real self, results showed that all architects in the study tended to think well of themselves, but the quality of the self-image differed from one sample to the next. The highly creative subjects more often stressed their inventiveness, independence, individuality, enthusiasm, determination, and industry. The less creative ones tended to be most impressed by their own virtue and good character and by their rationality and sympathetic concern for others. As for their descriptions of the ideal self, the most creative architects were recognizable by their wish for greater personal attractiveness, self-confidence, courage, adventure, masculinity, optimism, strength, and daring. Socially, they would like to be more generous, considerate, forgiving, friendly, sympathetic, affectionate, patient, tactful, and warm. What emerges from these studies of architects is an association between their levels of creativity and the distinctiveness of their self-images. The most creative ones thought better of themselves and differently about themselves, in contrast to those who were less endowed. Moreover, their images were extremely realistic. As MacKinnon (1963) notes, "one is struck by the accuracy of self-perception, by the degree to which architects see themselves as they really are, and by the remarkable consistency with which they conform in their thought and in their behavior to the type of person they see themselves as being" (p. 276).

There is also empirical evidence on the self-concepts of children judged to be creative. Milgram and Milgram (1976b) investigated the relationship of self-concepts to divergent thinking skills and tested intelligence in a sample of 159 Israeli children, from grades four through eight with WISC IQs ranging from 125 to 140. A modified version of the Wallach-Kogan Test was used to measure divergent thinking, and an Israeli adaptation of the Tennessee Self-Concept Scale was used to assess several aspects of self-esteem. For purposes of data analysis, estimates of general intelligence were made from the Ortar Milta test, an instrument normed on Israeli population.

Of the twenty-nine correlations between the Milta and Self-Concept measures, only four were statistically significant, in contrast to the ten significant relationships between self-concept and divergent thinking scores. According to Milgram and Milgram, the relatively low correlations between IQ and self-concept were not due to restrictions in the IQ range. As evidence, they reported that standard deviations for IQ as well as divergent thinking scores were as great for the study sample as they are for the general population. Instead, they explained their results on the basis of different competencies denoted by intelligence and creativity and the effects of these competencies on self-concept. They believe that children who score as high as IQ 150 do not necessarily solve problems more effectively than do those with IQs around 125; therefore, those with better scores will not receive more positive social reinforcement to provide an extra boost to their self-concept. On the other hand, the kinds of problem-solving skills that are demonstrated by exceptionally creative children may be so imaginative and attractive that they tend to maximize social reinforcement and thereby enhance their images of themselves.

This explanation of the data is highly speculative, but it is the one preferred by the researchers. An alternative line of reasoning would suggest that a low correlation between IQ and self-concept was an artifact of sample and test selection. Since IQ scores are less reliable at the upper extreme of the distribution than they are close to the mean, coefficients for a group of high-IQ children could be depressed even while IQ and self-concept correlate highly across the total IQ range. Nevertheless, the high correlations between divergent thinking and self-concept scores help us to understand what kinds of children perform well on such measures.

Further insight into the relationship between self-concept and divergent thinking skills was reported by Sisk (1980) in a large-scale study involving a random sample of fifteen classes of sixth-graders (N = 400). The major purposes of the study were to assess the influence of the self-concept and general ability on creative thinking and to determine whether children benefit from a specially designed series of exercises in self-knowledge. These exercises were designed to free the children's own ideas, to help them to express themselves, and to explore their separate identities through a series of oral and written tasks. Teachers working with the experimental groups received prior instruction on how to conduct the discussion and writing sessions, each of which lasted twenty minutes, once a week, for the five-week experimental period. In order to evaluate the effects of the program under controlled conditions, each of the fifteen classes was randomly assigned to one of three treatment groups, as follows:

1. Those who participated in writing exercises and discussions on topics encouraging self-knowledge.
2. Those who participated in writing exercises and discussions on topics that were general in scope.
3. Those who were given the tests on creative thinking and self-concept without any intervening treatments.

At the end of the five weeks of treatment, criterion measures were administered to all children. Self-concept was tested by the Bills Index of Adjustment Values, which provides a measure of self, acceptance of self, and ideal self. Divergent production was assessed by selected portions of Guilford Tests of Creative Thinking (i.e., Names for Stories and Ways to Use It), which were scored for fluency, flexibility, and originality. In addition, data on general ability were gleaned from the children's cumulative records, which contained scores on the California Test of Mental Maturity (CTMM).

Results confirm the general positive relationship between divergent thinking and self-concept. Scores on the Bills Instrument correlated significantly with measures of flexibility and fluency, though not with originality. In addition, training in self-knowledge seemed to have a significant effect on the children's flexibility scores, not on fluency and originality. Other findings show a positive relationship between tested intelligence and two out of the three divergent thinking measures: flexibility and originality. These findings are important not only because they show evidence of IQ, divergent thinking, and self-concept going hand in hand to some extent, but also because of the possible benefits of training in self-knowledge. Only a short series of writing exercises and guided discussions seemed to have a perceptible effect on the children's divergent performance. Perhaps more intensive and extensive efforts would increase our knowledge of how educators could enhance children's productivity by building up their pride in themselves.

TRAITS ASSOCIATED WITH HIGH/LOW CREATIVITY AND INTELLIGENCE

Children categorized by their performance on divergent and convergent thinking tests have provided important information not only about their cognitive powers but also their nonintellective traits. The Getzels and Jackson (1958) study comparing high-IQ, low-creative versus high-creative, low-IQ adolescents yielded clear personality differences.

For the high-IQ group, the correlation between the qualities they would like for themselves and the qualities they believed would lead to success in life was .81, as compared with only .10 for the high creatives. The correlation between personal qualities they would like to possess and those they believed teachers would favor was .67 for the high-IQs, in contrast to minus .25 among those scoring relatively high in creativity and low in IQ. The high-IQs exceeded the high creatives in wanting to possess such qualities as "pep," "character," "goal-directedness," and "high status." On the other hand, the high creatives wanted to possess wide ranges of interest, emotional stability, and a sense of humor. As for their career aspirations, 62 percent of the high creatives and only 18 percent of the high-IQs made unconventional choices. Finally, the high creatives showed more imagination than did the high-IQs in written stories based on projective test material, making significantly greater use of stimulus-free themes, unexpected endings, humorous turns of thought, playful styles, and incongruities.

Wallach and Kogan (1965) extended the Getzels and Jackson study by comparing personality characteristics associated with all possible combinations of high- and low-IQ and creativity in a sample of 151 fifth-graders. In order to test for general intelligence, ten indicators were utilized, including measures of scholastic aptitude and achievement. There were also ten creativity indicators derived from the Wallach and Kogan battery. Reliabilities on both sets of instruments proved to be high, as were the subtest intercorrelations within each battery. However, the correlations between creativity and intelligence tests were extremely low. Since separate analyses were made on boy and girl subsamples, it was possible to discern several personality differences between them, but in general, the patterns of variations associated with high and low creativity and intelligence were the same regardless of sex membership.

In summarizing the most consistent findings of the study, the researchers state that the four types of children can be described briefly as follows:

- *High Creativity-High Intelligence*: These children can exercise within themselves both control and freedom, both adult-like and child-like kinds of behavior.
- *High Creativity-Low Intelligence*: These children are in angry conflict with themselves and their school environment and are beset by feelings of unworthiness and inadequacy. In a stress-free context, however, they can blossom forth cognitively.
- *Low Creativity-High Intelligence*: These children can be described as "addicted" to school achievement. Academic failure would be perceived by them as catastrophic, so that they must continually strive to make excellent grades in order to avoid the possibility of pain.
- *Low Creativity-Low Intelligence*: Basically bewildered, these children engage in various defensive maneuvers, ranging from useful adaptations such as intensive social activity to regression such as passivity or the development of psychosomatic symptoms (p. 303).

As if to reinforce the findings of Wallach and Kogan (1965) on an older population, Welsh (1975, 1977) conducted a fairly similar study of adolescents that revealed generally similar clusters of nonintellective traits associated with the four creativity-IQ combinations. This study was conducted on a sample of more than one thousand boys and girls attending the Governor's School for the Gifted in North Carolina. IQ was determined by the Terman Concept Mastery Test (CMT), and the creativity measures consisted of the Revised Art Scale (RA) of the Welsh Figure Preference Test, a nonverbal personality measure. Trait descriptions for the subjects in the study were obtained from the Gough and Heilbrun Adjective Check-List (ACL), the Minnesota Multiphasic Personality Inventory (MMPI), and the Strong Vocational Interest Blank (SVIB). The students were then categorized as (1) high-RA, low-CMT, (2) high-RA, high-CMT, (3) low-RA, low-CMT, and (4) low-RA, high-CMT.

From an analysis of the data, two hypothetical personality dimensions emerged to account for differences in the four types of students. One such dimension is called "Intellectence," which describes individual predilections ranging from the concrete to the abstract. People characterized as low in Intellectence will relate best to "literal and specific events which may be expressed in concrete terms and that may have practical or pragmatic applications for the usual experiences of life" (Welsh, 1977). Those representing high Intellectence are more interested in abstractions, especially if it is figurative or symbolic. While Intellectence is associated with performance on the IQ-type measures, the second personality dimension, "Origence," is associated more directly with scores on creativity tests. Those at the low extreme of Origence feel comfortable with explicit and well-defined phenomena that can be grasped with the help of objective rules, whereas high-Origence people tend to be nonconforming and unconventional in their ways of dealing with the world and show an interest in artistic, literary, and aesthetic matters that allow great latitude for personal expression and interpretation. Table 16-1 summarizes the traits associated with high and low Intellectence and Origence.

In a study of adults focusing on every possible combination of high and low creativity and high and low IQ, Hitt and Stock (1965) sampled ninety-six engineers and scientists and found consistent variations in personality characteristics among all four types. Researchers scoring above the average in originality and logical reasoning tests proved to be exceptionally innovative thinkers who were not overly inhibited or too cautious in their work. They were able to identify problems and work energetically and responsibly. Those who were above average in originality but below average in logical reasoning were less cautious and less dependable in their work and enjoyed mixing with people and acting assertively toward them. Those who were below the average in originality and logical reasoning proved to be trusting of others and not strongly self-assertive. Finally, those who were above average in logical reasoning but below average in originality appeared to be emotionally stable, exceptionally cautious, and not self-assertive in group situations.

The studies by Wallach and Kogan (1965), Welsh (1975, 1977), and Hitt and Stock (1965) conducted separately on three age groups suggest that perhaps measures of creativity *do* help us to understand how people function, primarily with respect to their personal habits, attitudes, values, and life styles rather than special aptitudes. Other investigations of high school groups likewise show dis-

Table 16-1. Summary of Characteristics Associated with Dimensional Types

	High Origence, Low Intellectence	High Origence, High Intellectence	Low Origence, Low Intellectence	Low Origence, High Intellectence
Intrapersonal orientation	*Extroversive:* exhibitionistic, acting out	*Introverted:* withdrawing, ruminative	*Extroverted:* outward-directed, responsive	*Introversive:* inward-directed, speculative
Direction of activity	*Interactive:* interdependent, responder	*Proactive:* autonomous, detached viewer	*Reactive:* dependent, follower	*Active:* independent leader
Cognitive style	*Imaginative:* fantasy, improvisation, simile	*Intuitive:* insight, meditation, metaphor	*Customary:* industry, persistence, allegory	*Rational:* logic, deliberation, analogy
Attitudes and beliefs	*Irregular:* uncommon, "don't conform"	*Unorthodox:* unconventional, "take risks"	*Orthodox:* common, "play safe"	*Regular:* conventional, "follow rules"
Interpersonal conduct	*Sociable:* outgoing, many acquaintances, amicable	*Asocial:* isolative, few friends, impersonal	*Social:* friendly, indiscriminate sociality, benevolent	*Unsocial:* shy, guarded sociality, humanitarian
Nature of self-concept	*Self-seeking:* egocentric	*Self-centered:* egotistic	*Self-effacing:* allocentric	*Self-confident:* egoistic
Cognitive development	*Proto-integration without differentiation:* diffuse, global, imprecise	*Integration with differentiation:* synthesis, organization, composition	*Proto-differentiation without integration:* fragmented, detailed, unrelated	*Differentiation with integration:* analysis, specification, resolution
Vocational interests	*Histrionic:* action, performing and dramatic arts, sales occupations	*Intellectual:* ideas, arts and humanities, related occupations (e.g., journalism)	*Pragmatic:* practical problems, commerce and business, service occupations	*Scientific:* concepts, sciences and mathamatics, related occupations (e.g., statistician)

Source: G. S. Welsh, "Personality Correlates of Intelligence and Creativity in Gifted Adolescents," in J. C. Stanley, W. C. George, and C. H. Solano, eds., *The Gifted and the Creative* (Baltimore, Md.: Johns Hopkins University Press, 1977), pp. 200–201.

tinctive personality patterns associated with scores on creativity and IQ tests (Holland, 1961; Iwata, 1968; Damm, 1970). In the aggregate, these investigations show that people are different from each other, depending on how they perform on tests of creativity, and they may vary more predictably in their belief systems and the behavior codes than in their abilities to solve or find problems. The questions remains, however: Does so-called "creativity" reveal potential for original thinking or clues to the Origence dimension of personality?

Chapter 17 _____

Creativity and Mental Health

The creative person is sometimes seen as a "free spirit" who ignores conventional behavior codes or is unable to conform to them because of emotional deviance. We will never know just how much sanity, insanity, and supersanity is needed to make the creative act possible. The shyness of an Einstein and the moodiness of a Faulkner may be signs of deviance to be tolerated in geniuses but intolerable in ordinary mortals. Or perhaps the behavior of an Einstein and a Faulkner should be judged by special standards; what most people consider eccentricity could be a normal reaction to the world as only the creative person can see it. Conventional behavior codes may actually thwart creatives from producing or performing to the limits of their potentialities.

Psychoanalytic theory seems conflicted on the relationship between creativity and psychopathology. At one extreme is the Rank theory (1932, 1958), which suggests that neurosis itself contains creative elements that can stimulate the production of great art. At the other extreme, neoanalytic theory has maintained that "creative talent can be mediated within the conflict-free sphere of ego functions" (Suler, 1980, p. 159). However, both camps agree that a psychopathological defense against primary process thinking or a psychopathological surrender to it is a deterrent to creative thinking. Too much defense results in a rigid and conventional reality orientation and an absence of creative freedom and spontaneity. An easy surrender to primary process thinking, as demonstrated by psychotics, results in a highly subjective, fantasy-ridden perception of the world and a confusion of creativity with impulsivity.

It is possible that the effects of psychopathology on creativity depend on the area in which a person excels. For example, artists may derive creative power from their skill in gaining access to unconscious conflicts and incorporating these conflicts in their artistic work. On the basis of his clinical diagnosis of artist-patients,

Niederland (1973) found that traumatization during early development yielded a good portion of the content that was later absorbed into their creative products. Scientists, on the other hand, relate more directly to objective phenomena and therefore need not confront their own irrational impulses. This artist-scientist distinction is as yet speculative, but it is worth exploring, as it would shed light on the question of whether there are different typologies of creativity, each associated with a different area of competence.

Existing evidence on the connection between mental health and creativity is difficult to interpret since both phenomena are defined and nurtured in a variety of ways. There is also some difficulty in generalizing from different kinds of sample populations. Nevertheless, the research is worth examining for the few insights that it does provide. Spotts and Mackler (1967) report a study of 138 undergraduate males who were examined on parts of the Guilford and Torrance batteries as well as on several measures of field dependence-independence. Results showed a positive correlation between divergent thinking and field independence. The researchers also cited evidence from several previous studies that field-independent individuals may have adjustment problems since they tend to be rebellious, nonconforming, emotionally cold, tough, overambitious, overintellectualized, and overcontrolled. These findings are apparently in accord with MacKinnon's (1965) discovery that highly creative architects often defy convention and are so immersed in their work that they do not see the need to adapt socially.

In another study of college students, including males (N = 81) and females (N = 112) selected predominantly from arts and architecture programs, Taft and Gilchrist (1970) compared creativity ratings with scores on various personality measures. Creativity was measured by self-reports of productivity and also on the Creative Interests Scale of the Zimmerman-Guilford Interest Inventory. The correlation between the two assessments of creativity was .28, which indicates a relatively small degree of overlap between creative attitudes and productivity in the sample. Those who only scored high on the creative attitudes measure turned out to be pleasant, self-actualizing, extroverted, enthusiastic, quick-witted, and interested in theoretical and academic pursuits. On the other hand, subjects considered creative on the basis of productivity turned out to be more disorderly, impractical, and lacking in self-control than were those students who were distinguished by their creative attitudes. They also showed unusual interest in daydreaming, the use of imagination and a retreat from reality. Finally, creative production was frequently associated with unhappiness in childhood and neurotic disorders requiring medical attention.

A study of still another kind of adult population relied partly on clinical methods to determine whether a relationship exists between creativity and mental health. Cohen, Garfield, and Roth (1969) chose as their sample forty-seven male college students, ages 18 to 24, who were experiencing academic achievement problems that placed them in danger of dismissal from school. Three psychologists examined the men and rated them for their mental health. This was then followed by ratings from group therapists on two creativity indicators, Uses for Things (e.g., "How many uses can you think of for a brick?") and the Barron-Welsh Art Scale, which consists of sixty-two black-and-white drawings to be rated as being "liked" or "disliked" by the respondent. The creativity ratings obtained by the group therapists were then compared with the mental health diagnoses by the psychologists. Results showed positive, and in most cases, significant, correlations between creativity and mental health, although the coefficients were much higher for the Art Scale than for the Uses test. Researchers hypothesize that dynamic aspects of creativity may be associated more closely with mental health than are cognitive attributes of creativity.

The difficulty of determining whether or how mental health figures in creativity is reflected in the Barron and Harrington (1981) review of evidence on thought disorders and creativity. Studies report a similarity between schizophrenics and divergent thinkers in the way in which they respond to projective and trait list measures of personality. For example, a study by Barron (1972) showed that schizophrenics and artists resemble each other in their reports of sensory and perceptual experiences, a preference for solitude, rejection of common social values, and feelings of restlessness leading sometimes to impulsive outbursts. Yet the similarities may be superficial and therefore deceptive. What may count most is how these traits are used, either for productive or self-indulgent purposes. As Pickering (1974) suggests, a neurosis may provide not only the novel idea but also the necessary drive that helps see the idea through to completion, as in the cases of Joan of Arc, Mary Baker Eddy, Sigmund Freud, and Marcel Proust.

Studies of mental health and creativity in children produce a more encouraging picture than does the evidence on adults. Sussman and Justman (1975) offer evidence from previous research to show that a large number of traits associated with creativity in college-aged men and women have unfavorable connotations. However, their own study of 210 fourth-, fifth-, and sixth-grade boys employed a method similar to the one cited for adults and produced seemingly different results. Fourteen teachers were asked to indicate whether or not each of the fifty-nine adjectives on the Gough and Heilbrun Adjective Check List applied to their former students. The teachers also rated each child's creativity on the basis of their own subjective impressions. The 210 subjects were then divided into two groups, creatives and noncreatives, and compared on the fifty-nine traits.

The outcomes apparently contradicted evidence obtained for adults. The thirty-eight traits that differentiated the two subgroups all favored the creatives. Of these traits, thirty-four had desirable and four undesirable connotations. The researchers concluded that teachers seem to be more positive in their feelings about children they consider creative and they are negative about those they regard as noncreative. However, considering the nature of the research design, it is impossible to determine whether the teachers' responses were to creativity per se or to a mixture of attributes, some of them relevant and some irrelevant, but all of them regarded by teachers as "typifying" the creative personality.

Nevertheless, these positive results confirm Ogden's (1964) findings in a study of 2,516 fourth-graders. On the basis of uniform records kept by schools throughout the county where the investigation was made, there was evidence to show a significantly smaller proportion of children rated emotionally handicapped among those with high-creativity, high-IQ, or high-achievement scores than among those ranking lower in these characteristics.

Another issue addressed by researchers is the relationship between creativity and anxiety both for children and adults. In a study of 215 seventh- and eighth-graders, Hadley (1965) divided his sample into five subgroups, ranging from "very low" to "very high" in anxiety on the basis of scores on the Sarason Test Anxiety Scale for Children and the Sarason General Anxiety Scale for Children. Creativity was measured by parts of the Torrance battery and by Barron's Anagrams Test. Results showed a curvilinear relationship between tested creativity and anxiety, as hypothesized. However, another study of seventh- and eighth-graders using a similar design and instrumentation with a comparable-sized sample showed no significant relationship between anxiety and creativity (Feldhusen et al., 1965). When other kinds of anxiety measures are used and another age group is sampled, the results seem to be somewhat more consistent. For example, a study of two hundred male college freshmen measured anxiety through the 16 PF Questionnaire and creativity on two Guilford tests (White, 1968). Results showed high divergent thinking scores associated with low anxiety. Similar though far less dramatic results were obtained by Dentler and Mackler (1964) in their investigation of 120 high-achieving college students who took Torrance's Tin Can Uses and the Cattell and Scheier Test of Paranoid Anxiety.

Thus we see that the evidence on creativity and mental health relationships among children is not yet conclusive. Problems derive from variations in defining the concepts, characterizing adjustment and maladjustment, measuring creativity and psychopathology, selecting ability and age group samples, and employing methods of data analysis. Considering these diverse ways of approaching the central issue, it would be surprising if research produced a clear picture of the dynamic interaction between creativity and mental health.

But even if the evidence were consistent, it would be difficult to interpret in a practical sense. Comparable traits in two people can be used in ways that are not comparable. For example, it is known that schizophrenics and creatives both tend to absorb external stimuli indiscriminately. For the schizophrenic, it denotes a faulty filtering process that prevents distinguishing between relevant and irrelevant sensory experiences and contributes to the confusion between reality and unreality. For the creative, it is interpreted as openness to experience, a willingness to combine and recombine stimuli in unconventional ways to produce novel ideas. The same trait can therefore bring on a variety of behaviors, depending on who possesses it. Yet the fact that creatives sometimes share the same traits with emotionally handicapped people can give the impression that there is a streak of psychopathology in creativity. A streak may be there, but it cannot be inferred from superficial resemblances between creative and emotionally disturbed people. More clinical evidence is needed before any generalizations can be drawn.

Chapter 18

Concluding Thoughts About Creativity

The large body of theory and research on creativity is valuable in the sense that it has alerted educators of the gifted to locate children who are proficient in divergent thinking and to emphasize these thought processes in the classroom. However, as a psychological phenomenon, it is hard to evaluate its contribution to the understanding of human diversity, mainly because there is no universal agreement on how to recognize or measure it.

Hudson (1966) notes that some psychologists seem to regard "creativity" as a word of general approbation referring to human qualities that they admire. Like justice and morality, it is a universally acceptable virtue, but there is no universal agreement as to what it means. Nevertheless, there are at least four assumptions relating to creativity that Hudson considers influential, imprecise, and often misleading, and they still remain popular, though unsubstantiated. These myths may be summarized as follows: (1) we now have valid and reliable instruments to measure creativity; (2) those who score well on divergent thinking tests are potentially creative, but those who excel on convergent thinking measures are not; (3) divergent thinking gives people easier access to their unconscious impulses, thus enabling them to achieve good mental health, whereas convergent thinking is a form of neurotic defense against deep emotions; and (4) educators tend to be apathetic and sometimes hostile toward the divergent thinker, which jeopardizes the cultivation of creativity in schools.

Clearly, there is at least as much conflict and confusion about the meaning of creativity as there is about intelligence. In the research literature, creativity is defined by what so-called "creativity" tests measure just as intelligence is defined by its instruments for assessment. The problem is, however, that the instruments designed to measure creativity in children have not yet proven to be reliable and valid. We do not even have a clear understanding of how the psychological entity evaluated by these tests fits into the scheme of human potential. No matter how we characterize creativity, it probably consists of intellective and nonintellective attributes, and any instrument that assesses either one rather than both is probably insufficient. Yet there will always be a question as to whether it is realistic to expect any creativity test to be reliable, considering how mercurial creative inspiration seems to be. The "Aha!" sensation is sudden and transitory, and test performance may depend on whether it is administered near the moment of a person's peak experience or in more prosaic times.

There are other questions about creative thought processes that have to be addressed since they relate directly to problems of measurement. The following four are among the more salient ones:

1. Is the intellective aspect of creativity a kind of general ability? Or is it a catch-all term for special abilities that are essentially independent of each other? Great debates revolving about a g factor versus special and group factors in intelligence have no parallel in the literature on creativity. Judging from the allusions made to it by laypersons and behavioral scientists alike, it would appear that it is a unitary factor. Even Guilford often seems to refer to creativity as if it were a global phenomenon, something he would be far more reluctant to claim with respect to intelligence—even though he argues for the existence of differentiated divergent thinking aptitudes (Guilford, 1967). At stake here is our understanding of how a person manages to demonstrate productivity in one field rather than in another. If the same *kind* of creative power is used in composing music and in conducting scientific research, then creativity helps to determine the *extent*, not the *nature*, of individual potential. The educator's task is to enable creative children to take separate paths toward excellence by exposing them to many fields of inquiry and allowing their own predilections to determine which they will pursue. On the other hand, if creativity is specific in nature, children who show signs of it by writing poetry are no more apt than are any of their classmates to have original ideas in mathematics no matter how much special mathematics enrichment they receive. Each child would then be encouraged to specialize even in the early grades without focusing so narrowly as to exclude other possible interests.

2. A related question is whether "creativity" is an umbrella term for various intellective processes that are basically dissimilar. Does it figure in such accomplishments as *discovery* (as in the case of a Jonas Salk), *invention* (as in the case of a Johannes Gutenberg), and *composition* (as in the case of a William Shakespeare)? Does the creator of great art songs, such as Franz Schubert, use the same kind of creative powers as does a great singer (i.e., re-creator) of his songs, such as Lotte Lehmann? Except for a rich imagination, it is hard to name another intellective attribute that is common to all these forms of creativity. Unless there are more underlying similarities, it will be difficult to conceive of a single test that can measure creative potential in all its diversity. The problem can be even more serious if there are variations *within* the various types of creative functioning, no matter how they are categorized. For example, whatever it takes to be inventive in science may bear little resemblance to the requisites for invention of new art forms.

Perhaps the only way in which to find out where there are similarities and differences in the many realms of creativity is to monitor precisely how creative people function when they are in the process of being productive, as Getzels and Csikszentmihalyi (1976) did in their study of talented art students.

3. Are divergent thinking skills the important signs of creativity? Apparently so, judging from the popular measures of fluency, flexibility, elaboration, and originality. Yet it seems strange to think of a creative product or performance without considering its quality. People can be prolific, innovative, and sensitive to details and still never rise above mediocrity because their work lacks aesthetic appeal and whatever else it takes to please a discerning audience. And those who achieve immortality are appreciated for being more than just divergent thinkers. Wordsworth produced a larger body of poetry than did Coleridge, but it did not necessarily make Wordsworth a better Romantic poet; Rembrandt expressed himself through fewer art media than did Picasso without suffering by comparison as an artist; and although Beethoven and Mahler completed the same number of symphonies, Mahler's larger-scale orchestration and complexity of themes are not enough to qualify his compositions as more precious in the symphonic literature. As for the criterion of originality, it merely means that the product or performance is unique, not better than the commonplace. A chunk of coal is shaped differently from any one that has ever existed, and yet it fails to be included in our sculptural treasures. Of course, assessing the quality of creative work is far more subjective and difficult to quantify reliably than is testing for fluency, flexibility, elaboration, and originality. Indeed, there may never be a foolproof way of getting at the qualitative dimension. But it is too important to ignore in attempts at identifying creative potential, and any battery that omits it is probably bound to have trouble in achieving its objectives.

4. Is manifest creativity normally distributed? However we define the concept, one fact seems clear: there is little stress on cultivating it either in or out of school. Because of the neglect, it may be difficult to distinguish between high and low potential on performance tests of essentially unpracticed skills. It is perhaps comparable to conducting a nationwide assessment of ability in dart throwing or archery when the vast majority of people have never before thrown a dart or handled a bow and arrow. We would expect the distribution on such a measure to resemble a reversed "J curve" in which most people's scores would be bunched at the lower end of the distribution and the relatively few who perform at higher levels would probably have had some previous instruction and practice in the skills being measured. However, if we could possibly assess something akin to innate potential, "uncontaminated" by relevant experience or the lack of it, we would expect to see a normal distribution of scores in contrast to the inverted "J curve" as in Figure 18-1. The same may be true for creativity, which can only be measured through some kind of performance. It seems clear that the only way in which potential for creativity and mastery learning can be assessed equally well is for educators to stress the nurturance of new ideas as much as the retrieval of existing ideas.

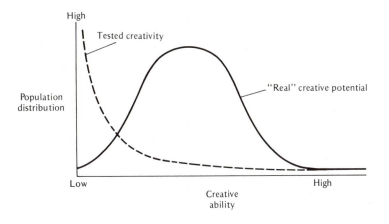

High

Tested creativity

Population
distribution

"Real" creative potential

Low   High

Creative
ability

Figure 18-1 Hypothesized distributions of manifest and innate creative abilities in our society

In the last analysis, the problem of defining and discovering creativity in children is part of the broader issue of how to conceptualize giftedness for this age group. Giftedness is revealed through productivity or performance at levels of excellence reached by only a few adults and hardly ever by children. Those who are regarded as potentially gifted in elementary or secondary school stand out only in comparison with their schoolmates. We see in them what we suspect are latent qualities that may someday flourish into distinction, given the right circumstances. Whatever tentativeness and uncertainty surround the concept of giftedness in children also apply to childhood creativity. The various attempts at measurement through tests of divergent thinking are still only experimental probes, not yet proven as reliable or valid. A considerable amount of theory building and research remain to be done before creativity can take its place as a clearly conceptualized psychological construct. Probably, the work done to date in this field is a greater boon to education than to psychology. Teachers are beginning to help children see the importance of questions that have no single convergent answers and to become fluent, flexible, original, and elaborative in dealing with such types of questions. What may seem to be a "creativity craze" among psychologists is producing dividends in the classroom as children learn the skills of brainstorming alternative solutions to problems in various fields of study. These developments are still only weak and scattered, but they promise to add an exciting new dimension to the content as well as the methods of instruction. Eventually, as divergent thinking becomes more prominent in education, we should expect the instruments that measure these processes to become more relevant to school achievement and consequently more valid.

Finally, there is the question as to why creativity is not listed among the linkages between promise and fulfillment, alongside general intelligence, special aptitudes, nonintellective facilitators, environmental influences, and chance or luck, as described in Part III of this volume. The answer is that it is not an additive to these factors but rather is integrated in each of them. To the best of our knowledge, it consists of a not yet known combination of general and specific abilities and personality traits associated with high potential that can be realized in a stimulating environment with the help of good fortune. Creativity is judged by two criteria: the *extent* and the *quality* of its innovativeness. Too often, the quality dimension is overlooked in favor of the offbeat and the profuse, and we forget that what is rare is not necessarily valued. Because it denotes rare and valued human accomplishment, creativity may be regarded as synonymous with giftedness. For after all, giftedness is reflected in productivity and performance, both of which are creative acts, rather than absorption and retention, which probably depend more heavily on other mental processes.

References

Aliotti, N. C., and W. E. Blanton. "Creative Thinking Ability, School Readiness, and Intelligence in First Grade Children." *Journal of Psychology*, **83-85**:137-143 (1973).

Anderson, H. H. "On the Meaning of Creativity." In H.H. Anderson, ed., *Creativity in Childhood and Adolescence*, pp. 46-61. Palo Alto, Calif.: Science and Behavior Books, 1965.

Anderson, R. C., and R. M. Anderson. "Transfer of Originality Thinking." *Journal of Educational Psychology*, **54**:300-304 (1963).

Ansbacher, H. L., and R. Ansbacher, eds. *The Individual Psychology of Alfred Adler*. New York: Basic Books, Inc., 1956.

Arici, H. "Brainstorming as a Way of Facilitating Creative Thinking." *Dissertation Abstracts*, **25**:6381-6382 (1965).

Arieti, S. *Creativity*. New York: Basic Books, Inc., 1976.

Austin, J. H. *Chase, Chance, and Creativity*. New York: Columbia University Press, 1978.

Bachtold, L. M. "Effects of Learning Environment on Verbal Creativity of Gifted Students." *Psychology in the Schools*, **11**:226-228 (1974).

Barron, F. "The Needs for Order and Disorder as Motives in Creative Activity." In C.W. Taylor and F. Barron, eds., *Scientific Creativity: Its Recognition and Development*, pp. 153-160. New York: John Wiley & Sons, Inc., 1963. (a)

———. *Creativity and Psychological Health*. Princeton, N.J.: D. Van Nostrand Company, 1963. (b)

———. *Creative Person and Creative Process*. New York: Holt, Rinehart and Winston, Inc., 1969.

———. *Artists in the Making*. New York: Seminar Press, 1972.

———, and D. M. Harrington. "Creativity, Intelligence, and Personality." *Annual Review of Psychology*, Vol. 32, pp. 439-476. Palo Alto, Calif.: Annual Reviews, Inc., 1981.

Bartlett, M. M., and G. A. Davis. "Do the Wallach and Kogan Tests Predict Real Creative Behavior?" *Perceptual and Motor Skills*, **39**:730 (1974).

Barton, K., T. E. Dielman, and R. B. Cattell. "Personality and I.Q. Measures as Predictors of School Achievement." *Journal of Educational Psychology*, 63:398-404 (1972).

Beittel, K. R. "Creativity in the Visual Arts in Higher Education." In C.W. Taylor, ed., *Widening Horizons in Creativity*, pp. 379-395. New York: John Wiley & Sons, Inc., 1964.

Bentley, J. C. "Creativity and Academic Achievement." *The Journal of Educational Research*, 59:269-272 (1966).

Bloom, B. S. "Report on Creativity Research by the Examiner's Office of the University of Chicago." In C.W. Taylor and F. Barron, eds., *Scientific Creativity: Its Recognition and Development*, pp. 251-264. New York: John Wiley & Sons, Inc., 1963.

————, and L. A. Sosniak. "Talent Development vs. Schooling." *Educational Leadership*, 39:86-94 (1981).

Bruininks, R. H., and D. H. Feldman. "Creativity, Intelligence and Achievement Among Disadvantaged Children." *Psychology in the Schools*, 7:260-264 (1970).

Bruner, J. S. *The Process of Education*. Cambridge, Mass.: Harvard University Press, 1960.

Chambers, J. A. "Relating Personality and Biographical Factors to Scientific Creativity." *Psychological Monographs*, Vol. 78, no. 7 (whole no. 584), 1964.

Cicirelli, V. G. "Form of the Relationship Between Creativity, IQ, and Academic Achievement." *Journal of Educational Psychology*, 56:303-308 (1965).

Clark, B. *Growing Up Gifted*. Columbus, Ohio: Charles E. Merrill Publishing Company, 1979.

Cohen, D., J. R. Whitmyre, and W. H. Funk. "The Effect of Group Cohesiveness and Training upon Thinking." *Journal of Applied Psychology*, 44:319-322 (1960).

Cohen, H. A., S. J. Garfield, and R. M. Roth. "Creativity and Mental Health." *The Journal of Educational Research*, 63:147-149 (1969).

Colgrove, M. "Stimulating Creative Problem Solving: Innovative Set." *Psychological Reports*, 22:1205-1211 (1968).

Covington, M. V., R. S. Crutchfield, L. B. Davies, and R. M. Olton. *The Productive Thinking Program: A Course in Learning How to Think*. Columbus, Ohio: Charles E. Merrill Publishing Company, 1972.

Crockenberg, S. "Creativity Tests: A Boon or Boondoggle for Education?" *Review of Educational Research*, 42:27-45 (1972).

Cropley, A. J. "Creativity and Intelligence." *British Journal of Educational Psychology*, 36:259-266 (1966).

————. "A Note on the Wallach-Kogan Tests of Creativity," *British Journal of Educational Psychology*, 38:197-200 (1968).

————. "A Five-Year Longitudinal Study of the Validity of Creative Tests." *Developmental Psychology*, 6:119-124 (1972).

Dacey, J. S., and G. F. Medaus. "Relationship Between Creativity and Intelligence." *Journal of Educational Research*, 64:213-216 (1971).

Damm, V. "Creativity and Intelligence: Research Implications for Equal Emphasis in High School." *Exceptional Children*, 36:565-569 (1970).

Datta, L. E., and M. B. Parloff. "On the Relevance of Autonomy: Parent-Child Relationships and Early Scientific Creativity." *Proceedings of the Seventy-fifth Annual Convention of the American Psychological Association*. Washington, D.C.: American Psychological Association, 1967.

Dave, R. "Effects of Hypnotically Induced Dreams on Creative Problem Solving." *Journal of Abnormal Psychology*, 88:293-302 (1979).

Dellas, M., and E. L. Gaier. "Identification of Creativity: The Individual." *Psychological Bulletin*, **73**:55-73 (1970).

Dentler, R. A., and B. Mackler. "Originality: Some Social and Personal Determinants." *Behavioral Science*, **9**:1-7 (1964).

Dewey, J. *How We Think*. Lexington, Mass.: D.C. Heath & Company, 1910.

Domino, G. "Creativity and the Home Environment." *Gifted Child Quarterly*, **23**:818-828 (1979).

Drevdahl, J. E. "Factors of Importance for Creativity." *Journal of Clinical Psychology*, **12**:21-26 (1956).

———, and R. B. Cattell. "Personality and Creativity in Artists and Writers," *Journal of Clinical Psychology*, **14**:107-111 (1958).

Dudek, S. Z. "Creativity in Young Children—Attitude or Ability?" *Journal of Creative Behavior*, **8**:282-292 (1974).

Dunnette, M. D., J. Campbell, and K. Jaastad. "The Effect of Group Participation on Brainstorming Effectiveness for Two Individual Samples." *Journal of Applied Psychology*, **47**:30-37 (1963).

Edwards, M. P., and L. E. Tyler. "Intelligence, Creativity, and Achievement in a Nonselective Public Junior High School." *Journal of Educational Psychology*, **56**:96-99 (1965).

Elliott, J. M. "Measuring Creative Abilities in Public Relations and in Advertising Work." In C.W. Taylor, ed., *Widening Horizons in Creativity*, pp. 396-400. New York: John Wiley & Sons, Inc., 1964.

Feldhusen, J. F., T. Denny, and C. F. Condon. "Anxiety, Divergent Thinking, and Achievement." *Journal of Educational Psychology*, **56**:40-45 (1965).

———, S. Hobson, and D. J. Treffinger. "The Effects of Visual and Verbal Stimuli on Divergent Thinking." *Gifted Child Quarterly*, **19**:205-209 (1975)

———, D. J. Treffinger, and S. J. Bahlke. "Developing Creative Thinking: The Purdue Creativity Program." *Journal of Creative Behavior*, **4**:85-90 (1970).

———, D. J. Treffinger, and R. M. Elias. "Prediction of Academic Achievement with Divergent and Convergent Thinking and Personality Variables." *Psychology in the Schools*, **7**:46-52 (1970).

Feldman D. H., B. Marrinon, and S. Hartfeldt. "Unusualness, Appropriateness, Transformation and Condensation as Criteria for Creativity." Paper presented at the Annual Meeting of the American Educational Research Association, New York, February 1971.

Flescher, I. "Anxiety and Achievement of Intellectually Gifted and Creatively Gifted Children." *Journal of Psychology*, **56**:251-268 (1963)

Foreman, S. G., and J. D. McKinney. "Creativity and Achievement of 2nd Graders in Open and Traditional Classrooms." *Journal of Educational Psychology*, **70**:101-107 (1978).

Freud, S. "The Relation of the Poet to Day-Dreaming." In *Collected Papers*. Vol. II. London: Hogarth, 1908.

———. "The Unconscious." In J. Strachey, ed. and trans., *The Standard Edition of the Complete Psychological Works of Sigmund Freud*. Vol. 14. London: Hogarth, 1958. Published originally in 1915.

Fromm, E. "The Creative Attitude." In H.H. Anderson, ed., *Creativity and Its Cultivation*, pp. 45-54. New York: Harper & Bros., 1959.

Getzels, J. W., and M. Csikszentmihalyi. *The Creative Vision: A Longitudinal Study of Problem Finding in Art*. New York: John Wiley & Sons, Inc., 1976.

———, and P. W. Jackson. "The Meaning of 'Giftedness'—An Examination of an Expanding Concept." *Phi Delta Kappan*, **40**:75-77 (1958).

————, and P. W. Jackson. *Creativity and Intelligence*. New York: John Wiley & Sons, Inc., 1962.

Ghiselin, B. "The Creative Process and Its Relation to the Identification of Creative Talent." In C.W. Taylor and F. Barron, eds., *Scientific Creativity: Its Recognition and Development*, pp. 355-364. New York: John Wiley & Sons, Inc., 1963.

Gilchrist, M. B., and R. Taft. "Creative Attitudes and Creative Productivity—A Comparison of Two Aspects of Creativity Among Students." *Journal of Educational Psychology*, **61**:136-143 (1970).

Goertzel, M. G., V. Goertzel, and T. G. Goertzel. *300 Eminent Personalities*. San Francisco: Jossey-Bass Publishers, 1978.

Goertzel, V., and M. G. Goertzel. *Cradles of Eminence*. Boston: Little, Brown and Company, 1962.

Gough, H. G. "Techniques for Identifying the Creative Research Scientist." In *Conference on the Creative Person*. Berkeley: University of California, Institute of Personality Assessment and Research, 1961.

Gowan, J. C. "The Relationship Between Creativity and Giftedness." *Gifted Child Quarterly*, **15**:239-244 (1971).

————. "The Development of the Creative Individual." In J.C. Gowan, J. Khatena, and E.P. Torrance, eds., *Educating the Ablest*, pp. 58-79. Itasca, Ill.: F.E. Peacock, 1979.

Guilford, J. P. "Traits of Creativity." In H.H. Anderson, ed. *Creativity and its Cultivation*, pp. 142-161. New York: Harper and Bros., 1959.

————. "Measurement and Creativity." *Theory into Practice*, **5**:186-189 (1966).

————. *The Nature of Human Intelligence*. New York: McGraw-Hill Book Company, 1967.

————. *Intelligence, Creativity and Their Educational Implications*. San Diego, Calif.: Knapp, 1968.

————. "Varieties of Creative Giftedness, Their Measurement and Development." *Gifted Child Quarterly*, **19**:107-121 (1975).

————, and P. R. Merrifield. "The Structure of Intellect Model: Its Uses and Implications." *Report from the Psychological Laboratory, No. 24*. Los Angeles: University of Southern California, 1960.

Gur, R. C., and J. Rayner. "Enhancement of Creativity via Free-Imagery and Hypnosis." *American Journal of Clinical Hypnosis*, **18**:237-249 (1976).

Gutman, H. "The Biological Roots of Creativity." *Genetic Psychology Monographs*, **64**:417-458 (1961).

Hacker, F. J. "Creative Possibilities for a Consideration of Creativity." In H.H. Anderson, ed., *Creativity in Childhood and Adolescence*, pp. 35-45. Palo Alto, Calif.: Science and Behavior Books, 1965.

Haddon, F. A., and H. Lytton. "Teaching Approach and the Development of Divergent Thinking Abilities in Primary Schools." *British Journal of Educational Psychology*, **38**:171-180 (1968).

————, and H. Lytton. "Primary Education and Divergent Thinking Abilities—Four Years On." *British Journal of Educational Psychology*, **41**:136-147 (1971).

Hadley, D. J. "Experimental Relationships Between Creativity and Anxiety." *Dissertation Abstracts*, **26(5)**:2586 (1965).

Halpin, G. "The Effect of Motivation on Creative Thinking Abilities." *The Journal of Creative Behavior*, **7**:51-53 (1973).

————, D. A. Payne, and C. D. Ellett. "Biographical Correlates of the Creative Personality:

Gifted Adolescents." *Exceptional Children*, **39**:652-653 (1973).

Hasan, P., and H. J. Butcher. "Creativity and Intelligence: A Partial Replication with Scottish Children of Getzels and Jackson's Study." *British Journal of Psychology*, **57**:129-135 (1966).

Hattie, J. A. "Conditions for Administering Creativity Tests." *Psychological Bulletin*, **84**:1249-1260 (1977).

———. "Should Creativity Tests Be Administered Under Test-Like Conditions?" *Journal of Educational Psychology*, **72**:87-98 (1980).

Hershey, M. "The Effect of Guided Fantasy on the Creative Thinking and Writing Ability of Gifted Children." *Gifted Child Quarterly*, **23**:71-79 (1979).

Hitchfield, E. M. *In Search of Promise*. London: Longman Studies in Child Development, 1973.

Hitt, W. D., and J. R. Stock. "The Relation Between Psychological Characteristics and Creative Behavior." *Psychological Record*, **15**:133-140 (1965).

Holland, J. L. "Creative and Academic Performance Among Talented Adolescents." *Journal of Educational Psychology*, **52**:136-147 (1961).

Huber, J., D. Treffinger, D. Tracy, and D. Rand. "Self-Instructional Use of Programmed Creativity Training Materials with Gifted and Regular Students." *Journal of Educational Psychology*, **3**:303-309 (1979).

Hudson, L. "Intelligence, Divergence, and Potential Originality." *Nature*, **196**:601-602 (1962).

———. *Contrary Imaginations: A Psychological Study of the Young Student*. New York: Schocken Books, Inc., 1966.

Institute for Behavioral Research in Creativity. "Preliminary Administration and Research Manual, Biographical Inventory—Form U." Salt Lake City, Utah: The Institute, 1978.

Iwata, O. "Some Relationships of Creativity with Intelligence and Personality Variables." *Psychologica*, **11**:211-220 (1968).

Johnson, D. M., and M. L. Fogel. "Creative Aptitudes in a High Intelligence Population." *Journal of General Psychology*, **91**:93-104 (1974).

Jordan, L. A. "Use of Canonical Analysis in Cropley's 'A Five-Year Longitudinal Study of the Validity of Creativity Tests'." *Developmental Psychology*, **11**:1-3 (1975).

Jung, C. G. "Psychological Types." In *Collected Works*. Vol. 6. Princeton, N.J.: Princeton University Press, 1971.

Kane, M., and N. Kane. "Comparison of Right and Left Hemispheres Functions." *Gifted Child Quarterly*, **23**:157-167 (1979).

Katz, A. N. "Creativity and the Right Cerebral Hemisphere: Towards a Physiologically Based Theory of Creativity." *Journal of Creative Behavior*, **12**:253-264 (1978).

Khatena, J. "Training College Adults to Think Creatively with Words." *Psychological Reports*, **27**:279-281 (1970).

———. "A Second Study Training College Adults to Think Creatively with Words." *Psychological Reports*, **28**:385-386 (1971a).

———. "Teaching Disadvantaged Preschool Children to Think Creatively with Pictures." *Journal of Educational Psychology*, **62**:384-386 (1971b).

———. "Creative Level and Its Effect on Training College Adults to Think Creatively with Words." *Psychological Reports*, **32**:336 (1973).

Koestler, A. *The Act of Creation*. New York: Macmillan Publishing Co., Inc., 1964.

Kogan, N., and E. Pankove. "Creative Ability over a Five-Year Span." *Child Development*, **43**:427-442 (1972).

———, and E. Pankove. "Long-Term Predictive Validity of Divergent-Thinking Tests:

Some Negative Evidence." *Journal of Educational Psychology*, **66**:802-810 (1974).

Krippner, S. "Consciousness and the Creative Process." *Gifted Child Quarterly*, **12**:141-147 (1968).

Kris, E. *Psycholoanalytic Explorations in Art*. New York: International Universities Press, 1952.

Kubie, L. S. *Neurotic Distortion of the Creative Process*. Lawrence: University of Kansas Press, 1958.

MacDonald, J. B., and J. D. Raths. "Should We Group by Creative Abilities?" *Elementary School Journal*, **65**:137-142 (1964).

MacKinnon, D. W. "The Highly Effective Individual." *Teachers College Record*, **61**:367-378 (1960).

———. "The Study of Creativity and Creativity in Architects." In *Conference on the Creative Person*. Berkeley: University of California, Institute of Personality Assessment and Research, 1961.

———. "The Personality Correlates of Creativity: A Study of American Architects." In G.G. Nielson, ed., *Proceedings of the Fourteenth International Congress of Applied Psychology, Copenhagen (1961)*, Vol. II, pp. 11-39. Copenhagen: Munksgaard, 1962.

———. "Creativity and Images of the Self." In R.H. White, ed., *The Study of Lives*, pp. 250-278. New York: Atherton, 1963.

———. "Personality and the Realization of Creative Potential." *American Psychologist*, **20**:273-281 (1965).

———. "IPAR's Contribution to the Conceptualization and Study of Creativity." In I.A. Taylor and J.W. Getzels, eds., *Perspectives in Creativity*, pp. 60-89. Chicago: Aldine Publishing Company, 1975.

Mansfield, R. W., T. V. Busse, and E. J. Krepelka. "The Effectiveness of Creativity Training." *Review of Educational Research*, **48**:517-536 (1978).

Marsh, R. W. "Statistical Re-Analysis of Getzels and Jackson's Data." *British Journal of Educational Psychology*, **34**:91-93 (1964)

Maslow, A. *Motivation and Personality*. New York: Harper & Bros., 1954.

———. "Creativity in Self-actualizing People." In H.H. Anderson, ed., *Creativity and Its Cultivation*, pp. 83-95. New York: Harper & Bros., 1959.

May, R. "The Nature of Creativity." In H.H. Anderson, ed., *Creativity and Its Cultivation*, pp. 55-68. New York: Harper & Bros., 1959.

———. *The Courage to Create*. New York: W.W. Norton & Company, Inc., 1975.

Mayhon, W. ·G. "The Relationship of Creativity to Achievement and Other Student Variables." Unpublished doctoral dissertation. The University of Mexico, Mexico City, 1966.

McCurdy, H. G. "The Childhood Pattern of Genius." *Horizon*, **2**:33-38 (1960).

McKinney, J. D., and S. G. Forman. "Factor Structure of the Wallach-Kogan Tests of Creativity and Measures of Intelligence and Achievement." *Psychology in the Schools*, **14**:41-44 (1977).

McNemar, Q. "Lost: Our Intelligence. Why?" *American Psychologist*, **19**:871-882 (1964).

Mead, M. "Creativity in Cross-Cultural Perspective." In H.H. Anderson, ed., *Creativity and Its Cultivation*, pp. 222-235. New York: Harper & Bros., 1959.

Mednick, M. T., and F. M. Andrews. "Creative Thinking and Level of Intelligence." *The Journal of Creative Behavior*, **1**:428 (1967).

Merrifield, P. R., S. F. Gardner, and A. B. Cox. "Aptitudes and Personality Measures Related to Creativity in Seventh-Grade Children." *Report from the Psychological Laboratory*, No. 28. Los Angeles: The University of Southern California, 1964.

————, J. P. Guilford, and A. Gershon. "The Differentiation of Divergent-Production Abilities at the Sixth-Grade Level." *Report from the Psychological Laboratory*, No. 27. Los Angeles: The University of Southern California, 1963.

Michael, W. B. "Cognitive and Affective Components of Creativity in Mathematics and the Physical Sciences." In J.C. Stanley, W.C. George, and C.H. Solano, eds., *The Gifted and the Creative: A Fifty-Year Perspective*, pp. 141-172. Baltimore, Md.: Johns Hopkins University Press, 1977.

Milgram, R. M., and N. A. Milgram. "Creative Thinking and Creative Performance in Israeli Students." *Journal of Educational Psychology*, **68**:255-259 (1976)(a).

————, and N. A. Milgram. "Self-concept as a Function of Intelligence and Creativity in Gifted Children." *Psychology in the Schools*, **13**:91-96 (1976)(b).

Moustakas, C. *Creativity and Conformity*. New York: Van Nostrand Reinhold Company, 1967.

Murphy, G. *Human Potentialities*. New York: Basic Books, Inc., 1958.

Murphy, J., D. Dauw, R. Horton, and A. Fredian. "Self-actualization and Creativity." *Journal of Creative Behavior*, **10**:39-44 (1976).

Myers, R. E., and E. P. Torrance. *Invitations to Thinking and Doing*. Lexington, Mass.: Ginn and Company, 1964.

————, and E. P. Torrance. *Invitations to Speaking and Writing Creativity*. Lexington, Mass.: Ginn and Company, 1965.

————, and E. P. Torrance. *For Those Who Wonder*. Lexington, Mass.: Ginn and Company, 1966. (a).

————, and E. P. Torrance. *Plots, Puzzles, and Ploys*. Lexington, Mass.: Ginn and Company, 1966. (b).

————, and E. P. Torrance. *Stretch*. Minneapolis, Minn.: Perceptive Publishing Company, 1968.

Nichols, R. "Parental Attitudes of Mothers of Intelligent Adolescents and Creativity of Their Children." *Child Development*, **35**:1041-1049 (1964).

Niederland, W. G. "Psychoanalytic Concepts of Creativity and Aging." *Journal of Geriatric Psychiatry*, **6**:160-168 (1973).

Odgen, J. A. "A Study of the Interrelationships of High Creativity, Curiosity, Intelligence, and Achievement and Emotional Handicap." *Dissertation Abstracts*, **63**:7292 (1964).

Osborn, A. F., Jr. *Applied Imagination*. New York: Charles Scribner's Sons, 1953.

————. *Applied Imagination*. rev. ed. New York: Charles Scribner's Sons, 1957.

————. *Applied Imagination*. 3rd rev. ed. New York: Charles Scribner's Sons, 1963.

Parnes, S. J. "The Effects of Extended Effort in Creative Problem Solving." *Journal of Educational Psychology*, **52**:117-122 (1961).

————. *Creative Behavior Guidebook*. New York: Charles Scribner's Sons, 1967.

Patrick, C. "Creative Thought in Poets." *Archives of Psychology*, **26**:1-74 (1935).

————. "Creative Thought in Artists." *Journal of Psychology*, **4**:35-73 (1937).

————. "Scientific Thought," *Journal of Psychology*, **5**:55-83 (1938).

Petrosko, J. "Measuring Creativity in Elementary School: The Current State of the Art." *Journal of Creative Behavior*, **12**:109-119 (1978).

Pickering, G. *Creative Malady*. London: George Allen & Unwin Ltd., 1974.

Pressey, S. L. "Concerning the Nature and Nurture of Genius." *Scientific Monthly*, **81**:123-129 (1955).

Raina, M. K. "A Study into the Effect of Competition on Creativity." *Gifted Child Quarterly*, **12**:217-220 (1968).

Ramey, C. I., and V. Piper. "Creativity in Open and Traditional Classrooms." *Child Development*, **45**:557-560 (1974).

Rank, O. *Art and Artists: Creative Urge and Personality Development*. New York: Alfred A. Knopf, Inc., 1932.

———. *Beyond Psychology*. New York: Dover Publications, Inc., 1958.

Rekdal, C. K. "Genius, Creativity, and Eminence." *Gifted Child Quarterly*, **23**:837-854 (1979).

Reynolds, C. R., and E. P. Torrance. "Perceived Changes in Styles of Learning and Thinking (Hemisphericity) Through Direct and Indirect Training." *Journal of Creative Behavior*, **12**:247-252 (1978).

Roe, A. *The Making of a Scientist*. New York: Dodd, Mead & Company, 1953.

———. "Painters and Painting." In I.A. Taylor and J.W. Getzels, eds., *Perspectives in Creativity*, pp. 157-172. Chicago: Aldine Publishing Company, 1975.

Rogers, C. R. "Toward a Theory of Creativity." In H.H. Anderson, ed., *Creativity and Its Cultivation*, pp. 69-82. New York: Harper & Bros., 1959.

Rossman, J. *The Psychology of the Inventor: A Study of the Patentee*. Washington, D.C.: Inventors Publishing Co., 1931.

Rothenberg, A. *The Emerging Goddess: The Creative Process in Art, Science, and Other Fields*. Chicago: University of Chicago Press, 1979.

Rotter, D. M., L. Langland, and D. Berger. "The Validity of Tests of Creative Thinking in Seven-Year-Old Children." *Gifted Child Quarterly*, **15**:273-278 (1971).

Schachtel, E. G. *Metamorphosis: On the Development of Affect, Perception, Attention, and Memory*. New York: Basic Books, Inc., 1959.

Schaefer, C. E. "The Self-concept of Creative Adolescents." *Journal of Psychology*, **72**:233-242 (1969).

———. "Follow-up Study of a Creativity Scale for the Adjective Check List." *Psychological Reports*, **30**:662 (1972).

———. "A Five-Year Follow-up Study of the Self-concept of Creative Adolescents." *The Journal of Genetic Psychology*, **123**:163-170 (1973).

Schafer, R. "Regression in the Service of the Ego." In G. Lindzey, ed., *Assessment of Human Motives*, pp. 119-148. New York: Holt, Rinehart and Winston, Inc., 1958.

Siegelman, M. "Parent Behavior Correlates of Personality Traits Related to Creativity in Sons and Daughters." *Journal of Consulting and Clinical Psychology*, **40**:43-47 (1973).

Sisk, D. A. "The Relationship Between Self-concept and Creative Thinking of Elementary School Children: An Experimental Investigation." *Gate*, **2**:47-59 (1980).

Skager, R. W., S. P. Klein, and C. B. Schultz. "The Prediction of Academic and Artistic Achievement in a School of Design." *Journal of Educational Measurements*, **4**:105-117 (1967).

Spotts, J. V., and B. Mackler. "Relationships of Field-Dependent and Field-Independent Cognitive Styles to Creative Test Performance." *Perceptual and Motor Skills*, **24**:239-268 (1967).

Stein, M. I. "Creativity and Culture." *Journal of Psychology*, **36**:311-322 (1953).

———. "A Transactional Approach to Creativity." In C.W. Taylor, ed., *The 1955 University of Utah Research Conference on the Identification of Creative Scientific Talent*, pp. 171-181. Salt Lake City: University of Utah Press, 1956.

Storr, A. *The Dynamics of Creation*. New York: Atheneum Publishers, 1972.

Stratton, R. P., and R. Brown. "Improving Creative Thinking by Training in the Production and/or Judgment of Solutions." *Journal of Educational Psychology*, **63**:390-397 (1972).

Suler, J. R. "Primary Process Thinking and Creativity." *Psychological Bulletin*, **88**:144-165 (1980).

Sussman, G., and J. Justman. "Characteristics of Preadolescent Boys Judged Creative by their Teachers." *Gifted Child Quarterly*, **19**:310-316 (1975).

Taft, R., and M. Gilchrist. "Creative Attitudes and Creative Productivity: A Comparison of Two Aspects of Creativity Among Students." *Journal of Educational Psychology*, **62**:136-143 (1970).

Tart, C. T. *Altered States of Consciousness.* New York: John Wiley & Sons, Inc., 1969.

Taylor, C. W. "Clues to Creative Teaching: The Creative Process and Education." *Instructor*, **73**:4-5 (1963).

———, and J. Holland. "Predictors of Creative Performance." In C.W. Taylor, ed., *Creativity: Progress and Potential*, pp. 15-48. New York: McGraw-Hill Book Company, 1964.

Taylor, D. W., P. C. Berry, and C. H. Block. "Does Group Participation When Using Brainstorming Facilitate or Inhibit Creative Thinking?" *Administrative Science Quarterly*, **3**:23-47 (1958).

Taylor, I. A. "Creative Production in Gifted Young Adults Through Simultaneous Sensory Stimulation." *Gifted Child Quarterly*, **14**:46-55 (1970).

———. "An Emerging View of Creative Actions." In I.A. Taylor and J.W. Getzels, eds., *Perspectives in Creativity*, pp. 297-325. Chicago: Aldine Publishing Company, 1975.

Thorndike, R. L. "The Measurement of Creativity." *Teachers College Record*, **64**:422-424 (1963).

———. "Some Methodological Issues in the Study of Creativity." In A. Anastasi, ed., *Testing Problems in Perspective*, pp. 436-448. Washington, D.C.: American Council on Education, 1966.

Torrance, E. P. *Guiding Creative Talent.* Englewood Cliffs, N.J.: Prentice-Hall, Inc., 1962.

———. *Education and the Creative Potential.* Minneapolis: University of Minnesota Press, 1963.

———. "Education and Creativity." In C.W. Taylor, ed., *Creativity: Progress and Potential*, pp. 49-128. New York: McGraw-Hill Book Company, 1964(a).

———. *Rewarding Creative Behavior.* Englewood Cliffs, N.J.: Prentice-Hall, Inc., 1964(b). (b).

———. *Torrance Tests of Creative Thinking.* Lexington, Mass.: Personnel Press, 1966.

———. "Can We Teach Children to Think Creatively?" Journal of Creative Behavior, **6**:114-141 (1972).

———. "Creativity Research in Education: Still Alive." In I.A. Taylor and J.W. Getzels, eds., *Perspectives in Creativity*, pp 278-296. Chicago: Aldine Publishing Company, 1975.

———. "Dyadic Interaction as a Facilitator of Gifted Performance." *Gifted Child Quarterly*, **14**:139-143 (1970).

———. "Creatively Gifted and Disadvantaged Gifted." In J.C. Stanley, W.C. George, and C.H. Solano, *The Gifted and the Creative: A Fifty-Year Perspective*, pp. 173-196. Baltimore, Md.: Johns Hopkins University Press, 1977.

———. "Predicting the Creativity of Elementary School Children (1958-80)—and the Teacher Who 'Made a Difference'." *Gifted Child Quarterly*, **25**:55-61 (1981).

———, and C. R. Reynolds. "Images of the Future of Gifted Adolescents: Effects of Alienation and Specialized Cerebral Functioning." In J.C. Gowan, J. Khatena, and E.P. Torrance, eds., *Educating the Ablest*, pp. 431-445. Itasca, Ill.: F.E. Peacock Publishers, 1979.

———, and T. Wu. "A Comparative Longitudinal Study of the Adult Creative Achievements of Elementary School Children Identified as Highly Intelligent and as Highly Creative." *Creative Child and Adult Quarterly*, **6**:71-76 (1980).

Toynbee, A. J. *A Study of History.* London: Oxford University Press, 1934.

Turner, W. M., and J. D. Rains. "Differential Effects of 'Brainstorming' Instruction upon High and Low Creativity Subjects." *Psychological Reports,* **17**:753-754 (1965).

Vernon, J. D. "Creativity and Intelligence: Research Implications for Equal Emphasis in High School." *Exceptional Children,* **36**:565-569 (1970).

Vinacke, V. E. *The Psychology of Thinking.* New York: McGraw-Hill Book Company, 1952.

Von Fange, E. K. "Understanding the Creative Process." *General Electric Review,* **2**:54-57 (1955).

Wallach, M. A. "Creativity." In P.H. Mussen, ed., *Carmichael's Manual of Child Psychology,* Vol. I, pp. 1211-1272. New York: John Wiley & Sons, Inc., 1970.

———, and N. Kogan. *Modes of Thinking in Young Children.* New York: Holt, Rinehart and Winston, Inc:, 1965.

———, and C. W. Wing, Jr. *The Talented Student: A Validation of the Creativity-Intelligence Distinction.* New York: Holt, Rinehart and Winston, Inc., 1969.

Wallas, G. *The Art of Thought.* London: C.A. Watts, 1926.

Wallbrown, F. H., and C. B. Huelsman, Jr. "The Validity of the Wallach-Kogan Creativity Operations for Inner-City Children in Two Areas of Visual Arts." *Journal of Personality,* **43**:109-126 (1975).

———, J. D. Wallbrown, and R. J. Wherry, Sr. "The Construct Validity of the Wallach-Kogan Creativity Test for Inner-City Children." *Journal of Genetic Psychology,* **92**:83-96 (1975).

Wallinga, C., and J. C. Sedahlia. "Parental Influence on Creativity of Fifth Grade Children." *Gifted Child Quarterly,* **23**:768-777 (1979).

Warburton, F. W. "The Measurement of Personality. I." *Educational Research,* **4**:2-18 (1961).

———. "The Measurement of Personality. II." *Educational Research,* **4**:115-132 (1962)(a).

———. "The Measurement of Personality. III." *Educational Research,* **4**:193-206 (1962)(b).

Ward, W. C. "Creativity and Impulsivity in Kindergarten Children." Unpublished doctoral dissertation. Duke University, Durham, North Carolina, 1966.

Ward, W. D., and P. R. Barcher. "Reading Achievement and Creativity as Related to Open Classroom Experience." *Journal of Educational Psychology,* **67**:683-691 (1975).

Weckowicz, T. E., et al. "Effect of Marijuana on Divergent and Convergent Production Cognitive Tests." *Journal of Abnormal Psychology,* **84**:386-398 (1975).

Welsh, G. S. *Creativity and Intelligence: A Personality Approach.* Chapel Hill: Institute for Research in Social Science, University of North Carolina at Chapel Hill, 1975.

———. "Personality Correlates of Intelligence and Creativity in Gifted Adolescents." In J.C. Stanley, W.C. George, and C.H. Solano, *The Gifted and the Creative: A Fifty-Year Perspective.* pp. 75-112. Baltimore, Md.: Johns Hopkins University Press, 1977.

White, K. "Anxiety, Introversion-Extroversion and Divergent Thinking Ability." *Journal of Creative Behavior,* **2**:119-127 (1968).

Williams, F., ed. *Creativity at Home and in School.* St. Paul, Minn.: Macalester Creativity Project, 1968.

Wilson, F. S., T. Stuckey, and R. Langevin. "Are Pupils in the Open Plan School Different?" *Journal of Educational Research,* **66**:115-118 (1972).

Wodtke, K. H. "Some Data on the Reliability and Validity of Creativity Tests at the Elementary School Level." *Educational and Psychological Measurement,* **24**:399-408 (1964).

———, and N. E. Wallen. "Teacher Classroom Control, Pupil Creativity, and Pupil Classroom Behavior." *The Journal of Experimental Education,* **34**:59-65 (1965).

Wright, R. J. "The Affective and Cognitive Consequences of an Open Education Elementary School." *American Education Research Journal*, **12**:449-468 (1975).

Yamamoto, K. "Threshold of Intelligence in Academic Achievement of Highly Creative Students." *Journal of Experimental Education*, **32**:401-405 (1964)(a).

———. "Role of Creative Thinking and Intelligence in High School Achievement." *Psychological Reports*, **14**:783-789 (1964)(b).

———. "Effects of Restriction of Range and Test Unreliability on Correlation Between Measures of Intelligence and Creative Thinking." *British Journal of Educational Psychology*, **35**:300-305 (1965).

———, and M. E. Chimbidis. "Achievement, Intelligence, and Creative Thinking in Fifth Grade Children: A Correlational Study." *Merrill-Palmer Quarterly*, **12**:233-241 (1966).

Ziller, R. C., R. D. Berringer, and J. D. Goodchilds. "Group Creativity Under Conditions of Success or Failure and Variations in Group Stability." *Journal of Applied Psychology*, **46**:43-49 (1962).

Ziv, A. "Facilitating Effects of Humor on Creativity." *Journal of Educational Psychology*, **68**:318-322 (1976).

PART V

Nurturing High Potential

To accomplish programmatic enrichment, it is necessary to recognize how the various steps toward this goal fit together. Identification procedures and curriculum planning have a reciprocal, mutually facilitating relationship. On the one hand, enrichment can be most effective if it is designed with the qualifications of its beneficiaries in mind. Conversely, the qualifications of children for special enrichment can be assessed best on the "proving ground" of such a program, if it is well taught. This kind of interdependence between locating and nurturing talent is vital to the integrity of our efforts on behalf of the gifted. Once we clarify *what* we are trying to do for them and that it is *worthwhile* doing, we can then proceed to evaluate *how well* we are doing it.

Chapter 19

Identifying the Gifted

High potential in children means different things to different people. But no matter what definition we accept, identifying it has to be counted among our inexact sciences, partly because the methods and instruments available for that purpose are imprecise. Besides, childhood is usually too early in life for talent to be full blown, so we have to settle for dealing with talent-in-the-making and keep in mind the uncertainties about the future. Identification is, therefore, a matter of locating children who possess high potential in comparison with other children, with no guarantees that they will eventually excel by universal standards as adults, even with proper nurturance. In creating a pool of "hopefuls," it is best to admit any child who stands a ghost of a chance of someday making it to the top in the world of ideas. Of course, most of those we think are "hopefuls" are really "doubtfuls," but nobody can know for sure in advance. Bringing them into the pool under liberal admission criteria cannot be helped if we want to increase the chances of uncovering hidden talent.

Although we are hardly out of the primitive stages of recognizing the many varieties of talent in their early stages of development, there is no doubt that methods exist to identify a few kinds of human potential fairly well. For example, as part of their Human Talent Project, McGuire, Hindsman, King, and Jennings (1961) found that the following measurable factors accounted for a large portion of the variance in scholastic achievement:

P = the potentialities of the person, pertinent to the behavior, in terms of variables representing significant aspects of cognitive structure, perceptual strategies, psychomotor skills, deeper elements of personality, and other relevant attributes;

E = the kinds of motivation and other elements of personality which govern the person's expectations regarding the supportive or non-supportive behavior of others . . ., phrased in terms of pertinent attitudes or motivations such as "to attain success and approval" or "to avoid failure and disapproval" with reference to parents, age mates, and teachers;

R = the pressures imposed upon the person by these cultural agents and the probable responses of the individual to them, or the selective reinforcements of some aspects of the person's behavior . . . (p. 5)

The research team developed a battery of tests to represent the P, E, and R factors and administered them to 1,242 seventh-graders in four different communities. Using grade-point average and achievement scores in reading, language, arithmetic, social studies, and science as dependent variables in a multiple regression analysis, they discovered that the coefficients varied from one achievement area to the next and that the multiple predictors explained no less than 43 percent of the variance (in arithmetic) and as much as 55 percent of the variance in grade-point average. Taking into account the fact that none of the instruments had perfect reliability, the amount of variance explained by the independent variables is indeed impressive. Thus we see that potential for performing well at school can be identified with reasonable accuracy in some children.

PROBLEMS AND ISSUES IN IDENTIFICATION

The success reported by McGuire and his associates in determining significant correlates of achievement was limited since the predictors related only to scholastic success within a short period of time. No attempt was made to forecast a variety of accomplishments in later periods of life. The impressive results were also due to the fact that the instruments used were not just measures of cognition; they also assessed several personality and environmental factors. But even the extensive data collected by the research team left large portions of the variance unexplained. Tests chosen to measure potential, and for that matter any such instruments available to us, are not reliable or valid enough to provide foolproof information on who is destined to achieve excellence. We are dealing, at best, with modest degrees of probability, since childhood is a stage in which only promise is shown, not even the beginnings of fulfillment. It is therefore prudent for us to "hedge our bets" in employing any known strategy for identification.

Cautions in the Use of IQ and Creativity Tests

Because of its longer history, far more is known about the value of the IQ than of creativity tests in identifying high potential. We therefore have to be cautious in interpreting creativity scores until some basic questions about reliability and validity are settled. Indeed, these tests may prove virtually useless if the enrichment program neglects to emphasize divergent thinking skills. But even the IQ can be misleading if it is accepted uncritically, despite the great amount of supportive data. Ever since Terman initiated his *Genetic Studies of Genius*, the IQ has been regarded by educators as the *single* most prominent and pervasive indicator of precocity in childhood. The reason for its popularity (and perhaps overpopularity) is that it evaluates some of the most persistently cultivated abilities in the school curriculum. It focuses on skills developed in the course of a person's experience that are critical to achievement in school and, to a lesser extent, beyond school. In other words, past success in learning whatever it is that the intelligence test measures is regarded as something of a forerunner of future success in the classroom and in higher-level occupations.

Thus, the extent to which IQ can predict achievement depends on how closely the achievement criteria resemble the kinds of cognitive operations tapped by IQ instruments. For example, in a large-scale study of educational and psychosocial consequences of school segregation in California, Gerard and Miller (1975) reported a modest correlation of .21 between IQ and individual reading and arithmetic grades for approximately thirteen hundred elementary school children. Goldman and Hartig (1976) examined this same population and found a similarly weak correlation of .27 between WISC IQ and a subsequent two-year grade point average. Even lower correlations were noted for low-SES black and Mexican-American subsamples. In the Gerard and Miller as well as the Goldman and Hartig studies, the low correlations may be explained partly by the occasional irrelevance of teacher evaluations as criterion measures. In fact, Goldman and Hartig included teacher grades on such unlikely subjects as physical education, instrumental music, and health.

On the other hand, when criterion variables are fairly similar to those measured on IQ tests, the relationships are understandably better. Messé, Crano, Messé, and Rice (1979) examined the school records of fifty-two hundred British children and found that IQ correlates between .5 and .6 with teachers' ratings of pupil performance in class. (The teachers were given explicit instructions on how to rate the children in reading and arithmetic.) Messe et al. indicated that their findings conform with those of other studies that examine the relationship between IQ and performance in traditional academic areas of study provided, of course, that both are measured reliably. However, as long as there are radical differences among instructors in grading standards, and students are allowed to choose most of their classes freely, no predictor can be expected to correlate more than moderately with overall grade-point average.

Goldman and Slaughter (1976) suggest a way in which to overcome the problem with college-age populations, but since it involves a statistical conversion of grades to make it possible to equate scholastic records from one college to the next, it is unlikely that college administrators will accept it. Without such adjustments, it will seem that poor predictive validity is to blame for the low correlations with grade-point average when in reality the fault can often be traced to an unstable, far too subjective grade-point average.

IQ-type measures will be particularly inadequate in forecasting performance at schools where lower-ability students gravitate toward classes where grades are inflated and the brighter students drift toward courses where marking is more stringent. In that case, too much dependence on the IQ for identifying the potentially gifted would produce many false-negative selection errors (i.e., rejection of students who would have succeeded).

There are other ways in which IQ test scores have been misinterpreted and misused in assessing children's potential. One frequent pitfall is the assumption that an impressive IQ obtained when a child is young will be confirmed in subsequent testing. A study by Schmeding (1964) shows that high IQ scores are anything but stable. In this investigation, the targeted group consisted of 199 eleventh- and twelfth-graders with scores at or above IQ 120 on the California Tests of Mental Maturity, the Pintner-Cunningham Primary Test, or the Pintner General Ability Test. After examining the cumulative records, Schmeding found that students with IQs of 120 or above at some point in the sequential testing seldom maintained this level in subsequent testing and that there was little basis for expecting trustworthy high IQs early in the children's lives. The fault can lie in test error, regression toward the mean, or even a change in the children's functioning levels as a result of their learning experiences. It is therefore clear that a single indicator of high potential is seldom adequate for such purposes.

Another source for concern is the use of IQ as a universal language, regardless of the test from which it is obtained. High scores on one instrument are not often substantiated on another instrument. The extent of discrepancy is illustrated in a study by Kincaid (1969) involving 561 children from kindergarten through sixth grade with IQs of 150 and above as measured by the Stanford-Binet. When a group intelligence test was administered to this sample, over 85 percent of the children scored below 150. Nearly half were between 130 and 149, and about 40 percent were below 130. Not only are there discrepancies between individual and group test scores but even between two individually administered instruments measuring the same kinds of ability. It is well known, for example, that high-IQ children obtain better scores on the Stanford-Binet than on the Wechsler Intelligence Scale for Children. The reader of test results therefore has to look beyond the IQ per se and consider carefully the source of the information.

IQ also seems far more closely associated with some signs of giftedness than with others. In one of a series of studies dealing with the predictive power of the so-called "11-plus" examination administered to children completing elementary school in Great Britain, an effort was made to determine how well these tests correlate with performance in various content areas covered in the General Certificate of Education Examination that is taken mostly by grammar school students at about the age of 16 (Emmett and Wilmut, 1952). The 11-plus battery consisted of an IQ-type test and a standardized measure of skills in English and arithmetic. The population sample chosen for this study was skewed toward the top in scholastic achievement, and this would tend to reduce the correlations between selection and criterion measures.

Table 19-1 shows that IQ was a better predictor than the other instruments but that it does not correlate equally well with all subjects. For example, much lower coefficients were obtained for biology and art than for English language and mathematics. Furthermore, there does not seem to be a relationship at all between

Table 19-1. Correlations, Uncorrected for Selection, of 11+
Tests with Different School Certificate Subjects

School Certificate Subject	N	Correlations with		
		IQ	E.Q.*	A.Q.†
English language	153	.505	.498	.204
English literature	153	.296	.298	.266
History	153	.383	.336	.328
French	153	.451	.463	.359
Mathematics	153	.514	.299	.429
Physics	96	.401	.224	.319
Chemistry	105	.386	.254	.366
Latin	81	.443	.388	.396
Geography	139	.285	.101	.071
Biology	67	.124	.038	.046
Art	66	−.020	.115	−.048

*E.Q. = English quotient.

†A.Q. = Arithmetic quotient.

Source: W. G. Emmett and F. S. Wilmut. "The Prediction of School Certificate Performance in Special Subjects." *British Journal of Educational Psychology,* 22:59 (1959).

IQ and art, although this may be due to the fact that the IQ range was fairly restricted. Nevertheless, it makes sense to expect that certain areas of accomplishment, particularly in the performing and visual arts, require basic abilities that are not closely related to those measured by the IQ. In that case, the only recourse for identifying high potential is to find some way to measure special aptitudes.

Cautions in the Use of Special Ability Tests

We can reasonably speculate that children who score at the ninety-fifth percentile or above in IQ will be among the top academic achievers at school. However, as Robinson (1977) points out, to be qualified as gifted, a child has to demonstrate superiority in something that has clear, productive significance, not just in taking IQ tests.

Among the better known measures for identifying high-level special abilities is Meeker's (1975) battery, based on Guilford's Structure of Intellect (SOI) theory (1967). Meeker (1969) contends that an IQ could have more meaning if educators were given access to assessments of the separate abilities entering into that score. She first analyzed children's performance on the Stanford-Binet in order to create strength-weakness profiles against the background of SOI factors. This kind of mapping procedure was then repeated for other general ability tests, thus enabling psychometrists to translate g factor protocols into SOI terms. The functional diagnostic information could then serve as a means of prescribing appropriate educational experiences for precocious children in much the same way that competency-based instruction is applied to handicapped learners.

Since measures of specific aptitudes shed some light on the subject areas in which the high-IQ child is likely to excel, it makes sense to administer such tests in the search for extraordinary potential. As might be expected, the validity varies from the test of one aptitude to that of another. For example, Shinn (1956) found that, by using a multiple correlation to predict scores on each of the Iowa subtests from the total PMA battery, all the coefficients hovered around .60 even though the correlations among separate PMA and Iowa subtests ranged from .73 to as low as .13.

It would seem, therefore, that the whole battery is more valid than are many of its separate parts. However, success in some courses of study relates more closely to total battery scores than do others. This was borne out in an investigation of scholastic performance of college students (Goldman and Slaughter, 1976). The researchers obtained SAT scores and high school grade-point averages for 254 undergraduates enrolled in courses in psychology, biology, chemistry, physics, and sociology. It was found that the multiple correlations with grades in the separate courses ranged from .32 for physics to .64 for sociology.

The extent to which different and combined aptitude scores relate to achievement in various subject matter areas is illustrated in Figure 19-1. The figures shown are summaries of more than thirteen hundred validity coefficients for the Academic Promise Tests (APT), which include measures of Abstract Reasoning (AR), Numerical (N), Verbal, (V), and Language Usage (LU). In addition to reporting the correlations for each test, the charts also indicate coefficients for two combination scores—V + LU and AR + N—and a total score for the battery. Note that the median correlations between the separate APT scores and English grades range from .33 for AR to .61 for LU. On the other hand, the median correlation for LU with mathematics grades is only .36. As expected, N correlates higher with mathematics and science than it does with English grades.

Evidently, there are different degrees of predictive validity for the separate aptitude tests in relation to the different subject matter areas. At the same time, it should be noted that the median validity coefficient for the total battery is often as high or higher than for any of the subtests. Obtaining factor profiles may therefore be a matter of convenience rather than an advantage in predicting achievement in an academic subject.

Predictions for Childhood versus Adulthood

In sobering essays on the use of tests to forecast various kinds of performance, McClelland (1973) and Wallach (1976) argued that measures of human potential have been validated on success at school but tell us little about accomplishment after graduation. The usual supportive data provided by test manuals pertain to classroom-type performance, and the evidence is often impressive. But it means

APT Scores and English Grades

r	AR	N	V	LU	AR + N	V + LU	Total
.70 and up		1	1	5	1	8	8
.60–.69	2	5	7	22	6	17	11
.50–.59	6	12	10	12	8	13	20
.40–.49	7	15	19	9	17	10	6
.30–.39	18	12	7	3	12	3	4
.20–.29	9	3	5		4		1
Below .20	9	3	2		3		1
Median	.33	.44	.45	.61	.44	.59	.56

APT Scores and Mathematics Grades

r	AR	N	V	LU	AR + N	V + LU	Total
.70 and up		3	1	1	3	1	6
.60–.69	3	7	4	3	5	6	7
.50–.59	3	19	7	10	14	10	18
.40–.49	9	11	11	11	14	13	7
.30–.39	19	11	9	13	10	9	8
.20–.29	9	1	9	9	6	7	7
Below .20	12	3	14	8	3	9	2
Median	.34	.50	.35	.36	.46	.42	.52

Figure 19-1 The academic promise tests: Studies of predictive validity (*Test Service Bulletin*, No. 55, Psychological Corporation, Dec. 1963, p. 10)

APT Scores and Science Grades

r	AR	N	V	LU	AR + N	V + LU	Total
.70 and up	1	1	2	3	1	6	4
.60–.69		5	10	7	5	10	15
.50–.59	3	16	9	11	14	12	11
.40–.49	13	13	14	12	10	8	5
.30–.39	13	3	4	3	6	3	3
.20–.29	3	3	1	5	3	3	4
Below .20	10	2	3	2	4	1	1
Median	.37	.50	.47	.49	.49	.55	.58

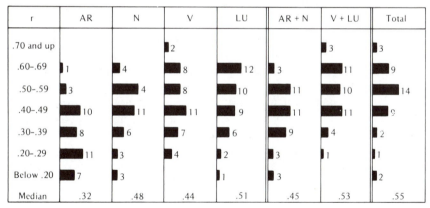

APT Scores and Social Studies

r	AR	N	V	LU	AR + N	V + LU	Total
.70 and up			2			3	3
.60–.69	1	4	8	12	3	11	9
.50–.59	3	4	8	10	11	10	14
.40–.49	10	11	11	9	11	11	9
.30–.39	8	6	7	6	9	4	2
.20–.29	11	3	4	2	3	1	1
Below .20	7	3		1	3		2
Median	.32	.48	.44	.51	.45	.53	.55

Figure 19-1 (continued)

little from a lifetime perspective except that those who excel scholastically have a better than average chance of achieving well in some unspecified high-level work in adulthood. In other words, no existing battery of measures can predict with much confidence (1) who will qualify for *what* prestigious occupation and (2) how those who manage eventually to qualify for *any* of them will perform at their jobs.

Terman's (1959) follow-up study of some fifteen hundred children with average IQs of over 150 revealed a tendency to occupy positions that could only be achieved through advanced academic or professional training. However, the data should not lead us to conclude that success in all of these types of work *requires* childhood IQs at or beyond the ninety-ninth percentile. Nor do their IQs suggest which specific careers each of these children would eventually pursue. Even the vast amount of data about the children's developmental histories, the environments in which they matured, and their formal educational experiences were not adequate to forecast the kinds of jobs they would someday hold and whether they would excel in their work during the productive years of life.

Measures of special aptitude are not of much help, either. The tests developed for children have not been evaluated as predictors of success in any particular field. And the best that can be said for adult batteries is that they seem to have more retrospective than prospective value. In their study of ten thousand careers, Thorndike and Hagen (1959) had access to scores on the Air Force battery of cadet classification tests administered during World War II. They then obtained follow-up information on ten thousand individuals in 1956, approximately thirteen years after the test had been administered. Results show that aptitude measures administered in early adulthood distinguished the successful persons in one field from those in another. For example, architects had rated highest on tests of perceptual speed administered thirteen years earlier; college professors, physical scientists, and engineers had the best records in reading comprehension; chemical, mechanical, and aeronautical engineers performed best in arithmetic reasoning; engineers and physical scientists excelled in mathematics; company treasurers and comptrollers were superior in numerical operations; and mechanical and aeronautical engineers and farmers were advanced in mechanical principles, and machinists in two-hand coordination. Thus, we find post hoc differences associated with aptitude tests administered more than a decade before the talents came to fruition. However, nobody could have anticipated that individuals scoring well on the tests would go on to excel in a specific occupation over another.

Even if aptitude scores could or should guide people in making career choices, there are still decisions to be made on how to use the test data to qualify them to go through the necessary preparations. Suppose, for example, that the minimum scores on measures of intellectual potential required for success in medical school were at the ninety-eighth percentile in IQ, reading comprehension, and verbal and mathematical reasoning. Imagine also that twice as many people as are needed in the field meet these qualifications and want to study medicine when they finish college. How should the one out of two be selected for admission ? Is it wise and fair to admit the higher-scoring half of those ranking at or beyond the ninety-eighth percentile on the qualifying measures? Could we assume that those who score best among the qualifiers are likely to become the most competent medical practitioners? Such assumptions seem to have been made by medical schools, judging from the dramatic year-to-year rise in undergraduate grade-point averages and aptitude scores among students in their programs.

One comprehensive survey reported by the American Medical Association (1975) shows that 39.3 percent of new first-year medical students in 1974 had premedical grade-point averages of "A" (3.6 to 4.0 on a four-point scale) as compared with only 12.3 percent of the entering freshman in 1963. Grade inflation may account for some of the difference, but not all of it, since there were also notable improvements in performance on the standardized Medical College Admission test during that decade.

Depite the widespread practice of accepting freshmen into medical school on the basis of rank-ordered scores on various scholastic measures, the results of a large-scale study of physician performance (Price et al., 1964) suggest that this is not the way in which to locate students with the highest potential for excellence as medical practitioners. Three independent variables pertaining to academic standing (i.e., grade-point average in college, grade-point average during the first two years in medical school, and grade-point average during the last two years of medical school) and seventy-seven criterion variables related to on-the-job performance in practice were intercorrelated. Of the resulting 849 coefficients, 97 percent were of zero-order magnitude, and most of the remaining 3 percent were negative. The senior author concluded,

This is a somewhat shocking finding for a medical educator like myself who has spent his professional life selecting applicants for admission to medical school, and in teaching and grading students after admission. It is true that a strong suspicion that grades have been weighted much too heavily in predicting performance in medical school and after graduation from medical school is what led to the initiation of this whole study in the first instance; but to have that suspicion so forcefully corroborated has led me to question the adequacy of some of our traditional admission policies, as well as the reliability of conventional grades as a measure of progress of the student during his medical course, or as the sole criterion for promotion, or as a dependent predictor of future success in practice. (p. 209)

Corroborating evidence is suggested in a study of SAT scores among people listed in *Who's Who* (Chauncey and Hilton, 1965). As indicated in Table 19-2, the scores are skewed toward the upper extreme with 3.8 times as many people as expected earning 696 and above (see the O/E column). However, the figures also reveal that fully 25 percent of those making it into *Who's Who* scored in the *lower* fifty percent of college students (i.e., 499 and below). Indeed, there were as many coming from the lower 50 percent as from the upper 10 percent of the SAT distribution for college students. On the other hand, Roe's (1953) distinguished scientists could easily be recognized by their scores on tests that correlate highly with school achievement. Table 19-3 shows that their IQs were impressive enough to label them "gifted" in many schools and to qualify them for special enrichment programs. Obviously, then, it is easier to identify through conventional measures of potential the kinds of gifted examined by Roe than many of those listed in

Table 19-2. Aptitude Scores and Proportion of Eminent Individuals at Each Level of SAT College Population

SAT Score Interval	% Expected in Each Interval (E)	% in *Who's Who* Group (O)	O/E
696 and above	2.6%	10%	3.8
629–695	7.3	15	2.1
563–628	18.9	25	1.3
500–562	21.2	25	1.2
450–499	19.1	15	.8
Below 450	30.9	10	.3

Source: H. Chauncey and T. L. Hilton, "Are Aptitude Tests Valid for the Highly Able?" *Science* 148:16 (1965).

Table 19-3. Range and Median of Test Scores (IQ Equivalents) of Outstanding Scientists Studied by Roe

Subtest	Score			N
	Highest	*Median*	*Lowest*	
Verbal	177	166	121	59
Spatial	164	137	123	57
Mathematical	194	154	128	39

Source: A. Roe, *Making of a Scientist* (New York: Dodd, Mead & Company, 1953).

Who's Who. Besides, gifted performance in science and mathematics at school is a good forerunner of excellence in these disciplines after graduation because there is a similarity between the problem-solving experiences in the classroom and those in the professions and industry. This is not true for those who appear in *Who's Who* because of their contributions to the world of business, politics, or entertainment. The careers in which they make their reputations are hardly given much attention in the elementary and secondary curricula, thus making it difficult for educators to recognize such talent.

To improve identification procedures for long-term prediction, McClelland (1973) and Wallach (1976) have offered a variety of suggestions that may be summarized as follows:

1. *Rely heavily on criterion sampling.* If we are looking for children who may turn out to be exemplary mechanics, observe them in the way in which they take apart, put together, and repair increasingly complicated machinery. Potential social leaders have to be watched for the manner in which they interact with peers. This principle applies to each area of talent that the school wants to nurture.

2. *Select tests designed to reflect changes in what the individual has learned.* Not only should we rely on monitoring children's performance, as in the cases of

mechanics and social leadership, but we should also determine how well the children sharpen their skills as a result of training and experience.

3. *Use tests that involve operant as well as respondent behavior.* Many of the popular instruments are designed to show how well people *can* rather than *will* perform. One is not necessarily a good predictor of the other. McClelland offers as an example the assessment of a person's *capacity* to drink beer as a poor indicator of how much that individual *actually* consumes. It is therefore necessary to look at motivational factors to determine the excitation values of various tasks for each child.

In effect, there is a need to rely less on tests made up of content that is only remotely relevant to the curriculum and more on measures of "in-context" potential. "In-context" tests are administered routinely to actors in the form of auditions, artists in the form of portfolio reviews, and athletes in the form of trials under competitive conditions. Schools might do well to apply similar procedures in locating other kinds of talent as well.

Identifying the Culturally Different

One of the most persistent difficulties in the identification process has been to find ways of locating representative numbers of gifted children in lower-status ethnic and social class groups. Conventional screening methods identify a much higher proportion of the gifted among majority than among minority populations. This fact has reinforced the charge that various measures of potential, especially IQ tests, are biased against the disadvantaged and create de facto segregation when children performing well on such measures are placed in special programs for the gifted. This assumption of difference *ergo* bias was questioned by Lorge (1953) and Tannenbaum (1965) who argued that the social system rather than the test instrument is guilty of prejudice, not only against racial and socioeconomic minorities, but also against groups classified by sex, age, education, geographic origin, and mental health. The test scores are sensitive to these differences. As such, they reflect one of the consequences of prejudice in our society by showing that its victims are denied a fair chance to achieve excellence. Nevertheless, ways have to be found to recognize hidden potential among minority subcultures as a first step toward helping them cultivate it and thereby combatting some of the bigotry in our society.

Several attempts have been made to search for special traces of giftedness among the disadvantaged. Davidson et al. (1962) conducted a large-scale study of high- and low-achieving black fifth-graders living in poverty. They found that the more able children in this group resembled those coming from more advantaged backgrounds. Compared with the low achievers, they were more willing to conform to adult demands, displayed greater self-confidence, had superior analytical and organizational ability, and excelled in tasks requiring memory, attention, and verbal facility. These results suggest that there are no characteristic differences between minority and majority children who succeed at school and that perhaps the only way in which to "make it" in the dominant culture is to adopt its success-oriented values and behaviors.

Other studies of potentially gifted minority children tend to confirm the existence of nonintellective traits similar to those of their majority counterparts. Bernal (1974) compared potentially gifted and nongifted Mexican-American bilingual children, ages 5 to 9, on a series of characteristics commonly associated with intellectual precocity. Nine of these items had high discrimination power. Similarly, in an investigation of Asian-American elementary school children, Chen and Goon (1976) found that the potentially gifted possessed such behavioral "trademarks" as initiative, enthusiasm, willingness to work, reliability, industry, good school attendance, and ability to do sustained work. When compared with the precocious non-Asians, they seemed to get along even better with others, particularly adults; they were able to work more diligently; and they demonstrated an exceptionally good sense of humor that was devoid of sarcasm or viciousness.

All in all, the personality traits associated with giftedness appear to be consistent across subcultural barriers. This seems especially true for nonintellective characteristics. However, the picture may be different for cognitive organization. In their studies of children representing different ethnic minority groups, Lesser, Fifer, and Clark (1965) found that each sample had a distinctive performance profile on the Verbal, Reasoning, Number, and Space criterion tests. The researchers interpreted these variations to reflect different emphases among ethnic groups on the specific intellectual functions to be cultivated. Yet, when each ethnic sample was subdivided into middle versus lower socioeconomic classes, there were sharp differences in performance on each test, as expected, but equally noteworthy, the performance profiles across the tests were virtually identical. It appears evident, therefore, that Cazden (1968) is correct in suggesting that ethnicity affects the *pattern* of mental ability, whereas socioeconomic status influences the *level* of performance on tests of specific mental abilities.

Several efforts have been made to modify testing instruments and procedures to assess the abilities of children with hidden potential. Bruch (1971) reported an attempt to analyze the performance of black elementary school children on the Stanford-Binet. Her method was to isolate those tasks on which the children perform best, using Guilford's Structure of Intellect model to describe these mental operations. On the basis of her findings, she developed an abbreviated form of the Stanford-Binet that assesses only those ability areas in which blacks are proficient. The strengths turned out to be problem-solving skills with visual and auditory content, memory operations, and convergent production. The weaknesses included cognition of semantic units (i.e., vocabulary) and, surprisingly, divergent production. Bruch concluded that the pattern of cognitive powers revealed in this study is distinctive and indicates that cultural experiences affect the development of cognitive strengths. The educator's task is to capitalize on these strengths so that blacks may be well represented in the talent pool.

In an innovative departure from conventional methods of testing potential, Feuerstein (1979) has rejected the IQ test as an appropriate indicator of human potential. He regards it as a "static" measure in that it assesses only the status, not the modifiability, of a person's functioning. The underprivileged are at a particular disadvantage in this kind of testing because their "static" performance is depressed by a lack of what he calls mediated learning experiences in the form of help from others to frame, clarify, and interpret their interaction with the environment and to strengthen their motivation to learn. The examiner therefore tries to make up for these deprivations by orienting the child to the test experience, not just taking account of test responses objectively. Administering the test involves, among other things, providing instruction on how to approach and solve problems similar to those used in assessing general intelligence. It is essentially a two-step, test-retest procedure designed to "stretch the mind" as far as possible beyond the level of functioning it manifests under nonmediating conditions. The degree to which this kind of modification can be accomplished in a child represents a more meaningful assessment of cognitive capacity, or potential.

Mercer (1977) took a different approach to nullifying the sociocultural contaminants by applying her System of Multicultural Pluralistic Assessment (SOMPA). Through this method she advocated combining the formal input from measures of intelligence, perceptual-motor skills, and visual-motor gestalt with information from parents about the child's performance of various social roles, social, cultural, and economic characteristics of the family, and health conditions that may be related to learning difficulties. Since nonintellective and environmental factors assessed through SOMPA figure prominently in the identification plan, they would account for the poor showing of socially disadvantaged children. The intention is to obtain better evidence of "true" potential by weighing these various kinds of evidence about the child.

In addition to modifying existing tests and procedures to uncover hidden talent among the disadvantaged, a popular approach is to amalgamate a wide range of information about the child, usually from different sources. This is the method advocated by Kranz (1978) through her Multi-Dimensional Screening device, which she devised and field tested (Gustafson et al., 1975). Following a staff training program on how to use the instrument, teachers rate the children in their class in ten talent areas: (1) ability in the visual arts; (2) ability in the performing arts; (3) demonstrated creative or productive thinking; (4) academic ability in a particular discipline; (5) general intellectual ability at or above the ninety-ninth percentile; (6) leadership qualities: organizing and decision making; (7) psycho-motor history and ability; (8) history and use of spatial and abstract thinking; (9) high discrepancy between performance and general intellectual ability; and (10) talent associated with the child's cultural heritage.

Each of the talents is evaluated in three ways: *frequency*, or the number of times the behavior is demonstrated in proportion to opportunities to do so; *intensity*, or the amount of intellectual, emotional, or physical energy the child invests in it; and *quality*, according to some standard of excellence, especially in the academically/ socially desirable categories of behavior.

Each teacher rates every pupil in class, and children scoring above the cutoff point specified in the manual in at least four areas of talent are then processed for further review by the school principal who sends the list to the Local Screening Committee (LSC) for final selection. The LSC is composed of approximately five people, usually a teacher of the gifted, a counselor, a librarian, a speciality teacher, and the principal. This group evaluates the teacher ratings, along with other information obtained from parents, teachers, and children themselves. The LSC may also request scores on standardized measures of general ability and achievement. Thus, decisions are made with the help of wide-ranging data culled from a variety of sources.

Kranz's comprehensive approach has been generally supported by Bernal (1980) who reaches the following conclusion from his review of literature on methods of identifying gifted minority students: "Contrary to popular and some professional opinion, the state of the art in measurement does not seem to support the tacit position that traditional indicators of ability identify enough of the gifted students to warrant their exclusive use" (p. 18). He argues that, aside from their limitations in measuring the potentialities of *any* children, they are particularly inappropriate with minorities, either because they lack experience in taking such tests or because their family traditions and life experiences affect the organization of their abilities in ways that penalize performance on tests of this kind. He also rejects the idea of "doctoring" traditional measurement techniques by adding points to compensate for social disadvantage or by using only those subtests in the battery that minority children understand best. These practices, along with the outright establishment of quota systems, tend to stigmatize minority students while still failing to recognize many who are gifted among them.

Instead, he advocates a wide-ranging data base to include tests of creativity; nominations from parents, teachers, peers, and community sources; behavioral inventories, interviews, self-reports, autobiographies, and case histories; and students' products or performances. He also suggests the possible usefulness of Piagetian tests and measures of language proficiency. To measure cognitive ability, he would consider using several experimental tests in which questions are more oriented to "What do you know?" rather than "Do you know what I know?"

Of course, even multiple means of identification are inadequate unless the educational follow through is just as dedicated and imaginative. Bernal argues strongly for periodic reassessment of students who had not been selected previously. He also agrees with Witty (1978) that minorities' intellectual strengths and learning styles have to be addressed by intelligent and caring teachers and that parents and educators should reinforce each other's efforts on behalf of the gifted. One might add that these basic principles are sound enough to apply to all children, including the advantaged.

Nominations by Teachers and Parents

It is not easy to determine the accuracy of teachers and parents in identifying giftedness in their children since the standards against which their judgments can be evaluated are themselves imprecise. Usually, investigators establish a cutoff point in IQ and presume that children scoring above that level are gifted. The next step is to determine how well teachers and parents can recognize with their naked eyes the ones who belong in that special category. In a large-scale study of fifty thousand children from grades four through eight, Lewis (1940) organized four comparison groups. The first consisted of children scoring in the upper 10 percent in IQ based on Kuhlmann-Anderson scores; a second group, taken from the first, represented the upper 2 percent in IQ; a third group was composed of children labeled as "geniuses" by their teachers; and the fourth was a normative group selected at random to represent the total school population. Results may be summarized as follows:

1. The median IQ for the girls designated as "genius" by their teachers was 118 while for the boys it was 114. The median IQs for the upper 10 percent as determined by the Kuhlmann-Anderson test was 121 for both boys and girls, and the median for the upper 2 percent was 129 for the girls and 130 for the boys.
2. On tests measuring achievement in reading, geography, arithmetic problems, and language usage, the "genius" group surpassed both test-selected samples in every subject and in every grade. These discrepancies were statistically significant in practically every case.
3. The teachers rated the "geniuses" as possessing more desirable personality traits than the test-selected and normative samples. They also rated the normative sample as having fewer desirable personality traits than did the others.

Despite the superior scholastic achievement of the teacher-selected group, Lewis concluded that teachers are ineffective in detecting intellectual superiority in children. He evidently considers IQ a better indicator of giftedness than achievement test scores. It would have been interesting to follow up the experimental samples into adolescence and adulthood to see how well they compared with each other in latter accomplishment.

In another study involving teacher judgments and test scores, Baldwin (1962) also defined giftedness as high IQ. The study focused on kindergarten children with IQs of 125 or above on the California Test of Mental Maturity and also those who were evaluated informally only for giftedness by their teachers after six weeks and again after seven months into the school term. Teachers nominated forty-six children in the first round and forty children in the second round. With IQ 130 on the Stanford-Binet as the criterion for giftedness, teachers were correct in 26 percent of the cases on their first judgments and 38 percent on their second judgments.

In determining the agreement between group and individual intelligence test scores, Baldwin found that 39 percent of the children with IQs of 125 and above on the California Test of Mental Maturity also scored at or above IQ 130 on the Stanford-Binet. The mean Stanford-Binet IQ for children screened by CTMM (121.75) was almost identical to the mean for children nominated as gifted by their teachers (121.30). Baldwin acknowledged that the criterion used to determine giftedness was narrow and placed limitations on his study. He also notes that a kindergarten teacher's ability to identify gifted children is unreliable, possibly because those entering kindergarten with only slightly above-average ability may demonstrate considerable readiness for school with the help of parents and older siblings.

Pegnato and Birch (1959) studied the relative accuracy of teacher nominations and various scholastic performance measures in locating high-IQ children. The experimental population consisted of 1,400 junior high school students, 781 of whom appeared on at least one of the following lists: (1) *teacher judgment* as "gifted"; (2) *honor roll listing*, which included children with a "B" average or higher on all subjects; (3) *creative ability in art or music*, based on ratings by teachers in these subjects; (4) *student council membership* selected in each home-room to represent their peers in this organization; (5) *superiority in mathematics*, as judged by teachers of arithmetic; (6) *group intelligence test results*, including those with IQs of 115 or higher on the Otis Quick Scoring Mental Ability Test; and (7) *group achievement test results*, including those who scored at least three grade levels above average in reading and arithmetic.

Of the 781 students on these seven lists, 91 had Stanford-Binet IQs of 136 and above, and they were designated as gifted. Pegnato and Birch then calculated how well each of the seven criteria "hit the mark" in identifying the 91 gifted children (with a percentage of "hits" called an index of *effectiveness*) and the extent to which it excluded the 690 nongifted (with the ratio of "hits" to total nominations called an index of *efficiency*).

The results, shown in Table 19-4, indicated that it is difficult to achieve both high efficiency and effectiveness. In fact, success in raising one seems to be at the expense of reducing the other. For example, a low cutoff point on the group intelligence test (IQ 115) enabled the researchers to locate 84 out of the 91 gifted children, producing a high effectiveness index of 92.3 percent. These 84 children were among a large group of 450 who met the 115 IQ criterion, thus producing a low efficiency index of only 18.7 percent. On the other hand, when the group IQ criterion was 130, the efficiency ratios rose to 55.5 percent, while effectiveness plunged to 21.9 percent. As for teacher judgment, the record was particularly unimpressive since only 45.1 percent of the gifted received nominations. Not only were more than half of the gifted missing on this list, but the researchers report that almost a third (31.4 percent) of those chosen by the teachers were in the *average* IQ range on the Stanford-Binet.

Comparisons have also been made between teachers' and parents' recognition of giftedness in their children. Jacobs (1971) evaluated 654 kindergarten children and found 19 with IQs of 125 and above on the Wechsler Pre-School and Primary Scale of Intelligence (WPPSI) and designated them as gifted. At the beginning of the school year, the parents of each of the 654 children were asked whether their child might possibly be intellectually gifted. After six months of school, the twelve kindergarten teachers were asked to name the intellectually gifted children in their classes. Neither the parents nor the teachers were told how to define giftedness. The parents nominated a total of twenty-six children, sixteen of whom were gifted and ten nongifted. By correctly nominating sixteen out of the total of twenty-one gifted children, including two who were added to the original nineteen after the

Table 19-4. Effectiveness and Efficiency of Screening Procedures

Screening Methods	No. Selected by Screening Method	No. Identified as Gifted by Stanford-Binet IQ	Effectiveness (% of Gifted Located; Total Gifted, N = 91)	Efficiency (Ratio of No. Selected by Screening to No. Identified as Gifted, as a %)
Teacher judgment	154	41	45.1%	26.6%
Honor roll	371	67	73.6	18.0
Creativity	137	14	15.5	10.2
Art ability	(66)	(6)	6.6	9.1
Music ability	(71)	(8)	9.9	11.2
Student council	82	13	14.3	15.8
Mathematics achievement	179	50	56.0	27.9
Group intelligence tests				
Cutoff IQ 115	450	84	92.3	18.7
Cutoff IQ 120	(240)	(65)	71.4	27.1
Cutoff IQ 125	(105)	(40)	43.9	38.1
Cutoff IQ 130	(36)	(20)	21.9	55.5
Group achievement tests	335	72	79.2	21.5
Total	781			

Source: C. W. Pegnato and J. W. Birch. "Locating Gifted Children in Junior High School: A Comparison of Methods." *Exceptional Children*, 23:303 (1959).

experiment began, the parents had an effectiveness score of 76 percent. Teachers identified a total of forty-six children, forty-four of whom had average IQs ranging from 97 to 118; and the remaining two qualified as gifted, giving the teachers an effectiveness score of only 9.5 percent. It appears, therefore, that teachers of kindergarten children are not as accurate as parents in recognizing IQ-defined giftedness.

The poor showing of kindergarten teachers relative to parents in identifying the children who had high IQs was confirmed in a study by Ciha, Harris, Hoffman, and Potter (1974). A total of 465 children were evaluated using the Slosson Intelligence Test and two subtests of the WISC-R (Block Design and Picture Completion). Two subgroups were then formed; the "gifted," with IQs of 132 or above on the Slosson (N = 58) and the "hidden potential," based on IQs of 120 or above on the WISC-R but below 132 on the Slosson (N = 36). The parents nominated a total of 276 children: 39 out of the 58 "gifted", all 36 "hidden potential," and 201 nongifted by either criterion. Their effectiveness score for the "gifted" category was 76 percent. The kindergarten teachers nominated 54 children, including 13 of the "gifted," 7 of the "hidden potentials," and 34 nongifted, a 22 percent record of effectiveness. These results are comparable to the ones obtained by Jacobs (1971) for kindergarten parents and more encouraging for teachers, although both investigations favor the parents by a wide margin.

The failure of teachers to "divine" which of their children had high IQs is not as sad as it seems. Basically, we are dealing with a guessing game that is played under the rules of effectiveness and efficiency. It presupposes, naïvely, that a high IQ is itself perfectly effective and efficient in designating who belongs in the charmed circle of gifted children. No psychometrician would ever make such a claim for a score on any kind of test. Who cares, then, if teachers are uncanny in "unmasking" high-IQ children? Why worry about revealing a secret flawlessly when the secret is flawed in the first place? Besides, what is the point in having teachers speculate about children's IQ levels when all we have to do is look at the test results? In fact, it borders on insult for teachers to learn that the only purpose they serve in discerning giftedness is to verify subjectively what is known or knowable objectively about a child's tested intelligence.

The use of nomination to help locate the gifted should not be an exercise of solving riddles without clues. Instead, it means helping the nominator capitalize on a special relationship with children in order to see traces of talent that could not be detected otherwise. The classroom is an excellent place in which to find such evidence because of the many social and educational interactions that occur there. Still, teachers do not always seek out the significant evidence, and even when they are able to recognize it, they often do not trust their own impressions.

For example, a teacher recently called this author to describe a boy who seemed to have extraordinary leadership ability. He watched the boy relate to other children in the school building and in the playground and felt that there was something charismatic about him. His schoolmates always gravitated to him for direction in all kinds of social activities, curried favor with him, asked for his advice on various personal and group matters, and generally deferred to his judgment above all others, often even above their own. After relating anecdotes of this kind, the teacher then asked if there are any formal pencil-and-paper tests to assess this boy's leadership potential—as if these observations were unimportant unless confirmed "definitively" by a standardized measure!

Existing evidence seems to show that, with proper direction, teachers can provide independent evidence of their students' potentialities. The direction can come in the form of a guiding checklist of characteristics usually associated with the gifted or a series of training seminars to advise teachers about such attributes. There are many checklists, but the one that is probably used most widely is the Scale for Rating Behavior Characteristics of Superior Students (SRBCSS).

Developed by Renzulli and Hartman (1971), SRBCSS consists of a series of short, descriptive statements that characterize gifted children, as revealed in previous research. These descriptors are divided into four categories: Learning, Motivation, Creativity, and Leadership. Renzulli, Hartman, and Callahan (1971) report that the instrument is reliable, based on the consistency of ratings among judges and the stability of scores over a three-month period for a group of fifth- and sixth-graders. As for its concurrent validity, the researchers report that teachers were able to use the scale to discriminate between groups of children who had previously been classified as gifted versus average.

Comparisons were also made between ratings on the SRBCSS and scores on standardized tests of intelligence and achievement as well as the Torrance Tests of Creative Thinking (TTCT). Results show that the Learning and Motivation Scales correlate fairly well with measures that are generally used to identify the academically gifted. The Creativity Scale compared favorably with the verbal subscores of the TTCT but not with the nonverbal sections. The Leadership Scale showed impressive validity when teachers' assessments were compared with peer ratings obtained through standard sociometric techniques. However, another validity study by Lowrance and Anderson (1977) reported that only the Learning Characteristics Scale correlated significantly with the WISC-R, while the other three sections did not. These results may mean that the SRBCSS and the WISC-R measure separate but equally important aspects of human ability. Further evidence is needed to test such a hypothesis. Generally, teachers should exercise caution in using checklists of this kind until more evidence of their validity is reported.

There are other studies of teacher judgments that show promising results when teachers are alerted to children's traits that are associated with eventual success at school. Keogh and Smith (1970) identified eleven "educationally high-potential" and fifteen "high-risk" kindergarten children, based on whether they scored above or below the mean on the Bender Gestalt Test, and asked the teachers of these children to rate them on a five-point global scale of readiness. Subsequently, the pupils took standardized achievement tests in reading and mathematics as they progressed through the fifth-grade. Relationships between teacher assessments and eventual performance were impressive, considering the time gap between them. None of the children receiving the highest possible readiness rating of five in the kindergarten scored below grade level in reading or math in the fifth grade. Of the seven children with low readiness ratings of 1 or 2, five were below grade level in reading and three in math when they were in the fifth grade. Overall, the correlations between teacher ratings and reading achievement in grades two through five ranged from .45 to .69. These results show that teachers' kindergarten ratings can be useful in forecasting children's educational development.

Further confirmation of the value of teachers' judgments was reported in a larger-scale study of kindergarten children (N = 117) with an average IQ slightly above 100, for whom data were collected through grade three (Stevenson et al., 1976). Teachers rated the children on a large number of traits three months and then nine months into the kindergarten year and again in the spring of grades one, two, and three. Results showed that, after only three months of observation and interaction in kindergarten, teachers were able to make ratings that would predict how well the children would achieve at school more than forty months later. The teacher judgments after nine months of kindergarten were even more closely related to later performance.

Interestingly, the traits considered most predictive were *effective learning* (i.e., "catches on" quickly; assimilates new material easily; grasps new principles readily; seems to understand explanations easily); *vocabulary* (i.e., high-level vocabulary, always uses precise words; conveys abstractions); *following instructions* (i.e., unusually skillful in remembering and following instructions); and *retaining information* (i.e., superior memory for details and content). Correlations between these variables as a group and scholastic achievement in kindergarten through grade three ranged from .43 to .54. *Not* figuring prominently as predictors were such traits as *intellectually independent, hardworking, reflective, comprehending discussions*, and *adapting to new situations*, all of which would appear to be associated with special instruction in higher-level thinking skills and high-volume productivity in programs for the gifted. Seemingly, the emphasis in classes for average-ability children is mostly on acquiring information and communication skills; hence, the higher validity of the aforementioned mastery, memory, and work habit traits in predicting early school achievement.

In an even larger study involving 888 kindergarten children with IQs of 90 and above, Feshbach, Adelman, and Fuller (1977) allowed kindergarten teachers an eight-week period in which to observe and rate children's behaviors classified as follows: attention and behavioral control, language skill, visual-auditory perceptual discrimination, memory, and perceptual-motor coordination. Results are extremely impressive. With IQ partialed out, the correlation of teachers ratings with third-grade reading achievement was .33. Again we see that, when teachers are alerted to attributes children need for school achievement, they can make the proper discriminations and thus help to identify various levels of potential. Nevertheless, more research is needed with gifted populations to determine clearly how teachers' judgments can be sharpened in spotting a variety of potentialities that are at least partially unrecognizable through formal measures.

Peer and Self-nominations

Children themselves may provide valuable insight into who is gifted and in what ways. A study by Granzin and Granzin (1969) sought to detemine whether fourth-grade children were able to recognize characteristics associated with the gifted and whether these pupils could discern such traits in their peers. Specifically, they hypothesized (1) that the fourth-graders would be able to discriminate traits of giftedness from traits applying to children in general; (2) that high-IQ children were the most proficient in recognizing potential giftedness; and (3) that fourth-graders' judgments of peers would agree with ratings from other sources.

The children were presented with a checklist of thirty characteristics, fifteen of which pertained primarily to the gifted and the rest to children in general. Instructions were to indicate for each trait whether it represented giftedness. A month later, the children were asked to list which of their classmates were best represented by any of the fifteen gifted traits. Results show that all the children distinguished the characteristics of high-IQ peers from others in the classes but that those with IQs of 120 or higher were able to do so more readily than were students in general. In addition, peer rankings correlated significantly with IQ and teacher rankings. The researchers concluded that fourth-graders can understand the concept of giftedness and are able to indicate the relative levels of their peers' intellectual abilities. There was no indication, however, of the children's ability to recognize signs of talent that are overlooked by formal measures.

Children may also be able to perceive their own special qualities as precocious individuals. Drews (1961) asked more than a hundred adolescents with IQs of 120 and higher to indicate individually which of three possible descriptions character-ized them best. One of the choices was labeled "creative intellectual," defined as the kind of student who is motivated to deal with intellectual and philosophical matters and to be both contemplative and independent. Such a person is also oriented toward scholarly, theoretical, aesthetic, complex, humanistic, and original approaches to the world of ideas. Another choice was "studious," defined as having a strong drive to perform with distinction in the areas recognized by parents and teachers as "school learning." Such a person also has a powerful desire to get high marks and measure up to the expectations of those in authority. The final choice was "social leader" who is motivated to acquire power and money as well as other material comforts. This type of person feels the need to be popular among peers, to exercise authority in social situations, and to engage in entre-preneurial activity.

After dividing themselves into the three categories, the students were compared on several intellective and nonintellective measures to determine if there were consistent differences among the groups. Results showed that, even though the students describing themselves as "creative intellectuals" had lower grade-point averages than did those who believed they resembled "studious" types, they scored higher on IQ and critical thinking tests, chose higher-level occupations, wanted graduate training, were less inclined toward dogmatism and attitudinal rigidity, and showed the strongest interest in values associated with discovering "truth." Nevertheless, teachers rated "creative intellectuals" lower in creativity, intellect, and social acceptance and thought that they were *more* prone to dogmatism and attitudinal rigidity.

Drews's study is a rare example of high-ability children defining their own identities and differentiating among themselves in ways that formal measures cannot accomplish. It gives credence to the frequently ignored fact that the gifted constitute a widely heterogeneous group, their only commonality being that each of them has some kind of high potential.

The use of biographical inventories likewise gives students an opportunity to reveal aspects of themselves that may not be easy to discover through formal means. This is particularly relevant to giftedness in the arts and social leadership, which are so difficult to assess directly with any degree of reliability and validity.

Ellison, Abe, Fox, and Coray (1976) assembled biographical information to determine the extent to which it correlates with artistic talent, academic perform-ance, and social leadership. Their experimental sample consisted of eleventh- and twelfth-graders from two special schools: The Leadership School, which offers advanced leadership training, and The Governor's School of North Carolina, a summer residential honors program with advanced training in the arts and in academics. Also participating in the experiment were students from two regular high schools, thus raising the total number of subjects to more than a thousand. The instrument used was an adaptation of the Biographical Inventory, developed by the Institute for Behavioral Research in Creativity, and consisting of three hundred multiple-choice items that enabled respondents to describe themselves with respect to the targeted areas of accomplishment.

Results showed that the biographical information correlated highly with other estimates of the students' special aptitudes. The reseachers concluded that self-reports of this kind can help in selecting candidates for enrichment programs. Not only were the ratings accurate in predicting performance, but they also had less racial bias than did more traditional measures. Furthermore, the biographical inventory can help teachers to become more aware of different kinds of students who have high potential in various specialized areas. It remains to be seen whether students' estimates of themselves are independent of other sources of information about their abilities or are these self-conceptions mostly reflections of what parents, teachers, and peers have previously known and expressd to the students. If a self-report is basically a version of others' estimates of the individual, then it adds little information that is unobtainable elsewhere. Even so, it encapsulates the information in a convenient form for educators to interpret easily when they are searching for gifted children. It would be interesting to know whether kindergarten and elementary school children are old enough to have clear images of their own potentialities.

AN OUTLINE OF STEPS TOWARD IDENTIFICATION

From all existing evidence, it is obvious that identifying the gifted is far from an exact science. The extent of its inexactness varies with the person's age, special abilities, and subcultural membership. It is easier to predict children's performance at school than it is to predict their accomplishments following graduation; it is easier to recognize early potential in physics, chemistry, and mathematics than it is in art, social work, and playwriting; and it is easier to find talent among the privileged than among the underprivileged. To compound the problem, children are rarely gifted by universal standards of productivity or performance. They can only show the promise of excellence, but the likelihood of fulfillment usually ranges from fair to good, only sometimes perfect.

Considering the various problems associated with identification, the best we can do is to find a relatively small pool of children with high potential from which the gifted will emerge. There is something of a Hobson's choice between being too *inclusive*, and allowing excessive numbers of nongifted children in the pool, or being too *exclusive*, and overlooking those who rightfully belong there. The preferable option between the two is to err on the side of inclusion, with the understanding that further discriminations will have to begin soon afterwards.

These follow-up assessments should be based on the child's performance in

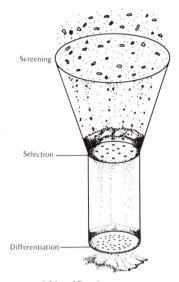

Figure 19-2 Three steps toward identification

enrichment and enrichmentlike activities, not just on tests similar to the ones that created the original talent pool. This implies a radical departure from the two-step, diagnosis-and-then-treat process advocated in medicine and in the education of the handicapped. The recommended approach is an oscillating one (not vacillating!) between diagnosis and treatment: not only do we identify the gifted *and then* educate them, but we also identify them *through* education. In other words, *prescribed enrichment becomes a vehicle for identification as much as identification facilitates enrichment, the relationship being reciprocal.*

Identification should begin as early as possible in the child's life, and it should go on for as long as possible, because there are always opportunities for discovering new insights and correcting old errors of judgment. The process is in three stages that can be depicted in the shape of a funnel—wide at the receptive end, becoming sharply narrower toward the middle, which has a built-in filter, and tapering off until the drainage end, which also has a sievelike attachment. As illustrated in Figure 19-2, the stages are (1) *screening*, (2) *selection*, and (3) *differentiation*. This sequence is reported continuously for children not yet screened and also for those who had previously not "made it" into the first stage.

Screening

At the wide mouth of the funnel, the criteria for inclusion are liberal, and many of the instruments used at this stage assess remote and sometimes far-fetched indicators of potential, not just actual performance at school. The purpose here is to include even those children who only show vague hints of giftedness in order to determine later if they possess real potential. Eventually, however, the identification process will limit itself only to those content areas that the school elects to emphasize in its enrichment program. It would be wasteful, for example, to seek out children who have a flair for creative writing unless plans were completed or at least underway to cultivate these skills in the overall program for the gifted. Therefore, the identification procedures have to conform to the scope and objectives of the curriculum. To obtain the proper kinds of initial information, it is necessary to consult multiple sources, including but not limited to the following:

Evidence of General Ability. If the program is geared exclusively to the academically gifted, then the major pool would probably be found among children scoring beyond one standard deviation above the mean on an IQ-type test. For disadvantaged groups, the cutoff point may have to be even lower, and Feuerstein's (1979) mediated approach to testing will undoubtedly be useful in measuring the child's potential rather than status. Much will depend also on other sources of information about the child's special abilities, work habits, and motivation, as suggested by Bernal (1980). A lowering of the cutoff point on scholastic aptitude measures and more confidence in other indicators of talent will also help to prevent overlooking the artistically and socially gifted.

Evidence of Specific Aptitudes and Achievement. Tests of special skills are useful in assessing children's progress in particular content areas. Such measures are useful because there is good reason to assume that a student performing better than expectation in a particular subject will continue to do so at least in the near future. However, such instruments probably work best for identifying high potential in some subjects such as language arts and mathematics; they are somewhat less suited for the sciences; and they are usually inadequate for the social studies. Aptitude tests generally provide better information about academic strengths than about artistic or musical abilities, thus limiting the areas in which such instruments are appropriate. A serious problem can arise when schools play mostly to the strengths of these kinds of tests and restrict their enrichment programs only to the academically talented because these abilities are easiest to measure. In such cases the instrument exercises power over the program and does not serve its intended purpose as a tool to help implement the program.

Evidence from "Creativity" Measures. The most popular of these tests measure divergent thinking and their reliability and validity remain yet to be fully confirmed. Regardless of how doubtful, cautious, or enthusiastic people may be about measuring creativity this way, all would probably agree that these instruments are most (and perhaps only) appropriate if the enrichment program is designed to emphasize divergent thinking. Otherwise, such a procedure amounts to auditioning people for their singing talent to qualify for the *corps de ballet*. It is necessary for divergent thinking skills to be emphasized as much in the school curriculum as in plans for identifying the gifted.

Evidence from Noncognitive Traits. Limitations in the predictive validity of performance measures should encourage educators to correct the underemphasis on personality variables and behaviors, including self-directedness, pride in accomplishment, persistence, dedication, work habits, and other traits associated with achievement. In a questionnaire developed by the Bureau of Educational Research and Service at the University of Kansas for aspiring Merit Scholarship winners, the following items distinguished most consistently between the eventual winners and also-rans: "How would you rate yourself in terms of intellectual curiosity?" "How would you rate yourself in terms of willingness to stand discomfort (a cold, illness, etc.) in completion of a school task?" "How would you rate yourself in terms of willingness to spend time, *beyond the ordinary schedule* in completion of a given school task?" "How would you rate yourself in terms of *questioning* the absolute truth of statements from textbooks, newspapers, and magazines or of statements made by persons in positions of authority such as teachers, lecturers, and professors?" (personal communication). These are examples of the kinds of information that can be obtained not only from the children about themselves, but also from their peers, parents, and teachers. Since these people see the children from different perspectives, it can be helpful to obtain their ratings through an identical list of traits. They will thus serve as a check on each other from their respective vantage points. A large number of trait lists now exists, and although they are not all fully validated for a wide range of talents, even the "soft signs" they reveal at the screening stage can be highly enlightening.

Evidence of Productivity or Performance. It is important for teachers to keep constant records of children's accomplishments in or out of school. A cumulative file that shows samples and other evidence of such projects may reveal unusual potential in an area of work that society values but is not necessarily emphasized in the classroom. The child prodigy is an obvious example of someone who builds up an early record of achievements, but for other children the evidence of talent may be more obscure and harder to elicit. A source of information is often outside the school, usually in the home, but not always so. Parents and peers can certainly help to keep a child's record up to date, and teachers ought to be eager to obtain and record whatever information can help to build a case for high potential in a child.

Table 19-5 lists various instruments used for screening the gifted. The list is based on responses to a nationwide inquiry on practices conducted by Richert and her associates (1982).

Selection

After the screening stage, it is necessary to move toward the narrow end of the funnel and reduce the proportion of nongifted children in the pool. This requires moving from the remote indicators to those more clearly in the context of the curriculum. All children in the pool are then given a chance to "prove themselves" in real and simulated enrichment activity to show how well they respond to the

Table 19-5. Measures Used in Screening the Gifted

Instrument	Talent Category					Population		Age			
	General Intellectual	*Specific Academic*	*Creativity*	*Leadership*	*Visual and Performing Arts*	*Advantaged*	*Disadvantaged*	*Early Childhood*	*Grades 4-8*	*High School to Adult*	*K-12*
A.S.S.E.T.S.	+	+	+		+	+		+	+		
Barron-Welsh Art Scale					+	+		+	+	+	+
Biographical Inventory–Form U (IBRIC)		+	+	+	+	+			+	+	
California Achievement Tests		+				+					+
Cartoon Conservation Scales	+						+	+	+		
Cattell Culture Fair Intelligence Series	+						+	+	+		
CIRCUS	+	+				+	+	+			
Cognitive Abilities Test	+					+		+	+	+	
Columbia Mental Maturity Scale	+					+	+	+	+		
Comprehensive Tests of Basic Skills		+				+					+
Creativity Assessment Packet			+			+		+	+	+	
Creativity Tests for Children			+			+			+	+	
Design Judgment Test					+	+			+	+	
Differential Aptitude Tests	+	+				+			+	+	
Feuerstein Learning Potential Assessment Device	+						+		+	+	
Gifted and Talented Screening Form	+	+	+	+	+	+		+	+	+	
Goodenough-Harris Drawing Test	+					+	+	+	+	+	
Group Inventory for Finding Creative Talent (G.I.F.T.)			+			+		+	+		
Group Inventory for Finding Interests (G.I.F.F.I.)			+			+				+	
Guilford-Holley Leadership Inventory						+				+	
Guilford-Zimmerman Aptitude Survey		+				+				+	
Henmon-Nelson Tests of Mental Ability	+					+					+
Horn Art Aptitude Inventory					+	+	+			+	
Iowa Tests of Basic Skills		+				+		+	+	+	
Kranz Talent Identification Instrument		+		+	+		+				+
Khatena-Torrance Creative Perception Inventory			+			+			+	+	
Lorge-Thorndike Intelligence Tests	+					+					+
Meier Art Judgment Tests					+	+			+	+	
Metropolitan Achievement Tests		+				+		+	+		
Musical Aptitude Profile					+	+	+		+	+	+
Otis-Lennon Mental Ability Test	+					+		+	+		+
Peabody Individual Achievement Test		+				+					+
Pennsylvania Assessment of Creative Tendency			+			+			+	+	

Table 19–5. (Continued)

Instrument	Talent Category					Population		Age			
	General Intellectual	*Specific Academic*	*Creativity*	*Leadership*	*Visual and Performing Arts*	*Advantaged*	*Disadvantaged*	*Early Childhood*	*Grades 4–8*	*High School to Adult*	*K–12*
Piers-Harris Children's Self-Concept Scale						+			+	+	
Preschool Talent Checklists	+	+	+	+	+	+	+	+			
Primary Measure of Music Audiation					+	+	+	+			
Raven Progressive Matrices–Advanced	+					+	+			+	
Raven Progressive Matrices–Standard	+					+	+	+	+		
Mednick Remote Associates Test			+			+			+		
Ross Test of Higher Cognitive Processes	+					+			+		
Scales for Rating Behavioral Characteristics of Superior Students	+		+	+	+	+	+				+
Seashore Measure of Musical Talents					+	+	+		+	+	
The Self-concept and Motivation Inventory (SCAMIN)						+	+	+	+	+	
Sequential Tests of Educational Progress (STEP)		+				+			+	+	
Short Form Test of Academic Aptitude	+	+				+		+	+	+	
Slosson Intelligence Test	+					+		+	+	+	
SOI Gifted Screening Form		+	+			+	+	+	+	+	
SOI Learning Abilities Test		+	+			+	+	+	+	+	
SRA Achievement Series		+				+					+
Stallings[1] Environmentally Based Screen	+						+	+			
Stanford Achievement Test		+				+		+	+	+	
Stanford-Binet Intelligence Scale	+					+		+	+	+	
System of Multicultural Pluralistic Assessment (SOMPA)	+						+	+			
Tennessee Self-concept Scale						+			+	+	
Test of Creative Potential			+			+		+	+		
Tests of Achievement and Proficiency		+				+					
Thinking Creatively with Sounds and Words			+			+		+	+	+	
Torrance Tests of Creative Thinking			+			+	+				+
Vane Kindergarten Test	+	+				+					
Watson-Glaser Critical Thinking Appraisal	+					+			+	+	
Wechsler Intelligence Scale for Children Revised (WISC-R)	+					+		+	+	+	
Wechsler Preschool and Primary Scale of Intelligence (WPPSI)	+					+		+			
Cumulative grades	+	+	+	+	+	+	+	+	+	+	+
Informal observation	+	+	+	+	+	+	+	+	+	+	+

Table 19-5. (Continued)

Instrument	Talent Category					Population		Age			
	General Intellectual	*Specific Academic*	*Creativity*	*Leadership*	*Visual and Performing Arts*	*Advantaged*	*Disadvantaged*	*Early Childhood*	*Grades 4–8*	*High School to Adult*	*K–12*
Parent essay—why child needs program	+	+	+	+	+	+	+	+	+	+	+
Parent nomination	+	+	+	+	+	+	+	+	+	+	+
Peer nomination	+	+	+	+	+	+	+	+	+	+	+
Products	+	+	+	+	+	+	+	+	+	+	+
Self-nomination	+	+	+	+	+	+	+	+	+	+	+
Student interview	+	+	+	+	+	+	+	+	+	+	+
Teacher nomination	+	+	+	+	+	+	+	+	+	+	+

Source: E. S. Richert. *National Report on Identification.* Sewell, N.J., Educational Improvement Center–South 1982.

challenge. For example, if a unit on the writing of psychodrama is part of the program for those gifted in language, it is obvious that no existing test of verbal skills or social intelligence can possibly reveal who will excel in such a unit. The only way in which to make the proper identification is to allow children in the pool who show any signs of unusual language development to try out for the psychodrama unit. This is what is meant by an oscillating process between identification and enrichment. The special curriculum is not a privilege for a predetermined group of children labeled "gifted"; it is initially a testing ground on which the gifted sort themselves out from the nongifted. The quality of identification therefore depends to a great extent on the quality of the program.

In the course of exposure to enrichment experiences, a child will reveal potential giftedness by a variety of behaviors that Hagen (1980) alerts teachers and parents to monitor. They include the student's sophisticated use of language; the quality of the student's questions; the quality of illustrations or elaborations that a student uses in communicating an idea; the student's ability to adopt a systematic strategy for finding or solving problems and to change the strategy if it does not work; the student's innovative use of materials found in or out of the classroom; the student's breadth or depth of information relevant to a particular learning experience; the student's persistence on uncompleted tasks; the extensiveness of the student's exploratory behaviors; the student's preferences for complexity, difficulty, and novelty in learning tasks; and the student's criticalness of his or her own performance. These selection criteria are more demanding than are those used at the screening stage, but even here mistakes can be made if we adhere to them too rigidly. There are still possibilities of accepting some who do not qualify and rejecting others who do qualify as potentially gifted. It is therefore important to refine the process further in the next stage, which is necessarily the longest lasting of the three.

Differentiation

We now come to the lower end of the funnel, which has a sievelike attachment that separates the gifted from the gifted as well as the gifted from the nongifted. This process should continue indefinitely, with several sifting and sorting attachments to help along the way. The main objective is to begin distinguishing potential mathematicians from potential literary critics, engineers from composers, historians from scientists, and so on, until the student's performance at school becomes more aligned with intelligent career choices. Much depends on the breadth and inspirational quality of the enrichment program because the gifted need exposure to a variety of possibilities to avoid being locked into an area of specialization too early in life.

Thus, we make the final transition from the screening stage, with its heavy reliance on measures that are indirectly related to life in the classroom, to the differentiation stage, where we identify mainly through the curriculum itself. If enrichment is continuous throughout the children's schooling, differentiation should never really end as long as they are in the program. In the last analysis, identification of the gifted is related not only to systematic observation and intelligent interpretation of test data but to the development of the right kinds of educational opportunities that facilitate self-identification. As Hagen (1980) points out, "When combining data on various indicators of potential giftedness to arrive at a decision, you should always give major weight in your decision-making to demonstrated achievement because it is the best single predictor of future achievement" (pp. 39-40).

Chapter 20

Enrichment Paradigms

Program enrichment for the gifted requires a unique curriculum distinguishable from the general scope and sequence of studies at school. As are other forms of special education, it is designed to meet the needs of an exceptional subpopulation in our schools. It should therefore be regarded as part of a comprehensive plan for individualizing instruction for *all* children. Ward (1961) developed a body of psychological and epistemological principles of differentiated education for the gifted that consists of twelve axiomatic propositions and twenty-nine corollaries. These principles emphasize the importance of helping the gifted to explore generic concepts that enable them to understand the nature of all chief branches of knowledge. Clark (1979) adapted Ward's theory in her analysis of characteristics and needs of the gifted and suggested educational plans for five domains of inquiry: cognitive, affective, physical, intuitive, and social. Each of these substantive areas contains recommended studies that are not stressed in curricula for the general school population but are justified for the gifted on grounds that the nature of the learning experience matches the special nature of the learner.

There is always the need to defend a curriculum design that differentiates school activities for children with outstanding potential since it is subject to suspicion of promoting elitism. Professionals and laypersons frequently ask why enrichment should not be subsumed under quality education appropriate for every student, outstanding or mediocre. Indeed, is it not possible for the nongifted to benefit from school activities that are promoted exclusively for the gifted? How can our schools claim to be democratic and yet reserve imaginative and exciting experiences exclusively for one small group? The issue is understandably a sensitive one and can be faced best by examining the conceptual frameworks in which these experiences fit. Differentiated education is not just a grab-bag of extra goodies for those who can thrive on them. Instead, they have to be selected carefully to

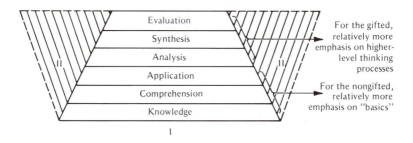

Figure 20-1 Cognitive domain: Emphasis based on Bloom's taxonomy

implement a comprehensive plan that has its own built-in rationale relating to the nature of the target population and the educational goals to be achieved. Educators have therefore created and adapted conceptual models of programs for the gifted as guides to curriculum development. These paradigms do not dwell especially on the specifics of a lesson nor do they necessarily give teachers cookbook-style instructions on what to do in the classroom. Instead, most of them serve as general blueprints for program design based on clearly stated or implied assumptions about the meaning of talent and the kind of nurturance it requires.

An example of a paradigm often used in developing enrichment for the gifted is Bloom's (Bloom et al., 1956) *Taxonomy: Cognitive Domain.* Although Bloom and his associates never intended to address the specific problems of curriculum content for potentially gifted children, the six-tier hierarchy of cognitive functions can be used as a conceptual framework for enrichment. Figure 20-1 depicts the different levels of functioning in the framework of a trapezoid. This would suggest that instructional time and effort are devoted mostly to the lower-level functions, which include helping children to build up their storehouse of knowledge and to sharpen their skills of comprehension, while the higher-level processes such as synthesis and evaluation receive the least attention.

Assuming that potentially gifted children can engage with relative success in synthesizing and evaluating ideas, the trapezoid would then be reversed to suggest that, for this group, it is possible and desirable to shift the major emphasis toward the top levels of the hierarchy, as indicated by the dashed lines. This adaptation is not made at the expense of the so-called "basics" of knowledge and comprehension. If such were the case, then the dashed lines would cut into these cognitive categories, thus implying that less attention be given to them in programs for the gifted than in the general curriculum for the nongifted. Rather, the idea here is that no children are to be short-changed in these fundamentals, except that enrichment for the gifted means devoting *relatively* greater stress on higher-level cognitive process-es. Educators who accept such a framework and its rationale would then proceed to fill in appropriate curriculum details to make the paradigm applicable in the classroom. Similarly, every enrichment model would have to be examined for its logical principles in differentiating education for the gifted and its relevance to program content and methodology.

Like most paradigms, the Bloom taxonomy leaves the task of designing instruction in the hands of practitioners while providing a framework within which such planning should take place. A far more prescriptive approach is taken by Meeker (1969) whose model is based on Guilford's (1967) Structure of Intellect (SOI). She has designed a battery of diagnostic tests covering 24 out of the 150 special abilities postulated by Guilford (SOI Institute, 1980). These measures make it possible to formulate an intellective profile for each child and to design appropriate enrichment accordingly. Further assistance is provided for teachers in the form of workbooks (SOI Institute, 1973) that contain instructional exercises categorized according to the abilities tested. For example, to give the child practice in Convergent Production of Semantic Classes (NMC), there is an exercise in composing synonyms for a list of verbal descriptions, the requirement being that each synonym consist of a pair of one-syllable, rhyming words (e.g., lengthy tune = long song; best policeman = top cop). Thus, the classroom teacher receives specific help from the diagnostic through the treatment stages of the program.

The Bloom taxonomy and the Meeker SOI are only two of several models now guiding enrichment plans for the gifted. To provide a more representative picture, this chapter presents a series of brief descriptions of other paradigms that are among the best known in the field. Obviously, these summaries cannot do justice to the full theory in each case, but they attempt to convey the essential frameworks, if not their details. For our purposes, it is hoped that an overview will give a sense of the kinds of enrichment that are favored for the gifted and of the varieties and consistencies of emphasis that characterize these models. The educator who wishes to translate any of the conceptual frameworks into a program obviously needs to consult the detailed writings of those who created them rather than to rely on the brief information sketched here. It is not necessary to choose a single model and exclude all features of all the others; there is enough that is unique and of value in each to make mixes and matches desirable in program planning. Even a "hybrid" model that is suitable in one school may be inappropriate in another, thus making it necessary to take local needs into account before putting together elements from different pre-existing plans.

THE ENRICHMENT TRIAD

The Enrichment Triad, designed by Joseph S. Renzulli (1977), is probably the best known and most widely applied curriculum model for the gifted in the nation's schools. It attempts to identify the kinds of learning experiences that can help gifted children to achieve excellence but would be excessively demanding on the nongifted. Teachers are offered a variety of specific suggestions on how to implement the model. Their role is to create an educational environment that encourages students with potential for superior performance to become contributors to knowledge through investigative activities dealing with real-life problems in contrast to scholastic exercises.

For Renzulli, the rationale for differentiated education grows out of his characterization of giftedness and of the ways in which eminent persons create products useful to society. He believes that a high IQ should not be the sole criterion for getting students into special enrichment programs; less than extraordinary cognitive ability can be an adequate qualifier, provided that there are also signs of exceptional creativity and task commitment. Children who meet these criteria require educational activities that are above and beyond the conventional curriculum. However, advanced coursework may not necessarily be sufficient or appropriate if it is simply a predesigned course of study for precocious children in general. Renzulli comments that under such a scheme "everyone ends up marching to the tune of the same drummer, albeit at a faster beat" (p. 16).

Educators have to appreciate the students' diverse learning interests and styles that can be accommodated only through encouragement of individual initiative. Self-designed, self-directed student learning activities therefore form the apex of the overall scheme. These projects can be carried out in the regular classroom, in special resource facilities, on a college campus, in the community, or even through a correspondence course in which there is no face-to-face interaction between the student and instructor.

To prepare themselves to plan and implement a program, teachers should equip themselves with the following understandings:

1. Gifted Children function best in an open learning environment where they can feel free to pursue their own interests extensively, in depth, and in a manner consistent with the learning strategies they prefer.
2. The program should be characterized by a systematic development of cognitive-affective potentialities, not merely an exposure to randomly stimulating events and materials.
3. Once the students decide on their fields of interest, the teacher is responsible to assist them to become firsthand inquirers in their respective domains. The instructional program has to allow for the developmental processes that are firmly rooted in the structures of various disciplines studied.
4. Learning should result from actual inquiry, and students need to be trained to work as professionals do in any given field. Since the children are capable of engaging in critical inquiry, their work is different from that of the professional in degree, not in kind.
5. The specific tasks of the teacher are to assist students in identifying realistic, solvable problems consistent with their interests, to help them acquire the strategies and logical thinking skills necessary for problem solving, and to find appropriate outlets for their products.
6. Since most gifted students learn rapidly, the basic skills curriculum can be telescoped to provide time for inquiry activity.
7. Learning should take place in a laboratory atmosphere, even if it means finding one away from school.

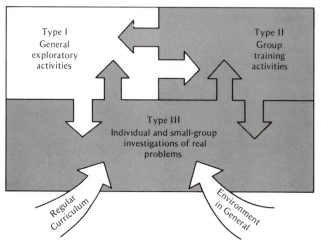

Figure 20-2　The Enrichment Triad model (Renzulli, 1977, p. 14)

After clarifying their role and objectives in educating the gifted, teachers can then proceed to guide qualified children through the three stages of the Enrichment Triad, which is depicted in Figure 20-2.

Type I Enrichment: General Exploratory and Group Training Activities

The purposes of the exploratory and training activities are to expose students to a wider variety of potential interests so that they can decide on which to explore in depth and to clarify appropriate training activities and resources needed for students to carry out productive work in their chosen fields. During this stage, there needs to be a good deal of exploratory freedom, but the children should understand that after a given period of time they will be required to analyze their experiences and decide upon a specific area for in-depth investigation. Students who show no desire to continue into specialized inquiry may have to be dropped from the program, not as a punishment, but because they are not likely to benefit from it. Thus, enrichment becomes a "revolving door" experience (Renzulli, 1980) that allows children to leave the program at odd times when they complete their explorations and re-enter new projects. Re-entry is then possible at any time since the timing and duration of a special learning experience is not predetermined by a fixed calendar.

One means of arousing student involvement is to develop categorical interest centers that represent broad areas of study. Material in these centers must be exciting enough to capture the children's attention and to stimulate them toward further research. Materials concentrating on history might deal with such topics as "What Is History?" "How Does the Historian Work?" and "The Historian as Detective." Materials in other parts of the interest center would be intended to evoke interest in literature, art, science, and other familiar curriculum areas, but some should also treat subjects not ordinarily included in the course of study, such as anthropology, psychology, aesthetics, the newer sciences, and various performing arts.

In giving background knowledge about these respected disciplines, the materials should be presented from the point of view of the professional—the artist, historian, or scientist. If the material is "packaged" in an interesting and informative way, it should inspire children to want to learn more about one of the disciplines and how its knowledge base can be enlarged. Ample time should be provided for students to browse through the center materials and to discuss them with other students and the teacher.

Focused field trips also help implement Type I enrichment. Such activities are suitable for all students, but those with exceptional abilities should be given the opportunity to go beyond the look-see level and become involved productively with what is on display, produced, or presented. They should also have opportunities to interact with such knowledge producers as artists, writers, historians, scientists, and other professionals who can provide insights on how they create ideas in their fields. Browsing in libraries, bookstores, and museums may also trigger interests, especially if teachers assist students in developing skills for high-level inquiry and criticism.

Also useful in stimulating special interest are such questions as "What would you like people to say about you at a retirement dinner given in your honor?" Renzulli's (1977) own Interest-A-Lyzer is a questionnaire designed specifically to assist students in focusing on areas of possible interest they wish to pursue through further inquiry. It contains such questions as, "Pretend that someday you will be the famous author of a well-known book. What type of book will it be (history, science, poetry, fiction, fashion, etc.) and what will the book be about?" (p. 76). "Pretend that a new time machine has been invented that will allow famous persons from the past to come back to life for a short period of time. If you could invite some of these persons to give a talk to your class, whom would you invite?" (p. 77).

During all exploratory activities, it is the teacher's job to monitor children's interests and to assist them in formulating solvable problems in relation to these interests. The teachers also have to help students structure their investigations and take note of the specialized training activities and materials needed to conduct such investigations. For instance, children immersing themselves in biological studies will require skills in classification, data analysis, and inference building. Students involved in producing a play may need creative dramatics training, special help in speech and writing, and possibly some puppet or scenery production skills. Thus, Type I activities provide a logical prelude to the next stages of the program.

Teachers should realize that student interests vary widely, and their ability to stay with a topic for a lengthy period is the exception rather than the rule. What inspires one child may bore another. What counts most for the child is the opportunity to come in contact with a rich, attractive array of subject areas so that alternatives could be weighed before choosing one for further investigation. Some children may benefit immediately from the knowledge they require; others will simply store the information for future use or neglect.

Type II Enrichment: Group Training Activities

Specialized group training can help in the development of the thinking and feeling processes. One aim is to enhance the powers of the mind through a variety of activities involving critical, creative, and productive thinking; problem solving; and inquiry training. Another aim is to promote affective growth through awareness development, sensitivity training, and other related exercises. The taxonomies of Bloom et al. (1956) and Krathwohl et al. (1958) and Guilford's Structure of Intellect model (1967) are valuable systems for organizing Type II enrichment activities. It is expected that the cognitive and affective training will enable students to deal effectively with many kinds of learning situations and help guide them toward a content area in which rich intellectual gratification can be achieved by applying these newly acquired skills. The specific cognitive and affective processes that are emphasized include

Brainstorming	Comparison	Elaboration
Observation	Categorization	Hypothesizing
Classification	Synthesis	Awareness
Interpretation	Fluency	Appreciation
Analysis	Flexibility	Value clarification
Evaluation	Originality	Commitment

For the gifted, exercises concentrate on developing higher-level thinking processes. Since the only constant in modern life is the rapid pace of change, it is difficult to know what subject matter will be of most use to students when they reach maturity. Moreover, since the explosion of knowledge makes it impossible to teach all the content available in even one subject area, it is better to instill in students effective thinking and problem-solving skills as tools for dealing with problems in any content area.

Teachers can learn to develop Type II enrichment activities by becoming familiar with a variety of curriculum packages that emphasize higher-level thinking processes out of the context of any specific curriculum. It is not always possible to relate these exercises to conventional subject matter, and there may be times when practice in "context-free" activities is appropriate. However, these exercises for exercise sake should be the exception rather than the rule. While Type II activities are an important part of the Enrichment Triad, the aims of the program will not be realized if students spend their time practicing process without regard to content. The program will then assume a "fun-and-games" character that is unrelated to real education and therefore not defensible.

Type II activities can be defended on at least three premises:

1. Process-oriented activities provide gifted students with advanced problem-solving skills. Such activities should represent a logical outgrowth of student interests and concerns rather than mere random involvement in whatever exercises happen to be available.
2. If they are selected appropriately, such open-ended experiences provide for a wide range of responses that enable children with superior thinking power to be challenged properly.
3. High-level cognitive processing prepares children to work productively in advanced fields of study.

Type III Enrichment: Investigations of Real Problems

At the third stage, gifted students are equipped with the appropriate methods of inquiry to investigate real problems. They study theoretical structures, examine raw data, and discover the generalizations in their chosen fields of inquiry.

Although most gifted students are not yet prepared to work on real problems at a high level, it is important for them to accomplish what they can even at this early stage of their development. As serious investigators, they have the ability to develop a variety of important insights into their chosen fields of study. Especially important is their appreciation for the work they are doing, which they can cultivate more easily by acquiring professional skill in their areas of investigation instead of simply completing exercises presented by their teachers. A crucial feature of this method of learning is that the children take active parts in formulating problems and methods of reaching solutions. Since real problems can be dealt with in a variety of ways, there are many opportunities for divergent thinking in areas of investigation that grow out of the students' sincerest interests. The children engage in such activities with the intention of making contributions to knowledge and communicating their findings in professionally appropriate manners.

Working toward the creation of new ideas is basically different from the usual practice of mastering ideas that already exist. Type III enrichment shifts the emphasis by opting for innovation rather than recapitulation in learning in the curriculum for potentially gifted children. Teachers are in a position to help the gifted to reflect the attitude and emulate the behavior of the professional investigator in several ways. They can expose students to a variety of interest areas and then assist in making choices for further study. They can also enable the gifted to acquire the necessary skills for problem finding and locating the methodological tools and techniques of inquiry that are needed for productive work. Finally, teachers can help children to find ways of communicating project outcomes to audiences that understand, appreciate, and react critically to these works. In short, the teacher's role in Type III enrichment is mainly that of a facilitator. Instruction for the gifted is not just a matter of dispensing knowledge; it also involves sensitizing the child to the logistics by which knowledge is acquired and created.

The student's product should not be merely a report to the teacher. Renzulli cites Roe's (1953) study of creative scientists to show that experiences in research were often decisive in shaping their future and that their discovery of how to work as productive thinkers came from experience in schools where teachers allowed them considerable self-direction. Not all students can benefit from that kind of independence. Advanced levels of inquiry should be initiated only by those who possess the requisite cognitive ability, task commitment, and creativity characteristics that distinguish productive thinkers from all others.

Types I and II enrichment are for all children, but such activities can also help teachers to identify those who are able and committed to pursue more advanced levels of investigation. Firsthand inquirers have a concern for the outcomes of their studies. Their work is almost always directed toward some kind of product, and this attitude toward a problem situation may be the essential difference between the scientist, who *discovers* areas of inquiry, and the technician, who deals with *presented* areas of inquiry. Most students should be given opportunities to engage in firsthand investigative studies, but it is the potentially gifted who can profit most from such activity. In fact, children's responses to enrichment opportunities enable the teacher to single out those individuals who can be educated to advance toward independent, innovative work. The children who benefit most from such opportunities will then, it is hoped, be able to reach out to any one of a variety of audiences, including professionals representing science, medicine, law, and mathematics, among others.

Developing and Managing Type III Activities

In essence, Type III enrichment emphasizes the following considerations:

1. The distinction between consumers and producers.
2. The role that task commitment plays in the work of creative and productive persons.
3. The distinction between presented exercises and investigative activity that is directed toward the solution of relatively real problems.
4. The role that products play in the *modus operandi* of creative and productive persons.
5. The distinction between investigating and reporting.
6. The importance of allowing students the freedom to select their own areas of interest for investigative study.

Since it is important that Type III enrichment grow out of the students' concerns, they have to spend a fairly large amount of time exploring possible areas of in-depth analysis. The extent to which a child is prepared to pursue a topic of interest has to be monitored closely since persistence is one of the keys to success. The child also needs help in finding various modes of entry to the study of a particular topic, especially where ability levels do not measure up to levels of interest. For example, a student who is enthusiastic about rock music but has no musical talent might study it from the standpoint of the producer of rock music concerts or a recording executive. Thus, the teacher assists not only in locating areas of interest but also in determining how gifted children can be most productive within their chosen fields. Not all expressions of interest will lead to innovative work. If the students' interests are essentially latent, it is best not to push them into investigative activity. Instead, they may use the self-directed experience simply for the sake of information gathering and storage for future application. They may even be inspired to fantasize about their interests and to see themselves as someday becoming great astronauts or artists. Such dreams should never be discouraged in potentially gifted children.

Identifying general patterns of interest is the first step in Type III activities. For this purpose, Renzulli has developed an "Interest-A-Lyzer" questionnaire to reveal the child's preferences and to help the teacher focus on areas in which real problems need to be identified. When the problem is formulated, the child will require assistance in developing appropriate methods for solving it and for evaluating the outcomes. Exemplary products deserve to be showcased, and teachers have been known to assist students in seeking publication outlets for their poetry and professional forums for reporting their scientific research. The kind of help that a teacher offers in disseminating high-quality student products may make a big difference in the way in which the gifted view their work and their continued involvement in it.

At the heart of Type III enrichment is the training of gifted children in methods of inquiry. Too often, the emphasis is on discovering a predetermined formula, a generalization, or an already established method. In the Triad program, the aim is to have students arrive at their own answers in their own ways. This requires investigative skills that go far beyond mastering the Dewey decimal system to use the library media and sources. It is wise to engage the aid of librarians, provided that they are informed about the advanced aims of the program for the gifted. Teacher trainers should also be aware of goals and methods of the Enrichment Triad to prepare specialists in their learning management role. Teachers need to know how to locate references related to various fields of inquiry and to judge the suitability of reference material for use in particular situations. As an independent investigator, rather than as just a lesson learner, the child requires a laboratory environment atmosphere in which to gather raw data and work with information to produce something that is new and valuable. The laboratory can be any room containing proper equipment for investigative or creative activity. Its proper use depends on the teacher's success in familiarizing gifted students with information processing strategies.

Renzulli (1977) suggests that strategic operations consist of two phases, one that relates to the selection and absorption of relative data (i.e., *input*) and the other that pertains to the treatment of data (i.e., *process*) to develop a product. Both phases may be accomplished through the following methods:

Input

A. The Input Operation
    1. The Identification of Information Sources

   2. The Acquisition of:
       a. Raw Data
       b. Summarized or Categorized Data
       c. Conclusions, Generalizations, Principles, Laws, Facts
       d. Opinion
   3. The Use of Person (Existing) Knowledge
B. The Input Procedures
   1. Empirical (First-Hand Experiences)
       a. Observing: Listening, Looking, Counting, Sketching, Note-taking, Charting
       b. Experimenting
       c. Interviewing
       d. Using Qustionnaires
   2. Normative or Authoritative
       a. Reading
       b. Listening
   3. Aesthetic
       a. Sensing
       b. Feeling
       c. Valuing
C. The Input Sources
   1. Reference Books
   2. Non-Book Reference Material
   3. People
   4. The Environment in General (p. 66)

Process

A. The Manipulative Processes of Inquiry
    1. Comparing and Verifying Sources of Data
    2. Establishing Connections Between Data
    3. Recognizing Bias in Informational Sources
    4. Classifying Data
    5. Categorizing Data According to Function
    6. Identifying Strong and Weak Arguments, Conclusions, etc.
    7. Distinguishing Fact from Opinion
    8. Recognizing
    9. Establishing the Credibility of a Data Source
   10. Discovering Trends, Patterns, Uniformities, and Discrepancies in Data
B. The Creative/Productive Processes
    1. Designing Experiments
    2. Constructing Data Gathering Devices
    3. Analyzing Data and Drawing Conclusions
    4. Perceiving Possible Solutions
    5. Making Probability Statements
    6. Stating Generalizations
    7. Redefining Problems
    8. Planning and Organizing
    9. Creating Testable Hypotheses
   10. Making Valid Inferences and Tracing Logical Implications

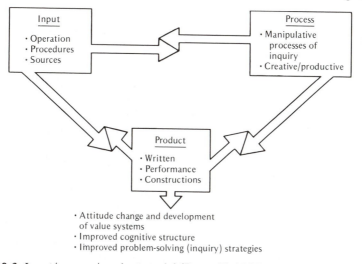

Figure 20-3 Input/process/product model (Renzulli, 1977, p. 65)

11. Specifying Evaluative Criteria
12. Evaluating According to Internal Criteria
13. Evaluating According to External Criteria
14. Building Theories and Models (p. 67)

Renzulli makes it clear that input, process, and product have a cyclical rather than a linear relationship (see Figure 20-3). While working on the product phase of an activity, the child may feel the need to go back and gather more data or subject existing data to more rigorous analysis. This would require a return to earlier phases of activity. But in the last analysis, all phases should be experienced in order to accomplish a truly differentiated program for the gifted. Higher-level thinking skills have to be applied to meaningful outcomes, not just as sterile exercises, as would be the case if the teacher failed or neglected to move from stage II to stage III in the Enrichment Triad.

SYNECTICS

Although designed originally to assist individuals in developing new products and processes in business and industry, aspects of synectics have been introduced into special enrichment programs for the gifted. These methods are designed to help students learn new concepts by making the strange appear familiar and to improve their creative skills by making the familiar appear strange. The key element in the process is metaphoric activity, which involves exercises in the use of analogies to release the flow of imaginative thought. This is usually done in a group setting where individuals can work collectively to find and solve problems by nonrational as well as rational means. Synectics theory suggests that the subconscious and preconscious minds make important contributions to the creative process and that genuine breakthrough ideas do not necessarily occur as a result of logical reasoning. An awareness of the importance of nonrational ideas and the attempt to engage them through the use of metaphor reflect the uniqueness of synectics as an approach to enrichment. These sources of creative possibilities are rarely applied systematically. However, despite the use of nonrational thought, the whole process is geared ultimately toward practical rational goals.

Developed by William J. Gordon (1971), an advertising executive, the synectics model represents a departure from the traditional view of creativity as a mystical process that cannot be described and can only be demonstrated by a few highly gifted individuals. It is in sharp contrast to the idea that any attempt to observe or analyze the process would automatically destroy it. However, Gordon felt that, if a person understands the psychological states involved in creativity, this knowledge can be translated into methods that would enhance the creative potential of individuals.

Convinced that creativity could be understood as a mental function, Gordon and his associates engaged in extensive study of the thought processes revealed in highly gifted individuals and groups pursuing creative solutions to problems. By recording carefully the ways in which people conduct high-level inquiry, Gordon and his collaborators were able to recognize semiconscious mental activity as figuring prominently in the creative process. A method was then developed to evoke the preconscious state of mind to include the benefit of irrational thoughts and ideas in problem solving. This practice is justified on the grounds that all the information one has ever gained is stored in the subconscious mind, which also acts as a censor that often prevents these thoughts from rising to consciousness. However, in meditative or dreamlike states, which occur during the incubation period of creativity, images can make their way into the conscious mind in the form of fantasy and imagination. Such imagery may then trigger new trains of thought that are useful in finding novel solutions to problems. Synectics methods try to bring the preconscious into play with the help of metaphoric techniques that tend to evoke new perspectives and insights.

As illustrated in Figure 20-4, there are several psychological states that are important in the creative process. One is called *detachment-involvement*, which denotes the fact that a creative individual can approach a problem with emotional investment and calculated objectivity at the same time. Another requisite is *deferment*, or the ability to withhold judgment on ideas until many alternatives have been brainstormed. A third element is *speculation*, involving the development of hypotheses. Another feature of the process is that the individual senses an *autonomy of object*, for as the solution develops there is a feeling that it is an entity that has its own independent quality. Finally, a *hedonic response* figures prominently in the creative act. As the individual plays with apparent irrelevancies, new views of the problem are generated. The hedonic response is a pleasurable sensation that accompanies a feeling of being right about a hypothesis that therefore deserves to be pursued further.

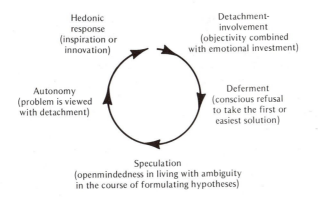

Hedonic
response
(inspiration or
innovation)

Detachment-
involvement
(objectivity combined
with emotional investment)

Autonomy
(problem is viewed
with detachment)

Deferment
(conscious refusal
to take the first or
easiest solution)

Speculation
(openmindedness in living with ambiguity
in the course of formulating hypotheses)

PSYCHOLOGICAL STATES
NECESSARY FOR CREATIVITY

Figure 20-4 Synectics: The ring of creativity

According to synectics theory, creativity exhibited even in dissimilar fields of specialization, such as the arts and sciences, emanates from the same psychic processes. Furthermore, the individual engaged in creative problem solving can function better as a member of a group than by working alone because of the multiplicity of ideas and support of fanciful thinking expressed by other group members. Creative activity is enhanced by jolting individuals out of their ordinary ways of viewing things in their environment, and it is only through the invention of new contexts in which to view the world that breakthroughs in any worthwhile field of endeavor can be achieved.

This does not mean that creative efficiency materializes spontaneously. Actually, it is a step-by-step process that begins with stating, defining, analyzing, and understanding a problem and then applying the operational mechanisms of metaphor and analogy in a brainstorming session in which judgment is deferred until many solutions have been produced and examined. When these steps are taken in a group setting, attempts are then made to reach a better understanding and a new view of the problem by fitting it into the solutions the group has devised. Sometimes, the group engages in force-fitting opposites, such as a "life-saving destroyer," which might suggest the idea of a vaccine containing deadly elements but useful in saving lives. Eventually, when the group arrives at a solution, attempts are made to render it practical and applicable; if this cannot be done, the entire process is repeated until a suitable solution is found. Thus, engaging in irrational thought is beneficial to the creative process, but it should be followed by a logical assessment of ideas that float up from the subconscious.

Metaphoric Activity

In the synectics model, creativity is stimulated by metaphoric exercises involving unfamiliar comparisons (i.e., "life is a river"). This practice of viewing the strange and abstract in a new light enables the individual to acquire "conceptual distance" or detachment from the topic in order to think more reflectively and produce better understanding. Since there are no "right" answers in imaginative thinking, it is easier for the student to become emotionally involved in the course of conjuring up original ideas that are acceptable in the brainstorming stage of the process, no matter how fantastic or bizarre they may be.

A lesson in remote associations might challenge children to compare a city with familiar things, such as their own bodies. In the course of brainstorming, they would perhaps see the city government as analogous to human brains, the press and other communications media similar in ways to people's eyes and ears, the transportation system as a cognate of legs in the process of locomotion, and the work force representing arms and hands in productive labor. Given an opportunity to detach themselves from the usual view of the city as a forest of houses and streets and to adopt instead an unfamiliar perspective, children are helped to acquire new understandings that may otherwise have been impossible.

Strategies used to implement the synectics system are easier to describe than to implement. The teacher states a problem or invites students to suggest one and then asks a variety of evocative questions to stimulate metaphoric activity that connects the old and familiar to the new and the unknown and past experiences to abstract ideas as the ways to search for a solution.

There are various kinds of exercises in analogous thinking that make up metaphoric activity. Direct analogy, which involves comparing two objects or ideas, is among the most frequently employed. The aim is to transpose the topical problem in order to get a new view of it (e.g., "the earth is like a ball"). There are levels of remoteness in analogies, and the greater the conceptual distance, the more likely they are to produce original ideas. To illustrate various degrees to which the imagination strains for uncommon images, Gordon (1971) indicates that the following objects have been compared with the rotating wheel of a car: the cutter on a can opener, the rotor of a helicopter, the orbit of Mars, and a spinning seed pod. Besides varying in remoteness and originality, these analogies are highly individual in metaphoric activity. It is also apparent that the ages of the students engaged in such exercises would affect the kinds of ideas that are generated.

Personal analogy involves detachment from self and empathic identification with another person, plant, animal, or inanimate object. Questions to evoke personal analogy might include "If you were an animal (or plant, or machine), what kind would you be?" "How do you feel as a poodle? an auto? a rosebush?" There are four levels of involvement in personal analogy:

1. *First-person description factor* (e.g., "If I were a poodle, I would whine and bark"). The student describes well-known facts, but there are no more imaginative ways of viewing the object expressed.
2. *First-person identification with emotion* (e.g., "If I were a car, I would feel powerful"). The student expresses a common emotion but no new insights.
3. *Empathic identification with a living thing* (e.g., "If I were a rosebush, I would feel like a strong parent protecting my children, the roses, with my thorns"). The student expresses human feelings under the circumstances.

4. *Empathic identification with a nonliving object* (e.g., "If I were a spring, I would get very angry when people push me down and compress me in a little space, and I would spring right back up and hit them"). The student engages in anthropomorphic fantasy.

Compressed conflict is a relatively difficult type of metaphor, a matching up of two words that seem to negate each other, such as "happy sadness" or "kind cruelty." The ability to see an object from these conflicting points of view requires considerable mental strain and, therefore, greater conceptual distance.

To reach toward remote associations, it is best to start with familiar and commonplace phenomena, often found in the world of biology, which do not ordinarily inspire flights of fantasy. This, it is hoped, will free students from their preoccupation with abstractions so that they can return to concrete organic data of the real world as a starting point for metaphors. If ideas are allowed to flow freely from the preconscious without the inhibition of criticism, many seemingly irrelevant thoughts will be revealed. But it is counterproductive to disregard commonplace ideas until the leap of creation is made. Judgment has to be suspended to allow for fancifulness and divergency until an idea emerges. Only then should rational judgment determine the value of what is produced in a brainstorming experience.

The Synectics Model in Education

Gordon believes that there are similar cognitive processes in learning and creativity and that the assumptions underlying the synectics model can help to promote better accomplishment at school. Practice in making the familiar strange and the strange familiar requires different sequences of problem solving. The following example illustrates the step-by-step procedures for making the familiar strange:

Phase 1: Describing the Condition. The teacher states a problem or asks students to describe the condition that causes the problem (e.g., a neighborhood gang harasses the children, beating them up, chasing them, stealing their belongings, and disrupting the school).

Phase 2: Direct Analogy. The teacher asks for direct inorganic comparisons to the gang. Students may suggest that it is like a plague, a destructive storm, a tornado, or other such threats to life and property. Students are then asked to choose one analogy and to explore it. Their choice is "tornado," and in discussing its properties, they comment that the tornado "swirls around," "gets dizzy," "catches up things," "blows them away," "destroys," and "makes people afraid."

Phase 3: Personal Analogy. At this point teachers ask the students to "be the tornado." How would they feel? Students answer that they would feel "twisted," "dizzy," "angry," "hateful," "like breaking up everything," "like scaring people," but they would also get tired of all this activity and feel isolated because people are likely to run away from them. They would like to stop their threatening motions, only they don't know how.

Phase 4: Compressed Conflict. The teacher then asks students to pick two words from their analogies that seem to be in conflict, such as "powerful tiredness" or "reluctant aggressor." This is in preparation to force-fitting the problem into the compressed conflict. In their attempt to do so, students might conjecture that, while the gang is powerful and hurtful, it may feel isolated from the rest of the students because gang members do not know how to get along with them, and their various pranks are the only way they know how to attract attention.

Phase 5: New Direct Analogy. The compressed conflict does not only facilitate exploration for its own sake but also serves as the basis for a new direct analogy. The teacher asks what machine might be suggested by powerful tiredness. One possible response is "a cement mixer," which goes round and round mixing everything up but does not have any control over itself. It gets tired and wants to stop, but it can only do so by breaking down. At this point the teacher asks students to try to force-fit the problem into the new analogy and asks for more information about it. Students might reply that people do not like the machine because it is noisy and it forces them to cover their ears and turn away from it. The machine cannot stop at will, but the gang members are different; they could learn to stop and thereby change their habits.

Phase 6: Re-examination of the Original Problem. The students are invited to look at the original problem again, using comparisons to find new insights. Some might comment that the gang needs and wants help in stopping its aggressive activity. At this point the teacher asks the students to write a paragraph describing the gang problem. As a result of metaphoric activity, students not only have a new perspective on the problem but they have acquired the power to write much more creatively. Moreover, they may have a new and more empathic insight into the problem, as evidenced by their willingness to include gang members in some of their activities to improve interpersonal relationships.

There are different approaches involved in making the strange familiar, and the strategies may be illustrated as follows.

Phase 1: Substantive Input. This stage involves the formulation of the problem, which in this case could be an understanding of causes of the American Revolution, based on events leading up to it.

Phase 2: Direct Analogy. In discussing why the colonists finally revolted, students might search for a nonorganic analogy to the situation. A volcano is a good possibility. As the analogy is explored, students learn how the various pressures brought about by rocks shifting from one place to another create heat and eventually produce magma and gas, which, in turn, cause the volcano to erupt. This process can then be compared with the events that made the colonists grow more and more hostile, until, like a volcano, they erupted in rebellion.

Phase 3: Personal Analogies. Students are now asked to "be the volcano" and to tell how they would feel as pressures built. Answers might include feeling "oppressed," "annoyed," "getting pushed around," "angry," "ready to explode," and "violent."

Phase 4: Comparing Analogies. Students now identify and explain the points of similarity between the new and analogous material. They show how various actions, such as the Stamp Act, the forced housing of British soldiers in colonists' homes, and the tea tax finally made the colonists so angry that they took action in the Boston Tea Party.

Phase 5: Explaining Differences. Students recognize that the accidental rock slip-pages causing heat and pressure to build in a volcano are not comparable to the deliberate actions of the British king in keeping the colonists under his control.

Phase 6: Exploration. Students explore the original topic on its own terms and discuss how the various acts taken by the king could cause once-loyal colonists to turn against him and their own homeland.

Phase 7: Generating Analogy. From their exploration of events in colonial times, the students generate their own contradictions, such as "disloyal citizen" or "hate-filled loyalty." The teacher then guides students back to a reconsideration of the original problem, the causes of the revolution, and has them try to force-fit it into the metaphor they have generated. Students can then identify more easily with the colonists who loved England and wanted to be loyal to the crown, but found their loyalty turn into hate and eventual rebellion against what they considered unbearable oppression. Thus, the analogy of volcanic action helps to produce better insight into the causes of the conflict in revolutionary days.

Gordon and his associates have produced a variety of materials, including programmed workbooks, for use by teachers and the students (Gordon, 1971; Gordon and Pose, 1971). The exercises are predicated on an assumption that making connections is basic to all learning and that the synectics process enables the students to rely less on intuition and more on step-by-step procedures for seeing relationships. Course outlines show the teacher how to use the materials to reach educational objectives in several subject areas.

As for empirical proof of the effectiveness of synectics, the little evidence that does exist seems to be encouraging. Industrial groups receiving such training have not only reported that they found satisfactory solutions to their problems, but also that they have learned techniques that have enhanced their personal and professional growth. Bouchard (1972) trained a group of introductory psychology students and compared them with controls engaged in standard brainstorming over three sessions and applying their contrasting methods to nine different problems. The synectics groups were superior to the brainstorming groups on all nine problems, although differences were statistically significant for only four. Bouchard concluded that synectics is a more effective group problem-solving strategy than is brainstorming. However, more studies have to be conducted not only to determine the efficacy but also the nature of the process.

Billow (1977) concludes from his review of the psychological literature on metaphor that the underlying cognitive processes are still unclear. He speculates,

Is metaphor a special form of response, or may it be subsumed under a general theory of learning, of cognitive development, or of psychoanalysis? Psychologists who are interested in cognition, motivation, imagery, language, memory, play, and even such seemingly unrelated areas as perception, sensation, and physiology have a rich and unexplored field of scientific inquiry. (p. 90)

Stein (1974) suggests that the psychological states used in synectics may be congruent with those observed in creative productivity. Metaphors seem to increase the associational range of responses that are important to innovative work. The synectics materials may also be useful in coping with the motivational problems of low-functioning students, especially the disadvantaged, since the children's own experiences figure prominently in the process. It would also be worthwhile to experiment with synectics in enrichment programs for the gifted.

When Gordon taught such a course to bright Harvard freshmen, they considered the experience extraordinarily valuable. It remains to be seen whether formal testing would bear out the students' reactions and whether such exercises would produce similarly positive results with younger bright students when it is taught by instructors who are trained for that purpose, not only by the inventor himself or his close colleagues. More evaluative research would certainly be welcome in determining the precise effects of metaphorizing on high-level performance and productivity.

CREATIVE PROBLEM SOLVING

The creative problem-solving model was designed originally to aid individuals in developing new products and processes in business and industry. It has also received increasing attention in school curricula. Among the people most responsible for the method in its early stages was Alex F. Osborn, an advertising executive, who approached creative problem solving through improved uses of the imagination. He emphasized the usefulness of brainstorming and then deferring judgment on the ideas it produces until a later stage in the problem-solving process. The aim is to stir up many creative solutions to prevent waste of energy in implementing hasty, ill-conceived ideas.

Osborn believed that the way in which to produce the best solutions is to generate the largest number of possible alternatives and to assess each of them afterward. This formed the basis of extensive research into the nature of creative strategies and into the development of educational programs that would enhance creativity. Osborn was convinced that the key to creative problem solving was to learn how to use the imagination, and he offered help through hundreds of techniques (Osborn, 1963). Out of this work he eventually developed a method for problem finding and solving that enables ideas to be produced at will without having to wait for inspiration from the muse or for a lengthy incubation period to pass.

At the outset, the problem is poorly defined and therefore appears in the form of a "mess" that causes discontent in the individual who has to address it (see Figure 20-5). The way in which to deal with such a situation is to follow a five-step process of creative problem solving: (1) *problem finding*, or the search for the nature of the real challenge from different perspectives; (2) *fact finding*, to understand the situation better and to imagine what the solution might be; (3) *idea finding*, aimed at

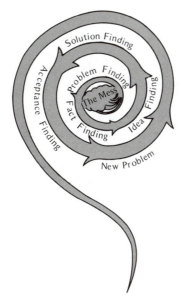

Figure 20-5 Creative problem-solving model

deliberately calling up ideas from the pre- and subconscious and to defer judgment of their quality until they have all been flushed out; (4) *solution finding*, at which point the ideas are evaluated for their relevance and applicability and the best one chosen for implementation; and (5) *acceptance finding*, or gaining an audience that is willing to support the idea and put it to practical use.

Osborn regards *idea finding* as a critical step in the creative problem-solving process, and he elaborates on several tactics necessary to implement it successfully. Among them is the use of checklists that can extend the ideas supplied by providing solution possibilities directly or by stimulating far-out thought that may turn out to be relevant. He devised some seventy-three idea-spurring suggestions to help brainstormers work on any kind of problem. Basic to this method are the following procedures:

Put to other use: Find new ways to utilize familiar objects.
Adapt: What other person, place, or thing is like this?
Modify: Change color, shape, form, size, odor, and so on.
Minify: Make it shorter, smaller, lower, split in two, etc.
Substitute: What can take the place of . . .?
Rearrange: Interchange components, transform, etc.
Reverse: Turn it backward, upside down, etc.
Combine: Units, purposes, colors, materials, etc.

Brainstorming is a technique to aid people in producing more and better ideas. The key to its success lies in suspending criticism in order to remove any inhibition to the free flow of thought. A skilled leader can help to maintain an informal atmosphere where brainstorming is most effective and where participants are encouraged to share any wild, improbable thoughts that come to mind or to "hitchhike" onto the thoughts of others.

Attribute listing starts with noting the characteristics of an object or problem and then moves on to suggesting changes of each attribute for improvement. The next step is to evaluate the suggestions before choosing those most consistent with the original objective and developing a plan for implementing the ideas. For example, in examining an ordinary telephone, one would list all its parts, including the mouthpiece, the receiver, and the container of the mechanism and then list as many ways as possible to improve each part. If holding the receiver to the ear is considered a nuisance because it prevents the hand from engaging in other work, one might substitute it with an amplifying device that could sit on a flat surface instead of being held to the ear.

Forced relationships is a tactic that involves triggering new associations by listing a number of words, objects, or ideas; numbering them; and then taking the first idea or word and juxtaposing it with the second, the third with the fourth, and so on through the entire list. For example, the combination of "house" and "money" may suggest thoughts of finding money to fix up the house or borrowing money on the house to take a trip. To facilitate this process, lists of words are made on separate strips of paper that are then matched in every possible combination, and each pair can be used for an exercise in relational thinking.

Morphological analysis consists of visualizing all possible elements relating to a given object or problem and then exploring various ways of combining and recombining these elements to produce different variations of a product. For example, a person preparing to build a cabinet visits a supply house where different designs and materials are showcased. For the substance of a chair, there is a choice among oak, walnut, maple, cherry, or some form of plastic. For style, there is colonial, French, rococo, contemporary, or dozens of other alternatives. The next step is to consider every possible combination of material and style that would best serve the purposes for which the chair is being made. Other techniques may be used, such as meditation and altered states of consciousness, as well as synectics, but brainstorming is the most widely used of all.

Creative Problem-Solving Programs

To disseminate his ideas and to stimulate research on creativity training and educational programs, Osborn founded the Creative Education Foundation in 1953 at the University of the State of New York at Buffalo. His assistant, Sydney J. Parnes, later became president of the foundation and expanded the program widely by introducing an eclectic approach to nurturing creative behavior. Using Osborn's model as a base, he tried to synthesize it with relevant parts of other existing programs to benefit from the important findings of research on creativity. The constantly evolving program in creative problem solving is an elaboration of the five-step model developed by Osborn and includes many new experiences with synectics, sensitivity training, art, fantasy, meditation, and a variety of other activities that relate to creativity or creative problem solving.

Along with Guilford, Parnes believes that creative ability represents learned skills that can be enhanced through mind-stretching exercises. He defines the creative process as an act of taking knowledge we already have and rearranging it into new and unusual configurations. The process is compared with what happens in a kaleidoscope when the drum is revolved and the colored pieces fall into many different patterns. Each piece is comparable to a bit of knowledge, and the number of patterns that can be made depends on how many pieces are in the drum. Thus, creativity is based on existing knowledge: the more bits of knowledge we have, the greater are the possibilities for new idea patterns.

Parnes points out that we all have the knowledge base for creative innovation but that we fail to develop new ideas because we are locked up in our conservative patterns of viewing our surroundings. Socialization experiences pressure us to conform to normative patterns of behavior and to be cautious about developing original ideas. Therefore, the first step to take toward becoming more creative is to increase sensitivity to seeing things in new ways, which requires upgrading the intake of perceptual stimuli.

Trainees in creative problem solving are exposed to a wide variety of exercises to promote heightened awareness of people, problems, and the environment. Emphasis is place on group interaction, art activities, relaxation, creative body movement, gathering data through all the senses, nonverbal awareness, and viewing films that stimulate new insights or reveal new perspectives on the creative process. Mind-stretching activities are designed along the lines of Guilford's tests of divergent thinking. Trainees concentrate on the ability to develop ideas more fluently, flexibly, and with greater originality, and to elaborate on an existing idea or figure. They also spend time on classifying objects or ideas, perceiving relationships, thinking of alternative outcomes, listing characteristics of a goal, and producing logical conclusions from presented data.

Groups in training work in an accepting atmosphere where all ideas are expressed freely during brainstorming sessions and the principle of deferred judgment is exercised. Participants are told how conservative thinking leads people to overlook potentially creative responses to situations. Specially designed exercises demonstrate the negative effect of habit and the need to make deliberate use of imagination for innovative ideas. Given a description of an ordinary problem, trainees consider habitual response patterns and evaluate their effectiveness. They then review many alternatives and select one as a basis for a plan of action. Before attacking the mess, they are told that problems are perplexing situations which should be viewed as challenges rather than as discouraging obstacles. To reach a solution, it is first necessary to find out what the real problem is and to study all aspects of the situation in order to find the best means of response. A checklist of initial strategies can be helpful in guiding the initial analysis.

Facilitating exercises are built into the five-step problem-solving process, as follows:

1. *Problem Finding*. An attempt is made to recognize the "hidden" or "real" problem that may underlie the situation. Crude methods of attack are designed to broaden, redefine, or reword the problem and to identify subproblems that are more manageable or can be solved more easily because they are easier to understand. For example, a speaker arrives at a hall to give a talk and is upset because there is no lectern. She requests that the custodian provide one for her, but none can be found. Spotting a rectangular wastecan, she rewords her problem from a need to find a lectern to a need to find some kind of platform on which to place her notes. She thereupon sets the wastecan on the table and this serves as an adequate substitute. Sometimes, changing key verbs makes a big difference, as in the case of a person trying to build a better mouse trap who asks instead, "How can I rid the house of mice?" Or, instead of wondering how to *invent* a better toaster, it may be easier to consider how to *brown* and dehydrate bread more successfully. Where the alternative definitions do not simplify the problem, it is helpful to identify subproblems that can be addressed more easily. For instance, a person expressing the need for a new car might be asked why, specifically, is the old one inadequate for further use. If the response is that the body is rusting and the windshield is broken, the problem then becomes one of finding a way to get the car refinished and where to purchase a new windshield. It is easier to proceed toward a solution of the two subproblems than it is to find the means of replacing the old car with a new one.

2. *Fact Finding*. After the real problem has been defined, it is time to search for all helpful facts related to it, to review and list the possible different angles of attack, and to locate other necessary information. The characteristics of the situation should be listed, as should the factors that might influence clear observation. Functions of the important aspects of the situation should be analyzed.

3. *Idea Finding*. At this stage the imagination is used to look in many directions for possible solutions. Rather than waiting passively for the subconscious to take over the problem, the trainee relies on a variety of techniques, including brainstorming and consulting checklists to spur the imagination to heighten its production of ideas. Indulging in fantasy and synectics may also help the individual to make unusual associations to bring the subconscious into play. For example, comparing a chair with a car leads to the obvious fact that both have seats, but it may also produce the idea of a wheelchair or a swivel chair. Such exercises in making remote associations are designed to increase the flow of innovative thinking and can be most effective if practiced repeatedly.

4. *Solution Finding*. After numerous alternatives have been generated, it is time to sort out the best from the also-rans. One effective way in which to do this is to judge each idea on the basis of some clear criteria, such as relationship to original objective, individuals or groups affected, costs involved, materials and equipment required, moral and legal implications, attitudes and aesthetic values involved, ease of implementation, repercussions of failure, and timeliness. Ideas should not be discarded just because they seem wild or silly, for they may be surprisingly helpful in modified form or intact in other problem-solving situations.

5. *Acceptance Finding.* Now that the idea is ready to be implemented, questions have to be asked about its "marketability." If an audience cannot be found, then the idea may have to be modified or discarded to make room for a new one. Practical concerns about distribution are given serious consideration perhaps because the creative problem-solving institutes assist business and industry in making products profitable through wide acceptance, not just in creating them. However, in the academic, artistic, and scientific arenas, the value of an innovative idea may depend less on the size than on the composition of an appreciative audience.

Most of the research on creative problem solving has been conducted at the Creative Education Foundation, and the results they report are generally positive (Biondi and Parnes, 1976). They conclude that imaginative thinking can be cultivated and that creative problem-solving courses can measurably improve the ability of students of average intelligence to produce ideas that are unique and useful. It is also alleged that such a course can produce significant gains in self-confidence, initiative, independence, and leadership potential. All in all, the research successes seem overwhelming.

Torrance (1972) reviewed twenty-two evaluations of the Osborn-Parnes approach to creativity training and concluded that as many as twenty of them produced salutary results. However, Stein (1974) suggests that more confirmation is needed since the subjects in previous studies had worked on problems similar to those used in the criterion measures. It is hoped that further research will reveal not only the generalizability of outcomes but also the relative impact of every key strategy in the training program.

Creative Problem Solving for the Gifted

While all students can probably benefit from the Osborn-Parnes program, it is especially suited to gifted children's high levels of curiosity, ability to use sophisticated thought processes, and need for mastery and innovation. The process is also suited for independent learning, which is sometimes regarded as an important part of education for the gifted. Brainstorming should work especially well in group sessions for the gifted who are able to spark each other with the richness of ideas relating to formal subject matter or to personal and social problems. Furthermore, the exercises are suited to almost any type of classroom organization regardless of whether it is open, self-contained, or departmentalized. According to advocates of creative problem solving, students who master the process may be equipped for a lifetime of creative approaches to problem solving.

Since there is a rapid growth of interest in creativity training for the gifted, it is worthwhile to consider the following strategies suggested by Parnes and his colleagues (1972, 1977):

Remove the Internal Blocks to Creativity. To prepare children for creative productivity, they must be helped to feel secure in their relationships with others without worrying about the acceptability of their ideas, even if they are extremely offbeat. However, freedom to think carries with it the responsibility for their mistakes.

Create an Awareness of the Role of the Subconscious. Even when a problem is removed from direct attention, the subconscious somehow keeps on working at it. Since ideas and fantasies about possible solutions surface only fleetingly, it is important to jot down these thoughts so that eventually they may be clarified and organized.

Defer Judgment. By so doing, the child can spend more time on acquiring a variety of perceptions about a problem and thereby increase the flow of ideas that lead to alternative solutions.

Create an Awareness of the Power of Metaphor and Analogy in Triggering New Connections and Associations. With the help of checklists and other devices, dealing with analogy and metaphor can be made easy if enough time is spent in practice.

Provide Experiences with Mind-Stretching Exercises. Forcing the mind to produce many alternative solutions to problems is uncomfortable at the beginning, but ideas flow more and more easily as children grow more comfortable with the task.

Keep Fantasy Alive. Fantasy is not only essential in helping children's mental growth and adjustment; it is also a vital ingredient in creativity. Every effort, therefore, has to be made to discourage the school and the home from communicating the belief to children that such flights of the imagination are signs of immature thinking.

Remove Mental Brakes: Encourage Freewheeling. Children have to feel assured that their ideas will not be ridiculed and that any far-out thought is worth expressing and sharing with others.

Discipline the Imagination. Although children should be encouraged to freewheel and fantasize, they need to realize that after the incubation period ideas will be reviewed critically. Some will be rejected, and those that are retained need to be implemented for humane and useful purposes.

Increase Sensitivity. Formal awareness training, art exercises, and in-depth discussions of literature can help to increase children's sensitivity to others and to their physical environment. It will also enable them to recognize incongruities as well as new relationships and connections that can prove to be meaningful.

Increase Knowledge. Creativity depends on knowledge previously absorbed. Increasing mastery of information and ideas can help children to see relationships that form the basis of new ideas. The point to remember, however, is that, while subject content is important, it does not constitute the entire learning experience. Learning to think, to solve problems, and to use knowledge should also become an essential part of the school experience.

Help Children to Understand Why They Engage in Various Exercises Related to Creative Thinking. Children, parents, and educators have to understand the importance of creative thinking and the exercises that facilitate it in order to maximize the effects of enrichment. Otherwise, such techniques may be seen mistakenly as "fun and games" that only embellish the curriculum rather than breathe life into it.

COGNITIVE-AFFECTIVE INTERACTION

The cognitive-affective interaction model created by Frank W. Williams (1972) is designed to help teachers stimulate creative thinking along with healthy emotional development in children. While educators are aware of the need to help children to develop worthy self-concepts, attitudes, and values, in practice little time is spent on affect in the curriculum. Subject matter and skills for acquiring it dominate the program, and there is room for little else. Williams contends that affective factors help provide the motivation essential for developing creativity. These feelings include intuition, openness to hunches, fantasy, and imagination, all of which are useful in sensing and solving problems. Unfortunately, this kind of thought tends to be squelched in the course of knowledge acquisition in school, and the result is that children cannot make the most of their abilities. A balanced educational diet provides for growth in cognition and also in creativity, with the understanding that thinking and feeling cannot be separated.

Although many schools attempt to combine cognitive and affective elements in what they call "humanistic education," these efforts are made only when the teacher can find time to design and implement such a program. Williams's model helps to systematize the planning for teachers by introducing cognitive and affective exercises into all subjects of the curriculum as a regular part of instruction. In developing the exercises, Williams asserts that (1) creativity is composed of a large number of skills that may be both intellectual and attitudinal; (2) every child has some creative potential, but individuals vary in how their creativity is expressed; (3) the creative process, whether in arts or sciences, is basically the same; (4) creativity may be nurtured and tested in a variety of ways; and (5) creative instruction results when the teacher stimulates children to think and feel creatively.

Cognitive-affective interaction concerns itself with divergent thought processes in which children reach out beyond what they know and engage in predicting, imagining, and fantasizing. Thus, different associations are formed among known facts, and the result is the production of new ideas. A storehouse of knowledge is basic to creative thinking since it is impossible to create in a vacuum. But it is also necessary to go well beyond merely assembling information. Divergent thinking requires exploration into the unknown to become involved in the production of a quantity and variety of ideas and then to try implementing the best of these ideas. Teachers should be aware of the intellectual factors related to creativity and provide students with exercises to trigger such thought. Practice in improvising, exploring, and synthesizing help children when they try to think divergently, but all these activities require considerable skill and must be taught and practiced regularly.

Williams observes that major theories of problem solving stress divergent thought as a key factor in creativity and even though these processes are hardly emphasized in the classroom they are highly prized outside of school. He also notes that IQ tests concentrate on convergent thinking, which represents only one kind of mental functioning, whereas creativity measures deal with a different kind of thinking ability pertaining to how children generate variety and originality in their ideas.

Both kinds of tests are useful since they complement each other, but it is well to remember that even the best of instruments are only crude tools for judging mental ability. In addition to formal assessments, the teacher should be aware that exceptionally able children show evidence of their talent in the course of classroom life. They are *curious* about the life they experience and ask many questions about it. They have wide-ranging interests and want to explore and know as much as they can and to toy with ideas. They are also *imaginative*, as evidenced by their ability to visualize things that never existed and to fantasize vividly about events that never happened. Intellectually, they *prefer complex problems*, especially those that stimulate them to seek order out of disorder and to explore the gaps between how things are and how they ought to be. Their efforts at unraveling intricate problems are reinforced by a *willingness to take risks*. They are prepared to engage in guesswork, test daring thoughts, make mistakes, and even face failure. These characteristics can be discerned and nurtured in the classroom, and it is vitally important for teachers to take them into account in stimulating childrens' creativity.

A Morphological Model

Some of the more popular models designed to teach thinking include derivatives from Bloom's taxonomy and Piaget's stage theory. Sometimes these constructs create the impression that thinking and feeling are separable in human beings. To correct this possible confusion, Williams has developed a morphological paradigm that enables teachers to see how affect and cognition interact. The purpose of the model is to aid teachers in uniting the global aspect of the intellect, or "head knowledge," with the personal, or "heart knowledge," in a type of education that

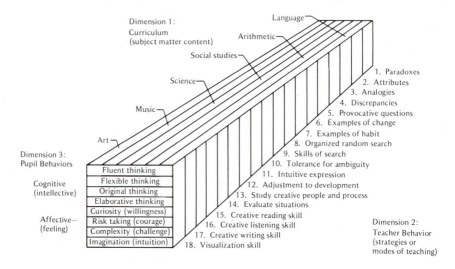

Figure 20-6 A model for implementing cognitive-affective behaviors in the classroom

can be described as humanistic. It differs from a cognitive taxonomy in that no hierarchical order of thinking or feeling processes is implied. Instead, three sets of considerations interact in every possible way, as illustrated in Figure 20-6.

Dimension 1, curriculum, lists the familiar subject matter areas of the elementary school curriculum. However, it is possible to substitute content from any other grade level or special courses for the gifted such as marine biology or cultural anthropology.

Dimension 2, teacher behaviors, includes the styles, strategies, tactics, or methods that can be employed during the instructional act. The eighteen alternatives that Williams lists are applied to each of the subject matter areas for purposes of fostering each of the thinking and feeling pupil behaviors.

Dimension 3, pupil behaviors, is deduced from theoretical studies of how children think and feel divergently. These behaviors are considered objectives to be attained in the classroom. If each of the 8 behaviors were taught through the 18 different strategies in each of the 6 areas of the curriculum illustrated in Figure 20-6, the total number of different kinds of lessons would be 864 (18 x 8 x 6), an ample variety that would bolster the teacher's repertoire in the classroom.

The Total Creativity Program

The cognitive-affective interaction model fits into Williams's Total Creativity Program, which includes the methodology for teacher training, instruments for diagnosing children's cognitive and affective strengths, and a wide variety of suggestions for educational enrichment. Teachers who receive training in the use of the model are helped thereby to recognize the various creative impulses in children and how to encourage them. Creativity does not flourish by chance; the teacher must make it happen by careful stimulation in an environment that balances intellectual freedom and discipline.

The Total Creativity Program provides a variety of checklists for teachers to use in gathering information on how children think and feel. These instruments can be helpful for prescriptive teaching. Other instruments tap children's feelings about themselves before and after exposure to creativity training. There are also questionnaires to help teachers to monitor their own classroom behavior to determine whether they are providing an educational climate that fosters creativity.

The teacher's workbook of the Total Creativity Program contains a form on which to record various kinds of information about children, including their cognitive and affective profiles. The purpose of such a record is to provide an overall picture of children's needs that have to be addressed in the classroom. Since the information is in profile form, it also alerts the teacher to many behaviors that are often overlooked but are valuable for diagnosing children's creative potential.

Creativity consists of many kinds of abilities, and no one test or focused observation can possibly make the teacher aware of all the talents children may possess. The creativity potential profile is therefore valuable in revealing children's strengths and weaknesses since the sources of data are varied and systematic. The profile should become part of children's cumulative record for teachers to use as a reference from year to year.

Among the personal attributes monitored and cultivated in the Total Creativity Program are children's feelings, which are vital to self-concept and motivation to learn. Feelings have to be nurtured through appropriate experiences that arouse curiosity, imagination, and risk-taking behavior, even in complex problem-solving situations. Learning can be sterile if its purpose is not clearly understood and appreciated by those engaged in it. Highly creative children have two sets of values, one based on aesthetic feelings and the other on rational processes. These children are often self-motivated and achievement oriented, but they can also be sensitive and introverted. They delight in challenge and have a high tolerance for ambiguity, but their adventure in the world of ideas must have meaning, and not simply be an exercise in discovery for discovery's sake. Among the feelings that deserve special encouragement are:

1. *Curiosity*, expressed through prolonged questioning, toying with ideas and materials, and intensive exploratory behavior.
2. *Imagination*, through flights of fantasy, dreams, and conjuring up events that never happened or places that never existed.
3. *Complexity*, as evidenced by an attraction to intricate problems and solutions, a determination to turn disorder into order, and the courage to explore gaps between how things are and how they ought to be.
4. *Risk taking*, or a willingness to make honest mistakes and face failure, which cannot be avoided in the course of being constructively venturesome.

Classroom climates that encourage creativity are not particularly permissive. Children must feel free to be creative, but at the same time they need guidance in using freedom responsibly. The classroom that fosters creativity keeps children's curiosity alive and sharpens it toward productive ends. The climate helps children to feel secure personally and not inhibited in expressing their ideas. It does not enforce excessive conformity, which can lead to boredom and resentment, especially among the highly creative; instead, there is an acceptance of each child's uniqueness. In short, the teacher's feelings toward children can be characterized best as concerned, cooperative, and most appreciative of diversity.

The Total Creativity Program provides a manual entitled *Classroom Ideas for Thinking and Feeling* (Williams, 1972) that offers a wide variety of suggestions of methods and materials that are useful in the classroom. The emphasis is on divergent thinking, which is considered central to creativity. Williams is aware that considerable lip service is given to developing self-concept and creativity, but he notes that few teachers really seem prepared to move children through a variety of thinking and feeling processes, divergent as well as convergent, yet at the same time help them to gain a strong sense of self-approval about their creative production. His program therefore tends to help teachers translate theory into classroom practice. Creativity training belongs in all subject areas, not just art, music, fiction, and poetry, and not as supplementary exercises in isolation from curriculum content.

Strategies for encouraging creativity are categorized among the eighteen teacher behaviors (Figure 20-6) and may be defined and illustrated as follows:

1. *Paradoxes.* Situations that seem hard to understand through common sense, self-contradictory statements, or discrepancies between beliefs and facts (for example, in studying poverty in the urban ghetto, help children to discriminate between popular myth and truth by evaluating the commonly held notion that hard work will solve any problem).

2. *Attributes.* Inherent properties, conventional symbols, or identities describing qualities (for example, ask children to observe the various aspects or individual parts of a common object such as a telephone, book, or pencil and to describe the uses of each part; then ask how each part could be changed to make the object better, more useful, or more beautiful).

3. *Analogies.* Situations of likeness, similarities between things, or corresponding circumstances (for example, consider how Bell's study of how the ear works inspired him to invent the telephone; compare how animals live and work with the way in which people live and work; look for analogies in poetry and use them in creative writing).

4. *Discrepancies.* Gaps in knowledge, missing links in information, or unknown elements in nature (for example, discuss what is meant by the "missing link"; study the development of the periodic table of elements and determine what is missing; list other gaps in knowledge, such as a total cure for cancer and the intricacies of how the brain functions).

5. *Provocative Questions.* Use of the inquiry method to trigger the search for knowledge and to bring forth meaning (for example, Why doesn't an igloo melt inside? What does petroleum mean to you?).

6. *Examples of Change.* Demonstrating how knowledge and the conditions of life are in a constant state of flux and how seemingly intact phenomena are amenable to alteration, modification, or reduction (for example, study a scientific principle and how it changed throughout history as men learned more; contrast the Ptolemaic theory to that of Copernicus; study the history of your community and how it has changed; investigate examples of metamorphosis).

7. *Examples of Habit.* Rigidity in ideas and fixation on customs, and their effects on innovative thinking (for example, discuss how religious ideas that cause people of certain religious sects in India to avoid killing insects can result in the spread of disease; also, how does failure to develop solar energy hurt countries that depend on the world's diminishing supply of fossil fuel?).

8. *Organized Random Search.* Practice in using a familiar structure to lead randomly to another structure (for example, establish ground rules for a classroom experience and allow children to explore freely various ways of participating in the experience within the ground rules; teach children to write cinquains and then have them invent other poetic forms).

9. *Skills of Search.* Methods used by scientists, explorers, historians, and others

to build knowledge (for example, control experimental conditions in a scientific study and report subsequent results; use trial-and-error methods to gain knowledge and describe the outcomes; gather data on past events and interpret their meaning).

10. *Tolerance for Ambiguity.* Provide encounters with open-ended situations that puzzle, challenge, or intrigue but do not force closure (for example, show a film, turn it off at a crucial point, and ask children to finish the story; then compare their endings with the real one).

11. *Intuitive Expression.* Encourage children to use all their senses to absorb stimuli from the environment; help them to develop skills to express their emotions; and allow them to brainstorm hypotheses in their quest for knowledge (for example, ask children to write or tell about their real feelings in reaction to an experience; point out how scientists often follow their hunches in developing new inventions or theories).

12. *Adjustment to Development.* Help children to understand how failures or accidents have paid off in the past (for example, the Wright brothers failed many times but eventually invented a plane that would fly; show other examples of how people learn from their mistakes).

13. *Study Creative People and Processes.* Study the biographies of great men and women, particularly the characteristics that may have contributed to their creativity (for example, study how physical and other handicaps have not prevented some people from doing creative work; learn about the creative process and what is meant by incubation and illumination as experienced by scientists, artists, writers, inventors, and other renowned personalities; stress the necessity for hard work and study in the creative process).

14. *Evaluate Situations.* Decide upon solutions in terms of their consequences (for example, extrapolate from the results of ideas and actions, such as the invention of DDT; anticipate possible developments in ongoing situations, and speculate about how a current event may eventuate in a particular outcome).

15. *Creative Reading Skills.* Encourage children to generate ideas from their reading experience by teaching them to read not only what it says but also the thought associations it inspires (for example, rather than merely asking children to recall details of plot and character, ask what new ideas they derived from the story or from a passage in it).

16. *Creative Listening Skills.* Instruct children to allow their listening experiences to transport them into new worlds of ideas in the same way that their reading does (for example, have children listen to music and ask them to write about the thoughts that are generated by the melodic pattern, tone, and mood).

17. *Creative Writing Skills.* Teach children how to express themselves through writing clearly and effectively (for example, give children ten words and ask them to write a story using the ten words in the order they were given; ask them to state an idea in a way no one else would express it).

18. *Visualization Skills.* Practice describing or portraying views from unaccustomed vantage points (for example, have children draw their room from the

viewpoint of an ant or other insect and then from the perspective of a giant or a plane overhead).

As noted earlier, teachers apply the various strategies to elicit thinking and feeling behaviors with respect to curriculum content. Many specific lessons are suggested by Williams, and they are coded to fit the appropriate teacher behavior, pupil behavior, and subject matter. The following are examples of how they are organized:

Pupils' Thinking Behaviors	Lesson Activities	Teacher Strategies
Flexible thinking	Show a picture of an inner-city slum adjacent to an affluent area. Have the class think of all the questions they might ask that cannot be answered by looking at the picture.	Pose a discrepancy.
Curiosity	Continue to seek questions from the class that might uncover hidden possibilities if more were known about the picture.	Build a tolerance for ambiguity.
Complexity	Ask the class to pose questions that would seek to uncover things that might have happened that caused the conditions shown in the picture.	Ask children to develop ideas from the picture, rather than report what is in it.
Flexible thinking	Ask the children to select their best questions and write them for the question box. A few days later, open the box and read the questions.	
Analytical thinking	Ask small groups to discuss all the different categories of questions submitted. Help them to classify the questions.	Categorize, classify.

Children's Feeling Behaviors	Lesson Activities	Teacher Strategies
Imagination	Small groups are asked to imagine what would have happened if critical moments in history had been different: if the Pilgrims had never settled in America; if the North had lost the Civil War; if Kennedy had not been assassinated; if the U.S. Constitution had never been written.	Ask provocative questions to stimulate imagniation. Brainstorm.
Fluent thinking	Each group considers one event. The children are asked to think of	Evaluate situations.

Children's Feeling Behaviors	Lesson Activities	Teacher Strategies
Prediction	as many consequences or implications as possible if the event had never happened. One pupil in every group records all of the ideas expressed in that group.	
Evaluation	All groups then select from their lists one consequence or implication that they feel would have the greatest and most lasting effect upon our lives today.	
Original thinking, imagination	After selecting the most influential consequence, each pupil composes an original story related to that projected outcome. Clever and original stories are encouraged, and they are discussed at length in class.	Develop creative writing skill. Encourage imagination and originality.

The Total Creativity Program systematizes the planning of a wide variety of educational experiences for gifted children. Neither the methodology nor desired outcomes are left to chance, since the teaching act is planned within a logical framework rather than by intuition. Teachers can thus be alerted to what works well, what fails, and what is neglected in alternative instructional procedures. They can also explain to children what kinds of methods are being used for thinking and feeling. However, the specific suggestions for lesson planning should be viewed as only starting points for developing a full-scale program that is adjusted to the unique needs of every child.

THE MULTIPLE TALENT APPROACH

Calvin W. Taylor (1973) has predicated his multiple talent approach to teaching and learning on the observation that traditionally schools have concentrated their efforts on nurturing only a few mental abilities, mostly scholastic, while ignoring other types of talent. He considers this narrow approach to education to be responsible for a waste of high-level human potential. Students who achieve well in academic areas are considered to have great promise while schoolmates with other kinds of special aptitudes are largely ignored. According to Taylor and Williams (1966) this traditional approach is based on the grossly oversimplified understanding of general intelligence and its representation in a single IQ score. He interprets research on intelligence tests to show that they measure only a fraction of an individual's mental abilities.

Taylor makes the following specific recommendations to educators:

1. Rather than cultivating one kind of talent, schools should gear programs to develop all of the country's resources; creative and productive thinking talents may be the most important resources to develop, considering the rapid rate of change in technological societies and the need for constant innovation.
2. More scientific research should be used to test the validity of educational approaches, and a greater amount of developmental activity by "educational engineers" should occur in conjunction with this research.
3. A closer relationship should exist among demands of the world of work, so-called "life requirements," and the school curriculum. Research related to on-the-job performance by scientists reveals that they had to unlearn many practices taught in school to do well on the job.
4. Creative thinking abilities cannot be ignored in the full development of a person's intellectual capacities and progress toward self-actualization. Moreover, many important abilities can be nurtured more easily through flexible methods than through an authoritarian approach.
5. More stress should be placed on the arts and humanities in education to nurture expressiveness as well as greater self-awareness and self-insight.

The multiple talent approach rejects the traditional, narrowly conceived uses of academic talent in the classroom and broadens the emphasis to include other thinking and learning processes. The teacher's role is to give children the various cognitive tools with which to approach subject matter. In that sense, teachers become talent developers and concentrate not only on academic skills but also on other important mental resources. Thus, the student gains both mastery of subject matter and improvement in various intellectual functions.

The contrast between conventional and multiple talent concepts in teaching is illustrated in Figures 20-7A and B. Figure 20-7A shows a systematic coverage of subject matter with all but one talent ignored. In contrast, Figure 20-7B shows a more balanced application of different talents, as students learn how to deal with the same subject matter content in different ways.

Considering the large number of mental abilities now identified empirically, the multiple talent approach would become extremely complex and unwieldly if all the known special aptitudes were taken into account. Taylor's model concentrates on six broad areas of talent, each of which has from ten to forty specific abilities within them. These classifications consist of talents in academics, creativity, planning, communicating, forecasting, and decision making. Verbal communication alone consists of more than thirty different types of abilities, and all of them are covered thoroughly in the sequence of learning experiences through the grades. The multiple talent totem poles (see Figure 20-8) illustrate how a child can rate differently in comparison with other children, depending on which of the six talent areas is being measured. One student may excel in communication skills but be less skilled in decision making and perhaps rate low in forecasting. Since various kinds of abilities are taken into account, not just academic skills, it is possible for every student to be outstanding in one way or another.

Two Extremely Different Ways of Distributing 24 Class Hours
(with an "x" for each class hour)

(A)

Different Talent Processes in Students

Content Acquired by Students	Academic talents	Creative talents	Communication talents	Planning talents	Decision-making talents	Forecasting talents	Other types of talents	
Language arts	xxx							xxx
Social studies	xxx							xxx
Humanities	xxx							xxx
Arts	xxx							xxx
Biological sciences	xxx							xxx
Physical sciences	xxx							xxx
Mathematics	xxx							xxx
Other subjects	xxx							xxx
Totals	xxxxxx xxxxxx xxxxxx xxxxxx							24 x's Grand Total

(B)

Different Talent Processes in Students

Content Acquired by Students	Academic talents	Creative talents	Communication talents	Planning talents	Decision-making talents	Forecasting talents	Other types of talents	
Language arts		x	xx					xxx
Social studies		x		x	x			xxx
Humanities	xx	x				x		xxxx
Arts		x	x				x	xxx
Biological sciences	x		x		x			xxx
Physical sciences	x	x		x				xxx
Mathematics	x				x	x		xxx
Other subjects				x	x			xx
Totals	xxxxx	xxxxx	xxxx	xxx	xxxx	xx	x	24 x's Grand Total

Figure 20-7 The two student-centered dimensions of content and process (Taylor, 1978, p. 145)

The multiple talent approach rejects the use of IQ measures as sole indicators of giftedness. Taylor notes that persons belonging to organizations that require a high IQ for membership rarely achieve distinction in their careers. While they tend to earn high grades in school, there is little correlation between scholastic standing and levels of success in the professions. Nevertheless, the traditional school program seems based on an assumption that many good things will happen to students if they become sufficiently knowledgable academically. In traditional programs, testing and teaching are confined to only a narrow band of intellectual abilities.

| Academic | Creative | Planning | Communicating | Forecasting | Decision-making |

Figure 20-8 Taylor's multiple talent totem poles (Taylor, 1978)

School systems are therefore unaware of the degree to which children possess other potentially high-level talents that deserve to be identified and cultivated.

When children are tested for a single talent, only about 10 percent or fewer can hope to excel at school. Viewing all students from this oversimplified point of view leads to the conclusion that at least 90 percent have only average or inferior ability, all on the basis of a test that assesses a small fraction of the known mental functions. Taylor rejects this restricted view of talent and, instead, takes into account the brain's wide-ranging intellectual powers. His multiple talent approach is the vehicle for schools to use in moving toward a goal of "zero reject," or in helping every child to find success in school. The assumption is that every child can excel in at least one area and that as many as 60 percent of all children will score above the median in some intellectual functions.

The six types of giftedness depicted on the multiple talent totem poles receive major emphasis in schools implementing the Taylor paradigm as a substitute for the more conventional teaching of past knowledge. In the early grades, teachers are trained to recognize children talented in any of the six specified areas by looking for formal and informal signs of the following traits:

Academic Talent. Ability to learn with ease, master advanced vocabulary, understand and remember complex ideas, and perform scholastically at a superior level. A child who excels in academic learning is able to pursue, locate, recognize, summarize, recall, and reproduce knowledge with exceptional skill.

Creative Talent. Tendency to produce offbeat ideas, novel expressions, unique solutions to problems, or some kinds of original projects. Such a child often has multiple interests and curiosities and shows tendencies to invent, compose, design, produce, create, and originate valuable thoughts or objects.

Planning Talent. Ability to understand the need for sequence and order, organize work and play, and deal with complexity in a systematic way. The child who shows real signs of talent in organization has special skills in arranging artistic ideas, social events, or theoretical abstractions.

Communicating Talent. The ability to use language for clear expression, make needs known, understand the needs of others, and relate and respond to people who function at high levels of thought. Such a child can state, explain, convey, and demonstrate ideas with exceptional skill.

Forecasting Talent. An understanding of human nature, associations of events, implications, and consequences. These reasoning abilities are useful in looking into the future and predicting outcomes. The child possessing such skills can anticipate, estimate, foresee, and "guess correctly" with unusual consistency.

Decision-Making Talent. Ability to gather information, weigh evidence, recognize influential conditions or events, make good generalizations, and demonstrate superior judgment in making decisions.

Among the various talent assessment instruments that Taylor and his associates have produced is the Biographical Inventory (Form U), which consists of about 150 items designed to measure the following six characteristics: (1) academic performance, (2) creativity, (3) artistic potential, (4) leadership, (5) career awareness and exploration, and (6) educational orientation versus dropout potential. One large-scale investigation reported by Hainsworth (1978) attempted to determine the incidence of at least one of several types of talent in an elementary school population. He tested 1,254 children on a battery that yielded six scores from the Biographical Inventory and four additional scores on tests designed to measure Realistic Decision Making, Remote Forecasting, Planning, and Non-verbal Originality. Results show that 91 percent scored above the fiftieth percentile, 74 percent above the seventy-fifth percentile, and 47 percent above the ninetieth percentile on one or more of the ten scores. Hainsworth concluded that such data can be used to "convince educators that almost every student in the school is gifted" (p. 88).

In addition to advocating a search for different kinds of abilities, the multiple talent approach also suggests a variety of ways in which to enrich programs for the gifted. Taylor (undated) recommends several kinds of enrichment, as follows:

1. *Knowledge enrichment,* which emphasizes thinking about knowledge and working with it, rather than merely learning it. The gifted should be taught to use their higher cognitive abilities to enhance their understanding of curriculum content. This is in contrast to dealing strictly with what the teacher and textbook already know, content that only restricts the gifted child's range of functioning.
2. *Talent enrichment,* designed to help the gifted to make use of many more competencies than are tapped in knowledge-focused education programs. The talent totem pole illustrates the possibilities of broadening the range of potential brainpower under the overall rubric of giftedness. Accordingly, "learning

centers" would be replaced by "thinking centers," which could then be divided into "talent centers," each covering appropriate domains of knowledge. The talent centers might also be known as "function junctions," where the gifted learn how to use their special abilities. The teacher's role is to be a talent igniter and developer who can help students take initiative in learning and thereby make the classroom an exciting place for creating and exchanging ideas.

3. *Nonintellectual talent enrichment*, which emphasizes affective and other supportive attributes of high-level functioning. For example, the research literature on creativity reports many personality factors that figure prominently in the creative act. These traits should be nurtured along with the requisite cognitive abilities as part of the plan for enrichment.

4. *Enrichment through experimental education*, designed to bring gifted children into direct contact with the phenomena they are studying. Experience forces the learner to develop insights that are meaningful and longlasting. It also enables them to make intuitive leaps into undiscovered realms of knowledge. It is therefore more efficient than learning complex generalizations that seem unrelated to the real world.

5. *Enrichment in intensity and depth of involvement*, designed to help the gifted function and produce on their own, without relying on external motivation imposed by the system that controls, manipulates, conditions, programs, and molds the child's educational experience. The students should become more self-made persons by being encouraged to participate in the planning and guidance of their activities.

6. *Environmental and situational enrichment*, involving the study of natural and fabricated environments and their effects on people's lives. Such an experience can help children to become better troubleshooters by sensing problems as early as possible. Furthermore, the ability to "read" situations prepares children to face up to contingencies more easily.

7. *Research participation enrichment*, engaging students in research activities long before they reach graduate school. This will enable them to identify problems on their own, make proper observations regarding the problems they find, learn how to collect data, and experience the satisfaction of deriving new knowledge out of research activity. The gifted have to learn how to use their own internal resources to the fullest extent and avoid relying mainly on outside authorities, such as instructors and textual material. Some of their research may take them along paths that others have followed earlier, but it is necessary to help the gifted seek out new directions for them to contribute something of their own, however difficult it may be.

8. *Multicultural enrichment*, enabling gifted children to benefit from exposure to the folkways of societies other than their own. The experience should be a direct rather than a vicarious, multicultural education, especially in songs, dances, crafts, and other distinctive aspects of life among various peoples, to provide a basis for children's understanding of their own media in global perspective.

9. *Enrichment through synthesis*, in which any or all of the previously described

types of special experiences are combined in appropriate situations for children who can derive the most benefit from them.

In summary, the newly formed and existing Gifted/Talented Programs have great opportunities for exploring, experimenting, and enriching their own experiences and contributions. A great diversity of programs and of contributions can occur during this expanding period of interest in talents and gifts. These contributions can range from those developing a best total program for a small percent of highly gifted and talented students to programs producing various powerful *demonstrations*, which could have a catalytic and leavening effect toward improving the total program for all students in all areas at all educational levels. (Taylor, undated, p. 17)

Taylor's plan goes a long way toward "democratizing" talent by suggesting that every measurable skill is as much a sign of excellence as any other. This means that the children ranking at the top of the illustrated totem poles (see Figure 20-8) are variously, *but equally*, gifted. And if we were to restrict our talent search to those showing outstanding promise in either academics or creativity, we would be overlooking four out of every six gifted children who possess comparable potential for greatness, albeit in other ways. It also means that the child depicted on the totem poles as rating highest in communicating and near the top in decision making qualifies as gifted even though her tested academic, creative, planning, and forecasting abilities range from fairly to extremely mediocre. Are these talents so independent of each other that whoever possesses one is unlikely to possess another in extraordinary measure? Is it possible to become widely appreciated as a "communicator" without having mastered much academically or produced much creatively that is worth communicating? These kinds of issues are critical in any multiple talent approach to identifying and educating the gifted. The answers will come only through longitudinal research comparable to follow-up studies conducted on high-IQ children.

THINKING SKILLS IN A CURRICULUM CONTEXT

During the 1960s, Hilda Taba collaborated with a group of teachers in Contra Costa County, California in an effort to improve the social studies curriculum in grades one through eight. Considering the rate at which knowledge has been expanding, the authors recognized that it becomes increasingly difficult to absorb more than a small fraction of existing factual information in a major discipline such as the social studies. They therefore concentrated on ways of dealing with concepts insightfully rather than on piling content upon content, thereby enabling children to sharpen their high-level thinking skills in a curriculum context. This is a departure from the familiar "training the mind" exercises in games, riddles, and puzzles that are supposed to help students think more deeply in any problem situation.

Taba's social studies curriculum involves the development of thinking skills through the following strategies in the classroom.

1. *Developing Concepts.* Students respond to questions that require them to enumerate an array of objects or events, find the basis for grouping them according to their similarities, identify additional common characteristics within each group, label the groups, and create final groupings under these labels. It is important that the children perform all these operations themselves in order to see the relationships between phenomena, recognize the basis by which to group them, and devise the categories. The teacher's questioning techniques figure prominently in the success of this method.

2. *Inferring and Generalizing.* Children are invited to examine data, explain what they see, arrive at generalizations by recognizing commonalities and discrepancies, and check their generalizations against particularisms in the data. The teacher should help pupils to realize the tentativeness and probabilistic nature of many generalizations.

3. *Applying Generalizations.* The last step involves applying facts and generalizations to explain unfamiliar phenomena or to infer consequences from known conditions. Students are required to support their generalizations or speculations with evidence and sound reasoning. For example, the teacher might ask, "What would happen to the way of life in a desert oasis if a government helped all the farmers to get tractors and they stopped using camels to pull the plows?" Two facts provide a starting point for any number of inferences: "obsolescence" of camels, "novelty" of tractors. In guiding the discussion, the teacher has to avoid the extremes of inhibiting offbeat ideas and accepting uncritically any fantasy-ridden thought. The practice of inviting reasons for observed phenomena and drawing inferences beyond the data is gradually expanded to include more and more aspects of the data and to reach more abstract generalizations.

Components of the Social Studies Curriculum

Several kinds of understandings are highlighted consistently and systematically in the program materials. Some studies revolve about key concepts, such as causality, conflict, cooperation, cultural change, differentiation, interdependence, modification, power, societal control, tradition, and values. These concepts are selected from a variety of social sciences and other disciplines that require the student to exercise exceptional powers of synthesis and organization. The challenge is repeated again and again at different levels of complexity, abstractness, and generality, thus providing for a developmental sequence from one grade to the next.

Each year's content is organized around six to eight main ideas selected on the basis of their significance, durability, balance, and scope. The main ideas are analyzed at several grade levels, albeit in different ways. An example of such a postulate might be, "As people grow, develop, and interact, conflict is inevitable.

There are approved and disapproved ways of resolving conflict. In most situations some form of compromise is necessary." For young children, the content developed around this main idea might involve conflict over a desired toy in kindergarten and primary-grade classrooms. In the higher grades, the idea might relate to the Civil War, affluence versus poverty, and capitalism versus communism. The generalization is not presented as a fact to be learned, but instead, the assumption is that a principle can be understood better by arriving at it inductively rather than by hearing it asserted before putting it to the test.

Feelings, attitudes, and values also have a great deal to do with the child's learning and socialization. Consequently, emphasis is placed on having children sensitize themselves to their own feelings, and to the sensibilities of others as well, while developing a sense of mutual empathy in the process. This leads them to analyze their own and their classmates' value structures. They explore conflict situations, their response to conflict, and the consequences of their actions to gain a deeper feeling of what it means to deal with dilemma and disagreement. Thus, the Taba curriculum systematizes both academic and social skills. Every objective is stated in terms of observable behaviors based on comprehension, analysis, attitude development, exploration of feelings, and a development of sensitivity and empathy, all of which are intended to move the child away from ethocentrism and toward true world citizenship.

The Taba curriculum model has been evaluated through various analyses of teacher strategies and tests of pupil performance (Taba, 1964, 1966). Results revealed that students made better inferences from given information, used more appropriately abstract concepts in summarizing data, appeared to be more "people oriented," and enjoyed the questioning strategies used by teachers in the program. But while the outcomes favoring experimentals over controls were statistically significant, the differences were not dramatic. This is not surprising since the experiment was conducted for only one year, and the new approaches to thinking and learning represent a sharp departure from the didactic teaching that the children had experienced during all their previous years at school.

Another study (Tennant, 1980) assessed the ability of one hundred gifted children, grades two through six, to identify the thinking strategies that ought to be used in different problem-solving situations. The experimental group had been exposed to a program called BASICS*, which is based substantially on the Taba model. Results show that children exposed to at least two hours of instruction were better able to recognize the appropriate thinking skills than were equally able children who spent less than two hours or no time at all in studying the special learning strategies. The best results were obtained from those who spent from six to fifteen hours in instruction.

BASICS not only expands on a number of the thought processes specified in the Taba model; it also provides teachers with detailed instructions on how to help

---

*Building and Applying Strategies for Intellectual Competencies in Students (Institute for Curriculum and Instruction, 1977)

children learn and apply each skill properly. These learning strategies are listed and defined in the program as follows:

Observing: Noting a variety of physical characteristics (e.g., indicating the size, color, and texture of a rock; the smell, taste, size, and other features of a fruit; kind and number of letters in a word; characteristics of a painting).

Recalling: Remembering what is known or has been experienced (e.g., what was observed on a field trip; how certain tools are used; details of a story; what certain words mean; findings of an experiment).

Noting Differences: Identifying observed and recalled differences (e.g., differences in certain occupations, word meanings, spellings, and types of government).

Noting Similarities: Identifying observed and recalled commonalities (e.g., what is alike about a group of insects, two or more communities, the characters in certain stories).

Ordering: Arranging items according to a given characteristic and explaining how rearrangement was determined (e.g., explaining the method used to determine which of five quantities was largest, which next largest; and chronological order of events).

Grouping: Putting items together and identifying a common characteristic or other relationship among them (e.g., explaining that "hat," "ran," and "cab" belong together because it is a short "a" that is pronounced; grouping meat and eggs together because they are rich in protein).

Concept Labeling: Providing names for items or classes of items and explaining why the labels are (or are not) appropriate (e.g., explaining what there is about the meaning of the word "triangle" that makes it an appropriate name for figures with three sides and three angles).

Classifying: Determining which items are additional members of a given class and the attributes that make them so (e.g., explaining that a spider is not an insect because it has eight rather than six legs).

Inferring Causes: Making inferences as to the causes of observed or recalled events and giving reasons for thinking that they are causes (e.g., explaining reasons for thinking that a method of production affected the price of the product).

Inferring Effects: Making inferences as to the effects of observed or recalled events and giving reasons for thinking that they are effects (e.g., explaining reasons for thinking that the change in location of the plant changed its growth patterns).

Inferring Feelings: Making inferences as to the feelings of people in given situations and given reasons for . . . these feelings . . . (e.g., explaining reasons for thinking that being with new people would make someone feel self-conscious).

Concluding: Synthesizing observations, recalled data, inferences, and so on, and giving the basis for the conclusion (e.g., explaining reasons for concluding that the main cause for a musunderstanding was unwillingness or inability to listen).

Questioning: Inquiring, asking questions, about new situations and explaining why the answers to the questions are needed (e.g., explaining why it would be important to find out when a book was written).

Anticipating: Predicting possible consequences of new or changed situations, giving reasons for expecting predicted events and conditions under which they would occur (e.g., predicting that if given seeds were planted they would grow into plants like the ones they came from and explaining the conditions needed for them to grow into healthy plants).

Making Choices: Deciding which of a number of alternatives would be best in a given situation and explaining why (e.g., explaining reasons for thinking a biography would be a better source of information about a person than an encyclopedia).

The mental operations combine in a variety of sequences to produce the following problem-solving strategies:

Concept Formation: Processing data about the characteristics of selected examples and nonexamples of a class, ultimately identifying the characteristics that distinguish one particular class from any other.

Concept Differentiation: Processing data about the characteristics of two similar classes, ultimately identifying the characteristics that distinguish one class from the other.

Concept Clarification and Extension: Processing data about the characteristics of a collection of items, all of which are members of a broad class, ultimately identifying subclasses.

Generalizing: Processing data about cause-effect relationships in sample situations, ultimately arriving at an idea of the general cause-effect relationship in any such situation.

Transfer of Knowledge: Confronting new problem situations and applying known concepts and generalizations to identify and test solutions.

Attitude Clarification: Processing data concerning one's own behavior in given situations, ultimately arriving at an understanding of one's attitude in situations calling for that behavior.

Attitude Formation and/or Change: Processing data concerning new opportunities to take action in given situations, ultimately developing a changed attitude toward situations calling for such behavior.

Skill Development and/or Refinement: Processing data concerning one's own proficiency level in the performance of a task as compared with a model performance, ultimately developing a higher level of proficiency in performing such tasks. (Institute for Curriculum and Instruction, 1977)

VALUES CLARIFICATION

Traditionally, schools have been as scrupulous in separating value systems from curriculum content as the country has been in separating church from state. Only the behavioral codes and judgments that are inherent in a democracy may be taught in the classroom to help children prepare for responsible citizenship. Any subject that seems to be sectarian or doctrinaire has to be ignored or else objectified as another course of study. Educators are often warned by school boards not to tamper with children's internal beliefs and to defer instead to the family as the primary source of influence. This separation of mentality from morals has affected standards of excellence, too. To this day, students are honored at school almost always for the superiority of their scholarship and almost never for the high-mindedness of their values. Credos are considered private matters, not to be examined too closely and critically. Even the gifted, who often show special interest in such matters, quickly learn that they are off limits from discussion in class. There is certainly no educational reward for polishing one's profoundest convictions as there is for honing one's scholarly aptitudes.

Although conscience will probably never compete strongly with intellect for attention at school, there are signs that it may not remain virtually neglected, either. Teachers allow children to recognize their emotions, thereby avoiding a sense of moral aimlessness and nihilism. The method used, known as *values clarification*, avoids indoctrinating children on what to believe but rather helps them develop and elucidate their own sense of beliefs. Raths, Harin, and Simon (1966) suggest methods that teachers can use to help students become aware of their beliefs and the behaviors they prize and would be willing to uphold in and out of the classroom. Students are encouraged to think of alternative beliefs, weigh the pros and cons of these options, and consider whether their actions match their stated beliefs, and if not, why not.

Guidelines for Values Clarification

Teachers who help children to define and act according to their belief systems are basically uncritical of these beliefs. They may correct students on facts, but they make it clear that there are no right or wrong answers. In offering their own points of view, they are careful to describe these opinions as their own judgments, not as final answers. Nobody is allowed to monopolize discussions or to act so authoritatively as to discourage children from being honest with themselves in formulating their values. The atmosphere has to be open and nonjudgmental to encourage diversity and to discourage censure for expressing opinions that may not be popular. Children can have a right to pass — that is, not to express any opinion — if they choose to safeguard their privacy that way. Such inhibitions may be overcome, however, if values clarification is conducted in an atmosphere free of criticism or excessive probing into reasons behind the opinions that individuals express.

The teacher should be especially careful to avoid asking questions that students may consider threatening, particularly in regard to controversial issues. Pointed "either/or" and "yes/no" questions are not easy for reluctant participants to handle; they often feel less intimidated if they are encouraged to consider a wide range of beliefs and the possible consequences of these points of view. Throughout the exercises in values clarification, the teacher has to demonstrate skills of probing and listening to convince all children that this is not a game of prying loose precious secrets but rather a way of dealing wisely with profound individual concerns and social issues.

Some Values Clarification Strategies

Voting provides a simple means by which every student can make a public affirmation on a variety of issues. It develops the realization that people often differ in the judgment of right and wrong. The children can recognize such disagreements among themselves if they are given the opportunity to vote on such questions as, "Are there times when cheating is justified?" "Would you raise your children more strictly than you were raised?" Voting can be used to explore such issues as race relations, ecology, geopolitics, energy conservation, and other present concerns. A list of issues is drawn up by teachers and students, and everybody is invited to render an opinion with or without supporting arguments. The teacher votes, too, but waits until after students have stated their views so as not to influence their decisions. Everybody is also given the right to "pass," and this privilege has to be respected at all times.

Rank ordering gives students practice in choosing from among alternatives as well as affirming and defending their choices. The children respond to questions by rank ordering the possible responses given to them by the questioner. For example, "Whose death through assassination would you consider the greatest loss?" (a) Martin Luther King (b) John F. Kennedy (c) Mahatma Ghandi (d) Abraham Lincoln; "Which of the following issues would you give the lowest priority today?" (a) space (b) poverty (c) defense (d) ecology. Students name their choices, ordering them by degree of importance, and the teacher then asks for alternative rankings. This exercise can be used to spark lively discussion, to clarify different points of view, and to give children an opportunity to reconsider their beliefs in the light of other possibilities.

Forced-choice exercises require students to distinguish between traits that characterize them and the ones that do not. A child might be asked, "With which do you identify most, a Cadillac or a Volkswagen?" The two alternatives are posted on separate sides of the room, and each child is asked to move either to the Cadillac or Volkswagen poster, thus dividing the class into two groups that differ in their self-perceptions. The children within each group then find partners with whom they can discuss the reasons for their sharing the same opinions. This forced-choice process may be repeated with five or six questions.

Listing twenty things you love to do is a familiar task to many children. After expressing their preferences on paper, the children may be asked to place various symbols next to each activity on the list, including a dollar sign for the ones that cost money, an "A" before the things they like to do alone, a "P" next to pipedreams, an "R" next to realistic expectations, and any other possibilities that help to reveal the details about children's tastes.

A values grid may help to clarify the fact that few of our beliefs and actions fit all the valuing processes. As the teacher names some general issues, such as population control, race relations, pollution, and international relations, students list them on these rows of a grid in which the columns are numbered from one to seven to indicate degrees of importance. The student then checks the appropriate cell for each issue to indicate how much concern should be invested in it. In this exercise, the children are not challenged to defend the content of their beliefs but rather to evaluate why they feel more strongly about some issues than others.

The forced-choice ladder exercise requires students to make choices among competing values. Since the list can contain more than a dozen items, considerable thought is required to evaluate the relative importance of given alternatives and their consequences as well. Sample item: "A man cheats on his income tax, but he gives to the church all of the monies he saves by cheating." The students then rank order the items on a ladder of importance to show the strength of their feeling about each issue.

A values continuum helps students to move away from dogmatic thinking and realize that in judging many issues there is good reason for moderation. For example, the teacher raises questions about the extent to which rents for apartments should be controlled. A line is then drawn on the chalkboard denoting the range of possible opinions from "complete control" to "no control," and students are asked to place a check somewhere along the line depending on how they feel about the issue. Children should examine the pros and cons carefully and fairly before rendering an opinion. It is important to encourage children to take a stand after weighing alternatives and not to avoid controversy by simply placing marks at the middle of the line. A variation of this technique, called *spread of opinion* helps students to see the wide range of possible positions they can take on any given issue. Small groups may discuss such controversial issues as the legalization of abortion or marijuana and then indicate where they stand on such matters. The purpose of the exercise is to free students from narrow, unimaginative, uninformed, or timid approaches to questions that are difficult to answer.

Through a strategy called the *public interview* students affirm and explain their stand on various value judgments in response to questions posed to them by their teacher in the presence of their peers. A sample interview sequence might be, "Will you be a cigarette smoker? If so, why? If not, why not?" A variation of this technique is the group interview in which the same process is used with small groups, thus giving students an opportunity to share their values on a more intimate basis. Children might also be asked to develop a series of statements of what they have learned (e.g., I learned that people_____) and things they wonder about (e.g., I wonder how come _____). The first type of question is intended to help the child to understand that learning takes place all the time; the second exercise is intended to vivify how much more there is to learn.

In an exercise called *partner risk*, students are asked to find partners who are not their close friends and to share with them the high and low points of their lives during the week. The teacher then attempts to determine how children feel about disclosing intimacies to strangers. It is also important to find out how much interest the listeners show in the information they are receiving and how much sharing occurs between partners. In addition to learning how to interact on sensitive matters, the children learn to develop a sense of openness and trust with each other.

A strategy called *risk ratio* is designed to help students determine what are the proper circumstances for affirming their ideas, feelings, and actions publicly. At times it would be self-defeating or counterproductive to reveal innermost feelings to anybody who is willing to listen; there are other times when excessive secrecy about such feelings is a sign of cowardice or defeatism. To help children tell the difference, the teacher asks them to write down any opinions that they think are risky to express. Each child then lists separately the benefits and risks involved in making no secret of such beliefs. After considering the lists of pros and cons and assigning numerical values to them, the children write essays describing how they feel about such a sensitive matter. They should be able to justify their positions if they have weighed both sides of the argument thoughtfully in advance.

In an exercise called *the pie of life*, students take an inventory of how they spend their time, money, or energy. The totality of expenditures is in the form of a pie, which may then be cut into different-sized wedges that are then labeled for the activities or possessions they represent. Thus, for example, some children may devote larger slices of time to socializing with peers than to watching television or studying school subjects, while the pie of life for others may show different allocation patterns. Any decision to make changes is up to each individual.

The *cave-in simulation* is a popular exercise for helping children discover critical feelings they have about themselves. Students pretend that they are trapped in a cave-in hundreds of feet below ground level, and there is only a narrow passageway leading to safety. The person at the head of the line has the best chance to escape, as further rock falls may occur at any moment. Each child is then asked to explain why he or she should be first in line. The reasons may center around the meaning and purpose of life or what the individual could contribute to the welfare of others. Much can be revealed about the children's self-images when they are forced to justify their continued existence as a precondition to surviving that cave-in.

Values Clarification Through Curriculum Content

While many teachers concentrate on values clarification as a separate experience, unrelated to the school's conventional course of study, it is also possible to incorporate the valuing process into various subject areas in the curriculum. Almost any discipline can be learned at the factual, conceptual, and values levels. For example, elementary school children are taught many facts about the Pilgrims' escape from religious intolerance in England, their sailing to Holland where they enjoyed freedom of worship, the reasons they chose to leave Holland and establish their own community in the Western hemisphere, the physical hardships they endured during their first venture in America, and the help they received from friendly American Indians in planting crops and reaping a rich harvest. The concepts involved in this study include prejudice, cultural assimilation, immigration, life in the wilderness, helping behaviors, and ritual ceremonies.

The teacher might ask such questions as, "Why did the Pilgrims have trouble practicing their religion in England? What are the meanings of religious freedom and prejudice against religious practice?" With the facts and concepts thus established, it is now possible to move to the values level where children relate the Pilgrims' story to their own lives. In so doing, they are encouraged to analyze, clarify, and affirm their own beliefs pertaining to issues that grow out of the Pilgrims' story. They talk about harboring and being victimized by prejudice and ways of combatting it. They also explore how membership in an ethnic minority can be viewed with pride by those who identify with its traditions, whereas others can see it as the cause of their being targets of bigotry. In clarifying their own attitudes toward other groups identified by language, religion, skin color, or geographic origins, the children might be asked to indicate their preferences (if any) for the kinds of people they would like to have as neighbors, friends, and even members of their family through marriage.

There are many other value-laden issues pertaining to prejudice that deserve review. Some represent a conflict of ideals, such as the choice between preserving cultural pluralism and creating a "melting pot" of nationalities; others involve a conflict of tactics, such as the choice between peaceful demonstration and violent protest on behalf of civil rights; and others still require new solutions to old problems such as "blockbusting" and "red-lining."

It is not always easy to deal with curriculum content at the values level, since much of what is taught at school is too remote from the intimate concerns of students. Sometimes well-intentioned teachers strain to create meaning in subject matter even where there is none that children can appreciate, and this leads to wasting time on counterfeit views. It may not be possible to graft values clarification onto every topic in a course of study, nor should every topic be judged for its importance solely on the basis of whether such a grafting is possible. Some subjects lend themselves to a clarification of personal values and others do not, and the teacher has to distinguish between them before planning classroom discussions. At times it is even worthwhile to develop a unit of content strictly for its potential in leading to personal issues. This would constitute a break in the general practice of building values clarification on subjects that are already in the curriculum.

Thus we see that dealing with moral and ethical issues in the classroom is beginning to gain some significance, possibly because educators see an erosion of traditional values and a realignment of social structures that are forcing people to redefine and reconsider their long-standing beliefs. Gifted children may someday exert an inordinate amount of influence on this rapidly changing world, and they need to support their leadership influence with a set of their own beliefs arrived at wisely and methodically. Much is at stake in their developing deep understanding of self and others and a social consciousness as well. For the gifted as well as the nongifted, ethical behavior arises neither out of psychological disposition nor instinct but, rather, from their learning what humanistic conduct means to them and then acting accordingly.

Chapter 21

A Proposed Enrichment Matrix

What has been summarized thus far is a sampling of educational paradigms from which programs for the gifted are often derived. The range is intended to be representative rather than exhaustive so that practitioners may become aware of the ideas that predominate in the field. There are, of course, instances where particular localities formulate enrichment designs around their own models. Unfortunately, however, only in rare instances do schools fit their plans for differentiated education into a conceptual framework such as the ones discussed here. Many so-called "enrichment" exercises consist of nothing more than brain twisters, conundrums, and puzzles that may be attractive to anybody whose mind craves such stimulation. But the effect is that of a quick fix, satisfying for the moment or even intoxicating for as long as the supply lasts, while the complex needs and capacities of the gifted child remain largely ignored.

The existing paradigms for enrichment offer educators a conceptual basis on which to build their programs. Most models stress the need for cultivating advanced competencies in cognition, especially divergent production in one form or another, and suggest the techniques for accomplishing this aim systematically. The assumption is that higher-level cognitive processes are vital to excellence in any area of productivity or performance and should therefore be featured in programs for the gifted. In short, it takes a thorough understanding of how the gifted mind works and how to train it to optimum efficiency to make enrichment comprehensive rather than haphazard.

There are other commonalities among various models worth considering before adopting any for local use. For example, most of them were not designed especially for the gifted in the sense that they address the question, "What ought to be special about curriculum for these children, and why?" Instead, they offer some thorough-going and imaginative ways of "stretching the minds" of people at *all* levels. Such popular paradigms as Gordon's Synectics and the Osborn-Parnes Principles of Creative Problem Solving are useful for any students who can benefit from the kinds of cognitive stimulation they outline, not just the gifted who need the exercises to help them realize their potential for excellence. In other words, differentiated education is what individuals derive from the *same* curriculum according to their separate capacities rather than a *separate* curriculum reserved for a select few.

Most children can probably benefit more or less from instruction on ways in which to think creatively and critically, except that the gifted succeed at it better than the others as a result of such training. However, the effects of training children to use complex cognitive skills is by no means clear. André (1979) concludes from his review of existing evidence that, when children receive exercises in answering higher-level questions related to written material, it probably deepens their knowledge of the content. The problem is that research methodology on the subject is often flawed, thus making it impossible to determine the conditions under which such facilitation occurs. None of the studies in André's review deals with the question of whether higher-level cognition should be emphasized more or differently in the education of children with higher cognitive abilities, or whether these students could be helped in some special way from such training.

But even if the gifted and the nongifted alike benefited most from stimulation of the same advanced thinking skills, what could be said about their respective courses of study? Is it unnecessary to provide gifted children with differentiated curriculum content? Can enrichment be characterized exclusively as something the gifted take out of their educational experience without the teacher's having to put anything special into it? There are, of course, instances where an instructional model is applied directly to subject matter, as in the case of Taba's system, which is reflected in a complete social studies program. However, the material is apparently designed for children at all ability levels, not just the brightest. One of the three dimensions of Williams's model incorporates the various common branch subjects of a curriculum, but here, too, there is no clear indication that the content should be adjusted according to children's ability levels. Still, it is expected that the gifted will accomplish more than the nongifted because they are better able to apply sophisticated thought processes to what is essentially the same substantive material.

The Enrichment Triad (Renzulli, 1977) seems to be one of the few paradigms to propose special content for the gifted. The topics are referred to as "real problems," selected by able and motivated students themselves, not by teachers or by a curriculum council. Renzulli seems to have little regard for an honors-type, "presented" curriculum on the grounds that it is too rigid and therefore cannot satisfy each child's personal tastes for knowledge and productive activity. One might add another benefit to this policy of student self-direction: by shifting the initiative from teacher to student in deciding what (if anything) should be an enriched learning experience, it is hard to accuse schools of practicing elitism. The only way in which they could possibly play favorites is by allowing some students and denying others the opportunity to pursue their separate interests. Yet these advantages may be bought at too high a price if it means sacrificing school-packaged enrichment entirely. To restrain educators from planning scholarly or artistic curricula for the gifted could amount either to short-changing these children or to denying that their teachers are qualified to offer them much of substance.

PRELIMINARY CONSIDERATIONS

Most of the best known models of enrichment give the impression that a teacher of the gifted is an educational facilitator whose job is primarily to help the children sharpen their thought processes and only secondarily to dispense knowledge. An alternative approach would be to establish a greater balance between the two roles, with the understanding that *what* to learn has to be given as much attention as *how* to learn. The proposed enrichment matrix is an attempt to bring about such a balance by amalgamating elements of existing paradigms and adding components that are deemed essential to differentiated programs for the gifted. The framework is predicated on some underlying assumptions or, more specifically, responses to questions concerning the nature of talent and the objectives of educational enrichment.

Who Qualifies as Gifted?

One basic premise is that gifted children are the tiny minority we suspect may someday produce important new theories, inventions, discoveries, artistic masterpieces, and solutions to monumental problems in order to enhance the human condition. Included also are those who show promise as exemplary performers in drama, medicine, teaching, politics and diplomacy, social and clinical service, and in any other way that preserves, prolongs, or adds meaning to life. Excluded are those who can do no better than consume and appreciate ideas, even though they score well on familiar measures of mastery and constitute the best known pool from which the gifted are most likely to be located.

It is therefore not enough for an enriched curriculum to consist of high-volume content to satisfy the needs of precocious children who are capable of absorbing large amounts of knowledge rapidly and efficiently. It also has to teach students how to tease out the subtleties and profundities of great ideas and how to mobilize their own creative impulses in order to produce new knowledge. Understandably, the gifted will benefit most from these kinds of emphases. Equally important, the way in which children respond to such nurturance will help to distinguish between those who are likely someday to become highly capable readers of history, philosophy, or literature and those who may develop into historians, philosophers, and literateurs. The latter require a great amount of exposure to their fields of competence and also special assistance in ways of expanding these fields.

What Qualifies as an Appropriate Curriculum?

A second premise is that a distinction has to be made between what may be called "enrichment provisions" and "enrichment programs." Although many schools claim to be doing something special for the gifted, what they really mean is that they are offering ad hoc provisions, defined here as fragmentary learning experiences lacking in complex form, long-range purpose, or clear directionality.

A teacher in the third grade who is committed to exposing children to extra subject matter may devote a half-year to teaching them the skills of raising chicks and then spend another half-year on an introduction to computer programming. The choice of topics reflects the special interest and knowledge of that teacher; another teacher of third-graders may have an affinity for the poetry of Edgar Allen Poe, in which case that would become the subject of enrichment. When these teachers have to be replaced for any reason, the newcomers will introduce different projects rather than duplicate the efforts of their predecessors. There is nothing in the second-grade classroom that prepares the gifted for what is to come a year later, and there is nothing in the fourth-grade curriculum that follows up the enrichment provisions of the preceding year. Nor are any of the special projects for gifted third-graders recorded anywhere in the school's curriculum outlines as part of the general scope and sequence. A lay board and a professional staff may be enthusiastic about the enrichment provisions in their schools, but this is not always a sign of commitment. It could mean only that the community is proud to have something extra and attractive in the curriculum and is willing to pay for the luxury for as long as there is enough popular support. When pressures to do something special for the gifted begin to moderate, or when budgetary cuts have to be made, enrichment provisions are seen as expendable ornaments to the general courses of study.

Many people who favor "extras" for the gifted are probably disappointed to see provisional offerings discarded; yet it is not considered nearly as calamitous as dropping science or literature from the curriculum. The "extras" are provisions, whereas science and literature are programs. There is never any question about whether a program should be retained. It is an educational imperative, declared so by tradition and popular acclaim and is therefore part of the lifeblood of the total curriculum. It is designed by a curriculum committee and codified in the school records as a comprehensive, sequential plan that commands attention by the lay board and professional staff and is supported solidly by a school budget. It is permissible to revise programs, as in the case of converting to a "new" mathematics, but it would be unthinkable to drop mathematics altogether. Whoever steps in to teach at any grade level can consult the curriculum plan to gain an impression of what the children had studied in the past, which leads up to what they are covering in the present and which, in turn, prepares them for what they will encounter in the future. On the other hand, provisions are educational electives that are never taken as seriously as imperatives, are rarely articulated from one grade level to the next, and are always vulnerable to extinction.

Unfortunately, most of what schools proclaim as their programmatic designs for enrichment are really provisional and probably shortlived. Even Renzulli's (1980) "revolving door" concept that allows the gifted to move into and out of the investigation of what he calls "real problems" can be interpreted and implemented more easily within the framework of enrichment provisions than enrichment programs, especially since these problems are taken as they come out of the interest patterns of children who happen to be at hand. The practitioner would have to remember to incorporate the procedure regularly into classroom instruction, even if the curriculum content keeps changing. The advantages are that moving gifted children into time-limited projects of their own choosing takes care of their individual enthusiasm, yet reduces the possible adverse effects of separating them from peers and conventional school activities. However, there is always the danger of regarding special projects as "icing on the cake" rather than as part of the basic meal for those capable of digesting it. Also, if the "revolving door" method is poorly administered, it will serve only the self-starting, independent-minded children who pursue their interests doggedly, while neglecting those who rely on external stimulation.

How Important Is Enrichment ?

A third premise is that enrichment for the gifted is as much an educational imperative as is the "common core" for the general school population. The curriculum design should resemble the flag of Japan, a large circle imposed on a larger rectangular field (see Figure 21-1). The circle represents the "common core" experiences for all children, gifted and nongifted. Included in the "common core" are skills, knowledge, insights, and opportunities for creative initiative that all students need in order to appreciate and function well in the world they inhabit. Unfortunately, the gifted are sometimes denied training in these competencies when teachers would rather plunge ahead to more advanced subject matter. The consequences can be embarrassing when some of these children have difficulty with everyday basics such as dealing with number combinations or putting together a grammatically correct sentence in their native tongue, to say nothing of writing with style and power. This "common core" is the fixed sine qua non of the school's offerings and therefore is programmatic rather than provisional.

The area beyond the circle represents enrichment experience open on a trial basis to any child suspected of having talent and reserved for those whose signs of talent are unmistakable. It is programmatic and therefore as much an educational imperative for the gifted population as the "common core" is for all children. As such, the real test of the school's commitment to educating the gifted is the extent to which the Japanese flag design remains intact as a rectangle without being cut back to the boundaries of the inner circle and then decorated with some temporary frills along the edge.

The idea of reserving educational experiences exclusively for the gifted may sound like favoritism, but it is not favoritism with prejudice. Instead, it represents

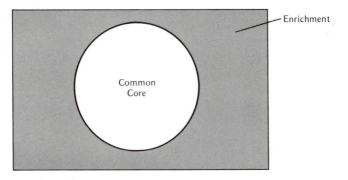

Figure 21-1 Framework of a program for the gifted

equal educational opportunity in the sense that it helps to meet the educational needs of all children without neglecting those who have the potential for excellence. The young athlete who shows promise of competing effectively in international sports deserves and receives special instructions, training gear, dietary adjustments, rest schedules, and practice sessions. Without these privileges, there is no chance for peak performance. Yet only the few with a potential for stardom can make the most of such a regimen or even withstand its rigors. That is why the coaching they receive is an equitable privilege for them. Similarly, plasma physics should be taught to the tiny number of students who can absorb it even though it "discriminates" against the huge majority who find it intellectually obscure. These are not violations of fair play but rather ways of individualizing instruction for children at the upper extreme of the ability continuum.

Where Should Enrichment Be Offered?

The final premise is that, to maximize enrichment for the gifted, it is necessary to enlist assistance beyond the school building, resources, and schedules. The range of abilities and interests of gifted children is so wide that the school is actually a restrictive environment for them. A fifth-grader who can benefit from experience in medical research or an introduction to law practice is not likely to find much help among the people and materials at school. In fact, the aggregate range of knowledge of gifted children in a single school is often broader and deeper than is that of the entire teaching staff in the children's fields of interests. What they need is an opportunity for apprenticeships with selected professionals in the community who are capable of elevating them to new heights of inquiry in their separate pursuits. This also opens up possibilities for career guidance in real-life settings where productivity is accomplished in the context of occupations. It does not mean that the school can divest itself of responsibility for the children by "shipping them out" to places where people are better qualified to take care of their needs during and after school hours. The community professional may be more steeped in knowledge, but it takes a trained educator to "package" it into a meaningful learning experience for children. School personnel have to be on hand to help gifted children understand the meaning of their encounter with the occupational world while accomplishing as much as they can in their off-campus studies.

THE ENRICHMENT MATRIX AND ITS APPLICATIONS

Based on the foregoing premises, it is possible to conceptualize an enrichment model in the form of a grid with the rows denoting content areas and the columns consisting of three sections labeled (1) *content adjustment*, (2) *cognitive processes*, and (3) *personal and social consequences* (see Figure 21-2). The task of planning differentiated education involves filling in the cells with a graduated sequence of activities that represent the best thinking and commitment of a duly appointed curriculum committee, not just a single teacher or an informal group of staff members whose ideas stand little chance of becoming official policy. One of the most serious matters that the committee has to consider is the time frame in which it is allowed to do its planning. Administrators are sometimes under pressure to develop a viable curriculum for the gifted practically overnight. In the rush to get something underway quickly, they find themselves settling for provisional enrichment that can materialize in short order and may be useful as a quick palliative, but anything so makeshift has no lasting strength.

Programmatic enrichment, on the other hand, takes a long time to plan, longer to implement, and much longer to fade. Designing it requires as much hard work and imagination as writing a new K-12 curriculum in a major subject area without having access to the old one or to any other for that matter as a source for ideas. The parent whose gifted child is bored in the fifth grade is understandably impatient and would rather settle for provisions than wait for a program that may not be ready for implementation until the child is already in high school. It is therefore suggested that the curriculum committee work on two plans simultaneously, one to deal with short-range needs (since doing something for the gifted is better than doing nothing) and another to be put into place at a later time (when doing something for the gifted can give way to doing what is best for them). The enrichment matrix is far more concerned with the longer perspective while taking some note of the shorter one as well.

Selection of Curriculum Content

Content areas include the conventional disciplines that make up the common core (e.g., language arts, mathematics, sciences, social studies, the performing arts) plus at least one supplemental area of study not generally included in the precollege curriculum (e.g., cultural anthropology, geopolitics, psychology, studies in ecology)

Content Areas/ Disciplines	Content Adjustments					Higher Level Cognitive Processes	Social and Affective Consequences
	Telescoping Common Core	Expansion of Basic Skills	Programatic Augmentation	Provisional Augmentation	Out-of-School Augmentation		
Language arts							
Mathematics							
Sciences							
Social studies							
Music							
Art							
Literature							
Supplementary area I							
Supplementary area II							
Interdisciplinary area I							
Interdisciplinary area II							
etc.							

Figure 21-2 The enrichment matrix

and interdisciplinary syntheses (e.g., humanities, aesthetics). Introducing supplementary and interdisciplinary content would demonstrate that the subject matter need not be reserved for college-level study. And if it ever is to infiltrate into the elementary or secondary school curriculum, it should start out in the form of educational enrichment that can then be adapted for study by all children. What is suggested here is part of a hypothesis that the education of exceptional children at both ends of the ability range is the forerunner of education for those who function closer to the norm. The *content* of programs for the gifted and the *methodology* of programs for the handicapped eventually affect "what" and "how" all children are taught at school.

The choice of supplementary and interdisciplinary content areas should be determined on two counts. First, so-called "newer disciplines," such as sociology, anthropology, and psychology have matured through vast amounts of research published in the present century and are ready to receive serious attention at all school levels. Second, there are topics of study, such as geopolitics and ecology, that are becoming more and more important in helping us understand the world in which we live. The gifted should not have exclusive access to any of these disciplines, but if they lead the way, the chances are that others will follow.

Enriching Curriculum Content

The first five columns of Figure 21-2 refer to *content adjustment* or the various approaches to curriculum enrichment. Each subject matter area requires its own plans according to guidelines indicated in the headings and legitimized eventually as a course of study designed in advance, accepted as an educational imperative, administered by teachers who are capable of working with the gifted, and sequenced from one grade level to the next, wherever appropriate. The grid may be used in at least two ways.

First, it is a framework for a master plan covering all disciplines to take care of the varieties of talent included in the program. This does not mean that every cell has to be filled before any action can be taken in the classroom. Quite the contrary, in the interest of saving time it is preferable to deal with only two or three content areas at the outset, and the choices may be made for the sake of convenience. Whatever subjects lend themselves to relatively quick, easy, and thorough enrichment planning are obvious first choices. It is also helpful if the talents chosen for nurturance are the ones that the community and staff clamor for most persistently and can be diagnosed with the least amount of error. For example, getting started with enrichment in academics is so much simpler and more popular than is formulating a K-12 sequence in social leadership, even though a case might be made for giving priority to the latter kinds of talent in our modern world. It would therefore be a waste of time to delay serving the needs of the academically gifted until the same could be done for young social leaders.

A second use of the matrix, every bit as important as the first, is for developing a contract with a single child who may be gifted in one or two areas and requires content adjustment only in them. Appropriate cells can then be filled in every case, thus making the overall program flexible enough to take individual differences into account. Although the contract has to be adjusted to each child's needs, whatever is written into it should come out of the master plan.

Suppose, for instance, that the master plan dealt with ways in which to enrich the program in the language arts, mathematics, the sciences, and social studies. Teachers would then have available to them a framework with details on how to adjust content for the gifted in these four subject areas. Once the total design is in hand, they can dole out parts of it in contracts with children possessing special talents. The matrix covering enrichment in mathematics would go to the mathematically gifted, and the same matching of subject area to gifted child would be arranged for language arts, the sciences, and social studies. Sometimes, the entire master plan might appear in a contract if the child in question shows enough all-around talent. Finally, the enrichment matrix encourages flexibility even within a single content area by nurturing individual student initiative as part of the overall scheme. In addition to being exposed to the same special subject matter and skills training, children possessing similar talents are helped in and out of school to pursue special topics of their own choosing. In some cases the gifted can be released to work by themselves; most often, however, they need some guidance and instruction to help them reach their goals.

One of the obvious ways of providing for individual differences between the gifted and nongifted and also among the gifted themselves is *telescoping the common core*, or teaching conventional subject matter in less time in order to move up to higher levels as quickly as possible. The logic is simple: since the pool from which gifted children tend to emerge consists mainly of rapid learners, they are likely to benefit from acceleration through courses of study in which they excel. In some curriculum areas, such as mathematics, it may be particularly important that they complete the basics in the least amount of time, thereby sparing themselves the tedium of dwelling on content that they either know already or can absorb in short order. Research evidence tends to support acceleration regardless of whether it is in the form of early admittance to school, rapid advancement through elementary, junior, or senior high school, or admittance to college with advanced standing (Gallagher, 1975). But the empirical evidence has had little impact on the schools, as educators find this type of administrative adjustment generally unattractive.

By far the strongest advocacy for acceleration has been in the field of mathematics, especially through the Study of Mathematically Precocious Youth at Johns Hopkins University. The evidence marshalled by that research team from a variety of studies has helped to focus attention on children who qualify for college-level mathematics even before they reach adolescence (George et al., 1979). Some disciplines, such as mathematics and perhaps foreign languages, probably lend themselves more readily to telescoping than do others. Literature and social studies, on the other hand, may be harder to justify because there is so much room for ancillary topics to almost anything that is covered in these subject areas. Still, the usual pace at which the nongifted are expected to progress through the common core is often too slow for gifted children, and there is no reason why they should be expected to mark time with the others when they could be accomplishing so much more at their own pace.

Another method of adjusting curriculum content for the gifted is to *expand basic skills and concepts* in preparation for important original work. Basic skills are often known as the tool subjects, relatively unimportant for their own sake, but indispensable for enabling the learner to gain access to substantive areas of study. Among the most familiar tools, of course, are reading, writing, and arithmetic. Learning how to read can be a waste of time unless it is applied to any number of situations such as understanding street signs, newspaper stories, great literature, and recorded history. Writing is also intended for any number of purposes, ranging from simple communication to composing memorable prose or poetry. Similarly, number facts have their use in the marketplace and as part of the language of higher mathematics. In short, tool subjects are necessary for mastering the conventional disciplines and for making original contributions to them and therefore serve as keys to knowledge.

It is important to keep in mind that basic skills are not uniform for all children. Even the three R's have to be modified and sometimes ignored in favor of other necessities to accommodate individual differences. For example, sign language is a tool for communication among some deaf people; the blind rely on a mastery of braille symbols, compressed speech, and various electronic devices to transact messages and on manipulating a walking stick for safe locomotion; and trainable mental retardates concentrating on a self-care curriculum need to engage in all kinds of activities for daily living through such exercises as manipulating buttons, zippers, spoons, forks, soap and water, and whatever else can help them to function independently. In these cases of exceptionality, the tool subjects are adjusted to fit the nature and needs of special populations and are understandably excluded from the curriculum of the nonhandicapped.

The same consideration should apply to the modification of basic skills and competencies for the gifted. If these children are to stand a chance of achieving excellence in the performing arts and in the service professions, or of producing knowledge in their chosen fields, not just consuming it, they need the tools for accomplishing what only they can accomplish. For example, those with unusual sensitivity to language structure can benefit from an introduction to linguistics and general semantics. Talented young writers need to learn how to express themselves in different forms of poetry, drama, and the familiar essay, in addition to mastering the conventional narrative and critical writing skills that the nongifted also study as part of the common core. And children with extraordinary reading comprehension and sensitivity to symbolism in language deserve to be taught the elements of literary criticism.

Basic skills for the young mathematician may be some extensive units in mathematical logic and the languages of computers. Children who show signs of someday becoming contributing scientists need to learn how to expand knowledge in their fields through the scientific method, which encompasses skills in finding and stating problems, developing rationales for investigating them, formulating operational hypotheses, designing plans for gathering data, and learning how to report and interpret findings. Similarly, the child with a potential for becoming an historian requires the skills of historiography, which would be wasted on a student who reads history for understanding but without any intention of creating theories about it. As for the young creative and performing artists, it is generally accepted that the basic skills training has to be special not only in the amount of time they devote to practice but also in the nature of instruction they receive.

Basically, then, the expansion of basic skills and competencies is a way of providing the gifted with the "tools of the trade" that they will need in their mature productive years. Few children can learn how to use these tools effectively, and they should not be denied that privilege even though they constitute only a minority in the schools. The potential benefits to them and to society easily outweigh any reservation people may have about enabling the relatively few gifted to excel, especially since so much has yet to be done in helping even greater numbers of children to function adequately in their studies. A program that is fair to all children does not sacrifice the needs of one subgroup for those of another. Nor should children functioning at either extreme of the ability continuum have to live up or down to the basic skills requirements that apply to the vast majority whose level of performance is closer to the mean.

A third type of curriculum adjustment is in the form of *programmatic augmen-*

tation. The term "programmatic" is used in a special sense, defined earlier as subject matter that is prescribed, sequential, and a permanent part of the curriculum, rather than an occasional frill. Telescoping the common core and expanding basic skills and competencies are also forms of programmatic adjustment, except that they deal with different kinds of content, the first with curriculum material required of all children and the second with tools of learning necessary to achieve excellence. Here, the reference is again to the common core, but this time the charge to the curriculum planning committee is to develop a course of study for each discipline that adds dimensionality to the conventional curriculum.

Thus, for example, the study of folk tales as literature might be supplemented by cross-cultural comparisons of the content of such stories and how they might reflect on the societies from which they originate. In mathematics and science, virtually every topic can be studied in greater depth with the help of supplementary material, instructions, and exercises. In history, an examination of causes of the Civil War may also include a parallel investigation of European policy toward the Union and the Confederacy during that period. Or the children may be helped to understand history through art, music, and literature instead of relying solely on the conventional political, military, and economic data contained in so many textbooks. Conversely, music, art, and literature might be better understood in the context of historical milieus.

The purpose of programmatic augmentation is to expand gifted children's knowledge base laterally to sharpen their perspectives and to help them determine what kinds of new knowledge should be developed. In many schools, this kind of enrichment is called an "honors program" or an "honors curriculum" and is presented by teachers as the scope and sequence open to those who can absorb it successfully. The rationale is that ideas often beget ideas and that children capable of learning more and better ones are most likely to create more and better ones.

However, programmatic augmentation should never be confused with "more of the same" exercises that fill up the child's time with busy work and little else. Teachers are sometimes misled by a gifted student's work habits that are disciplined enough to be applied devotedly even to unimportant activity. The problem in such a situation is that there are no signs of boredom to reveal there is something wrong. The only clues are in the augmented program itself, which has to be examined on its own merits, even if it seems to satisfy the child's desire to be preoccupied with some kind of educational activity, however trivial it may be.

A fourth type of content adjustment is *provisional augmentation*. The term "provisional" is used here in the special way in which it was defined earlier as referring to enrichment activities that are fragmentary, teacher bound, lacking in sequence, and transitory additions to the common core curriculum. Yet there is room for provisional augmentation for two reasons. First, teachers should serve as role models despite the real possibility of their having to profess a fair amount of ignorance in the fields that their gifted children excel. They can do it by cultivating their own passionate cultural interests in any field, be it raising chicks, learning computer technology, studying ancient Chinese pottery or Gustav Mahler's music, or examining anything that fires their imaginations and that they are willing to share enthusiastically with the gifted. They can thus show by example how important it is to possess knowledge, not just the skills to help others find it.

Second, if a teacher shows enthusiasm for a particular field of interest, it may have a contagious effect on some gifted children and inspire them to delve into those fields in the hopes of making a contribution to them someday. Almost any biography or autobiography of a celebrated individual contains some reference to the decisive influence of a teacher or mentor who had enough attachment to a particular subject area to stimulate the kind of inquiry that carried at least one person to greatness.

To introduce provisional augmentation, the teacher has to serve not only as a manager of learning activity who can help gifted children locate and generate ideas, but also as a possessor and dispenser of knowledge. The easiest first step toward building a program for the gifted is to allow such teachers to initiate provisions based on their own cultural strengths. Such plans can be made in short order without investment of new resources. Too often, however, the schools become complacent with provisions, especially if the effects are to satisfy the children and pacify the clamorers for enrichment. Under the circumstances, it is easy to forget that introducing special provisions is only the first of two goals and, by far, the easier one to reach; reaching the second goal of designing and implementing a full-scale program for the gifted is far more difficult. But the qualitative differences between provisions and programs make the effort worthwhile. Appendix A, prepared by Donald J. Treffinger, contains a listing of instructional resources that can help teachers to get enrichment provisions underway quickly and effectively.

Provisional augmentation may reflect the student's individual interests as well the teacher's. Either way, the possibilities should be open for children to engage in independent activity according to their respective enthusiasms and work habits. The gifted may engage in what Renzulli calls "real problems" on or off campus, and these projects can turn out to be important episodes in the children's education if enough care is given to the logistics of carrying out such goal-directed activity. Too often, practitioners assume that children who are highly motivated and qualified to embark on projects that reflect their areas of interest are necessarily capable of working their way through to the end without help or supervision. Gifted children who are left to their own devices frequently flounder and fail to finish their work, or if they manage to turn in a completed product or performance, the quality is embarrassingly low. There are, of course, exceptions among the gifted who are single-minded in their dedication to independent work and who can be relied on to take all necessary initiatives in assembling and organizing the best possible resources and to finish the job brilliantly. However, the gifted do not necessarily have that kind of self-discipline, and their initial enthusiasm is liable to wane unless they are kept on task every step along the way.

A fifth type of curriculum adjustment is accomplished through *out-of-school augmentation* and is programmatic in nature. Gifted children need opportunities to apprentice with outstanding producers and performers in the field at the sites where innovative work takes place. There are at least four kinds of benefits to be gained from such activity. An obvious one is the opportunity for in-depth learning in a setting and under instruction that cannot be matched at school. In a real sense, the gifted can use the field experience to extend their knowledge base through the use of higher-level thinking processes and advanced communication and study skills.

In one career exploration program for gifted students (Jefferson County Public Schools, 1978), children receive credit for working successfully in specific content areas related to the field experience. For example, a student seeking art credit for serving as an architecture intern negotiates learning objectives with an art teacher at school. This is done by ascertaining specific ways of applying the art objectives to satisfy both academic and internship requirements. This task is left to a "learning manager" who serves as liasion, coordinating activities between the school and the internship site. Such a person may be described best as a combination educator and counselor. The learning manager makes it possible for gifted children to receive the best possible help in and out of school in initiating and completing real-life projects that are worthy of potential leaders in various fields of inquiry.

A second benefit to be derived from working in the field with gifted people who are in midcareer is the opportunity to absorb various life skills that are important for productive work in many fields. Included are such personal and social competencies as leadership, conflict resolution, trust building, and collegiality with other productive people. There is also the need to learn special techniques for decision making, through brainstorming and flexible responses to obstacles, and to demonstrate steadily increasing independence through initiative, resourcefulness, and the management of time. As might be expected, the learning manager figures prominently as a personal counselor in facilitating life-skills growth among the gifted.

The third advantage of out-of-school augmentation, as suggested in the Jefferson County program (1978), is that the learning manager can help gifted children in their career development. Through guided experiences in the field, students clarify career interests and aptitudes and increase their knowledge of occupational opportunities. They also increase their familiarity with requirements for entering and progressing in the world of work. By improving the child's knowledge of career options and individual proclivities, it is hoped that the best possible match will be made between the person and the occupation.

There is a fourth benefit implied but not detailed in the Jefferson County program that is as important in its own way as are the other three. It has to do with all the psychosocial adaptations necessary to succeed in any area of work. Children serving as interns with people in high-level occupations realize immediately that each job has its own life-style requirements for success, regardless of ability. In addition, there are life-style norms that interns can examine from close-up to see how willing they are to live by them. For example, if the research scientist customarily engages in research projects lasting a year or two, or even longer, a certain capacity for delaying gratification is necessary. It may even involve frustration tolerance if results do not emerge as expected. Is the gifted young science student interning in the field laboratory able to live that way? If the mentor's kind of work is in fits and starts, in which around-the-clock activity alternates with a far less frantic schedule, what are the effects on such a person's married life? Would the young apprentice want to enter such a profession even if it may cause strains in the relationship with a spouse? What are the mentor's dress codes and how do they conform with those of colleagues in the profession? If the male tends toward pin-striped suits, button-down collars, a clean shaven face or a carefully cropped beard, neatly combed hair, a stylish tie, and polished shoes, does the intern see himself fitting such an image? Similar questions about conformity and dress codes can be asked of the females.

Sometimes, the realities associated with careers can lead to disillusionment, as in the case of a child who aspires to a career in veterinary medicine because of a love for animals, but is placed in an internship with veterinarians who do not share that love. The child sees them, instead, as occupying places in their profession only for the sake of financial security and social status. These perceived motives can be eye-openers to the young intern, and it takes an off-campus apprenticeship to help the child experience them at all.

Considering the conditions of success in high-level careers, it is obvious that the worlds of education and work are vastly different and that the qualifications for excellence in one do not always apply to the other. This has important implications for identifying talent. Instruments used for locating children with potentialities for excelling at school lay heavy stress on intellective strengths that are nurtured in the classroom. Nonintellective factors are also considered, but they focus on goal-directedness, persistence, self-reliance, and special interests that serve the school's purposes adequately. However, they are not sufficient to tease out the specific basic life skills, career interests and aptitudes, and life-style inclinations that are so intimately associated with excellence in high-level occupations.

It is therefore not easy to place gifted children in appropriate internships on the basis of their performance at school. The high-IQ, highly motivated honor student may show great interest in a career of serving innovatively the needs of adult mental retardates who are institutionalized. When placed in such a residential facility, the student quickly learns that many hours have to be spent in teaching the adults not to injure themselves. Can the high IQ be a sign that the young intern will *not* be bored or even discouraged by such a seemingly tedious instructional routine? Since it is so difficult to know in advance how to establish a goodness-of-fit between the child and the internship, the exploratory aspects of out-of-school augmentation become important ways of determining who qualifies for what kind of high-level work.

Combined with apprenticeship experiences, the study of biography and auto-biography can help to orient the gifted to careers and excellence in them. This material provides children with insight into the lives of the celebrated, with some emphasis on the joys and travails in the work they did. It is a vicarious "shadow-ing" experience that enables the reader to follow great people from one adventure to the next while learning about their innermost feelings in the process. Appendix B lists biographies, autobiographies, and works of fiction dealing with how it feels to be gifted in various fields of productivity and performance. The gifted should also be allowed to "shadow" highly able live people at their places of work in the community, including the college campus, law office, hospital laboratory, dance studio, editorial office, and wherever else productive activity takes place. It gives the child an opportunity to raise meaningful questions about the work being done and to explore different occupations as part of the preparation for an apprenticeship that involves on-site training.

Cultivating Cognitive Power

Out-of-school augmentation is one of the five proposed means of adjusting conventional curricula; the others include *telescoping common core subjects, expanding basic skills and competencies, programmatic augmentation*, and *provisional augmentation*. In addition to modifying *content*, there is also a need to emphasize high-level *cognitive processes* as they apply to each of the subject matter areas. Fortunately, the literature on educational enrichment is itself rich in designs for stimulating the gifted student's intellect. Each of the instructional models described in Chapter 20 places heavy emphasis on complex problem-finding and -solving strategies. All these approaches provide guidance for teachers and curriculum planners to nurture gifted children's cognitive strengths. In addition, they reflect what Newland (1976) called "a sensitivity to the importance of the progression from the perceptual or low conceptual level to the higher conceptual kinds of cognitive operations" (p. 154).

As important as it is to help the child deal successfully with complex intellectual processes, the methods of administering such assistance would have to be considered with special care in order to produce the desired effect on the child. Sometimes, teachers are content to deal with cognitive operations out of context in the hope that it will "train the mind." Unfortunately, there is no solid evidence to show a carry-over from proficiency in these exercises to more advanced mastery of subject matter in the curriculum. There is also no universal consensus as to what constitutes the cognitive hierarchy or where a given problem-finding or -solving operation belongs in such a hierarchy. It is therefore advisable that the teacher accept as reasonable many ideas for cultivating higher-level thinking processes, as suggested in the various paradigms for enrichment, without neglecting to apply them to the curriculum and without prejudging how complex each operation is in comparison to any other.

The following suggestions to teachers are intended as examples to illustrate, *not* to blueprint, activities in the classroom that may add meaning to the gifted child's learning experiences:

1. Ask children to look at the shoes they are wearing (or at any familiar sight) and perceive something physical or functional that they had never noticed before. The same exercise can be applied to the Bill of Rights or the Gettysburg Address, *after* the children have read it so many times that it would seem pointless to expect any more benefit to be derived from another reading. Well-known poetry, essays, stories, art, music, and even scientific and mathe-

matical phenomena lend themselves to rediscovery and reinterpretation. It is all part of making the familiar strange in order to take a fresh approach to its understanding.

2. Ask children how they would improve on the welfare of dogs, birds, the poor in their community, underdeveloped nations, their families, and perhaps even themselves. The purpose is to show that brainstorming can be deadly serious and is a skill that is often applied to solve some of the most critical problems in society.

3. Stimulate children to conjure up consequences of events that might have happened in the past and those that may happen in the future. Ask such questions as, "What would the world be like if the Nazis had conquered Great Britain in 1940 or 1941?" "What would America be like today if the South had won the Civil War?" "What might happen to our daily lives if all imports of petroleum from the Middle East were cut off tomorrow?" "Describe our society in the year 2000 if zero population growth were achieved by tomorrow and if the next day's headlines reported a breakthrough in medical research that could prolong the life span to 120 years." Here, too, it would become apparent that imagining consequences is not always a matter of fun and games.

4. Encourage children to develop skills in speculation by having them forecast possible changes in technology, politics, ecology, international relations, and any other area of concern. Ask them what problems would be created by the changes they foresee and how these problems might be overcome. It is important to discourage idle speculation that derives from ignorance and to emphasize, instead, the need for a solid knowledge base that can provide some support for speculation.

5. Have children reflect on what they would like to know more about in any realm of inquiry, even one that may be far removed from the curriculum. Schools often concentrate almost exclusively on problems that have been solved in the past, as if to suggest to students that it is enough for them to inquire into what is known without bothering about the unknown. Some children gain the impression that the unknown is unknowable, so why bother to explore it? Even with respect to existing knowledge, gifted children often sit back and wait for it to be served up to them instead of developing any seek and search initiatives of their own. Teachers can make up for this kind of intellectual complacency by focusing on the importance and methods of problem finding, disciplined curiosity, and stimulating independent interests.

6. Teachers might ask children, "Do you have an original idea about anything? Possibly something you thought about after reading a book, participating in a class discussion, watching a movie, doing an experiment, or just plain daydreaming? It may even be an idea that turns out to be original only with you, since others have thought about it before. That doesn't matter, so long as *you* think it's your own." Children have to be convinced that education is not just a matter of sponging on existing knowledge but also involves creating new

knowledge. It is startling sometimes to see students delving into subject matter without feeling the urge to draw any refreshing inferences, much less having an "Aha!" experience. The reason for it has nothing to do with their inability to make a creative leap from the subject matter at hand; they are simply not challenged to do so often enough. If the challenge were persistent, it would be easy for the gifted to develop a habit of making newness a by-product of every important learning experience. In fact, their response to such stimulation may well be one of the most important signs of how gifted they really are.

7. Children have to be trained to distinguish between essentials and embellishments. They can examine advertising and propaganda to learn how language is used to enlighten, entertain, promote, denigrate, and indoctrinate. Preparing to conduct an interview is also a good way in which to develop probing skills. Children might be asked to formulate what they think are the ten most important questions they would pose to a famous person of the past or present to get a better understanding of human and situational factors associated with fame. Finding the right questions to ask will also help children to understand the everyday world about them. They will come to realize that, while a city's historical landmarks are popular attractions, its survival depends far more on little known facts about the ways in which it disposes of garbage and sewage. Children ought to learn how to find the right questions so that these facts will come to light during an interview conducted with an engineer at the local waste disposal plant.

8. Teachers can help children to organize knowledge by asking not only the right questions but also enough of them to support the wisest possible judgment. This is essential for convergent thinking, especially when serious matters are at stake, as in the case of medical decisions. An intern in medicine might be presented with the case of a hypothetical patient who complains about a belly ache and seeks relief. The medical educator responsible for training the intern has put together a "case history" of the hypothetical patient and has "determined" the nature of the ailment. The intern, who has not seen any of the diagnostic data, is then invited to ask for any kind and amount of information about the patient's symptoms and to make a diagnosis based on the data requested. It is then possible to evaluate whether the facts obtained about the ailment are the right kind and in the right amount to help determine its true nature. In other words, has the intern asked *only* relevant questions? Are there any relevant questions that the intern has *not* asked? Some of the methods for sharpening search techniques can be conducted in any subject matter area where things have to be explained rationally.

9. Futurism is a popular subject in search of a methodology that will leave forcasting less and less to chance. Children might be asked to plan a house (or a city or a government) a hundred years from now. Such an exercise requires the child to have a formidable grasp of current information and enough imagination to project from the "what is" to the "what might be." Some influential factors are highly predictable,such as climate, geography, the phys-

iology of living organisms, and other "laws of nature." It would therefore be helpful to analyze how these "laws of nature" set consistent limitations on the design of a house, a city, or a government for all time.

10. Dealing with predicaments, imagined and real, is always a useful exercise. The teacher may have to start with brainstorming alternatives on matters of no consequence that pose no dilemmas either, such as imagining as many uses as possible of empty coffee jars. But eventually the technique has to be applied to practical dilemmas, plights, and quandaries. A group assembled on a playing field might be asked to devise a sports program with the understanding that they have no access to any kind of athletic equipment. At a more advanced and meaningful level, some students may be qualified to write scenarios for keeping the United States from being trapped into alliances with right- or left-wing dictatorships in South America. Life is filled with Hobson's choices, and children have to learn that it is necessary to live with them.

Enrichment with a Conscience

Finally, there is the matter of teaching gifted children the *social and affective consequences* of becoming a high-level producer or performer. Problems relating to self-concept, friendship and career choices, and emotional development have special meaning for gifted children because of their unique abilities and needs. Perhaps the worst possible outcome of an enriched program is that it will produce a cadre of technocrats who are brilliant in the work they do but have no conscience or commitment to a set of values and are willing to sell their talents to the highest bidder. Hitler's master architect, Albert Speer, is a notorious example of giftedness without a conscience, and there are many others in the annals of history. There are also extraordinarily inventive people who may be well meaning in their intentions but are extremely naïve about the impact of their work on the general well-being of society. The creators of DDT, for example, intended to save our crops from destruction by insects, but neglected the possible effects on the environment. They did not realize that shortsightedness is a human failing with varying consequences, depending on what is at stake. In ordinary human activity, it can produce annoyances and regrets; in highly sensitive work, it can bring on tragedy. It is therefore important for the gifted to learn that there is no self-evident virtue in possessing great brainpower and using it to its fullest extent. Creativity can be as lethal as it is constructive if there is no allegiance to a code of ethics to govern its expression. Values clarification therefore takes on special meaning inasmuch as it deals with the responsibilities of assuming some kind of leadership in the world of ideas.

Some children excel in their sensitivity to the human consequences of innovation and may someday be acclaimed as important social commentators. There is obviously a need for such specialists who can serve as the conscience of the people provided they are not seen as the sole arbiters of right and wrong and authoritative prophets of utopia or doom. Their presence can be a mixed blessing if it encourages people who are gifted in some way other than sagacity to defer only to the sages, thus absolving themselves from being accountable for any of their own innovations. This kind of indifference is displayed occasionally by young students talented in the sciences. When asked how they would feel about working on an invention that could someday be used to blow up the world, they reply simply that their job is to invent, while some amorphous entity called "society" and its social leaders take over all moral obligations for whatever happens with their product. They rationalize their detachment further by claiming that a conscience would only inhibit their freedom to innovate. This may be so, but it is well worth the risk.

The Enrichment Matrix therefore suggests that it is necessary for all gifted children, regardless of what their special talents may be to concentrate as seriously on the affective domain (Krathwohl et al., 1964) as they do on the cognitive domain (Bloom et al., 1956) in the taxonomy of educational objectives. This means developing an alertness to human values and judgments on life as experienced vicariously through reading and through everyday encounters with people. It also requires an acceptance of responsibility for developing a kinship with other human beings and caring for their needs. Values are to be examined for the purpose of developing a personal code of conduct, and the choice has to be guided to some extent by universal principles rather than just by personal taste. Among the universals are (1) faith in the power of reason and in methods of experiment and discussion, (2) the need to conserve human and material resources, and (3) the preference for the general welfare of the public over the benefits to specialized and narrow interest groups. But all of this soul searching should be combined with a commitment to action, for just as creative work without a regulating conscience leads to recklessness, contemplation without creative work leads to impotence. As John Dewey allegedly once said, "While saints engage in introspection, burly sinners rule the world."

Chapter 22

Evaluating Enrichment for the Gifted

A viable plan for enrichment has to run a middle course betwen two kinds of pitfalls. At one extreme there is the temptation to opt for *precision* in the choice of assessment methods and instruments at the expense of the *relevance* of these devices to program objectives. For example, a large school system offered the gifted a wide array of studies ranging from introduction to atomic physics to opera production and used conventional achievement and diagnostic tests to measure outcomes, the results showing that the experimentals outperformed the controls only in the "capitalization" and "punctuation" subtests! In this case the criteria tests were chosen because it is easier to measure communication skills than the complexities covered in the curriculum. At the other extreme there is an over-zealousness about relevance to program objectives. The data collected in this instance are merely samplings of work done at school that is hard to generalize to other kinds of accomplishment. For example, a researcher determined the value of a course in Sanskrit for the gifted by comparing experimentals and controls on a test of Sanskrit, and he discovered to nobody's surprise that those who took the course performed better than those who did not! No attempt was made to determine whether learning Sanskrit made a difference in their general language development or even whether it affected growth in other scholastic areas.

Finding ways to assess the impact of a special enrichment program is hampered by the fact that few ready-made measures are designed for such purposes. Even in cases where standardized tests are relevant, their ceiling scores may be too low to measure individual differences and comparative gains in the course of the program. Taking into account these serious problems that pertain uniquely to the gifted, we can proceed to conduct the assessment following guidelines that would apply to the nongifted as well.

Renzulli (1975) suggests several such principles in the form of "basic concepts" in program evaluation. According to him, there are two types of design that should be complementary rather than mutually exclusive. One is known as *formative evaluation*, which requires collecting data long enough before the end of the experiment in order to (1) discover deficiencies early, (2) provide continuous in-process feedback about these deficiencies, and (3) make midcourse corrections in the curriculum. The other type of design is *summative evaluation* in which data are collected at the end of the experiment, thus making feedback impossible until then. The purpose is to assess overall quality and effectiveness to help administrators decide whether the program ought to be adopted, modified, or dropped.

Three kinds of data are important in implementing the formative and summative evaluation designs. The most familiar is *product*, or pay-off, *evaluation*, which relies heavily on standardized and teacher-made tests, ratings of students' projects, and measures of morale at school and at home, all of which are supposed to reveal changes resulting from the children's exposure to enrichment. There is also *process evaluation*, which draws attention to the way in which students and teachers interact in the classroom, specifically the level of intellectual stimulation in the course of teaching, the instructional strategies used in transacting ideas, the allowances made for student-initiated topics of study, the extent of students' on-task and off-task behavior, and the degree of permissiveness and control exhibited by the teacher. Finally, there is *presage*, or intrinsic, *evaluation*, which allows for a systematic look at the program's logic, structure, elegance, imaginativeness, thoroughness, and overall integrity with the help of carefully prepared criteria for judgment.

Renzulli (1975) uses his basic principles of evaluation in general to formulate a step-by-step approach to assessing the effects of enrichment in particular. He starts with a front-end analysis to clarify key features of the program and to identify its prime interest groups. This requires a review of all pertinent documents, collecting interview and questionnaire data on feelings about the program as expressed by the prime interest groups and observing all aspects of the program directly.

The second step is to synthesize this information in a format designed to present the major concerns of each prime interest group and to classify these concerns topically as key features to be evaluated. One key feature that is almost certain to represent the concerns of some groups is "progress in academic studies." Another may be "students' social development." Instruments are then selected and created on the basis of their relevance to the key features as well as to the targeted population. Examples of such measures used in evaluating programs for the gifted have been assembled by Renzulli (1975), Renzulli et al. (1979), and Richert (1982).

The third step is data collection and analysis. Timing, planning, field testing, and scaling techniques are all extremely vital at this stage of the evaluation. The data may be examined informally to extract the "flavor" of outcomes or analyzed statistically to organize and draw inferences from the quantified results. Finally, there is the preparation of the evaluative report that has to be organized for maximum impact. It should begin with an overview to identify sections in which each prime interest group will find its concerns addressed. The succeeding sections ought to be planned around every key feature separately, with the data analysis techniques described as well. The last section is a summarizing chapter presenting a holistic view of the program and recommendations (if any) for improvement.

MONITORING AND ASSESSING COMMUNITY FEELINGS

The front-end analysis advocated by Renzulli (1975) includes an assessment of needs as perceived by various interest groups. There are several advantages to such a procedure, not the least of which is to determine the extent of agreement among these constituencies regarding every possible aspect of the program. Sometimes a highly vocal minority can give the impression of representing the concerns of a whole community. There may also be hidden disagreements or conflicts, albeit honest ones, between teachers and administrators, between administrators and parents, between parents of the gifted and parents of the nongifted, or between all parents and the school board. All shades of feeling ought to be brought to the surface before evaluation takes place; otherwise, the assessment may be based on criteria of a successful program as seen by some groups and not others.

An omnibus-type questionnaire such as the one appearing in Appendix C can help to elicit feelings about the gifted and the enrichment offered them in a single school or school system. The first part asks for information about the respondent and for some general impressions about how well the gifted are being served at school. Parts II through V consist of a series of statements about the gifted and their education, with each statement requiring three responses.

First, the respondent rates it with respect to "priority," or perceived importance of the idea being expressed. Thus, for example, a person can attach high, moderate, or low priority to an item such as "The search for gifted pupils at school is intense and thorough." The response reveals how intensely the need is felt for schools to conduct this kind of search. The reactions of one group of respondents can then be compared with those of another as part of the preliminary needs assessment in which the various constituencies reveal whatever differences may exist among them in their attitudes toward satisfying the needs of the gifted. It will also help clarify each group's feelings about where the emphasis (if any) in educating the gifted should be placed.

After rating the "priority" of the statement, the respondent then evaluates the school's or school system's "performance" with respect to it. In the example given, the assessment of performance can range from high to low on the intensity and thoroughness of the search for gifted pupils. "Performance" ratings should be weighted by "priority" ratings to determine how much importance we ought to attach to the respondent's judgement of the school or school system. On a scale of 5 to 1 (high to low) a moderate score of 3 for "priority" and a high score of 5 for "performance" would yield a weighted total of 15 for that item (3 x 5 = 15). Another person may give both "priority" and "performance" scores scores of 5, with a weighted total of 25 (5 x 5 = 25). This shows that, although both respondents gave the highest possible score for "performance," the second evaluation of the school or school system was more positive because the second respondent attached more importance to the criterion statement on which the assessment of performance was being made.

Finally, the respondent is asked to speculate as to the "prospects," or likelihood, that the idea represented in each statement will figure significantly in the policies or practices at school in the years to come. The purpose here is to test perceptions as to whether interest in educating the gifted is deeply rooted for longevity or is it a shortlived fad. Again, each "prospects" item can be weighted for its "priority," thus making it possible to see how much lasting power is anticipated for the school policies and practices that are regarded as most (and least) important. Assessments can also be made of projections into the future in areas of school performance rated high as well as those rated low.

Every type of analysis of "priority," "performance," and "prospect," and the interrelationships among them, should be conducted separately for the total sample and the various constituencies within it. This will prove helpful in understanding the general mood of the community along with the areas of consensus among interested subgroups. The data can be examined section by section as outlined in the questionnaire.

Part I would provide a preliminary hint of how people react to special opportunities for the gifted. Part II deals in some detail with the idea of individualizing instruction for children at any level of ability. Part III is devoted to specific concerns about the gifted. Part IV deliberately creates an artificial split between the gifted and the talented to test whether people are more concerned about one kind of excellence than another. Since the statements in Parts III and IV are mostly identical, it is then possible to compare reactions to the needs of children specializing in the arts (who are sometimes labeled "talented") with those concentrating in the academic disciplines (who are sometimes known as "gifted"). Part V combines the gifted and talented to assess the comprehensiveness of the enrichment program. Finally, Part VI contains only one statement, but it is probably the single most impotant one, because it asks the respondent to judge whether enrichment is programmatic in the sense of being part of the lifeblood of the total school curriculum or provisional in the sense of being an ad hoc, add-on luxury that lasts for only as long as it is considered attractive and affordable.

MONITORING AND ASSESSING ENRICHMENT IN THE CLASSROOM

Every program for the gifted has its own scope and objectives, which vary from one setting to the next. It is impossible to suggest guidelines that will fit them all. Evaluation makes sense if the methods and instruments relate directly to the educational objectives, even if it means sacrificing some precision for the sake of relevance. If the expected outcomes are extensive, it is necessary to monitor a wide variety of growth indicators in the intellective, nonintellective, and social domains. Wherever possible, comparison or control populations should be designated to assess the relative impact of enrichment and to determine whether the gifted are penalized in some way by their exposure to special curriculum content. In the last analysis, an evaluation serves educators best by helping them to improve their services to children.

Formative measures are therefore extremely important in calling attention to early signs of strengths and weaknesses in the program. This information can then be used to help make curriculum adjustments along the way rather than waiting until the end of the school year when evaluations can only suggest what might have been done in the past and what promises to be successful in the future.

Although the aims of enrichment ought to emerge from deliberations within the school and the community, there are some that seem appropriate in most programs and are presented here in order to illustrate how their attainment may be evaluated. These aims may be outlined as follows:

1. To extend, broaden, and deepen children's educational achievement beyond ordinary expectation.
2. To enable children to cultivate higher-level intellective processes for purposes of problem finding and solving.
3. To inspire children toward greater creative productivity.
4. To help children achieve a balanced commitment toward bettering themselves and bettering the human condition.
5. To create for children a wide-ranging encounter with the world of ideas, not just a narrow specialization in a single area of study.
6. To influence the extent and quality of children's out-of-school experiences in learning, producing, and performing in the world of ideas.
7. To enhance children's self-concepts and aspirations for self-fulfillment.
8. To raise children's social status among peers.
9. To create a climate of high morale in children's homes, schools, and classrooms.
10. To influence children's mental health in a positive way.

Each of these aims has to be clarified in considerable detail in order to eliminate any possibility of more than one interpretation. Concerned citizens in the community without training in educational jargon may not understand precisely what the professional has in mind unless the language is elaborated in terminology that makes sense to them. Even among themselves, professionals can interpret program aims in different ways if there are any traces of ambiguity in the language. Anything less than complete consensus as to the meaning of every expression will hamper efforts to evaluate the program, since people will disagree as to whether the data collected are on target.

Since the aforementioned ten aims are presented for illustrative purposes only, they are not yet explicated as they would be if they were considered for adoption in a program. The following sketch of how to evaluate their attainment derives therefore from only one person's interpretation of them.

Aim 1: Enhancing Pupil Achievement

There are often serious problems in the use of standardized achievement tests to assess programs for the gifted, even though their reliability and validity are impressive. They can be useful primarily if the curriculum stresses rapid progress in the acquisition of basic skills in the language arts and the mastery of facts in mathematics, sciences, and the social studies. Even here the evaluator has to be careful to use instruments with high enough ceiling scores to permit fair readings of the status and progress of every student. In many instances, however, the program features content that is rarely part of the regular school curriculum or tapped by conventional achievement tests. For example, if the children are studying general semantics as part of enrichment, it is hardly likely that they will improve their scores by much on the usual measures of skills in reading. The evaluation therefore has to forgo complete reliance on standardized achievement tests, precision made as they may be, and make heavy use of difficult-to-manage but far more appropriate teacher-made tests, work assignments, and special opinionnaires.

Many teachers schedule examinations in major subject areas periodically. These tests cover the enrichment content for the gifted, revealing more or less what they can be expected to have learned or created, and the results show how well they have succeeded in their work. It is difficult to quantify these outcomes so as to compare experimentals and controls, but they do help us to understand the nature and extent of differences between them. Topics covered consistently in an enrichment program are understandably mastered only by its participants. The number and depth of such topics tell us more about the children's achievement, provided that test scores exist to show the extent of coverage. Examinations designed and administered early in the school year can also provide material for formative evaluation. The children's performance on them will show whether the curriculum content is too deep or shallow, too extensive or not extensive enough, and too varied or too restricted. Whatever the results show in the first rounds of testing, there will be ample opportunity to use the test data to reflect on the overall program design.

While experimentals are expected to perform better than controls on topics covered only in the enriched curiculum, the question is whether enrichment is accomplished at the expense of more conventional content. In other words, are the gifted so preoccupied with special topics that they are forced to neglect the basics? One way to find out is to compare achievement in the general curriculum. This means developing a uniform examination of common core areas to which all children are exposed. Such data have to be collected repeatedly to avoid making overly easy assumptions about what the gifted accomplish at school. In our zeal to emphasize enrichment, we sometimes push the more commonplace learning requirements into the background not only for lack of time but because we think the gifted have already met them. Besides, there is not much glamor and excitement in the commonplace; in fact, the gifted are often bored by it. But boredom is not always a sign of belaboring the obvious. The gifted may have special difficulty in building up enthusiasm for exercises in spelling and grammar and absorbing facts in any course of study. Yet their indifference should not be interpreted to mean that they are able to express themselves clearly and with grammatical correctness in writing or to draw easily on a fund of knowledge in their memory banks. Too many teachers complain about gifted children's weakness in "fundamentals," thus making it necessary to assess the extent of educational neglect as well as accomplishment.

One of the more important benefits in relying on teacher-made tests, assignments, and special projects is that they provide evidence of children's progress that everybody can understand and appreciate. Instead of reporting differential gain scores between experimentals and controls on measures that are only vaguely relevant to what is happening in the classroom, we can now look at what the children have actually done in the course of the program. This is not just for the sake of public relations, or for "show-and-tell" sessions, although they are important, too. What counts most is to examine what actually went on in the classroom as reflected in student performance and productivity, the intention being to compare the general accomplishments of beneficiaries with nonbeneficiaries of differentiated education and to see how well the actualized program is fulfilling the expectations of various interest groups. These kinds of data will also help school officials to decide if (and how) the program in its present or modified form can be administered to the nongifted as well. By considering the adaptability of the program to a wider audience, the school will be less vulnerable to the charge of creating its own gifted elite.

Aim 2: Cultivating High-Level Intellective Processes

Few standardized instruments designed to measure complex thought patterns have enough of a "track record" to permit an evaluation of their validity. None has been validated sufficiently for children who perform near the top of the scale. We are therefore forced to rely on nonstandardized, nonvalidated measures derived from work in the classroom.

The evaluation can then be accomplished in two ways, both of which reveal *what kind* of thought processes are used most and least frequently in the classroom rather than *how effectively* they are used. One approach is through observing pupil-teacher interaction directly with a monitoring instrument designed to record pupils' intellective activity. Recordings can be made along a hierarchy of processes ranging from the least to most complex, with a conceptual model such as the Bloom et al. (1956) taxonomy serving as guide. The observer records each cognitive performance by a child by placing a checkmark for that pupil at one of the six cognitive levels that Bloom and his colleagues have posited. After a series of such observations, a count can be taken of the relative frequency with which the higher-level processes of synthesis and evaluation are represented in the classroom. An alternative to using a hierarchical model to guide classroom observation is to use a categorical model such as the one developed by Aschner and Gallagher (1965), which is based on the Guilford Structure of Intellect (1967) and depicts a variety rather than a hierarchy of human functioning. Such an instrument can show how many *kinds* of intellective processes are stressed in the program, whereas a Bloom-based recording device would show the complexity of such processes.

Direct observation may be difficult to manage, partly because it is time consuming and partly because observers of the same teaching act often disagree as to what kinds of thinking were displayed. An alternative approach, therefore, is to apply the same kinds of analysis to samples of pupils' homework assignments, special projects, and the examinations they take on their coursework. These materials probably give a faithful indication of the kinds of thinking encouraged by the teacher. It is therefore unnecessary to take the trouble of recording and analyzing such behaviors live in the classroom.

But regardless of whether gathering data is through direct observation of teachers and pupils or through a content analysis of work accomplished, the information should be used constructively, not judicially. Teachers welcome supervision, but abhor "snoopervision." If recordings are made early in the school year, they can contribute to the formative evaluation and thereby help to determine whatever adjustments in the program are indicated. This can be done on a periodic basis to reveal trends in the program as teachers become more and more aware of their instructional tactics. At the end of the experimental period, a summative evaluation of children's projects and performance on teacher-made tests will reveal the complexity, quality, and variety of cognitive stimulation featured in the enrichment program. It will also show how well children meet the challenge.

Aim 3: Broadening Cultural Interests at School

It is important to prevent children from being narrowly focused in their educational experience, spending most of their time on one or two subjects and virtually neglecting the others. Sometimes there is an imbalance in the quality of teachers or in the emphasis in the curriculum, so that the enrichment program develops a reputation of being strong, for example, in science and social studies and relatively weak in the language arts and mathematics. Children who are accepted into the program begin to specialize too early in their schooling if their strengths are in the sciences and social studies, whereas those who are equally precocious in the language arts and mathematics may be neglected. An exciting enrichment program may begin modestly in just one or two subject areas, but eventually it ought to range broadly with no weak spots in its offerings.

To evaluate the extensiveness and uniform strength of the program, the children's independent projects should be examined for subject area variation to see whether a range of interest has developed within a classroom and also within each child. A filing system should be developed to contain children's work specimens, projects in progress, completed reports and creative products, and whatever special assignments reflect on the content of the program. The *nature* and *variety* of these projects, no less than their *quality*, should reveal much about the range of interests pursued by the children and inspired by their teachers. The work files of children in the experimental program should also be compared with those in control group situations to obtain a better view of how (or whether) enrichment makes a real difference in the nature, variety, and quality of student accomplishments. The file should be started as early as possible in the school term to provide evidence for a formative evaluation.

Aim 4: Creative Productivity

Since the nurturance of creativity is featured in so many enrichment aims, it is important to determine how well they are realized. However, there are basic problems concerning what to assess and how to assess it. As is well known, standardized tests of creativity that measure pupil performance concentrate on divergent thinking, a special aptitude revealed in Guilford's (1950, 1967) Structure of Intellect, which may or may not be related to creativity in the arts, sciences, and letters. These kinds of instruments also need further proof of their reliability and validity before they can be used with much confidence in evaluating the effects of enrichment. Nevertheless, the test items reflect a kind of thinking process that educators ought to consider seriously, provided that it is exercised in the context of the curriculum rather than in unrelated mental gymnastics. It means little to be fluent, flexible, and original if children are given opportunities to practice these skills primarily in relation to the uses of the tin can or daily newspaper.

The effects of such practice are felt mostly in their own context but should not be expected to transfer from one context to another. In other words, if divergent thinking is to be demonstrated by children's resourcefulness in conjuring up ways to reduce poverty, pollution, or inflation, the teacher has to emphasize this kind of thinking in relation to such topics. The evaluation will therefore have to be conducted subject area by subject area, with the students' work at school serving again as the main source of data since there are no standardized measures to evaluate such accomplishments. Quantitative and qualitative assessments are then possible, the first deriving from a frequency count of divergent thinking exercises found in a sample of children's work, and the second based on quality judgments of that work.

In the more conventional domains of creativity, such as art, music, theater, writing, and the dance, evaluations are done routinely through critiquing sample projects rather than by relying on nonexistent or poorly validated measures. Unfortunately, divergent thinking measures are not scored for quality of responses. There are dangers, too, in proliferating performance and product reviews for assessing progress in creativity or anything else because of the extra responsibilities imposed on the gifted. Close physical proximity between the gifted and nongifted makes it easy for them to compare work loads and thus create resentment among those who carry the heavier burden. Such feelings are often close to the surface except in the few instances when children are out and out workaholics who welcome the special demands made of them. Otherwise, the pressures on teacher and students to pile up observable evidence of the success of the program can lead to open resistance to any enrichment experience.

It is not easy to know when the gifted stop being overawed and start becoming overwhelmed, or when their talents stop being showcased and start being exploited. Requiring them to develop extra samples of their work for the sake of evaluating it more closely can tip the balance and make their entire experience overwhelming and exploitative. It would be absurdly self-defeating to sacrifice morale in the program for the sake of making the data banks super rich. Moderation is necessary. The rule of thumb in conducting the evaluation is to make it parsimonious, preferably without any need for the children to show evidence of accomplishment beyond what they demonstrate in the course of the program.

Aim 5: Balancing Self-betterment with Social Consciousness

An effective enrichment program should help the gifted to avoid the extremes of self-indulgence and self-denial. On the one hand, they have the potential for contributing more than their share to the common good, and it would therefore be a tragic waste for them to become part of an "only-I-count" sect. On the other hand, by allowing others to dictate the development and use of their talents, they can lose their individuality and become part of an impersonal talent pool that exists only to serve society. One of the objectives of enrichment is to teach the gifted that they do not have to choose between egotism and dehumanization and that service to self can be balanced with service to society.

The instrument used to assess children's personal-social commitments could be in the form of a "preference-remembrance" questionnaire. It is a simple device in which they are asked to choose how they would like to be remembered by the world after they finish their occupational careers. Several possible choices could be ranked in the order of preference, each of them representing a different point of view of where the person wants to be placed in relation to society. One of them reflects extreme self-centeredness ("Someone who developed his or her abilities *mostly* for the sake of self-improvement rather than for the sake of serving society"). Another statement reflects extreme selflessness ("Someone who developed his or her abilities *mostly* for the sake of serving society rather than for the sake of self-improvement"). The middle choice is a balance between the extremes ("Someone who developed his or her abilities *equally* for the sake of self-improvement and *equally* for the sake of serving society"). Between the middle choice and each extreme there should be another option that is identical in wording to the extreme statement, except that "mostly" is replaced with "more."

Children might be asked to rank the characters twice: (1) in the order in which they *prefer* to be remembered and (2) in the order in which they *expect* to be remembered. This would show some possible discrepancies between their ideal and realistic perceptions of themselves. For each of the two rank orders, the children ought to write a short essay clarifying the reasons for their choices. If a matched control group responds to the same questionnaire, comparing experimentals with controls will make it possible to see how much change (if any) in attitudes results from exposure to the program and how much is due to maturation.

Aim 6: Broadening Cultural Interests out of School

The inspirational qualities of enrichment should extend beyond the school building into the child's everyday life experience in the community. Sometimes, the gifted show signs of quantitative rather than qualitative changes in their cultural habits, and these indicators may be misleading to parents and teachers. For example, increasing the number of books read during leisure hours could really be a sign of absorbing more of the same kinds of material that most children do at that age, not an elevation of taste and variety. The children's responses to art and music can also remain superficial even if they spend more time than ever in museums and concert halls.

Information about out-of-school cultural activities can be elicited through informal interviews or open-ended responses of parents and children to a questionnaire that is brief and to the point. Children who have enough time and interest to develop a log of such activities may be encouraged to record the titles of books they have read, activities connected with their hobbies, notes about any creative work they are doing, adventures in science or mathematics, descriptions of any apprenticeships they may have, facts and feelings about their efforts to improve community life, and impressions of their visits to art galleries, libraries, historical landmarks, and other points of cultural interest. It is hoped that some of these activities will be traceable to experiences in the classroom. Periodic discussions of them at school may also give children the impression that teachers are interested in every aspect of their learning experiences, not just in life within the school building.

Aim 7: Raising Self-concepts and Aspirations

Enhancing children's feelings about themselves and raising their sights for the future are essential to the success of enrichment. Two instruments may be used to assess change over time, one for elementary school and the other for high school gifted populations. The one designed for younger children is in the form of a series of pairs of statements, each pair referring to a personal characteristic of the respondent. The first statement of each pair always begins with the words "I am," which should produce a realistic self-rating, while the second statement starts with "I would like most people to consider me," pertaining to personal aspirations. A single adjective then follows the opening of the statement, which the respondent completes by indicating how accurate a self-description it is. A pair of such statements would appear as follows:

	Always	**Usually**	**Sometimes**	**Rarely**	**Never**
I am *sociable*	5	4	3	2	1
I would like most people to consider me *sociable*	5	4	3	2	1

For each statement, the child circles the number that signifies which ending to the statement makes the self-description most accurate. The numbers of pairs of statements appearing in the questionnaire will depend on how far ranging the adjectives or adjectival phrases are chosen to be. The school may want to include descriptors pertaining to school success, motivation, sociability, personal happiness, emotional status, and any other factors pertinent to human development. The realistic self-ratings (i.e., "I am") are quantified separately as are the children's aspirations (i.e., "I would like most people to consider me") for the entire instrument and separately for each group of adjectives, factor by factor. Then within each pair of statements the realistic self-rating is subtracted from the aspiration score and the within-pair differences are added together, thus revealing a third body of information concerning the extent to which aspirations may be unrealized. This would help to reveal degrees of inner tension (if discrepancies are great) and complacency (if discrepancies are minimal) felt by children in the course of the program.

For high school students, the instrument is more elaborate, with two uniform statements added to the pairs in the elementary school form. Each adjective is then preceded by the following four stems: (1) "I am," (2) "I would like most people to consider me," (3) "Most people think I am," and (4) "Most people are."

Such a questionnaire was developed originally by the Talented Youth Project of the Horace Mann-Lincoln Institute of School Experimentation Teacher's College, Columbia University (New York City) and was used extensively in evaluating programs for the gifted. Six kinds of comparisons can be made for each adjective: (1) "I am" vs. "I would like people to consider me," (2) "I am" vs. "Most people think I am," (3) "I am" vs. "Most people are," (4) "I would like people to consider me" vs. "Most people think I am," (5) "I would like most people to consider me" vs. "Most people are," and (6) "Most people think I am" vs. "Most people are." Comparisons can be made between experimentals and controls to reveal whether enrichment programs foster snobbery and inflated egos among gifted children.

Aim 8: Improving Social Status Among Peers

Since the morale of the school depends to a great extent on interpersonal relations among the children, it is important to assess how the gifted get along with each other and with the nongifted. A specially designed sociogram can be used to elicit the necessary data.

Each child receives a copy of the class list with introductory instructions as follows: "This is your class roster. Write a number next to each name to show how much you would like that person to become or remain your friend. The highest possible score you can give any classmate is a 5, and the lowest possible score is a 1. You may write any number from 1 to 5 next to each name to express how you feel about every person in your class. When you come to your own name, write the number that you think most of your classmates will give you, and draw a circle around it. Whatever you write will be held in strictest confidence."

When the data are assembled, a grid can be constructed in which the names of the children head the columns and also the rows. Thus, the entire class roster appears across the top of the page to head the columns, and the same listing appears along the left-hand side of the page as labels to the rows. Each of the children heading the rows has previously rated each of the children heading the columns, and the scores should be transferred from the children's individual rating sheets to the appropriate cells on the grid. The circled number denoting the score a child anticipates from the rest of the class should be entered in the cell where the child's name labels both the column and the row and should be circled in that cell. Thus, the scores appearing across a row denote a child's rating of classmates; scores appearing in a column denote the ratings a child receives from classmates. A mean score for each row is computed and entered in a box beyond that row at the right hand side of the page. Similarly, mean scores for the columns are entered in boxes along the bottom of the page. The sum of mean scores for the rows is the same as the sum for the columns, and that total divided by the number of children on the roster can be entered in a special box in the lower-right-hand corner of the page. It represents the general level of friendship feelings in the classroom. Progress in the way in which children rate others and are rated by others can be monitored over time and compared with similar records of the control group to determine the effects of enrichment. The ratings of and by individual children can also be compared to see if friendship status is related to friendliness. Finally, the circled scores, revealing how the children *think* they would be rated *by* others, can be compared with the *actual* mean ratings received *from* others.

To illustrate the use of the grid as a sociogram, Table 22-1 contains friendship ratings by and of a sample of five children, A, B, C, D, and E. Child A, for example, gives classmates an average rating of 3.25 and receives an average 3.25 rating from them, while expecting to be rated at a level of 3. The score of 3.4 in the extreme bottom, right-hand cell of the grid shows the general level of friendship within the group.

Aim 9: Stimulating Appreciation of the Program

An Opinionnaire that assesses feelings about enrichment in general and how well it is implemented at school is useful in monitoring the attitudes of those directly involved. Such instruments have been developed in many school systems and should reflect local concerns. Sample formats can be found in publications by Renzulli (1975), Renzulli et al. (1979), and Richert (1982) and are easily adaptable to highlight any issues raised during the needs assessment and enrichment planning

Table 22-1. Friendship Ratings By and Of a Sample of
Five Children

		Rated					
		A	*B*	*C*	*D*	*E*	*Mean Rating of Classmates*
	A	③	4	4	3	2	3.25
	B	3	⑤	4	4	2	3.25
Raters	*C*	4	5	④	4	3	4.00
	D	3	3	4	③	2	3.00
	E	3	3	4	4	④	3.50
Mean Rating by Classmates		3.25	3.75	4	3.75	2.25	3.4
Mean Rating of and by the Total Class: 3.4							

phases of the program. Separate forms should be administered to the children, their parents, and their teachers in order to elicit some impression of morale at different times during the school year. Wherever possible, items on the opinionnaire ought to be the same for the separate groups of respondents in order to facilitate easy and meaningful comparisons. Such an analysis lends itself both to formative and summative evaluation.

Aim 10: Fostering Mental Health

Some children may enter the special program with various psychosocial problems. Others may develop such problems in the course of the program. These children have to be watched closely in order to put together case studies based on data derived in the course of identification and formative evaluation. The purpose is to develop some hypotheses concerning positive or negative indicators of mental health status. Such in-depth case studies are time consuming and require considerable staff resources, but they add vital information that is often difficult to discern in mass data. Some children may react emotionally and behaviorally to being understimulated; others may be overwhelmed by the added burden of an enriched curriculum. Clinical specialists should make every effort to collaborate with the staff responsible for enrichment to adjust the program design to the needs of children so as to forestall emotional or interpersonal problems. Their working together may produce new understandings of what educational enrichment ought to be and new insights into the ways in which children respond to educational enrichment.

IN CONCLUSION . . .

An evaluation design that touches on all aspects of the program is enlightening to educators and noneducators alike. It helps to clarify the nature of young talent, the varieties of children who possess it, and the effects of its nurturance in and out of school. It especially reveals the "goodness-of-fit" among pupil, teacher, and curriculum and how to improve this match through refinements in the enriched program of study. In short, what we learn in the course of evaluation advances us closer to the goal set for this volume — an appreciation of the nature and needs of the gifted.

References

American Medical Association "Annual Report on Medical Education in the United States." *Journal of the American Medical Association* (whole issue) Vol. 234, Dec. 29, 1975.

Andre, T. "Does Answering Higher Level Questions While Reading Facilitate Productive Learning." *Review of Educational Research*, **49**:280-318 (1979).

Aschner, M. J., and J. J. Gallagher. *A System for Classifying Thought Processes in the Context of Classroom Verbal Interaction*. Urbana: Institute for Research on Exceptional Children, University of Illinois, 1965.

Baldwin, J. W. "The Relationship Between Teacher-Judged Giftedness, a Group Intelligence Test and an Individual Intelligence Test with Possible Gifted Kindergarten Pupils." *Gifted Child Quarterly*, **2**:153-156 (1962).

Bernal, E. M. "Gifted Mexican American Children: An Ethnoscientific Perspective." *California Journal of Educational Research*, **25**:261-273 (1974).

———. "Methods of Identifying Gifted Minority Students." ERIC Report No. 72. Princeton, N.J.: ERIC Clearinghouse on Tests, Measurement and Evaluation, Educational Testing Service, 1980.

Billow, R. M. "Metaphor: A Review of the Psychological Literature." *Psychological Bulletin*, **84**:81-92 (1977).

Biondi, A. M., and S. J. Parnes. *Assessing Creative Growth*, 2 vols. Great Neck, N.Y.: Creative Synergetics Associates, 1976.

Bloom, B. S., ed. *Taxonomy of Educational Objectives: Cognitive Domain*. New York: David McKay Co., Inc., 1956.

Bouchard, T. J. "Training, Motivation, and Personality as Determinants of the Effectiveness of Brainstorming Groups and Individuals." *Journal of Applied Psychology*, **56**:324-331 (1972)(a).

———. "A Comparison of Two Group Brainstorming Procedures." *Journal of Applied Psychology*, **56**:418-421 (1972)(b).

Bruch, C. B. "Modification of Procedures for Identification of the Disadvantaged." *Gifted Child Quarterly*, **15**:267-272 (1971).

Cazden, C. B. "Subcultural Differences in Child Language: An Interdisciplinary Review." In J. Helmuth, ed., *Disadvantaged Child: Head Start and Early Intervention*, pp. 217-256. New York: Brunner/Mazel, 1968.

Chauncey, H., and T. L. Hilton. "Are Aptitude Tests Valid for the Highly Able?" *Science*, **148**:1297-1304 (1965).

Chen, J., and S. W. Goon. "Recognition of the Gifted from Among Disadvantaged Asian Children." *Gifted Child Quarterly*, **20**:157-164 (1976).

Ciha, T. E., R. Harris, C. Hoffman, and M. Potter. "Parents as Identifiers of Giftedness, Ignored but Accurate." *Gifted Child Quarterly*, **18**:202-209 (1974).

Clark, B. *Growing Up Gifted*. Columbus, Ohio: Charles E. Merrill Publishing Company, 1979.

Davidson, H. H., J. W. Greenberg, and J. M. Gerver. "Characteristics of Successful School Achievers from a Severely Deprived Environment." Mimeo. New York: The City College of the City University of New York, 1962.

Drews, E. M. "A Critical Evaluation of Approaches to the Identification of Gifted Students." In E. Arthur, ed., *Measurement and Research in Today's School*, pp. 109-121. Washington, D.C.: American Council on Education, 1961.

Ellison, R. L., C. Abe, D. G. Fox, and K. E. Coray. "Using Biographical Information in Identifying Artistic Talent." *Gifted Child Quarterly*, **20**:402-408 (1976).

Emmett, W. G., and F. S. Wilmut. "The Prediction of School Certificate Performance in Special Subjects." *British Journal of Educational Psychology*, **22**:52-62 (1952).

Feshbach, S., H. Adelman, and W. Fuller. "Prediction of Reading and Related Academic Problems." *Journal of Educational Psychology*, **69**:299-308 (1977).

Feuerstein, R. *The Dynamic Assessment of Retarded Performers*. Baltimore, Md.: University Park Press, 1979.

Gallagher, J. J. *Teaching the Gifted Child*. 2nd ed. Boston: Allyn & Bacon, Inc., 1975.

George, W. C., S. J. Cohn, and J. S. Stanley, eds. *Educating the Gifted: Acceleration and Enrichment*. Baltimore, Md.: Johns Hopkins University Press, 1979.

Gerard, H. B., and N. Miller. *School Desegregation: A Long-Term Study*. New York: Plenum Publishing Corporation, 1975.

Goldman, R. B., and L. K. Hartig. "The WISC May Not Be a Valid Predictor of School Performance for Primary-Grade Minority Children." *American Journal of Mental Deficiency*, **80**:583-587 (1976).

Goldman, R. D., and R. E. Slaughter. "Why College Grade Point Average Is Difficult to Predict." *Journal of Educational Psychology*, **68**:9-14 (1976).

Gordon, W. J. J. *Synectics*. New York: Collier Books, 1971.

———, and T. Pose. *The Basic Course*. Cambridge, Mass.: Porpoise Books, 1971.

Granzin, K. L., and W. J. Granzin. "Peer Group Choice as a Device for Screening Intellectually Gifted Children." *Gifted Child Quarterly*, **13**:189-194 (1969).

Guilford, J. P. "Creativity." *American Psychologist*, **5**:444-454 (1950).

———. *The Nature of Human Intelligence*. New York: McGraw-Hill Book Company, 1967.

Gustafson, B., B. Kranz, and R. Riley. *The Multidimensional Screening Device (MDSD)*. Fairfax, Va.: Fairfax County Public Schools, 1975.

Hagen, E. *Identification of the Gifted*. New York: Teachers College Press, 1980.

Hainsworth, J. "A Teacher Corps Project on Multiple Talents." In C.W. Taylor, ed., *Teaching for Talents and Gifts, 1978 Status*, pp. 85-89. Salt Lake City: Utah State Board of Education, 1978.

Institute for Curriculum and Instruction. *BASICS: Teaching/Learning Strategies*, Books A, B, and C. Miami, Florida: The Institute, 1977.

Jacobs, J. C. "Effectiveness of Teacher and Parent Identification of Gifted Children as a Function of School Level." *Psychology in the Schools*, **8**:140-142 (1971).

Jefferson County Public Schools. *Career Exploration for Gifted and Talented Students*. Lakewood, Colo.: Jefferson County Public Schools, 1978.

Keogh, B., and C. E. Smith. "Early Identification of Emotionally High Potential and High Risk Children." *Journal of School Psychology*, **8**:285-289 (1970).

Kincaid, D. "A Study of Highly Gifted Elementary Pupils." *Gifted Child Quarterly*, **13**:264-267 (1969).

Kranz, B. *Multi-Dimensional Screening Device (MDSD) for the Identification of Gifted/Talented Children*. Bureau of Educational Research and Services Publication No. 9. Grand Forks: University of North Dakota, 1978.

Krathwohl, D. R., ed. *Taxonomy of Educational Objectives: Affective Domain*. New York: David McKay Co., Inc., 1964.

Lesser, G. H., G. Fifer, and D. H. Clark. "Mental Abilities of Children from Different Social-Class and Cultural Groups." *Monographs of the Society for Research in Child Development*, Vol. 30 (Whole No. 102), 1965.

Lewis, W. D. *A Study of Superior Children in the Elementary School*. Contributions to Education No. 266. Nashville, Tenn.: George Peabody College for Teachers, 1940.

Lorge, I. "Difference or Bias in tests of Intelligence." In G.K. Bennett, ed., *1952 Invitational Conference on Testing Problems*, pp. 76-83. Princeton, N.J.: Educational Testing Service, 1953.

Lowrance, D., and H. N. Anderson. "Intercorrelation of the WISC-R and the Renzulli-Hartman Scale for Determination of Gifted Placement." Paper presented at the Annual International Convention, Council for Exceptional Children, Atlanta, Georgia, 1977.

McClelland, D. C. "Testing for Competence Rather than for Intelligence." *American Psychologist*, **28**:1-14 (1973).

McGuire, C., E. Hindsman, and F. J. King. "Dimensions of Talented Behavior." *Educational and Psychological Measurement*, **21**:3-38 (1961).

Meeker, M. *The SOI: Its Interpretation and Uses*. Columbus, Ohio: Charles E. Merrill Publishing Company, 1969.

————, and R. Meeker. *SOI: Screening Form for Gifted*. El Segundo, Calif: SOI Institute, 1975.

Mercer, J. R., and J. F. Lewis. *System of Multicultural Pluralistic Assessment (SOMPA)*. New York: The Psychological Corporation, 1977.

Messé, L. A., W. D. Crano, S. R. Messé, and W. Rice. "Evaluation of the Predictive Validity of Tests of Mental Ability for Classroom Performance in Elementary Grades." *Journal of Educational Psychology*, **71**:233-241 (1979).

Newland, T. E. *The Gifted in Socioeducational Perspective*. Englewood Cliffs, N.J.: Prentice-Hall, Inc., 1976.

Osborn, A. F. *Applied Imagination*. 3rd rev. ed. New York: Charles Scribner's Sons, 1963.

Parnes, S. J. *Creativity: Unlocking Human Potential*. Buffalo: D.O.K. Publishers, 1972.

————, R. B. Noller, and A. M. Biondi. *Guide to Creative Action*. New York: Charles Scribner's Sons, 1977.

Pegnato, C. W., and J. W. Birch. "Locating Gifted Children in Junior High School: A Comparison of Methods." *Exceptional Children*, **23**:300-304 (1959).

Price, P. B., C. W. Taylor, J. M. Richards, and T. L. Jacobsen, "Measurement of Physician Performance." *Journal of Medical Education*, **39**:203-211 (1964).

Raths, L. E., M. Harin, and S. Simon. *Values and Teaching: Working with Values in the Classroom*. Columbus, Ohio: Charles E. Merrill Publishing Company, 1966.

Renzulli, J. S. *A Guidebook for Evaluating Programs for the Gifted and Talented*. Ventura,

Calif.: National/State Leadership Training Institute on the Gifted and Talented, 1975.

————. *The Enrichment Triad Model: A Guide for Developing Defensible Programs for the Gifted and Talented.* Mansfield Center, Conn.: Creative Learning Press, 1977.

————. "What Makes Giftedness? Reexamining a Definition." *Phi Delta Kappan*, **60**:180-184 (1978).

————. "Will the Gifted Child Movement Be Alive and Well in 1990?" *Gifted Child Quarterly*, **24**:3-9 (1980).

————, and R. K. Hartman. "Scale for Rating Behavioral Characteristics of Superior Students." *Exceptional Children*, **38**:243-248 (1971).

————, R. K. Hartman, and C. M. Callahan. "Teacher Identification of Superior Students." *Exceptional Children*, **38**:211-214 (1971).

————, et al. *Sample Instruments for the Evaluation of Programs for the Gifted and Talented.* Storrs: Bureau of Educational Research of the University of Connecticut, 1979.

Richert, E. S. *National Report on Identification.* Sewell, N.J.: Educational Improvement Center-South, 1982.

Robinson, H. B. "Current Myths Concerning Gifted Children." *Gifted and Talented Brief No. 5*, pp. 1-11. Ventura, Calif.: National/State Leadership Training Institute, 1977.

Roe, A. *Making of a Scientist.* New York: Dodd, Mead & Company, 1953.

Schmeding, R. W. "Group Intelligence Test Scores of Gifted Children: Degree of Consistency and Factors Related to Consistency." *Personnel and Guidance Journal*, **42**:991-996 (1964).

Shinn, E. O. "Interest and Intelligence as Related to Achievement in Tenth Grade." *California Journal of Educational Research*, 7:217-220 (1956).

SOI Institute. *SOI Workbook.* El Segundo, Calif.: The Institute, 1973.

————. *SOI-LA Basic Test: Technical Data.* El Segundo, Calif.: The Institute, 1980.

Stein, M. I. *Stimulating Creativity.* 2 vols. New York: Academic Press, Inc., 1974.

Stevenson, H. W., T. Parker, A. Wilkinson, A. Hegion, and E. Fish. "Predictive Value of Teachers' Ratings of Young Children." *Journal of Educational Psychology*, **68**:507-517 (1976).

Taba, H. *Thinking in Elementary School Children.* San Francisco: San Francisco State College, 1964.

————. *Teaching Strategies and Cognitive Functioning in Elementary School Children.* Washington, D.C.: U.S. Office of Education, 1966.

Tannenbaum, A. J. "A Review of the IPAT Culture Fair Intelligence Test." In. O. K. Buros, ed., *Sixth Mental Measurements Yearbook*, pp. 721-723. Highland Park, N.J.: The Gryphon Press, 1965.

Taylor, C. W. "Developing Effectively Functioning People." *Education*, **94**:99-110 (1973).

————. "How Many Types of Giftedness Can Your Program Tolerate?" Mimeo. (undated).

————, and F. E. Williams. *Instructional Media and Creativity.* New York: John Wiley & Sons, Inc., 1966.

Tennant, C. G. J. "The Identification of Thinking Skills by Students Participating in an Academically Gifted Program." *Dissertation Abstracts International*, **40**:4393A (1980).

Terman, L. M., and M. H. Oden. *The Gifted Group at Mid-Life.* Stanford, Calif.: Stanford University Press, 1959.

Thorndike, R. L., and E. Hagen. *Ten Thousand Careers.* New York: John Wiley & Sons, Inc., 1959.

Torrance, E. P. "Can We Teach Children to Think Creatively?" *Journal of Creative Behavior*, 6:114-141 (1972).

Wallach, M. A. "Tests Tell Us Little About Talent." *American Scientist,* **64**:57-63 (1976).

Ward, V. *Educating the Gifted: An Axiomatic Approach.* Columbus, Ohio: Charles E. Merrill Publishing Company, 1961.

Williams, F. E. *A Total Creativity Program Kit.* Englewood Cliffs, N.J.: Educational Technology Publications, Inc., 1972.

Witty, E. P. "Equal Educational Opportunity for Gifted Minority Group Children: Promise or Possibility?" *Gifted Child Quarterly,* **22**:344-352 (1978).

PART VI

Epilogue

As an underserved minority in our schools, gifted children merit an educational Bill of Rights to arouse concern about their special needs. But unlike other minorities who suffer neglect and hostility, the gifted are victimized by envy for what makes them unique in a crowd. Even well-meaning people may be reluctant to articulate "rights" for individuals whose superior mental endowment already gives them a coveted edge over their peers. In this case, "rights" can easily be misread as "privileges" conceived to encourage elitism by heaping favor upon the advantages of being gifted. It is therefore necessary to state, as a preamble, that *all* children deserve to be challenged to the limits of their abilities, thus denying any minority or even majority preferential treatment at school. A corollary would be that quality education for the nongifted is a precondition of enrichment for the gifted, although not a substitute for it. What is necessary and sufficient for the nongifted is necessary but *insufficient* for the gifted, who need more and different learning experiences commensurate with their potentialities. The proposed Bill of Rights calls attention to the gifted and to what qualifies as quality education for them.

Chapter 23

A "Bill of Rights" for the Gifted

1. *Children have a right to be identified as gifted at the earliest possible age.*

A disproportionately large number of children who show precocity even in the earliest years of life can go on to make outstanding contributions to the world of ideas as adults, provided that their education enables them to cultivate their high potential. Early promise and later productivity or performance are linked in the form of a complex web rather than a simple chain, and some of the filigrees of that web are spun at school. Given the right education, many of these children will grow up to be great patrons of our cultural heritage. Some will accomplish even more than that; they will make their own lasting contributions to that heritage and thereby enrich the lives of their generation and of succeeding generations as well.

2. *Children have a right to be identified as gifted long before they are able to achieve renown.*

The difference between gifted children and gifted adults is in the realm of productivity and performance as judged by universal rather than childhood standards. Gifted adults can be recognized by the quality of their contributions to the arts, sciences, and the human condition; children are too young to compete for such recognition. Under the best of circumstances, they reveal an extraordinary measure of precocity, which is a good, though far from perfect, precursor of later accomplishment. In other words, we can only *infer* eventual fulfillment from early promise, and the connections are difficult to control.

Identifying giftedness in our schools is far from foolproof, and we therefore have to rely on educated guesswork in our search for signs of it. Those who seem to show these signs should be educated in such a way as to make sure that no one is denied the encouragement and opportunity to excel. Unfortunately, however,

462

only a few of those who have what it takes to reach the top actually do so; sometime in the course of their development they are either distracted or discouraged from fulfilling their potentialities.

3. *Gifted children have a right to be regarded as precious human resources far out of proportion to their numbers.*

A single gifted child may have the potential to shake the world. Let us think of the example of Dr. Jonas Salk, a beneficiary of special programs for the gifted in his early school years. Can we fault the schools he attended for failing to produce masses of eminent people who could accomplish as much as he? Rather should we not ask ourselves whether the potential Jonas Salk in cancer research may be living in obscurity because of educational neglect? There is no doubt that the handful of seminal thinkers whose schooling was enriched appropriately have proven the value of special education for the gifted by virtue of their accomplishments. Thus, while our schools address their efforts to the total student population, they must not be allowed to neglect the unique needs of unique *individuals* in favor of the broader needs of the *masses*. Equality of educational experience was never meant to be sameness of educational experience for all children. Or, as Paul Brandwein, a gifted educator of the gifted has told his audiences so often, there is nothing more unequal than the equal treatment of unequals.

4. *Gifted children have a right to differentiated education that is especially appropriate for them.*

An enriched program for the gifted is special education, not simply an embellishment of education for all children. It does not mean doing more of the same things everybody does in the classroom. Instead, the gifted require exposure to content and basic skills that will enable them to make original contributions in their fields of excellence. Since we expect them to become producers of ideas, they should have the kind of training that is particularly beneficial to potential producers.

The child who shows promise as a concert artist or ballet virtuoso needs to have a training regimen that is basically different in content and in intensity from that of the student who is developing these skills just for self-enrichment. The same kind of differentiated training is applicable to the potential professional athlete versus sandlot athlete and also holds true for the playwright versus playgoer, the historian versus Civil War buff, and the scientist versus reader of science.

If we truly believe in individualized education, then we have to vary our educational objectives and programs to accommodate individual differences. For the trainable mental retardate, the aim of education may be to develop self-care and self-help skills, which are not contained in the curriculum of so-called normal children. The gifted also have their own special learning capacities that have to be honored. The national mean in educational accomplishment should never become our national ideal. If it does, then the handicapped will receive help to live up to that standard, while the gifted will be neglected because they can live up to it without any special help.

5. *Gifted children have a right to the kind of education that is the forerunner of education for all children.*

Education of the gifted is a vital cutting edge of innovative programs for the nongifted. What is enrichment today can, with adaptation, become general practice for tomorrow. In planning special educational experiences for our ablest, it is necessary to conjure up new and meaningful courses of study, new and meaningful out-of-school experiences, new and meaningful encounters with cultural resources, and new and meaningful attempts at creative productivity. When such programs are initiated, they inevitably stimulate educators to consider aspects of them for the general curriculum. Thus, if our elementary and secondary schools ever seriously consider studies of ecology, geopolitics, cultural anthropology, intergroup relations, and human psychology as possible areas of concentration that can benefit all children, the breakthrough will come when these disciplines are introduced to the gifted. That has been an historical pattern of curriculum revision in our schools. The so-called new mathematics started with the gifted and was later adapted for all children. The same is true for current curricula in science, social studies, and language arts.

Special education should therefore be recognized for its pioneering efforts in two ways: (1) special program *content* for the gifted influences the general program content and (2) special program *methodology* for the handicapped influences general educational methodology. We mistakenly think that the gifted are the only beneficiaries of our efforts on their behalf. For that reason, we worry about educational elitism and snobbery. Actually, whatever we do to benefit the gifted can and should spread to benefit every child.

6. *Gifted children have a right to be educated by teachers who are specially qualified to teach them.*

Gifted children require inspiring teachers with special competencies in curriculum enrichment. The teacher cannot succeed fully by simply being a "learning manager" who directs children to source material but is uninformed in any field of inquiry. A know-nothing classroom technician will have only limited influence on the gifted. They need a role model they can emulate in their own quest for new ideas. This does not mean that the teacher has to be as clever or knowledgable as the gifted in a variety of disciplines. In fact, no teacher can know as much as an aggregate of gifted children in a classroom, whose interests are highly diversified and advanced.

Nevertheless, teachers should communicate the feeling that they possess some active enthusiasm for cultural pursuits for two reasons: first, to be a living example of an educated person whom children can emulate and, second, to be a source of inspiration in a particular realm of ideas. Thus, by becoming extremely informed about cybernetics or Mahler's music or Yeats's poetry, they should share their understandings of these cultural legacies with children who may develop similar motivation to pursue their own interests or even those of their teachers. But serving as a role model is not enough. A teacher of the gifted should also understand the nature of giftedness, the objectives necessary for an enriched educational program, and the special methodology appropriate for implementing such a program. Education of the gifted is indeed a subspecialization of general education that deserves its own visibility and public support.

7. *Gifted children have a right to a formal eduation that originates in the total environment.*

The gifted child needs opportunities to encounter gifted adults at their professional sites that contain the materials and atmosphere for productive work. Career education has a special meaning for the gifted since it allows opportunities for apprenticeships at leadership levels. By seeking out special training resources outside of school during hours that accommodate the schedules of mentors, educators can broaden the gifted child's learning experiences in ways that the school is not equipped to provide. Nevertheless, the child should not be "farmed out" in an apprenticeship without establishing close cooperative relationships between the school and the community agency, research laboratory, art studio, or professional center where the field training takes place.

Educators should retain a strong influence over the child's learning experiences, even if these opportunities are located away from the school building, scheduled after or before school hours, and supervised by mentors who do not belong to the teaching profession. For, in the last analysis, educators are the ones who know the gifted child's needs best.

8. *Gifted children have a right to be nurtured in a school program, not just through school provisions.*

A program is an educational imperative, not an elective; it is essential, not luxurious. Thus, while schools plan programs in the major disciplines for all children, they are less serious about the needs of the gifted and offer them only temporary provisions that are basically extracurricular. Programs are everlasting, although they can undergo revision, whereas provisions survive only at the pleasure of the teachers who design and implement them. Education for the gifted can be truly meaningful only if schools make it programmatic, thereby incorporating it into the mainstream of individualized education for every child.

9. *Gifted children have a right to their own individualities.*

The gifted vary in talent, enthusiasm, and domains of interest. Enrichment means offering school experiences that address these individualities. Schools should take stock of the kinds of talents they are equipped to cultivate and begin their efforts within the limits of reality. It is useless to seek out children who are talented in the dance or in social leadership unless there are programs to educate these children at their levels of advancement. Schools should begin where their educational resources are strongest, but they should not end there. An expansion of offerings has to be a persistent possibility, not only because gifted children are so varied in their skills and curiosities, but also because the world of ideas is changing and new disciplines deserve attention especially from those who are equipped to contribute to these realms of knowledge.

10. *Gifted children have a right to social equality and freedom from harassment.*

A climate of social acceptance has to be created at school and in the community so that the gifted will want to realize their potential rather than suppress their exceptionalities. There is evidence to show that the gifted are influenced by their peers', parents', and teachers' feelings about their abilities. If they are seen as mental freaks, unhealthy personalities, or eccentrics simply because they are brainy or creative, many of them will avoid the stigma through conformity. Some would rather underachieve and be popular than achieve honor status and risk social ostracism.

It is not easy to make the school a place where the gifted want to excel. It requires real staff commitment to the purposes and benefits of special education for our ablest children and hard work to actualize these commitments through special programs that are exciting and meaningful. A school climate that fosters excellence is infectious. It influences the total substance and conduct of education, thereby reinforcing the idea that designing enriched programs for the gifted are essential steps toward our goals of individualizing quality education and indeed of honoring the individualities of *all* children.

Methods, Techniques, and Educational Programs for Stimulating Creativity: 1982 Revision*

Donald J. Treffinger

This list of methods and programs has been developed for two major purposes: first, to serve as a source of references for further study of particular methods and programs; and second, as an indication of the relationship of a wide variety of methods and programs to the common goals of creative development and expression.

No attempt has been made to provide detailed explanations of any of the methods or programs. Nor is the list intended to be completely comprehensive or critical; certainly, we have not uncovered every possible resource which might have been included. Neither is every item which has been included of equal quality or importance. This compilation attempts to provide merely a representative listing of the great range of available methods, resources, and programs.

AESTHETIC EDUCATION PROGRAM

The Central Midwest Regional Educational Laboratory (now CEMREL, Inc.) sponsored an aesthetic education project, in which a multi-media, multi-discipline program was developed for primary through middle school age children. The program, called *The Five Sense Store*, includes many kits designed to give the

*Previous versions of this bibliography appeared in the *Journal of Creative Behavior*, 1971, 5(2) (by Donald J. Treffinger and John Curtis Gowan), and in the First and Second Editions of the *Creative Behavior Guidebook* (by Sidney J. Parnes; New York: Scribners, 1967, 1977).

child the experience of discovering, using, and understanding h/sr senses and emotions.

(*For information*: Educational Sales Department, The Viking Press, 625 Madison Avenue, New York, N.Y. 10022.)

AFFECTIVE DOMAIN

Stimulation of the feelings and emotions of persons, to improve or enhance sensitivity to feelings, environments, and responses of others, as well as to develop values and release creative potential.

Borton, T. *Reach, Touch, and Teach.* New York: McGraw-Hill, 1970.

Brown, G. I. *Human Teaching for Human Learning.* New York: Viking, 1971.

Casebeer, R. L. *Project Prometheus: Education for the Technetronic Age* (1968). Jackson County Schools, 1133 South Riverside, Medford, Oregon 97501.

Casteel, J. D., and Stahl, R. J. *Values Clarification in the Classroom: A Primer.* Pacific Palisades, Calif: Goodyear, 1975.

Eberle, B., and Hall, R. *Affective Education Guidebook.* Buffalo, N.Y.: D.O.K., 1975

Eberle, B., and Hall, R. *Affective Direction.* Buffalo, N.Y.: D.O.K., 1979.

Greenberg, H. M. *Teaching with Feeling.* New York: Macmillan, 1969.

Gunther, B. *Sense Relaxation.* New York: Collier, 1968.

Johnson, J. L. and Seagull, A. A. "Form and Function in the Affective Training of Teachers." *Phi Delta Kappan*, 1968, **50**:166.

Krathwohl, D. R., Bloom, B. S., and Masia, B. B. *Taxonomy of Educational Objectives, Handbook II: The Affective Domain.* New York: David McKay, 1964.

Lyon, H. C., Jr. *Learning to Feel—Feeling to Learn.* Columbus: Merrill, 1971.

Mager, R. F. *Developing Attitude Toward Learning.* Palo Alto, Calif: Fearon, 1968.

Neill, A. S. *Summerhill: A Radical Approach to Child Rearing.* New York: Hart, 1960.

Rogers, C. R. *Freedom to Learn.* Columbus: Merrill, 1969.

Rogers, C. R. *On Becoming a Person.* Boston: Houghton Mifflin, 1961.

Shaftel, F. *Role Playing for Social Values.* Englewood Cliffs, N.J.: Prentice-Hall, 1967.

Simon, S. B., Howe, L. W. and Kirschenbaum, H. *Values Clarification: A Handbook of Practical Strategies for Teachers and Students.* New York: Hart, 1972.

Strom, R. D. and Torrance, E. P. (eds.) *Education for Affective Achievement.* Chicago: Rand McNally, 1973.

Spolin, V. *Improvisation for the Theater*. Evanston, Ill.: Northwestern University Press, 1967.

Weinstein, G., and Fantini, M. D. *Toward Humanistic Education: A Curriculum of Affect*. New York: Praeger, 1970.

ALTERED STATES OF CONSCIOUSNESS

Anderson, M., and Savary, L. *Passages: A Guide for Pilgrims of the Mind*. New York: Harper & Row, 1972.

Gowan, J. C. "Trance, Art, and Creativity." *Journal of Creative Behavior*, 1975, **9**:1-11. (A book by the same title is also available from Professor Gowan.)

Houston, J. "The Psychenaut Program: An Exploration into Some Human Potentials." *Journal of Creative Behavior*, 1973, 7:253-278.

Masters, R., and Houston, J. *Mind Games: The Guide to Inner Space*. New York: Viking, 1972.

Naranjo, C., and Ornstein, R. *On the Psychology of Meditation*. New York: Viking, 1971.

Rosenfeld, E. *The Book of Highs*. New York: New York Times/Quadrangle, 1973.

Tart, C. T. *Altered States of Consciousness*. New York: Wiley, 1969.

Weil, A. *The Natural Mind*. Boston: Houghton Mifflin, 1972.

ATTRIBUTE LISTING

Emphasizes the detailed observation of each particular characteristic or quality of an item or situation. Attempts are then made to profitably change the characteristic or to relate it to a different item.

Crawford, R. P. *Direct Creativity* (with attribute listing). Wells, Vt: Fraser, 1964.

Davis, G. A. "Idea Checklist for Stimulating Solutions." In A.M. Biondi (ed.), *Have an Affair with Your Mind*. Buffalo, N.Y.: D.O.K., 1974.

Feldhusen, J. F., Treffinger, D. J., Pine, P., et al. *Teaching Children How to Think*. West Lafayette, Ind.: Purdue Research Foundation, 1975.

Mettal, W. G. "Creative Solutions Through Attribute Listing." In A.M. Biondi (ed.), *Have an Affair with Your Mind*. Buffalo, N.Y.: D.O.K., 1974.

Pittman, K. L. "Morphological Analysis and Speculation." In A.M. Biondi (ed.), *Have an Affair with Your Mind*. Buffalo, N.Y.: D.O.K., 1974.

Stein, M. I. *Stimulating Creativity: I. Individual Procedures.* New York: Academic Press, 1974.

AWARENESS DEVELOPMENT

A program to increase the individual's sensitivity to what is going on within himself and how he relates to the here and now.

Fabun, D. *Three Roads to Awareness.* New York: Macmillan (Glencoe), 1970.
Otto, H. A. "The Human Potentialities Movement: An Overview." *Journal of Creative Behavior*, 1974, **8**:258-264.
Perls, F. S., Hefferline, R. F., and Goodman, P. *Gestalt Therapy.* New York: Julian Press, 1951.
Stevens, J. O. *Awareness: Exploring, Experimenting, Experiencing.* New York: Bantam, 1971.
(See also: *Altered States of Consciousness.*)

BIOGRAPHICAL FILM PROGRAM

An educational program of ten documentary biographical films and a flexible textbook. It provides filmed contact with exemplary personalities and opportunity to draw from students' own inner resources in expressing themselves. Designed for college-bound students. See: Drews, E. M. and Knowlton, D. The Being and Becoming series for College-Bound Students. *Audiovisual Instruction, 1963 (January),* **8**:29-32.

BIONICS

A technique that seeks discovery in the nature of ideas that are related to the solution of human problems. For example, attributes of the eye of a beetle have suggested new types of groundspeed indicators for aircraft. See: "Bionics." *Journal of Creative Behavior*, 1968, **1**:52-57.

Davis, G. A. *Psychology of Problem Solving: Theory and Practice.* New York: Basic Books, 1973, Chapter 9.

BLOCKS TO CREATIVITY

Frequently social, environmental, or emotional influences result in obstacles or "blocks" to creative effort. Strategies for overcoming such obstacles are discussed by:

Adams, J. *Conceptual Blockbusting.* San Francisco, Calif.: Freeman, 1974.
Alamshah, W. H. "Blockages to Creativity." *Journal of Creative Behavior*, 1972, **6**:105-113.
Biondi, A. M. (ed.). *The Creative Process.* Buffalo, N.Y.: D.O.K., 1972.

BRAINSTORMING

Promotes rapid and unfettered associations in group discussions through deferment of judgment.

Bouchard, T. J. "Whatever Happened to Brainstorming?" *Journal of Creative Behavior*, 1971, **5**:182-189.
Bristol, L. H., Jr. "Alternating the Mental Current with Brainstorming." In A.M. Biondi (ed.), *Have an Affair with Your Mind.* Buffalo, N.Y.: D.O.K., 1974.
Davis, G. A. *Psychology of Problem-Solving: Theory and Practice.* New York: Basic Books, 1973, chapter 7.
Osborn, A. F. *Applied Imagination.* New York: Scribners, 1963.
Parnes, S. J. "Toward a Better Understanding of Brainstorming." Originally published in *Adult Leadership* (April 1959); reprinted in Parnes and Harding, *Source Book for Creative Thinking* (New York: Scribners, 1962), and Biondi, *The Creative Process* (Buffalo, N.Y.: D.O.K. 1972).
Stein, M. I. *Stimulating Creativity: Volume II: Group Procedures.* New York: Academic Press, 1975.

CANDID CAMERA FILMS

The Cornell Candid Camera Collection, which includes films originally made for and used by the television program, has many delightful short films which illustrate principles of creative problem-solving and effective (as well as not-so-effective) thinking. Write for further information and catalog to: Du Art Film Laboratories, Du Art Film Building, 245 West 55th Street, New York, N.Y. 10019.

CHECKLISTS

Focuses one's attention on a logical list of diverse categories to which the problem could conceivably relate.

Davis, G. A. "Idea Checklists for Stimulating Solutions." In A.M. Biondi (ed.), *Have an Affair with Your Mind.* Buffalo, N.Y.: D.O.K., 1974.
Davis, G. A. *Psychology of Problem Solving.* New York: Basic Books, 1973, Chapter 8.
Osborn, A. F. *Applied Imagination.* New York: Scribners, 1963.
(See also *Think products.*)

CLASSROOM TEACHING AND CREATIVITY

Many articles and books have been addressed to the classroom teacher, providing ideas for encouraging creativity in the classroom. The following bibliography summarizes some useful resources.

Burton, W. H., Kimball, R. B., and Wing, R. L. *Education for Effective Thinking.* New York: Appleton-Century-Crofts, 1960. (pp. 323-326, 342-343 in partic.)
Callahan, C. *Developing Creativity in the Gifted and Talented.* Reston, Va.: CEC, 1978.
Carlson, R. K. "Emergence of Creative Personality." *Childhood Education,* 1960, **36**:402-404.
Cole, H. P. "Process Curricula and Creative Development." *Journal of Creative Behavior,* 1969, **3**:243-259.
Davis, G. A. *Creativity Is Forever.* Cross Plains, Wis.: Badger Press, 1981.
Denny, D. A. "Identification of Teacher-Classroom Variables Facilitating Creative Growth." *American Educational Research Journal,* 1958, **5**:365-383.
Diamond, J. *Picture Books for Creative Thinking: a Bibliography.* Cedar Falls: University of Northern Iowa, 1974.
Feldhusen, J. F., and Treffinger, D. J. *Creative Thinking and Problem Solving in Gifted Education.* Dubuque, Iowa: Kendall-Hunt, 1980.
Feldhusen, J. F., and Hobson, S. K. "Freedom and Play: Catalysts for Creativity." *Elementary School Journal,* 1972, **73**:149-155.
Givens, P. R. "Identifying and Encouraging Creative Processes." *Journal of Higher Education,* 1962, **33**:295-301.
Hallman, R. J. "Techniques of Creative Teaching." *Journal of Creative Behavior,* 1967, **1**:325-330.
Hughes, H. K. "The Enhancement of Creativity." *Journal of Creative Behavior,* 1969, **3**:73-83.

Hutchinson, W. L. "Creative and Productive Thinking in the Classroom." *Journal of Creative Behavior*, 1967, **1**:419-427.

Kranyik, R. D., and Wagner, R. A. "Creativity and the Elementary School Teacher." *Elementary School Journal*, 1965, **66**:2-9.

Rogers, C. R. *Freedom to Learn*. Columbus, Ohio: Merrill, 1969.

Rusch, R. R., Denny, D., and Ives, S. "Fostering Creativity in the Sixth Grade." *Elementary School Journal*, 1965, **65**:262-268.

Schaefer, C. S. *Developing Creativity in Children: An Ideabook for Teachers*. Buffalo, N.Y.: D.O.K., 1973.

Smith, J. A. *Setting Conditions for Creative Teaching in the Elementary School*. Boston: Allyn & Bacon, 1966. (Also: several companion paperbacks dealing with specific subject areas.)

Soar, R. S. "Optimum Teacher-Pupil Interaction for Pupil Growth." *Educational Leadership*, 1968, **26**:275-280.

Strang, R. "Creativity in the Elementary School Classroom." *NEA Journal*, 1961, **50**:20-22.

Taylor, C. W., and Harding, H. F. "Questioning and Creating a Model for Curriculum Reform." *Journal of Creative Behavior*, 1967, **1**:22-33.

Torrance, E. P. "Developing Creativity Through School Experiences." In S.J. Parnes and H. Harding (eds.), *A Source Book for Creative Thinking*, New York: Scribners, 1962, 31-47.

Torrance, E. P. *The Search for Satori and Creativity*. Buffalo, N.Y.: Creative Education Foundation, 1979.

Torrance, E. P. *Encouraging Creativity in the Classroom*. Dubuque, Iowa: Wm. C. Brown, 1970.

Torrance, E. P. *Guiding Creative Talent*. Englewood Cliffs, N.J.: Prentice-Hall, 1962.

Torrance, E. P. *Rewarding Creative Behavior*. Englewood Cliffs, N.J.: Prentice-Hall, 1965.

Torrance, E. P. "We Know Enough to Teach More Creatively Than We Do." *Gifted Child Quarterly*, 1965, **9**:59-63.

Torrance, E. P., and Myers, R. *Creative Learning and Teaching*. New York: Dodd, Mead, 1970.

Turner, R. L., and Denny, D. A. "Teacher Characteristics, Teacher Behavior, and Changes in Pupil Creativity." *Elementary School Journal*, 1969, **69**:265-270.

Wodtke, K., and Wallen, N. "Teacher Classroom Control, Pupil Creativity, and Pupil Classroom Behavior." *Journal of Experimental Education*, 1965, **34**:59-65.

COLLECTIVE NOTEBOOK

Participants record their thoughts about a problem several times daily, then review the list, selecting the most promising ideas for further investigation. See J. W. Haefele, *Creative Innovation*. New York: Reinhold, 1962.

CREATIVE ANALYSIS

A program of exercises designed to increase the college student's facility in discovering relationships within the knowledge s/he possesses, and thereby in creating new knowledge. Emphasizes words as tools of the mind and the thought process. See A. Upton, and R. Samson, *Creative Analysis*, New York: Dutton, 1964.

CREATIVE DRAMATICS

Involving students in creative dramatics may be an effective tool for stimulating imaginative, original thinking. Resources available to the educator include:

Crosscup, R. *Children and Dramatics.* New York: Scribners, 1966.
Davis, G. A., Helfert, C. J., and Shapiro, G. R. "Let's Be an Ice Cream Machine! Creative Dramatics." *Journal of Creative Behavior*, 1973, **7**:37-48.
Eberle, R. "Does Creative Dramatics Really Square with Research Evidence?" *Journal of Creative Behavior*, 1974, **8**:177-182.
Lease, R., and Siks, G. B. *Creative Dramatics in Home, School, and Community.* New York: Harper, 1952.
McCaslin, N. *Creative Dramatics in the Classroom.* New York: McKay, 1968.
Sanders, S. *Creating Plays with Children.* New York: Citation Press, 1970.
Woods, M. S. *Wonderwork: Creative Experiences for Young Children.* Buffalo, N.Y.: D.O.K., 1970.
Woods, M. S., and Trithart, B. *Guidelines to Creative Dramatics.* Buffalo, N.Y.: D.O.K., 1970

CREATIVE HELPING

Instruction concerned with creative thinking and problem-solving frequently implies new definitions for the traditional roles of "teacher" and "learner." The concern for "helping relationships" can be useful in examining and understanding modern approaches.

Combs, A., Avila, D., and Purkey, W. *Helping Relationships: Basic Concepts for the Helping Professions.* Boston: Allyn & Bacon, 1971.
Peavy, R. V. "Creative Helping." *Journal of Creative Behavior*, 1974, **8**:166-176.

CREATIVE INSTRUCTIONS

Emphasizes how instructions are given (problem presented, etc.) as a key determinant in stimulating individual or group production of creative responses. See unpublished doctoral dissertation (67-15607), Colgrove, Melba, Annetta, Stimulating Creative Problem Solving Performance Innovative Set. University of Michigan, 1967.

CREATIVE PROBLEM SOLVING

Ainsworth-Land, V. *Making Waves with Creative Problem Solving.* Buffalo, N.Y.: D.O.K., 1979

Eberle, B., and Stanish, B. *CPS for Kids.* Buffalo, N.Y.: D.O.K., 1980.

Noller, R. *Scratching the Surface of Creative Problem Solving.* Buffalo, N.Y.: D.O.K., 1977.

Noller, R., Treffinger, D., and Houseman, E. *It's a Gas to Be Gifted.* Buffalo, N.Y.: D.O.K., 1979.

Noller, R., Parnes, S., and Biondi, A. *Creative Actionbook.* New York: Scribners, 1976.

Parnes, S. J. *The Magic of Your Mind.* Buffalo, N.Y.: Creative Education Foundation, 1981.

Parnes, S., Noller, R., and Biondi, A. (eds.) *Guide To Creative Action.* New York: Scribners, 1977.

CREATIVE STUDIES PROJECT

Dr. Sidney Parnes and Dr. Ruth Noller conducted an extensive project evaluating the effectiveness of a four-semester Creative Studies program among undergraduate college students. The results provided an extremely comprehensive demonstration of the impact of instruction on creative problem-solving.

Noller, R. B., and Parnes, S. J. "Applied Creativity: The Creative Studies Project: Part III: The Curriculum." *Journal of Creative Behavior,* 1972, **6**:275-294.

Parnes, S. J., and Noller, R. B. "Applied Creativity: The Creative Studies Project: Part I: Development." *Journal of Creative Behavior,* 1972, **6**:11-22.

Parnes, S. J., and Noller, R. B. "Applied Creativity: The Creative Studies Project:

Part II: Results of the Two Year Program." *Journal of Creative Behavior*, 1972, **6**:164-186.

Parnes, S. J., and Noller, R. B. "Applied Creativity: The Creative Studies Project: Part IV: Personality Findings and Conclusions." *Journal of Creative Behavior*, 1973, 7:15-36.

Parnes, S. J., and Noller, R. B. *Toward Supersanity: Channeled Freedom*. Buffalo, N.Y.: D.O.K., 1973.

Parnes, S. J., and Noller, R. B. *Toward Supersanity: Channeled Freedom; Research Supplement*. Buffalo, N.Y.: D.O.K., 1974.

Parnes, S. J., and Treffinger, D. J. *Development of New Criteria for the Evaluation of Creative Studies Programs*. Buffalo: State University College, February 1973. Final Report of USOE Project No. 2B019, Grant No. OEG-2-2-2B019.

Reese, H. W., Parnes, S. J., Treffinger, D. J., and Kaltsounis, G. "Effects of a Creative Studies Program on Structure-of-Intellect Factors." *Journal of Educational Psychology*, 1976, **68**:401-410.

CREATIVE TEACHING GAMES

Many educators have found that simulation activities and games can be used to encourage creative learning in a variety of school subjects. Some basic resources on games are:

Heyman, M. *Simulation Games for the Classroom*. Bloomington, Ind.: Phi Delta Kappa Education Foundation, 1975.

Keith, B., and Hall, S. *Teacher-Made Games: Any Teacher Can*. Buffalo, N.Y.: D.O.K., 1974.

Kennedy, L., and Michon, R. *Games for Individualizing Mathematics Learning*. Columbus, Ohio: Merrill, 1973.

Kohl, H. *Math, Writing, and Games in the Open Classroom*. New York: New York Review (Random House), 1974.

Polon, L., and Pollitt, W. *Creative Teaching Games*. Minneapolis: T. S. Denison, 1974.

Stanford, G., and Stanford, B. *Learning Discussion Skills through Games*. New York: Citation Press, 1969.

CREATIVE THINKING WORKBOOK

A program for adults and college-level students; many exercises suitable for high school students. The exercises are designed to remove internal governors and to provide practice in stretching the imagination in problem-finding and problem-solving. Problems are included on product design and on presenting ideas. Can be self-instructional. Available from: W. O. Uraneck, 56 Turning Mill Road, Lexington, Mass. 02173 (1963).

CORT THINKING SKILLS

The Cognitive Research Trust (CoRT), founded by Dr. Edward deBono in England, has been actively involved in the development of many instructional programs to foster various aspects of effective, creative thinking.

deBono, E. *PO: Beyond Yes or No.* New York: Simon & Schuster, 1972.
deBono, E. *The Mechanism of Mind.* New York: Simon & Schuster, 1969.
deBono, E. *Teaching Thinking.* New York: Penguin, 1978.
deBono, E. *A Thinking Course for Juniors.* Dorset, U.K.: Direct Education Services, 1974.

CURRICULUM—GENERAL

Many recent developments in curriculum and instruction have been concerned with providing opportunities for creative growth. In this section, and the next six, several representative publications are listed in a variety of curriculum areas.

Bruch, C. B. and others. *The Faces and Forms of Creativity.* Ventura, Calif.: Ventura County Supt. of Schools, 1981.
Davis, G. A. *Psychology of Problem Solving: Theory and Practice.* New York: Basic Books, 1973.
Davis, G. A., and Scott, J. A. (eds.) *Training Creative Thinking.* New York: Holt, Rinehart and Winston, 1971.
Franco, J. M. *Project Beacon.* Public schools, Rochester, N.Y. 14608. (Concerned with the development of ego strength in primary grades.)
Gibson, J. S. *The Intergroup Relations Curriculum.* Medford, Mass.: Tufts University Press.
Gowan, J. C., Demos, G. D., and Torrance, E. P. (eds.) *Creativity: Its Educational Implications.* New York: Wiley, 1967.
Jaynes, R., and Woodbridge, B. *Bowman Early Childhood Series.* Glendale, Calif.: Bowman Publishing, 1969. (Designed to help develop positive self-awareness and identity, awareness of self as a person, ability to relate to others.)

Kresse, F. H. *Match Projects.* Boston: American Science and Engineering, Inc., 20 Overland Street. (Materials and activities across many areas for grades 4-6+.)

Massialas, B. G., and Zevin, J. *Creative Encounters in the Classroom.* New York: Wiley, 1967.

For anthologies dealing with educational and curricular implications of creativity studies: see also *Affective Domain; Creative Teaching Games; Learning Centers.*

CURRICULUM ENRICHMENT

Heuer, J., Koprowicz, A., and Harris, R. *M.A.G.I.C. K.I.T.S.* Mansfield Center, Conn.: Creative Learning Press, 1980.

Renzulli, J. S. *The Enrichment Triad Model.* Mansfield Center, Conn.: Creative Learning Press, 1977.

Smith, L. (ed.) *Triad Prototype Series.* Mansfield Center, Conn.: Creative Learning Press.

Stewart, E., and Dean, M. *The Almost Whole Earth Catalog of Process-Oriented Enrichment Materials.* Mansfield Center, Conn.: Creative Learning Press, 1980.

CURRICULUM—FINE ARTS

Hickok, D., and Smith, J. A. *Creative Teaching of Music in the Elementary School.* Boston: Allyn & Bacon, 1974.

Lowenfeld, V., and Brittain, W. L. *Creative and Mental Growth.* New York: Macmillan, 1982.

Ritson, J. E., and Smith, J. A. *Creative Teaching of Art in the Elementary School.* Boston: Allyn & Bacon, 1975.

CURRICULUM—MATHEMATICS

Davis, R. B. *The Madison Project.* Reading, Mass: Addison Wesley. (Five different curricula; grades 2-8.)

Kennedy, L. M. *Experiences for Teaching Children Mathematics.* Belmont, Calif.: Wadsworth, 1973.

Kennedy, L., and Michon, R. *Games for Individualizing Mathematics Learning.* Columbus: Merrill, 1973.

Kohl, H. *Math, Writing, and Games in the Open Classroom.* New York: New York Review (Random House), 1974.

Matthews, G. *Nuffield Mathematics Project.* New York: Wiley. (A British program for ages 5-13.)

Noller, R., Heintz, R., and Blaeuer, D. *Creative Problem Solving in Mathematics.* Buffalo, N.Y.: D.O.K., 1978.

Werntz, J. H. *Minnemast Project.* For grades K-6; write Minnemast Project, 720 Washington Avenue SE, Minneapolis, Minn. 55414.

Westcott, A. M., and Smith, J. A. *Creative Teaching of Mathematics in the Elementary School.* Boston: Allyn & Bacon, 1967.

CURRICULUM—PREPRIMARY

Dunn, L. M. *Peabody Language Development Kit.* American Guidance Publishers, Circle Pines, Minn. 55014.

Frostig, M. *Frostig Visual Perception Program.* Chicago: Follett.

Kaplan, S. N., Kaplan, J. B., Madsen, S. K., and Gould, B. T. *A Young Child Experiences.* Pacific Palisades, Calif.: Goodyear, 1975.

Khatena, J. *Training Preschool Disadvantaged Children to Think Creatively.* Huntington, W. Va.: Marshall University, 1969.

Schaefer, C. S. *Becoming Somebody: Creative Activities for Preschool Children.* Buffalo, N.Y.: D.O.K., 1973.

Stendler, C. *Early Childhood Curriculum: A Piaget Approach.* Boston: American Science and Engineering.

Woods, M. S. *Wonderwork.* Buffalo, N.Y.: D.O.K., 1970.

For research on creativity among preprimary children, contact Professor Elizabeth Starkweather, Oklahoma State University, Stillwater.

CURRICULUM—READING, LITERATURE, LANGUAGE ARTS

Armstrong, R. Q., and Merkelson, W. S. *Cards for Reading Response: I. Intermediate Level.* Monterey Park, Calif.: Creative Teaching Press, 1972.

Charles, C. M., and Church, M. *Creative Writing Skills.* Minneapolis: Denison, 1968.

Christensen, F. B. *Cards for Reading Response: II. Primary.* Monterey Park, Calif.: Creative Teaching Press, 1974.

Christensen, F. B. *Springboards to Creative Writing.* Monterey Park, Calif.: Creative Teaching Press, 1971.

Clymer, T. et al. *Reading 360.* Ginn and Company, 1969. (An innovative series in which E. Paul Torrance served as creativity consultant.)

DiPego, G., and Davis, G. A. *Imagination Express: Saturday Subway Ride.* Buffalo, N.Y.: D.O.K., 1973.

Medeiros, V. *The Voices of Man Literature Series.* Reading, Mass.: Addison-Wesley. High school literature series for disadvantaged students.

Moffet, J. *A Student Centered Language Arts Curriculum.* (Volume 1: K-6; Volume 2: K-13.) Boston: Houghton Mifflin, 1968.

My Weekly Reader: Creative Expression Series (Imagine and Write). Xerox Educational Publishing Co.

Sargent, R. *Discovery Stories.* Urban Media Materials, 212 Mineola Ave., Roslyn Heights, N.Y. 11577. (Filmstrips and tapes.)

Scholastic Magazines: Creative Expression Series.

Smith, J. A. *Creative Teaching of Language Arts in the Elementary School,* 2nd ed. Boston: Allyn & Bacon, 1973.

Smith, J. A. *Creative Teaching of Reading in the Elementary School,* 3rd ed. Boston: Allyn & Bacon, 1975.

CURRICULUM—SCIENCE

Anderson, R. D., DeVito, A., Dyrli, O. E., Kellogg, M., Kochendorfer, L., and Weigand, J. *Developing Children's Thinking through Science.* Englewood Cliffs, N.J.: Prentice-Hall, 1970.

Brown, R. R. *Elementary Science Study.* (Gr. K-6) Manchester, Mo.: Webster Division, McGraw-Hill.

DeVito, A., and Krockover, G. *Creative Sciencing.* Boston, Mass.: Little, Brown, 1976.

Karplus, R., and Thier, H. D. *Science Curriculum Improvement Study.* (Gr. K-6) Chicago: Rand McNally.

LaSalle, D. Write for information concerning an independent science center. *Talcott Mountain Science Center,* Montevideo Road, Avon, Conn. 06001.

Mayor, J. *Science: A Process Approach.* (Gr. K-6) New York: Xerox Corporation.

Piltz, A., and Sund, R. *Creative Teaching of Science in the Elementary School.* 2nd ed. Boston: Allyn & Bacon, 1974.

Stone, A. H., Geis, F., and Kuslan, L. *Experiences for Teaching Children Science.* Belmont, Calif.: Wadsworth, 1971.

Sund, R., Tillery, B., and Trowbridge, L. *Investigate and Discover Elementary Science Lessons. Boston: Allyn & Bacon, 1975.*

Washton, N. S. Teaching Science Creatively. Philadelphia: W. B. Saunders, 1967.

CURRICULUM—SOCIAL STUDIES

Bruner, J. S. *Man: A Course of Study.* Curriculum Development Associates, 1211 Connecticut Ave., NW, Washington, D.C. 20036.

EDCOM Systems, *Space, Time, and Life.* (Gr. 4-6) EDCOM Systems, 145 Witherspoon Road, Princeton, N.J. 08540.

Educational Research Council of America. *Concepts and Inquiry.* (Gr. K-8) Boston: Allyn & Bacon.

Lippitt, R. *Social Science Laboratory Units.* (Gr. 4-6) Chicago: Science Research Associates.

Muessig, R. *Discussion Pictures for Beginning Social Studies.* New York: Harper & Row, 1967.

Smith, J. A. *Creative Teaching of the Social Studies in the Elementary School.* Boston: Allyn & Bacon, 1967.

Taba, H., and Durkin, M. *Taba Social Studies Curriculum.* (Gr. 1-8) Reading, Mass.: Addison-Wesley, 1969.

Weitzman, D. *My Backyard History Book.* Boston, Mass.: Little, Brown, 1975.

Winks, R. *The Historian as Detective.* New York: Harper, 1968.

DELPHI TECHNIQUE

Polling procedure resembling an absentee "brainstorming" effort used to generate alternative futures for a particular topic or series of topics. See O. Helmer, *Social Technology.* New York: Basic Books, 1966. For additional references, contact Book Service, World Future Society, P. O. Box 19285, Twentieth Street Station, Washington, D.C. 20036.

DEVELOPMENTAL STAGE ANALYSIS OF CREATIVITY

See J. C. Gowan, *The Development of the Creative Individual* (1971). Robert Knapp Pub., Box 7234, San Diego, Calif. 92107

DOUBLING IDEA POWER

A packaged course for business, industrial, and governmental training programs on creative problem-solving. The modular format involves books, written exercises for participants, filmstrips, and cassette tapes.

The modules are: (1) Introduction and mental blocks; (2) Encouraging the creative process; (3) The creative problem-solving process; (4) Exercise in free association; (5) Application of the total process to participant's problems.

Edwards, M. O. *Doubling Idea Power: A Program in Creative Innovative Problem-solving and Decision-making.* Reading, Mass.: Addison-Wesley, 1975.

EXPERIMENTAL PSYCHOLOGY TECHNIQUES

Caron, A. J. "A Test of Maltzman's Theory of Originality Training." *Journal of Verbal Learning and Verbal Behavior*, 1963, **1**:436-442.

Duncan, C. P. "Attempts to Influence Performance on an Insight Problem." *Psychological Reports*, 1961, **9**:35-42.

Gallup, H. F. "Originality in Free and Controlled Association Responses." *Psychological Reports*, 1963, **13**:923-929.

Maltzman, I. "On the Training of Originality." *Psychological Review*, 1960, **67**: 229-242.

Maltzman, I., et al. "Experimental Studies of Associational Variables in Originality." *Psychological Monographs*, 1964, **78**:3. (Whole #580).

Maltzman, I., Bogartz, W., and Breger, L. "A Procedure for Increasing Word Association Originality and Its Transfer Effects." *Journal of Experimental Psychology*, 1958, **56**:392-398.

Maltzman, I., Brooks, L., Bogartz, W., and Summers, S. "The Facilitation of Problem-Solving by Prior Exposure to Uncommon Responses." *Journal of Experimental Psychology*, 1958, **56**:399-406.

Maltzman, I., and Gallup, H. F. "Comments on 'Originality' in Free and Controlled Association Responses." *Psychological Reports*, 1964, **14**:573-574.

Maltzman, I., Simon, S., Raskin, P., and Licht, L. "Experimental Studies in the Training of Originality." *Psychological Monographs*, 1960, **74**:(6). Whole #493.

FORCED RELATIONSHIP TECHNIQUES

Specific types of exercises designed to derive new combinations of items and thoughts.

deBono, E. *Think Tank: Instruction Booklet.* Toronto, Canada: Think Tank Corp., 1973.

Stein, M. I. *Stimulating Creativity: I. Individual Procedures.* New York: Academic Press, 1974.

Whiting, C. S. *Creative Thinking.* New York: Reinhold, 1958.

Whiting, C. S. "Forced Relationship Techniques." In A.M. Biondi (ed.), *Have an Affair with Your Mind.* Buffalo, N.Y.: D.O.K., 1974.

(See also *Management of Intelligence; Racking.*)

FUTURE PROBLEM SOLVING

The Future Problem-Solving Program provides opportunities for application of creative problem-solving skills in many problems of futuristics. There are also opportunities for interscholastic competition from the local through the national levels. *Contact*: Dr. Anne Crabbe, Future Problem-Solving Program, Coe College, Cedar Rapids, Iowa 52402.

Torrance, E. P. "Helping Your G/C/T Child Learn About the Future." *G/C/T Magazine*, 1978, **1**:5 .

Torrance, E. P., Bruch, C., and Torrance, J. P. "Interscholastic Futuristic Problem Solving." *Journal of Creative Behavior*, 1978, **10**:117-125.

FUTURISTICS

Predicting the future, with projections for five-, ten-, and fifty-year periods. Write Carl Gregory, California State College, School of Business, Long Beach, Calif. 90801. Also contact World Future Society, P. O. Box 19285, Twentieth Street Station, Washington, D.C. 20036.

Bleedorn, B. *Looking Ahead.* Buffalo, N.Y.: D.O.K., 1981.

Eggers, J. *Will You Help Me Create the Future Today?* Buffalo, N.Y.: D.O.K., 1981.

Kahn H., and Wiener, A. *The Year 2,000.* New York: Macmillan, 1967.

Maryanopolis, J. *The Leading Edge: A Futurist Workshop.* Logan, Iowa: Perfection Form Co., 1980.

Toffler, A. *Future Shock.* New York: Random House, 1970.

Weber, R. E. "Human Potential and the Year 2000: The Futures Project of the New Jersey Department of Education." *Journal of Creative Behavior*, 1973, **7(2)**:133-150.

Weber, R. E. "The Techniques of Futurology." *Journal of Creative Behavior,* 1973, **7(3)**:153-160.

GENERAL SEMANTICS

Approaches that help the individual to discover multiple meanings or relationships in words and expressions. For continuing current information, see ETC.: *A Review of General Semantics,* a quarterly journal with editorial offices at San Francisco State College, San Francisco, Calif. 94132. (Business office: 540 Powell Street, San Francisco, Calif. 94108).

Hayakawa, S. I. *Language in Thought and Action.* New York: Harcourt Brace Jovanovich, 1964.

Noller, R. B. "Some Applications of General Semantics in Teaching Creativity." *Journal of Creative Behavior,* 1971, **5(4)**:256-266.

True, S. R. "A Study of the Relation of General Semantics and Creativity." *Dissertation Abstracts,* 1964, **25(4)**:2390.

IDEABOOKS AND IMAGI/CRAFT SERIES

With his colleagues, Professor E. Paul Torrance of the University of Georgia (Athens, Ga. 30602) has developed numerous sets and programs for encouraging creative thinking, particularly among elementary school children.

The *Ideabooks* series, with Robert Myers, includes several booklets: "Can You Imagine?" "For Those Who Wonder," "Invitations To Thinking and Doing," "Invitations to Speaking and Writing Creatively," and "Plots, Puzzles, and Ploys."

The *Imagi/craft* series, with B. F. Cunningham, includes recorded exercises and stories, based on biographical sketches of famous people, and (also with Joe Khatena) "Thinking Creatively with Sounds and Words." (See also *Verbal Imagery.*)

For information, write to Ginn and Company, Waltham, Mass. 02154.

In 1972, Dr. Torrance compiled an excellent review of research on creativity training programs: "Can We Teach Children To Think Creatively?" *Journal of Creative Behavior,* 1972, **6**:114-143. Although Dr.Torrance's writings are considerably more numerous than can be included in this summary, some papers and books specifically related to encouraging creative thinking are:

Torrance, E. P. "Achieving Socialization without Sacrificing Creativity." *Journal of Creative Behavior,* 1970, **4**:183-189.

Torrance, E. P. *Encouraging Creativity in the Classroom.* Dubuque, Iowa: Wm. C. Brown, 1970.

Torrance, E. P. "Priming Creative Thinking in the Primary Grades." *Elementary School Journal,* 1961, **62**:34-41.

Torrance, E. P., and Myers, R. *Creative Learning and Teaching.* New York: Dodd Mead, 1970.

Torrance, E. P., and Torrance, P. "Combining Creative Problem-solving with Creative Expressive Activities with Disadvantaged Children." *Journal of Creative Behavior,* 1971, **6**:1-10.

IMAGINATION GAMES

Fantasy and imagination are important dimensions of creativity, but are frequently inhibited in the school setting. Some collections of games to help keep the "spark of imagination" alive, for both adults and children include:

deMille, R. *Put Your Mother on the Ceiling: Children's Imagination Games.* New York: Viking, 1973.

Eberle, R. F. *Scamper: Games for Imagination Development,* Buffalo, N.Y.: D.O.K., 1971.

Otto, H. A. *Fantasy Encounter Games.* New York: Harper & Row, 1972.

See also R. F. Eberle, "Developing Imagination through Scamper." *Journal of Creative Behavior,* 1972, **6**:199-203.

INCIDENT PROCESS

A problem-solving approach (and/or training program) developed at the college and adult level. It stresses multiple viewpoints and a wide search for problem-elements; applies many methods similar to the older Job Relations Training program. See P. W. Pigors, and F. C. Pigors, *Case Method in Human Relations: The Incident Process.* New York: McGraw-Hill, 1961.

INDEPENDENT, CREATIVE LEARNING

Treffinger, D. J. *Encouraging Creative Learning for the Gifted and Talented: A Handbook of Methods and Techniques.* Ventura, Calif.: Ventura County Supt. of Schools, 1980.

INDEPENDENT STUDY

Alexander, W., and Hines, V. *Independent Study in the Secondary Schools.* New York: Holt, Rinehart & Winston, 1967.

Atwood, B. *Building Independent Learning Skills.* Palo Alto, Calif.: Learning Handbooks, 1974.

Beggs, D., and Buffie, E. *Independent Study: Bold New Venture.* Bloomington: Indiana Univ. Press, 1965.

Doherty, E., and Evans, L. *Self-starter Kit for Independent Study.* Austin, Tex.: Special Education Associates, 1980.

Homeratha, L., and Treffinger, D. *Independent Study Folders.* Buffalo, N.Y.: D.O.K., 1980.

Kaplan, S., Madsen, S., and Gould, B. *The Big Book of Independent Study.* Santa Monica, Calif.: Goodyear, 1976.

Treffinger, D., Nash, D., and Homeratha, L. *Independent Study Folders-Secondary.* Buffalo, N.Y.: D.O.K., 1981.

KEPNER-TREGOE METHOD

An approach (or training program) that emphasizes "what a person *does* with information," how she/he interrelates facts in analyzing problems and making decisions. Developed at adult level. See C. H. Kepner, and B. B. Tregoe, *The National Manager.* New York: McGraw-Hill, 1965.

LATERAL THINKING

deBono, E. *Lateral Thinking.* New York: Penguin, 1970.

deBono, E. *The Use of Lateral Thinking.* New York: Penguin, 1967.

LEARNING CENTERS AND INDIVIDUALIZED INSTRUCTION

Many classroom teachers are discovering that classroom space can be used in many ways, and that creativity can flourish when many options are provided for active, participative learning by students. "Learning centers" provide useful ways of organizing such learning in the classroom. Some basic resources include:

Anderson, R. *Super Cards*. Monterey Park, Calif.: Creative Teaching Press, 1974.

Cooperman, B., Fischle, M. J., and Hochstetter, R. *Teacher, Let Me Do It: Learning Centers that Grow*. Buffalo, N.Y.: D.O.K., 1975.

Forte, I., Pangle, M., and Tupa, R. *Center Stuff for Nooks, Crannies, and Corners*. Nashville, Tenn.: Incentive Publications, 1973.

Hughes, M., and Dakan, P. *Creating Learning Centers. Set 2: Primary*. Monterey Park, Calif.: Creative Teaching Press, 1974.

Kaplan, S., Kaplan, J., Madsen, S., and Gould, B. *A Young Child Experiences*. Pacific Palisades, Calif.: Goodyear, 1975.

Kaplan, S., Kaplan, J., Madsen, S., and Taylor, B. *Change for Children*. Pacific Palisades, Calif.: Goodyear, 1973.

Kaplan, S. N., and Madsen, S. K. *Think-ins*. Monterey Park, Calif.: Creative Teaching Press, 1974.

Mummert, P. *Create Your Own Learning Centers*. Buffalo, N.Y.: D.O.K., 1974.

Mummert, P. *The Learning Center Smorgasbord*. Buffalo, N.Y.: D.O.K. (several volumes; undated).

Thompson, D., and Parker, S. *Creating Learning Centers-1. Intermediate Level*. Monterey Park, Calif.: Creative Teaching Press, 1973.

Yellow Pages of Learning Resources. Cambridge, Mass.: MIT Press, 1972.

MANAGEMENT OF INTELLIGENCE

A number of techniques for creative problem-solving, including negative ideation, 7 times 7 technique, and others, are included in: C. E. Gregory, *The Management of Intelligence: Scientific Problem Solving and Creativity*. New York: McGraw-Hill, 1967.

MENTORING

Boston, B. O. *The Sorcerer's Apprentice: A Case Study in the Role of the Mentor*. Reston, Va.: CEC, 1976.

Noller, R. B. *Mentoring: A Voiced Scarf*. Buffalo, N.Y.: Bearly Limited, 1982.

Runions, T. "The Mentor Academy: Educating the Gifted and Talented for the 80s." *Gifted Child Quarterly*, 1980, **24**:152-157.

MINI-BOOKS

The Creative Education Foundation has sponsored the development of several "mini-books," which focus upon various aspects of creative problem-solving.

Biondi, A. M. (ed.) *The Creative Process.* Buffalo, N.Y.: D.O.K., 1972.
Biondi, A. M. (ed.) *Have an Affair with Your Mind.* Buffalo, N.Y.: D.O.K., 1974.
Parnes, S. J. *Creativity: Unlocking Human Potential.* Buffalo, N.Y.: D.O.K., 1972.
Parnes, S. J. *Aha! Insights into Creative Behavior.* Buffalo, N.Y.: D.O.K., 1975.
(See also *Creative Studies Project.*)

MORPHOLOGY (OR MORPHOLOGICAL ANALYSIS)

A system involving the methodical interrelating of all elements of a problem in order to discover new approaches to a solution. See: M. S. Allen, *Morphological Creativity.* Englewood Cliffs, N.J.: Prentice-Hall, 1962.

See also K. L. Pittman, Morphological analysis and speculation. In A.M. Biondi (ed.), *Have an Affair With Your Mind.* Buffalo, N.Y.: D.O.K., 1974.

Treffinger, D. J. "50,000 Ways to Create a Gifted Program." *G/C/T/ Magazine.* January-February 1979.

MULTIPLE TALENT TEACHING

Recent psychological advances in the understanding of human talents have important implications for educational practice: we must no longer be content to define "talent" in an extremely narrow way. Children come to school with many different kinds of talents that must be nurtured and given opportunities for expression.

Eberle, R. F. *Classroom Cue Cards for Multiple Talent Teaching.* Buffalo, N.Y.: D.O.K., 1974.
Lloyd, B., Sghini, J., and Stevenson, G. *Igniting Creative Potential: II.* Jordan School District, 9361 South 400 East, Sandy, Utah 84070 (1974).
Taylor, C. W. "Be Talent Developers as Well as Knowledge Dispensers." *Today's Education,* 1968, **57**:67-69.
Taylor, C. W. "Developing Effectively Functioning People—the Accountability of Multiple Talent Teaching." *Education,* 1973, **94**:99-111.

Taylor, C. W. "The Highest Talent Potentials of Man." *Gifted Child Quarterly*, 1969, **13**:9-30.
(See also *Williams' Model*.)

NEW DIRECTIONS IN CREATIVITY

A program designed to assist teachers of middle-grade youngsters foster creative thinking abilities. The exercises included in each volume are based on several dimensions of the divergent-thinking category of Guilford's Structure of Intellect model. All exercises are presented as ditto masters that can be duplicated by the user. The volumes in the series are *Mark I* and *Mark II* (by Joseph S. Renzulli) and *Mark III* (by Joseph S. Renzulli and Carolyn Callahan). *New Directions in Creativity* is published by Harper & Row. (See also J. S. Renzulli and C. M. Callahan. "Developing Creativity Training Activities." *Gifted Child Quarterly*, 1975, **19**:38-45.)

OLYMPICS OF THE MIND

A program of creative competition for students in elementary through high school. Student teams are challenged to find unique and effective solutions for a variety of complex, realistic problems. Creative Competitions, Inc., P.O. Box 27, Glassboro, N.J. 80828.

OPPORTUNITY DISCOVERY

Ainsworth-Land, V., and Ainsworth-Land, G. *The Opportunity Discovery Process.* Buffalo, N.Y.: D.O.K., 1982.

PANEL CONSENSUS TECHNIQUE

A way to process a large number of ideas, circumventing organizational restraints to idea-creation, using extensive participation and emphasizing methods for selecting good ideas.

Taylor, C. W. "Panel Consensus Technique: A New Approach to Decision-making." *Journal of Creative Behavior*, 1972, **6**:187-198.

PEER TEACHING

Creative learning may be encouraged when children participate actively in helping younger children learn.

Lippitt, R., and Lippitt, P. "Cross Age Helpers." *Today's Education*, March 1968, 24-26.
Riessman, F., Kohler, M., and Gartner, A. *Children Teach Children*. New York: Harper & Row, 1971.
Strom, R. D., and Engelbrecht, G. "Creative Peer Teaching." *Journal of Creative Behavior*, 1974, **8**:93-100.

PERSONAL CREATIVITY

Davis, G. A. "Personal Creative Thinking Techniques." *Gifted Child Quarterly*, 1981, **25**:99-101.
Davis, G. A. *Creativity Is Forever*. Cross Plains, Wis.: Badger Press, 1981.

PROBLEM FINDING

Csikszentmihalyi, M., and Getzels, J. W. "Discovery-Oriented Behavior and Originality of Creative Products: A Study with Artists."*Journal of Personality and Social Psychology*, 1971, **19**:47-52.
Getzels, J. W. "Problem-finding and the Inventiveness of Solutions." *Journal of Creative Behavior*, 1975, **9**:12-18.
Getzels, J. W. *Problem-finding*. The 343rd convocation address, University of Chicago; *University of Chicago Record*, November 21, 1973 (vol. 7), 281-283.
Getzels, J. W., and Csikszentmihalyi, M. "Scientific Creativity," *Science Journal*, 1967, **3**:80-84.

PROBLEM-SOLVING IMPROVEMENT

A self-instructional program, including two audio tapes, for simulated problem-solving experiences, with applications for business and industry as well as for education.

Samson, R. W. *Problem Solving Improvement.* New York: McGraw-Hill, 1970.

PROCESS EDUCATION

A survey of materials and resources that can be utilized in process education:

Cole, H. P. "Process Curricula and Creative Development." *Journal of Creative Behavior,* 1969, 3:243-259.
Cole, H. P. *Process Education.* Englewood Cliffs, N.J.: Educational Technology Publications, 1972.
Seferian, A., and Cole, H. P. *Encounters in Thinking: A Compendium of Curricula for Process Education.* Buffalo, N.Y.: Creative Education Foundation, Occasional paper #6.

PRODUCTIVE THINKING PROGRAM

A self-instructional program for the upper elementary grades. It attempts to help children improve their creative problem-solving ability. The program is authored by Martin Covington, Richard S. Crutchfield, Robert Olton, and Lillian Davies. It was published in 1972 by Charles E. Merrill, Inc., Columbus, Ohio. Considerable research has been conducted in which the original version of the *Productive Thinking Program* was used; much of this research is reviewed in: Treffinger, D. J. and Ripple, R. E. "Programmed Instruction in Creative Problem-solving." *Educational Leadership,* 1971, **28**:667-675. Other published reports include:

Covington, M. V. "Some Experimental Evidence on Teaching for Creative Understanding." *The Reading Teacher,* 1967 (Feb.), 390-396.
Covington, M. V., and Crutchfield, R. S. "Facilitation of Creative Problem-solving." *Programmed Instruction,* 1965, **4**:3-5, 10.

Crutchfield, R. S. "Creative Thinking in Children: Its Teaching and Testing." In H. Brim, R. Crutchfield and W. Holtzman (eds.), *Intelligence: Perspectives 1965*. New York: Harcourt Brace Jovanovich, 1966 (pp. 33-64).

Crutchfield, R. S. "Instructing the Individual in Creativity." In Educational Testing Service's *Individualizing Instruction* (Princeton, N.J., 1965); also in Mooney and Razik's *Explorations in Creativity* (1967), pp. 196-206.

Crutchfield, R. S., and Covington, M. V. "Programmed Instruction and Creativity." *Programmed Instruction*, 1965, **4**:1-2, 8-10.

Davis, G. A. *Psychology of Problem Solving: Theory and Practice*. New York: Basic Books, 1973, chapter 11.

Evans, D., Ripple, R. E., and Treffinger, D. J. "Programmed Instruction and Productive Thinking: A Preliminary Report of a Cross-national Comparison." In W.R. Dunn, and C. Holyroyd (eds.) *Aspects of Educational Technology*, London: Methuen, 1968 (115-120).

Olton, R. M. "A Self-instructional Program for the Development of Productive Thinking in Fifth- and Sixth-grade Children." In F.E. Williams (ed.), *First Seminar on Productive Thinking in Education*. St. Paul, Minn.: Macalester College, 1966, 53-60.

Olton, R. M. "A Self-instructional Program for Developing Productive Thinking Skills in Fifth- and Sixth-grade Children." *Journal of Creative Behavior*, 1969, **3**:16-25.

Olton, R. M., and Crutchfield, R. S. "Developing the Skills of Productive Thinking." In P. Mussen, J. Langer, and M. Covington (eds.), *New Directions in Developmental Psychology*. New York: Holt, Rinehart, and Winston, 1969.

Olton, R. M., Wardrop, J., Covington, M., Goodwin, W., Crutchfield, R., Klausmeier, H., and Ronda, T. "The development of Productive Thinking Skills in Fifth-grade Children." Technical report #34. Madison: University of Wisconsin, Rand D Center for Cognitive Learning, 1967.

Ripple, R. E., and Dacey, J. S. "The Facilitation of Problem-solving and Verbal Creativity by Exposure to Programmed Instruction." *Psychology in the Schools*, 1967, **4**:240-245.

Schuler, G. The Effectiveness of the Productive Thinking Program. Paper presented at American Educational Research Association, Chicago, April 1974.

Shively, J., Feldhusen, J., and Treffinger, D. "Effects of Creativity Training Programs and Teacher Influence on Pupils' Creative Thinking Abilities." *Journal of Experimental Education*, 1971, **41**:63-69.

Sporburg, A. "The Effect of Programmed Productive Thinking Materials on the Divergent and Convergent Thinking Scores of Sixth-grade Students." Paper presented at American Educational Research Association, New York, February 1971.

Torrance, E. P. "Can We Teach Children to Think Creatively?" *Journal of Creative Behavior*, 1972, **6**:114-143.

Treffinger, D. J., and Ripple, R. E. "Developing Creative Problem-solving Abilities and Related Attitudes through Programmed Instruction." *Journal of Creative Behavior*, 1969, **3**:105-110.

Treffinger, D. J., and Ripple, R. E. *The Effects of Programmed Instruction in Productive Thinking on Verbal Creativity and Problem-solving among Elementary School Children.* Ithaca, N.Y.: Cornell University, 1968. Final Report of USOE Research Project OEG-0-8-080002-0220-010.

Treffinger, D. J., and Ripple, R. E. "The Effects of Programmed Instruction in Productive Thinking on Verbal Creativity and Problem-solving among Pupils in Grades Four through Seven." *Irish Journal of Education*, 1970, **4**:47-59.

Treffinger, D. J., Speedie, S. M., and Brunner, W. D. "Improving Children's Creative Problem Solving Abilities: The Purdue Creativity Project." *Journal of Creative Behavior*, 1974, **8**:20-30.

Wardrop, J. L., Olton, R., Goodwin, W., Covington, M., Klausmeier, H., Crutchfield, R., and Ronda, T. "The Development of Productive Thinking Skills in Fifth-grade Children." *Journal of Experimental Education*, 1969, **37**:67-77.

PSYCHODRAMATIC APPROACHES

These include a variety of techniques such as role-playing and role reversal. In psychodrama the attempt is made to bring into focus all elements of an individual's problem; whereas in sociodrama the emphasis is on shared problems of group members. Elements of these techniques have been used in various types of educational settings and training programs. See J. L. Moreno, *Who Shall Survive?* New York: Beacon House, 1953. For current reading, see the quarterly journal *Group Psychotherapy* by the same publisher.

PSYCHOLOGY OF PROBLEM-SOLVING AND THINKING

Bourne, L. E., Jr., Ekstrand, B. R., and Dominowski, R. L. *The Psychology of Thinking.* Englewood Cliffs, N.J.: Prentice-Hall, 1971.

Davis, G. A. *Psychology of Problem Solving: Theory and Practice.* New York: Basic Books, 1973.

Duncan, C. P. *Thinking: Current Experimental Studies.* Philadelphia: Lippincott, 1967.

Farnham-Diggory, S. *Cognitive Processes in Education.* New York: Harper & Row, 1972.

Johnson, D. M. *Systematic Introduction to the Psychology of Thinking.* New York: Harper & Row, 1972.

Maier, N. R. F. *Problem Solving and Creativity in Individuals and Groups.* Belmont, Calif.: Brooks Cole, 1970.

Newell, A., and Simon, H. A. *Human Problem Solving.* Englewood Cliffs, N.J.: Prentice-Hall, 1972.

Vinacke, W. E. *The Psychology of Thinking, 2nd ed.* New York: McGraw-Hill, 1974.

PURDUE CREATIVITY TRAINING PROGRAM

The *Purdue Creativity Training Program* consists of 28 audio tapes and accompanying printed exercises, for the development of creative thinking and problem-solving abilities among elementary school pupils. For further information, write: John F. Feldhusen, Educational Psychology Section, Purdue University, South Campus Courts G, West Lafayette, Ind. 47907. Published descriptions and research reports include:

Bahlke, S. J. *A study of the Enhancement of Creative Abilities in Elementary School Children.* Unpublished master's thesis, Purdue University, 1967.

Bahlke, S. J. *Componential Evaluation of Creativity Instructional Materials.* Unpublished doctoral thesis, Purdue University, 1969.

Davis, G. A. *Psychology of Problem Solving: Theory and Practice.* New York: Basic Books, 1973, chapter 11.

Feldhusen, J. F., Bahlke, S. J., and Treffinger, D. J. "Teaching Creative Thinking." *Elementary School Journal,* 1969, **70**:48-53.

Feldhusen, J. F., Speedie, S. M., and Treffinger, D. J. "The Purdue Creative Thinking Program: Research and Evaluation." *NSPI Journal,* 1971, **10**:5-9.

Feldhusen, J. F., Treffinger, D. J., and Bahlke, S. J. "Developing Creative Thinking: The Purdue Creativity Program." *Journal of Creative Behavior,* 1970, **4**:85-90.

Feldhusen, J. F., Treffinger, D. J., and Thomas S. J. B. *Global and Componential Evaluation of Creativity Instructional Materials.* Buffalo, N.Y.: Creative Education Foundation, 1971.

Robinson, W. L. T. *Taped-Creativity-Series versus Conventional Teaching and Learning.* Unpublished master's thesis, Atlanta University, 1969.

Shively, J., Feldhusen, J., and Treffinger, D. "Effects of Creativity Training Programs and Teacher Influence on Pupils' Creative Thinking Abilities." *Journal of Experimental Education,* 1971, **41**:63-69.

Speedie, S. M., Treffinger, D. J., and Feldhusen, J. F. "Evaluation of the Components of the Purdue Creative Thinking Program: A Longitudinal Study." *Psychological Reports, 1971,* **29**: 395-398.

Torrance, E. P. "Can We Teach Children to Think Creatively?" *Journal of Creative Behavior,* 1972, **6**:114-143.

Treffinger, D. J. "The Purdue Creativity Training Program: Recent Research and Evaluation." In C. W. Taylor (ed.), *Proceedings of the Eighth International Creativity Research Conference.* Salt Lake City: University of Utah, 1974 (mimeo).

Treffinger, D., Speedie, S., and Brunner, W. "Improving Children's Creative Problem-solving Abilities: The Purdue Creativity Project." *Journal of Creative Behavior,* 1974, **8**:20-30.

WBAA. *Creative Thinking: The American Pioneers.* (A manual for teachers.) West Lafayette, Ind.: Purdue University, 1966.

RACKING TECHNIQUES

(also 7 x 7 technique and other forcing techniques)
See C. E. Gregory, *Management of Intelligence: Scientific Problem-solving & Creativity.* New York: McGraw-Hill, 1967.

REACH EACH YOU TEACH

Any classroom unit of instruction can provide many opportunities for students to use creative thinking skills, if the unit is carefully designed. Specific strategies for individualized unit planning are given.

Treffinger, D., Hohn, R., and Feldhusen, J. *Reach Each You Teach.* Buffalo, N.Y.: D.O.K., 1979.

REAL TIME

Two catalogues of ideas and information concerning new models and approaches to problems from many disciplines.

Brockman, J., and Rosenfeld, E. *Real Time 1.* Garden City, N.Y.: Anchor/ Doubleday, 1973.
Brockman, J., and Rosenfeld, E. *Real Time 2.* Garden City, N.Y.: Anchor/ Doubleday, 1973.

RELAXED ATTENTION

McKim, R. H. *Experiences in Visual Thinking.* Belmont, Calif.: Brooks-Cole, 1972.

McKim, R. H. "Relaxed Attention." *Journal of Creative Behavior*, 1974, **8**:265-276.

SELF-CONCEPT ENHANCEMENT

Felker, D. W. *Building Positive Self-concepts.* Minneapolis: Burgess Publishing, 1973.

Grimm, G. D. *It's Me— You'll See.* Buffalo, N.Y.: D.O.K., 1973.

Hamachek, D. E. *Encounters with the Self.* New York: Holt, Rinehart, and Winston, 1971.

Purkey, W. W. *Self-concept and School Achievement.* Englewood Cliffs, N.J.: Prentice-Hall, 1970.

SELF-ENHANCING EDUCATION

Emphasis on basic principles of creative problem-solving, including education for setting as well as solving one's own problems. See: Randolph, Norma & Howe, W. A. *Self-enhancing Education, a Program to Motivate Learners.* Sanford Press, Sanford Office, 200 California Avenue, Palo, Alto, Calif., 1967.

SELF-INSTRUCTIONAL COURSE IN APPLIED IMAGINATION

Programmed set of 28 self-instructional booklets. For complete curriculum No. 015677 or microfiche of report EDO-10382 write to ERIC Document Report Service, 4936 Fairmont Ave., Bethesda, Md. 20014.

SENSITIVITY ("T GROUP")

A training program designed to help a person gain insight into h/self and h/sr functioning in a group. It attempts to increase the person's openness to ideas and viewpoint. See L. P. Bradford, J. R. Gibb, and K. Benne (eds.), *T Group Theory and Laboratory Method.* New York: Wiley, 1964. (See Affective Domain; Altered States; Awareness Development; and Self-Concept Enhancement.)

STRUCTURE OF INTELLECT

A model devised by J. P. Guilford giving organization to the various factors of intellect, and arranging them into three dimensions: contents, operations, and products.

Guilford, J. P. "Intellect and the Gifted." *Gifted Child Quarterly*, 1972, **16**:175-184 239-243.

Guilford, J. P. *Intelligence, Creativity, and Their Educational Implications.* San Diego: Knapp, 1968.

Guilford, J. P. *The Nature of Human Intelligence.* New York: McGraw-Hill, 1967.

Guilford, J. P. "Varieties of Creative Giftedness, Their Measurement and Development." *Gifted Child Quarterly*, 1975, **19**:107-121.

Guilford, J. P. *Way Beyond the IQ.* Buffalo, N.Y.: Creative Education Foundation, 1977.

Guilford, J. P., and Hoepfner, R. *The Analysis of Intelligence.* New York: McGraw-Hill, 1971.

Meeker, M. N. *The Structure of Intellect: Its Interpretation and Uses.* Columbus: Merrill, 1969.

Meeker, M., Sexton, K., and Richardson, M. *SOI Abilities Workbook.* Los Angeles: Loyola-Marymount University, 1970.

SYNECTICS (OR OPERATIONAL CREATIVITY)

A training program that stresses the practical use of analogy and metaphor in problem-solving. The synectics mechanisms "force new ideas and associations up for conscious consideration rather than waiting for them to arise fortuitously." Developed at adult level.

Gordon, W. J. J. "On Being Explicit about Creative Process." *Journal of Creative Behavior*, 1972, **6**:295-300.

Gordon, W. J. J. "Some Source Material in Discovery-by-Analogy." *Journal of Creative Behavior*, 1974, **8**:239-257.

Gordon, W. J. J. *Synectics: The Development of Creative Capacity.* New York: Harper Bros. 1961.

Gordon, W. J. J., and Poze, T. "SES Synectics and Gifted Education Today." *Gifted Child Quarterly*, 1980, **24**:147-151.

Gordon, W., Poze, T., and Reid, M. *The Metaphorical Way of Learning and Knowing*. Cambridge, Mass.: SES Synectics, Inc., 1971.

Making it Strange. Prepared by Synectics, Inc. New York: Harper & Row, 1968.

Prince, G. *The Practice of Creativity*. Cambridge, Mass.: Synectics, 1969.

TEACHING CHILDREN HOW TO THINK

In 1975, the National Institute of Education provided support for a project to synthesize, interpret, and evaluate research and development on creative problem-solving. These project reports include information on specific methods and techniques (checklists, forced relationships, brainstorming, etc.), how to set up a program to encourage creativity in the classroom, and written descriptions about a large number of published curriculum resources for fostering creative problem-solving. For information, write to Dr. John F. Feldhusen, Purdue University, Educational Psychology Section, West Lafayette, Ind. 47907.

Feldhusen, J. F., and Treffinger, D. J. *Creative Thinking and Problem Solving in Gifted Education*. Dubuque, Iowa: Kendall-Hunt, 1980.

Feldhusen, J. F., Treffinger, D. J., Pine, P. A., et al. *Teaching Children How to Think*. West Lafayette, Ind.: Purdue University, March 1975. (Final Report of Project NIE-G-74-0063.)

Feldhusen, J. F., Treffinger, D. J., Pine, P. A., et al. *Teacher's Edition: Teaching Children How to Think*. West Lafayette, Ind.: Purdue University, 1975. (An abbreviated edition of the completed report.)

THEORETICAL ISSUES

The question, "Can creativity be developed?" has interested many scholars, and the literature, both supportive and critical, contains many stimulating papers. Among them are:

Anderson, H. H. "Creativity and Education." *College and University Bulletin*, 1961, 13.

Arieti, S. *Creativity: the Magic Synthesis*. New York: Basic Books, 1976.

Ausubel, D. P. *Educational Psychology: A Cognitive View*. New York: Holt, Rinehart and Winston, 1968. (Ch. 16, partic. pp. 549-555, 559-562).

Ausubel, D. P. "Fostering Creativity in the School." *Proceedings of the Centennial*

Symposium, How Children Learn. Toronto, Ontario, Canada: Phi Delta Kappa and O.I.S.E., 1967, 37-49.

Ausubel, D. P., and Robinson, F. *School Learning.* New York: Holt, Rinehart and Winston, 1969. (Ch. 17, partic. pp. 523-540, 543-544.)

Bruch, C. and others. *The Faces and Forms of Creativity.* Ventura, Calif.: Ventura County Supt. of Schools, 1981.

Danziger, K. "Fostering Creativity in the School: Social Psychological Aspects." *Proceedings of the Centennial Symposium, How Children Learn.* Toronto: Phi Delta Kappa and O.I.S.E., 1967, 50-59.

deMille, R. "The Creativity Boom." *Teachers College Record,* 1963, 54, 199+.

Gagne, R. M. *The Conditions of Learning.* New York: Hold, Rinehart, Winston, 1965. (partic. pp. 166-170.)

Getzels, J. W. "Creative Thinking, Problem-solving, and Instruction." In NSSE Yearbook, *Theories of Learning and Instruction,* 1964, 240-267.

Guilford, J. P. "Factors that Aid and Hinder Creativity." *Teachers College Record,* 1962, **63**:391.

Hallman, R. J. "Can Creativity Be Taught?" *Educational Theory,* 1964, **14**:15 .

Parnes, S. J. "Can Creativity be Increased?" In S.J. Parnes and H.F. Harding. *A Source Book for Creative Thinking.* New York: Scribner's, 1962, pp. 151-168.

Parnes, S. J. *Creative Potential and the Educational Experience.* Buffalo, N.Y.: Creative Education Foundation, 1967. Occasional paper no. 2.

Taylor, C. W. (ed.) *Creativity: Progress and Potential.* New York: Wiley, 1964, chapters 3 and 4.

Taylor, C. W., and Williams, F. E. (eds.) *Instructional Media and Creativity.* New York: Wiley, 1966.

White, W. E. *Psychosocial Principles Applied to Classroom Teaching.* New York: McGraw-Hill, 1969. (Ch. 7, partic. pp. 136ff.)

THINK PRODUCTS

A series of materials for teachers and industry to stimulate creative performance. Included is a series of TNT materials for teachers (techniques and tips) and a little magazine called *The Creative Thinker.* Available from Think Products, 1209 Robin Hood Circle, Towson, Md. 21204.

THINKING CREATIVELY

Gary A. Davis, Department of Educational Psychology, University of Wisconsin, Madison, has been active in research on the development of creative thinking abilities, and in constructing instructional programs and materials as well. He has also published with Joseph A. Scott, an anthology entitled, *Training Creative Thinking*. New York: Holt, Rinehart, and Winston, 1971. Related articles and materials include:

Davis, G. A. *Psychology of Problem-solving: Theory and Practice*. New York: Basic Books, 1973.

Davis, G. A. "Training Creativity in Adolescents: A Discussion of Strategy." *Journal of Creative Behavior*, 1969, 3:95-104.

Davis, G. A., and Houtman, S. E. *Thinking Creatively: A Guide to Training Imagination*. Madison: University of Wisconsin Res. and Devel. Center for Cognitive Learning, 1968.

Davis, G. A. Houtman, S., Warren, T., and Roweton, W. "A Program for Training Creative Thinking: I. Preliminary Field Test." Madison: University of Wisconsin, Res. and Devel. Center for Cognitive Learning, 1969.

Davis, G. A., and Manske, M. "An Instructional Method of Increasing Originality." Psychonomic Science, 1966, 6:73-74.

Davis, G. A., and Roweton, W. "Using Idea Checklists with College Students: Overcoming Resistance." *Journal of Psychology*, 1968, 70:221-226.

Manske, M., and Davis, G. "Effects of Simple Instructional Biases upon Performance on the Unusual Uses Tests." *Journal of General Psychology*, 1968, 79:25-33.

TRANSACTUALIZATION

Taylor, I. A. *A Theory of Creative Transactualization*. Buffalo, N.Y.: Creative Education Foundation, 1972. Occasional paper no. 8.

Taylor, I. A. "A Transactional Approach to Creativity and Its Implications for Education." *Journal of Creative Behavior*, 1971, 5:190-198.

Taylor, I. A., Sutton, D., and Haworth, S. "The Measurement of Creative Transactualization: A Scale to Measure Behavioral Disposition toward Creativity." *Journal of Creative Behavior*, 1974, 8:114-115.

TRANSLIMINAL EXPERIENCE

An examination of creative behavior in relation to the processes of experience at differing levels of consciousness.

MacKinnon, D. W. "Creativity and Transliminal Experience." *Journal of Creative Behavior*, 1971, **5**:227-241.

UNIVERSAL TRAVELER

The Universal Traveler is an entertaining, stylishly presented introduction to the basic principles of creative problem-solving. It includes sections on blocks to creativity (and overcoming them), creativity games, and a variety of specific methods and techniques to stimulate creative problem-solving.

Koberg, D., and Bagnall, J. *The Universal Traveler*. Los Altos, Calif.: William Kaufmann Co., 1974. (Distributed by Crown Publishers, New York, as a Harmony Book.)

VALUE ENGINEERING (OR VALUE ANALYSIS, VALUE INNOVATION, VALUE MANAGEMENT, ETC.)

Training programs applying general principles of creative problem-solving to group efforts toward reducing costs or optimizing value. Adult level. See L. D. Miles, *Techniques of Value Analysis and Engineering*, New York: McGraw-Hill, 1961; also Value Engineering Handbook, H111, U.S. Department of Defense, March 29, 1963 (U.S. Government Printing Office, Washington, D.C.). For current information, conference reports, bibliographies, etc., write Society of American Value Engineers, Windy Hill, Suite E-9, 1741 Roswell Street, Smyrna, Ga. 30080.

VERBAL IMAGERY

Research on the facilitation of verbal imagery and imagination has been conducted by Professor Joe Khatena, of Marshall University in Huntington, West Virginia.

Khatena, J., and Torrance, E. P. *Thinking Creatively with Sounds and Words: Norms and Technical Manual*. Lexington, Mass.: Personnel Press, 1973.

Torrance, E. P., Khatena, J., and Cunnington, B. F. *Thinking Creatively with Sounds and Words.* Lexington, Mass.: Personnel Press, 1973.

The development and evaluation of materials for the assessment and encouragement of imagination through verbal imagery has been the focus of many reports:

Khatena, J. "Children's Version of Onomatopoeia and Images: A Preliminary Validity Study of Verbal Originality." *Perceptual and Motor Skills*, 1971, **33**:26.
Khatena, J. "Creative Imagination Imagery and Analogy." *Gifted Child Quarterly*, 1975, **19**:149-160.
Khatena, J. "Imagination Imagery by Children and the Production of Analogy." *Gifted Child Quarterly*, 1973, **17**:98-102.
Khatena, J. "Onomatopoeia and Images: Preliminary Validity Study of a Test of Originality." *Perceptual and Motor Skills*, 1969, **28**:235-238.
Khatena, J. "Training College Adults to Think Creatively with Words." *Psychological Reports*, 1970, **27**:279-281.
Khatena, J. "The Use of Analogy in the Production of Original Verbal Images." *Journal of Creative Behavior*, 1972, **6**:209-213.

VISUALIZATION

Eberle, B. *Visual Thinking.* Buffalo, N.Y.: D.O.K., 1982.
McKim, R. *Experiences in Visual Thinking.* Belmont, Calif.: Wadsworth, 1972.
Samuels, M., and Samuels, N. *Seeing with the Mind's Eye.* New York: Random House, 1975.
Torrance, E. P. *The Search for Satori and Creativity.* Buffalo, N.Y.: Creative Education Foundation, 1979.

WFF'N PROOF

A symbolic logic game designed to increase one's ability to discover new relationships in a logical manner. Portions applicable at elementary level, proceeding through adult levels. Available from author, L. E. Allen (*WFF'N PROOF, the game of modern logic*), P.O. Box 71, New Haven, Conn. 06501.

WILLIAMS' MODEL

Frank E. Williams has developed an approach for helping teachers integrate the teaching of cognitive and affective skills with the presentation of subject matter. Other published reports include:

Cole, H. P., and Parsons, D. E. "The Williams Total Creativity Program." *Journal of Creative Behavior*, 1974, **8**:187-207.

Williams, F. E. *A Total Creativity Program for Individualizing and Humanizing the Learning Process*. Englewood Cliffs, N.J.: Educational Technology Press, 1972.

Williams, F. E. *Classroom Ideas for Encouraging Thinking and Feeling*. Buffalo, N.Y.: D.O.K., 1972.

Williams, F. E. *Creativity Assessment Packet*. Buffalo, N.Y.: D.O.K., 1981.

Williams, F. E. "Fostering Classroom Creativity." *California Teachers Association Journal*, March 1961.

Williams, F. E. *Media for Developing Creative Thinking in Young Children*. Buffalo, N.Y.: Creative Education Foundation, 1968. Occasional paper no. 3.

Williams F. E. "Models for Encouraging Creativity in the Classroom by Integrating Cognitive-Affective Behaviors." *Educational Technology*, 1969, **9**:7-13.

Williams, F. E. "Perspective of a Model for Developing Productive-Creative Behaviors in the Classroom." In F. E. Williams (ed.), *First Seminar on Productive Thinking in Education*, St. Paul: Macalester College, 1966, 108-116.

Williams, F. E. "The Search for the Creative Teacher." *California Teachers Association Journal*, January 1964, **60**:14-16.

Williams, F. E. "Stabilizing the Swings—A Synergistic Approach Toward More Creativity in Education." *Journal of Creative Behavior*, 1973, **7**:187-195.

Williams, F. E. "Training Children to Be Creative may Have Little Effect on Original Classroom Performance, Unless. . . ." *California Journal of Educational Research*, 1966, **17**:.

WORK SIMPLIFICATION

An industrial training program that applies some of the general principles of creative problem-solving to the simplification of operations or procedures. Provides opportunity for personnel to use their mental resources in helping improve organizational operations, using simple industrial engineering pricniples. ("Job Methods Training," as well as other similarly named programs of World War II and thereafter, applied the basic concepts of this program.) See H.F. Goodwin, "Work Simplification" (a documentary series of articles), *Factory Management and Maintenance*, July 1958. Briefer but more recent information may be obtained from Work Simplification Conferences, P.O. Box 30, Lake Placid, N.Y. 12947, and from an article on Work Simplification by Auren Uris in the September 1965 issue of *Factory*.

YOUNG THINKER (1964)

For children between five and ten years of age. A series of more than fifty projects and exercises that can be used by the individual or by groups. These have been used in the home and in schools. Available from W.O. Uraneck, 56 Turning Mill Road, Lexington, Mass. 02173.

Books About the Joys and Travails of Achieving Excellence

Addams, Jane. *Twenty Years at Hull-house*. Chautauqua, N.Y.: Chautauqua Press, 1911; Reprint ed., New York: New American Library, 1961.

Bell, Eric T. *Men of Mathematics*. New York: Simon & Schuster, Inc., 1937.

Beveridge, Albert J. *The Life of John Marshall*. 4 vols. New York: Houghton Mifflin Company, 1919; reprint ed., Marietta, Ga.: Larlin Corp., 1974.

Binger, Carl. *Revolutionary Doctor: Benjamin Rush, 1746-1813*. New York: W.W. Norton & Company, 1966.

Cannon, Walter B. *The Way of an Investigator, A Scientist's Experiences in Medical Research*. New York: W.W. Norton & Company, 1945.

Cole, Jonathan R. *Fair Science: Women in the Scientific Community*. New York: The Free Press, 1979.

Coolidge, Olivia E. *Gandhi*. Boston: Houghton Mifflin Company, 1971.

Darrow, Clarence S. *The Story of My Life*. New York: Charles Scribners' Sons, 1932.

DeCamp, L. Sprague. *The Ancient Engineers*. New York: Ballantine Books, 1980.

DeMille, Agnes. *Dance to the Piper*. Boston: Little, Brown and Company, 1952.

Dyson, Freeman. *Disturbing the Universe: A Life in Science*. New York: Harper & Row, Publishers, 1979.

Fonteyn, Margot. *Margot Fonteyn: Autobiography*. New York: Alfred A. Knopf, Inc., 1976.

Goertzel, Victor, and Mildred Goertzel. *Cradles of Eminence*. Boston: Little, Brown and Company, 1962.

Goertzel, Mildred, Ted Goertzel, and Victor Goertzel. *Three Hundred Eminent Personalities: A Psychosocial Analysis of the Famous*. San Francisco: Josey-Bass, 1978.

Greer, Germaine. *The Obstacle Race: The Fortunes of Women Painters and Their Work*. New York: Farrar, Straus & Giroux, Inc., 1979.

Hart, Moss. *Act One*. New York: Random House, Inc., 1976.

Highet, Gilbert. *Man's Unconquerable Mind*. New York: Columbia University Press, 1954.

Hoffman, Banesh, and Helen Dukes. *Albert Einstein, Creator and Rebel*. New York: New American Library, 1973.

Jaffe, Bernard. *Crucibles: The Story of Chemistry From Ancient Alchemy to Nuclear Fission*, rev. ed. New York: Simon & Schuster, Inc., 1948.

Lewis, Sinclair. *Arrowsmith*. New York: Harcourt Brace Jovanovich Inc., 1949.

Marcus, Stanley. *Quest for the Best*. New York: The Viking Press, Inc., 1979.

Maugham, W. Somerset. *The Summing Up*. New York: Penguin Books, Inc., 1978.

Medawar, Peter B. *Advice to a Young Scientist*. New York: Harper & Row, Publishers, 1979.

Meir, Golda. *My Life*. New York: G.P. Putnam's Sons, 1975.

Meltzer, Milton *Langston Hughes: A Biography*. New York: Harper & Row Publishers, 1968.

Nolen, William A. *The Making of A Surgeon*. New York: Random House, Inc., 1970.

Osen, Lynn M. *Women in Mathematics*. Cambridge, Mass.: The MIT Press, 1974.

Parks, Gordon. *A Choice of Weapons*. New York: Harper & Row, Publishers, 1973.

Pines, Maya. *The Brain Changers*. New York: Harcourt Brace Jovanovich, Inc., 1975.

Roe, Anne. *The Making of a Scientist*. New York: Dodd, Mead & Co., 1953; reprint ed., Westport, Conn.: Greenwood Press, Inc., 1974.

Russell, Bertrand. *Autobiography of Bertrand Russell*. London: George Allen & Unwin Ltd., 1975.

Sayre, Anne. *Rosalind Franklin and DNA*. New York: W.W. Norton & Company, Inc., 1975.

Schwartz, Helene E. *Lawyering*. New York: Farrar, Straus & Giroux, Inc., 1976.

Speer, Albert. *Inside the Third Reich: Memoirs of Albert Speer*. New York: Macmillan Publishing Co., Inc. 1970.

Stanislavski, Constantin *My Life in Art*. New York: Theatre Arts, 1952.

Taper, Bernard *Balanchine: A Biography*. New York: Macmillan Publishing Co., Inc., 1974.

Terkel, Studs. *Working*. New York: Avon Books, 1975.

Watson, James D. *Double Helix*. New York: New American Library, 1969.

White, Theodore H. *In Search of History*. New York: Warner Books, 1979.

Wiener, Norbert. *Ex-Prodigy: My Childhood and Youth*. Cambridge, Mass.: The M.I.T. Press, 1964.

Wilson, Mitchell A. *Passion to Know: The World's Scientists*. Garden City: Doubleday & Company, Inc., 1972.

Zuckerman, Harriet. *Scientific Elite: Nobel Laureates in the United States*. New York: The Free Press, 1977.

Survey of Feelings About the Gifted and Their Education

This questionnaire is designed to elicit important impressions concerning children in your school or school district who have been identified as gifted or talented. Please answer each question candidly and accurately.

PART I: GENERAL INFORMATION

1. Name ——————————————————————————————
   (*Confidential*: To be used only for purposes of verification, if necessary)

2. Present position (check one)
   _____ Teacher, elementary level
   _____ Teacher, secondary level
   _____ Member, pupil personnel services (e.g., counselor, psychologist, social worker, remedial specialist)
   _____ Member, supervisory or administrative staff
   _____ Special teacher of the gifted
   _____ Lay member of the board of education
   _____ Parent of child at school who may be gifted or talented
   _____ Parent of child at school who is probably not gifted or talented
   _____ Taxpayer with no children at school
   _____ Other (explain)——————————————————————

3. Have you taken time out to study gifted children, through formal coursework, attending conferences, or reading books on the subject?

    Yes _____ No _____

4. Does your school/system offer special enrichment opportunities of any kind to gifted or talented pupils, *other than* athletes? (Fill in one.)

    Yes □
    No   □

5. If "yes," how long ago were these enrichment offerings initiated? (Fill in one.)

    Within the last five years   □
    Approximately six to ten years ago   □
    More than ten years ago   □

6. Indicate the *additional* outlay (if any) per pupil that is earmarked in your budget for these enrichment offerings. (Fill in one.)

    No additional outlay earmarked   □
    Approximately 1%-5% of general per pupil cost   □
    Approximately 6%-10% of general per pupil cost   □
    Approxmiately 11%-20% of general per pupil cost □
    Approximately 21%-33% of general per pupil cost □
    Approximately 34%-50% of general per pupil cost □
    More than 50% of general per pupil cost   □
    Don't know   □

7. How would you assess your community's feeling about special enrichment opportunities for the gifted or talented? (Fill in one.)

    Strongly supportive □
    Mildly supportive   □
    Indifferent   □
    Mildly opposed   □
    Strongly opposed   □
    Don't know   □

8. How would you assess the *professional* school staff's feelings about special enrichment opportunities for gifted or talented? (Fill in one.)

    Strongly supportive □
    Mildly supportive   □
    Indifferent   □
    Mildly opposed   □
    Strongly opposed   □
    Don't know   □

9. Please indicate the amount of *special* effort your school/system exerts in locating

and cultivating exceptionally high potential among socially disadvantaged children. (Fill in one.)

Maximum *special* effort	☐
Considerable *special* effort	☐
Moderate *special* effort	☐
Little *special* effort	☐
No *special* effort	☐
Don't know	☐

PART II: INDIVIDUALIZING THE LEARNING PROCESS

Please fill in the appropriate spaces in columns I, II, III, and IV as follows:

A. For column I, indicate on a scale from *High to Low* (H to L) the PRIORITY you would assign each statement below in terms of its *importance* for educational policy or practice in school systems *in general.*

B. For column II, indicate on a scale from *High to Low* (H to L) how you would rate *your own school's system's* PERFORMANCE with respect to each statement below:

C. For column III, indicate on a scale from *High to Low* (H to L) how you would rate the PROSPECTS, or likelihood, that each statement below will represent a significant feature of *your own school's system's* policy or practice five years from now.

D. If a statement *does not pertain* to the kind of school/system you represent (e.g., it is meant for high schools whereas you are responding for an elementary school) omit columns I, II, III, and fill in the space marked IRRELEVANT in column IV.

Example

Column I Priority	Column II Performance	Column III Prospects	Column IV Irrelevant
H L	H L	H L	
☐ ☐ ☐ ☐ ☐ Rich varieties of in-service training courses are available to any teacher tho wants them.	☐ ☐ ☐ ☐ ☐	☐ ☐ ☐ ☐ ☐	☐

Note: Respondents consider rich varieties of in-service training courses among the highest priorities for quality education in general. They give their own school/system a moderate rating for its in-service training program. Finally, projecting into the future, they give their own school/system a fairly low rating with respect to the likelihood of its having a significant program of in-service training five years from now.

(I) Priority			(II) Performance		(III) Prospects		(IV) Irrelevant
H L			H L		H L		
☐☐☐☐☐	1.	To the educational staff, success means every pupil measuring up to his or her own individual potential, *not* up (or down) to a fixed standard for his or her age group.	☐☐☐☐☐		☐☐☐☐☐		☐
☐☐☐☐☐	2.	Every pupil plays a significant role in planning his or her learning expriences at school.	☐☐☐☐☐		☐☐☐☐☐		☐
☐☐☐☐☐	3.	Pupils undergo careful testing to diagnose individual abilities or aptitudes.	☐☐☐☐☐		☐☐☐☐☐		☐
☐☐☐☐☐	4.	The pace of instruction is varied to accommodate the full range of individual aptitudes or abilities at each age level.	☐☐☐☐☐		☐☐☐☐☐		☐
☐☐☐☐☐	5.	The *subject areas* of the curriculum are varied to accommodate the full range of individual abilities or aptitudes at each age level.	☐☐☐☐☐		☐☐☐☐☐		☐
☐☐☐☐☐	6.	Each pupil is given ample opportunity to interact freely with his or her teachers concerning his or her *individual* learning experiences.	☐☐☐☐☐		☐☐☐☐☐		☐
☐☐☐☐☐	7.	Pupils often work independently and in small groups in the classroom.	☐☐☐☐☐		☐☐☐☐☐		☐
☐☐☐☐☐	8.	Resource materials in the classroom are abundant and varied enough to facilitate individualized learning experience.	☐☐☐☐☐		☐☐☐☐☐		☐
☐☐☐☐☐	9.	Pupils often move freely within and outside the classroom to seek resource materials they need in their individualized learning experience.	☐☐☐☐☐		☐☐☐☐☐		☐
☐☐☐☐☐	10.	Pupils undergo frequent testing through which they monitor their individual progress continuously.	☐☐☐☐☐		☐☐☐☐☐		☐

PART III: THE GIFTED

Note: The term "gifted pupil" as used in this survey is defined as meaning any pupil who is considered by his or her school to be worthy of special consideration because of his or her *academic* or *intellectual* abilities. These pupils may be referred to locally as academically talented, advanced, able, high ability, and so on.

(I) Priority		(II) Performance		(III) Prospects		(IV) Irrelevant
H	**L**	**H**	**L**	**H**	**L**	

Priority (H L)	Item	Performance (H L)	Prospects (H L)	Irrelevant
☐☐☐☐☐	1. The search for gifted pupils at school is intense and thorough.	☐☐☐☐☐	☐☐☐☐☐	☐
☐☐☐☐☐	2. Generally speaking, there is great emphasis on the quality of enrichment experiences for the gifted at school.	☐☐☐☐☐	☐☐☐☐☐	☐
☐☐☐☐☐	3. The school/system offers prestigious honors to the exceptionally gifted for their special accomplishments.	☐☐☐☐☐	☐☐☐☐☐	☐
	4. In identifying gifted pupils, the school system uses the following criteria:			
☐☐☐☐☐	a. Group IQ	☐☐☐☐☐	☐☐☐☐☐	☐
☐☐☐☐☐	b. Individual IQ	☐☐☐☐☐	☐☐☐☐☐	☐
☐☐☐☐☐	c. Standardized achievement test scores	☐☐☐☐☐	☐☐☐☐☐	☐
☐☐☐☐☐	d. Teacher opinions	☐☐☐☐☐	☐☐☐☐☐	☐
☐☐☐☐☐	e. School marks	☐☐☐☐☐	☐☐☐☐☐	☐
☐☐☐☐☐	f. "Creativity" tests	☐☐☐☐☐	☐☐☐☐☐	☐
☐☐☐☐☐	g. Product review	☐☐☐☐☐	☐☐☐☐☐	☐
☐☐☐☐☐	h. Parent nominations	☐☐☐☐☐	☐☐☐☐☐	☐
☐☐☐☐☐	i. Peer nominations	☐☐☐☐☐	☐☐☐☐☐	☐
☐☐☐☐☐	j. Self-nominations	☐☐☐☐☐	☐☐☐☐☐	☐
☐☐☐☐☐	5. The school/system has a policy of early admission of gifted children to kindergarten or first grade.	☐☐☐☐☐	☐☐☐☐☐	☐
	6. Gifted pupils are allowed to skip grades at the following levels:			
☐☐☐☐☐	a. K-3	☐☐☐☐☐	☐☐☐☐☐	☐
☐☐☐☐☐	b. 4-6	☐☐☐☐☐	☐☐☐☐☐	☐
☐☐☐☐☐	c. 7-9	☐☐☐☐☐	☐☐☐☐☐	☐
☐☐☐☐☐	d. 10-12	☐☐☐☐☐	☐☐☐☐☐	☐
	7. Gifted pupils are allowed to compress two or more years' work into less time at the following levels:			
☐☐☐☐☐	a. K-3	☐☐☐☐☐	☐☐☐☐☐	☐
☐☐☐☐☐	b. 4-6	☐☐☐☐☐	☐☐☐☐☐	☐
☐☐☐☐☐	c. 7-9	☐☐☐☐☐	☐☐☐☐☐	☐
☐☐☐☐☐	d. 10-12	☐☐☐☐☐	☐☐☐☐☐	☐
	8. Gifted pupils are placed into honors or advanced sections at the following levels:			
☐☐☐☐☐	a. K-3	☐☐☐☐☐	☐☐☐☐☐	☐
☐☐☐☐☐	b. 4-6	☐ ☐ ☐ ☐	☐☐☐☐☐	☐
☐☐☐☐☐	c. 7-9	☐☐☐☐☐	☐☐☐☐☐	☐
☐☐☐☐☐	d. 10-12	☐☐☐☐☐	☐☐☐☐☐	☐
	9. Gifted pupils at the following levels are offered subjects usually studied in higher grades:			
☐☐☐☐☐	a. K-3	☐☐☐☐☐	☐☐☐☐☐	☐
☐☐☐☐☐	b. 4-6	☐☐☐☐☐	☐☐☐☐☐	☐
☐☐☐☐☐	c. 7-9	☐☐☐☐☐	☐☐☐☐☐	☐
☐☐☐☐☐	d. 10-12	☐☐☐☐☐	☐☐☐☐☐	☐

10. Gifted pupils are placed in ungraded classes to facilitate their optimum development at the following grade levels:
 □□□□□   a. K-3   □□□□□ □□□□□   □
 □□□□□   b. 4-6   □□□□□ □□□□□   □
 □□□□□   c. 7-9   □□□□□ □□□□□   □
 □□□□□   d. 10-12   □□□□□ □□□□□   □

11. Gifted pupils are offered enrichment experiences and individual attention in regular classes at the following levels:
 □□□□□   a. K-3   □□□□□ □□□□□   □
 □□□□□   b. 4-6   □□□□□ □□□□□   □
 □□□□□   c. 7-9   □□□□□ □□□□□   □
 □□□□□   d. 10-12   □□□□□ □□□□□   □

12. Partial grouping* is arranged for the gifted at the following levels:
 □□□□□   a. K-3   □□□□□ □□□□□   □
 □□□□□   b. 4-6   □□□□□ □□□□□   □
 □□□□□   c. 7-9   □□□□□ □□□□□   □
 □□□□□   d. 10-12   □□□□□ □□□□□   □

13. Complete grouping** is arranged for the gifted at the following levels:
 □□□□□   a. K-3   □□□□□ □□□□□   □
 □□□□□   b. 4-6   □□□□□ □□□□□   □
 □□□□□   c. 7-9   □□□□□ □□□□□   □
 □□□□□   d. 10-12   □□□□□ □□□□□   □

14. Gifted pupils are offered enrichment experiences in school after hours (i.e., evenings or Saturdays) at the following levels:
 □□□□□   a. K-3   □□□□□ □□□□□   □
 □□□□□   b. 4-6   □□□□□ □□□□□   □
 □□□□□   c. 7-9   □□□□□ □□□□□   □
 □□□□□   d. 10-12   □□□□□ □□□□□   □

15. The school/system encourages gifted pupils at the following grade levels to engage in special study on a college campus:
 □□□□□   a. K-3   □□□□□ □□□□□   □
 □□□□□   b. 4-6   □□□□□ □□□□□   □
 □□□□□   c. 7-9   □□□□□ □□□□□   □
 □□□□□   d. 10-12   □□□□□ □□□□□   □

 □□□□□   16. Gifted pupils in high school have an opportunity to apply for early admission to college.   □□□□□ □□□□□   □

17. Advanced placement courses (CEEB) are offered in the following subjects:
 □□□□□   a. American history   □□□□□ □□□□□   □
 □□□□□   b. European history   □□□□□ □□□□□   □
 □□□□□   c. English   □□□□□ □□□□□   □
 □□□□□   d. French   □□□□□ □□□□□   □
 □□□□□   e. Spanish   □□□□□ □□□□□   □
 □□□□□   f. German   □□□□□ □□□□□   □
 □□□□□   g. Latin   □□□□□ □□□□□   □
 □□□□□   h. Mathematics   □□□□□ □□□□□   □
 □□□□□   i. Physics   □□□□□ □□□□□   □

| □ □ □ □ □ | j. Chemistry | □ □ □ □ □ □ □ □ □ □ | □ |
| □ □ □ □ □ | k. Biology | □ □ □ □ □ □ □ □ □ □ | □ |

*Partial grouping: gifted pupils are placed in special groups for only part of the day or for only those academic subjects in which they are most able.

**Complete grouping: gifted pupils are grouped together all day for all academic subjects.

PART IV: THE TALENTED

Note: The term "talent" is defined here as exceptionally high potential in any one of the nonacademic areas of productivity, including the performing and fine arts, crafts, music, social leadership, and the like, but *excluding* sports. Also, such "extracurricular" activities as glee clubs, art clubs, school orchestras, and so on may be counted among the special enrichment experiences for the talented, *only* if they include *special* enrichment experiences for the talented.

(I) Priority		(II) Performance		(III) Prospects		(IV) Irrelevant
H	**L**	**H**	**L**	**H**	**L**	
□ □ □ □ □	1. The search for talented pupils at school is intense and thorough.	□ □ □ □	□ □ □ □ □			□
□ □ □ □ □	2. Generally speaking, there is great emphasis on the quality of enrichment experiences for the talented at school.	□ □ □ □	□ □ □ □ □			□
□ □ □ □ □	3. The school/system offers prestigious honors to the exceptionally talented for their special accomplishments.	□ □ □ □	□ □ □ □ □			□
	4. The talented are offered special enrichment opportunities in the following areas of productivity:					
□ □ □ □ □	a. Fine arts	□ □ □ □ □	□ □ □ □ □			□
□ □ □ □ □	b. Performing arts	□ □ □ □ □	□ □ □ □ □			□
□ □ □ □ □	c. Crafts	□ □ □ □ □	□ □ □ □ □			□
□ □ □ □ □	d. Music	□ □ □ □ □	□ □ □ □ □			□
□ □ □ □ □	e. Social leadership	□ □ □ □ □	□ □ □ □ □			□
	5. The following measures are used in identifying talented pupils:					
□ □ □ □ □	a. Tests of creativity	□ □ □ □ □	□ □ □ □ □			□
□ □ □ □ □	b. School-designed performance tests	□ □ □ □ □	□ □ □ □ □			□
□ □ □ □ □	c. Commercially produced performance tests	□ □ □ □ □	□ □ □ □ □			□
□ □ □ □ □	d. Teacher assessment	□ □ □ □ □	□ □ □ □ □			□
□ □ □ □ □	e. Subjective assessment by specialists	□ □ □ □ □	□ □ □ □ □			□
□ □ □ □ □	f. Parent nominations	□ □ □ □ □	□ □ □ □ □			□
□ □ □ □ □	g. Peer nominations	□ □ □ □ □	□ □ □ □ □			□
□ □ □ □ □	h. Self nominations	□ □ □ □ □	□ □ □ □ □			□
□ □ □ □ □	6. The talented are placed in special ability groups at school to facilitate their optimum development.	□ □ □ □	□ □ □ □ □			□

☐ ☐ ☐ ☐ ☐ 7. The talented are encouraged to join vol- ☐ ☐ ☐ ☐ ☐   ☐ ☐ ☐ ☐ ☐   ☐
untary special interest clubs at school to
facilitate their optimum development.

☐ ☐ ☐ ☐ ☐ 8. The talented are offered enrichment ex- ☐ ☐ ☐ ☐ ☐   ☐ ☐ ☐ ☐ ☐   ☐
periences and individual attention in reg-
ular classes.

☐ ☐ ☐ ☐ ☐ 9. The talented are offered special enrich- ☐ ☐ ☐ ☐ ☐   ☐ ☐ ☐ ☐ ☐   ☐
ment experiences *in school* after hours
(i.e., evenings or Saturdays).

☐ ☐ ☐ ☐ ☐ 10. The school/system encourages the talent- ☐ ☐ ☐ ☐ ☐   ☐ ☐ ☐ ☐ ☐   ☐
ed to receive advanced instruction and
guided practice at a local cultural center
(e.g., university, museum, conservatory).

PART V: GIFTED AND/OR TALENTED

(I) Priority			(II) Performance		(III) Prospects		(IV) Irrelevant
H	L		H	L	H	L	
☐ ☐ ☐ ☐ ☐		1. Virtually all pupils designated as gifted and/or talented at school are benefiting from some kind of educational enrichment there.	☐ ☐ ☐ ☐ ☐		☐ ☐ ☐ ☐ ☐		☐
☐ ☐ ☐ ☐ ☐		2. At least one person is assigned to spend a major part of his/her time coordinating special enrichment experiences for the gifted and/or talented at the school or system wide level.	☐ ☐ ☐ ☐ ☐		☐ ☐ ☐ ☐ ☐		☐
		3. The school/system places responsibilities for identifying gifted and/or talented pupils upon:					
☐ ☐ ☐ ☐ ☐		a. Teachers	☐ ☐ ☐ ☐ ☐		☐ ☐ ☐ ☐ ☐		☐
☐ ☐ ☐ ☐ ☐		b. School psychologists	☐ ☐ ☐ ☐ ☐		☐ ☐ ☐ ☐ ☐		☐
☐ ☐ ☐ ☐ ☐		c. Guidance counselors	☐ ☐ ☐ ☐ ☐		☐ ☐ ☐ ☐ ☐		☐
☐ ☐ ☐ ☐ ☐		d. School principals	☐ ☐ ☐ ☐ ☐		☐ ☐ ☐ ☐ ☐		☐
☐ ☐ ☐ ☐ ☐		e. Special resource people	☐ ☐ ☐ ☐ ☐		☐ ☐ ☐ ☐ ☐		☐
☐ ☐ ☐ ☐ ☐		f. Parents	☐ ☐ ☐ ☐ ☐		☐ ☐ ☐ ☐ ☐		☐
☐ ☐ ☐ ☐ ☐		g. Peers	☐ ☐ ☐ ☐ ☐		☐ ☐ ☐ ☐ ☐		☐
☐ ☐ ☐ ☐ ☐		4. The school/system has published special curriculum guides for enriching the education of the gifted and/or talented.	☐ ☐ ☐ ☐ ☐		☐ ☐ ☐ ☐ ☐		☐
☐ ☐ ☐ ☐ ☐		5. The school/system engages outside resource people to help enrich the experiences of the gifted and/or talented.	☐ ☐ ☐ ☐ ☐		☐ ☐ ☐ ☐ ☐		☐
☐ ☐ ☐ ☐ ☐		6. Teachers of special classes of the gifted and/or talented require special preservice training before they can qualify for such an assignment.	☐ ☐ ☐ ☐ ☐		☐ ☐ ☐ ☐ ☐		☐

☐ ☐ ☐ ☐ ☐   7. Teachers of special classes of the gifted   ☐ ☐ ☐ ☐ ☐   ☐ ☐ ☐ ☐ ☐   ☐
and/or talented are required to undergo
special in-service training for such an
assignment.

☐ ☐ ☐ ☐ ☐   8. When the gifted and/or talented are ready   ☐ ☐ ☐ ☐ ☐   ☐ ☐ ☐ ☐ ☐   ☐
to enter the next higher school, the send-
ing school arranges to have them placed
in an appropriate program.

☐ ☐ ☐ ☐ ☐   9. The school/system conducts careful stud-   ☐ ☐ ☐ ☐ ☐   ☐ ☐ ☐ ☐ ☐   ☐
ies to evaluate its special enrichment of-
ferings to the gifted and/or talented.

☐ ☐ ☐ ☐ ☐ 10. The school/system disseminates widely a   ☐ ☐ ☐ ☐ ☐   ☐ ☐ ☐ ☐ ☐   ☐
considerable amount of information re-
garding its special enrichment offerings.

PART VI: PROGRAMS VERSUS PROVISIONS

In this final section there is only a single question, but a most important one, which enables you to characterize special enrichment offerings at your school/ system primarily as *programs* or *provisions*.

A program is a comprehensive offering, sequenced over a long period of time, usually designed as a requirement, and very much a major part of the total school curriculum. Thus, the school offers *programs* in mathematics, literature, art, social studies, and the like.

A *provision*, on the other hand, is more fragmentary, an ad hoc offering, relatively brief in duration, often designed by an individual teacher with special abilities rather than by a curriculum committee, and supplemental to the major offerings, not integral with them. Thus, a teacher who is interested in electronics will initiate a special *provision* in that subject for a selected group of qualified pupils. Another teacher may be interested in incubating chicks, or in writing psychodrama, or in opera production and designs special *provisions* in any of these areas for selected groups accordingly.

Please review the overall enrichment offerings in your school/system and characterize it *primarily* as a collection of the programs or provisions (fill in one space for each grade level).

	Grades			
	k-3	*4-6*	*7-9*	*10-12*
Programs	☐	☐	☐	☐
Provisions	☐	☐	☐	☐
No programs or provisions	☐	☐	☐	☐
Irrelevant	☐	☐	☐	☐

Author Index

517

Subject Index

527